Mike Ashley is an author and editor of over seventy books, including many Mammoth titles. He worked for over thirty years in local government but is now a full-time writer and researcher specializing in ancient history, historical fiction and fantasy, crime and science fiction. He lives in Kent with his wife and over 20,000 books.

Also available

The Mammoth Book of 20th Century Science Fiction
The Mammoth Book of Awesome Comic Fantasy
The Mammoth Book of Best New Erotica 3
The Mammoth Book of Best New Horror 14
The Mammoth Book of Best New Science Fiction 16
The Mammoth Book of British Kings & Queens
The Mammoth Book of Celtic Myths and Legends
The Mammoth Book of Fighter Pilots
The Mammoth Book of Future Cops
The Mammoth Book of Great Detective Stories
The Mammoth Book of Great Inventions
The Mammoth Book of Hearts of Oak
The Mammoth Book of Heroes
The Mammoth Book of Historical Whodunnits
The Mammoth Book of How It Happened
The Mammoth Book of How It Happened: America
The Mammoth Book of How It Happened: Ancient Egypt
The Mammoth Book of How It Happened: Ancient Rome
The Mammoth Book of How It Happened: Battles
The Mammoth Book of How It Happened: In Britain
The Mammoth Book of How It Happened: Everest
The Mammoth Book of How It Happened: Naval Battles
The Mammoth Book of How It Happened: WWI
The Mammoth Book of How It Happened: World War II
The Mammoth Book of International Erotica
The Mammoth Book of Jack the Ripper
The Mammoth Book of Maneaters
The Mammoth Book of Mountain Disasters
The Mammoth Book of Native Americans
The Mammoth Book of New Terror
The Mammoth Book of Private Eye Stories
The Mammoth Book of Prophecies
The Mammoth Book of Pulp Action
The Mammoth Book of Roaring Twenties Whodunnits
The Mammoth Book of Roman Whodunnits
The Mammoth Book of SAS & Elite Forces
The Mammoth Book of Science Fiction Century Volume 1
The Mammoth Book of Seriously Comic Fantasy
The Mammoth Book of Sex, Drugs & Rock 'n' Roll
The Mammoth Book of Sorcerers' Tales
The Mammoth Book of Space Exploration and Disasters
The Mammoth Book of Special Forces
The Mammoth Book of Shipwrecks & Sea Disasters
The Mammoth Book of Short Erotic Novels
The Mammoth Book of Sword and Honour
The Mammoth Book of The Edge
The Mammoth Book of Travel in Dangerous Places
The Mammoth Book of True War Stories
The Mammoth Book of UFOs
The Mammoth Book of Vampires
The Mammoth Book of War Correspondents
The Mammoth Book of Women Who Kill
The Mammoth Encyclopedia of Extraterrestrial Encounters
The Mammoth Encyclopedia of Modern Crime Fiction
The Mammoth Encyclopedia of Unsolved Mysteries

THE MAMMOTH BOOK OF

King Arthur

Mike Ashley

ROBINSON
London

Constable & Robinson Ltd
3 The Lanchesters
162 Fulham Palace Road
London W6 9ER
www.constablerobinson.com

First published in the UK by Robinson,
an imprint of Constable & Robinson Ltd 2005

A copy of the British Library Cataloguing in Publication Data is available from the British Library.

ISBN 1-84119-249-X

Printed and bound in the EU

1 3 5 7 9 10 8 6 4 2

CONTENTS

Section 3: The Big Picture

TABLES AND CHARTS

Maps

PREFACE: PEELING BACK THE LAYERS

What's it all about?

You may ask: why do we need another book on King Arthur? Aren't there enough already?

It's the very fact that there *are* so many that makes this book necessary. There is such a profusion of material that it's all become a little confusing, and anyone trying to understand the Arthurian world has problems knowing where to start and what it all means. Add to that books about the Arthurian legend, Merlin, Lancelot, Guenevere and the Holy Grail, and you have a library of books, articles and academic studies vast enough to daunt even the most dedicated enthusiast.

In this book I will bring everything together – the facts, the theories, the legend – and try and make some sense of them all. I'll even present a few theories of my own, and provide maps, family trees and a chronology. That way not only can you see how I arrive at my conclusions but it will allow you to draw your own.

The book is divided into three main parts. The first covers the historical Arthur. It looks at the world in which Arthur lived (roughly between 400 and 600AD), and explores what evidence has survived to prove or disprove his existence. It also looks at the many theories that have been put forward to identify Arthur and sets them against the historical background in the hope that the real Arthur will stand out. You might think it ought to be straightforward. If Arthur existed, if he was as famous as he's supposed to have been, whether under that name or another, then he'll appear in the historical record, just like Alfred the Great or Canute or Macbeth, other great kings from a thousand years ago whose existence is easily provable and not in doubt and whose exploits have become as much a part of legend as Arthur's. But it's far from straightforward and there's a lot of work needed to peel back the layers and reveal Arthur in all his glory.

The original Arthur dates back to those Dark Ages in the fifth and sixth centuries when the people of Britain were fighting for their lives against invaders, famine, plague and civil war. No one had much time to keep written records, and those that may have been kept have not survived the centuries. The single sobering fact is that there is not one single piece of genuine historical evidence to support the existence of someone called King Arthur.

Ironically, it is this lack of evidence that makes the search for the real Arthur so compelling, because there is a fair amount of circumstantial evidence to show that someone who was a great leader must have existed. That someone was the man who defeated the Saxons at the Battle of Badon so decisively that the Saxon invasion was held at bay for at least a generation. Whoever did that – and for simplicity's sake I shall call him Arthur of Badon – had to exist because his victory at Badon is a certain historical fact.

I believe that the original stories about Arthur are based on several historical people, at least three of whom were also called Arthur. Their lives, which only show dimly through the veils of history, soon became submerged into the oral tradition that created the Arthur of legend, a whole amalgam of historical and legendary characters spread across a wide period of history. That is one of the reasons why there are so many theories about the real Arthur and why he is so difficult to pin down.

The second part of this book, therefore, takes us into the legend, the Matter of Britain as it's become known. We follow the story of Arthur as it was created by the poets and bards through the Welsh and Breton tales, into the Norman world, culminating in Thomas Malory's famous *Morte d'Arthur*. This section looks at each of the legends in turn and sifts the facts from the fiction. It will help us identify not just further aspects of King Arthur, but the world of the Round Table, of Merlin and of the Holy Grail. The Arthur of legend has been constantly recreated and reborn, a multiple personality composed of a myriad of historical Arthurs. This section retells his story, and those of his companions, allowing us to identify the originals.

The final section looks at the modern interpretation of the Arthurian legend in both fiction and cinema. Although these works are pure fiction, many authors have brought their own interpretation to the legend, advancing theories every bit as intriguing as those of the historical scholar. The twentieth century passion for fantasy fiction has seen a remarkable growth in the number of books about the Arthurian world, from the pioneering works of T.H. White and Mary Stewart, to the blockbusters of Marion Zimmer Bradley, Bernard Cornwell and Rosalind Miles. This section includes a "Who's Who" and a Gazetteer to the Arthurian world to provide you with a complete picture.

Fifteen hundred years of legend is a lot to cover in one book, but before launching into the hunt we need to ponder for a moment the problems and pitfalls ahead.

The great puzzle

Arthur lived at that one period of British history when historians looked the other way. In fact, apart from a few Continental writers who commented briefly upon the state of Britain in the fifth century, there is only one possible contemporary of Arthur whose work survives – Gildas, who is discussed in detail in Chapter 5. Unfortunately, Gildas was not interested in recording history, and certainly not in noting dates, being more concerned with reprimanding the aberrant rulers whose waywardness had brought down the wrath of God by way of the Saxon invasion. Even more unfortunately for the Arthurian scholar, Gildas doesn't mention Arthur at all.

Nothing significant by any other contemporary writer survives, apart from a few church writings which tell us virtually nothing about the state of Britain. Even the surviving text of Gildas's work dates from the eleventh century, five hundred years after he wrote it. The same is true for other surviving texts, especially the Welsh Annals and the Anglo-Saxon Chronicle, as the copies we have were created several centuries later from long-lost sources. No matter how diligent the copyists were, mistakes could have crept in – in fact, some mistakes are all too obvious, as we shall see.

Then there is the problem of names – both personal and place names. Any individual could be known by a title, a personal name or a nickname. For instance, the name of the British king Vortigern is possibly not a name at all but a title meaning High King. Likewise the names of the Saxon chieftains, Hengist and Horsa, were probably nicknames; both names mean horse (or, more precisely in Hengist's case, stallion). This is more common than you might think. "Genghis Khan" was actually a title meaning "very mighty ruler"; the great Mongol ruler's real name was Temujin. Perhaps the same happened with Arthur. It's fine if we know the alternative names and titles for people, but hopeless if we don't. How do we know when we come across a new name that it isn't someone we already know? In the time of Arthur and in later writings about his period, the name could be recorded in Celtic (both British and the later Welsh variant), Latin or Anglo-Saxon. If these variants are also used for titles, real names and nicknames, then it means one individual could be called by nine different names, and that doesn't allow for misspellings, copyists' errors or mistaken identity. The same applies to place names, which are further complicated by their having evolved over time, and by many places throughout Britain having the same name. Just think how many rivers are called Avon or towns called Newtown. If original Celtic or local names have died out and been superseded by Saxon or Norman names, and no documentation survives to identify the place, then tracking it down is as likely as winning the lottery.

The biggest problem is one of dates. The method of recording years from the birth of Christ may seem simple today, but it wasn't in the fifth century and had only really been introduced a few decades before. Copyists trying to update records from ancient documents encountered several problems. Firstly, they could not be sure whether the year recorded was calculated from the birth of Christ or from his baptism, usually treated as twenty-eight years later, or from his death and resurrection, variously thirty-three or thirty-five years later. Thus a year recorded as, say, 460 years from the "incarnation" of Christ could, by our reckoning, be 432, 427 or 425.

Some annals recorded events on an Easter cycle. The dates for Easter more or less repeat themselves every nineteen years. But it was entirely possible, if working from an incomplete manuscript, to lose track of which Easter cycle was being covered. The copyist would use his best judgement, but could be out by 19 years. This is certainly evident in early entries in the Anglo-Saxon Chronicle, as we shall see.

Finally, the copyist might simply misread a figure, especially if working from a crumpled or charred document all but destroyed in a Viking raid. Years were usually recorded in Roman numerals, but it's easy to make a mistake, copying *ccclxviii* (368), for example, as, perhaps, *ccclxxiv* (374). Once the mistake is made and the original lost, who is there to correct it?

This problem about dates, which will keep resurfacing, is crucial to identifying Arthur, because we need to know when he lived and how his life related to other events. Imagine a future historian trying to understand events if the outbreak of World War II were placed 28 years earlier, in 1911, or 28 years later in 1967? How could you possibly relate it to individuals' lives?

The events of the fifth century were every bit as critical to those living then as World War II is to us. The Roman Empire, which had existed for over 400 years, was crumbling and so-called "barbarians" were taking over Europe. To individuals at that time the world was collapsing about them and chaos reigned. To help us interpret it and get back to what really happened, we need to understand the complete history and geography of those times. The secret to identifying Arthur is to find the right name in the right place at the right time, and it's those three criteria which we need to tackle at the start of this book.

Where do we start?

The search for the real Arthur – and the legendary one – will take us through a mass of material, some of it detailed and much of it complicated. Piecing together the Arthurian world is like trying to complete a jigsaw in which a lot of the pieces are missing. Many of those that remain may have only a partial picture, some may have the picture re-drawn, and some belong to another jigsaw entirely. We have to look at each piece in detail and see what it is, whether it fits and, if so, where it fits.

First, let's start by looking at the big picture. It will help us keep things in perspective and give us a framework within which to fit the pieces.

If we are to find the real Arthur, we need to look somewhere in the two hundred years between the end of Roman administration of Britain, a date usually assigned as 410AD, and the emergence of the Saxon kingdoms, which were taking a strong hold by the start of the seventh century.

The general history of those two centuries can be described fairly easily, and that is our big picture. After the passing of Roman authority Britain sank into a period of decline. There were civil unrest, plague and famine, and Britain – i.e., the territory south of Hadrian's Wall – was constantly under threat of invasion by Germanic forces from the east, the Irish (Scotii) from the west and the Picts from the north. By the middle of the fifth century the Saxons and other tribes had gained a hold on territory in the east, and progressively, over the next hundred years or so, infiltrated Britain, pushing the British nobility west, primarily into Wales and Cornwall, and Brittany. The British, though weakened by their own strife, put up a resistance under various leaders. One Briton in particular managed to defeat the Saxons so significantly at Badon, sometime towards the end of the fifth century, that the Saxon advance was halted. For a period of at least twenty-five years the British held their ground, and the Saxons did not advance further for at least a generation. From the middle of the sixth century, the Saxons advanced again and – presumably after the death of Arthur – began to win territory in the west. After a series of battles in the west (Dyrham in 577 and Chester in 615) and the north, the British were divided. Soon after 600 the powerful warlord Athelfrith established his own kingdom of Northumbria, stretching across northern Britain. The heartland of Britain, where a few Celtic enclaves struggled on, was also crushed by the Northumbrians and the next wave of Angles, who created the kingdom of Mercia under Penda. By 625, the territory later to be called England was under Saxon control.

During these two hundred years several British kingdoms emerged. We know some better than others, depending on what records have survived. Perhaps not surprisingly, the best known were those in Wales, which survived beyond the Arthurian age and well into the Middle Ages. The major kingdoms were Gwynedd (originally called Venedotia) in the north, Powys along the Welsh Marches, Dyfed (originally Demetia) in the south-west and Gwent in the south-east. There were several smaller Welsh kingdoms, such as Ceredigion, Builth and Brycheiniog, all of which will feature in our explorations, but the history of Wales is really the history of those four main kingdoms.

In the south-west of Britain was the kingdom of Dumnonia, primarily Devon and Cornwall but also, for much of the fifth century, covering parts of Dorset and Somerset.

There were also several kingdoms in the north. The Scottish Highlands remained the domain of the Picts, but between Hadrian's Wall and the Antonine Wall further north there were three main British kingdoms: the Gododdin (originally called the Votadini) in the east, with centres at Traprain Law and Din Eityn (Edinburgh), Strathclyde (originally Alclud) in the west, with its centre at Dumbarton, and Galloway in the south-west. At some stage Galloway seems to have become part of the kingdom of Rheged, which at its height stretched from Galloway, down through Cumbria and into Lancashire, probably as far as Chester, and thus bordering onto Gwynedd and Powys.

These were the main Celtic kingdoms to survive through the Dark Ages. There were further kingdoms in the east of Britain, but we know much less about these, because they were the first to be overrun by the Saxons and the cultures soon merged. The main eastern kingdom in the north was York (originally Ebrauc). To the north of York was Bryneich, in Northumbria; to the south was Lindsey (originally Linnuis), which covered much of Lincolnshire and Norfolk. To the west of Lindsey was Elmet, based around Leeds, one of the last British kingdoms to survive in England. There were other smaller kingdoms north of Elmet, in the Pennines, one of which will prove of some interest to us, but no formal record of them survives.

To the south was a kingdom stretching from London into Essex and parts of Suffolk. There was also a kingdom in Kent, though this hardly seems to have started before it was snuffed out. Beyond these it is probable that there were kingdoms based

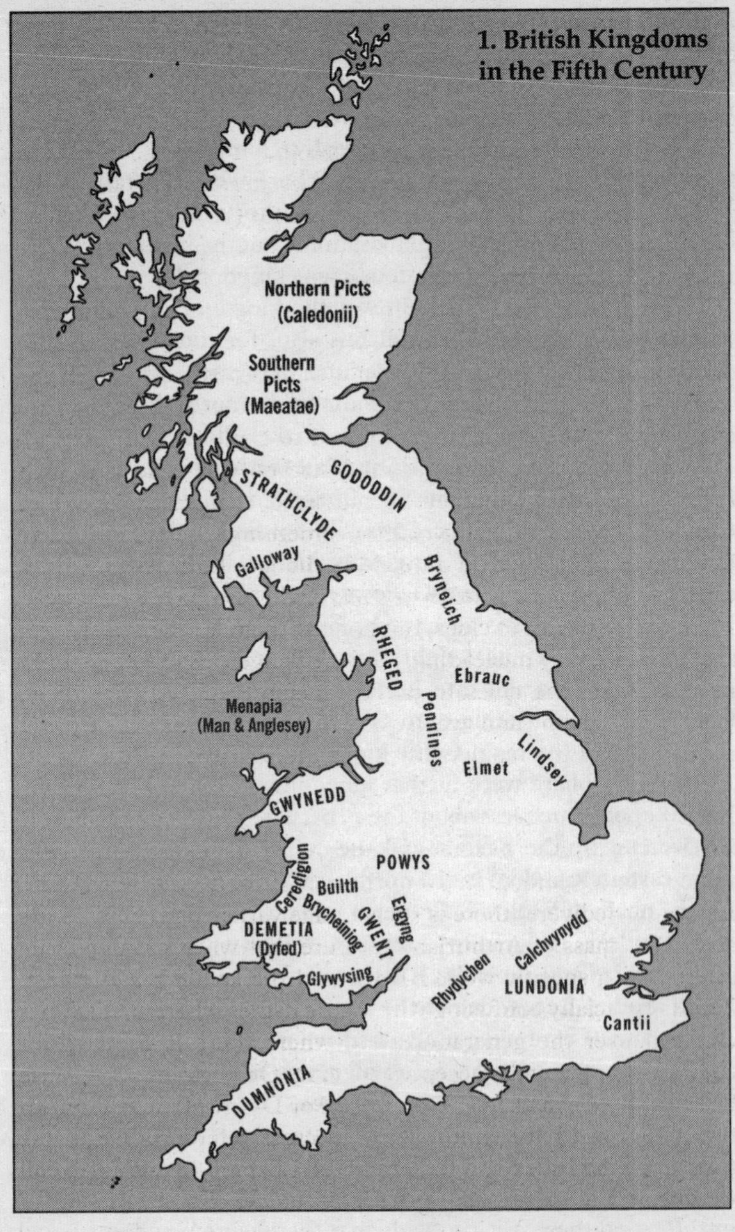
1. British Kingdoms in the Fifth Century
Northern Picts
(Caledonii)
Southern
Picts
(Maeatae)
GODODDIN
STRATHCLYDE
Galloway
Bryneich
RHEGED
Ebrauc
Menapia
(Man & Anglesey)
Pennines
Lindsey
Elmet
GWYNEDD
Ceredigion
POWYS
Builth
Brycheiniog
Ergyng
GWENT
DEMETIA
(Dyfed)
Calchvynydd
Glywysing
Rhydychen
LUNDONIA
Cantii
DUMNONIA

in the Chilterns, Oxford, Gloucester, Sussex and so on. The map opposite shows the approximate location of these kingdoms, but we do not know for certain their extent. Their boundaries remained fluid depending on the individual warlord's power.

The importance of these kingdoms is that if Arthur really was a king, then he must have ruled one of these territories. Not all the pedigrees survive; the best preserved are for the Welsh kingdoms and those of the North. We do not know the names of any of the rulers of London, for instance, and even the one name for a ruler of Kent is somewhat dubious. We will encounter several people with a name like Arthur in the pedigrees, all of whom I outline in the first chapter, but whether any of them is the real Arthur, or whether the real Arthur was a composite of them or of any other characters, is something that we need to explore.

At this stage we can think of Arthur solely as a British resistance leader. Whether he mustered that resistance from Cornwall, Wales or the North is something else we will have to consider. Whether he did this in the late fifth or early sixth century, or perhaps another time, we will also have to deduce.

There are plenty of clues, but none of them is straightforward, and some are very misleading. And it's dangerous to leap straight in and expect the clues to declare themselves. We have to go looking for them, and we have to go armed with some basic information. First we need to consider the name Arthur itself.

Note on Spelling

Whilst I have tried to retain a consistent and generally recognizable form of spelling for all of the names used (e.g. Guenevere, Lancelot, Bedivere) there is such a huge variance in these names across the mass of Arthurian literature that when citing a character from a specific work I have used the spelling used there. This is especially confusing with Celtic names where spelling has changed over the generations and where there is not really a consistent or generally accepted spelling. On occasions I may use both forms of names (e.g. Dumnagual or Dyfnwal) depending on the source but have endeavoured to cross reference within the text. Both the Index and the entries in Chapter 23 and 24 list all variants.

SECTION 1

THE HISTORICAL ARTHUR

1

AN INTRODUCTION TO ARTHUR – WHAT'S IN A NAME?

1. Myth, History and Mystery

You will find in the course of this book that we encounter several Arthurs. There's not just one Arthur of legend, for a start, and there's certainly not one Arthur of history.

The Arthur we remember from our childhood reading is, for the most part, a fiction. Most of us know the basic legend from Sir Thomas Malory's *Morte Darthur*. Arthur was born of a deceitful relationship. With the help of the magician Merlin, Arthur's father Uther Pendragon, king of Britain, was able to take on the guise of Gorlois, duke of Cornwall, and seduce Gorlois' wife Ygraine. After Uther's death, there was a contest to find the next king, who would be the one who could pull the sword out of the stone. All the champions and dukes tried and failed but young Arthur, still only fifteen, succeeded. Not all of the dukes and other rulers were happy about this, and Arthur had to fight for his kingdom. But he won and, for a while, ruled happily and wisely. Thanks to Merlin, Arthur acquired the sword Excalibur from the Lady of the Lake, the scabbard of which protected him from harm. He established the Round Table of brave and valorous knights, including Sir Kay, Sir Bedivere, Sir Gawain, Sir Bors, Sir Tristram and, of course, Sir Lancelot. We learn of the adventures of these knights, saving damsels and fighting villains, and we follow the quest for the Holy Grail. But there is a dark side. Arthur's queen, Guenevere, fell in love with her champion, Lancelot, and those knights who disliked Lancelot plotted against him. These included Arthur's illegitimate son Sir Mordred, whose mother, Margawse, was the wife of King Lot of Orkney and Arthur's half-sister. Mordred, caught up in the scheming of other knights, especially Sir Agravaine, revealed the truth about Lancelot to Arthur, and Guenevere was sentenced to burn at the stake. She was rescued by Lancelot, but in the fracas Gawain's brothers were killed. Lancelot exiled himself to France, but Arthur, urged on by Gawain, followed, allowing Mordred to usurp the kingdom. Arthur returned to do battle with Mordred and was mortally wounded at the battle of Camlann. The heroes of the Round Table not already killed in the war with Lancelot lay dead, all but Bedivere who returned Arthur's sword to the Lady of the Lake. Arthur was taken to the Isle of Avalon where his wounds would be cured, and one day he will return. Thus he is remembered as the Once and Future King.

That, in a nutshell, is how we remember Arthur.

Myth? Well, mostly. History? Well . . .

Malory took this story from earlier accounts, mostly from the so-called *Vulgate Cycle*, which drew on the work of Chrétien de Troyes. Chrétien got his stories from local tales and legends in France and Brittany, including some of the Welsh tales later collected under the title *The Mabinogion*. It was Chrétien who invented the name Camelot and created the character of Lancelot. In his stories we find much of the original of Malory's Arthur, but his sources, the Welsh tales, portray a different, earlier Arthur, an Arthur of legend, far removed from the world of Plantagenet chivalry. This Arthur's world is still one of fantasy and magic, but beneath that surface is a sense of history. The Celtic Arthur feels as if he really belonged in his own time, unlike Malory's Arthur who is rooted in a contemporary Britain ravaged by plague and war.

But there is yet another Arthur of legend, the creation of Geoffrey of Monmouth. Three hundred years before Malory, Geoffrey set out to write (or, according to him, translate) a history of Britain from a mysterious and ancient book. The result, the *Historia Regum Britanniae* (*The History of the Kings of Britain*), contains a huge section on the exploits of King Arthur, which proved so popular that Geoffrey's *History* became a medieval best-seller. It was Geoffrey who created the fascination with Arthur and who created most of the myth, though his story differs in certain parts from Malory's later version and significantly from the Welsh tales. Yet both Geoffrey's and the Welsh Arthurs have some basis in history. Or at least a memory of history.

Geoffrey also had his sources. These included Nennius, a ninth-century collector of old documents and chronicles, and a sixth-century monk called Gildas. Both writers furnish some historical background to the story. Nennius provides a list of Arthur's battles whilst Gildas, without naming Arthur, refers to the most famous battle associated with him, Badon, and mentions Arthur's illustrious predecessor Ambrosius Aurelianus. When you dig around other ancient documents, like the Welsh Triads and the *Welsh Annals* (*Annales Cambriae*), and the various pedigrees of the ancient British kings, you find further references to Arthur.

Now you feel that you've moved out of legend into history, but Arthur doesn't quite fit into this history. A chronology proves difficult. By all accounts the original Arthur, that is, Arthur of Badon, ought to be living in the period between 490 and 520, but he's difficult to find there. The *Welsh Annals* place him a little later, around 510–540, but he's difficult to find there as well. Historical Arthurs pop up in the period 540–620, but these dates are too late for Badon. Does that mean that these later Arthurs became credited with the exploits of an earlier hero? Or does it mean that the chronology is all wrong and that these events happened a century later? Or does it mean that these exploits were really by a number of people spread over a much longer period of time?

That's what we need to unravel.

2. The Historical Arthurs

You will encounter several Arthurs in this book and rather than introduce them one by one, which becomes confusing, I'll mention them now so you'll know who they are when they appear and how I shall refer to them.

(1) Lucius Artorius Castus, the Roman Arthur, who lived from about 140–197AD.

(2) Arthwys ap Mar, sometimes called Arthur of the Pennines, who lived around 460–520.

(3) Artúir ap Pedr, known as Arthur of Dyfed, who lived around 550–620.

(4) Artúir mac Aedan, prince of Dál Riata, who lived around 560–596, but who never survived to become king.

(5) Athrwys ap Meurig, known as Arthur of Gwent, who lived around 610–680 by my calculations, but is given an earlier date by others. He may be the Arthur of the *Mabinogion*.

(6) Arthfoddw of Ceredigion, or Arth the Lucky, who lived about 550–620.

(7) Artúir ap Bicor, the Arthur of Kintyre, who also lived about 550–620.

(8) Armel or Arthmael, the warrior saint, who lived about 540–600.

(9) Arzur, the Arthur of Brittany, who may or may not be the same as,

(10) Riothamus, or Rigotamus, a military leader in Brittany last heard of in 470.

These are not the only contenders, but they are the primary ones called Arthur. As we explore the many old documents and pedigrees I shall frequently refer to these names as well as, of course, the original Arthur of Badon, who may be one, some or all of the above.

3. The name of Arthur

Much is made of Arthur's name, one argument being that there was a sudden flush of people in the late sixth century being named Arthur after some hero of the previous generation or two. In fact Arthur isn't that uncommon a name and it has its origins in two primary sources.

First and foremost, it is an Irish name, Artúr, derived from the common name Art, meaning "bear", which is well known from the Irish ruler, Art the Solitary, son of Conn of a Hundred Battles, and his son, the more famous Cormac mac Art, High King from 254–277. There are several diminutives (Artan, Artúr, Artúir), and these names passed into Wales with the Irish settlers during the fourth and fifth centuries. These were descendants of

Art Corb, or Artchorp, the ancestor of the Déisi, a tribe who were exiled from Ireland and settled in Demetia, now Dyfed, in west Wales, and include the Artúir ap Pedr listed above. Other Irish, from the Dál Riatan kingdom in Ulster, settled in Kintyre and Argyll at around the same time, and Artúir mac Aedan is descended from them.

The other source is the Roman family name Artorius. It is not certain when or from where this family originated, but it may well have been Greece. The earliest known member was Marcus Artorius Asclepiades, physician to Octavian, the future Caesar Augustus. The Artorii lived in Campania in Italy, but also occupied southern Gaul and Spain. Apart from Lucius Artorius Castus, they seem to have had little impact in Britain, but the memory of his name may have lingered on, becoming adopted by the Celtic tribes in Gaul and gradually leeching into Britain. The name would have evolved to Arturius, and then to Artur, and would more likely have been used within the highly Romanised parts of southern Britain than in Wales or the North, where the name more probably came from the Irish.

There may be other sources. One is Artaius, a minor Romano-Celtic deity rather like Mercury, whose cult may have helped popularise a form of the name. Another slightly more tortuous derivation may be based on the Celtic for High King, *Ardd Ri*. The Brythonic *dd* is pronounced *th*, so that the title, pronounced *Arth-ri*, may later have been remembered as a name.

There is, though, a danger in looking at any name beginning with "Art" and assuming it has some Arthurian connection. It doesn't, and in any contemporary documents would otherwise be ignored, just as we would not confuse Tony with Tonto or George with Geoffrey. But we can't ignore the possibility that scribes working from inferior documents several centuries after the event might have misread, misinterpreted or miscopied names, so that an Arthwyr – a name which means "grandson of Arth" – became Arthur. The excitement in the press in 1998 over the discovery of a stone at Tintagel bearing the name Artognou, is a case in point. Artognou means "descendant of Art" and has no direct connection with Arthur, but because it was found at Tintagel, there was an immediate assumption that the two had to be connected.

Our quest is to find an Arthur whose credentials fit as much of the history as we know. In order to understand the world of Arthur, we have to understand the state of Britain from the arrival of the Romans, five hundred years before. So let us first explore Roman Britain and see what it has to tell us about the Arthurian world that followed.

2

BEFORE ARTHUR – THE ROMAN BACKGROUND

1. The First Empire

When Julius Caesar took his first tentative and rather wet steps into Britain in 55BC, he learned that the native British were a challenging foe. He later wrote that there were separate tribal states in Britain between which there had been almost "continual warfare", but in order to oppose the Roman forces most of the states had united behind one king, the powerful Cassivelaunos, or Caswallon. Caesar eventually got the measure of the Britons, but his incursion into Britain was little more than that, and by no means a conquest. It would be nearly a hundred years before the emperor Claudius headed a successful invasion of Britain in 43AD and brought the island into the Roman Empire.

Even so, Britain remained an outpost. No one from Rome wanted to go there. It had a cold and forbidding reputation even though, by the second and third centuries, it had become a prosperous part of the empire, supplying much of the grain for Rome. Those Romans who did live in Britain attained heights of luxury, although, in truth, they were Romans only by name. They were, for the most part, Britons, although continuing to aspire to the aristocratic lifestyle of the Romans, and remaining loyal to Rome. This siding with Rome was evident even in Caesar's day. Mandubracius, son of the king of the Trinovantes, promised to give Caesar inside information to help the invasion. Likewise Cogidubnus, because of the aid he had given the Romans, became a client king and received the tribal territory of the Regnii in Hampshire, together with a magnificent palace at what is now Fishbourne, near Chichester. Cogidubnus was a shining example of the benefit of working with the Romans.

Other sympathetic tribal leaders included Prasutagus, ruler of the Iceni, and Cartimandua, queen of the Brigantes. Both retained their power and territory in return for aiding Rome. Cartimandua even turned over to Rome the rebel leader Caratacus, who had sustained a guerrilla-style opposition to the imperial forces for seven years.

Prasutagus may not be so well known today, but his wife certainly is. She was Boudicca (or Boadicea), who, because of her treatment by the Romans after her husband's death, led a revolt, catching them unawares and destroying Colchester and London. But she was unable to defeat the might of the main Roman army under Suetonius Paulinus and died, probably by her own hand, in 61AD.

After Boudicca's revolt the process of Roman colonization continued but it was never simple and never straightforward. For a start, the Romans never got a firm grip on Scotland, despite the defeat of the chieftain Calgacus of the Caledonii in 84AD. In 122AD, the emperor Hadrian commissioned the construction of a wall across northern Britain, from the Solway Firth in the west to what is now Wallsend in the east. It contained the northern frontier, and recognized that it was not worth the effort to try and defeat the tribes to the north – the tribes that came to be known collectively as the Picts.

Roman occupation of Wales was also rather limited, and there was not the same civic development as in England. The Roman towns were mostly in the south, and Wales was held under control by several powerful forts. Relationships were not helped by the attempts of Suetonius Paulinus to annihilate the Druids in their retreat on the island of Anglesey, only halted by Paulinus being called to deal with Boudicca's revolt.

The rebellious nature of the British was one of the few facts known to the Romans at the core of the empire. Writing at the time that Claudius was planning his invasion, Pomponius Mela, who lived in southern Spain and probably knew the British, wrote in *De Chorographia* (43AD):

> It has peoples and kings of peoples, but they are all uncivilised and the further they are from the continent the less they know of other kinds of wealth, being rich only in herds and lands . . . Nevertheless, they find occasions for wars and do fight them and often attack each other, mostly from a wish for domination and a desire to carry off what they possess.

Tacitus, writing in 98AD about the campaigns of his father-in-law Agricola, saw these internecine struggles as an advantage:

> Once they paid obedience to kings, but now they are divided by warring factions among their leading men. Nothing has been more helpful to us in dealing with these powerful tribes than the fact that they do not co-operate. Seldom is there a combination of two or three states to repel a common danger; so, fighting separately, all are defeated.

This inability of tribes to live in harmony will re-emerge as a major factor in the Arthurian world. The number of hill forts throughout Britain is a testimony to how often the tribes fought each other, resulting in a need to build defences. Tacitus also recognised the impact upon the British of Roman civilization. Comparing the British to the Gauls in his *Life of Agricola*, he wrote:

> . . . the *Britanni* display more fierceness, seeing that they have not been softened by protracted peace. For we know that the Gauls were once distinguished in warfare, but later sloth came in with ease and valour was lost with liberty. The same thing has happened to those [southern] *Britanni* who were conquered early; the rest remain what the Gauls once were.

This was the first recognition of a North-South divide in Britain.

There were over twenty different tribes in Britain. The Romans used the tribal divisions as the bases for their *civitates*, mostly in what is now England, each of which had a capital town. There were sixteen in total, mostly established within a century of the invasion in 43AD. These towns remained throughout the Roman occupation and into the early post-Roman period, and because they are relevant to the Arthurian story, it's worth noting them here. The following table lists them in sequence, from the southern coast of Britain rising north.

These *civitas* capitals were rather like present day county towns. They were essentially self-governing, run by elected magistrates. Although all too few of these magistrates' names survive, it is entirely likely that they came from the ruling families of the tribes and that the pre-Roman mini-kingdoms effectively continued, now reconstituted in Roman form (*see* Map 2).

Table 2.1. The Roman Civitas

Tribe (Civitas)	*Capital*	*Present-day name*
Cantii (*Cantiacorum*)	Durovernum	Canterbury (*Kent*)
Regnii (*Reginorum*)	Noviomagus	Chichester (*West Sussex*)
Belgae (*Belgarum*)	Venta Belgarum	Winchester (*Hampshire*)
Atrebates (*Atrebatum*)	Calleva	Silchester (*Hampshire*)
Durotriges (*Durotrigum*)	Durnovaria	Dorchester (*Dorset*)
Dumnonii (*Dumnoniorum*)	Isca	Exeter (*Devon*)
Trinovantes (*Trinovantium*)	Caesaromagus	Chelmsford (*Essex*)
Catuvellauni (*Catuvellaunorum*)	Verulamium	St. Albans (*Hertfordshire*)
Dobunni (*Dobunnorum*)	Corinium	Cirencester (*Gloucestershire*)
Silures (*Silurum*)	Venta Silurum	Caerwent (*Monmouth*)
Demetae (*Demetarum*)	Moridunum	Carmarthen (*Carmarthenshire*)
Cornovii (*Cornoviorum*)	Viriconium	Wroxeter (*Shropshire*)
Iceni (*Icenorum*)	Venta Icenorum	Caistor St. Edmund (*Norfolk*)
Coritani (*Coritanorum*)	Ratae	Leicester (*Leicestershire*)
Parisii (*Parisorum*)	Petuaria	Brough-on-Humber (*Yorkshire*)
Brigantes (*Brigantium*)	Isurium	Aldborough (*Yorkshire*)

The capitals were not the only important towns in Roman Britain. Of more significance were the *coloniae*. Initially these were independent towns with their own surrounding territory (separate from the *civitates*) and city council, occupied only by Roman citizens, usually retired soldiers and administrators. There were originally three *coloniae*: Camulodunum (Colchester), Lindum (Lincoln) and Glevum (Gloucester). Eboracum (York), one of the most important cities in Roman Britain, was later granted the status of *colonia* by the emperor Septimius Severus, who used it as his imperial capital from 208 until his death in 211, while he was involved in campaigns against the northern tribes.

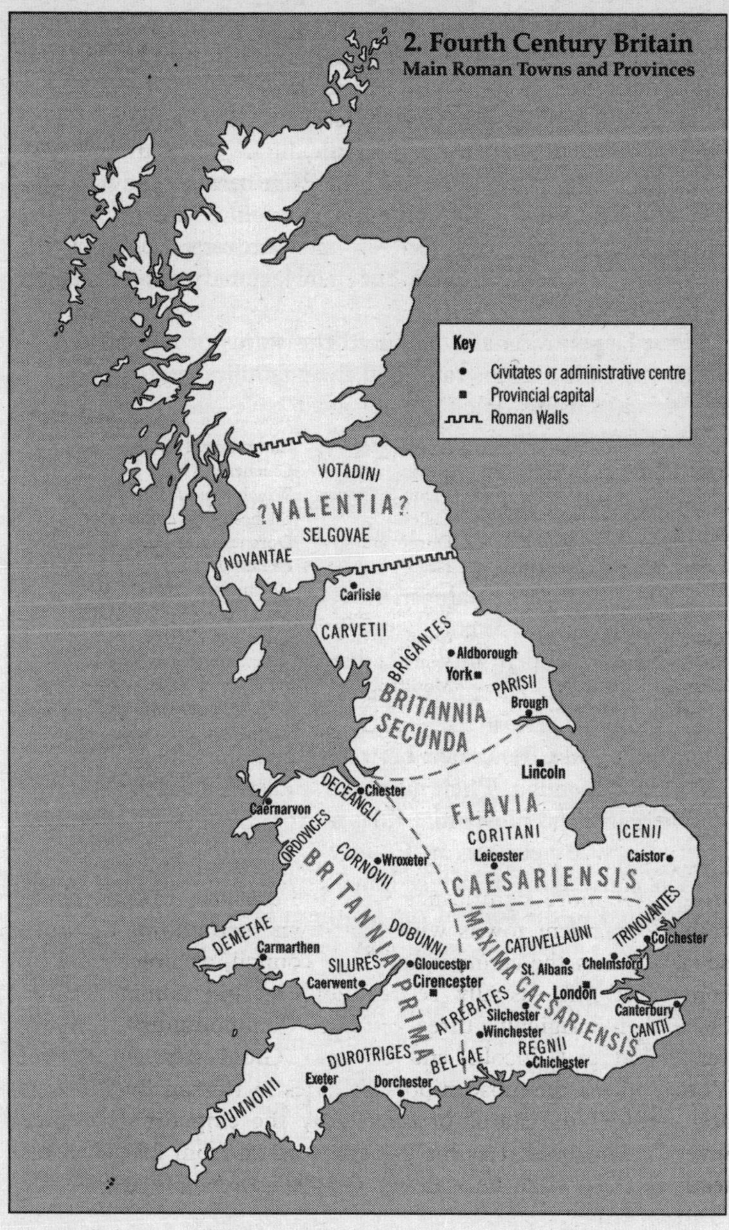
2. Fourth Century Britain
Main Roman Towns and Provinces
Key
Civitates or administrative centre
Provincial capital
Roman Walls
VOTADINI
?VALENTIA?
SELGOVAE
NOVANTAE
Carlisle
CARVETII
BRIGANTES
Aldborough
York
PARISII
Brough
BRITANNIA SECUNDA
Lincoln
DECEANGLI
Chester
Caernarvon
ORDOVICES
F.LAVIA
CORITANI
ICENII
Leicester
Caistor
CORNOVII
Wroxeter
BRITANNIA PRIMA
CAESARIENSIS
DEMETAE
Carmarthen
DOBUNNI
MAXIMA CAESARIENSIS
CATUVELLAUNI
TRINOVANTES
Colchester
SILURES
Gloucester
St. Albans
Chelmsford
Caerwent
Cirencester
London
ATREBATES
Silchester
Canterbury
CANTII
Winchester
REGNII
DUROTRIGES
BELGAE
Chichester
Exeter
Dorchester
DUMNONII

York had been one of the three legionary fortresses at the start of the Roman occupation. It was home first to the IX Hispana Legion and then, from around 122, to the VI Victrix Legion. The other two fortresses were Isca (Caerleon), the home of the II Augustan Legion, and Deva (Chester) home, from around 87AD onwards, of the XX Valeria Victrix. Each became known as the City of the Legion. Before becoming a *colonia*, Lincoln had also briefly been a legionary fort, as had Wroxeter before it was developed as a *civitas* capital, but their legionary days were over by around 87AD.

Some large towns also acquired the status of *municipium*, in which the ruling magistrates and their families were all granted Roman citizenship. Each *colonia* must have been a *municipium* before rising in status. It is known that Verulamium (St. Albans) was later granted this status, and it is likely that Londinium (London) and Venta Belgarum (Winchester) were similarly rewarded. There were other smaller towns and forts, but those listed above were the primary centres of Roman Britain. They gave their occupants a status in the Roman world, although not all freeborn Britons were automatically granted Roman citizenship (that did not happen until 212, during the reign of Caracalla).

There were also countless villas dotted around the countryside. The majority were in the south, with concentrations around Gloucester and Cirencester, between Silchester and Winchester, and around London. Their number rapidly thinned to the north, and there were no substantial villas north of Vinovium, a fort near what is now Binchester, in County Durham. These villas, the Roman equivalent of stately homes, were also working farms, more suited to the soils of the southern lowlands.

North of Vinovia was essentially a military zone, running up to Hadrian's Wall and beyond to the Antonine Wall, an earth rampart with a series of forts built between the Forth and the Clyde. An advance under emperor Antoninus Pius in 139 was maintained for barely twenty years, and after Pius's death in 161 there was an effective withdrawal to Hadrian's Wall.

Between the walls lay the Scottish lowlands, inhabited by three major tribes (four if you count the Damnonii who lived in the area of what is now Glasgow). To the east were the Votadini, whose territory stretched from what is now Edinburgh down as far as

Newcastle. To the west, in the area of Galloway, were the Novantae. In the centre, inhabiting the vast wooded uplands, were the Selgovae. The Romans never conquered these tribes, but did reach a peace with the more amenable Votadini. The largest forts that the Romans established in the Scottish lowlands, at Bremenium (High Rochester) and Trimontium (Galashiels) were in the territory of the Votadini, and were as much to protect the Votadini as to serve the Roman advance.

Further north, beyond the Antonine Wall, was the heartland of the peoples who were to become known as the Picts. Writing at the start of the third century, the Roman historian and governor Cassius Dio recognised two main groupings of tribes: the Caledonii, far to the north, and the Mæatae, or Miathi, a confederation of Pictish tribes who lived just north of the Antonine Wall, near Stirling. In fact, both the Caledonii and Mæatae were confederations of tribes who united against the Romans, and in time they came to be ruled by separate Pictish kings.

There were many fortresses along Hadrian's Wall, and at the western end was the fortress town of Luguvalium (Carlisle). In later years this was raised to the status of a capital of the *civitas* of Carvetiorum, the homeland of the Carvetii tribe, an offshoot of the Brigantes. Luguvalium remained a military town, and was the largest of any administrative significance in northern Britain.

All of these towns, fortresses and villas were linked by a system of roads that remains the basis for the country's existing network, fourteen centuries later (*see* Map 3). The roads were kept in good repair by the army, certainly into the fourth century, and would still have been in good condition in Arthur's day. They were essential for Arthur's forces (and those of other war leaders) in moving quickly across country. The Romans regarded a day's steady march as twenty miles and as a consequence staging posts and refreshment establishments appeared at roughly twenty-mile intervals along all of the major routes. These did not vanish overnight at the end of the Roman era. As archaeology is still rediscovering, Britain was a thriving society throughout the Roman period and it was not until some time afterwards that the major towns were abandoned and the native Britons returned to their hill forts and encampments.

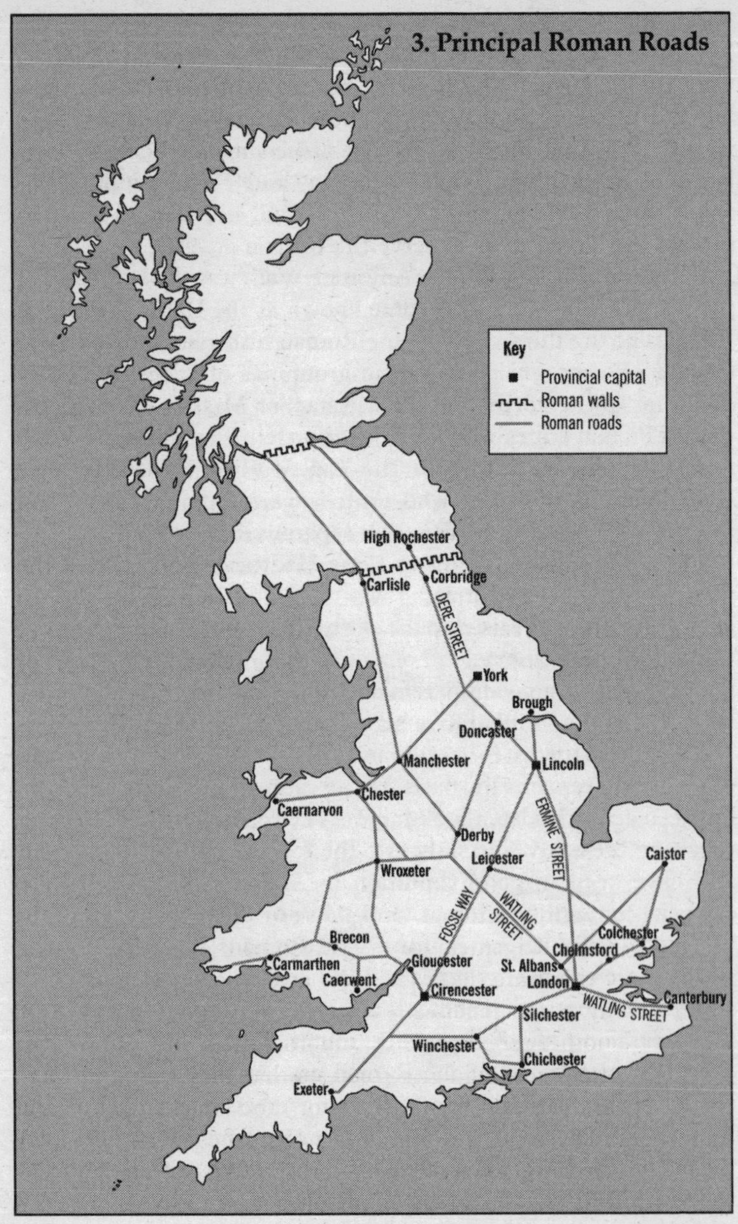
3. Principal Roman Roads
Key
Provincial capital
Roman walls
Roman roads
High Rochester
Carlisle
Corbridge
DERE STREET
York
Brough
Doncaster
Manchester
Lincoln
Chester
Caernarvon
ERMINE STREET
Derby
Leicester
Caistor
Wroxeter
FOSSE WAY
WATLING STREET
Brecon
Colchester
Chelmsford
Carmarthen
Gloucester
St. Albans
Caerwent
London
Cirencester
Canterbury
WATLING STREET
Silchester
Winchester
Chichester
Exeter

2. The first Arthur?

Despite the Romans having stamped their authority on Britain, the undercurrent of rebellion was always there. After the Boudiccan revolt, the southern tribes learned to adapt to the Roman way of life, recognising the benefits, though that did not mean that they lost their individual identity. The creation of the *civitas* perpetuated the original tribal structure, and this remained throughout the Roman occupation.

The northern tribes were less compliant. Hadrian's Wall was built as much to separate the north's two main troublemakers, the Brigantes and the Selgovae, as it was to contain the Empire. It was almost certainly at this time that the Brigantian *civitas* was created, with the capital at Isurium. At the same time a more extensive network of forts was developed in the west, suggesting that although the eastern Brigantes were calming down, the western Brigantes remained less trustworthy. Amongst these forts was Bremetennacum, modern-day Ribchester, which was significantly developed at the start of the second century. Over the next hundred years or so a large civilian settlement developed around the fort, making it a town of some note.

When the Roman forces moved north to man the Antonine Wall, with the inevitable reduction in troops along Hadrian's Wall, the equally inevitable rebellion happened. Although evidence is thin, it looks as if the western Brigantes, perhaps in a concerted action with the Selgovae, rose up against the Romans in 154AD, with widespread destruction, so that troops came back from the Antonine Wall and a new governor, Julius Verus, was brought in with additional troops. Verus regained control by 158AD, and the Brigantes were deprived of their *civitas*. It was probably at this time that the *civitas* at Carlisle was created.

An uneasy peace remained. A generation later, around 183, there was another rebellion, this time from the tribes north of the wall. Archaeological evidence suggests that they broke through the wall near the fort of Onnum (Halton) and attacked the forts at Cilurnum (Chesters) and Vindobala (Rudchester), their army probably marching down the Roman road of Dere Street, attacking Coriosopitum (Corbridge). Just how far south they reached is not clear. There's some suggestion they may have reached York.

Cassius Dio reported that they "did a great amount of damage, even cutting down a general together with his troops." David Breeze, in *The Northern Frontiers of Roman Britain*, has suggested that the officer killed may have been a legate from York, or a provincial governor. It may be pertinent that the term of office of the governor, Quintus Antistius Adventus, ceased in 183, suggesting that he was either recalled to face the wrath of the emperor Commodus or was killed.

A new governor, Lucius Ulpius Marcellus, who had served in Britain ten years earlier, was despatched to Britain. Commodus must have felt it was important to have a man who knew the territory and was noted for his discipline and severity. According to Cassius Dio, Marcellus was "a temperate and frugal man and when on active service lived like a soldier . . . but he was becoming haughty and arrogant." Apparently Marcellus needed little sleep and was forever issuing commands and orders, ensuring that his soldiers also slept little. So although he might have endeared himself to some, he must have made many enemies. He inflicted major defeats on the Picts, but the soldiers were in disarray, and Marcellus was recalled. A new governor, Publius Helvius Pertinax, was sent to Britain in 185 to sort out the mess.

The army may not have rebelled solely against Marcellus. In Rome, Commodus, alarmed by an assassination attempt, had withdrawn into his palace, leaving the government of the Empire to one of his favourites, Perennis, who instituted a number of unfavourable changes. The last straw seems to have been his meddling with the command structure of the legionary forces, replacing the senatorial command with one of lesser rank, called equestrians, similar to senior civil servants. This was so unpopular that the British army took the unprecedented measure of sending a deputation of 1,500 men to Rome in 185. Their ploy was to warn Commodus of another assassination attempt, this time by Perennis. It worked. Perennis was executed and it was then that Pertinax was sent to Britain to satisfy the troops.

Pertinax could be as severe as Marcellus, and the army mutinied against him, leaving him for dead. He recovered, however, and dealt with the army "with signal severity", as one chronicler recorded. Although he quelled the mutiny, Pertinax never gained the full respect of the army, even though they wanted him as their next candidate for emperor. Pertinax refused and after two or three years of an uneasy relationship between him and the army, he asked to be relieved of his duties, and became governor of Africa. When Pertinax was governor of Britain, a conflict erupted in Armorica (Brittany). Pertinax turned to a soldier who has since been swept into the debate as a possible candidate for Arthur: Lucius Artorius Castus.

Lucius Artorius Castus (140–197) was prefect of four legions. When the Sarmatian tribes from Hungary invaded the empire in 170, a five-year war, in which Castus would have been involved, ensued. In 175, as part of the peace deal, 8,000 Sarmatian cavalry were handed over to serve in the Roman army. 5,500 of these were sent to Britain, and settled at Bremetennacum (Ribchester). Castus oversaw the transfer and returned to Rome, but returned to Britain in 181 as prefect of the VI Victrix Legion, based at York. Linda Malcor and C. Scott Littleton have suggested that it was Castus who led his legion, perhaps including the Sarmatian contingent, against the Caledonii in 183, chasing them back north of the border. These battles, they suggest, could equate to the series later attributed to Arthur by Nennius (*see* Chapter 7). Castus was promoted to the rank of *dux* in about 185, almost certainly as a reward for his service in Britain. After being sent back to Armorica by Pertinax in the same year for another campaign, Castus retired from the army and spent his last days as a procurator of the province of Liburnia, in Dalmatia. Malcor has speculated that Castus may have been called back from retirement by the new emperor Septimius Severus at the time of the revolt by Clodius Albinus, and may have died in battle at Lugdunum (Lyon) in 197. He would then have been about 57 years old. Castus's sarcophagus has been found at Stobrec, near Split, on the Adriatic coast.

3. The revolting British!

Over the next ten years there was an uneasy peace in Britain, but in 207 rebellion erupted again of sufficient magnitude that the emperor Septimius Severus came to Britain with his sons Caracalla and Geta. Cassius Dio records that Severus was determined to conquer the whole of Britain once and for all, but as ever the tactics of the enemy north of the wall made this impossible. Cassius Dio reports that Severus lost up to 50,000 men, which, though surely an exaggeration, shows the scale of the problem.

The campaign stretched out over three years until Severus's death in York in February 211. His son Caracalla, who had hated this enforced stay in Britain, was anxious to return to Rome to secure the transfer of power. Somehow he reached peace terms with the Caledonii. The exact nature of this is not known, but he was able to secure a handover of more territory, possibly the area of Fife, where a new fort was secured at Carpow. The area between the walls seems to have come under Roman command even if it was never formally part of the Empire. It was probably patrolled by the Votadini, who remained loyal to Rome.

Caracalla also enacted plans prepared by his father to divide Roman Britain in two. This meant there were now two governors rather than one, with less power and less troops at their command. Severus had been determined not to see a repetition of the Albinus affair. From 211 onwards Britain was divided into Britannia Superior in the south, with its capital at London, and Britannia Inferior with its capital at York. The dividing line ran from the Wash to the Dee, skirting south to avoid the Pennines. Britannia Superior was the larger area, as well as the more wealthy and peaceful, and had two legions, whereas Britannia Inferior was essentially a military zone with a minimum of settled civilian life, and had one legion augmented by many auxiliary troops. Although Caracalla has passed into history as a brutal and wayward emperor, his peace arrangements in Britain were effective, allowing Britain to develop and prosper over the next seventy years.

We can skim over the next fifty years or so, pausing only to mention that whilst Britain experienced a period of unusual calm, the rest of the Roman empire was plunged into turbulence with a succession of minor and short-lived emperors. During this period there was an off-shoot Gallic Empire, which included France and Britain, and which lasted from 260–274. A brief stability was restored under the dual control of Diocletian and Maximian, from 285, but soon after the Empire faced another rebel who used Britain as his base. This was Carausius.

During the third century, and especially from 260 onwards, the

Roman borders became subject to raids and incursions from Germanic tribes. It led to several British cities being walled, and stronger defences created around the British coast, with new forts at Reculver in Kent and Brancaster in Norfolk. This was the start of what later became known as the "Saxon shore". The port of Dover was also rebuilt and the Roman fleet was strengthened to patrol the Channel against Saxon and Frankish pirates. Carausius, based in Gaul, at Boulogne, was placed in charge of that fleet, and was thus the prototype of a later official post called the Count of the Saxon Shore. He was a canny individual, popular with his troops, and not averse to a little piracy of his own. He often waited until after the barbarian raid and then captured the ships, keeping the booty for himself. When Maximian learned of this he ordered Carausius's arrest, but Carausius used his popularity and declared himself Emperor in 286, shifting his base to Britain. Carausius seems to have been readily accepted by the British, perhaps because he was a Celt rather than a Roman. In any case the British had by now built a reputation for supporting any rebel against Rome. Carausius may well have intended to restore the Gallic Empire, since he kept a hold on Boulogne for as long as he could.

Archaeological evidence seems to suggest that Britain prospered during Carausius's reign. He not only completed the fortification programme already initiated but built further forts and castles, such as Portus Aderni (Portchester) and Cardiff Castle, and probably started work on the massive fort at Anderida (Pevensey). He also established the first mint in London. Unfortunately, he also apparently withdrew troops from Hadrian's Wall to defend the Saxon shore and the Welsh coast, allowing the Caledonii to take advantage for the first time in nearly a century.

Because of his defences and his fleet, attempts to capture Carausius proved difficult, and Maximian suffered heavy losses. In 293 he delegated the problem to his new caesar, Constantius. After a long siege, Constantius regained Boulogne and was able to blockade Britain. Though still popular, Carausius became weakened and was murdered by his second-in-command Allectus, who proclaimed himself Emperor. Allectus had been Carausius's treasurer, ensuring that the troops were paid, and thus was able to retain their support. He remained independent for a further three years until Constantius mounted a major invasion on two fronts. Allectus was killed in battle, either near Farnham in Surrey, or near Silchester, by Constantius's second in command Asclepiodotus. Allectus's troops fled to London where they met Constantius's army and were defeated. Legend has it that many were executed and their bodies thrown into the Walbrook.

Both Carausius and Asclepiodotus left their mark in British myth, though in reverse. By the time Geoffrey of Monmouth produced his *History*, Carausius had become the enemy of the British, an invader and usurper, who killed Bassianus (Caracalla's original name) and ruled in his place. Geoffrey correctly has him killed by Allectus and then Allectus murdered by Asclepiodotus, but identifies the latter as a Briton and Duke of Cornwall. Geoffrey states that Asclepiodotus reigned for ten years before being in turn killed by King Coel, the Old King Cole of the nursery rhyme. Coel will feature again in our history, though in his rightful place, but this story serves to show how soon oral history and legend transmute facts into pseudo-history. With Carausius we are, in fact, a little over a hundred years away from the start of the Arthurian period, yet that is sufficient time for history to mutate into myth. Such mutation is something we have to bear in mind throughout this book.

The truth is that Carausius's rebellion had a more significant impact upon Britain. The caesar, Constantius, having rid Britain of Allectus, undertook a lightning tour to check defences, especially on the northern frontier. Contemporary accounts refer for the first time to the tribes as the Picts, though there's little reason to believe they are any other than the Caledonii and other northern tribes. Constantius ordered some refurbishments and then returned to Rome to celebrate his triumph.

He returned to Britain ten years later, in 305, this time as Emperor. He was later joined by his son Constantine. The intervening decade had seen Diocletian introduce a series of sweeping reforms to the administration of the Empire, though precisely when they were enforced in Britain is not clear. Diocletian divided the Empire into twelve dioceses, each with a *vicarius* in charge. Every diocese was divided into provinces, each with its own governor. Britain was one diocese and now had four provinces. The former northern province of Britannia Inferior was divided in two from the Mersey to the Humber. The northernmost province became Britannia Secunda, with its capital at York, whilst the southern half became Flavia Caesariensis, with a capital at Lincoln. The former southern province of Britannia Superior was also split in half by a line heading almost straight north from Southampton. The west, including Wales and the south-west, became Britannia Prima, with the capital at Cirencester. To the east was Maxima Caesariensis, with the capital at London. London also seems to have been the overall diocesan capital. This further division was to have consequences a century later with the re-emergence of British kingdoms. These reforms also separated the civic administration from the military. Whilst Britain was administered by a *vicarius* based in London, the northern forces were controlled by the *dux Britanniarum*, based in York. Diocletian was going to have no more rebellious usurpers able to call upon vast armies though, as we shall soon see, this did not work in Britain.

Diocletian also issued a violent edict against Christianity. It was probably at this time that Britain saw its first martyr in Alban, who was executed at Verulamium (St Albans). Christianity had a strong hold in Britain, and was a factor in how the provinces developed distinct from the rest of the Empire.

Constantius undertook a series of campaigns in northern Britain against the Picts. Little is known about this, but it seems to have been successful as there was comparative peace for another fifty years. For Constantius, alas, there was little time to appreciate his achievement. He was seriously ill, possibly with leukaemia (his nickname was Constantius the Pale), and he died in York in July 306, aged 56.

Under Diocletian's reforms, Constantius should automatically have been succeeded as emperor by his nominated caesar, Flavius Valerius Severus. In fact, Constantius had not selected his successor; it had been done for him by Galerius, his co-emperor in the east. Not everyone wanted Severus as emperor, least of all the British, and true to tradition the British troops promptly nominated their own successor, Constantius's son Constantine. Galerius begrudgingly made Constantine the successor to Severus, but it was a far from simple succession, and it would be eighteen years before Constantine became sole emperor.

Because Constantine became such a great emperor and, most significantly, made Christianity the official religion of Rome, and because his cause had been promoted by the British, he was well remembered in Britain and entered popular folklore.

Constantine's mother Helena was a native of Bithynia (in present-day northern Turkey) and never, apparently, came to Britain. Later beatified, Helena became a devout Christian and undertook a pilgrimage to Palestine in 326, founding several churches. She is supposed to have found the True Cross in Jerusalem, though dates conflict; she died in about 330 whilst the legend of the discovery of the Cross dates from about 335, during the construction of Constantine's basilica. At some stage the legend grew that Helen was British, the daughter of King Coel of Colchester, whom we have already met in myth as the murderer of Asclepiodotus. This legend took a firm hold in Britain, because it made Constantine a Briton and the grandson of Coel. It is probable that later chroniclers, especially Geoffrey of Monmouth, confused Helena with Elen, wife of a later British usurper-emperor, Magnus Maximus, who also had a son called Constantine. Elen was the daughter of the British chieftain Eudaf (of whom more later).

But the legend refuses to die. As we have seen, myths have a habit of ousting history, and we have to be on our guard.

4. The End of Empire

By good organisation, strength of character and sheer charisma, Constantine kept the Roman empire together, but thereafter the empire was on the decline. His successors fought each other, crumbling the empire at its heart and weakening it at its frontiers, making it vulnerable to barbarian attack. This was as evident in Britain as elsewhere in the empire.

One mystery related to Britain at this time is worth mentioning, as it may have later relevance. By the 340s the empire was split between Constantine's two surviving sons: Constans, who ruled the west, including Britain, and Constantius II who ruled the east. In 343 Constans made an impulsive visit to Britain. His visit remains a mystery, yet the fact that he risked crossing the English Channel during the winter suggests that it was something serious. The contemporary chronicler Libanius, who recorded the visit (but seemed equally at a loss to explain it), noted that "affairs in Britain were stable", thereby ruling out the likelihood of a rebellion.

So what prompted it? Was it a religious matter? We shall see later that Britain was one of the rebel nations when it came to Christianity, supporting pagan worship and later encouraging dangerous interpretations of Christian teachings such as Pelagianism. Would this be enough to tempt Constans across the waves at such a dangerous time? Possibly, but I am not convinced.

Further incursions by the Picts in the north is a possible explanation, but the winter was not a great period for warfare, and although British defences to the north were not as thorough as they had been, they were still sufficient to cope with any activity that had not come to the notice of the chroniclers.

Was it, perhaps, an enclave of support for Constantius against Constans, or perhaps a lingering support for their dead brother Constantine II, who had ruled Gaul and Britain until his murder just three years earlier?

This seems more likely. Diocletian had set up an extremely efficient intelligence agency, known as the *agentes in rebus*, who were good at sniffing out areas of unrest. Britain was always a hotbed of rebels, and the fact that Libanius reports that Britain's affairs were "stable" might only mean that word had not got out and any rebellion had been nipped in the bud by Constans's surprise visit.

Support for this interpretation comes from events just a few years later. In 350 Constans was murdered following an uprising in support of his army commander Magnentius. Although Magnentius was born in Gaul, his father was believed to be British and was probably a high-ranking official. Did Constans learn of a plot, perhaps by Magnentius's father in 343, which he was able to stifle? Magnentius had a brief but mostly successful period as rival emperor until a series of defeats led him to commit suicide in 353. Constantius lived to fight another day, and sent the heavies into Britain to root out any remaining supporters of Magnentius. His envoy was an over-zealous martinet from Spain called Paul who tortured, killed and imprisoned many British officials, regardless of their guilt or innocence. So vicious were Paul's measures that the *vicarius* of Britain, Flavius Martinus, tried to assassinate him but, when he failed, killed himself.

Soon after Paul's inquisitorial rampage another usurper rose in Britain, the mysterious Carausius II. Continental writers seem to know nothing about him, not even the ever-vigilant Ammianus Marcellinus, whose *History* is one of the best records of this period. Unfortunately, most of the early part of his work has been lost, so we know of the existence of Carausius II only from surviving coinage. Some historians have even dismissed the very existence of Carausius. However, he has been adopted into Welsh legend as the son-in-law of the patriarchal Eudaf Hen ("the Old"), from whom most of the British kings were descended.

Even more mysteriously, amongst the British coinage is a record of someone called Genceris, who may have ruled elsewhere in Britain at the time of Carausius. Analysis of these coins can only tell us so much, but it suggests that rival rulers did emerge in Britain in the period 354–358. They were seeking not to proclaim themselves rival emperors but, like Carausius I, to rule Britain independently. Britain in the fourth century was at her wealthiest. Profits from grain exports and other native industries, plus unprecedented periods of comparative peace, had allowed the Romano-British to become comfortable, and to think thoughts of independence. Constantine's successors were fighting so much amongst themselves, and drawing troops away from the borders, that Britain was becoming increasingly vulnerable. Saxons were continuing to harry the western coasts, the Irish were raiding the east, and the Picts were once again invading from the north. The Romano-British aristocracy did not feel that the Empire was providing sufficient protection

From 360, Roman Britain was overrun by a massive Pictish invasion, with further uprisings in 364 and 367. Ammianus Marcellinus, who lived through these times, recorded the 367 revolt with dramatic effect in his *Res Gestae* in 378,

> At this time, with trumpets sounding for war as if throughout the Roman world, the most savage tribes rose up and poured across the nearest frontiers. At one and the same time the Alamanni were plundering Gaul and Raetia, the

> Sarmatae and Quadri Pannonia; the Picts, Saxons, Scots and Attacotti harassed the Britons with continual calamities.

The Attacotti (or Attecotti) were another tribe in the far north of Scotland. Later in his narrative, Ammianus provides amplification of the above:

> . . . at the time in question the Picts were divided into two tribes, the Dicalydones and the Verturiones. These, together with the warlike Attacotti and the Scots, were ranging over a wide area causing much devastation, while the Franks and their neighbours the Saxons ravaged the coast of Gaul with vicious acts of pillage, arson and the murder of all prisoners . . .

We also learn that the *areani* who, rather like present-day police informants, were relating intelligence of barbarian activities back to the military, had turned traitor and allied themselves with the Picts and Scots in revealing troop movements. As a consequence, the barbarians captured the *dux Britanniarum* Nectaridus, and killed the Count of the Saxon Shore, Fullofaudes.

The new emperor, Valentinian, sent a general to deal with the problem, but he was soon recalled because of the enormity of the situation. Eventually, a much bigger force was despatched, under the command of the brilliant general and tactician Theodosius. Upon his arrival, he discovered bands of marauding barbarians as far south as Kent and London. The Roman army was also in disarray, many having deserted or forsaken their posts. The remaining force was demoralised and lacked co-ordination. The barbarians had by now no central command, and it was easy for Theodosius and his troops to pick them off. He arrived at London in triumph and soon restored morale, pardoning deserters and encouraging the return of others. He spent the next two years not only recovering the diocese, but undertaking a major programme of repair and refortification. Old forts were strengthened, towns were rebuilt and fortified, and a new series of watchtowers and signal stations was built along the north-east coast to serve as advance guard against sea-borne attacks. Theodosius also nipped one possible revolution in the bud when he arrested one Valentinus, a criminal exiled to Britain from Pannonia, who was apparently planning some sort of takeover in Britain. Most interestingly, Ammianus refers to Theodosius recovering an existing province, which had fallen into the hands of the enemy, and restoring it to its former state, renaming it Valentia in honour of the Emperor. Unfortunately he does not say where Valentia was, presumably having described it in one of his earlier, lost, books. The fact that Theodosius restored a former province means either that one of the four existing provinces had been lost to Roman control and was now recovered, or that a fifth province had previously been created. Evidence that it was a fifth province comes from the glorious document of the Roman civil service, the *Notitia Dignitatum*, a compendium of the various offices of state throughout the Empire, which lists Valentia separately. Although this document came into being during the reign of Constantine the Great, it was continually amended and updated and the version in which we know it today dates to some time around the end of the fourth century. Therefore we don't know exactly when Valentia was created or where it was.

In the *Notitia*, Valentia is grouped with Maxima Caesariensis, the southeastern province based around London, as being governed by a consul rather than a *praesides*. This could suggest either that Valentia had been created by dividing Maxima Caesariensis in two – though then giving both halves consular governors was perhaps a little top heavy – or that Maxima Caesariensis had been renamed Valentia. If that is the case, it means that one of the more senior provinces had somehow been wrested from Roman control, and the chances of this being in the south are remote. We do not know if this was related to the rebel Valentinus, or where he was located, though in all likelihood he would have been in one of the southern provinces. Ammianus states that "it had fallen into the hands of the enemy," which probably means it had been taken over by the barbarian Picts. This would suggest it was a province in the north, the most obvious one being Britannia Secunda, based at York. It may well be, therefore, that Valentia was a province split from Britannia Secunda. As we have seen in the past, the most difficult area to control had been the western Pennines, and it has been suggested that Valentia could have been created in what is now Cumbria and which, in Arthurian times, was part of Rheged.

It is just possible that Valentia was the territory between the Walls, not strictly a "province" but a buffer zone, and was the easiest province to lose to the Picts.

The separate reference to Valentia in the *Notitia Dignitatum* rules out the suggestion that Valentia was the name given to the whole of the diocese of Britain, an interpretation that could be read into Ammianus's text, and which would certainly have made sense. The fact that it was either a renamed fourth province or a new fifth province that was, albeit briefly, taken away from Roman control, makes identification important, because it shows the abilities of the Picts, perhaps in collaboration with any rebellious indigenous population. This becomes important when mapping out the Arthurian world in the next century.

Theodosius confirmed a number of new officers in various posts at this time. It's possible that some of the people who were ancestors of the British kings may have been installed now, such as Paternus, the grandfather of Cunedda, as a commander of the Votadini. One other appointment is worth mentioning. A short while after these events, Valentinian transferred a Germanic king, Fraomar, to Britain as a military tribune in command of an existing contingent of Alamanni troops. It is not recorded where he was placed but it is a reminder that a high-ranking Germanic commander was in Britain in the fourth century, in charge of Germanic troops, and he may well not have been the only one.

Theodosius's campaign and reforms were successful in improving British morale and restoring Roman command and also, as a consequence, improving the quality of life in Britain. Archaeological evidence, especially in the south, has identified plenty of places where high quality villas were extended or rebuilt at this time. Theodosius did not, however, stop continued attempts by the Picts to undermine control in the north. This was especially so after the death of Valentinian in 375. He was succeeded by his two sons, Valentinian II, who was only four, and Gratian, who was sixteen. Though Gratian grew into a passable soldier, he was no good at government and soon lost the confidence of the army. Once again the time was right for another usurper.

This came in the shape of Magnus Maximus, the "greatest of the great." He was of Spanish descent and had served in Britain with Theodosius in 367. He had remained with Theodosius, serving in Raetia from 370, against the Alamanni, and in Africa from 373, before returning to Britain in 380, possibly as *dux Britanniarum*. In 382 there was another incursion by Picts and Scots which Maximus repulsed, bringing him great acclaim. He was popular amongst the troops and knew how to use this to his advantage, especially in denigrating the work of Gratian. In 383 the ever-rebellious British soldiers declared Maximus their emperor.

Maximus took his army into Gaul and defeated Gratian after a protracted skirmish outside Paris. Gratian fled, but was murdered. Maximus knew better than to go after Valentinian, who was still only 13. An agreement was reached with Theodosius whereby Valentinian remained emperor in Italy, but Maximus controlled the western empire north of the Alps.

And so it remained until Maximus became too sure of himself. His fate was an early example of the Christian faith being used by rulers to further their own ends. Valentinian, heavily influenced by his mother, had passed an act legitimizing Arianism, a creed that held Jesus to be human and not divine. Maximus, who purported to be a devout Christian, and who had been the first to have a non-orthodox Christian bishop executed for heresy, used Valentinian's act as a cause to invade Italy and confront the young emperor. He took with him a large army, including further troops from Britain. It was a foolish act. Maximus found himself trapped by the army of Theodosius, who had come to Valentinian's aid, and he was killed. Maximus's son, Flavius Victor, whom he had appointed as caesar and left behind in Gaul, was also killed.

Maximus was bad news for Britain. He could have been a good emperor, but his belief in his own self importance got the better of him and he drained many troops from Britain, seriously weakening its defences. These troops did not return. Many settled in Armorica (Brittany) and became the core of a British settlement.

Curiously, however, Maximus has entered British legend as something of a hero, and his march upon Rome has become subsumed into Arthurian myth, as we shall later see. To the Celts he was Macsen Wledig – *wledig* means "leader". They claimed he was the grandson of Constantine the Great, through a daughter. This would fit into the chronology – Maximus was born about 330 – though there is much uncertainty about his father. It is also claimed that Maximus was married twice: firstly to Ceindrech ferch Rheiden, who claimed descent from Caswallon, and secondly to Elen, daughter of Eudaf. By his first wife he had two children – the unfortunate Victor, and Owain, who will feature again shortly. By his second wife he had five children, including Constantine, a name which becomes drawn into the Arthurian legend, and Severa, who became the wife of Vortigern, the future ruler of Britain. There is no reason to doubt that these children of Maximus existed. A tomb, which may be Constantine's, has been found near Segontium (Caernarvon), a place strongly associated with Maximus. Future kings and usurpers all liked to claim descent from Maximus, especially as he himself claimed descent from Constantine the Great, but one has to treat these genealogies with caution. I shall discuss all of them in much detail later. All we need note at the moment is that despite having weakened Britain's defences, Maximus was hailed a British hero and his life is a prelude to the story of Arthur.

Following the death of Maximus, Roman control over events in Britain was virtually lost. As Gildas later expressed it, "The island was still Roman in name, but not by law and custom." Maximus's son Victor was killed by a soldier called Arbogast, who set up his own puppet emperor, Eugenius, and sought to make himself king of France. Arbogast, a pagan, encouraged the return to pagan worship in Britain and Gaul. Theodosius's two sons, Honorius and Arcadius, were both too young to rule so the Vandal general Stilicho governed the western empire as regent for Honorius. Stilicho prevailed and, after the deaths of Eugenius and Arbogast, sought once again to shore up defences in Britain. Around the years 395–396, Stilicho sent a force against the Picts, but it was too little too late. Soon after, in 401–402 Stilicho withdrew further troops from Britain to help fight against Alaric, the Visigoth governor of Illyria, who had invaded Italy.

Hadrian's wall was now undefended and all troops had been withdrawn from Wales. Only one legion remained in Britain, at

Chester. The Irish now secured a grip on the fringes of Britain. The chieftain Eochaid, ruler of the Déisi in present-day Waterford, established a base in south-west Wales, in the territory then known as Demetia (later Dyfed). Meanwhile the descendants of Cairbre Riata, founder of the territory of the Dál Riata in Northern Ireland, had established settlements in what are now Argyll and Kintyre.

No new Roman coinage entered Britain after 402. Feeling abandoned, and having lost all hope in any further support from Rome, Britain once again chose its own emperors. The first two – Marcus, a Roman official, and Gratian, a British official – scarcely lasted a few months before both were murdered. This was between December 406 and May 407. The third choice was more promising, even though he was apparently an ordinary soldier from the ranks. This was Flavius Claudius Constantine, later Constantine III. Constantine marshalled what few troops remained in Britain and marched on Gaul, winning over the troops both there and on the Rhine. The latter desertion was a disaster for Rome, as the barbarian armies had already crossed the borders of the Empire and the defences were crumbling. Nevertheless Constantine proved a surprise. His presence seemed to deter the Vandals and other armies, and there was a brief respite in hostilities.

The problem for Britain, though, was that Constantine was now in Gaul. He seemed to have lost interest in Britain, and once again Britain became subject to increasing attacks from Picts and Saxons. By 408 Constantine had lost his grip on affairs, and the Vandals were again on the move. Britain had enough, and, in 409, expelled all Roman officials. The Greek historian Zosimus, who lived only a few years after these events, tells the story in his *Historia Nova* (*c*500).

> The barbarians beyond the Rhine, attacking in force, reduced the inhabitants of Britain and some of the Celtic tribes to the point where they were obliged to throw off Roman rule and live independently, no longer subject to Roman laws. The Britons therefore took up arms and, braving the danger on their own behalf, freed their cities from the barbarians threatening them. And all Armorica

> and the other Gallic provinces followed their example, freed themselves in the same way, expelled their Roman rulers and set up their own governments as far as lay within their power.

But it proved difficult. There were continued attacks, and in 410 the British wrote to the emperor Honorius (son of Theodosius) pleading for help. Honorius, however, had enough to contend with, what with the barbarians overrunning the empire and Constantine III seeking to destroy him. According to Zosimus, he replied telling them to look to their own defence. A.L.F. Rivet and Colin Smith, in *The Place-Names of Roman Britain*, have suggested that Zosimus somehow mistook the town of Bruttium in southern Italy for Britannia – the names in Greek are very similar – which may mean that Honorius did not officially dismiss the British. However, the British had certainly dismissed the Romans, and Honorius was in no position to respond. Whether by design or default, and no matter how temporary it may have seemed at the time, Britain was no longer under direct Roman rule.

It now had to defend itself and needed strong men to do so. The Age of Arthur was about to begin.

3

THE DARKNESS DESCENDS

1. British Authority

I have dwelt for some time on the Roman background to the Arthurian age because it is important to understand the state of Britain at the start of the so-called "Dark Ages". We have seen that the British had increasingly sought independence during the third and fourth centuries and, as troubles beset the rest of the Roman Empire, had grown wealthy and financially resilient. Though Germanic, Scottish and Pictish invaders continued to trouble the periphery of Britain, even in the late fourth century, the Romano-British lived in style, in grand villas with expensive goods imported from elsewhere in the Empire.

The years 409/410, with the apparent end of Roman control in Britain, were part of a process of independence that stretched for over a century. It should not be seen as Britain being abandoned by Rome, with the sudden desertion of the army leaving Britain at the mercy of the Saxons waiting to pounce. Britain had been steadily deprived of its forces at intervals over the last thirty years or more. The native British had been well trained and conditioned in Roman ways for nearly four centuries, and British officials would have ensured continuity with the training of their own troops. The British forces, which no doubt included Germanic mercenaries, may not have been as disciplined as the Roman legions, nor as numerous, but we cannot discount them.

Moreover, there were already plenty of Germanic settlers and retired soldiers in Britain. The Roman Empire was multicultural, allowing the free movement of people throughout Europe. Many of the soldiers stationed in Britain were not of strict Roman stock, but from Germanic and other tribes, as we have already seen with the Sarmatians at Bremetennacum. There were many Friesian cavalry units posted in Northern Britain, such as at Vinovia (Binchester) and Derventio (Papcastle). They even feature in the Arthurian legends.

The dismissal of the Roman administration was no doubt part of a power struggle in Britain, both secular and religious. The British appeal to Honorius had come from the heads of the *civitates*, not the provincial heads or the *vicarius*. Some historians believe this means that the British usurpation of power had come from the provincial governors who had overthrown the *vicarius*, leaving the *civitates* in a degree of confusion. With no overall diocesan control it meant that after 409 Britain was no longer one single diocese but four provinces, each with its own governor.

Throughout the Roman occupation, the tribal structure within Britain had led to continuous rivalry and conflict between the British. The Roman administration had stifled this to a degree, particularly in the south, but it was always there, and would have reasserted itself after the Romans left. In our own time we have seen a similar resurgance of tribalism in Eastern Europe following the fall of Communism.

To this must be added a conflict in religious views. The Christian faith was still evolving and various sects were emerging throughout the Roman world. At the dawn of the fifth century, the strongest voice of Christian understanding, and the one regarded as orthodox, was that of Augustine of Hippo. His interpretation of doctrine, including the concept of predestination (that mankind's fate is controlled by God and that original sin is inherited) was upheld by Pope Innocent, the most powerful pope of the period. As a consequence, any opposing views were seen as heretical. One such came from the British monk Pelagius, who had studied law in Rome but turned to the Church around the year 386. Pelagius's strong opinions apparently made ready enemies. He held the viewpoint that individuals had free will and could have a one-to-one relationship with God, not requiring the channel of a priest. Pelagius and Augustine were vehemently opposed, and it was Augustine whose doctrine held sway. Pelagius was first condemned by the Pope in 411, again in 416, and threatened with excommunication by Innocent in 417. Pelagius did not reform and, in 418, solely through the forcefulness of Augustine, was excommunicated. Pelagius died soon afterwards, in 419, but his views lived on, especially in Britain, where they seem to have found favour with the aristocracy.

So, not only were there pro-Roman and pro-British views of governance, there was also a pro-Catholic/pro-Pelagian divide in Britain. Effectively Britain would have split into two political factions, whilst various military leaders established themselves to repel invaders and take over control in their own territories. Combine this with external threats from hostile forces and you have a Britain where, over a period of time, the social structure cracked through the lack of strong central control.

It is that central control which is so fundamental to the Dark Age history of Britain and where the Arthurian legend has its roots. Even though the British had dismissed the Roman administrators, it does not mean that the system of administration in Britain ceased overnight. The existing officials, except perhaps the dismissed *vicarius* and his retinue, were probably already British, being part of the original tribal aristocracy.

In the pre-Roman days, at times of civil upheaval, the tribes would have looked to a High King, usually the most powerful of the tribal rulers. In effect, whoever might take on the role of the *vicarius* in Britain would become the equivalent of a High King.

You might wonder what role the usurper emperor Constantine III played in this, and the answer is very little. Constantine had effectively been dismissed along with all the other Roman officials after 409. Despite his British origins, he had virtually turned his back on Britain by trying to establish himself within the Empire from his base in Gaul, at Arles. The British officials must have held a dim view of Constantine as they had appealed not to him, but directly to Honorius. Evidently the appeal was from the pro-Roman faction. In 410, soon after the British expelled the Roman officials, Rome was itself entered and sacked by the Visigoths under Alaric. The Empire was in turmoil. Constantine's general, Gerontius, an able man who might have been a capable leader in Britain, deserted him and changed his allegiance. He killed Constantine's son Constans, and raised another general, Maximus, as a rival Emperor. Maximus and Gerontius took control of Spain and parts of Gaul and Constantine found himself isolated. Unable to function, Constantine surrendered and was executed in September 411. Gerontius, unable to capitalise on events, was betrayed by his troops and forced to kill himself.

With no help from Europe, Britain was left to its own devices. The approach within each of the four provinces was probably different. With no surviving written record we do not know what happened and can only surmise from a vague knowledge of later history, all too much of which has to be viewed through the haze of myth. It becomes apparent, however, from the archaeological record, that every effort was made to continue with Roman life as much as normal. The area most affected was the heavily militarized zone in the north, in Britannia Secunda. Never really acquiring the civilized benefits of the south, it had been occupied and run by the legions and settled by legions' families, who dominated and controlled the local British. If there was anywhere where the old native rivalries would surface, it was going to be in the north.

2. Northern Britain

Britannia Secunda contained the tribes of the Carvetii, Parisii and Brigantes, the last of which was the biggest and most rebellious. This was also the area under the control of the *dux Britanniarum* who would need to stamp his authority, not only in marshalling troops to fight back the Picts, but also to quell any internal rebellions. We do not know the name of the *dux Britanniarum* at this time, but a name that rapidly comes to the fore is Coel, or "Old King Cole." The real Coel is so wrapped in legend that it is difficult to get at the truth.

If Coel was not formally appointed as the Northern *dux Britanniarum* – and he might have been by Constantine III before the latter's departure for Gaul – he almost certainly filled that role. His official base was at York, but the flimsy evidence that survives, most of it circumstantial, suggests that he operated primarily from Carlisle. It's quite possible that Coel took over control of the old Roman province of Valentia if, as has been surmised, this was based in the north-west around Carlisle. Valentia had already shown a strong disposition to independence in the late Roman period, and would certainly have sought to re-establish itself as an independent state soon after the end of Roman authority.

Genealogists would establish a pedigree for Coel, identifying descent from the early pre-Roman kings, with a line direct from Caswallon (*see* Table 3.2). Some genealogies identify his father as Guotepauc or Godebog, but most authorities now believe that Guotepauc was an epithet. In the old Brythonic tongue it means "protector" or "defender", a title that fits the role of *dux* admirably.

We do not know Coel's tribal affiliations. Regardless of the genealogies, which suggest a descent from the pre-Roman Catuvellauni tribe, his forefathers could have come from any where, having been posted to help command Hadrian's Wall. Coel, if not from the local Brigantes, may have been a seventh or eighth generation settler along the Wall. Coel is also associated with Kyle in Galloway – indeed some believe Kyle's name comes from Coel, though really it comes from the gaelic word *caol* meaning 'strait' – so he may have been from the Novantae tribe.

By all accounts Coel had rivals in the area between the walls. This area had never been under direct Roman control (unless it was Valentia), though the Votadini had been friendly towards Rome and probably provided a policing role. The territory of the Votadini stretched around the eastern coast from the Forth estuary to Hadrian's Wall. The north-western part of their lands was known as the Manau Gododdin. Gododdin was, in fact, a Brythonic variant of the name Votadini, and later the whole tribe became known as the Gododdin. Over time, they became divided between the Manau in the north and the southern Gododdin, later Bryneich.

The earliest known ruler of the Manau is Cunedda, grandson of Paternus who may have been a commander placed in control of the territory by Magnus Maximus. Cunedda was evidently something of a thug. An elegy to him, *Marwnad Cunedda*, attributed to Taliesin, calls him a "relentless raider," and implies that he had control of all the lands between the walls and perhaps even south into Cumbria. At some stage Coel and Cunedda must have reached a treaty. The elegy describes how Cunedda's warhounds "will constrain the Coeling in a truce of peace." The genealogies state that Cunedda married Coel's daughter Gwawl, which doubtless sealed the treaty. The rivalry between the Coelings and Cunedda is hinted at in another poem, *Y Gododdin*, which I will discuss in more detail later. This poem describes how the Gododdin "used to defend their land against the sons of Godebawc, wicked folk." A picture of open and continuous warfare in the north with Coel seeking to stamp his overall authority becomes apparent.

One other name emerges in the north via the writings of St. Patrick. He refers to a king Coroticus, who was slave trading with the Irish. Coroticus is believed to be Ceretic, who became a ruler of Strathclyde, the old tribe of the Damnonii, at about the same time that Cunedda ruled in the Manau. The genealogies suggest that Ceretic, like Cunedda, was descended from Romano-British who were probably military commanders in northern Britain (*see* Table 3.4).

We do not know Coel's precise dates, but it is probable that he was dead by the year 430. His territory was divided between his "sons" (if the genealogies are correct), though some of these may have been military deputies whom Coel appointed as a successor. One of these, Germanianus (called Garbanion by the British), although identified as a son, was almost certainly a high ranking military commander, whose name suggests either a Germanic origin or that he was a commander of Germanic troops. He probably received command of territory east of the Pennines, including York and the southern Gododdin, whilst another "son", Ceneu, received the land west of the Pennines, including the territory of the Carvetii, later known as Rheged and which may have been Valentia. There was a third son, Dydrwr, who may have pre-deceased Coel, as we know no more about him, but otherwise we must presume he took command of some territory, possibly the Manau or land to the south that later became the kingdom of Elmet.

At some stage, perhaps as part of a treaty with Coel, Cunedda went south, to North Wales, to lead the resistance against the Irish raiders. Cunedda's son Tybion remained in the Manau but did not establish a dynasty, and it is probable that his territory was fought over by the sons of Coel. Cunedda's shift to Wales is mentioned by Nennius in an infuriating section which has rankled scholars ever since.

We will discuss Nennius's *Historia Britonum* in detail later, but this part is best discussed here. In Section 62 he says:

> Maelgwn the Great King ruled the British in Gwynedd, for his ancestor [*atavus*] Cunedda, with his eight sons, had come from the North, from the country called Manaw Gododdin, 146 years before Maelgwn reigned and expelled the Irish from these countries with immense slaughter, so that they never again returned to inhabit them.

If the 146 years runs from the start of Maelgwyn's reign, usually regarded as 534, then it takes us back to 388AD. This means that Cunedda came down from the North to fight the Irish in Wales at the same time as the death of Maximus, and while Britain was still part of the Empire. We know that Eochaid had established a base in south-west Wales, in Demetia, at around this same time and it may be that, with a power vacuum left by Maximus's death and that of his eldest son, the officials in Britain brought further troops down as a defence. This would make Cunedda a contemporary with Coel, but the likely dates of his descendants means that this date is too early.

The genealogies list Maelgwyn as Cunedda's great grandson. If we allow 25–30 years to a generation, that means that if Maelgwyn was at the height of his powers in the 530s, then Cunedda was probably most active in the 450s. This could be stretched back to the 430s. The alternative is that the genealogies are wrong. The word used to describe Cunedda's relationship with Maelgwyn is *atavus*. As Leslie Alcock explains in *Arthur's Britain*, this word can be used loosely to describe an ancestor, or more precisely to describe a great-great-great-grandfather. This adds two further generations, or another 50–60 years, exactly what is needed to fill the gap.

The time span of 146 years is so precise that whoever first calculated it clearly had something specific in mind. It cannot be a copyist's error because the years are written out in full – *centum quadraginta sex*. It could, of course, just be a false figure to reinforce the authority of Cunedda's descendants over North Wales in their rivalry with the rulers of Powys and Gwent. If it is, then we have no real guidance.

But as we have seen, errors exist elsewhere relating either to the Easter cycle of 19 years, or to the gap between the incarnation and passion or death of Christ. The 146 years could have been calculated with a built-in error. The likeliest is the difference between the birth and passion of Christ, noted by Nennius as 35 years. Deducting this brings the gap to 111 years which, if deducted from 534, gives 423. This might suggest that Cunedda moved south after reaching an agreement with Coel. There might also have been an arrangement with Ceretic of Alclud, because by the mid fifth century there is a clear spread of control. Ceretic and his descendants ruled the land between the walls, the Coelings ruled northern Britain (sometimes called Brigantia), and Cunedda ruled Venedotia, with its base at Anglesey but spreading across North Wales.

3. Southern Britain

The position in the south was far less clear. There were three provinces: Maxima Caesariensis, the original base for the *vicarius*, with its capital at London; Flavia Caesariensis, with its capital at Lincoln, and the first (from the archaeological record) under major threat from the Saxon settlers; and Britannia Prima, which included Wales. North Wales was uncertain territory, not unlike Northern Britain. It was primarily a militarized zone with minimal Roman settlement, despite the legionary fortress at Chester and another major fort at Segontium (Caernarvon). This had been the area of the Deceangli and Ordovices tribes, both of whom, like the Brigantes in northern Britain, had been hostile to Rome. South-west Wales, the area of the Demetae, was the main focus for Irish settlement, and it is evident that with the withdrawal of troops by Magnus Maximus the Irish had succeeded in settling in Demetia and had established what became the kingdom of Dyfed. It is interesting that the name in the pedigrees at about the time of the Roman withdrawal is Tryphun, a Brythonic version of "tribune", which may have been a rank and not a name.

This arc, from Demetia through west and north Wales, rapidly shifted away from centralised Roman control. When Cunedda came down from Manau Gododdin to North Wales in the 420s, he was able to establish various territories for himself and his sons, that subsequently became the kingdoms of Gwynedd (Venedotia), Ceredigion and Meirionydd plus the smaller chiefdoms of Rhos and Dunoding. The tables at the end of this chapter show the emergence of these kingdoms and attempt to provide a chronology of their rulers.

South Wales was another matter. Despite the original hostility of the Silures to the Romans, south Wales had become heavily Romanized as had the area later known as the Welsh Marches. This territory included the Severn basin and was the rich heartland of Roman Britain. Here were the towns of Gloucester, Worcester and Wroxeter, plus Cirencester, the biggest city in Britain after London.

Just what happened here, both within this territory and between it and Maxima Caesariensis, is not entirely clear but, according to the accounts left by Gildas and Nennius, there was discord between various factions. Two names become prominent, Vitalinus and Ambrosius. Vitalinus, according to Nennius's genealogies, came from the city of Gloucester, but is described by Geoffrey of Monmouth as the archbishop of London. Whether Geoffrey meant archbishop or someone in a senior magisterial role is not clear, but it may well be that Vitalinus made himself head of the province of Maxima Caesariensis, whilst Ambrosius took control of parts of Britannia Prima. Vitalinus, though, may have belonged to the Cornovii *civitas* as his grandson, whom we shall come to know as Vortigern, was regarded as the ancestor of the rulers of Powys, the kingdom that grew out of that *civitas*. Ambrosius, on the other hand, may have belonged to the Dobunni tribe which occupied the Severn estuary and parts of Somerset and Wiltshire. Their power struggle seems to have had consequences for both the provinces of Britannia Prima and Maxima Caesariensis and, in due course, for Arthur.

The leading official in the *civitas* of Caerwent, out of which would emerge the kingdoms of Gwent and Glywysing, was probably Owain Finddu, another of the sons of Magnus Maximus. His name is given in one of the Welsh Triads, ancient triplets of verse used to memorise people and events (*see* Chapter 8). Triad 13 lists the "Three Chief Officers of the Island of Britain":

Caradawg son of Bran
And Cawrdaf son of Caradawg
And Owain son of Macsen Wledig.

Owain was not Maximus's eldest son – that was Victor, who was murdered soon after Maximus's death in 388. Owain was Victor's younger brother and, though we do not know his age, he may still have been quite young at the time of his father's death, perhaps only in his early teens. This means he would have been in his thirties around the year 410 and, because of his parentage and seniority, may well have been appointed as deputy by Constantine III when he left for Gaul. The very phrase "chief officer", rather than king or ruler, suggests a senior administrative role, such as provincial governor or possibly vicarius.

It has been suggested that Owain (the British version of the Roman Eugenius), was the same person as the puppet emperor set up by Arbogast in 392. But Zosimus recorded the execution of Eugenius after the battle of Frigidius in 394, an event he is not likely to have got wrong.

Through his mother, Owain was a grandson of Eudaf Hen, who could claim descent from Caratacus. Eudaf, the Brythonic version of Octavius, was almost certainly a high-ranking Romano-British official, who had held command in Gwent in the fourth century. Geoffrey of Monmouth calls him a duke of the Gewisse, and I shall explore what that means in more detail later. According to tradition, Eudaf married the daughter of the usurper Carausius, which is unlikely, as that would push his lifetime back to the dawn of the fourth century. His own daughter is supposed to have married the shadowy Carausius II, which may well be how the Carausius connection arose, and places Eudaf more satisfactorily in the middle of the fourth century. He was almost certainly dead by 410, but his power and influence had been strong, and many of the later rulers of southern Britain, including Arthur, would claim descent from him (*see* Table 3.1).

Table 3.1 The Arthurian Patriarchs

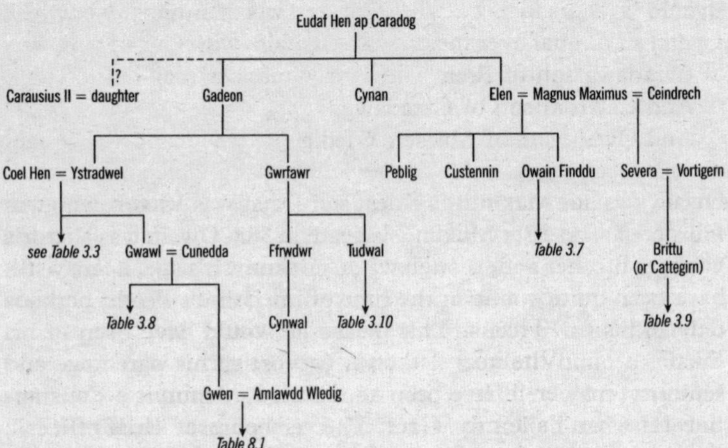

So it is possible that, in the decade after 410, the three leading officials in Britain were all based in Britannia Prima: Vitalinus in Wroxeter (though bishop of London), Ambrosius in Gloucester or Cirencester, and Owain in Caerwent.

Eudaf's own sons and grandsons were also active at this time, though not necessarily in Britain. Two of his sons, Cynan and Gadeon, had apparently supported Maximus in his bid for Empire in the 380s. In reward, Maximus made Cynan leader of the British who settled in Brittany around the end of the fourth century. The earliest known chieftain of Brittany was Cynan Meriadoc, and there is some confusion between him and Cynan ab Eudaf. Meriadoc is usually assigned dates towards the middle of the fifth century, whereas Cynan ab Eudaf must have been born in the mid fourth century, and was perhaps in his forties when he fought alongside Maximus.

Gadeon joined Cynan in Brittany, and the two brothers may have ruled jointly. Almost certainly Cynan was dead by 410, and Gadeon may have been too. His successor Saloman has been accorded the dates 405–412 for his reign. Gadeon was old enough to have a daughter, Ystradwel, who allegedly married Coel, and if he had also fought alongside Maximus in the 380s, he must have been in his sixties by 405. Geoffrey of Monmouth, who frequently gets his facts back to front, reports of animosity between Cynan and Eudaf over the crown of Britain, with Cynan believing he was the rightful heir. This may mask a real tension that developed between Owain and Cynan.

Legend remembers Owain as a strong, virile man, who fought the giant Eurnach, with both wielding tree trunks. The same legend records that although Owain defeated Eurnach the giant fell on Owain, killing him. This may all be fanciful, but at the core it may be a folk memory of Owain struggling against a greater authority whom Owain weakened, but who ultimately defeated him. That greater authority could well have been Vitalinus, or Vitalinus's grandson Vortigern, who was also Owain's brother-in-law, having married Maximus's daughter Severa. Owain's tomb is recorded as being at Beddgelert in Snowdonia, which was near one of Vortigern's strongholds. There is no further reference to Owain after Vortigern's rise to power.

As we have seen, the British gave their military leaders the title *wledig*. Magnus Maximus, for instance, was Macsen Wledig, and the title was also applied to Ceretic of Strathclyde, Cunedda of the Manau and Ambrosius the Younger (son of Vitalinus's rival), who was called Emrys Wledig. There were about a dozen *wledig*s from the fifth and sixth centuries, some of whom are remembered only in later tales and legends, and it is difficult to know what part they played in the emergence of these kingdoms. One in particular stands out – Amlawdd Wledig. I shall discuss him in more detail later, but because he married a daughter of Cunedda, he must also have been fairly active around this period. Legend makes him the grandfather of Arthur's wife Guinevere. He is associated with territory in South Wales and it is possible that he filled the vacuum left by Owain.

There is no reason to believe that any other kingdoms emerged in the south at this time. Both the archeological evidence and, to a degree, the written record – primarily that left by Gildas – suggest that Roman life continued much as before for at least a generation. Whilst northern Britain and parts of west Wales were the scenes of fighting and increasing devastation, it was not until the 430s and 440s that the south began to be threatened by the more serious incursion of the Saxons. It was then that the seeds were sown for the Arthurian legend with the stories of Vortigern, Ambrosius and Uther Pendragon.

In order that we can see how this legend emerged I want to follow through all of the surviving ancient documents that cover this period, no matter how dubious.

The principal documents are the *De Excidio et Conquestu Britanniae* (*The Ruin of Britain*) by Gildas, the *Welsh Annals (Annales Cambriae)*, the *Historia Brittonum*, usually credited to Nennius, and the *Anglo-Saxon Chronicle*. There are also the genealogies, a few ancient poems such as the *Y Goddodin*, and the lives of the saints, none of which is contemporary and few of which are reliable. More reliable are ancient inscriptions on stones, but these have been subject to weathering and destruction.

There may well have been more documents at some stage. When Geoffrey of Monmouth wrote his *History of the Kings of Britain* in the 1130s, he referred to a "certain very ancient book" which he had consulted. But such chronicles as may have been kept in the fifth or sixth centuries would mostly have been compiled and retained in monasteries, and these were subject to regular attack from the Vikings for over two hundred years, let alone the ravages of time and other dangers such as fire and flood. The library at Glastonbury Abbey was all but destroyed by fire in 1184 and one can but weep at what irreplaceable documents were lost.

The Venerable Bede, regarded as the father of British history, was a dedicated researcher and may have had access to some of these lost documents, but he relied heavily on Gildas for his coverage of the fifth and sixth centuries and, like Gildas, makes no mention of Arthur. That may by itself seem significant, but Bede was not that interested in events before the arrival of St. Augustine, and would not have looked further into ancient British history. He was, however, the first to provide the name Vortigern. His primary research relates to later years, which means that England's foremost historian of the Dark Ages can provide no help with the story of Arthur.

One can live in hope that some long lost document may surface in an ancient archive, but until then we have to work with what we've got and hope that archaeology may help substantiate or further define the world in which the events took place. I shall look at each of these sources over the next few chapters, which will also help flesh out a chronology so we know where in time to place Arthur.

Before doing that, though, it is worthwhile listing here the various pedigrees that survive in the ancient records. These are far from reliable – in fact at times they are wholly misleading – and they are almost impossible to date. But we will encounter many of these people as we travel through the other documents so it is worth acquainting ourselves with them here and trying to get at least a rough chronology. This will also show where the various individuals named Arthur or Artúir or Arthwyr appear.

GENEALOGIES AND KING LISTS

One of the key essentials to identifying Arthur is to place him in a specific period of time, along with his contemporaries. Without that we will get nowhere. In the next few chapters I will go through the various chronicles and see what timeline they suggest. Here, in order to acquaint ourselves with the names and territories that later emerged in Britain, I shall set out the various "royal" pedigrees and make some attempt to date them. Several authorities, not least Dr David Dumville, one of the undisputed experts on the Dark Ages, have demonstrated the difficulty in trying to get any chronology from the pedigrees for reasons I shall cover in a moment. So I start with a huge caveat that of all the sources covered in the next few chapters, these are amongst the most unreliable. But it seems to make sense to start with the data which is the least in focus and fine tune it as we go along.

The British pedigrees and regnal lists are extensive and survive in a wide variety of ancient documents, though none contemporary with Arthur's period. There are three major sources and many minor. The major ones are known as the Harleian MS. 3859, Jesus College MS. 20 and *Bonedd y Saint*. The Harleian manuscript is part of the text which also includes Nennius's *Historia Brittonum*, but the oldest surviving copy with the genealogies dates from about 1100. The name Harleian comes from the original collection, now housed in the British Library, established by Robert Harley (1661–1724), first Earl of Oxford. The surviving copy of Jesus College MS. 20 (now in the Bodleian Library in Oxford) has been dated to around 1340, and was probably drawn from a copy completed about a century earlier. The *Bonedd y Saint*, or "Lineage of the Saints", survives in many copies and versions, but the oldest dates from the end of the thirteenth century. This is held in the National Library of Wales and is known as Peniarth MS. 183. Both the *Anglo-Saxon Chronicle* and Nennius also provide a number of pedigrees.

The pedigrees start with a contemporary descendant and work backwards through the generations. For instance, the first genealogy of the kingdom of Gwynedd listed in Harleian MS. 3859 begins:

> Uen map iguel map catell map Rotri map mermin map etthil . . .

. . . "Owen son of Iguel son of Catell" and so on. For the purposes of this book I want to reverse them into the order we usually understand genealogies, reading from earliest to latest.

Clearly these genealogies are so far removed in time from the Arthurian period that their accuracy is spurious. This is not simply because they may have been corrupted by scribal errors, but because there has been ample time for genealogies to have been fabricated. The primary reason for producing a pedigree is to identify a priority of descent, and thereby a claim to a title or land, and later rulers would have no compunction in having their scribes create a false genealogy. It is only by comparing the many hundreds of documents that survive that we can identify variances and attempt to correct them.

The other problem is that all too few of these genealogies contain identifiable dates. The only way to create a chronology is by working backward or forward from known dates and for that reason I take many of the following lists beyond our period of 400–600AD in order to get a firm footing. But dating pedigrees has an inherent problem. There is a general rule of thumb that a generation covers 25 to 30 years. We can easily test that. In the *Mammoth Book of British Kings & Queens*, I list a pedigree for Queen Elizabeth II from Beli Mawr, the first known British king who lived in about 100BC. It consists of 73 generations covering approximately 2050 years, equalling 28 years per generation. However, it is a very approximate yardstick. We do not always know if a name in a genealogy is a first born or last born, and a man could father a son at any time from, say, age 15 to 65. It is quite easy to have a youngest son who is younger than his own nephew. Unless we have some corroborating dates it is easy to be out by an entire generation.

In the following pedigrees I alternate generations by 25 and 30 years to keep the average to around 28. I use the term *floruit* to denote the period of an individual's prime of life, from about age 20 to 50. The dates given for *floruit* therefore are not birth-death. Where any real dates are known I provide them. In some cases I list generations from brothers and because you have to allow ten or more years between a range of brothers I have extended the generational span accordingly from 30 to 40 years. Clearly all of this is very approximate but, if the pedigree itself is in any way accurate, it will give us a bearing on an individual at least to within thirty to forty years. Even so, some displacements in time do occur, which suggests corruption within the pedigree.

I am indebted to the work of P.C. Bartrum who has collected and assimilated many of these surviving pedigrees in *Early Welsh Genealogical Tracts* (1966) and explored them further in *A Welsh Classical Dictionary* (1993). Without his work the following would have been extremely difficult. However I have not always followed the dates that Bartrum has assigned to individuals, preferring to follow my own logic as consistently as I can.

Following the sequence I discussed above, starting with the kingdoms in the north, the following charts begin with the ancestry of Coel and Cunedda and work through the Men of the North to Wales, the south-west and finally Brittany. I also include the Saxon pedigrees, such as they are.

This first table lists the two pedigrees in Harleian MS. 3859

Table 3.2 The ancestors of Cunedda and Coel

		Floruit	
Beli	Beli	BC/AD	Son of Bran the Blessed and husband of Anna, cousin of the Virgin Mary
Amalech/Aballac	Aballac	1–30	Also known as Afallach or Evelake
Eugein [Owain]	Eudelen	25–55	
Brithguein [Brychwain*]	Eudos	55–85	* also called Prydein, the original Celtic name for the Picts
Dubun [Difwng]	Ebiud [Eifudd]	80–110	
Oumun [Onwedd]	Outigirn [Eudeyrn]	110–140	
Anguerit [Amwerydd]	Oudecant [Euddigan]	135–150	
Amguoloyt [Afloyd]	Ritigirn [Rhydeyrn]	165–195	Lucius Artorius Castus in Britain 181–185
Gurdumn [Gwrddwfn]	Iumetel [Rhifedel]	190–220	
Dumn [Dwfn]	Grat [Gradd]	220–250	
Guordoli [Gwrddoli]	Urban	245–275	
Doli	Telpwyll	275–305	revolt of Carausius, 286
Guorcein [Gwrgain]	Teuhant [Deheuwaint]	300–330	Constantine the Great declared emperor, 306.
Cain	Tecmant [Tegfan]	330–360	Constans visits Britain, 343
Tacit [Tegid]	[Guotepauc] (*probably an epithet for Coel and not a separate generation*)	355–385	Time of Carausius II and Genceris; Pictish invasion, 360; Magnus Maximus emperor, 383–388
Patern [Padarn]	Coel Hen	385–415	Roman administration ends, 410
Atern [Edern]	Garbanion	410–440	
Cunedda	Dumnagual Moilmut	440–470	

that show the descent of both Cunedda and Coel through collateral lines from Beli. The names given are first the Latin names, as per the pedigree, followed by their Celtic equivalent, as per Bartrum.

The table shows the limitations of the 25–30 year average for each generation, especially when the starting point is also vague. If we assume that Amalech in the first column is a duplication of Aballac, then there are 15 generations to Coel and 17 to Cunedda, which gives us roughly 410 and 465 respectively. That gives a reasonable mid-life *floruit* for Coel, but the extra generation places Cunedda too late. Since Cunedda is supposed to have married Coel's daughter, he must have lived a generation earlier, in the 420s. Although Coel's dates seem about right, if the name listed as his father, Guotepauc, was really the title "Protector", it would push him back a generation, making him too early.

It shows that though the generation calculation may get you to roughly the right period, you need other data to fine tune it, albeit still approximately. The more we work through the pedigrees, the more the chronology will come into focus.

Table 3.3 introduces the second "Arthur" after Artorius. Because Coel's descendants are so numerous, I have grouped them by generation, giving an idea of their territories. I have excluded Coel's daughter Gwawl who married Cunedda, who appears in a later chart, and Coel's third son Dydrwr, whose descendants are not known. Because each line includes older and younger sons, I've lengthened the prime-of-life "floruit" to forty years, and averaged the generation span to about thirty years.

This table is a synthesis of several pedigrees, not all of which concur. Presenting them in a chronological form opens up even more queries. For instance, the few certain dates we know are the life of Kentigern and the fall of Ceredig, last king of Elmet, who was expelled by Edwin of Northumbria around 619/620. Ceredig is usually regarded as the son, or successor, of Gwallawg, who was involved in battles with the early kings of Bernicia (northern Northumbria and the southern territory of the Goddodin) in the 580s. But Gwallawg is recorded as the son of Llenauc, great-grandson of Coel, and thus could only have lived around the early 500s. It is possible that the sons were born in their father's older years, but that raises the question of older sons more likely to succeed (or, if they were killed in battle, to be

Table 3.3 The descendants of Coel

Floruit												
385-415	Coel. *Married* Ystradwel, daughter of Gadeon ap Eudaf Hen.											
410-450	Ceneu											Garbanion
440-480	Maeswig the Lame	Mar (*Mar and Maeswig may be the same person. He and his descendants may have ruled the Southern Pennines.*)					Pabo, Pillar of Britain (*He and his descendants may have ruled the Borders and Northern Pennies*)		Gwrwst the Ragged			Dyfnwal Moelmud (Dumna-gual Moilmut)
470-510	Llenauc	Arthwys (*this would give a life-span of roughly 450-520AD*)			Einion	Morydd	Samyl the Humble (*daughter married Maelgwyn; had sister called Arddun*)	(*? missing generation?*)	(*missing generation?*) Merchiaun the Lean *He and his descendants ruled Rheged*			Cyngar (*and brother Bran Hen*)
500-540	(*? missing generation*)	Ceidyaw	Eliffer of the Great Host	Cynvelin	Rhun the Wealthy	Madog Morfryn	Guticern	Dunod (*died 590*)	Elidyr the Stout	Cinmarc or Cynfarch the Dismal		Morcant Fwlch
530-570	Gwallawg (*fought Bernicians in 580s*)	Gwenddo-lau (*died at Arfder-yddin 573*)	Peredur and Gwrgi (*both died 580*)	Cynwyd	Perweur (*married Rhun ap Mael-gwyn*)	Myrddin	Cadwallon	Deiniol (*died 584*)	Llywarch Hen	Urien of Rheged (*killed c590*)	*possibly* Lleuddun (Loth)	Coledauc or Clydog
560-600	Ceredig (*last king of Elmet died c620*)			Cadrod *and* Cynfor Host-Protector						Owain (*killed c592*) and Rhun (*alive in 620s*)	*possibly* Gwrfan (Gawain?)	Morcant (*possible assassin of Urien*)
590-630										Kentigern (*lived 550-614*) and Rhoeth		

remembered in the poems). It suggests there may be a missing generation. The same applies to Dunod, who is always listed as a son of Pabo, yet the annals give his death as 590, suggesting either that he lived a very long time or that there is a generation missing.

The most confused genealogy belongs to the children of Mar (also called Mor) and Maeswig, grandsons of Coel. Indeed, Bartrum conjectures that Mar and Maeswig may have been the same person, as they feature commonly in the ancestry of their descendants. Mar's son Einion is sometimes listed as a son of Arthwys, but we know that Einion's son Rhun must have been contemporary with Maelgwyn Gwynedd (i.e. 500–540) because Rhun's daughter married Maelgwyn's son. Eliffer is sometimes listed as a son of Gwrwst, but the earlier pedigrees treat him as a son of Arthwys and this best suits the chronology.

This table should not be set in stone. It is an approximation of descendants and chronology but it is unlikely to be out more than 25/30 years either way. It places Arthwys somewhere in Yorkshire in the period 470–510 which, as we will see, ties in with the probable dates of Arthur of Badon. It does not mean that he is the same as King Arthur, but it raises the question as to whether some activities attributed to Arthwys in now-lost ancient records were picked up by Nennius and Geoffrey. We have tentatively recognised a part of the jigsaw.

These were not the only descendants of Coel and Cunedda, or "Men of the North". There were also the British rulers of Alclud (Strathclyde), with their capital at Dumbarton. Only one of the ancient records lists their pedigree, so we have no corroboration. Some of the other Men of the North, who ruled amongst the Votadini at Din Eidyn (Edinburgh) also belong to this pedigree, through Dyfnwal Hen rather than Coel, so I have amalgamated all of them below. The only change I have made is that, in the pedigrees, the future rulers of Strathclyde (Neithon and Bili), are listed as descended from Dyfnwal's son Gwyddno, but that is impossible according to the time scale. I believe this was a scribal error mistaking their descent from a later Gwyddno, descended from Garwynwyn. This is supported by the later Gwyddno having another son called Alpin who is recorded amongst the princes of Strathclyde.

Table 3.4 The descendants of Ceretic of Strathclyde

						Floruit
Cluim [Clemens]						340–370
Cinhil [Quintilius]						365–395
Cynloyp [Cynllwyb]						395–425
Ceretic guletic [Ceredig wledig]						420–450
Cinuit [Cynwyd]						450–480
Dumnagual Hen [Dyfnwal Hen] (whose daughter married Brychan of Manau)						475–505
Clynog	Cynfelyn	Cedig		Garwynwyn	Gwrwst	500–540
Tutagual	Clydno Eidin (*ruled Votadini*)	Serwan	Senyllt	Cawrdaf	Elidir the Wealthy (*killed c*555)	530–570
Rhydderch (*ruled Alclud c580–c614*)	Cynon (*may have survived Catraeth*)	Mordaf the Generous	Nudd the Generous	Gwyddno "Long-shanks"		560–600
Constantine				Neithon (*ruled Alclud 614–621*)		590–630

To complete the North, we need to match all of the above against the rulers of Dál Riata in Argyll, and the Pictish kings. The chronology of the kings of the Picts at this time is extremely confused and complicated, and is further aggravated by their kingship passing through the female line, making paternity difficult to track. The table below shows both sets of rulers as a list of kings, rather than a pedigree. This includes our third "Arthur".

Table 3.5 The rulers of Dál Riata and the Picts

Picts	**Dál Riata**
Talorc (400–424)	
Drust (424–453)	
Talorc (453–457)	
Nechtan Morbet (457–468)	
Drest (468–498)	
Galanan (498–513)	Fergus (498–501)
Drest mac Drust (513–516 and 521–529)	Domangart (501–507)
Drest mac Girom (513–521 and 529–533)	Comgall (507–538)
Gartnait and Cailtram (533–541)	Gabhran (538–558)
Talorg (541–552)	
Drest (552–553)	
Cennalath (553–557)	
Brude (556–584)	Conall (558–574)
Gartnait (584–602)	Aedan (574–608) and his son **Artúir** (*c*560–596)
Nechtan/Neithon (602–621) (*same as Neithon of Alclud in Table 3.4*)	

We now move our attention to Wales. Table 3.6 lists the pedigree of the kings of Dyfed. They were descended from the Irish tribe of the Déisi, who were driven out of Leinster in the fourth century and settled in Demetia in south-west Wales, under Eochaid mac Artchorp.

Table 3.6 The rulers of Dyfed

Irish pedigree	**Welsh pedigree**	**Floruit**	**Notes**
Artchorp	[Cyngar]	320–350	
Eochaid Almuir	[Ewein]	350–380	may be first to settle in Demetia
Corath	[Cyndwr/Kyndeyrn]	375–415	
Aeda Brosc	[Ewein "the Stout"]	405–435	
[Tryffin]	Tryphun	430–460	Contemporary with Vortigern
Aircol	Ayrcol	460–490	Contemporary with Ambrosius
	Erbin	485–515	may be a brother of Vortipor
Gartbuir [Vortipor]	Gwrdeber/Guortepir	490–520	Gildas noted was old in the 530s.
Congair [Cyngar]	Cyngar	515–545	
Retheoir [Pedr]	Peder	545–575	
Artúir	**Arthur**	570–600	This suggests a life-span of 550–620
Nowy	Nennue/Nougoy	600–630	also ruled Brycheiniog
Cloten [Gwlyddien]	Clothen	625–655	also ruled Brycheiniog
Cathen	Cathen	655–685	also ruled Brycheiniog
Cadwgan	Catgocaun/Gwgawn	680–710	also ruled Brycheiniog
Rhain	Regin/Rein	710–740	lived at the time of Seisyll of Ceredigion conquered part of Dyfed in *c*730

This is a rare example where there is both a Welsh pedigree and an independent Irish one. The latter, from the *Book of Uí Maine*, is listed in the first column, as reprinted by Bartrum from a twelfth century document held in the Bodleian Library (MS. Rawlinson B.502). The second column is the Welsh version from Jesus College MS.20. The Welsh list is dubious for the first five generations where at some stage a different pedigree has been fused on to Tryphun to create a descent from Magnus Maximus. I have placed those names in brackets but they are best ignored. From Tryphun on the two pedigrees agree. This pedigree is important because the third Arthur is our first "real" Arthur.

The chronology looks reliable. It allows for Eochaid to settle in Demetia in the mid to late fourth century, which fits in with known events. It allows Vortipor to be an old man at the time of Gildas (the above would give Vortipor's life-span as 470–540), and it terminates at the known dates assigned to Rhain. Allowing for an error of maybe no more than 20 years, we can fix Arthur of Dyfed firmly in the late sixth century.

The pedigree of the rulers of Gwent and Glywysing (Table 3.7), which includes our fourth "Arthur", is both complicated and confusing. Unlike in Gwynedd (Table 3.8), where a strong hereditary kingship became established early on, in Gwent this proved harder to do. Leslie Alcock, who undertook a major archaeological study at Dinas Powys in Glamorgan, has suggested that because Gwent and Glamorgan had been strongly Romanized, Gwent clung more tenaciously to the Roman way of life and no single hereditary kingship emerged for some time. Instead, there were competing administrators and governors, no doubt many from the old Silurian nobility, all of whom sought overall authority but few of whom achieved it. When chroniclers tried to piece this back together two or three centuries later the key records were lost. The position is not helped by Gwent incorporating three or four small kingdoms, which began independently and at various times merged or regained independence. Gwent and Glywysing were the two main kingdoms. Part of Glywysing was originally called Cernyw and became Gwynllwg. In later years when Glywysing merged with Gwent it was called Morgannwg. To the east of Gwent was Ergyng, which later became a sub-kingdom of Gwent.

The following table depicts all of these parallel and sometimes overlapping dynasties, and tries to rectify some of the obvious errors in the old genealogies. For instance, the Jesus College manuscript shows a descent from Caradog Vreichfras, placing him so far back as to be contemporary with the Emperor Constantine. Yet other sources we will encounter show him as a companion of King Arthur. A study of the pedigree shows that two recurring names (Meurig and Erb) have become repeated, conflating two pedigrees into one and doubling the span of time.

Table 3.7 The rulers of Gwent and Glywysing

Glywysing	**Gwent**	**Ergyng**	**Floruit**	
Owain Finddu			385–415	son of Magnus Maximus
Nor	Caradog		410–440	
Solor [Filur]	Ynyr [Honorius]		440–470	
Glywys	Caradog*		465–495	* may be *Vreichfras*
Gwynllyw (*married Brychan's daughter*)	Erb		495–525	
Cadog	Nynnio	Peibio	520–550	Cadog gave the kingship of Glywysing to Meurig
Meurig ab Enhinti	Llywarch or Teithfall	Cynfyn and Gwrgan	550–580	
Erbic	Tewdrig (*killed at Tintern in mid-620s*)	Caradog*	575–605	* more likely to be *Vreichfras*
Glywysing merged with Gwent	Meurig	Cawdraf	605–635	
	Athrwys	Medrawd	630–660	equates to a life span of 610–680
	Morgan (*died 665?*)	Gwrfoddw	660–690	
	Ithel [Einudd]		685–715	
	Ffernfael (*died 775*)		715–745	
	Athrwys		740–770	

Dates for some of the reigns are more reliable by the eighth century, and the death of Ffernfael ap Ithel is recorded as 775 in the *Welsh Annals*. We also know that Meurig's father, Tewdrig, died after the battle of Tintern when he was already of an advanced age. That battle has been variously dated between 577 and 630, with around 626 being the most likely. However, Morgan ap Athrwys is believed to have died in 665, which is too early for his position in the chart. We know that many of these kings lived to an advanced age, even the later ones not listed here. Hywel ap Rhys died in around 885, well into his eighties; Tewdrig ap Llywarch was also into his eighties. So we may find a 25–30 generation span insufficient in this instance. However, that makes it even more difficult to count back from Tewdrig, as it would push Owain Finddu, son of Magnus Maximus, back too far. Meurig's mother Enhinti is identified as either the daughter or sister of Urien of Rheged, so I have placed him in the mid sixth century, even though he was probably of the same generation as Cadog.

The table is nevertheless within a reasonable degree of accuracy and provides a life span for Arthur of Gwent of around 610–680, perhaps slightly earlier to accommodate his son and the known longevity of his grandfather. This will seem late for those who have theorised that he is the Arthur of

Badon. This Arthur's primary advocates are Alan Wilson and Baram Blackett and, in *Artorius Rex Discovered*, they give Arthur's dates as 503–575, or a *floruit* of 525–555, a century earlier than the above. I find it difficult to accept such a date if the above pedigree is even approximately accurate. I suspect we may be missing a generation or two, even assuming the lines of succession are correct.

One of the curiosities of this table is that it identifies a person called Medrawd (or Mordred) as a grandson of Caradog, contemporary with Arthur.

In order to set these chronologies against the main powerbase in Wales, it will be useful here to set out the ruling dynasty of Gwynedd, where the chronology is better understood. It will help us understand who else was active at the time of Badon, and during the lifetimes of the other Arthurs so far identified.

Table 3.2 provided dates for Cunedda of 440–470 but, as discussed, he almost certainly belonged to an earlier generation which I have adjusted here. These pedigrees are taken from Harleian MS. 3859; though I have modernised the names where possible for easier understanding. Also, as with Table 3.3, because I am charting brothers and cousins, I have allowed a 40–year *floruit*, rather than 30, and used an average generation span of 30 years rather than 25–30.

The chronology throws up a few anomalies, especially in the line of Ceredigion. We know that Seisyll conquered parts of Dyfed sometime in the eighth century, probably in 730. To accommodate this I have had to move Seisyll, his father and descendants down by two generations. However, as we have no independent dates to confirm Clydog's ancestors it is impossible to know when these missing generations occur. Something has to be adrift. There are nine generations from Cunedda to Arthwen, who died in 807. Taking the average 25–30 years per generation, that gives 250 years, which would put Arthwen's mid-life at around 675, suggesting we are missing four generations. It means we cannot be sure where to place Arthfoddw, which may prove important later.

Table 3.8 The rulers of Gwynedd and other descendants of Cunedda

Floruit	**Gwynedd**	**Rhos**	**Ceredigion**	**Meirionydd**	**Dunoding**
410–440	Cunedda				
440–480	Einion the Stricken		Ceredig	[Tybion, *stayed in Manau*]	Dunaut
470–510	Cadwallon Longhand	Owain White-tooth	Usai	Meirion	Eifion
500–540	Maelgwyn (*died c549*)	Cynlas the Red (*the Cuneglasus of Gildas*)	Serwyl	Cadwaladr	Dingad
530–570	Rhun the Tall	Maig	Boddw	Gwrin Cut-Beard	Meurig
560–600	Beli	Cangan or Aeddan	**Arthfoddw**	Clydno	Eifion
590–630	Iago (*died c615*)	Cadwal (*possibly killed at Chester c615*)	Arthlwys	Gwyddno	Isaac
620–660	Cadfan	Idgwyn	*missing generation?*	Idris (*died 632, allegedly killed by Arthur*)	Pobien
650–690	Cadwallon (*died 634*)	Einion	*missing generation?*	Sualda or Yswalt	Pobddelw
680–720	Cadwaladr (*died 664 or 682*)	Rhufon	Clydog	Brochwel	Eifion
710–750	Idwal the Roebuck	Meirion	Seisyll (*conquered part of Dyfed in c730*)	Einudd	Brochwel
740–780	Rhodri the Bald (*died 754*)	Caradog (*killed 798*)	Arthwen (*died 807*)	Ednyfed	Eigion
770–810	Cynan (*died 816*) *His daughter Essyllt married Gwriad of Man*	Hywel (*died 825*)	Dyfnwallon	Brochwel	Ieuanawl

Table 3.9 The rulers of Powys, Gwrtheyrnion and Brycheiniog

Floruit	Powys (primary line)		Powys (subsidiary lines)		Builth and Gwrtheyrnion	Brycheiniog
420–450	Gwrtheyrn [Vortigern]					
450–480	Categirn (died *c*455)				Pascent	Brychan
480–510	Cadell Gleaming-Hilt		Brittu [Brydw]		Riagath/Riocatus	Rhain the red-eyed
510–540	Cyngen the Famous		Camuir	Thewer *married* Casanauth Wledig	Idnerth	Rhigeneu
540–570	Brochwel of the Tusks		Millo	Cynan	Pawl	Llywarch
570–600	Cynan of the White Chariot	Mawn	Cynan	Cenelaph	Elaed	Idwallon
600–620	Eiludd	Llemenig (Lancelot?)	Elfoddw	Rhun	Morvo	Rhiwallon
630–660	Beli		Gurhaiernn [Gwrhearn]	Madog	Gwyddaint	Ceindrech *married* Cloten of Dafyd, *fl* 625–655
660–690	Gwylog		Hesselis	Merin	Pascen	Cathen, ruled Brycheiniog and Dyfed
690–720	Elisedd			Tudwal	Gloud	Cadwgon
720–750	Brochwel			Sandde	Brawstudd, *wife of* Arthfael ap Rhys	Rhain
750–780	Cadell (*died 808*)			Madog	Rhys	Tewdwr
780–810	Cyngen (*died 855*)			Noë	Hywel	Nowy

In the house of Gwynedd, we find that around the time of Cadwallon and Cadwaladr, the chronology shifts out of sync, suggesting an earlier date. This may mean that they were descended from the older sons and thus the generation span should be reduced to 20–25 years. However, by the time of Cynan this has righted itself, suggesting that some younger sons must have inherited, perhaps through the deaths of older brothers in conflict.

We know virtually nothing about the rulers of the other three kingdoms to be able to corroborate their dates although the death dates for Idris of Meirionydd and Cadwal of Rhos, taken from the Annals, do fit the pattern. There is a legend about the giant Idris, after whom the mountain Cader Idris is supposed to be named, that says he was killed by Arthur. The ruler Idris was called Idris the Tall, and the date of his death would be roughly contemporary with Arthur of Gwent, or just possibly Arthur of Dyfed.

There are two other major Welsh kingdoms that we have not yet charted and, because they are related, I shall list their rulers together. These were Powys and Brycheiniog. Hemmed between the two was the small but historically significant kingdom of Buellt and Gwrtheyrnion, whose later rulers inherited Glywysing and Brycheiniog.

The pedigrees for Powys are highly corrupted and virtually no two agree. Bartrum has, however, detected a reasonable pattern which may reflect the original. There is still much confusion over the immediate descendants of Vortigern, and, although the general consensus is that Cyngen the Famous was the son of Cadell Gleaming-Hilt, there are sufficient other pedigrees that show an additional generation between them. However, we know that Eiludd survived the Battle of Chester in 615 in which his brother Selyf was killed. It is also fairly certain that Elisedd, whose memory is commemorated in Eliseg's Pillar, erected by his great-grandson Cyngen, was active in the early 700s.

The table above includes a secondary but otherwise unknown cadet line of Powys, descended from Brittu, variously treated as a son of Vortigern, Cattegirn, or Cadell. I've shown him here as Cadell's brother because otherwise his descendants shift too far out of sync.

* * *

The pedigrees of Armorica are also vague and frequently confused with the pedigrees of Dumnonia. Part of the problem is that when the Britons migrated to Armorica in the fifth century, they took local names with them, and two of the principalities of Armorica were called Domnonée and Cornouaille. The latter should not be confused with Cernow, which later became Cornwall, or Cernyw which, as we shall see, was part of Glywysing. Just to add to the confusion, the Welsh name for Armorica was Llydaw, and it seems that name also had its equivalent in south-east Wales, probably on the borders of Brycheiniog and Gwent, and perhaps bordering Ergyng. Caradog Vreichfras was associated with Llydaw, possibly suggesting that he ruled Brittany, but which probably means he ruled territory from Brycheiniog to Ergyng, including Llydaw.

Most of these pedigrees trace their descent from Eudaf Hen. However, unlike the Welsh pedigrees, the Breton and Cornish ones have become greatly corrupted and merged with legend, to the point that the two have become almost indistinguishable. The following presents a reasonable picture whilst recognising the non-historicity of much of it. We shall need to sift through the data very carefully.

Table 3.10 The rulers of Dumnonia and Armorica [Brittany]

fl 340–370	Eudaf Hen (*his daughter Elen married Magnus Maximus*)			
fl 370–395	Cynan and Gadeon (*sons of Eudaf*)			
fl 395–425	Gwrfawr or Morfawr (*son of Gadeon*)			
	Dumnonia	**Armorica**	**Domnonée**	**Cornouaille**
fl 425–455	Tudwal	Cynan Meriadoc		
fl 450–480	Cynfor	Grallo/ Gradlonus		Iahan Reeth (*possibly Riothamus*)
fl 475–505	Custennin *Fendigiad*	Saloman	Riwal	Daniel
fl 505–535	Erbin and Meirchion *(cousins) ruled separately*	Aldroenus	Deroch	Budic
fl 530–560	Geraint ab Erbin and Mark ab Meirchion *ruled separately*	Budic ——— *Kingdom usurped by Canao*	Riatham then his brother Ionas *Conmor seized power during his rule*	Meliau or Macliau *Title usurped from his brother Rivold*
fl 560–590	Cadwr	Macliaw	Iudwal or Judhael	
fl 585–615	Peredur	Waroch	Iuthael	
fl 615–645	Tewdwr	Canao (II)	Haelog	
fl 640–670	Erbin	Alanus		
fl 670–700	Geraint (who fought the Saxons in 710)	Budic		

Table 3.11 The ancestors of the Saxons

Floruit	Kent	West Saxons	Bernicia	Deira	East Angles	East Saxons	Mercia	Lindsey
360–390		Freawine	Beornic	Saebald	Tytmon	Gesecg	Wermund	Finn
390–420	Wecta	Wig	Gechbrond (*ASC reverses Beornic and Brond*)	Saefugl	Trygils	Antsecg	Offa	Friodulf
415–445	Witta	Gewis	Alusa (*ASC has Aloc*)	Soemil (*not in ASC*)	Rothmund	Swebba	Angengeot	Frealaf
445–475	Wihtgils	Esla	Ingui (*ASC adds extra generation Angenwit*)	Swaerta (*Nennius*) Westerfalca (*ASC*)	Hryp	Sigefugel	Eomer	Woden
470–500	Hengist	Elesa	Esa *ASC* Athelbert (*Nennius*)	Wilgsil	Wilhelm	Bedca	Icel	Winta
500–530	Octa	Cerdic	Eobba	Wyscfrea	Wehha or Guechan	Offa	Cnebba	Cretta
525–555	Ossa or Oisc	Cynric or Creoda	Ida	Yffi	Wuffa	Aescwine	Cynewald	Cueldgils
555–585	Eormenric	Ceawlin	Athelric (*died* 593?)	Aelle (*died c599*)	Tytill	Sledda	Creoda (*died c*593)	Cædbæd
580–610	Athelbert (*died c*618)	Cutha	Athelfrith (*died* 616)	Athelric (*died* 604)	Redwald (*died 625*)	Saebert (*died c616*)	Pybba (*died c*606)	Bubba

Not all the names in the line of Armorica are related. Cynan's line was interrupted after Budic when the kingdom was usurped by Canao, whose descendants ruled until Cynan's line was restored under Alanus (*see* Chapter 14 for further discussion on the implications of this for the Tristan legend).

The above has covered the Welsh pedigrees, but we also need to consider the early Saxon royal pedigrees, as listed in Nennius and the *ASC*. The *ASC* takes its ancestries back to the god Woden, but though we can ignore that, that is not a reason for treating the whole of the ancestries as fabrication. They are equally as reliable or suspect as the British ones. The *ASC* pedigrees do not always agree with those in Nennius, so where they vary I have noted accordingly. Nennius provides no pedigree for the West Saxons, East Saxons, South Saxons or Lindsey. Indeed the *ASC* is also silent on the South Saxons, yet their chieftain, Aelle, was regarded by Bede as the first Bretwalda, or overlord of the Saxons. Nennius identifies Soemil as the first to separate Deira from Bernicia, and with his *floruit* of around 440, he must remain the earliest named Angle in Britain. Nennius also credits Wilhelm as being the first to rule over the East Angles, showing that in those two generations the Angles had moved from being mercenaries and invaders, to settlers with established territories. Icel and Hengist both fall into that same generation, and although logic would suggest that Hengist must have reigned earlier, if he really was the first Saxon to be invited over by Vortigern, the record suggests something different. We will explore this in more detail later.

The purpose of exploring these pedigrees in such detail has been to try and ascertain an approximate chronology as a backcloth against which we can paint in some detail. Now we can start our exploration for Arthur amongst the ancient chronicles.

4

THE CHRONICLERS

1. The early chronicles

Now that we have some idea of who lived when, it would be helpful to explore the few relevant chronicles that exist in relation to Britain to see what they can tell us about what was going on. In order to fix a date for Arthur we need to chart the events leading to Badon.

A good starting place is not in Britain, but in Gaul, with the *Gallic Chronicle*, one of the few contemporary documents that give us a firm, if contestable, date. We do not know who compiled the *Chronicle*, but it was a continuation of an earlier chronicle established by the scholar Jerome, finished in 378AD. In fact there are two *Gallic Chronicles*, one of which stops at the year 452, whilst the other continues to 511. The 452 *Chronicle* was once attributed to Prosper of Aquitaine, who also produced his own continuation of Jerome's *Chronicle*, but whoever compiled the 452 *Chronicle* – and there is a surprising candidate somewhat closer to home whom we shall encounter later – held ecclesiastical views that differed from Prosper's. Prosper's work shows him as a supporter of the views of Augustine of Hippo, whilst the Gallic chronicler was sympathetic towards the Pelagians. His *Chronicle* is important because it was a contemporary record by someone who knew Britain.

The dates within the *Gallic Chronicle* are not without their problems as the compiler used more than one system. However, the supporters of the *Chronicle* have, to a large degree, reconciled the dates, especially in the later years, and the two that interest us are accurate to within a year or two.

The *Chronicle* has two entries relating to Britain in the post-Roman period.

> *Honorius XVI* [410AD]. At this time the strength of the Romans was completely reduced by [a host of enemies] who were gaining strength. The British provinces were devastated by the Saxons. The Vandals and the Alans devastated part of Gaul; what remained the tyrant Constantine occupied. The Sueves occupied the better part of Spain. Finally, Rome itself, the capital of the world, suffered most foully the depredations of the Goths.

> *Theodosius XVIII* [441AD]. The British, who to this time had suffered from various defeats and misfortunes, are reduced to the power of the Saxons [i.e. the Saxons held sway].

The 511 *Chronicle* records the last event in similar words, though with one interesting addition: "Britannia, lost to the Romans, yields to the power of the Saxons."

These two entries are of great significance. The first makes clear that the Saxon incursions into Britain were of some strength, sufficient to "devastate" the provinces, though whether it means some or all four (five?) provinces, is not clear. Some authorities have preferred to treat this entry as relating to the year 408, suggesting a build-up of Saxons within Britain and that the lack of help by Rome against the Saxons is what caused the British to eject the Roman administration. It also adds reason to why, around this time, the British were so keen to appoint their own emperor. As the record shows, though, "the tyrant Constantine" (Constantine III) moved away from Britain to occupy Gaul, leaving Britain further bereft of forces.

The second entry is the more remarkable. The wording "yields to the power" implies that by 441, Britain was under the control of the Saxons, an event usually placed in the second half of the century. Likewise, the 511 *Chronicle*'s phrase "lost to the Romans" implies that it was not until the year 441 that Britain formally passed from Roman control to Saxon. Even though

Honorius had apparently told the British to look to their own defences in 410, he had probably not meant to sever Britain from the Empire. For thirty years it remained in limbo.

Another entry of interest appears in the chronicles maintained by Prosper of Aquitaine, which ran parallel to the *Gallic Chronicles*. Prosper lived throughout this period, about 390–465, and had a keen awareness of events, especially during his role as notary to Pope Leo the Great. He records the following event for the year 429:

> Agricola, a Pelagian, the son of the Pelagian bishop Severianus, corrupted the British churches by the insinuation of his doctrine. But at the persuasion of the deacon Palladius, Pope Celestine sent Germanus, bishop of Auxerre, as his representative and, having rejected the heretics, directed the British to the catholic faith.

Prosper is the only source for the date of Germanus's visit to Britain, placing it right in the middle of that period from the end of Roman administration in 409 to the apparent domination of Britain by the Saxons in 441. Germanus was a native of Auxerre, in north-central Gaul, and came from an aristocratic family. Trained in law, he became a governor of Armorica and was raised to the rank of *dux*. In 418, he was appointed Bishop of Auxerre.

Constantius of Lyon wrote a "life" of Germanus, *Vita Sancti Germani*, around the year 480. Although it was written while those who knew Germanus were still alive, the *Vita* shows little evidence of research. Any factual reliability is buried beneath a welter of hyperbole and hagiophily.

Constantius confirms Germanus's visit, saying that it had arisen following "a deputation from Britain". We do not know who in Britain sent the deputation, but it shows that Britain was not isolated, and that there was traffic to and from Gaul, and probably the rest of the Mediterranean world.

Constantius tells us that Germanus, with Bishop Lupus, crossed the Channel during winter. They were beset by a great storm, but through prayer arrived safely in Britain. We do not know where Germanus landed, but it was probably at Richborough in Kent, where there was a strong Christian community. Constantius reveals that they were met by "great crowds" who had come "from many regions", and that news of their arrival spread far and wide. Eventually the Pelagians, who had gone "into hiding" for fear of Germanus, reappeared, "flaunting their wealth" and prepared for a debate at a "meeting place". Constantius does not tell us where this was, but as he tells us that soon after the debate Germanus visited the shrine of St Alban, we may presume that they met at the Roman amphitheatre at Verulamium. Verulamium was the third largest town in Britain and remained fully functioning throughout the fifth century.

During the debate, Germanus, through his inspired responses, out-manipulated the Pelagians and received the accolades of the crowds. Constantius goes on to say that a man "of high military rank" gave his young blind daughter to the bishops to heal. Germanus suggested that the tribune take his daughter to the heretics, but the heretics blanched at the idea and begged the bishops to cure the girl, which they did. Germanus and Lupus won the day and "this damnable heresy had been thus stamped out."

After visiting the shrine, Germanus tripped, injuring his foot, and had to be taken to a house where he was confined to a bed for several days. A fire broke out, burning several houses "roofed with reeds", and the wind carried the flames towards the house where Germanus lay. Although the flames engulfed the surrounding houses, Germanus's was spared.

What Constantius tells us next is most revealing:

> Meanwhile, the Saxons and the Picts had joined forces to make war upon the Britons. The latter had been compelled to withdraw their forces within their camp and, judging their resources to be utterly unequal to the contest, asked the help of the holy prelates. The latter sent back a promise to come and hastened to follow it.

Constantius does not tell us where this "camp" was situated, but does say that it was during Lent and that upon the arrival of the bishops the soldiers eagerly sought baptism. A small chapel was built out of branches, and Easter was celebrated. In the absence of any other military leader, Germanus offered himself as their general. Constantius continues:

> He chose some lightly-armed troops and made a tour of the outworks. In the direction from which the enemy were expected he saw a valley enclosed by steep mountains. Here he stationed an army on a new model, under his own command.
>
> By now the savage host of the enemy was close at hand and Germanus rapidly circulated an order that all should repeat in unison the call he would give as a battle-cry. Then, while the enemy were still secure in the belief that their approach was unexpected, the bishops three times chanted the Alleluia. All, as one man, repeated it and the shout they raised rang through the air and was repeated many times in the confined space between the mountains.
>
> The enemy were panic-stricken, thinking that the surrounding rocks and the very sky itself were falling on them. Such was their terror that no effort of their feet seemed enough to save them. They fled in every direction, throwing away their weapons and thankful if they could save their skins. Many threw themselves into the river, which they had just crossed at their ease, and were drowned in it.

This became known as the Alleluia victory and entered legend. For Constantius, writing fifty or so years later, it would have been a noted event, and therefore it is all the more surprising that he does not say where it took place. Indeed, throughout his biography of Germanus, Constantius's description of Britain is woefully lacking, suggesting he had not visited Britain himself. There is a site in what was north Powys, called Maesgarmon, just outside Mold in Flintshire, where the River Alun runs through a steep valley. If this was the site then the combined Pict/Saxon army had sailed along the River Dee, suggesting the army may also have included Irish warriors. This area has several Arthurian sites, including Moel Arthur and particularly Moel Fenlli (*see* Chapter 6).

What is perhaps most surprising about this account is that the British forces had no competent battle leader of their own.

Germanus was a *dux* in his own right and could have been the most senior official at the "camp", and been offered the command through respect. Or it could have been a purely nominal gesture, with Germanus being the spiritual leader of the troops, whilst the temporal commander is conveniently forgotten. It may even be that this battle had nothing to do with Germanus, who may have become confused with the British holy man Garmon, of whom more later.

We may wonder, though, whether by the year 429 the British troops had become demoralised and lacked training, even though this was not long after Cunedda's forces had been restationed in North Wales. Gildas has some comments on the state of the British defences, as we shall see in the next chapter.

In summing up the victory Constantius remarks:

> Thus this most wealthy island, with the defeat of both its spiritual and its human foes, was rendered secure in every sense.

No matter how much Constantius embellishes this text, he was writing within only a generation or two of the real events and his readers would know exactly how Britain had fared over those years. Thus we must give some credence to his account that at this time Britain was wealthy and still unconquered by the Saxons.

Constantius reveals that some years after this visit there was a resurgence of Pelagianism, and Germanus was again called upon to visit Britain, this time accompanied by Severus, bishop of Trier. The decision to return to Britain must have been sudden (despite another synod of bishops) because British officials were unaware of it. An official called Elafius, described as "one of the leading men in the country", hurried to meet Germanus. Otherwise the visit is all too similar to the earlier one. The resurgence of Pelagianism seems to have been restricted to just a few, who were quickly identified and condemned. In order to prevent any further growth of Pelagianism, the leading heretics were taken by Germanus into exile on the continent.

There is no separate record of Elafius in the pedigrees, but that would not be surprising if he were a church, rather than civic, official. Amongst the descendants of Coel is the Latinised name of Eleutherius (Eliffer in British), and although he lived a century later, in northern Britain, the name was not uncommon. I conjecture more on Elafius later.

Constantius does not provide a date for this second visit or give any indication of how long it was after the first. The only clue is that Germanus died soon after his return. His death is usually dated to around 448, but that contradicts other known events. Most significant is that upon his return to Gaul, Germanus was sent to Ravenna to plead with the Emperor about the rebellious Bretons, but the 452 *Chronicle* records the downfall of their leader Tibatto by the year 437. This would place Germanus's second visit in the year 436, a date which has growing support.

At the core of Constantius's account is a picture of a wealthy Britain, at least in the south. It was subject to surprise attacks from the Saxons and Picts but, by 436, the officials had regained some level of control and Britain was, perhaps, in a period of relative calm.

2. The Welsh Annals

The *Welsh Annals*, or *Annales Cambriae*, is a list of events, recorded year by year, which was kept by the British chroniclers. Over the years copies were made of copies and none of the original documents survives. The earliest copy (Manuscript A) dates from the end of the tenth century, but the earliest date entered relates to the year 447. Another version (Manuscript B) is of a later date although the entries go back far earlier. They are believed to have been copied from another document, most likely one of the Irish Annals, which runs until 1203, as does a third version (Manuscript C). Where A, B and C overlap, they are fairly consistent, with just an occasional variance of a few years.

Unfortunately, there are only six entries for the fifth century and eighteen for the sixth century. Clearly either the original *Annals* were in such a poor state that later copyists were unable to interpret records against certain years or, more likely, the records were not commenced until much later. In fact a regular sequence of dates does not start until the year 807. The Welsh ruler Merfyn the Freckled, whose reign began in 825, encouraged the study of

British history, and it is likely that during his reign the *Annals* as we know them were brought together from a variety of earlier documents. Therefore none of the fifth and sixth century records is likely to be contemporary. Moreover, it is impossible to tell whether entries were copied correctly from originals, or were distorted by error.

There is an added problem in knowing which dates apply. The *Annals* do not record a standard date. Written in Latin, and thus recorded in Roman numerals, the entries begin from Year 1. Assuming that each individual year is accurately recorded, we need to find a year in which the event is recorded against a verifiable time line, and count back. The usual event selected is against Year 9, "Easter altered on the Lord's Day by Pope Leo." This happened at Easter 455, which makes Year 1 equal 447, the generally accepted date. Originally it was believed Leo had adjusted Easter earlier, in 452. Therefore, some sources list the *Annals* as starting in 444. There are other entries which help us identify dates, especially in relation to St Columba (Columcille), whose life was written by Adomnán, one of his followers, and who was excommunicated from Ireland in 561 and died on 9 June 597. The following *Annals* concur with this timeline, which allows some degree of confidence.

Listed below are the relevant entries from the fifth and sixth centuries. The key dates are those for 518, 539 and 575.

447 Days as dark as night
459 St Patrick raised to the Lord
460 St David born thirty years after Patrick left Menevia
518 The Battle of Badon in which Arthur carries the Cross of Our Lord Jesus Christ for three days and three nights on his shoulders and the Britons were the victors
523 St Columcille born. The death of St Brigid
539 The battle of Camlann, in which Arthur and Medraut fell: and there was plague in Britain and Ireland
549 A great plague in which Mailcun king of Venedotia died
560 The death of Gabran son of Dungart
564 Columcille leaves for Britain
565 The voyage of Gildas to Ireland

572 Gildas, the wisest of Britons, died
575 The battle of Armterid between the sons of Eliffer and Guendoleu, son of Keidiau, in which battle Guendoleu fell; Myrddin became mad
581 Gwrgi and Peredur, sons of Eliffer, died
591 The conversion of Constantine to the Lord
594 Edilburt reigned in England
597 The death of Columcille. The death of king Dunaut, son of Pabo. Augustine and Mellitus converted the English to Christ

Apart from the references to Arthur and Myrddin (Merlin), what strikes me most about these *Annals* is what little reference is made to other secular rulers. You would expect entries on such major church figures as Patrick and Columba, for example, but the only individuals actually designated as king (*rex*) are Mailcun (Maelgwyn) and Dunaut, and the Saxon ruler Edilburt (Athelbert). There is no mention of such well-attested rulers as Cadwallon or Rhun, let alone the more shadowy figures of Vortigern or Ambrosius Aurelianus. Most amazing of all, there is no mention of the domination of the Saxons. The monks may not have wanted to record the activities of pagan invaders, but it is surprising that there is no mention of Hengist or Cerdic or Aelle, names that figure strongly in Arthurian history. All of this suggests that not only were the *Annals* compiled at a later date, when the only reliable dates available to the chroniclers were a few well remembered events in church history, but that they came from a source, such as the Irish Annals, for which these secular British events were of no interest.

With this in mind, one wonders just where the entries for Arthur and Merlin came from. Are these genuine or merely added by a later scribe who enjoyed the heroic tales? All the other entries are brief references to births, deaths and disasters, but the Arthurian and Myrddin entries are longer. The Badon entry almost feels like an echo of Germanus's Alleluia victory (which is conspicuously missing), as if there were a folk memory of some distant battle of religious significance. We will encounter a similar reference amongst the list of Arthur's battles rescued by Nennius.

I do not believe that a monk would deliberately invent a record, though I believe he could include one in good faith. The other entries are known from other records, and no one would doubt their existence. To believe that the Arthur and Merlin entries were the only fabricated ones is to suggest a conspiracy, and there is no reason to suspect that of a ninth century annalist. However, they could have been copied from a document, now lost, which was erroneous, suggesting that both the names and the dates must be suspect.

We may accept that the *Welsh Annals* provide hearsay evidence that someone called Arthur achieved a major victory at Badon, and that another Arthur (not necessarily the same one) "fell" at the battle of Camlann. They provide similar evidence for the existence of Merlin, even though this Merlin lived over thirty years after Arthur's passing.

3. The Anglo-Saxon Chronicle

As with the *Welsh Annals*, there are no copies of the *Anglo-Saxon Chronicle* (*ASC*) contemporary with the fifth or sixth centuries. The oldest surviving copy, known as the Winchester Manuscript, seems to have been compiled during the reign of King Alfred, around 890, and continued by others into the tenth century. There are other variants of the *ASC*, most of much later date. As a consequence the reliability of the early entries is always open to question. It is evident that the compilers of the *ASC* drew upon other sources such as Bede for the entry for 449. Bede himself had relied heavily on Gildas for the early part of his history, so much of the *ASC* information is third hand. Unlike the *Welsh Annals*, however, the *ASC* tends to include more complete entries, sometimes adding anecdotes not available elsewhere.

Once again I've selected records from the period 410–600, focusing on areas of importance. The translation comes primarily from Manuscript A, the oldest of the surviving versions of the *ASC*, but I've included any additional or variant data from the other versions within [square] brackets. I've kept place names in the original Saxon and show them in italics. Any brief interpretations by myself are in [square] brackets and italics.

418. The Romans gathered all the gold-hoards there were in Britain; some they hid in the earth, so that no man might find them, and some they took with them to Gaul.

443. The British sent men over the sea to Rome, and asked for help against the Picts, but they never got it, because [the Romans] were on an expedition against King Attila the Hun. They sent then to the Angles, and the Anglian Aethelings, with the same request.

449. Mauricius [Martianus] and Valentinian succeeded to the kingdom and ruled seven years. And in their days Hengist and Horsa, invited by Vortigern, king of the Britons, came to Britain [in three ships] landing at the place which is named *Ypwines fleot*, at first to help the Britons, but later they fought against them. [The king Vortigern gave them land in the south-east of this land on condition that they fought against the Picts.] They did so and had victory wherever they went. They then sent to Angeln, requesting more aid, and commanded that they should be told of the Britons' worthlessness and the choice nature of their land. They soon sent hither a greater host to help the others. Then came the men of three Germanic tribes: Old Saxons; Angles; and Jutes. [. . .] Their war-leaders were two brothers, Hengist and Horsa, who were Wihtgil's sons. First of all, they killed and drove away the king's enemies; then later they turned on the king and the British, destroying through fire and the sword's edge.

455. Hengist and Horsa fought against Vortigern the king in the place which is called *Ægælesþrep*, and his brother Horsa was killed. And after that Hengist, and Æsc his son, succeeded to the kingdom.

456. Hengist and Aesc fought against the Britons in the place called *Crecganford*, and there killed 4,000 men [4 troops]; and the Britons then abandoned *Centlond* and in great fear fled to *Lundenbyrg*.

465. Hengist and Aesc fought against the Welsh *[i.e. British]* near *Wippedesfleot*, and there killed 12

Welsh chieftains and one of their thegns, whose name was Wipped, was killed there.

473. Hengist and Aesc fought against the Welsh and seized countless war-loot, and the Welsh fled from the English like fire.

477. Aelle and his three sons came to Britain with three ships at the place which is named *Cymenes ora*, and there killed many Welsh and drove some to flight into the wood which is named *Andredes leag*.

485. Here Aelle fought against the Welsh near the margin of *Mearcrædes burnam*.

488. Here Aesc succeeded to the kingdom and was king of the inhabitants of *Cantwara* 24 years [34 years].

491. Here Aelle and Cissa besieged *Andredes cester* and killed all who lived there; there was not even one Briton left there.

495. Here two ealdormen, Cerdic and Cynric his son, came to Britain with five ships at the place called *Cerdices ora*, and on the same day fought against the Welsh [and were victors in the end].

501. Here Port and his two sons, Bieda and Mægla came with two ships to Britain at the place which is called *Portesmuþa* and immediately seized land] and killed a certain young British man – very noble.

508. Here Cerdic and Cynric killed a certain British king, whose name was Natanleod [Nazanleod] and five thousand men with him, after whom the land as far as *Cerdices ford* was named *Natanleag*.

514. Here the West Saxons came to Britain with three ships at the place called *Cerdices ora*, and Stuf and Wihtgar fought against the Britons and put them to flight.

519. Here Cerdic and Cynric succeeded to the kingdom of the West Saxons; and the same year they fought against the Britons at the place they now name *Cerdices ford*. And the royal family of the West Saxons ruled from that day on.

527. Here Cerdic and Cynric fought against the Britons at the place which is called *Cerdices leag*.

530. Here Cerdic and Cynric took the Isle of Wight and killed a few [many] men at *Wihtgaræsbyrg*.
534. Here Cerdic passed away and his son Cynric continued to rule 26 years; and they gave all Wight to their two *nefa [*i.e. *nephews or grandsons]* Stuf and Wihtgar.
538. Here on 16 February the sun grew dark from early morning until *undern [9.00 a.m.]*.
540. Here on 20 June the sun grew dark and the stars appeared for well-nigh half an hour after *undern*.
544. Here Wihtgar passed away and they buried him at *Wihtgaræsbyrg*.
547. Here Ida, from whom originated the royal family of the Northumbrians, succeeded to the kingdom and ruled twelve years. And he built Bamburgh which was first enclosed by a stockade and thereafter by a wall.
552. Here Cynric fought against the Britons at the place which is named *Searo byrg* and put the Britons to flight.
556. Here Cynric and Ceawlin fought against the Britons at *Beran byrg*.
560. Here Ceawlin succeeded to the kingdom in Wessex, and Aelle succeeded to the kingdom of the Northumbrians, Ida having died, and each of them ruled 30 years.
565. Here Columba the priest came from Ireland to Britain to teach the Picts, and made a monastery on the island of Iona. Here Athelberht succeeded to the kingdom of Kent and held it 53 years.
568. Here Ceawlin and Cutha [Ceawlin's brother] fought against Athelberht and drove him into Kent; and they killed two ealdormen, Oslaf [Oslac] and Cnebba, on *Wibbandun*.
571. Here Cuthwulf [Cutha] fought against the Britons at *Biedcanford* and took four settlements: *Lygeanburg* [Limbury], *Ægelesburg* [Aylesbury], *Benningtun* [Benson?], *Egonesham* [Eynsham]; and in the same year he passed away.
577. Here Cuthwine and Ceawlin fought against the Britons and they killed three kings, Coinmail, Condidan

and Farinmail, in the place which is called Dyrham; and took three cities, Gloucester, Cirencester and Bath.

584. Here Ceawlin and Cutha fought against the Britons at the place which is named *Fetham leag*, and Cutha was killed; and Ceawlin took many towns and countless war-loot.

588. Here King Aelle passed away and after him Aethelric ruled for five years.

591. Here Ceol ruled for five [six] years.

592. Here there was great slaughter at *Woddes beorge* and Ceawlin was driven out. Gregory succeeded to the papacy in Rome.

593. Here Ceawlin and Cwichelm and Crida perished; and Aethelfrith succeeded to the kingdom of the Northumbrians.

595 [596] Here Pope Gregory sent Augustine to Britain with very many monks who preached God's word to the English nation.

597. Here Ceolwulf began to rule in Wessex and he continually fought and strove either against the Angle race or against the Welsh or against the Picts or against the Scots.

601. Here Pope Gregory sent the pallium to Archbishop Augustine in Britain and very many religious teachers to help him [and among them was] Paulinus who turned Edwin, king of Northumbria, to baptism.

603. Here Aedan, king of the Scots, fought with Dæl Reoda and against Aethelfrith, king of the Northumbrians, at *Dægsanstan* and they killed almost all his raiding army; [there Aethelfrith's brother, Theobald, was killed with all his troop. After that no king of the Scots dared lead a raiding army into his nation. Herin, son of Hussa, led the raiding army there.]

There is no mention of Arthur, but that is perhaps not too surprising. The Saxons liked to record their victories and ignore their defeats. It is a shame that the *Welsh Annals* are not as complete, so that we had a more adequate view of both sides of the same story, although, arguably, the two chronicles are not telling the same story. The *Welsh Annals* are primarily church history with some secular references, whilst the *ASC* concentrates on the conquest of Britain. The only events to appear in both lists are the start of Columba's mission and that of Augustine's. Fortunately, both dates agree.

If we assume, for the moment, that the dates in both chronicles are correct, then we can see that at the time of the Battle of Badon in 518 Cerdic was in the thick of his conquest of what would become Wessex, establishing himself as king the following year, in 519. These two records raise a serious question. Arthurian legend has it that Arthur's victory at Badon was so complete that the Saxons had to retreat and that for at least twenty-five years there was a relative peace. The *ASC* does show this to some extent. We get a significant increase in the West Saxon offensive from 552 onwards, and arguably from 547 if Ida's rise to power also involved conflict, though this was in the North. There is a gap of around thirty years in which the *ASC* records no Saxon conquest except for the exploits of Cerdic.

Cerdic is one of those fascinating enigmas. His name is not Saxon but British, the same as Caradoc or Ceretic. Because of this he is regarded as possibly a renegade British chieftain who might have fought against Arthur, perhaps with Saxon mercenaries. Alternatively, if he came to power after Badon, he might previously have fought on Arthur's side and benefited subsequently with lands in Wiltshire. Some even go so far as to suggest that Cerdic *was* Arthur. I won't go that far, but he is crucial to fixing a date for Arthur's life.

If we look closer, the entries relating to Cerdic raise further questions. The entry for 495 seems to duplicate that of 514, except that Cerdic and Cynric have become Stuf and Wihtgar. 501 also appears to be a repetition of the same event, whilst 501 and 508 also have some elements in common – the "very noble young Briton" of 501 might be the same as the Natanleod of 508.

It's as if there were a standard story, known to all West Saxons: that the founder of their kingdom had arrived with his son and fought against the British, and that places involved with that arrival and battle are named after them.

If we look elsewhere in the *ASC* we find two further pieces of information that help us unravel this. Not surprisingly for a Chronicle brought together at the time of Alfred the Great, the *ASC* includes a genealogy of Alfred. Manuscript A incorporated this in a "Preface", which begins by saying:

> In the year when 494 winters had passed since Christ's birth, Cerdic and Cynric his son landed at *Cerdices ora* with five ships. [. . .] And 6 years after they landed, they conquered the West Saxons' kingdom; and these were the first kings who conquered the West Saxons' land from the Britons. And he held the kingdom 16 years, and then when he departed his son Cynric succeeded to the kingdom and held it 26 years . . .

The other surviving manuscripts for the *ASC* place this note under the year 855, and insert the name Creoda between Cerdic and Cynric.

This Preface tells us that Cerdic arrived "after 494 winters" [the year 495], took six years to attain the kingdom and then ruled for 16 years, which brings his death to the year 517 – just before (maybe even *at*) the Battle of Badon. But let's not jump to conclusions. In the Introduction I discuss the problems faced by annalists copying from old records in which entries may be grouped by the Easter cycle, which repeats itself every nineteen years.

If we look again at the near-duplicate entries for 495 and 514, we find that these are nineteen years apart. The "Preface" to the *ASC* notes that Cerdic "obtained the kingdom after six years". 519 is the sixth year after 514 (if you count the years as inclusive), and the adjacent entries between 495 and 501 and 508 and 514 are also six years apart. There is a pattern here, suggesting that the annalists knew certain time spans and perhaps an end date, but did not quite know how to get there. Entries thus became duplicated.

The problem we have is determining which dates are correct. We cannot know, because the only way we can verify it is to rely further on the dates within the *ASC*. If, for the moment, we accept that the dates closer in time to the final compilation of the *ASC* are more likely to be accurate, particularly in relation to the length of reigns of the later rulers, then we can work backwards. The "Preface" lists the rulers and years down to King Aethelwulf. His father Egbert died in 839, a date well attested by other documents. If we add up the total lengths of the reigns of all the West Saxon kings from the start of Cerdic's to the end of Egbert's, we get 310 years. Deducting this from 839 gives 529 as the start of Cerdic's reign. This clearly contradicts the entry for 534 which records Cerdic's death after, we are told, a reign of 16 years.

This total of 310 years does not include Creoda, who is not otherwise mentioned. However, the *ASC* also gives two different reign lengths – 17 years or 30 – for Cerdic's grandson Ceawlin. The missing 13 years could belong to Creoda without disrupting the grand total.

At present, therefore, we have three possible dates for Cerdic's reign. The Preface states 501–517, the individual entries support 519–534, whilst the total reign lengths give 529–545. Table 3.11, based on the pedigrees, supports a later date, suggesting a death around 550.

It is important to confirm Cerdic's reign because of its implications for Arthurian history, but how do we resolve this problem? Various people have tackled the matter. In *The Historic King Arthur* Frank D. Reno undertook an exercise similar to mine, but added Creoda's reign, allocating him 17 years (on the basis that Creoda's reign is wrongly assigned to Ceawlin) and resolving some other anomalies. He determined that the Preface dates of 500–516 were accurate. In "*The West Saxon Genealogical Regnal List*" (1985), the most detailed study of this issue, David Dumville analysed all the surviving documents of the *ASC* and other supporting data and concluded that the West Saxon regnal list had been corrupted with the purpose of pushing back the founding of the West Saxon line as far as possible. He believes that the annalists compiling the *ASC* in Alfred's time recognised this but could do little about it, so fudged the issue, which is why so many contradictions arise. He produced his version of the regnal list which has Cerdic's reign starting in 538, a date that I also used when I compiled my *Mammoth Book of British Kings & Queens* though, curiously, I arrived at it by a different method based on the Easter cycle (two cycles of 19 years from 500). This agrees with Table 3.11. It also means that if the *Welsh Annals*' date for Camlann is correct then Cerdic may have benefited from the death of Arthur. This date would support a period of peace during Arthur's reign – a *Pax Arthuriana* – and may therefore suggest an end-date of 538/9. We need other evidence to confirm this, but it's something to orientate upon.

So, setting dates aside for the present, let us reflect on what the *ASC* tells us. We learn that the Britons first appealed to Rome for help against the Picts, and, when that was not forthcoming, turned to the Angles for help. There seems to be a distinction between this first appeal and that of Vortigern six years later, though this frequent leaping of six years is further evidence of uncertainty. Following Vortigern's invitation, the Angles arrived, led by Hengist and Horsa, and in payment for fighting the Picts Vortigern gave them land in the "south-east". This is usually interpreted as being in Kent, more specifically the Isle of Thanet, but this is not necessarily accurate. I explore this in more detail in Chapter 6.

Hengist and Horsa were successful and brought more mercenaries over, comprising Saxons, Angles and Jutes. Trouble brewed, Hengist and Horsa fought against Vortigern, and the British were defeated, fleeing to *Lundenbyrg* (usually interpreted as London but more on that later). A series of conflicts now occurred, spread over several years, whilst further waves of Saxons arrived, including those led by Aelle and Cerdic. The Saxon victories were not decisive and, as mentioned above, apart from the Cerdic anomaly, the Saxons made no further significant advances until after 547, but from then on the writing was on the wall, especially following the victories of 571, 577 and 584. It is evident from this that Arthur's victorious days must have been before 547, to allow for his 21 years (or more) of peace. Even though these dates remain suspect, they do not contradict the *Welsh Annals*' dates of 518 for Badon and 539 for Camlann. In fact they fit into the sequence rather neatly, especially if we have resolved the Cerdic question.

One other date from this period is worthy of further thought. The entry for 540 refers to the sun growing dark, as does the entry for 538. These could simply refer to solar eclipses. Chroniclers frequently record eclipses and they are very useful for confirming dates, as eclipses can be precisely calculated. However, research has shown that these records refer to something far more significant. David Keys, in *Catastrophe*, has demonstrated that the decade starting in 535 saw the consequences of a worldwide catastrophe, with cold summers, freezing winters, crop failures and plague. It is recorded in virtually every ancient civilization. He believes the cause was a volcanic eruption in 535, pointing the finger at Krakatoa. Mike Baillie, however, in *Exodus to Arthur*, is more convinced that the disaster arose following a near collision with a comet, resulting in cometary debris in the atmosphere.

Whatever the cause, it remains clear that there was a major catastrophe, maybe two, that led to a decade or more of suffering, a scenario which sounds remarkably like the Waste Land of Arthurian legend. Moreover, Keys notes that "great natural catastrophes often induce political instability, administrative dislocation and the consequential collapse of regular record keeping in affected societies." Be it a comet or volcano, it could well have been a disaster such as this that tipped the balance in Britain after 540, with the battle-hardened Saxons taking the upper hand, being better able to endure the plague and pestilence than the now weakened Romano-British.

A period for Arthur's "reign" between 516 and 539 seems to be appearing, but we have a long way to go, and the comparative simplicity of the above is about to become very complicated.

5

GILDAS – THE MAN WHO KNEW ARTHUR

1. Gildas

We have already encountered Gildas via the *Welsh Annals*. The year 565 lists his voyage to Ireland and his death is recorded under the year 572. Whether these dates are correct is something we'll need to consider. Gildas's writings are perhaps the most important in relation to the authenticity of Arthur, and yet they are annoyingly vague and obtuse.

We know few genuine facts about Gildas. His life became the subject of two books, one by a monk of Rhuys in Brittany, where Gildas is believed to have died, and another by Caradog of Llancarfan. The first was written at least five hundred years after Gildas's death and the second another sixty years or so after that. What's more, Caradog was a close friend of Geoffrey of Monmouth, so the fact that Arthur features prominently in Caradog's *Life of Gildas* and not once in the earlier biography, speaks for itself.

The two biographies have only a few events in common. According to these sources, Gildas was born in Alclud (Dumbarton), one of the many children of Caw or Caius, who was probably a Romano-British official. When he was born is crucial, in fact the most important date in all Arthurian studies as we shall see. In his youth in south Wales, Gildas studied under Illtud, whom legend makes a cousin of King Arthur. Gildas also studied in Ireland. According to Caradog, while Gildas was in Ireland several of his brothers rebelled against Arthur. During the confrontation, Arthur killed one of the brothers, Huail, leading to a rift between Arthur and Gildas, although they later made peace. Later, Gildas apparently travelled to Rome, and lived in Brittany for several years where he probably died.

The many tales about Gildas have led some to believe that there were at least two people of this name, Gildas son of Caw, and the Gildas who wrote *De Excidio Britanniae* (*The Ruin of Britain)*, but this only confuses the issue. It may, though, explain why the *Welsh Annals* chose to describe him as Gildas the Wise, as if to distinguish him from another, but we may simply accept that as an endearment written by one who knew him.

What makes Gildas important is that his writings, principally *De Excidio*, are the only works that survive from the sixth century, providing a first-hand witness to the events of the preceding fifty years, the period, if the *Welsh Annals* are correct, when Arthur was alive. In other words, here is a book by someone who would certainly have known Arthur, or known of him. However, Gildas chose not to write about Arthur. And although his work does include a history of Britain, it was not Gildas's intention to write a history. *De Excidio* takes the form of a very long letter, most of which is filled with complaints about the church and about the wicked rulers of Britain. Gildas believed that the fate of Britain at the hands of the Saxons was directly due to the corruptness of the British, their laziness and inability to fight for themselves. It was a sentiment picked up by the *ASC*, which refers to the "worthlessness of the Britons" (year 449). Gildas was thus something of a Jeremiah, bewailing the fate of the British, and quoting events and scriptures as appropriate to make his case. He worries little about dates or historical characters, which is what makes his *De Excidio* so infuriating. Here was the one man who could have told us exactly what happened, but instead he chose to moan – probably from the safety of Brittany – about the corruptness of the British.

2. De Excidio

Despite his moaning, as the lone voice from that time we must pay attention to what he says. I won't quote *De Excidio* in full, but will refer to the relevant sections set after the fall of Roman authority in Britain and will also quote his complaints against the British kings who were his contemporaries. Hidden in the following should be further clues about Arthur, provided we can find them.

In Sections (§) 18 and 19 Gildas provides a graphic picture of the horrors of Britain after the Romans left. He gives the impression that before the Romans departed they did what they could to improve the island's defences and train the people. He seems to believe that the Wall (presumably Hadrian's) was built at this time, rather than nearly 300 years earlier, which shows how poor the surviving records in Britain were. He may be recounting a memory of the strengthening of the Wall during the fourth-century struggle with the Picts. He also refers to the Saxon shore defensive forts, and he may be remembering other defences built at this time, such as the Wansdyke in Somerset and Wiltshire, which dates from the mid fifth century.

He tells us that the British forces were "too lazy to fight and too unwieldy to flee." The men were apparently "foolish and frightened," and they "sat about day and night rotting away in their folly." Leaving aside Gildas's hyperbole, his comments could support the problem Germanus had faced of a wealthy country where the people were unprepared for the horrors to come. And come they did. He talks of the "foul hordes" of Scots and Picts who massacred the British. Death was apparently preferable to the "miserable fate" (possibly slavery) of those that were snatched away. A few years later (probably in the 440s, though some say the 470s), St Patrick wrote to Ceretic (usually treated as the ruler of Alclud), complaining about the slave trade between Ireland and Britain, which had clearly been prevalent for many years.

At the end of §19 Gildas tells us:*

> Our citizens abandoned the towns and the high wall. Once again they had to flee; once again they were scattered, more irretrievably than usual; once again there were enemy assaults and massacres more cruel. The pitiable citizens

* All excerpts from Gildas are adapted by the author from previous translations by J.A. Giles (1891) and Hugh Williams (1901).

were torn apart by their foe like lambs by the butcher; their life became like that of beasts of the field. For they resorted to looting each other, there being only a tiny amount of food to give brief sustenance to the wretched people; and the disasters from abroad were increased by internal disorders, for as a result of constant devastations of this kind the whole region came to lack the staff of food, apart from any such comfort as the art of the huntsman could procure for them.

§ 20. So the miserable remnants sent off a letter again, this time to the Roman commander Agitius, in the following terms: "To Agitius, thrice consul: the groans of the British." Later came this complaint: "The barbarians push us back to the sea, the sea pushes us back to the barbarians; between these two kinds of death we are either drowned or slaughtered." But they got no help in return. Meanwhile, as the British feebly wandered, a dreadful and notorious famine gripped them, forcing many of them to give in without delay to their bloody plunderers, merely to get a scrap of food to revive them. Not so others: they kept fighting back, basing themselves on the mountains, in caves, heaths and thorny thickets. Their enemies had been plundering their land for many years: now for the first time they inflicted a massacre on *them*, trusting not in man but in God, for, as Philo says, "when human help fails, we need the help of God." For a little while their enemies' audacity ceased, but not our people's wickedness. The enemy retreated from the people, but the people did not retreat from their own sins.

§ 21. It was always true of this people that it was weak in beating off the weapons of the enemy but strong in putting up with civil war and the burden of sin: weak, I repeat, in following the banners of peace and truth, but strong for crime and falsehood. So the impudent Irish pirates returned home (though they were shortly to return); and for the first time the Picts in the far end of the island kept quiet from now on, though they occasionally carried out devastating raids or plunder. So, in this period of truce the desolate

> people found their cruel scars healing over. But a new and more virulent famine was quietly sprouting. In the respite from devastation the island was so flooded with abundance of goods that no previous age had known the like of it. Alongside there grew luxury. It grew with a vigorous growth, so that to that time were fitly applied the words: "There are actually reports of such fornication as is not known even among the Gentiles."

Up until now Gildas has only been telling us about the onslaught of the Picts and Scots, and that after an appeal to Rome, which brought no help, some of the British fought back. They inflicted such a "massacre" that there was a respite. The Picts and Irish went "home". Now Britain prospered, and there was an abundance of wealth, as Germanus witnessed. But with it came civil war:

> Kings were anointed not in God's name, but as being crueller than the rest; before long, they would be killed, with no enquiry into the truth, by those who had anointed them, and others still crueller chosen to replace them. Any king who seemed gentler and rather more inclined to the truth was regarded as the downfall of Britain: everyone directed their hatred and their weapons at him, with no respect.

Amidst this political strife Gildas tells us that rumours reached the British of "the imminent approach of the old enemy, bent on total destruction and (as was their wont) on settlement from one end of the country to the other." Yet the British did nothing and, as if by way of punishment:

> §22 [. . .] . . . a deadly plague swooped brutally on the stupid people and in a short period laid low so many, with no sword, that the living could not bury all the dead. But not even this taught them their lesson . . .

Gildas emphasises how hopeless the British were and how that sealed their fate. Now he comes to the crucial part:

§22 [. . .] And they convened a Council to decide the best and soundest way to counter the brutal and repeated invasions and plunderings by the people I have mentioned.

§23. Then all the members of the Council, together with the *superbo tyranno* "proud tyrant", were struck blind. As protection for our country, they sealed its doom by inviting in among them, like wolves into a sheep-fold, the ferocious Saxons, hated by man and God, to beat back the peoples of the North. Nothing more destructive, nothing more bitter has ever befallen the land. How utter the blindness of their minds. How desperate and crass the stupidity. Of their own free will they invited under the same roof a people whom they feared worse than death even in their absence.

Then a pack of cubs burst forth from the lair of the barbarian lioness, coming in three keels, as they call warships in their language. The winds were favourable; favourable too the omens and auguries which prophesied, according to a sure portent among them, that they would live for three hundred years in the land towards which their prows were directed and that for half that time, a hundred and fifty years, they would repeatedly lay it waste. On the orders of the ill-fated tyrant they first of all fixed their dreadful claws on the east side of the island, ostensibly to fight for our country, in fact to fight against it. The mother lioness learned that her first contingent had prospered and she sent a second and larger troop of satellite dogs. It arrived by ship and joined up with the false units. [. . .] The barbarians who had been admitted to the island asked to be given supplies, falsely representing themselves as soldiers ready to undergo extreme dangers for their excellent hosts. The supplies were granted and, for a long time, "shut the dog's mouth." Then they again complained that their monthly allowance was insufficient, purposely giving a false colour to individual incidents, and swore that they would break their agreement and plunder the whole island unless more lavish payment was heaped upon them. There was no delay: they put their threats into immediate effect.

§24. In just punishment for the crimes that had gone before, a fire heaped up and, nurtured by the hand of the impious easterners, spread from sea to sea. It devastated town and country round about and, once it was alight, it did not die down until it had burned almost the whole surface of the island and was licking the western ocean with its fierce red tongue. [. . .] All the major towns were laid low by the repeated battering of enemy rams, laid low too all the inhabitants – church leaders, priests and people alike – as the swords glinted all around and the flames crackled. It was a sad sight. In the middle of the squares the foundation-stones of high walls and towers that had been torn from their lofty base, holy altars, fragments of corpses covered with a purple crust of congealed blood, looked as though they had been mixed up in some dreadful wine press. There was no burial to be had except in the ruins of houses or the bellies of beasts and birds – [. . .].

§25. So a number of the wretched survivors were caught in the mountains and butchered wholesale. Others, their spirit broken by hunger, went to surrender to the enemy; they were fated to be slaves forever, if indeed they were not killed straight away, the highest boon. Others made for lands beyond the sea [. . .]. Others held out, though not without fear, in their own land, trusting their lives with constant foreboding to the high hills, [. . .] to the densest forests and to the cliffs of the sea coast.

After a time, when the cruel plunderers had gone home, God gave strength to the survivors. Wretched people fled to them from all directions, as eagerly as bees to the beehive when a storm threatens, and begged whole-heartedly that they should not be altogether destroyed. Their leader was Ambrosius Aurelianus, a gentleman who, perhaps alone of the Romans, had survived the shock of this notable storm: his parents, who had certainly worn the purple, were slain in it. His descendants in our day have become greatly inferior to their grandfather's excellence. Under him our people regained their strength, and challenged the victors to battle. The Lord assented and the battle went their way.

§26. From then on, victory went now to our countrymen, now to their enemies, so that in this people the Lord could make trial of his latter-day Israel to see whether it loved him or not. This lasted right up to the year of the siege of Badon Hill, pretty well the last defeat of the villains, and certainly not the least. That was the year of my birth; as I know, one month of the forty-fourth year since then has already passed.

But the cities of our land are not populated even now as they once were; right to the present they are deserted, in ruins and unkempt. External wars may have stopped, but not civil ones. For the remembrance of so desperate a blow to the island and of such unlooked for recovery stuck in the minds of those who witnessed both wonders. That was why kings, public and private persons, priests and churchmen, kept to their own stations. But they died; and an age succeeded them that is ignorant of that storm and has experience only of the calm of the present.

At this point Gildas launches into his tirade against the present-day kings, but before considering that, let us consider what Gildas has told us so far. It's wrapped up in hyperbole, but tucked away in these nine sections is a history, and most of it we can match to the chronicles already noted.

The start of §20 is a rare moment when Gildas gives us the opportunity to verify a date. He refers to a letter written to the Roman commander Agitius, referring to him as "thrice consul." Although Agitius would more accurately translate as Aegidius, most historians believe that Gildas meant Aëtius, who did indeed hold the consulship three times. In fact, he was the only Roman (excluding emperors) to have done so for over three hundred years. Aegidius (d. 464), on the other hand, was never consul. He was a Roman general, who was appointed the *magister militum* of northern Gaul by the Western Roman emperor Avitus in 457, and later became king of the Franks, establishing a small kingdom around Soissons.

Aëtius became consul for the third and fourth times in 446 and 453, so the letter, if Gildas remembered it correctly, had to be written between 446 and 452. The *ASC* records this as happening in 443, and notes that the Romans were coping with Attila the Hun and thus could not help the British. In fact the first major confrontation between Aëtius and Attila was in 451, which could be the date the letter was sent.

As Gildas quotes from the letter, it is possible that a copy may have survived to his day, although of course it's easy to reconstruct an apparent text from hearsay. This means that the previous section, concerning the conflict with the Picts and Scots, covers a period of over thirty years, from 410 to at least 446AD.

Even when we get to the letter to Aëtius, an apparent moment of certainty instantly becomes uncertain. Gildas tells us that no help came from the Romans and that a famine descended upon Britain until at last the British fought back and achieved a major victory. At this stage, Gildas is still referring to the Picts and Scots, not the Saxons.

The period 446 to 454 seems a bit short for the British to weaken, lapse into famine, fight back against the Picts and Scots and, as we learn in §21, become "flooded with abundance." Evidently Gildas has become confused again. The British may well have written to Aëtius in 446 or soon after, but that was almost certainly in relation to the Saxon incursions. The victory over the Picts and Scots is more likely to be the Alleluia victory of Germanus. Gildas, bewailing the wretchedness of the British in §19, is recalling the decline into Pelagianism, and the appeal he refers to in §20 was probably the one to the church leaders in Gaul that resulted in Germanus's visit to Britain. It is noticeable that when Constantius referred to Germanus's second visit, he described Britain as a "wealthy island", precisely as Gildas recalls it here. What probably happened was that Gildas knew of the appeal to Aëtius, but confused it with the earlier appeal, so that the events in §19 really relate to 410–429, a far more probable period, whilst §20 and §21 relate to 429–446, or perhaps 441. The *Gallic Chronicle* had referred to Britain "yielding to the power of the Saxons" in 441. This is close enough to 446 (though one might hope it could have been closer) to suggest that from the late 430s the Germanic incursions had grown stronger, and that by 441, insofar as was apparent to the chronicler in southern Gaul, the Saxons had taken hold of Britain.

This would also explain why the British should write to Aëtius.

After all, if they had been independent of Rome for 30 years, why should they suddenly write to a Roman commander and expect help? Admittedly they got none, perhaps a sign that Rome had no further hold on Britain. It seems to confirm what I suggested earlier, that Britain was not really "expelled" in 410, but that Honorius and the empire simply had rather too much to contend with. Technically Britain remained in the Empire, appointing their own officials, but by 441–446 those final slender threads were cut. Aëtius sent no help, the Saxons were overrunning Britain, and Britain now regarded itself as independent. This would explain why, in §21, Britain anoints "kings". Evidently the turnover was rapid as "before long they would be killed".

Once again, Gildas is probably recording a tradition of a great number of petty rulers, suggesting that by the 440s the old provincial boundaries had broken down. The British, fleeing from the Saxons, had taken refuge in the mountains. The archaeology shows a resettling of a number of ancient hill-forts, mostly in the west and south.

In Gildas's eyes all kings were usurpers, hence his term "tyrants". There was a particular outbreak of them from the 440s onwards, once the first generation of leftover Romans, like Ambrosius, had died out.

In §21, therefore, Gildas records his account of the rise of a series of lawless usurper kings, whose successors are to become the subject of his later condemnation. This is the central point of *De Excidio*, namely that this lawlessness was to be punished by God and the form of that punishment is shown in §22 with the return of the "old enemy", the Picts and Scots. Gildas tells us that the British did not learn from the return of these enemies but continued to sink into further corruption until laid low by a plague. Europe was regularly devastated by plagues during the fifth and sixth centuries, and although there is not a specific record of one in Britain around this time, it is known that in 452 the Huns were struck by plague, one which could have spread to Britain.

In §23 Gildas refers to the most crass decision the British could have made. The Council, "together with the *superbo tyranno*", chose to invite the Saxons into Britain to fight the Picts. This is recorded in the *ASC* as happening sometime between 449 and

455, which ties in with 451–452 suggested above. Gildas does not name his "proud tyrant," but the *ASC* tells us it was Vortigern, so it's likely that's who he meant. The name Vortigern means "supreme king", and Gildas's *superbo tyranno* is a pun on that. Nennius (*see* Chapter 6) has much more to say about Vortigern, so I shall save my comments about him until then.

Gildas reports that the Saxons soon turned upon the British, and those Britons who were not enslaved retreated into the mountains or fled abroad. There was another wave of refugees from Britain to Armorica about this time. Around this time, too, emerges the mysterious character of Riothamus, a "king of the Britons" fighting in Gaul, who has been suggested as another candidate for Arthur (*see* Chapter 6). Gildas paints a desolate picture of abandoned Roman towns and the British hiding in their hill forts, cut down wherever they met the Saxons. The archaeological record also shows that many Romano-British cities were deserted by this time. Only St Albans, Wroxeter, Silchester, Chester, Gloucester, London and Caernarvon show signs not only of continued occupation, but also of new development. It also shows that several pre-Roman hill forts were reoccupied, the major ones being South Cadbury, Cadbury-Congresbury, Glastonbury, Tintagel, Deganwy, Dinas Emrys, Dinas Powys, Dumbarton and the Mote of Mark.

Interestingly, in §25 Gildas comments, "after a time, when the cruel plunderers had gone home . . .", the implication being that this wave of Saxon invaders was out for plunder and not for settlement. The *ASC* makes no reference to the Saxons returning home, but does state that they sent for reinforcements, after which successive waves of Saxons invaded Britain over the next sixty years. But then perhaps the *ASC* would not want to record a retreat. There are sufficient gaps in the years to allow a return, such as between 456 and 465. There is something a little suspicious about the *ASC*'s record of events from 449 to 477. It drags on too long. For a period of twenty-eight years we only learn about Hengist and his son fighting the Britons, or the Welsh. In fact the change in terminology from Britons (456) to Welsh (465) itself gives pause for thought. The Saxons began to call them the Welsh, or *Welisc* (later *Wealhas*), meaning "foreigners", which is rather audacious for an invader. (The British, incidentally, called the Saxons the *Sais*, which in Gaelic became *Sasunnach*, or Sassenach.)

It is as if the records after 465 come from a genuine Saxon source whereas the earlier entries were derived from a British, or at least non-Saxon, source. Could it be that the later chroniclers were embarrassed by a gap in the record from, say, 456 to 477, and so pushed back some events to fill the gap? They could not push back entries relating to Aelle or Cerdic, but they could add extra events for Hengist, or extend the time during which he really was in Britain. The events recorded against 465 and 473 may have taken place in the late 450s, after which the majority of the "plunderers" returned to Saxony and Angeln. The British were able to regroup under a new leader and drive the Saxons back to their settlements along the east. For a time, until around 477, the British could breathe again.

Gildas is discussing a period that would have been remembered clearly by his parents, certainly his grandparents, and be well known amongst the older churchmen with whom Gildas associated. Although his history may be weak on the events and chronology of a century earlier, there is no reason for him to get more recent history wrong. We therefore have to accept that perhaps during the early 460s most of the Saxons marauders returned home (presumably to Germany, though by "home" Gildas may mean the few Saxon settlements along the east coast), allowing the British to regain control. This was when Britain rallied under a new leader.

And who was the new leader who rallied the British? For once Gildas names him, and it isn't Arthur. It's a man whom Gildas clearly reveres, Ambrosius Aurelianus. Gildas calls him a "gentleman" and refers to him as a "*duce*", a senior official. What's more, his parents, who had been slain during the hostilities, had "worn the purple". Gildas really does mean "parents", not forebears, as he refers to their deaths during the recent hostilities. Ambrosius's father may not have literally worn the purple, in terms of the rank denoted by his toga, but the phrase itself would certainly have meant that he had held a very senior position. In the later Roman Empire consuls were also allowed to wear the purple, usually a purple-fringed toga. In the previous chapter I referred to the *Notitia Dignitatum*, a catalogue of official posts which was still valid at the time of Britain's "departure" from the Empire. This listed the four or five provinces of Britain, two of which had governors of consular rank, Maxima Caesariensis, based on London, and the mysterious Valentia. We do not know the name of the consular governors in Britain at the start of the fifth century, so it is entirely possible that one might have been Ambrosius's father.

Incidentally, it is worth noting here that the venerable Ambrose (339–397), Bishop of Milan, later beatified as St Ambrose, was himself a consular governor in Italy, based at Milan. His father, who was the Praetorian Prefect of Gaul, at Arles, and to whom the *vicarius* of Britain reported, was also called Ambrosius Aurelianus. He was descended from a notable senatorial family possibly related to the emperor Aurelian (215–275), one of the more successful emperors of his day, who earned the title *Restitutor Orbis* ("Restorer of the World") for reuniting the Empire in 274AD. If Gildas's Ambrosius Aurelianus could count these amongst his antecedents and be the son of a consular governor, no wonder Gildas emphasised his name, and regarded him as special.

§25 of Gildas would seem to take place during the 470s when Ambrosius led the British in a series of battles against the Saxons, which eventually led to the momentous victory at Badon. This was the battle recorded in the *Welsh Annals* as the "victory of Arthur" in 518. It does seem a little surprising that, having named Ambrosius and sung his praises, Gildas chooses not to name Arthur, whose victory over the Saxons he describes as "pretty well the last defeat of the villains and certainly not the least." Gildas does not mention Arthur anywhere in *De Excidio*. Why not?

There are at least six possible reasons:

(1) Arthur didn't exist. We have to consider that the reference in the *Welsh Annals* might have been added by a later chronicler, based on the growing Arthurian legend, and that the victor was someone else, possibly Ambrosius himself.

(2) Gildas had no need to mention Arthur. As we have seen, Gildas does not mention many names at all, not even Vortigern's. He mentions Ambrosius Aurelianus because he was clearly one of Gildas's heroes, the man who turned the tide against the Saxons during Britain's darkest days.

(3) Arthur's name was superfluous. Gildas is referring to events within living memory, only forty-three years in the past. If Badon was such a glorious victory, everyone would remember who the victor was.

(4) Gildas disliked Arthur and did not want to glorify him. If Caradog's life of Gildas has any basis of truth, Arthur was responsible for the death of Gildas's brother Huail. Whilst having to admit that Badon was a crucial victory, he did not see fit to go further and name him as the victor. It's even possible that Arthur is named, but as one of the "tyrants" Gildas later castigates. He would not want to praise him whilst also vilifying him.

(5) Arthur was not yet born. It could be that the real Arthur, to whom the various legends and triumphs became attached, lived later than the time Gildas was writing. Someone else was the victor at Badon, but Arthur was retrospectively given the credit.

(6) Gildas did not know who the victor was. This seems the unlikeliest of reasons, but although Arthur seems such a major character to us today, he may not have been in Gildas's day. His legend had yet to grow, and despite the triumph of Badon, the victor's name may not have been that well remembered.

Whatever the reason, Gildas's omission of Arthur's name is not proof that Arthur did not exist, but the onus is on us to find that proof elsewhere.

Gildas's account tells us that the siege of Badon happened in the year of his birth, 43 years and 1 month before the time of writing. Such precision, so unusual for Gildas, might have helped us date Badon and provide corroboration for the year 518 in the *Welsh Annals*. Unfortunately, we don't know when Gildas wrote *De Excidio*.

There are, however, clues within *De Excidio* itself. Most telling is the final paragraph quoted from §26, in which he refers to the "calm of the present." He is writing in a time when external wars have stopped, and a whole generation has grown up that is now ignorant of the "storm" with the Saxons. He makes no mention of plague or famine, and yet if the evidence presented by David Keys in *Catastrophe* and Mike Baillie in *Exodus to Arthur* is true – and there is no reason to doubt it – from 535 onwards Britain was subject to bitterly cold winters and summers. A plague swept through Europe during the 540s, one of the worst ever. Had Gildas experienced this at the time of writing *De Excidio* there is little doubt that he would have referred to it, because it was further support for his argument – another punishment from God for the wicked ways of the kings. This suggests that Gildas must have written *De Excidio* before 540, possibly even before 535. If so, then 43 years earlier would place Badon at 492–497 at the latest, suggesting that the entry in the *Welsh Annals* is wrong. The gap from 497 to 518 is 21 years, and we have seen already that later annalists, copying from earlier documents, may have confused entries dated only by Easter cycles of 19 years.

A date of 497 for Badon is more consistent with Gildas's narrative. We deduced earlier that Ambrosius led the resistance to the Saxons during the 470s, and Gildas tells us that victories went both ways until the time of Badon. If Badon took place in 518, then the Saxon war continued for some forty years. Not impossible, of course, but Gildas's narrative does not suggest that long a period. Also, in §25, Gildas remarks that Ambrosius's descendants "in our day" were greatly inferior to their "grandfather's" excellence. He would not have used the term "grandfather" unless he genuinely meant two generations. This gives us some 60 years from the 470s, which brings us to the 530s. On this basis *De Excidio* was written in the mid to late 530s; thus Gildas was born in the early 490s, placing Badon between 492 and 497.

An alternative translation of Gildas §26 by Bede appeared in his *Ecclesiastical History of the English People*, completed in 731. Bede's research was impeccable, his understanding of Latin first class and, living just two centuries after Gildas, he was close enough to have had access to an original or early copy of Gildas's work, one less prone to error. The following extract, from Chapter 16 of Bede's *History*, is clearly lifted from Gildas:

> When the army of the enemy had exterminated or scattered the native peoples, they returned home and the Britons slowly began to recover strength and courage. They emerged from their hiding places and with one accord they prayed for the help of God that they might not be completely annihilated. Their leader at that time was a certain Ambrosius Aurelianus, a discreet man, who was, as it

> happened, the sole member of the Roman race who had survived this storm in which his parents, who bore a royal and famous name, had perished. Under his leadership the Britons regained their strength, challenged their victors to battle and, with God's help, won the day. From that time on, first the Britons won and then the enemy were victorious until the year of the siege of Mount Badon, when the Britons slaughtered no small number of their foes about forty-four years after their arrival in Britain.

Bede has read Gildas's reckoning of 43 years and one month as being from the arrival of the Saxons, the so-called Saxon *adventus*, and not related to Gildas's birth at all. Bede actually gives a year for the *adventus*, 449, a date later adopted by the *ASC*. This gives us a date of 492–493 for Badon which, by pure coincidence, fits into the timeframe cited above.

If Arthur was the battle leader at Badon, and not someone simply added by an overzealous annalist, then he was in his heyday at the end of the fifth century. And, if the *Welsh Annals* have the date for Badon wrong, then the date for Camlann may also be out by the same degree. Instead of 539 it could have been during the 510s, certainly no later than the year 520. However, we must not assume that the victor of Badon and the victim of Camlann are the same "Arthur", and thus the *Annals* entry for Camlann might still be accurate.

There is one other reference in this first part of Gildas's work which is easily overlooked, but which will prove crucial to our later research. In his earlier discussion about Britain under the Roman Empire, he refers to Britain's martyrs: "St Alban of Verulam, Aaron and Julius, citizens of the City of the Legions, and the others of both sexes who, in different places, displayed the highest spirit in the battle-line of Christ." In referring to their shrines, Gildas says, in §10:

> Their graves and the places where they suffered would now have the greatest effect in instilling the blaze of divine charity in the minds of beholders, were it not that our citizens, thanks to our sins, have been deprived of many of them by the unhappy partition with the barbarians.

In other words, in the time that Gildas was writing, the mid to late 530s, there was a partition between the British and the Saxons which denied the British access to these sites. These shrines must have been in the east, because we know from both written and archaeological records that the Saxons had not advanced far to the west by this time. Verulam (St Albans) was north-west of London. The City of the Legions, as we will discuss in Chapter 7, could apply to at least three sites, but as two of those, Caerleon and Chester, were in the west, Gildas must have meant York. York was part of the Angle kingdom of Deira, later part of Northumbria, and Nennius tells us (*see* Chapter 6) that the start of this Saxon colony was in the mid fifth century under Soemil. By Gildas's time presumably Yffi, father of Aelle, was established as the ruler.

The two big questions are where this partition ran and when it came into being. Fitting York into the division is less of a problem than St Albans. It is known that there were significant British enclaves in both London and St Albans throughout most of the fifth century, with no evident Saxon infiltration until the late sixth century. The battle of *Biedcanford* entered in the *ASC* for 571 shows that Cuthwulf succeeded in capturing the towns of Limbury, Aylesbury, Benson and Eynsham. If those locations are correct, then Cuthwulf captured a small British kingdom known as Calchvynydd, usually treated as covering the Chilterns, mostly Bedfordshire and Oxfordshire (*see* Map 1). Limbury, now part of Luton, was within 20km of St Albans, suggesting that St Albans must have been right on this frontier. The resident population may have remained primarily British, hence the archaeological evidence, but under Saxon control, hence the access problem.

Normally one might expect divisions to be decided by rivers, but few rivers in eastern England flow north-south. However, there is another obvious boundary. The Roman road of Dere Street ran from the eastern end of the Antonine Wall, past Hadrian's Wall near Corbridge, continuing just west of York and on to Lincoln. From there, now renamed Ermine Street, it ran direct to London. A confluence of roads there allows a switch along the Lower Icknield Way to St Albans, and from there south, skirting London to the west and terminating, presumably, at the Thames (*see* Map 3).

This boundary, which follows the route of today's A1 trunk road, would contain all the nascent Anglo-Saxon settlements along the east coast. The kingdom of Kent, tucked away at that time in the far south-east of the island, was to a large extent separated by the natural boundary of the Weald.

As to when, the obvious answer must be the Battle of Badon. That victory allowed the British to contain the Saxons within a fixed area, just as Alfred's victory over the Danes resulted in the same division, the Danelaw, four centuries later.

We will return to this partition in Chapter 7.

2. The Tyrants

We have not yet finished with Gildas. Having presented us with his understanding of the history of Britain, he then launches into an attack on five kings whom he sees as wicked and the enemies of God. I will not transcribe these in full, colourful though they are, as his lengthy condemnation of their lives and actions adds little to our quest for Arthur. But there are some factors that are relevant.

"Britain has kings, but they are tyrants," Gildas begins (in §27). The first he castigates is Constantine, "tyrant whelp of the filthy lioness of Dumnonia" (§28). Constantine is evidently alive at this time, as Gildas writes: "This same year after taking a dreadful oath not to work his wiles on our countrymen . . . he nevertheless, garbed in the habit of a holy abbot, most cruelly tore the tender sides of two royal children and their two guardians." Constantine apparently killed these children in a church, with sword and spear, whilst they clung to the altar. Gildas also accuses Constantine of adultery and sodomy. Constantine appears in the Arthurian story as Arthur's appointed successor, and he is described as the son of Cador, duke of Cornwall. Dumnonia was the Celtic kingdom in south-west Britain, including Cornwall and Devon, although just to add to the confusion it was also the name of a province in Brittany. When Gildas states that Constantine had sworn not to act against "our countrymen", he could be talking about the men of Brittany. However, this Constantine does not feature in the Welsh pedigrees and thus is not in Table 3.10, although he would be a contemporary of Geraint and Mark.

Geoffrey of Monmouth repeats this story, making the princes that Constantine kills the sons of Mordred. This happened soon after the battle of Camlann, which, as Gildas tells us, had happened only within the last year. If Gildas was writing in the period 535–540, perhaps Camlann's date really was 539, and not subject to the 19–year error. This heightens the idea of an Arthurian Golden Age lasting from 500 to 540. Gildas seems to support this as in §26 he speaks of the "calm of the Present" and of "an age" ignorant of past violence. This seems more like forty years than twenty.

The next king to be excoriated by Gildas is Aurelius Caninus, who, according to Geoffrey, later murdered Constantine. Gildas states that Caninus is "engulfed by the same slime" as Constantine, and accuses him of "parricide, fornications, adulteries" and of being a warmonger (§30), but does not say where he ruled. Some authorities have equated him with Cynan Garwyn (Cynan of the White Chariot, or Cynan the Cruel), a prince of Powys who was noted for his battles. However, this Cynan ruled towards the end of the sixth century and would not be a contemporary of Gildas. There is also no indication that Cynan Garwyn killed his father, the famous Brochwel of the Tusks. Another Cynan appears in the genealogies, five generations in descent from Vortigern, but he was a contemporary of Cynan Garwyn and was thus unlikely to have been born when Gildas was writing.

The name Caninus is more likely an epithet applied by Gildas. He was fond of nicknames, calling all of the kings he identified after animals. "Caninus", or "little dog", would mean "the whelp", and the king's name was therefore Aurelius, suggesting that he may have been one of the grandchildren of Ambrosius Aurelianus, whom Gildas had described as "greatly inferior" to their forebear. If this is so, the father that Aurelius Caninus killed was either Ambrosius's son or son-in-law. Such an action would be sure to raise Gildas's wrath.

Aurelius may not have inherited a kingdom, but usurped one through murder. If so, this is likely to have been in the south, possibly in the Severn Valley.

It's possible that Caninus is the same as Conmor, sometimes called Comorus, or Conomorus, the ruler of Leon in Armorica and later usurper of the whole territory. Conmor had killed the ruler, Ionas, forcibly married Ionas's widow, and imprisoned their son, Iudwal. Conmor was an exact contemporary of Gildas – indeed the usurpation had happened while Gildas was deliberating over writing *De Excidio* (he put it off for ten years). Conmor is sometimes identified with Mark (or March), a king of Dumnonia associated with the Tristan legend. This may explain Gildas's remark than Caninus was "engulfed by the same slime", meaning that Caninus and Constantine ruled in the same territory. Interestingly, Conmor called for a holy man, Paul, a pupil of Illtud, to spread the Christian faith through Brittany. This Paul is called Paul Aurelian, and though the epithet is believed by some to refer to the fact that Paul's remains were later moved to Orleans, it is possible that Paul was related to the Aurelian family.

The next to feel the bite of Gildas's tongue was Vortipor, "tyrant of the Demetae" (§31). We know something about him because his tombstone was discovered in 1895 in the churchyard at Castelldwyran in Dyfed. It bore the inscription MEMORIA VOTEPORIGIS PROTICTORIS. "Protector", the title also given to Coel, was a genuine title bestowed on barbarians who, in the latter days of the Roman Empire, helped patrol the Empire's frontiers. Vortipor appears in the genealogies of Dyfed/Demetia as the son of Aircol Lawhir ("the long-hand"). Aircol is the Brythonic version of Agricola, suggesting that Vortipor's father was a Romano-Briton. Gildas clearly thought well of Aircol, calling Vortipor the "bad son of a good king". Vortipor is charged with having divorced and possibly even murdered his wife and then raping her daughter (presumably by a previous marriage, though Gildas does not say). Vortipor may not have been all bad. Gildas calls him "spotted with wickedness", and it is likely that he was a once strong king who descended into wickedness in his final years. Gildas remarks that "the end of your life is gradually drawing near" and that his "head is already whitening", so we may presume Vortipor was well into his sixties. This is borne out by the analysis of the Demetian pedigree in Table 3.6, which suggests a lifetime for Vortipor of 470–540. If so then Vortipor would have been a young man at the time of Arthur's triumphs and his father,

Agricola, would certainly have known, and possibly fought alongside Ambrosious Aurelianus.

Incidentally, the name by which Vortipor is known in the Irish pedigrees is Gartbuir. If a later chronicler came across this written in Gaelic script as *Gartbuir*, might he have misread the 'b' as an 'h' and red *Garthuir*? A thought.

The fourth of Gildas's kings is Cuneglasus, the "tawny butcher" (§32). Cuneglasus's sin, in addition to waging war "with arms special to yourself", was to reject his wife and lust after her sister, a widow who had retired to a convent. This king is most likely Cynlas Goch, a cousin of Maelgwyn and ruler of the small cantref of Rhos (Table 3.8). Gildas reports that Cuneglasus had been a wicked man ever since his youth, and refers to him as "driver of the chariot of the Bear's Stronghold." Knowing Gildas's delight in puns, we can interpret "Bear's Stronghold" into Welsh as "Din-arth" (*din* for fortress and *arth* for bear); Dinarth is a small village near Llandrillo in North Wales. Others have taken the reference to "the Bear" as relating to Arthur, as the prefix *Arth* means "the Bear", and have suggested that Cuneglasus was Arthur's charioteer or even Arthur himself.

What did Gildas mean by referring to Cuneglasus as having "arms special to yourself"? What did he have that no one else did? A specially trained army, perhaps, or a huge arsenal of weapons? Yet Gildas's phrase sounds more personal, as if Cuneglasus had his own particular weapon. It makes one think of Excalibur. Would a sword that invoked awe and wonder, and which the owner believed protected him, be "special"? Probably, but unless Cuneglasus had somehow acquired Arthur's own sword, I find it hard to believe that Cuneglasus, a violent, psychotic despot, could ever be remembered as the heroic Arthur.

Gildas saves the worst for last: Maglocunus, better known as Maelgwyn, whom Gildas refers to as "first in evil." The catalogue of Maelgwyn's crimes takes up as much space as all the others put together. In his youth, Maelgwyn murdered his uncle, the king. This might have been Owain Danwyn ("white-tooth"), ruler of Rhos and father of Cuneglasus, but according to Peter Bartrum in *A Welsh Classical Dictionary,* the word used for uncle, *avunculus*, means strictly "his mother's brother". We do not know who his mother's brother was, so cannot be sure which kingdom Maelgwyn usurped. He seems to have repented and sought penance in a monastery. But this was short-lived. He subsequently murdered his wife, and, determined to marry his nephew's wife, had his nephew murdered as well.

Gildas must have felt very sure of himself. Castigating one or other of the first four kings was risky enough, but to take on Maelgwyn was like Thomas More taking on Henry VIII. As Gildas describes him, Maelgwyn was "dragon of the island", the Pendragon or High King. Arthur was also described as the Pendragon, a title steeped in historical lore which I shall explore later. Maelgwyn was the most important ruler in Britain, although Gildas did not see it this way: "The King of all kings has made you higher than almost all the generals of Britain, in your kingdom as in your physique." (§33). Maelgwyn was called "the Tall", and we can imagine him as a well built, powerful man, towering over all others. Gildas does not say what he means by "almost all the generals," but he clearly believed that there was one more powerful than Maelgwyn in Britain. Gildas had decried most of the kings of Wales and the West and had made no comment on the kings of the North. Perhaps he is alluding to one of them. Or perhaps this is Gildas's one cryptic reference to Arthur. We know the names of most of Maelgwyn's contemporaries, and possibly only Eliffer of the Great Host or his sons Peredur and Gwrgi might otherwise be classified as great generals. Once again Gildas masks his facts.

As the best attested ruler mentioned by Gildas, Maelgwyn's reign has been used to help date when Gildas wrote *De Excidio*. I have already used other factors to deduce that it must have been written in the mid to late 530s. The *Welsh Annals* note the death of "Mailcun" in 549, and Maelwgyn's reign is usually allocated to 534–549. This suggests that Gildas was writing early in Maelgwyn's reign, but the catalogue of crimes Gildas lists, including three marriages, suggests a good few years have passed. However 534 relates to the death of Cadwallon and that date is far from certain, and Cadwallon could have died in the 520s. Also the throne Maelgwyn usurped by murdering an uncle relates to a smaller chiefdom, not the main line of Gwynedd that he later inherited. In all probability, Maelgwyn's post-monastic catalogue of crimes began in the 520s, perhaps even earlier, allowing plenty of opportunity for Gildas to vilify him in the late 530s.

Gildas was the major witness to early sixth century events, and if Arthur existed he would have known about him. The fact that he does not name him is frustrating but in itself proves nothing. What Gildas does do is prove that a battle of Badon took place, but he also casts doubt on the dating in the *Welsh Annals*, forcing us to consider an earlier date, during the 490s. He also provides useful details on Ambrosius, Vortigern and Arthur's contemporaries, but any other clues about Arthur, despite ingenious interpretations, are very circumspect. We must continue our search, but now we enter the murky waters of Nennius's *Historia Brittonum*.

6

NENNIUS'S OLD PAPERS

1. Historia Brittonum

Nennius is both the saviour and the curse of Arthurian research. The works attributed to him provide considerable background to early British history that is missing from other sources. Nennius claimed to "heap" together those records that other historians and church fathers had rejected. Like a jackdaw, he assembled a miscellany of writings known as the *Historia Brittonum*, which, on the surface, seems a goldmine of information, but on close analysis poses more questions than it answers. After working our way through Nennius, the path we have carved with the help of the *Welsh Annals*, the *ASC* and Gildas will have lost some of its definition.

Nennius tells us in his opening section that "from the passion of Christ 796 years have passed; from the Incarnation 831 years." In fact, the date, as evident from various references within the papers, was closer to 828/9. Nennius's figures show that he believed the life of Christ was 35 years, whereas most scholars treat it as 33, and we will need to bear this in mind in the computations arising from Nennius's work.

Nennius benefited from that flowering of research at the court of King Merfyn "the Freckled" of Gwynedd, which also encouraged the compilation of the *Welsh Annals*. However, it is evident that there were several revisions to the original *Historia Brittonum*, and only one of these incorporates a preface ascribing the work to Nennius. Whilst there's no reason to doubt it, we must consider that the attribution may have been a guess by a later scholar. Nevertheless, for the sake of convenience, I will continue to refer to Nennius as the author.

That same preface refers to extracts found by Rhun. If this is accurate then it is significant, for it means that amongst the papers found by Nennius were some going back to the century following Gildas. The son of Urien of Rheged, Rhun was alive in the 620s (*see* Table 3.3), and entered the church in his later years, retiring to live in Powys. He was on good terms with the Angles (even credited with baptising King Edwin of Northumbria), and is a logical candidate for producing a Northern Chronicle.

Nennius's papers go back to the settlement of the Roman consul Brutus, a story told in greater detail by Geoffrey of Monmouth. We need not concern ourselves with his pre-history, but there are occasional chronological references. For instance, §16 states*

> From the year when the Saxons first came to Britain to the fourth year of king Mervyn, 429 years are reckoned; from the birth of the Lord until the coming of Patrick to the Irish are 405 years. From the death of Patrick to the death of Saint Brigit are 60 years; from the birth of Columba to the death of Brigit are 4 years.
> 23 cycles of 19 years from the Incarnation of the Lord until the coming of Patrick to Ireland; these years number 438. From the coming of Patrick to the present 19 year cycle there are 22 cycles, that is 421 years, two years in the Ogdoad until this present year.

Clearly Nennius – or the author of the paper he was editing – had access to a set of annals, but not the same as those from which the *Welsh Annals* were compiled, as the latter cite the birth of Columba and the death of St. Brigid in the same year (523). The key date noted here is the first one, relating to the coming of the Saxons. King Merfyn's reign is generally accepted to have begun in 825. His fourth year, therefore, is 828/829, the

* All extracts from Nennius are adapted by the author from the translation by J.A. Giles (1891).

date believed to be when Nennius compiled his *Historia*. That makes the first Saxon *adventus* the year 400, loosely tying in with the entry in the *Gallic Chronicle* under 410 when the British provinces were "devastated" by the Saxons, but clashing with another date I shall come to shortly.

The start of his next paragraph contradicts the previous one, though in fact the year cited for the mission of Patrick to Ireland, 438, is close to the traditionally accepted date of 432. The gap between 438 and 405 is 33 years, the generally accepted lifetime of Christ. Adjusting the number 405 to running from the death of Christ, rather than from his incarnation, reconciles the dates. Moreover, if we add the 405 years in the first paragraph to the 421 in the second and then add on the two years of the Ogdoad (an ogdoad is a set of eight years), that gives us 828, consistent with the reference to Merfyn's reign. This kind of confusing consistency runs throughout Nennius.

The next inconsistency appears between §28 and §30. First Nennius says:

> Hitherto the Romans had ruled the British for 409 years. But the British overthrew the rule of the Romans and paid them no taxes and did not accept their kings to reign over them and the Romans did not dare to come to Britain to rule any more, for the British had killed their generals.

The year 409 at first seems fairly accurate, close to Zosimus's date of 410, when the British expelled the Roman officials. However, the Claudian conquest of Britain was in 43AD, meaning that Nennius's 409 years begins then, bringing us to the year 452, which seems far too late. Before contesting this further, let's see what it says in §30:

> The Romans came with a great army to help them and placed emperors in Britain; and when the emperor was established with his generals the armies went back to Rome, and came and went in alternation over 348 years. But the British killed the Roman generals, because of the weight of the empire, and later asked their help. The Romans came to bring help to the empire and defend it, and deprived Britain

> of her gold and silver and bronze and all her precious raiment and honey, and went back in triumph.

348 years from 43AD is 391, soon after the death of Magnus Maximus. It is, however, worth noting that the gap from 391 to 409 inclusive is 19 years – one Easter cycle. Nennius's source may simply have missed (or lost) one set of records.

Elsewhere in his Miscellany, in §66, Nennius has this to say:

> From the reign of Vortigern to the quarrel between Vitalinus and Ambrosius are 12 years, that is Guoloppum, or *Catguoloph* [the battle of Wallop]. Vortigern, however, held the empire in Britain in the consulship of Theodosius and Valentinian, and in the fourth year of his reign the English came to Britain, in the consulship of Felix and Taurus, in the 400th year from the incarnation of our Lord Jesus Christ.

The first joint consulship of Theodosius and Valentinian was in 425AD, although they also held the title jointly in 426, 430 and 435. However, Felix and Taurus held the consulship only once, in 428, which was indeed the fourth year after 425. Nennius, though, equates that year to the 400th since Christ's birth, but may have meant from the baptism of Christ, at age 28, when he received the Holy Spirit, sometimes referred to as Christ's true "incarnation".

Thus we can see that Vortigern came to power in 425, that the Saxons first arrived in 428 and that in 437 was a battle between Ambrosius and Vitalinus, which I shall explore in more detail shortly.

All this gives the impression that the information is there, but one has to work hard to find it. With that in mind, let us run through the *Historia Brittonum* from §31 onwards, which follows from the death of Magnus Maximus:

> It came to pass that after this war between the British and the Romans, when their generals were killed, and after the killing of the tyrant Maximus and the end of the Roman Empire in Britain, the Britons went in fear for 40 years. Guorthigirnus [Vortigern] then reigned in Britain. He had

cause for dread, not only from the Scots and Picts, but also from the Romans, and a dread of Ambrosius.

In the meantime, three ships, exiled from Germany, arrived in Britain. They were commanded by the brothers Horsa and Hengist, sons of Wihtgils. [. . .]. Vortigern received them as friends, and delivered up to them the island which is in their language called Thanet, and, by the Britons, Ruym.

Gratianus Æquantius at that time reigned in Rome. The Saxons were received by Vortigern, three hundred and forty-seven years after the passion of Christ [and, according to the tradition of our ancestors, from the period of their first arrival in Britain, to the first year of the reign of king Edmund, five hundred and forty-two years; and to that in which we now write, which is the fifth of his reign, five hundred and forty-seven years].

The opening paragraph is ambiguous. It could be interpreted as meaning that the fearful 40 years occurred directly after the fall of Maximus in 388AD, during which time Vortigern ruled, or that Vortigern came to power at the end of the forty year period. If the latter, then Vortigern's rule began in 428, close to the date of 425 extrapolated from §30.

It is pertinent that Nennius records Vortigern as afraid not only of the Picts and Saxons, but also of the Romans, specifically Ambrosius. This reference to the Romans may mean that Vortigern feared they might try to reclaim Britain for the Empire, but I believe it has to be read in conjunction with the reference to Ambrosius, namely that Vortigern was in fear of the Roman faction in Britain, led by Ambrosius. Can this be the same Ambrosius that led the British rally against the Saxons in the 460s? It seems unlikely, especially when we check §66, which refers to Ambrosius's battle with Vitalinus in 437. If we read this in conjunction with Gildas's description of Ambrosius's parents as having "worn the purple", and therefore being Roman, we can more logically deduce that Vortigern was in dread of Ambrosius the Elder. But who was Vitalinus?

This brings us to the matter of Vortigern's real name. The name Vortigern, as mentioned earlier, means "supreme king", hence Gildas's pun on "superb tyrant." It may well have been the name by which Vortigern was always known. In §49 Nennius provides a genealogy for Vortigern, telling us that "Guorthegirn Guortheneu was the son of Guitaul, son of Guitolion of Gloui." Latinized, this reads "Vortigern, the Third son of Vitalis, son of Vitalinus of Gloucester." Vitalinus was thus Vortigern's grandfather and it is possible that Vortigern's real name was also Vitalinus or Vitalis.

There is, however, more to Vitalinus. An ancient list of archbishops of London, believed to have been compiled by the twelfth-century Jocelin of Furness and incorporated by John Stow into his *Annales of England* (1580), includes the name Guetelinus as the twelfth to hold that office. No date is attached to him, but intriguingly Geoffrey of Monmouth, in his *History of the Kings of Britain*, also mentions this Guetelinus as the archbishop of London at the time of the Roman withdrawal. He attributes to Guetelinus the writing of the letter, which we know to have been written in about 446, to the Roman commander Aëtius, seeking help against the invaders. Although it is entirely possible for Guetelinus to have survived that long, I believe that both Geoffrey and Nennius's sources were confusing father and son, or grandson. The elder Vitalinus would have been bishop in 410, and either Vitalis or Vortigern fought Ambrosius the Elder at Guoloph in 437, and wrote the appeal in 446.

Nennius tells us that Vortigern granted Hengist and Horsa territory on Ruym, which in other copies of the manuscript is spelled Ruoichin. *Ruoichin*, or *Ruithin*, is sometimes translated as "river-island", and is taken to mean the Isle of Thanet in Kent, separated from the mainland by the Wantsum Channel, and long regarded as the landing place of the Saxons and their first settlement in Britain. But this does not wholly accord with Nennius's record. In fact, there is no reference to Kent in this paragraph. For a start he states that Ruym is called "Tanet" in "their [the Saxons'] language", but the Isle of Thanet's name is of Celtic origin, *Tanat*, meaning "fire island", perhaps because there was a beacon there.

Ruym, on the other hand, is more likely derived from *rhwym*, meaning a bond or obligation. In other words, this land, wherever it was, was granted to the Saxons in return for their services. The town of Bonby in the North Lincolnshire Wolds has a similar origin, *Bond-by*, usually interpreted as "peasant's farmhouse", but meaning literally a farmland worked under bond. Bonby is on the edge of the Ancholme river valley which was regularly flooded until extensive drainage works were built in the seventeenth century. Moreover, just north of Bonby is Saxby, "Saxon's farmhouse", and just north of that, near Barton on Humber, is Beacon Hill, which was almost certainly an island in Saxon times and may also have been called Tanet by the British. This is not to say that Bonby was the original Saxon settlement, but its location is significant for two reasons. Directly across the Ancholme valley from Bonby are the villages of Winteringham and Winterton, the names of which are both from an Angle, Winta. J.N.L. Myres has suggested in *The English Settlements* that this is the same Winta as in the ancestry of the kings of Lindsey (*see* Table 3.11), a contemporary of Hengist and Icel, and thus one of the first settlers after the initial forays. Additionally, the archaeology has identified early Saxon settlements with mixed British and Saxon burial customs throughout this area.

§32–35 of Nennius' *Historia* tells a story about Germanus's visit to Britain, a story that does not relate to any other life of Germanus of Auxerre. It tells how Germanus tries to seek audience with the wicked king Benli, who refuses to see him. He is welcomed instead by one of Benli's servants, Cadell. Germanus warns Cadell to leave the fortress, and that night it is destroyed by a bolt from heaven. Cadell was the grandson of Vortigern and became the forefather of the kings of Powys. Table 3.9 assigns him the dates 460–530, which is too late for St Germanus. Most scholars believe that Nennius has confused Germanus with the Irish-born St Garmon, who may have been a nephew of St Patrick, and who preached throughout Wales, especially Powys, in the late fifth century. The hill fort of Moel Benlli is near Maesgarmon, the suggested site for the "Alleluia" victory. It is possible that both sites should be associated with St. Garmon.

In the next section Nennius returns to the Saxon invasion of Britain, although, as with the Cadell episode, he seems now to be recounting folklore rather than true history.

In §36 he tells us that after the Saxons had been settled on Thanet for "some time", Vortigern promised to supply them with provisions if they would fight the enemy, the Picts and Scots. But as the barbarians had "greatly increased in number", the Britons could not keep up with demand and told the Saxons they were no longer needed and could go home.

We don't know how long Nennius meant by "some time." It could mean an entire generation, possibly suggesting two different folk memories that have become jumbled. The first Saxon *adventus*, around 428, led to them being granted land at Ruym. The next stage may be after that settlement has grown through children and fresh settlers. We could now have moved on to the period described in the *ASC* as starting in 449.

In §37 Nennius contradicts himself. He reports Hengist as saying, "We are indeed few," and promising that if Vortigern agrees, Hengist will go home and return with more men. He returns with sixteen ships and his daughter, with whom Vortigern becomes besotted. Hengist agrees that Vortigern can marry her in exchange for the "province" of Kent. Vortigern grants Kent to the Saxons, much to the annoyance of the native ruler Gwrangon. Hengist continues with his grand plan and, in §38, says to Vortigern:

> If you approve, I will send for my son and his brother [cousin], both valiant men, who at my invitation will fight against the Irish, and you can give them the countries in the north, near the wall called Guaul."

Vortigern agrees, and Octa and Ebissa arrive with forty ships. The two sail to the land of the Picts, lay waste to the Orkneys and take possession of territory "beyond the Frenessican Sea", a contrived name for the Solway Firth.

One other point to note from this section is that Nennius says Vortigern had an interpreter called Ceretic. This was a common Celtic name, so one should not jump to conclusions, but one wonders why Nennius (or his chronicler) should name the interpreter at all, as he appears nowhere else but here. It suggests a connection with Cerdic, the later West Saxon leader, but since we have already determined that Cerdic's reign may not have started until 538, he is unlikely to be with Hengist in the 440s.

Nennius's narrative turns to another reason to condemn Vortigern. In Section §39 he reveals that Vortigern married his own daughter. As he had only just married Hengist's daughter this seems to be another folktale inserted well out of sequence. Nennius tells us that Vortigern has had a son by his daughter whom he tries to deny, and that Germanus (or St. Garmon) condemns Vortigern for this. It may be that Vortigern married a widowed daughter-in-law or step-daughter. The child of this union is believed to have been called Faustus, of whom more shortly.

The next section takes us into the legend of how Vortigern first met the young Ambrosius. Vortigern seeks the counsel of his wise men who tell him to retire to the "remotest boundaries of your kingdom," and there build a city to defend himself from the Saxons who, they say, intend to slay him. Vortigern sets off, and, reaching the province of "Guined" (clearly Gwynedd), finds a suitable site on the summit of Hereri, or Snowdon.

Building work commences, but each morning the previous day's work is found to have vanished over night. Vortigern again consults his counsellors, who tell him he must find a "child born without a father", who can be sacrificed to satisfy the gods. Despite Vortigern's professed Christianity, certain pagan rituals had clearly resurfaced. Excavations at several hill forts have found evidence of human sacrifice.

Vortigern's men search the land and we learn that:

> 41. [. . .] they came to the field of Elleti, in the district of Glevissing, where a party of boys were playing at ball. And two of them quarrelling, one said to the other, "O boy without a father, no good will ever happen to you." Upon this, the messengers diligently inquired of the mother and the other boys, whether he had had a father. Which his mother denied, saying, "In what manner he was conceived I know not, for I have never had intercourse with any man;" and then she solemnly affirmed that he had no mortal father. The boy was, therefore, led away, and taken before King Vortigern.

The next day the boy asks Vortigern why he has been taken. Vortigern reveals the problem with his citadel and the boy, as if by inspiration, reveals the reason for the problem.

> 42. [. . .] "There is," said he, "a pool; come, dig and you will find." They did so, and found a pool. "Now," he continued, "tell me what is in it", but they were ashamed, and made no reply. "I," said the boy, "will show you. There are two vases in the pool." They looked, and found it so. Continuing his questions the boy said, "What is in the vases?" They did not know. "There is a tent in them," said the boy. "Separate them, and you shall find it so." This being done by the king's command, there was found in them a folded tent. The boy, going on with his questions, asked the wise men what was in it. But they did not know what to reply. "There are," said he, "two serpents, one white and the other red; unfold the tent." They obeyed, and two sleeping serpents were discovered. "Consider attentively what they are doing," said the boy. The serpents began to struggle with each other; and the white one, raising himself up, threw down the other into the middle of the tent, and sometimes drove him to the edge of it; and this was repeated thrice. At length the red one, apparently the weaker of the two, recovering his strength, expelled the white one from the tent; and the latter being pursued through the pool by the red one, disappeared.
>
> Then the boy, asking the wise men what was signified by this wonderful omen, and they expressing their ignorance, said to the king, "I will now reveal to you the meaning of this mystery. The pool is the emblem of this world, and the tent that of your kingdom: the two serpents are two dragons; the red serpent is your dragon, but the white serpent is the dragon of the people who have seized many lands in Britain, almost from sea to sea. At length, however, our people shall rise and drive away the Saxon race across the sea, whence they originally came. But you must depart from this place, where you are not permitted to erect a citadel. I, to whom fate has allotted this mansion, shall remain here; whilst to you it is incumbent to seek other provinces, where you may build a fortress."

> "What is your name?" asked the king: "I am called Ambrosius (in British Embreis Guletic)," returned the boy; and in answer to the king's question, "What is your family?" he replied, "A Roman consul is my father."
>
> Then the king gave him that city, with all the western provinces of Britain; and departing with his wise men to the sinistral district, he arrived in the region named Guunnessi, where he built a city which, according to his name, was called Cair Guorthegirn.

This story is best remembered in the version retold by Geoffrey of Monmouth, in which he transforms Ambrosius into Merlin. The important matter here is that despite being called a boy without a father, Ambrosius reveals he is the son of a consul. Perhaps by now the elder Ambrosius was dead, killed, as Gildas wrote, in the Saxon wars or in the battle of Guoloph in 437. If the younger Ambrosius was at his height in the 460s, he was perhaps born in the 430s, and therefore still a child at the time of the Saxon settlement.

The fortress is usually taken to be Dinas Emrys, in Snowdonia, one of the major hill forts of North Wales. The name has obvious associations with Ambrosius, who was also called Emrys Wledig. Though it is unlikely that he lived here, it is possible that he (or his father) ordered that it be rebuilt as a safe retreat from Segontium during the raids by the Irish and Picts.

It is interesting that Ambrosius is found in Glevissing (Glywysing), one of the early Welsh kingdoms in Gwent, the territory of the Silures. This area was heavily Romanised, but also clung steadfastly to its British roots. Glywys, the traditional founder of Glywysing, was the great-grandson of Owain, son of Maximus. We do not know the precise dates of Glywys but, as shown in Table 3.7, they were probably around 445–515. This means he was active throughout the Arthurian period.

The name *Glywys* means "a man of Glevum", the Roman name for Gloucester. Vortigern was descended from one of four brothers attributed with founding Gloucester. Though Gloucester is not in Glywysing, it is close to the borders of Gwent, in the territory of the Gewisse. Glywysing itself was not established until around 470, so although Nennius records Ambrosius as having been found there, the chronicler was simply using a later name for a traditional site. This ties in with the theory that the Ambrosius family was connected with Gloucester.

Glywys is sometimes called Glewys Kerniw, or Glywys Cernyw, and some commentators have connected him to Cornwall (Cernow). However, Cernyw is also the name of a place in south Wales, a strip of territory along the coast between Chepstow and Cardiff. Glywys founded a church here towards the end of his life and the name lives on in the present-day Coedkernew, four miles south-west of Newport.

Finally, Nennius tells us that, unable to build his original fortress, Vortigern sets off to the "sinistral" part of Wales, where he establishes his citadel at Caer Gwrthegirn. "Sinistral" means "left", and Vortigern evidently moved west from Snowdonia towards the Lleyn Peninsula. There is still today a Nant Gwrtheyrn on Lleyn, in the extreme west of Gwynedd, and Lleyn Peninsula has several sites of Arthurian interest (*see* Chapter 24). However, Vortigern is also associated with Gwrtheyrnion, which later formed part of Brycheiniog and southern Powys, whilst Geoffrey places his final fortress at Ganarew in Gwent.

After this detour about Vortigern and the young Ambrosius, Nennius returns to the main story about the Saxons, and for once we may have some real history.

> 43. Meanwhile Vortimer, the son of Vortigern, valiantly fought against Hengist, Horsa, and his people; drove them back to the Isle of Thanet, and thrice enclosed them within it, and besieged, attacked, threatened and frightened them on the western side. The Saxons despatched envoys to Germany to summon reinforcements, with an additional number of ships with many men: and after he obtained these, they fought against the kings of our peoples and princes of Britain, and sometimes extended their boundaries by victory, and sometimes were conquered and driven back.
>
> 44. Four times did Vortimer valorously encounter the

> enemy; the first has been mentioned, the second was upon the river Derguentid, the third at the Ford, in their language called Episford, though in ours Rithergabail, there Horsa fell, and Categirn, the son of Vortigern; the fourth battle he fought was near the Inscribed Stone on the shore of the Gallic sea, where the Saxons, being defeated, fled to their ships and were drowned.
>
> Soon after Vortimer died; before his decease, anxious for the prosperity of his country, he charged his friends to bury his body at the entrance of the Saxon port, viz. upon the rock where the Saxons first landed. "For though," said he, "they may inhabit other parts of Britain, yet if you follow my commands, they will never live again in this island." They imprudently disobeyed this last injunction, and neglected to bury him where he had appointed [for he is buried in Lincoln].

This episode of Vortimer's battles against the Saxons sounds like the precursor to the campaign of Ambrosius as told by Gildas, and could explain Gildas's account that the Saxons had returned home. It also echoes the *ASC*'s description of the battles between Vortigern and the Saxons, although only one seems to be specifically cited in both accounts. Nennius records that Horsa was killed in the battle of Episford, which would seem to equate with the *ASC* entry under the year 455, which notes that Horsa was killed at *Ægælesþrep*. The name *Ægælesþrep* has long been translated as Aylesford on the river Medway in Kent, though a proper translation would be Aylesthorp. Because it has long been believed that all these battles were fought in Kent, antiquarians have looked for likely Kentish names. In fact *Ægælesþrep* would more likely evolve into Addlethorpe or Althorp, both villages in Lincolnshire. The first is near Skegness, but Althorp is on the Trent, almost within site of Bonby, where I suggested the Saxons may have first settled (*see* Map 4).

Nennius, who calls this battle Episford, says its British name is *Rithergabail*, or *Rhyd-yr-ceffyl* in modern Welsh, the "ford of horses". As *epi* means horse, Nennius may have believed that the name Episford commemorated the death of Horsa, rather than

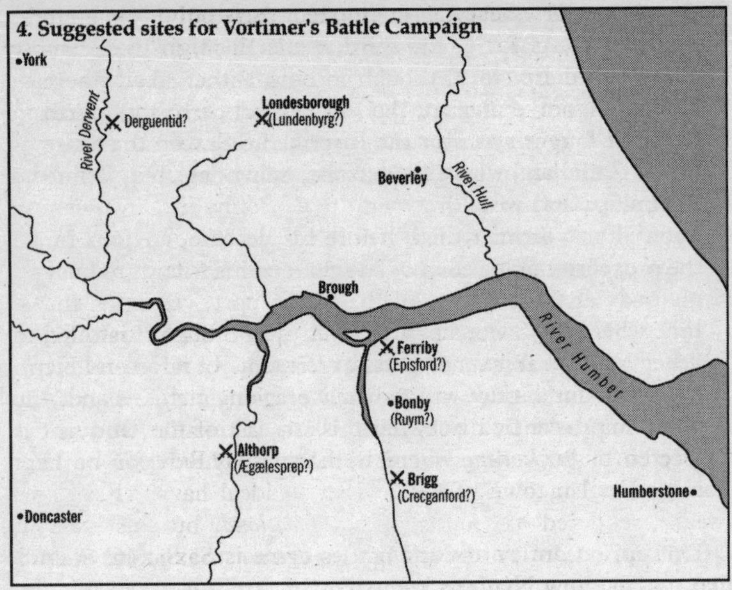

simply signifying a ford where horses gathered. However, in the *Brut Tysilio* (*see* Chapter 9), Episford is treated as Fishford, which is apparently a literal translation of the original Welsh version, *Rhyd y pyscod*. *Pyscod* is sufficiently similar to Episford to suggest an error in translation or copying. But the translator of *Tysilio*, Peter Roberts, maintains that Nennius's source did not state *Rithergabail* but *Sathnegabail*, more properly *Syddyn-y-ceubal*, "the station of the ferryboat". This is still reflected in the towns of North and South Ferriby, on either side of the Humber, just north of Bonby.

The river *Derguentid* is usually translated as the Darent in Kent, and is therefore equated with the battle at *Crecganford* in 456. *Crecganford* itself is usually translated as Crayford, in northwest Kent, though this is not on the Darent, but the neighbouring river Cray. Though Darent is an accurate translation of *Derguentid*, which means "river where oak trees grow", that name must once have applied to scores of rivers, and is still plentiful in such modern names as Derwent, Darwen, Dart or Derwen. Of these the Yorkshire Derwent joins the

Ouse just at its estuary with the Humber, only 25km (16m) from Althorp. As for *Crecganford*, whilst it might conceivably be Crayford, there may be another explanation. The name may be derived from the original Celtic word *chrecwen*, meaning laughter and revelry. The same word in Saxon is *gleam*, as reflected in Glanford Bridge, now known as Brigg, in the Ancholme Valley, just 10km (6m) from Bonby in Lincolnshire. *Gleamford* was where people gathered for games. It could be that this is also the location of Arthur's first battle in Nennius's battle list (*see* Chapter 7).

The *ASC* entry says that after their defeat the British fled to *Lundenbyrg* from *Centlond*, usually treated as London and Kent. However if this battle was at Brigg or along the Derwent the British must have fled elsewhere. 10km east of the Derwent is Londesborough (*Lodenesbyrg* in the Domesday Book). Near here was the Roman town of Delgovitia, an ideal haven. Kent was usually rendered as *Cantwara* not *Centlond*, but just east of Doncaster is Cantley and though its name is Saxon (*Canteleia*) that may be how Nennius knew it.

Finally, the Gallic Sea was the standard name for the sea between Gaul and Britain, which continued round the coast of Essex and East Anglia until it merged with the Germanic Sea somewhere around Lincoln. No inscribed stones survive in this area. In fact, they are extremely uncommon in eastern England and are found mostly in the west, but this is because so many of these stones were destroyed and plundered by generations of farmers and settlers. However, at the point where the Humber enters the sea is a town called Humberston where there used to be a boundary stone.

Vortimer's victory over the Saxons was short-lived because, as Nennius tells us, they did not bury him where he requested. Nennius recounts the consequences in §45 and §46. With Vortimer dead, Hengist regathers his strength. He knows he now has Vortigern under his thumb, and asks Vortigern and his nobles to come to a meeting to ratify a treaty. When they have been wined and dined, Hengist's men draw their knives and murder all 300 of Vortigern's noblemen. Only Vortigern is spared, and, in return for his life, grants the Saxons the territories of Essex, Sussex and Middlesex, as well as others of their choosing.

The story of how Hengist killed Vortigern's men is the stuff of legend, and similar tales appear in other countries' myths. It may well have a basis in fact, but the nub of it suggests that the Saxons had overrun south-east Britain by this time, probably in the 460s before Ambrosius's counterattack.

According to Nennius (§47), Vortigern flees to his fortress in Gwrtheyrnion, where Germanus prays for his sins. Curiously, it is at this point that Nennius recounts the story of the Alleluia battle, with Germanus leading the army and driving the "enemies" back into the sea.

Vortigern now flees to his castle of Caer Gwrthegirn in Demetia, followed by Germanus. But after three days and nights the castle is destroyed by fire from heaven, killing Vortigern, his wives and all the inhabitants. This sounds like a repetition of the Benli episode, in reverse. It could have been Vortigern and not Benli who died by fire and allowed Cadell to succeed to the throne of Powys.

After providing a summary of Vortigern's wickedness, Nennius tells us that Vortigern:

> 48. [Vortigern] had three sons: the eldest was Vortimer, who, as we have seen, fought four times against the Saxons, and put them to flight; the second was Categirn who was slain in the same battle with Horsa; the third was Pascent, who reigned in the two provinces Builth and Guorthegirnaim, after the death of his father. These were granted him by Ambrosius, who was the great king among the kings of Britain. The fourth was Faustus, born of an incestuous marriage with his daughter, who was brought up and educated by St. Germanus. He built a large monastery on the banks of the river Renis, called after his name, and which remains to the present period.

Categirn is a variant of Catotigirn which, according to Peter Bartrum, means "war-lord" or "battle-king". This Categirn is recorded as being the father of Cadell. With their deaths it is the

Table 6.1 The Family of Vortigern

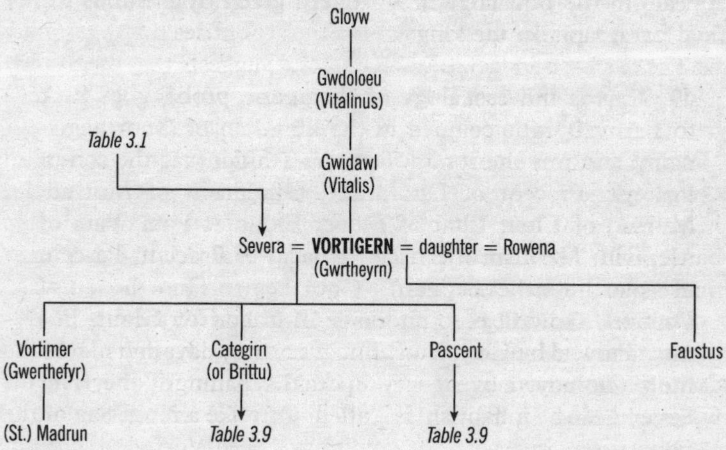

third son Pascent, who becomes king, ruling the territories of Builth and Gwrtheyrnion as vassal to Ambroisus.

The final reference is to the fourth, incestuous son, who was educated by Germanus and established a monastery at Renis. This sounds very similar to Faustus, bishop of Riez, who is usually accorded the dates 405–490, though if he really were a later son of Vortigern he must have been born in the early 410s and would have been an adolescent when Germanus visited Britain in 429. Faustus was known as "the Briton", and accounts of his life make much reference to his mother but none to his father. If Nennius's account is true, then we may believe that Faustus and his mother were sent by Vortigern to Armorica, where he was taken into the care of Germanus.

Faustus was probably sent to Armorica when he was a young child, perhaps soon after the end of Roman administration in 410. Germanus was then the governor of Armorica. Faustus trained as a lawyer but entered the monastery at Lérins in the 420s, becoming head of the monastery in 433, and bishop of Riez around 462. What is intriguing about Faustus is that in a surviving letter his friend, the Roman aristocrat Sidonius, refers both to "your Britons" and to a friend of Faustus called Riocatus, who is returning some of Faustus's books to Britain. Riocatus appears in the genealogy of Vortigern given by Nennius in his final paragraph on the king:

> 49. This is the genealogy of Vortigern, which goes back to Fernvail, who reigned in the kingdom of Guorthegirnaim, and was the son of Teudor; Teudor was the son of Pascent; Pascent of Guoidcant; Guoidcant of Moriud; Moriud of Eltat; Eltat of Eldoc; Eldoc of Paul; Paul of Mepurit; Mepurit of Briacat; Briacat of Pascent; Pascent of Guorthegirn (Vortigern); Guorthegirn Guortheneu of Guitaul; Guitaul of Guitolion; Guitolion of Gloui. Bonus, Paul, Mauron, Guotelin, were four brothers, who built Gloiuda, a great city upon the banks of the river Severn, and in British is called Cair Gloui, in Saxon, Gloucester.

Riocatus is the name copied in error as Briacat, from the original *map Riacat* ("son of Riocatus"). This makes Riocatus the son of Pascent, and thus nephew of Faustus. Riocatus possibly succeeded Ambrosius as commander of the British forces and probably succeeded Pascent in the territories of Builth and Gwythernion. The name Riocatus means "king of battles" which strikes a chord with Arthur's title as "duke of battles". Table 3.9 gives Riocatus the dates 460–530 making him an exact contemporary of Arthur of Badon. It makes a convincing connection and suggests there may be some truth to the legend. It also raises the tempting idea that Faustus could have been the anonymous compiler of the *Gallic Chronicles*. He certainly would have had knowledge of events in Britain at that time and a clearer understanding of their import than his contemporaries.

Since we have touched on Armorica and mentioned the like-sounding Riocatus, it is appropriate here to consider Riothamus and his Arthurian connections.

2. Riothamus

In 1019, a Breton monk called William wrote a life of St. Goeznovius, *Legenda Sancti Goeznovii*, in which he refers to Vortigern and Arthur, "King of the Britons". William stated that his information came from a now lost book called *Ystoria Britanica*, the only known reference to this source:

> In due course the usurper, Vortigern, to strengthen the defence of Britain, which he held unrighteously, summoned warriors from the land of Saxony and made them his allies. Since they were pagans and possessed by Satan, lusting to shed human blood, they brought much evil upon the Britons.
>
> Presently their pride was limited for a while through the great Arthur, king of the Britons. They were largely expelled from the island and reduced to subjection. But when this same Arthur, after many glorious victories which he won in Britain and in Gaul, was summoned at last from human activity, the way was open for the Saxons to again enter the island and there was great oppression of the Britons, destruction of churches and persecution of saints. This persecution went on through the times of many kings, Saxons and Britons fighting back and forth.

In spirit this agrees closely with Gildas's passage in §25 and §26, but without mention of Ambrosius. In William's summary Arthur follows on from Vortigern, separated only by the key word "presently". In the original language this was *postmodum*, meaning "soon afterwards" or "shortly", certainly not after twenty or thirty years. William is unlikely to have confused Arthur and Ambrosius as they must have been identified by name in the original document. This could suggest that Arthur and Ambrosius were the same person – but if so, then Arthur/Ambrosius must have been very young in the 460s to have fought so victoriously at Badon in the 490s and still be fighting at Camlann twenty years after.

This summary is also significant because it identifies Arthur as "king", not *dux*, and states that Arthur won victories in Britain and Gaul, possibly the source for Arthur's European campaign against Rome that we will find in Geoffrey's account. This could suggest that there were two major campaigns, one by Ambrosius and a separate one by Arthur, which brought him to Gaul.

This is where the shadowy figure of Riothamus rides briefly into the light. During the mid fifth century Gaul, like Britain, was subject to attacks from Germanic tribes and after 466 was under threat by the new Visigoth king Euric. The newly appointed Emperor, Anthemius, was determined to restore order. He brought in mercenaries, including a a sizable force under the command of Riothamus. The account of this is recorded by the sxith century historian, Jordanes in *De Rebus Gothicis*.

> Euric, king of Visigoths, aware of the frequent change of Roman Emperors, endeavoured to take Gaul by his own right. The Emperor Anthemius, hearing of this, asked the Brittones for aid. Their king Riotimus came with 12,000 men into the state of the Bituriges by way of Ocean, and was received as he disembared from his ships. Euric, king of the Visigoths, came against them with an innumerable army and, after a long fight, he routed Riotimus, king of the Brittones, before the Romans could join him. So, when he had lost a great part of this army, he fled with all the men he could gather together and came to the Burgundians, a neighbouring tribe then allied to the Romans. But Euric seized the Gallic city of Arverna, for the emperor Anthemius was now dead.

Anthemius was killed in 472, so Jordanes's account must take place between 467 and 472. Ian Wood in *The Merovingian Kingdoms* dates the battle in 469.

Riothamus is called "king of the Brittones", which probably means the British in Armorica. This is supported by the fact that the Roman senator Sidonius had written several letters to Riothamus appealing for help over some rebellious Bretons. Yet, if Riothamus was in Armorica, why did Jordanes say that he arrived in ships "by way of the Ocean"? Riothamus travelled into the "state of the Bituriges" (now Bourges) which is near the river Arnon a tributary of the Loire which marked the southern border of Armorica. 12,000 troops is a large force and it is likely that Riothamus brought in reinforcements from others fleeing Britain, who would have sailed around Armorica and down the Loire valley.

It seems that William's Arthur is Riothamus. But if that is so, why did William call him Arthur, a name he presumably took from the *Ystoria Britanica*? Like Vortigern ("supreme ruler") Riothamus is an epithet, meaning "great king". Arthur, in the Brythonic, as *Ardd-ri*, also means "High King". The author of *Ystoria Britanica*, knowing the meanings of both *Rio-thamus* and *Ardd-ri*, may have assumed they related to the same ruler.

Somehow this explanation feels unsatisfactory. If Riothamus' real name was Arthur, we might have to recognise that someone old enough to be king and to command troops – let us say 25 – in 469 could still have been victorious at Badon in around 493x497 – aged about 50 – and perhaps have fought at Camlann in 514x518 at the age of 70. The bigger question, though, is: why would a king in Armorica, already defeated by the Goths, re-emerge in Britain over 20 years later? And, if he were a king of Armorica, why does his name not appear in the king lists? The names of the rulers of Armorica (*see* Table 3.10) during the fifth century are confusing because there were waves of settlers whose chieftains claimed princedoms in various parts of Armorica, in particular Dumnonée in the north and Cornouaille in the south. However, there are some clues that may help clarify the problem over names.

The Cartulary of Quimperlé lists four early *comes*, or counts, of Cornubia (Cornouaille), amongst whom is Iahann Reeth or Regula (king). Iahann is an early version of John and two generations later lived another John or Ionas Riotham. The second one died in 540, while the first, Iahann Reeth, had come to Armorica with a large fleet of ships in the 450s. He could easily have been the king who fought against Euric and whose name became confused with Ionas Riotham, who lived so soon afterwards.

3. A Tentative Chronology

So we come back full circle to the lifetime of Vortigern. By all accounts he was banished and killed soon after the death of his son Vortimer which means he must have died around the year 460. Into the vacuum, so Gildas tells us, stepped Ambrosius, who d the British and fought against the Saxons, leading to the jor British victory at Badon. In studying these events, it seems increasingly likely that Badon had to come at the end of the fifth century, most likely around 493–497 and not the later date (518) listed in the *Welsh Annals*. According to the annals, it was Arthur who was the victor at Badon. By now Ambrosius must have been an old man, and a new general was leader.

This appears to be the background to Arthur, and it is only now in Nennius's miscellany that Arthur appears. Nennius provides a battle list which is one of the most discussed and analysed sections in all Arthurian lore. It appears as a separate section and I discuss it fully in the next chapter.

Nennius makes only two other brief references, both in his catalogue of the wonders of Britain and both of which really belong in the section of Welsh tradition. He tells of a stone at Carn Cafal, in the province of Builth, that apparently bears the imprint of Arthur's hound. The other is a tomb in the province of Ergyng, which is called Llygad Amr. According to legend, Amr (or Amhar) was Arthur's son, whom he killed and buried there. These two sites, along with the statement in the battle list that Arthur alone had cut down over nine hundred men, show that already Arthur's status had taken on the trappings of legend. The sites also help us locate associations with Arthur in both Builth and Ergyng, territories in south-east Wales already linked with events we have discussed. A pattern is emerging of activities linking Arthur to south Wales and to earlier connections with Vortigern and Ambrosius, stretching across southern Britain, especially around Gloucester and Hampshire. But we also have to recognise the conflicts in the north, especially in Lindsey, and that Ambrosius's and Arthur's theatre of operations was far broader than southern Britain.

Table 6.2. Chronology from Roman withdrawal to Badon

From the last few chapters, we can piece together a chronology which gives us a framework to fifth century Britain, and see where Arthur fits.

410	Britain secedes from Roman Empire. Incursions by Picts and Saxons on the increase.
410–425	Coel serves as *dux*. Wars in North. Remaining Romans hide their wealth. Rise to power of Vitalinus in rivalry with Ambrosius the Elder. Clergy support Pelagianism.

425–430	Treaty reached between Coel and Cunedda. Cunedda moves south to Wales. Vortigern rises to power. Conflict with Ambrosius the Elder continues.
428	Possible first major Saxon *adventus*. Perhaps under Gewis.
429	Visit of Germanus of Auxerre. Possible date for the Alleluia victory over the Picts and Saxons.
436	Possible second visit of Germanus, though this may be confused with mission of Irish monk Garmon.
437	Conflict between Vortigern/Vitalis and Ambrosius culminates in Battle of Guoloph. Vortigern now takes on full power and becomes *superbus tyrannus*.
441	Saxon infiltration into Britain now so complete that Gallic chronicler (Faustus?) believes Britain has fallen to the Saxons. Continued civil wars and plague lead to poor harvests and famine. Further waves of British settle in Armorica.
446–452	Vortigern appeals to Aëtius to send reinforcements to Britain. None is forthcoming.
449–455	Vortigern negotiates with Saxons to provide mercenaries to help fight Picts.
455–460	Saxons under Hengist revolt against Vortigern and mount campaign to win territory in Britain. Vortigern is expelled. Vortimer leads British resistance but is killed in battle, as is his brother Categirn. Horsa killed. Saxons are driven back and there is a brief respite. Further waves of settlers in Armorica, amongst them Iahann Reeth/Riothamus.
460s	Saxon forces return. Massacre of British nobles. Vortigern flees and is killed. Start of counter campaign, perhaps initially by Garmon and then Ambrosius the Younger, supported by Aircol of Dyfed. Rise to power of Pascent and Brychan.
469/470	Riothamus and army of "Brittones" fight the Visigoths. Defeated, Riothamus survives the battle but disappears from recorded history.
470s-485	Further waves of Saxon warriors. Ambrosius's campaign has mixed results. Main opponents are Octa and Aelle.
480s	Dyfnwal Hen, Lord of Strathclyde and Arthwys, Lord of the Pennines.
485	Aelle fights British at *Mearcraedes burn*. Start of possible new campaign under Arthur. Rise to power of Cadell and Riocatus.
488	Octa succeeds to the kingdom of *Cantwara*.
491	Massacre at Anderida by Aelle. Rise to power in Dyfed of Vortipor.
493x497	Victory of Arthur at Mount Badon. Death of Aelle and perhaps of Octa. Partition of Britain.
495x516 *or* 538	Arthur's reign, *Pax Arthuriana*.
514x518 *or* 535x539	Battle of Camlann; Cerdic assumes power over West Saxons.
536x540	Gildas writes *De Excidio*.

7

ARTHUR'S BATTLES – SEEKING THE SITES

1. Nennius's Battle List

One of the most discussed items in all Arthuriana is Nennius's list of twelve battles. It is a list which seems to offer so much, and yet reveals so little. Clearly identifying the battle sites should enable us to pinpoint Arthur's theatre of operations, and ultimately identify him. Unfortunately the sites almost defy interpretation. Despite valiant and ingenious efforts by scholars over two centuries there is not a single site on which there is universal agreement. It is yet another mystery within a web of mysteries, making it all the more fascinating.

As we shall see, suggested locations are scattered the length and breadth of Britain. One might imagine that if Arthur were fighting a common foe such as the Saxons, then the battles would be along a frontier. Alternatively, if he were a ruler of a specific territory then those battles might be within or around its borders. However, if Arthur were fighting several enemies, either as High King or *dux bellorum*, the scattering of sites would be more random. We also have to consider whether or not the list is of the battles of several kings, which might reveal a different pattern.

Nennius's battle list is his first and – bar the two items in his "wonders" – only reference to Arthur. Here is what he says:

> 56. At that time, the Saxons grew strong by virtue of their number and increased in power in Britain. Hengist having

died, his son Octha came from the northern part of Britain to the kingdom of the Kentishmen and from him are descended the kings of Kent. Then Arthur, with the kings of Britain, fought against them in those days, but Arthur himself was the *dux bellorum.* The first battle was at the mouth of the river which is called Glein. The second, third, fourth, and fifth battles were above another river which is called Dubglas and is in the region of Linnuis. The sixth battle was above the river which is called Bassas. The seventh battle was in the forest of Celidon, that is Cat Coit Celidon. The eighth battle was at the fortress of Guinnion, in which Arthur carried the image of holy Mary, the ever-lasting virgin, on his shoulders [shield]; and the pagans were put to flight on that day. And through the power of our Lord Jesus Christ and through the power of the blessed Virgin Mary his mother there was great slaughter among them. The ninth battle was waged in the City of the Legion. The tenth battle was waged on the shore of a river which is called Tribruit. The eleventh battle was fought on the mountain which is called Agned. The twelfth battle was on Mount Badon in which there fell in one day 960 men from one charge by Arthur; and no one struck them down except Arthur himself, and in all the wars he emerged as victor. And while they [the Saxons] were being defeated in all the battles, they were seeking assistance from Germany and their numbers were being augmented many times over without interruption. And they brought over kings from Germany that they might reign over them in Britain, right down to the time in which Ida reigned, who was son of Eobba. He was the first king in Bernicia, that is, in Berneich.

As many commentators have noted, Arthur is called not a king but a *dux bellorum*, a "duke of battles". We are in a Britain being carved up by petty kings, but they still look toward an overall military command.

This happens, according to Nennius, after Hengist dies (in 488, according to the *ASC*). Octha [Octa] comes down from northern Britain, probably either from Lindsey or the territory by the Wall, triggering the start of a campaign of twelve notable battles between the British and the Saxons, culminating, as Gildas also cites, in Badon. We have already dated Badon to around 493–497, allowing Arthur's campaign to last for five to ten years, a believable span of time for twelve battles which are unlikely to have been crammed into one season.

There were probably other battles. Nennius's list almost certainly comes from a now lost battle-song commemorating the victories and ignoring the defeats. John Koch, in *The Celtic Heroic Age*, believes that it is possible to reconstruct the rhyming scheme of the original poem. He adds that the reference to Badon fits into that rhyme, and therefore was part of the original list and not added later due to Arthur's prestige. Arthur was associated with Badon from whenever this poem was first told, possibly during his lifetime. However, if it was composed a century or two later, the memory of Badon and the other battles may have become blurred.

We know that Gildas wrote of Ambrosius's campaign, so we cannot discount the possibility that the battle list belonged primarily to Ambrosius. Or it may have been a catalogue of major victories over the Saxons, regardless of commander, and thus could include Vortimer's campaign. One factor in favour of this theory is the reference to four battles taking place on the river Douglas, which could mean either a concentrated campaign in one area, or that several battles spread over time took place on more than one river Douglas.

The third sentence seems to suggest that all of Arthur's battles were against the Saxons, and, more specifically, against Octha and the men of Kent. It may, however, be that this sentence did not originally follow on from the previous two, but began a new section. "Them" may not refer solely to the Saxons, but to a more general enemy. The list does not suggest a civial war.

The title *dux bellorum* has been discussed extensively. Although its literal translation is "duke of battles", a tremendous amount has been read into it. Firstly, because Arthur fought "with the kings of Britain", many have suggested he was not a king himself, but a military commander. The title *dux*, of course, was one previously owned by the *dux Britanniarum*, the commander based in the north but having control over all of Britain's military. It was doubtless appropriated by Coel and possibly passed on through his descendants, one of whom was Arthur of the Pennines.

Does Nennius's phrasing preclude Arthur from also being a king? Clearly he is set apart; fighting alongside kings suggests equal, or superior, rank. *Dux Britanniarum* was a very senior role, almost equal to *vicarius*, and if that role had continued in some form the rulers of the smaller kingdoms would certainly have looked up to the *dux* as their senior commander. He may not have held the title of High King, but he could have wielded the same authority.

Perhaps we should not take the title *dux* too literally. By Nennius's day, the understanding of the role of *dux* may have been lost, so only the title survived. It may have had some vestigial prestige attached, so that any military commander who brought various kings together to fight a common foe might have been given this title without it meaning anything specific. This means Arthur need not have been stationed in the north (where the battle-hardened Men of the North probably didn't need a commander), but may have been based in Wales or in the south. Indeed, if the southern factions had had no kings of stature since the old Roman provinces crumbled, they probably needed a commander to bring them together.

In some ways it does not matter. The *dux* would have to be of royal blood in order to command kings, as they would not serve alongside someone whom they regarded as inferior. We might not find Arthur ruling a kingdom, but he'll be in the pedigrees. So if Nennius's battles provide us with locations and we can fine tune the time, we should be able to identify him.

1. *The first battle was at the mouth of the river which is called Glein*
The name Glein is derived from the Celtic *glan*, meaning "pure" or "clean." No river is called Glein today, but two are called Glen, in Lincolnshire and Northumberland. The Lincolnshire Glen flows through the Fens and today joins the River Welland near Spalding, but in the fifth century Spalding was on a hard ridge of land virtually on the shoreline of the Wash, which then reached further inland. Interestingly, the origin of the name Welland is uncertain, but it is also a Celtic word and could mean

"good" or "holy" stream, thus the names Glen and Welland may be connected and the mouth of the Glen may, at one time, have been at the mouth of the Welland. This is a possible site, because the area to the north, in Lindsey, was one of the first to be settled by the Angles. The Fens do not lend themselves to major battles but, as Hereward the Wake proved five centuries later, they are suited to a covert guerrilla operation in territory which would be known by the British but highly dangerous to the unwary invader. There is, however, no significant base nearby from which Arthur could have launched his attack. There may be another appropriate site in Lincolnshire at Brigg, originally Glanford Bridge, which I discussed in the last chapter. The river, now called the Ancholme, was a major estuary, before drainage works reduced much of the surrounding marsh.

The Glen in Northumbria also flows into another river, meeting the Till near Doddington. This confluence is close to Yeavering Bell, the largest Iron Age hill fort in Northumberland. It was a significant site of over a hundred dwellings, and a major archaeological dig in 1960 showed that it had been reoccupied after the Roman period. Yeavering has an unspoilt view down to Bamburgh and Lindisfarne and would have been a major defensive site against the early Germanic invaders in the fifth century. The site was of such importance that after the conquest of the area by the Angles, Edwin of Northumbria established his own palace here at the foot of the hill. If Nennius's list is in chronological order, Yeavering Bell is also a suitable location for the first conflict. However, considering how important this site would have been to the British and Saxons, it is surprising the battle list refers to the river and not to the fort.

There are other suggestions. In 1867, in *Chronicles of the Picts and Scots*, W.F. Skene suggested Glen Water, a small stream running down to the river Irvine at Darvel in Strathclyde, near Kilmarnock. His suggestion was based on local legend, which even supplies a date for the battle, 542AD. However, since that was the year that Geoffrey of Monmouth said Arthur of Badon died, it would seem an unlikely date for the first of his battles.

Josephus Stevenson suggested, in notes to his 1838 translation of Nennius, either the River Lune, in Westmorland, or the Leven in Cumberland. The Lune is of special interest. The name is derived from *glein*, likewise meaning "pure and healthy". The river has a major estuary at Lancaster where there was a small Roman fort, strengthened in the 340s as a coastal defence against the Irish. Of all the *glein* rivers it is the only one with a mouth to the sea and a significant fortification.

Other suggestions include the River Glyme in Oxfordshire, Glynch Brook near Bewdley, and Gleiniant near Llanidloes, in west Wales. The Glyme is an intriguing possibility. The name means "bright one", so is not immediately related to *glein*, but its confluence, where it joins the River Dorn at Wootton, north of Oxford, is at the southern end of the little known British enclave of Calchvynydd, which ran up through the Chilterns between Oxford and Northampton. Nearby is Ambrosden, a town which is suggestive of Ambrosius Aurelianus, and a likely spot for one of his battles.

Gleiniant has the distinction of retaining the name *glein*. The stream at Gleiniant meets the Trannon at Trefeglwys in present day Powys, close to the old borders with Gwynedd and Ceredigion. It is also close to one of the suggested sites for Camlann. Gleiniant would suit an internal struggle, but is far out of the conflict zone for the Saxons.

One final possibility is the Glynde Reach in Sussex, one I'm not aware has previously been suggested. This small stream was originally the Glynde Bourne – indeed it flows right below the famous Glyndebourne Opera House – and Glynde is derived, according to some etymologies, from the Celtic for valley, *glen*. Others say it comes from the Saxon *glind*, for enclosure. Either way it has a striking similarity to the first in Nennius's list, made all the more intriguing as this could be the site of one of Aelle's battles listed in the *ASC* as happening at *Mearcrædes burnam* in 485, exactly when I have suggested that Arthur's battle campaign may have started.

Of all the suggestions the best possibilities are the Northumbrian Glein, the Cumbrian Lune and the Sussex Glynde.

2–5. *The second, third, fourth, and fifth battles were above another river which is called Dubglas and is in the region of Linnuis.*

Dubglas is the original of the name Douglas. It is usually translated as meaning "black water", but a more strict interpretation is "black-blue" or even "black-green" (*dub*+*glas*). *Glas* means that blue-green colour seen in glass – the name Glasgow means "green hollow". So we're really looking for a dark, probably deep, river that reflected blue-black, or green-black. Unfortunately, that could apply to many, not helped by the fact that the name Douglas survives as one English river, two Scottish rivers and twelve called Dulas in Wales. Doubtless there would have been plenty more called Dulas in England, which changed their name under Saxon domination to such variants as Dawlish or even Blackwater (there's a tempting site in Hampshire that I discuss separately on page 162). It was probably because of this abundance of names that the original chronicler qualified the description by adding that it was in the region of Linnuis.

In 1945, Kenneth Jackson, in an article in *Modern Philology*, determined that *Linnuis* derives from *Lindenses*, meaning "the people of Lindum", or Lincoln. This at first seems promising, because we know that the area around Lincoln, which was Lindsey, was one of the earliest areas settled by the Angles. Unfortunately, no river in that area has a name remotely like Douglas. The primary river is the Witham, and some have suggested that the Witham might originally have been called the Douglas, on the assumption that Witham is a Saxon name, derived from "Witta's ham." However, Kenneth Cameron, in *English Place Names*, states that the Witham is probably one of a group of rivers the names of which go back before Celtic times into unrecorded history, so it was probably never known as the Dubglas.

There is another candidate for Linnuis. The Roman geographer Ptolemy used that word to describe the area now known as Lennox, covering the territory north of the Clyde and Firth around Loch Lomond. Just east of Loch Lomond is Glen Douglas, where the Douglas Water gushes down through the glen to enter the loch at Inverbeg. Beyond, across Loch Long, but still clearly visible from Glen Douglas, is the strangely shaped peak of Ben Arthur, which may well be connected with the Dál Riatan king's son, Artúir mac Aedan. The old road from the Dál Riatan capital at Dunadd, in Argyll, skirts the southern fells of Ben Arthur before descending into Glen Douglas. There could certainly have been a battle here involving Artúir mac Aedan, probably against the Picts. Otherwise it is far too distant for a battle of a southern or even a northern British Arthur against the Saxons.

Leslie Alcock has suggested that *Linnuis* may have been copied wrongly and that the original word was *Lininuis*, which would have derived from the peoples known as the Lindinienses, who lived in Dorset and parts of Wiltshire, Somerset and Hampshire, the area that later became Wessex. The Roman name for Ilchester was Lindinis. Here the river Divelish runs from Bulbarrow Hill at Woolland, to Sturminster Newton in Dorset. Just south of Bulbarrow Hill is the Devil's Brook, running south to Burleston where it enters the River Piddle. En route it passes through Dewlish, a village which also means "dark stream". Although these two watercourses are minor, they do form a north-south barrier. Bulbarrow Hill is the site of a Celtic hill fort, and the rivers run through a triangle formed by Cadbury Castle, the Badbury Rings and the Cerne Giant, all significant Celtic landmarks. This could certainly be a location for a confrontation between the British and the West Saxons.

August Hunt on the Vortigern Studies website draws attention to the Devil's Water, a stream in Northumberland that passes through Linnel Wood and joins the River Tyne near Corbridge, at Dilston. Linnel is probably derived from *llyn-elin* ("lake-elbow"). It is an interesting combination of the two names in an area that would have been rich for conflict during the fifth and sixth centuries.

Of the many Dulas rivers in Wales, Steve Blake and Scott Lloyd in *Pendragon* suggest the Dulas that flows into Liverpool Bay at Llandulas, just east of Colwyn Bay. Another Dulas worth noting is now called Dulas Brook, and runs parallel to the Golden Valley in northern Ergyng, eventually joining the River Dore at Ewyas Harold. This is in the same area as part of Arthur's hunt of the giant boar Twrch Trwyth, as told in the story of *Culhwch and Olwen* (*see* Chapter 8). That story, as we shall see, may well represent a series of battles conducted by Arthur across southern Wales and it is possible that at least some of the battles in Nennius's list equate to it. We shall encounter another later.

One other Dulas, or Dulais, worthy of note flows through Pontarddulais in Glamorgan, where it joins the River Neath.

Near its source it flows through Cwm Dulais, above which is Craig y Bedw, or Bedwyr's Crag. This area was known for its groves and bushes. The Welsh for grove is *llwyn*, and there are places called Llwyngwenno, Llwynadam, Llwyn-y-domen, and so on. The area might have been known locally as the land of groves, or Llwyni, which might have evolved into *Linnuis*.

6. *The sixth battle was above the river which is called Bassas.* This is one of the more baffling locations and even the most dedicated Arthurians have declared it impossible to identify. The more intrepid have suggested sites as far afield as Bass Rock off North Berwick in the Firth of Forth, and the River Loddon in Old Basing in Hampshire, suggesting that the Loddon was once known as the river of Basa's people. The etymology for Basing is Saxon, and though this makes it unlikely to appear in what was originally a Celtic battle song, it may refer to an area so long occupied by the Saxons that their name had superseded the original.

The same problem affects Basford, the name of three places in Cheshire, Staffordshire and Nottinghamshire. All seem to be derived from the Angle *Basa's ford*. Blake and Lloyd's suggestion, Basingwerk, in Shropshire, is also of Saxon origin ("Basa's stronghold"), and its Celtic name was *Maesglas* ("Green field"). Equally frustrating is Bassingbourne in Cambridgeshire, for although of Angle origin, it does at least mean "Bassa's stream". It is, however, in an area long occupied by the Saxons.

In the 1860s, Skene suggested Dunipace, the site of two hillocks at Falkirk in Scotland, near the Roman fort of Camelon. He proposed that the name was originally *Duni-Bass*, meaning "two mounds." However the origins of Dunipace are not clear, with suggestions that it came from *Dun-y-pax* ("hills of peace") or *duin-na-bais* ("hills of death"). John Stuart Glennie, writing in *Arthurian Localities*, whilst recognising this as a possibility felt there was an even better site across the river where a huge rock precipice may be the *bass* (or rock). Neither of the rivers in the area (the Bonny and the Carron) is called Bassas, but there is a ford across the Carron, and the Celtic name for ford, or shallows, is *bais*. But all this seems to be clutching at straws. The same concept of *bais* for shallows would work even better at the Fords of Frew on the Tribruit, discussed under battle 10.

The most likely suggestion is Baschurch in Shropshire, put forward by Graham Phillips and Martin Keatman in *King Arthur, The True Story*. The name derives from the churches of Bassa, mentioned in a poem by Taliesin as the burial place of the kings of Powys. Situated near the Welsh Marches, Baschurch could well have been the site of forays by the West Saxons. It is within a day's march of the Gewisse territory to the south, and close to the site for Badon (Caer Faddon) given in the Mabinogion story *The Dream of Rhonabwy* (*see* Chapter 8). The nearest river is the Perry, but this name may be of Norman origin, derived from the Peveril family who controlled the area after the Norman conquest. We do not know the original Celtic name.

One other possibility concerns the Roman cognomen Bassus. One of the consuls at the time of Julius Caesar was Ventidius Bassus, and there were two noted poets at the time of Nero, Caesius Bassus and Saleius Bassus. Several inscriptions have been found in Britain, mostly in the north, bearing the name Bassus. One at Black Carts, halfway along Hadrian's Wall, notes that part of the wall here was built by Nas . . . Ba[ssus] of the First Cohort. Most significantly, at the fort of Alavana at Kendal in Cumbria, there is a tombstone to the centurion Publius Aelius Sergius Bassus Mursa of the Twentieth Legion. Alavana stood on what is now the River Kent, though the original name for this river is not known. Might Publius Aelius Bassus have earned such a reputation that the area around his burial would be remembered by his name?

7. *The seventh battle was in the forest of Celidon, that is Cat Coit Celidon.*

Unlike Bassas, most scholars pounce on this site as straightforward and unchallenged. Leslie Alcock says it is the battle "about which we can have the most confidence", adding that "there is full agreement that this was in Scotland." But if there was full agreement when he wrote that, there isn't now.

Cat Coit Celidon means "battle in the forest of Celidon", which Nennius had already said in Latin. It seems strange that he should restate it in Celtic unless he wished to emphasize the original Welsh name as something specific, rather than another Forest of Celidon which had become better known in the intervening years. If so, then it suggests there are at least two Celidons, which immediately complicates the matter.

The usual interpretation is that this refers to the Caledonian Forest, which is a very widespread location. Caledonia was the Roman name for Scotland. Sometimes it was used to specify the Highlands, north of the Antonine Wall, but generally it applied to the whole country. Stories about the bard Myrddin, which we will explore later, record that after the battle of Arderydd he fled into Coed Celyddon, where he ran wild and went mad. Arderydd is the modern Arthuret, a few miles north of Carlisle. Just beyond, up Liddesdale, is the start of the present day Border Forest, which runs through to the Kielder Forest in Northumbria. There is no specific spot within this forest called Celidon, so if this is the same forest where Arthur's seventh battle occurred it could have happened almost anywhere across the north-west, perhaps as far as High Rochester, where the Roman fort of Bremenium stood. Nikolai Tolstoy, following clues in the Scottish Arthurian romance *Fergus of Galloway*, has determined that the battle probably took place near Hart Fell.

There is an ancient inscribed stone here, near the village of Yarrow. Dating from the early sixth century, it commemorates the burial of two princes, Nudus and Dumnogenus (Nudd and Dyfnwal), sons of Liberalis. *Liberalis* may be a Roman cognomen but it is as likely an epithet suggesting he was generous, a nickname that appears as *Hael* in British. It is tempting to think this refers to Nudd Hael, the grandson of Dyfynwal Hen (*see* Table 3.4), but he lived in the late sixth century, too late for this inscription. Nudd/Nudus was involved in a raid on Anglesey against Rhun ap Maelgwyn to avenge the death of Elidir the Wealthy. Rhun retaliated with a march across Britain to York, and up as far as the Clyde, so he would have passed through this area. Possibly Nudd was killed in this show of force, which might have been the real Battle of Celidon.

The Caledonian Forest is too generalized a description to pinpoint Nennius's battle, and yet he seems to be trying to be specific. He does not say the "Caledonian Forest" but the "Forest of Celidon", which may be something different, even personalised. In the Mabinogion story *Culhwch and Olwen*, we learn that Culhwch is the grandson of Celyddon Wledig, an important local chieftain. The story is set chiefly in Gwent. Celyddon is not otherwise identifiable, so we cannot verify his territory, but it would not be far removed from Gwent. This is the area of Arthur's capital, Gelliwig, as we will explore later. There are several towns and localities in this area bearing the prefix *gelli-*, derived from *celli* for a woodland grove, including Gellideg, Gelligaer and Gellinudd. Though no Gelliddon survives, the other names are testament to a special wood around Caerphilly, and it is quite possible that the Forest of Celyddon was once there. Blake and Lloyd have used similar logic but different etymological trails to fix Celidon in North Wales, between the rivers Clwyd and Conway.

Frank Reno follows a different route, reminding us that *coed* is a contraction of *Argoed*, the proper Brythonic word for forest, and that the phrase "Men of Argoed" was a phrase used to describe the Men of Powys. The main forest in Powys is the Clun, in present day Shropshire, and is relatively close to Baschurch and Caer Faddon. Intriguingly the derivation of Clun is the same as for Glein.

Earlier in his *History* Geoffrey refers to the Forest of Calaterium, where one of his pre-Arthurian kings, Archgallo, wanders dejectedly after being deposed. Archgallo is almost certainly based upon Arthwys ap Mar (Arthur of the Pennines), and I'm convinced that Geoffrey had access to a Northern Chronicle which covered the exploits of Arthwys, some of which he may have confused with Arthur of Badon's. Calaterium is sufficiently similar to Celidon to cause possible confusion. Some experts, including J.A. Giles, have suggested that Calaterium was the old Royal Forest of Galtres, north of York, around Sutton-on-the-Forest and Easingwold. This was a rich area much treasured by the later kings of Northumbria. We will see in Chapter 9 that, according to Geoffrey, Arthur pursued the Saxons from Lichfield to the Forest of Caledon. It is over 300km to the Caledonian Forest, but about half that to the Forest of Galtres.

8. *The eighth battle was at the fortress of Guinnion, in which Arthur carried the image of holy Mary, the everlasting virgin, on his shoulders [shield]; and the pagans were put to flight on that day.* This is the only battle that carries a description and is not unlike

the *Welsh Annals* reference to Badon, suggesting that the reference to the Virgin Mary must be significant. Why did Arthur carry the image of the Virgin Mary at this battle rather than any of the earlier ones? The usual answer is that the battle occurred at a church or other holy place, and that Arthur may have been protecting a church from the heathen invaders. We should not overlook the fact that the Celts were Christians whilst the Saxons and Angles were pagans. One legend attached to Arthur, but linking him to the Crusades, tells that Arthur brought back with him from Jerusalem a splinter of the Holy Cross, which was kept at Wedale. Wedale is in the Scottish Borders and the main town is Stow. Stow is the Saxon for "holy place" and the church there is dedicated to St. Mary.

Connecting Stow with a fort called Guinnion is not straightforward. Skene and others simply based it on the fact that a Roman fort was known to be nearby, and that this must have been Guinnion ("White Fort"). The nearby Gala Water tumbles at high spate along the valley and is sometimes called the "White Strath" or *Gwen-y-strad*, though this seems rather convoluted. Alistair Moffat, in *Arthur and the Lost Kingdoms*, follows a more convincing route. He reminds us that *gwen*, or more properly *gwyn*, means not only "white" but also "holy", in the sense of "pure". Thus the name Stow may simply have been a Saxon translation of an earlier Celtic name. Some etymologists suggest that Wedale was originally Woe-dale, or "dale of woe", remembering a Saxon defeat, whilst Moffat suggests the name derived from *Guidh-dail*, the Valley of Prayer, but had previously been the Holy Valley or *Gwyn-dail*, possibly corrupted into *Gwyn-ion*. This all seems rather tenuous to me.

In fact as Gwynion the name is quite common in Wales. There are at least four noted hills, or crags, called Carreg Gwynion, near Pembroke, Rhayader, Rhos and in the Berwyn Mountains at Llanarmon. This last is the site of a well preserved Celtic hill fort, which seems more likely to have been the "fortress of Guinnion" than at *Guidh-hail*. This locale would better suit a battle between Welsh factions, but it is less than a day's ride from Chester and cannot be ruled out. The fact that the name is fairly common in Wales suggests that at one time it was probably equally common across the rest of Britain. If so the name may have adapted to

Wenbury or Winbury or Whitsbury, near Fordingbridge, a site I discuss later in relation to Cerdic's battles.

A more intriguing possibility is Wanborough, just outside Swindon. The name was once *Wenbeorge*, which is usually treated as "wenn beorge," meaning the "place at the tumour-shaped mounds", as *wenn* is Saxon for tumour. However, *wen* could as easily be derived from the Welsh *gwyn* for "white", a theory strengthened by the fact that nearby are two sites, White Hill, renowned in Roman times for its pottery production, and Whitefield Hill, near the site of some ancient earthworks. The surrounding hillsides are covered by the many famous chalk carvings, such as the White Horse at Uffington. Wanborough was the site of the Roman fort Durocornovium, the Fort of the Cornovii, and this may well have been known locally as the White Fort. What adds to the intrigue of this site is that a little way to the south is Liddington Castle, one of the most favoured sites for the battle of Badon.

There have been other suggestions, including Burgh Castle (Gariannonum) in Norfolk, Winchester (Caer Guinn), and the Wrekin (Caer Guricon) in Shropshire, but the only other one that has some merit is Binchester, near Durham. Here was the Roman fort of Vinovium, one of the earliest in Britain which was later refortified and remained in use until the early fifth century. The origin of the fort's name is uncertain, most suggesting "the Way of the Wine" or similar. One suggestion is that it meant "pleasant spot", which may link back to the Celtic word *gwyn*, which could have been Latinized to *vin*. The Celtic spelling of Vinovium is *Uinnouion,* becoming *Gwinnouion.* It was the largest fort in the north-east and held a contingent of Germanic soldiers. Its location must have been important to later settlers because they also buried their dead here, showing that it became a sustained community. At nearby Escomb is the oldest surviving Saxon church in England, and it may be that, once converted, the Saxons were drawn to what had long been a holy and venerated area, as Arthur's battle in the name of the Virgin Mary might imply.

9. *The ninth battle was waged in the City of the Legion*

This ought to be reasonably straightforward but unfortunately isn't. There were three main legionary towns, Caerleon, Chester and York. With the construction of Hadrian's Wall, Carlisle also became a legionary town but not in the conventional sense, and, unless it was the capital of Valentia and its status changed, not at the end of the Roman period. Although Caerleon remained a legionary base, the legion was seldom there, beyond a skeletal force. It was involved in the construction of Hadrian's Wall, but by the third and fourth centuries was assigned elsewhere, including Richborough in Kent. So whilst Caerleon can rightly claim the name City of the Legion, it was far less significant than either York or Chester.

York was not only the home of the VI Legion, it was the military capital of Britain, and the fortress remained permanently manned and strengthened throughout the Roman period. The headquarters of the Fort was such a major building that it remained in use well into the ninth century.

Like Caerleon, Chester's XX Valeria Victrix legion was often stationed elsewhere, especially during the third century, but Chester was refortified in the fourth century and remained so until the end of the Roman period. Nennius refers to the city in the singular, as *urbe Legionis*, "city of *the* Legion", as if by the time of this battle all but one legion had left Britain. Gildas, in describing York, used the plural *Legionum urbis cives*, "the city of the Legion*s*". Unless this was too subtle for Nennius's source we are evidently talking about a different place. The XX Valeria Victrix was the last legion to leave Britain.

So whilst York was the major legionary fortress, and more likely to have been a focus for Anglo-British confrontation, Chester was the centre of the last legion, and is known to have been the site of a major Anglo-British battle in about 615. Both therefore have an equal case to argue. Which one Nennius meant can only be solved by identifying the other localities in the list.

10. *The tenth battle was waged on the shore of a river which is called Tribruit.*

Like Bassas, this river has almost defied analysis, and most authorities admit defeat. The early analysts, Skene and Glennie, considered the Celtic version of Tribruit, *Tryfrwyd*, a name which also appears in the poem *Pa Gur* (*see* Chapter 8), where it is spelled *Trywruid*. In a study of Scotland written in 1165, they found that the old British name for the Firth of Forth was *Werid*, derived from *Gwruid*, meaning "men of the forth". The word "shore" is significant as it suggests more of a sea-shore than a river bank. The Celtic word is *traeth* and the word *Tribruit* or *Trywruid* may have originally been a combination of *Traeth* and *Gwruid*, with the "g" dropped, becoming *Traewruid*. It sounds plausible, albeit tortuous, and the site suggested is the Links of Forth between the river and the heights of Stirling Castle, a site better known for the Battle of Bannockburn in 1314.

O.G.S. Crawford, the pioneer of aerial surveys in archaeology, also suspected that this battle was waged on the Forth, but further east at the Fords of Frew, between Gargunnuck and Kippen. This was one of only two safe crossing places on the Forth, used most notably by Bonnie Prince Charlie in 1745. Two other streams join the Forth at the point of the Fords, the Boquhan Burn to the west and the Goodie Water to the east. Crawford believed that the old name for the Frew was the *Bruit*, so that the Fords of Frew, marking the stretch of three streams, was the *Tribruit*. The site seems more likely than its explanation, as it was a key crossing point, regarded as the gateway between the Lowlands and the Highlands. It was doubtless a frontier for many engagements between the British and the Picts.

Others who reject this derivation, including Kenneth Jackson whose essay "Once Again Arthur's Battles" (1945) is considered one of the cornerstones of Arthurian research, do not necessarily reject the location. He notes that *tryfrwyd* could be used to describe something pierced or broken, and that Nennius's location is not necessarily a river's name but a description of a shoreline as "the broken place". This could still refer to a ford, particularly one where the river is very shallow, leaving sandy and stony banks breaking the surface of the river.

For another possible location, Barber and Pykitt looked to the story of *Culhwch and Olwen*, which tells of the hunt for the Irish Boar, the Twrch Trwyth. They suggest that this tale involves a play on words with the River Twrc (also called the Troggy) and *trwyth* as a variant of *traeth*. Twrch Trwyth therefore not only meant the Irish Boar, but the "shores of the Twrc", becoming, over time, *Try-Troit*, and later *Trywruid*. They also believe that the story of the Irish Boar hunt is the retelling of a battle between the British and the Gewisse with the final decisive battle at the mouth of the river Twrc on the Severn estuary near Caerleon. If the Dulas Brook mentioned above also corresponds to one of the twelve battles, then these two sites may relate to Arthur's conflict with the Twrch Trwyth.

One other suggestion of interest is the River Ribble. The Ribble is known as the "roaring river", a name adopted by the Roman fort at Ribchester, known as Bremetennacum. The *Bre-* prefix comes from the Celtic *breffw,* which means "to bellow". The original river name may therefore have been something like *Breffwrd,* from which the "b" was eventually dropped, becoming *Reffwrd.* The Ribble meets the Douglas from the south and the Dow from the north at what is now called Hutton and Longton Sands. Because of this confluence of three rivers it has been conjectured that the locality may have been known as *Trireffwrd,* which could easily mutate into *Tryfrwyd.* With the Lune and Douglas in this vicinity, this might suggest a series of battles against the Irish marauders.

11. *The eleventh battle was fought on the mountain which is called Agned.*

This battle has the added confusion that there is an alternative entry. A later version of the Nennius manuscript calls this site Breguoin, and other manuscripts have other spellings, including Bregnion and Bregomion. One manuscript even combines the two as *Agned Catbregomion,* implying that the two names mean the same site: that is, the battle (*Cat*) of Bregomion on Mount Agned. Just as with Dubglas and Linnuis, bringing the two together is not easy, though the fact that Breguion and Agned are such rare names means that if we can identify the two we would almost certainly have a unique site.

Mount Agned is referred to by Geoffrey of Monmouth, though not in connection with Arthur's battles. He says that the British ruler Ebrauc founded the cities of Kaerebrauc, Alclud and Mynydd Agned. John of Fordun, in his fourteenth-century *Scotichronicon,* states that Agned was an old name for Edinburgh. Edinburgh was usually called Eidyn and the fortress there, on top of what is now called Arthur's Seat, was Din Eidyn. It would require some philological contortions to convert Eidyn into

Agned, and even more to make it convincing. August Hunt suggests the two are a play on words. Eidyn could relate to the Greek *eidon*, meaning "to behold or envision", similar to the Latin *agnitio*, which means "recognition or understanding." Both would suggest that Din Eidyn might have been called Mount Agned because both could mean the "Mount of Understanding". It's a romantic notion, but one not even hinted at in folklore.

Geoffrey of Monmouth says that Mount Agned was known as "The Castle of the Maidens". This relates to the Picts. The right to kingship passed through the female line, and, according to legend, the Picts kept all the eligible royal maidens in the Castle for their security and education. However, Eidyn was a British stronghold and though it was briefly captured by the Picts, it was never settled by them. The Picts had several strongholds along the Forth in the area of the Manau, especially at Myot Hill to the west of Camelon. Their territory was at Stirling and one might imagine the rock of Stirling Castle being an equally suitable site for a "Castle of the Maidens". However, in the Middle Ages, the Castle of Maidens was always believed to refer to Edinburgh, regardless of any historical accuracy.

Geoffrey also called Mount Agned the Dolorous Mountain, which may be appropriate as one understanding of the word *agned* is that it is related to the Welsh *ochenaid* meaning "sigh". This makes an interesting connection to the possibility of Wedale as the eighth battle at Guinnion, since the Eildon Hills near Wedale are referred to as the Dolorous Mountains in the Arthurian romance *Fergus of Galloway*. This may link with the location of Breguoin, which has been shown to derive from Bremenium, the Roman fort at High Rochester, a day's ride to the south, perhaps suggesting a continuation of the first battle.

The philologist Alfred Anscombe demonstrated that had Breguoin been spelled *Breguein*, it would have derived from Bravonium, the Roman fort at Leintwardine, in Herefordshire. This is just west of Ludlow and within hurling distance of the Clun Forest, one of the candidates for the Celidon battle. Bravonium appears in one Roman itinerary as Branogenium. Kenneth Jackson has suggested that Branogenus means "born of the raven", but it can equally mean "born of the king" or, taking *genus* in its more general sense, "people of the king." This could suggest that the original Celtic site of Bravonium/Branogenium was a hill fort occupied by royalty or descendants of royalty.

Linda Malcor has shown that Bremetennacum, the name of the fort at Ribchester which has the same prefix as Bremenium, would also adapt to Breguoin. Bremetennacum was the fort at which Lucius Artorius Castus was based, and would be a natural candidate during the period when the Picts were attacking the forts south of the wall.

One other intriguing suggestion arose from a marginal note in an old translation of Nennius found by Joseph Ritson in 1825, suggesting that the site was Cathbregyon, in Somerset. Barber and Pykitt identified this as Catbrain in Bristol, now at one end of Filton airfield. It has also been suggested that this might be Cadbury, where the Saxon *Caddesbyrig* was derived from the Celtic *Cat-bregyon*. Cadbury has long been associated with Arthur, as a possible site for Camelot, but not with this battle. However, the name is derived from the personal name *Cada*, not from *Cat* for battle.

12. *The twelfth battle was on Mount Badon in which there fell in one day 960 men from one charge by Arthur; and no one struck them down except Arthur himself, and in all the wars he emerged as victor.* This is the one battle for which we have irrefutable historical support because Gildas mentioned it, and said that it happened in the year of his birth. We have already tentatively dated it to some time in the 490s, probably between 493 and 497. We have also seen that both the original battle poem and the *Welsh Annals* connect Badon with Arthur. Unfortunately Gildas does not tell us who the commander was at Badon, or where it was fought. Why did he need to? In his day, the audience for his *De Excidio* would have remembered Badon or have heard of it, and the location was well known.

The fact remains that Badon was the decisive battle which forced back the Saxons, resulting in a period of comparative peace in Britain. Whoever was the victor at Badon became the Arthur of legend. Tying Badon into the landscape is thus vital in helping identify Arthur.

Gildas would have referred to the place by its British name, and *Badon* or *Baddon* is British for "bath". Nennius had the same view. In his historical miscellany is a reference to "the Hot Lake, where the baths of Badon are, in the country of the Hwicce." (§67). The passage then describes what are clearly Roman baths, and the obvious assumption is that the reference is to Bath itself.

The territory of the Hwicce centred upon Worcester and its main town Winchcombe, but included Gloucester and Cirencester, and thus were the lands opened up to the Saxons following the battle of Dyrham in 577. Bath was tucked in at the southern end of the Hwicce, and the southern boundary follows the River Avon to the coast and along part of the Wansdyke defensive earthwork. However, the Hwicce people must have roamed because their name is remembered as far afield as Whiston (formerly *Hwiccingtune*), east of Northampton.

Bath continued to be known as the city of the "Hot Baths" long after the Roman period and into the Saxon. It was called *aet Badum* in the foundation charter for Bath Abbey in 676AD. Just when the original of Nennius's list of wonders was compiled is not known. The baths would have to have survived in sufficiently useable condition to be regarded as a "wonder". Barry Cunliffe, in his excavations at Bath in the 1980s, confirmed that whilst there was considerable stone-robbing in the post Roman period, efforts were made to maintain other buildings well into the fifth and even sixth centuries. The likelihood is that Bath was still a functioning British city at the time of the Battle of Dyrham, and the baths there must still have been held in awe.

This would seem to prove that Badon must be Bath, but we need to be cautious. To begin with, Gildas does not refer specifically to the town of Bath. His phrase is *obsessionis Badonici montis*, "the siege of Mount Badon" or "Badon Hill". Bath isn't on a hill – quite the contrary. The area of the hot spring which fed the baths was originally in a marshy valley. Bath is, however, surrounded by hills, and most authorities assume that Gildas meant one of those, but which one?

All other references to Badon date from several centuries later, and they give us three other pieces of dubious information. Firstly, that Arthur fought at Badon carrying the Cross of Jesus on his shoulder, or shield. This presumably refers to an emblem, unless it is meant figuratively, in that Arthur is defending a church, or fighting in the name of Christ, as at Guinnion. Secondly, Nennius tells us that the siege lasted for three days and nights. Thirdly, Nennius also states that Arthur killed 960 of the enemy. This does not mean Arthur killed them single-handedly, but that he led the charge that resulted in such whole-sale, and doubtless exaggerated, slaughter.

If Badon Hill is one of the hills surrounding Bath, it could be one of several. The most favoured are either Bannerdown Hill or Little Solsbury Hill, both at Batheaston. Analysis by John Morris, for instance, suggests that the Saxon forces were almost certainly infantry, perhaps no more than a thousand strong, whilst the British forces were probably cavalry. Little Solsbury Hill has a major hill fort on its plateau-like summit, which was certainly large enough to house a cavalry unit, but a difficult site for a cavalry charge. It is unlikely that the Saxons would take the hill fort and then be besieged by the British from below. However, the Saxons could have been hemmed in on Bannerdown Hill, less than a mile to the east, which has no hill fort.

Such speculation, however, takes us no nearer to identifying the location precisely. There are certainly many who do not believe that Badon does equate to Bath and presume that Badon Hill is a specific location. Kenneth Jackson demonstrated that if Badon was the site of a hill fort, and therefore known as Din Badon to the British, it would convert into the Saxon *Baddanbyrig*, evolving into the English Badbury. Badbury in Wiltshire, Badbury Rings in Dorset and Badby in Northamptonshire are all recorded as *Baddanbyrig* in tenth century records. There is also Badbury Hill in Oxfordshire, near Faringdon.

All of these sites except Badby have Celtic hillforts associated with them. That at Badbury, in Wiltshire, is now called Liddington Castle, a name I shall use to avoid confusion. Although an interesting case could be made for each of the sites, Liddington seems the most suitable by virtue of its location. It stands just above the Ridgeway, the ancient British trackway that runs through the Chilterns to the Marlborough Downs, towering above the neighbouring land. Over 277m (900 feet) at its highest point, it had a strong vantage point over the neighbouring territory, and was within sight of other major hill forts, including Barbury Castle. Liddington stands as the frontal defence against a northern or eastern attack, with its back line of defence at the Wansdyke. It allows for greater flexibility than Solsbury Hill at Bath, which would not only have to have conceded a significant Saxon advance, but is also a highly restricted site.

Like Liddington, Badbury Rings in Dorset is an open site, and would have been a primary focus for any Saxon advance from the coast around Poole Bay. However, it is not a focal point for a major breakthrough. Badon was decisive because it repulsed the Saxons in their advance into the west. The Saxon target would have been the rich territories of Cirencester and Gloucester, and their advance would have been either from the south, where Aelle had established his base in Sussex, or from the east, around Lindsey. Aelle's base after 491 was at Pevensey, but there were no major Roman roads in that area. So if Aelle were to strike toward Cirencester he would have had to move along the coast to Chichester, then follow the Roman road to Silchester and from there to Cirencester. That road goes right past Liddington. This is far more likely than working all the way along the coast as far as Badbury Rings, and then striking north for Bath along the Ackling Dyke, with the intention of taking the Fosse Way up to Cirencester.

A Saxon advance from Lincoln towards Cirencester would have taken a direct route along the Fosse Way. However, the *ASC* tells us that though the Saxons had been making steady territorial gains in the south, and archaeological evidence reaches the same conclusion for East Anglia, Lindsey and further north along the coast, central Britain was untamed territory. The Angles would have needed to make far more gains towards the Midlands before risking an assault on the golden lands of the Cotswolds. The alternative would have been to march from East Anglia down Icknield Street to Verulamium (St. Albans), and then either follow Ackeman Street to Bicester and then to Cirencester, or follow the Ridgeway to Swindon and up to Cirencester. The latter route would, again, take them right past Liddington. There are no other logical routes that would take them past the alternative sites of Badbury Rings or Badbury Hill, and certainly not to Badby in Northamptonshire.

It would of course have been possible for the Saxons to sail round the coast and up the Severn Estuary, a daring tactic considering the treacherous currents around Land's End, though one of which they were capable. Then they would either strike directly at Gloucester or divert along the Avon towards Bristol and Bath. But why go to such lengths when they could have marched to Bath from the south anyway?

Not everyone accepts that Liddington is Badon, or that Badon need necessarily be in the south. Alternative suggestions run from Dumbarton in Strathclyde and Bowden Hill in the Lothians, to the Wrekin in Shropshire or Caer Faddon near Welshpool. Dumbarton is a difficult one to accept if we believe that the battle was between the British and the Saxons in the 490s. The Gaels, the Irish Scotii of Dál Riata, called it *Din Brithon* (the "Fortress of the Britons"), certainly not Din Badon. In any case Gildas, who allegedly came from this area, would call it by its British name, Alclud.

Bowden Hill, near Linlithgow, relies on little other than the similarity of the name and the fact that, like Bath, it is on a River Avon, albeit six hundred miles away. In 1710, the antiquarian Sir Robert Sibbald identified it in his *Account of Linlithgowshire* as having been the site of a major battle, and thereafter fancy took over. There is another Bowden in the Scottish Borders, a village on the southern slopes of the Eildon Hills. Since a possible site for the previous battle at Agned is also in the Eildon Hills, and since this held the major British hill fort in the area, it begs closer inspection, although it would seem strange for such a notable battle to be named after Bowden and not Eildon.

There is also a Bowden in County Durham, between the towns of Willington and Crook. It has all but vanished today, and the location is only worth noting because it is close to Vinovium/ Binchester.

Caer Faddon is the locale for Badon given in the Celtic tale *The Dream of Rhonabwy* (*see* Chapter 8) but its tradition as the site for a key battle may have derived from later conflicts.

The Wrekin is championed by Frank Reno, who also draws upon *The Dream of Rhonabwy*, but interprets the directions differently. The Wrekin was a major hill fort outside present-day Telford, near the old Roman town of Viriconium. This was the fourth largest town in Roman Britain and continued to be occupied, in various stages of disintegration and repair, well into the seventh century. What is significant about Viriconium is that it had a major set of baths which almost certainly survived into the seventh century. Indeed, part of the outer wall, known now as the Old Work, is still standing after 1800 years. Though it seems scarcely creditable that Gildas would refer to Viriconium as Badon, it is possible that in his delight for word-play he would nickname the Wrekin as the Hill of the Baths. He may also have been alluding to the Breidden Hills, one of the probable sites for Caer Faddon, which can be seen from the Wrekin.

Another suggestion is Mynydd Baidan in mid Glamorgan, south of Maesteg. Alan Wilson and Baram Blackett suggest that the name *baidan* is derived from the Celtic for "to dare", which is *beiddio* in modern Welsh. North of Mynydd Baidan is Maescadlawr, which they translate as the "area of the battle field". They believe this may be the site of the second battle of Badon in the year 667, but it's one worth considering for the original battle.

For completeness I should mention Laurence Gardner's suggested site at Dun Baetan, near Carrickfergus in Ulster. In *Bloodline of the Holy Grail*, Gardner refers to the conflict between the Scotii kings of Dál Riata and their Irish overlords. In their battle for independence, the Scots defeated the Irish at Dun Baetan in 516, but were defeated there in 575. It was this second battle, according to Gardner, at which the young Artúir mac Aedan was present. Despite the internal logic and consistency of Gardner's argument, there is an inherent problem in accepting that the British would celebrate a victory in Ireland by Irish settlers in Britain, and Gildas specifically states that the victory at Badon was against the Saxons, not the Irish.

Before plotting the locations, let us turn to Arthur's final battle.

2. Camlann

Camlann is not included in Nennius's list. This may be because the original compiler did not want to sing of a defeat but of Arthur's victories, ending at the triumph of Badon, or because the original list was compiled during Arthur's reign, and therefore before Camlann. Its absence from the list is not necessarily critical, although it will inevitably raise doubts about whether it was fought by the same Arthur who fought the others. Curiously, Camlann is not mentioned anywhere else by Nennius, nor is it referred to by Gildas. Its first appearance is in the *Welsh Annals* under the year 93 (539AD), the year "in which Arthur and Medraut fell." It also appears in several of the Welsh Triads, where the clear implication is that it arose out of a quarrel between Gwenhwyfar, Arthur's queen, and Gwenhwyfach, Gwenhwyfar's sister and the wife of Mordred, and, in the way of such things, a quarrel led to a battle. Geoffrey of Monmouth typically took it out of all proportion and has Mordred abduct and seduce Gwenhwyfar and seize the kingdom while Arthur is away. The Triads regard it as one of the "Three Futile Battles", emphasising that it mushroomed out of nothing. This has the feel of authenticity, a memory of Britain's greatest hero brought low by a pointless quarrel.

Geoffrey of Monmouth places the battle at Camelford in Cornwall, based on no more than the name – the river Camel was known as Cambla – and possibly the proximity to Tintagel. The bridge over the Camel here is known as Slaughterbridge, though this probably refers to a battle between the British and Saxons during the reign of Egbert of Wessex in 823. In fact, the name may not refer to a battle at all as it could be derived from the old Saxon word *slaggy* for muddy, as in Slaggyford in Northumberland. In 1602 the antiquarian Richard Carew, one time High Sheriff of Cornwall, developed the Arthurian connection in his *Survey of Cornwall* by identifying a stone near the Camel as being the spot where Arthur died. This stone, however, bears the inscription *Latini ic jacit filius Mogari*, recording the burial of Latinus, son of Mogarus, and was probably brought to the site years before to form part of a footbridge across the river. Although many Arthurian legends have developed in this area, it is difficult to find any basis for them.

The word Camlann means either "crooked bank" (*cam glan*) or "crooked enclosure" (*cam llan*), a phrase which must describe thousands of locations across Britain. The River Cam in Somerset is a likely contender. It is a tributary of the Yeo and flows from the hills near Yarlington to join the Yeo just outside Yeovilton, near Ilchester. En route it passes by the impressive hill fort of Cadbury Castle, long believed to be the original

Camelot. Excavations by Leslie Alcock in the late 1960s showed that Cadbury Castle was significantly refortified from 470 onwards, for at least two generations. It was both a defensive fort and an inhabited village right through the Arthurian period. If it were occupied by Arthur then Camlann may have been fought right on his doorstep. The Cam twists through a vigorous series of bends about a kilometre away at Sparkford.

In 1935 O.G.S. Crawford proposed that the name was originally *Camboglanna*, a Roman fort along Hadrian's Wall at what is now Birdoswald. It is certainly true that here the river Irthing twists its way around the site in a very crooked glen but, as Geoffrey Ashe has highlighted, the name Camboglanna, in evolving towards Camlann, would for centuries have been known as *Camglann*, and that ought to be how it is recorded in the *Welsh Annals* and any other near-contemporary sources. The fact that every source records it as Camlann suggests a much older name. Nevertheless, Camboglanna has another connection of interest. Some thirty kilometres to the west, at what is now Burgh-by-Sands, was the fort of Aballava, which became Avalana by the sixth century. The legend has Arthur taken to Avalon to heal his wounds after Camlann. Intriguingly, there are dedications at several of the forts along Hadrian's Wall, including Aballava, to Latis, the goddess of lakes and water. August Hunt has suggested she may be the basis for the Lady of the Lake legend.

Another northern site frequently suggested is Camelon, near Falkirk in the Lothians, just north of the Antonine Wall. It has also been suggested as the original for Camelot, most recently in David Carroll's *Arturius, A Quest for Camelot*. Laurence Gardner has Artúir mac Aedan fight at both Camelon and Camboglanna, in his battles against the Picts. Camelon was a significant Roman fort which had been strengthened in the 140s at the time the Antonine Wall was built. The Roman name of the fort is no longer known, although the village that grew up around it gained the British name of *Caermawr* ("Great Fort") so is unlikely to be confused with Camelot. It is difficult to know when it was abandoned, because the site was substantially robbed and subsequently built over. The presence of a nearby Romano-British temple, now called Arthur's O'en, suggests a stable period of occupation. Nevertheless, the fort was almost certainly abandoned by the mid third century and steadily fell into ruin.

There are several locations in Wales still called Camlan today. Two of these are near Dolgellau, near the village of Mallwyd, a name which may mean "battle ground". This is the area advocated by Blake and Lloyd in *Pendragon* and by Alan Wilson and Baram Blackett in *Artorius Rex Discovered.* It is close to other locations connected with Vortigern and Ambrosius, and to several of the suggested sites from the battle list, especially the rivers Glen and Dubglas. It is also close to one of the suggested sites for Llongborth (discussed below), showing that it might fit a pattern of struggles within the Welsh princedoms. There is also a stream called Afon Gamlan just north of Dolgellau, emphasising how common the name is in the area.

Another site is also associated with the battle. This is Cwm Llan, a valley on the southern flanks of Snowdon, close to the fort of Dinas Emrys. Peter Bartrum draws attention to the legend about this battle as recorded in *Y Brython.* It tells how Arthur and his men were heading from Dinas Emrys towards the pass over Snowdon at Cwm Tregalan, and met the enemy in Cwm Llan ("the Valley of the Lake"). Arthur was able to push the enemy back but at the top of the pass they were ambushed in a hail of arrows. Arthur was killed and buried where he fell at a cairn called Carnedd Arthur, and the pass is still called Bwlchysaethau, "the Pass of the Arrows". A steep climb down from the pass takes you to Llyn Llydaw, supposed to be the home of the Lady of the Lake. Nearby is supposed to be Ogof Llanciau Eryri ("The Cave of the Young Men") in which, rather like the Christian legend of the Seven Sleepers of Ephesus, the seven who survived Camlann are supposed to be sleeping, awaiting their call to fight again for Arthur.

The Welsh sites are tempting because of the continuity of the name, but we should not forget that the name would have been just as common throughout Britain before the Saxon settlement. Nevertheless, the Welsh sites suggest a link with Arthur of Dyfed, who probably had conflicts with Gwynedd in this region. These sites do not, however, fit comfortably with any for Badon, raising again the question of whether the battles were fought by two different Arthurs.

3. The Saxon sites

Before we map out all of the above locations, we need to remind ourselves of the known Saxon battles during the Arthurian period. If Arthur's twelve battles were all against the Saxons or Angles then, although the *ASC* was not given to recording defeats, there may yet be some hints.

We have determined that the Arthurian period ran from about 480–520, and the *ASC* lists these battles during and around those years.

477. Aelle fought Welsh at *Cymenes ora*, [who] fled into the wood *Andredes leag*.
485. Aelle fought Welsh near the margin of *Mearcrædes burnam*.
491. Aelle besieged *Andredes cester*.
495. Cerdic fought Welsh at *Cerdices ora*, which is on or near the coast.
501. Port landed at Portsmouth and killed a noble young Briton.
508. Cerdic killed the British king Natanleod, after whom the land as far as *Cerdices ford* was named Netley.
514. Stuf and Wihtgar fought the Britons at *Cerdices ora*.
519. Cerdic fought the Britons at *Cerdices ford*.
527. Cerdic fought the Britons at *Cerdices leag*.
530. Cerdic took the Isle of Wight at *Wihtgaræsbyrg*.

Only a few of these provide much help, especially since we know that some of the names may arise retrospectively, such as Port and Portsmouth. However, even though the individual's names may be suspect, the locations are probably more accurate, if they can be traced. Thankfully a few are easier to identify than others.

Cymenes ora (*ora* meaning shore) appears in a charter of Selsey Abbey as *Cumeneshore* relating to a grant of land by Caedwalla, king of Essex, to the abbey in 673. The surviving copy is not contemporary, leading some authorities to term it a forgery, but regardless of whether or not the abbey owned the land, the description must still be accurate. It states that *Cumeneshore* was a stretch of coast between Pagham and Selsey Bill, now known as The Owers, much of which has long since eroded away. The *Andredes leag* is taken as the vast forest of Anderida, the Weald, which at that time densely covered much of Sussex and west Kent. Its western extremity was just north of Selsey, around Midhurst and Petersfield, so the *ASC* entry does hold together. In 491 Aelle besieged *Andredes cester*, the Roman fort at Anderitum [Pevensey]. Pevensey, some 80km east along the coast from Selsey, is the same spot that William the Conqueror chose to land nearly six hundred years later.

These first three entries seem to make clear the spread of Aelle's territory. The archaeology, however, does not wholly support this. The Saxons made little inroad into what became Sussex, and certainly not in the area around Selsey. One would expect a successful landing there to result in Aelle capturing the Roman town of Noviomagus [Chichester], but not only is there no mention of this, there have been no archaeological discoveries of any fifth-century Saxon sites there. The main area of Saxon settlement in the fifth century was between the rivers Ouse and Cuckmere, and by the sixth century it had expanded westward into the area between the Ouse and the Adur. There must be some significance in the battle of 485 "near the margin of *Mearcrædes burnam*". This name has been interpreted as "the river of the frontier agreed by treaty", suggesting that Aelle had an agreement with the British that the Saxons could settle on one side of a river only. We do not know which river, but it must be either the Cuckmere or, more probably, the Ouse. A major hill fort, Mount Caburn, rises above the Ouse where it is joined by the Glynde Reach. Caburn is one of the few Celtic names surviving in Sussex, originally *Caer Bryn*: "strong fort". It seems likely that the original Saxon settlers, despite their initial victory at Cymen's shore, must have settled between the Ouse and the Cuckmere, where they were guarded on the west by the fort at Caburn and on the east by the fort at Anderida. In 485 the Saxons sought to break out across one of the rivers, probably the Ouse at Caburn. Unusually for the *ASC,* this is not recorded as a victory. It simply says, "they fought the Welsh". No doubt they were contained and pushed back across the river and later, in 491, broke out across the Cuckmere and slaughtered the British at Pevensey.

What it most interesting about Mount Caburn is the Glynde Reach. This small stream was originally the Glynde Bourne, thus bearing a striking similarity to the first battle of Nennius's list at the River Glein. If it is the same battle, then it may have been the first Arthurian victory. We do not know how accurate the date is, but 485 fits perfectly with the likely date for the start of the Arthurian campaign, culminating in Badon in 493 or so. It appears that Aelle was contained by the defeat at *Mearcrædes* until he defeated the British at Anderida. After that he was able to move further west. It is perhaps telling that the hill that faces Mount Caburn, just to the north, is now called Saxon Down, possibly a memory of where the Saxons gathered in readiness for their battle against the British.

Aelle is something of a mystery amongst the early Saxon settlers. The earlier Hengist and his successor Octha have been remembered in the story of Vortigern and Ambrosius, whilst the later Cerdic became the founder of a dynasty. Aelle exists between these two almost as an aside, as if he were battling away in Sussex whilst the main action was happening elsewhere. He doesn't appear in any of the Arthurian foundation stories, and after his passing we know nothing more about Sussex for over 150 years. Yet Bede cites Aelle as the first of the Saxons "to rule over all the Southern kingdoms". He was the first to be regarded as the *Bretwalda*, a form of High King, to whom all the other chieftains offered their loyalty. We have no reason to doubt Bede. He tells us that he gathered his information about Sussex from Bishop Daniel of Wessex who knew the people of Sussex intimately. Somehow Aelle, although seeming to have been confined to the shores of Sussex, became paramount chief of the Saxons.

This suggests that whilst his people may have remained closeted in Sussex, Aelle was in contact with the British leaders, almost certainly with Ambrosius and probably with Arthur. The evidence has shown that the Saxons had been held in check by the resistance under Ambrosius and that for nearly a generation the Saxons and Angles remained in their coastal settlements. This peace had become strained by the late 480s, and then broke, perhaps when Ambrosius was too old to govern, and Aelle led a Saxon revival. The assault on Anderida may have been the start of this revival, which culminated at Badon.

Thus it would seem that Aelle was the Saxon leader at Badon, even though tradition names Octha (or Osa/Eossa). Octha may have been the commander under Aelle. The British victory at Badon would seem to be a suitable retaliation for the slaughter at Anderida, wiping out the Saxon army. In all likelihood Aelle and his sons were killed in the battle, which is why we hear no more of him, and why he left no dynasty to rule Sussex. Thereafter Sussex survived as a small insignificant enclave, hemmed in by the British in the Weald. If this is true – and Aelle's high rank would strongly suggest it – then it would argue that Badon, and probably most of Arthur's battle campaign, was in the South.

Octha may also have been killed at Badon or, if he survived, it was now that he was assigned a small territory in Thanet in the far east of Kent, keeping the Saxons at arm's length from the British heartland. Octha is usually equated with Aesc, but we cannot be sure they are the same individuals. Aesc is supposed to have ruled the *Cantwara* for 34 years, from 488 to 522, which almost parallels the Arthurian period, but we cannot accept those dates without question. I am not convinced that the Octha who fought at Badon, according to the story in *The Dream of Rhonabwy*, is the same as Aesc (or Oisc) from whom the rulers of Kent were descended.

The remaining battles listed at this time all relate to Cerdic and his nephews, Stuf and Wihtgar. We have already discussed the uncertainty of Cerdic's reign (*see* Chapter 4) and that his arrival in Britain could have been any one of a series of dates – 495, 514, 523 or 532. Remember that the *ASC* states that Cerdic "succeeded to the kingdom" six years after his arrival, so that he could have assumed the kingship in 501, 520, 529 or 538. Intriguingly, two of those dates show that he could have arrived either at the time of Badon (493×497) or at the time of Camlann (*circa* 520).

It is hard to imagine that Cerdic's rise to power is not in some way connected to either Arthur's triumph or his downfall. Badon was supposed to have instigated a period of peace, a *Pax Arthuriana*, in which all conflicts with the Saxons ceased. Indeed, Gildas still recalled this remarkable calm while writing *De Excidio* in the 530s. If Cerdic arrived in 495, then his sequence of battles would have disrupted that calm unless they were confined to an area not under Gildas's consideration. Alternatively, if Cerdic did not arrive until 532 and his battles fell into the period 532–538, Gildas may not have considered them worth commenting on, especially as Cerdic was British. Cerdic's rise to power must have come as a consequence of Arthur's fall, unless he was in league with Arthur. But because Cerdic was British, Gildas might have regarded his battles as yet another of the civil wars that continued in Britain through this period of peace. However, if Cerdic was alive and ruling when Gildas was writing, he would have seen him as the greatest traitor of them all, and would undoubtedly have mentioned him. This means Cerdic was either already dead or not yet in power. Thus we have two scenarios:

(1) Cerdic was a young Briton, born around the time of the major Saxon revolt in the 440s. He may well have had a Saxon mother and thus knew the language and became an interpreter. He sought personal gain during the subsequent British retaliation, but failed and retreated to Gaul, possibly Armorica, returning in 495 to curry favour with Arthur and, as a consequence, was granted command of the Gewisse. Wanting more power he fought against the British and took control of land in Hampshire and Wiltshire, setting himself up as king in 501 and ruling to 517. His death is close to the probable date for Camlann and we might conjecture that Cerdic was involved in the wars with Arthur and was a supporter of Medraut/Mordred. Cerdic's usurpation would thus fit into the category of Gildas's civil wars but because Cerdic was dead by the 530s, Gildas did not single him out for comment.

(2) Cerdic fits into the later wave of chieftains who established control in the 540s. Cerdic's campaign ran from 532 to 538 when he assumed control of the West Saxons. This makes a stronger case for Cerdic being the military commander of a group of confederate Saxons and Britons. The West Saxons were not yet a unified whole, and during the mid sixth century were a number of separate units carving out territory across the south and the Thames Valley. After a few battles Cerdic managed to unify an area of Saxons and Britons. Gildas would doubtless dismiss Cerdic's initial forays as part of the continuing civil unrest and not see it as a re-emergence of the Saxon onslaught which gathered pace in the 540s. What's more, if Camlann did occur just before Gildas wrote *De Excidio* (as suggested by his comments about Constantine), then Cerdic may have benefited from

Arthur's death, taking territory in the inevitable chaotic aftermath. If he did not already have control of the Gewisse, he certainly took command now.

Of these two options (2) best fits the overall time frame for the chronology of the rulers of the Wessex. (1) has a romantic appeal that makes Cerdic an ally and then an enemy of Arthur, and has some substance in some of the later tales that claims Cerdic was a friend of Arthur's until they argued. However, as we have seen, there were so many people called Ceredig/Ceretic/Cerdic that the tradition probably relates to someone else – most likely Caradog Vreichfras – and was later identified with Cerdic. This solution concurs with our earlier analysis based on the *ASC*, and convinces me that Cerdic was not contemporary with Arthur but rose to power in the vacuum left by Arthur's death.

If we look at Cerdic's battles as listed in the *ASC*, regardless of other chieftains such as Port or Stuf, we find only four sites mentioned – *Cerdices ora*, *Cerdices ford*, *Cerdices leag* and *Wihtgaræsbyrg*. No firm location is known for any of these. It has been suggested that *Cerdices ora* may be the same as Calshot, a spit of land that juts out at the end of Southampton Water, though other sources suggest this was named after the chalky deposits in the area – *celces ora*. O.G.S. Crawford puts forward a theory that the Saxons landed at Totton, at the head of Southampton Water, based purely on a logical route rather than any philological data. However, Crawford believed that the Saxons followed an ancient trackway known as the Cloven Way, which passes through two other possible sites. The *ASC* tells us that *Cerdices ford* was on the far side of Netley Marsh, and if we assume this reference to be correct, it would place it somewhere just north of the New Forest. The chronicler Athelweard identified it as being on the River Avon, but since *afon* is the Celtic for any river this does not necessarily help. The Hampshire Avon flows through Charford, just north of Fordingbridge, and Crawford suggested that this was *Cerdices ford*. However, most etymologists believe the name Charford (and there are several villages with that name) is derived from either *Ceorl's-ford*, named after another individual, or *cyric forda* meaning "ford by the church". Interestingly, just to the east of Charford is the source of the River Blackwater, which flows into the Test near Netley Marsh (*see* Map 5).

5. Possible sites for Cerdic's battles.

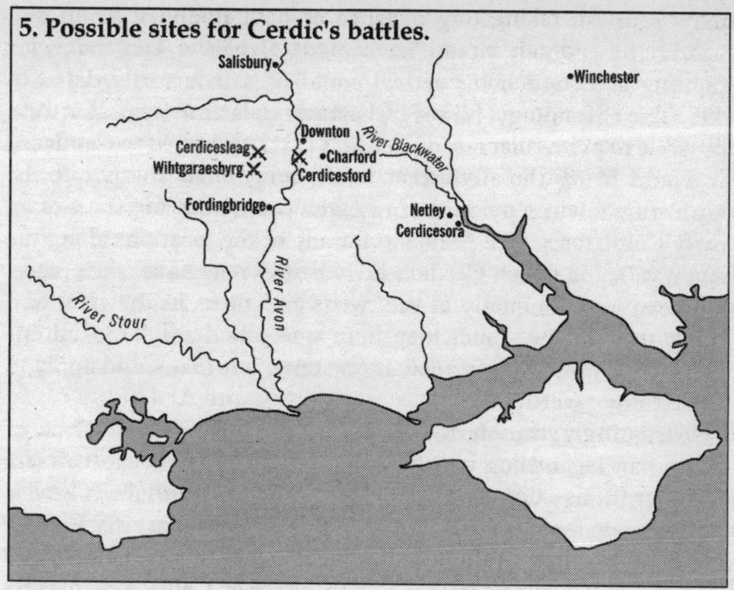

These four battles (*Cerdicesora*, *Cerdicesford*, *Cerdicesleag* and *Wihtgaræsbyrg*) could be the four fought on the *Dubglas* if the British were fighting Saxons arriving via Southampton Water.

Continuing along the Cloven Way, Crawford identifies a site to the west of Charford, near the ancient earthworks known as Grim's Ditch, listed in a charter as *fyrdinges lea*. Fyrding refers to an army on full war footing, and he suggests this could have been the site of *Cerdices leag*. There is a logic to this route. It may also be significant that at Downton, the village that adjoins Charford to the north, is a feature called The Moot, or Moot Hill, believed to have been a meeting place for Saxon councils. It would seem only natural that, if the Saxons under Cerdic first established themselves in this area, they would have a meeting place for their *witan* which, as the first in that area, would have become held in high esteem. Perhaps even more intriguingly, the part of the Moot that abuts the River Avon has been called for centuries Natanbury, and is believed to have been the burial mound of Natanleod.

It is worth noting that if Cerdic's confederates did establish themselves in the basin of Southampton Water around Charford, they were within striking distance of both Badbury Rings and Liddington, which would have made Cerdic a contender for fighting at Badon if his arrival could be satisfactorily dated to 495. The chronology, however, best suits a later arrival. If it were possible to prove that one of Cerdic's battles equated to Camlann, it would bring the Arthurian world into much sharper focus. Unfortunately, no amount of research can detect any trace of an early Celtic name like Camlann for any of the locations along the Avon valley in which Cerdic's early battles may have taken place. One can look longingly at the twists and turns in the river and think that maybe somewhere here was called the 'crooked enclosure' or something similar at one time, but that could apply to almost any river.

Intriguingly, the *Mort Artu*, part of the early Vulgate Cycle of Arthurian legends on which Malory based his famous work (*see* Chapter 9), has Camlann take place on Salisbury Plain. There is no evidence for this at all. Possibly this reflects some distant folk memory, but that could be a dim recollection of any major battle near Salisbury, such as that in 715 between Ceolred of Mercia and Ine of Wessex.

Despite these suggestions, no firm location can be made for any of Cerdic's battles. That also applies to *Wihtgaræsbyrg*, presumed to be a hill fort on the Isle of Wight. The only such fort is at Carisbrooke, but neither archaeological nor linguistic evidence can show any relationship between this and *Wihtgaræsbyrg*. The obvious place, based on the other Cerdic locales, is Whitsbury, less than 10 km (6 m) west of Charford, and set amongst a maze of valleys and ancient earthworks. However, most etymologies note that Whitsbury evolved from *Wiccheberia*, from *wice* for "wych elm", thus meaning the "fort where wych elms grow."

Trying to identify any other possible places associated with Cerdic is complicated by the abundance of the name Cerdic/Ceretic, and also, being a Celtic name, it was doubtless superseded by a Saxon name in due course. In this sense Cerdic is unusual amongst the early Saxon leaders in that he did not have places named after him. Creoda of Mercia, for example, is remembered in Credenhill in Herefordshire, and Icel, his forebear, in Ickleton near Cambridge. For some reason Cerdic did not leave his mark on the landscape as much as he did on history.

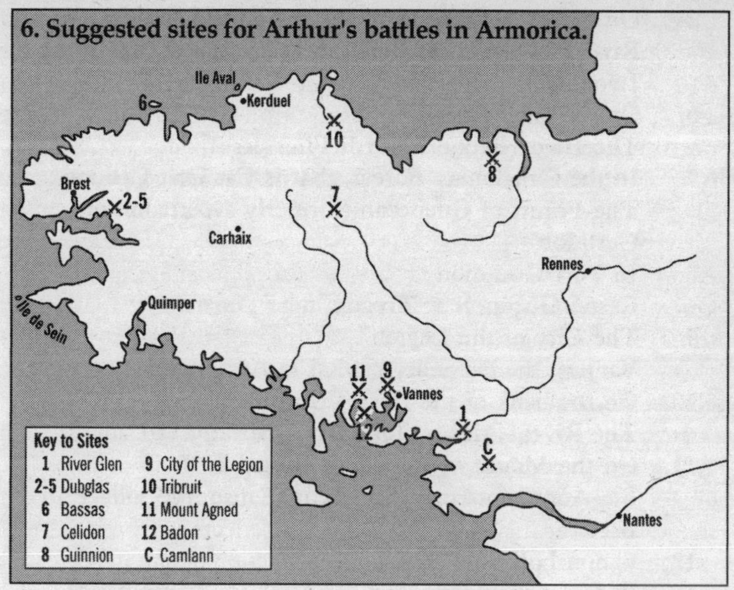

6. Suggested sites for Arthur's battles in Armorica.

4. The Breton angle

Ronald Millar, in *Will the Real King Arthur Please Stand Up?* (1978), has enterprisingly managed to find sites for all of Arthur's battles in Brittany (*see* Map 6, and below). Some people have dismissed this book as a spoof, or simply as a humorous read, but it raises some interesting points.

Millar reminds us that the Arthurian story also thrived in Brittany, and indeed much of the Arthurian story as we now know it developed there. In later centuries Arthur's name had mutated to Arzor, perhaps remembered in the name of the town Arzal, in the south near the mouth of the river Vilaine. Further along the coast is Arzon, which looks over the Golfe du Morbihan to the cliffs at Baden.

Below is a list of the possibilities identified by Millar:

1. At the mouth of the river Glein
   River Vilaine (formerly Gwilen), at Arzal

2–5. On the river Dubglas in the region of Linnuis
River Daoulas, near Brest, in Leon (called Linnuis or Lyonesse)

6. On the river Bassas
The Ile de Batz off North Finisterre

7. In the Caledonian Forest, that is Cat Coit Celidon
The Forest of Quenecan (formerly Guerledon or Gerlidon)

8. In Fort Guinnion
Castel Guennon at Tregon, near Dinard

9. The City of the Legion
Vannes, the legionary capital in Armorica

10. On the bank of the river Tribruit
The River Trieaux (formerly Trifrouit) at Lanleff

11. On the Mount of Agned, at Breguoin
Ste-Anne (formerly Ste-Agned) near the village of Brech

12. Badon Hill
Baden, near Vannes, on the Golfe du Morbihan

and Camlann
Camerunn, near St-Nazaire

Millar is able to get a compellingly close similarity with most of the battles, except Bassas, Badon and Camlann. Perhaps this should not be too surprising. It is known that when the British migrated to Armorica and established new settlements, they brought their old names with them, naming territories Cornouaille and Leon, for example. What this demonstrates is that place names in Brittany have remained relatively unchanged. Millar's research is an interesting snapshot of how names might have been identifiable in Britain had not so many changed under successive settlers.

Having identified a name is one thing, but are they necessarily appropriate settings? Millar himself admits that Baden, atop the cliffs overlooking the massive estuary of the river Vilaine, does not really fit the description of a *Mons Badonicus*. The monastery of St Gildas is only the other side of this bay, near Arzon, so one would expect Gildas's description of it to be more accurate. Likewise, Millar's suggestion of Camerunn in the marshland near St-Nazaire is really a throwaway at the end of his book, and not a serious proposal.

The Breton dimension, however, raises the question of whether Arthur's battles started in Armorica and he then came to help the British at Badon. The Breton historian Leon Fleuriot suggested that one reason why the British were able to maintain a resistance against the Saxons around the turn of the fifth/sixth centuries was partly due to "the support of continental Bretons" and that the collapse of the British defence in the late sixth century was because the Bretons were involved in their own war against the Franks. If the British saviour was Arthur then possibly he either came from Armorica or he was able to command Breton mercenaries, a concept that Geoffrey of Monmouth utilizes in his own story of Arthur, which I explore in Chapter 9. It is also the basis of Geoffrey Ashe's case for propósing Riothamus as Arthur though, as we have seen, the dates undermine this.

A variant on this idea comes from Chris Barber and David Pykitt in *Journey to Avalon* where they suggest that Arthur survived Camlann and retired to Brittany as a religious hermit, adopting the name Arthmael or Armel. Barber and Pykitt believe that he was Athrwys of Gwent, whom they date from 482–562. Little is known about Arthmael. He is believed to have been born in Gwent, near Llantwit Major but not one knows when. He was a contemporary of and probably related to St Samson and St Cadfan. He appears in Armorica around the year 538, the same year as Camlann according to the *Welsh Annals*. He died sometime between 552 and 570. The church of Saint-Armel-des-Boscheaux is on the Golfe du Morbihan, close to the monastery of St Gildas.

Barber and Pykitt's dates coincide with those in the *Welsh Annals* for Badon and Camlann, but are too early for Athrwys of Gwent whom I believe lived from around 600–660. The name change from Athryws to Arthmael also seems strange. Arthur of Badon is hardly likely to have kept his identity hidden after Camlann, not with Gildas living nearby.

All the evidence suggests that Badon was in Britain – that's where Gildas set it. The battle campaign that ended in Badon was therefore also going to be in Britain. The commander might have previously fought in Armorica. He might even have been a son of

Riothamus, and so could have retired to Armorica afterwards. But otherwise we can exclude Armorica from our battle zone.

5. The overall picture

Map 7 brings together the full distribution of battles. Apart from a few isolated proposals in Lincolnshire and Cambridgeshire the concentration of sites is in the North, the West, the South and North Wales. This may be an accident of language, in that old names survived longer in these areas and thus can be made to fit the sites, whereas sites in the east and Midlands have been too long influenced by later settlers and the old names have been lost. Nevertheless, they suggest three possible frontiers, as well as an agglomeration in North Wales. Nor should we ignore a possible eastern frontier, to include the partition mentioned by Gildas.

Table 7.1 groups the more likely sites for these battles by those five areas. In plotting these sites (*see* Map 8) several patterns emerge. The southern, eastern and western sites form clear frontiers. The northern frontier is more problematic. The pattern suggests a focus around the territory of the Gododdin, with the eastern line presenting a barrier to the Angles whilst the northern and western lines are a barrier against the Picts or Britons of Strathclyde. The southern line more or less follows Hadrian's Wall and would also be a frontier against the Angles and the Coelings.

The Welsh sites plot a fluctuating border between Gwynedd and Powys. These sites could, at a push, be interpreted as dealing with Irish raiders, but if that was so you would expect a stronger distribution in Dyfed, yet few sites have been proposed for Nennius's list in either Ceredigion or Dyfed. Whilst accepting the limitations imposed by a selective interpretation of battle sites, the sparsity of other options somewhat speaks for itself.

There is always the possibility that the battle sites did not follow a frontier but were opportunist strikes against local threats. If so, this would suggest that the battles were fought by local chieftains and not one overall commander. No sensible commander would stretch his resources across Britain, even though the capability was there, but would focus them against the main threats. These were Aelle in the south or the Angles in the North, suggesting that the campaign could have been in two halves.

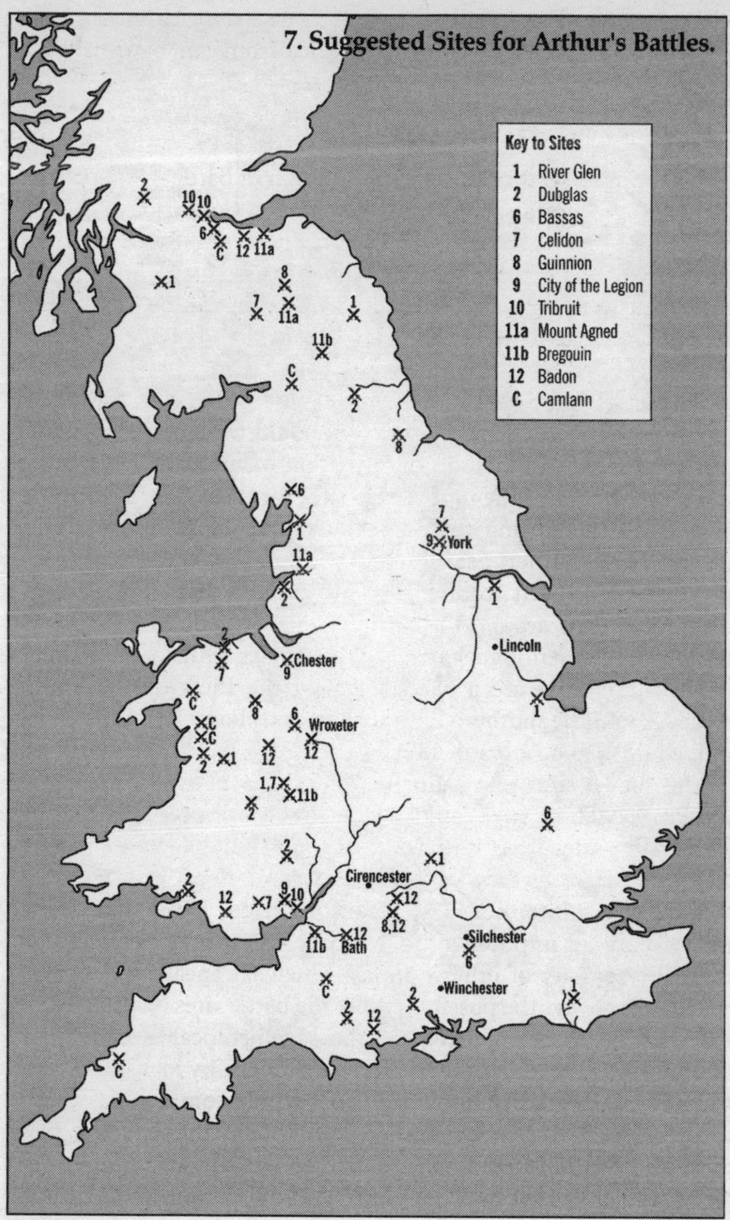
7. Suggested Sites for Arthur's Battles.
Key to Sites
1 River Glen
2 Dubglas
6 Bassas
7 Celidon
8 Guinnion
9 City of the Legion
10 Tribruit
11a Mount Agned
11b Bregouin
12 Badon
C Camlann
York
Lincoln
Chester
Wroxeter
Cirencester
Bath
Silchester
Winchester

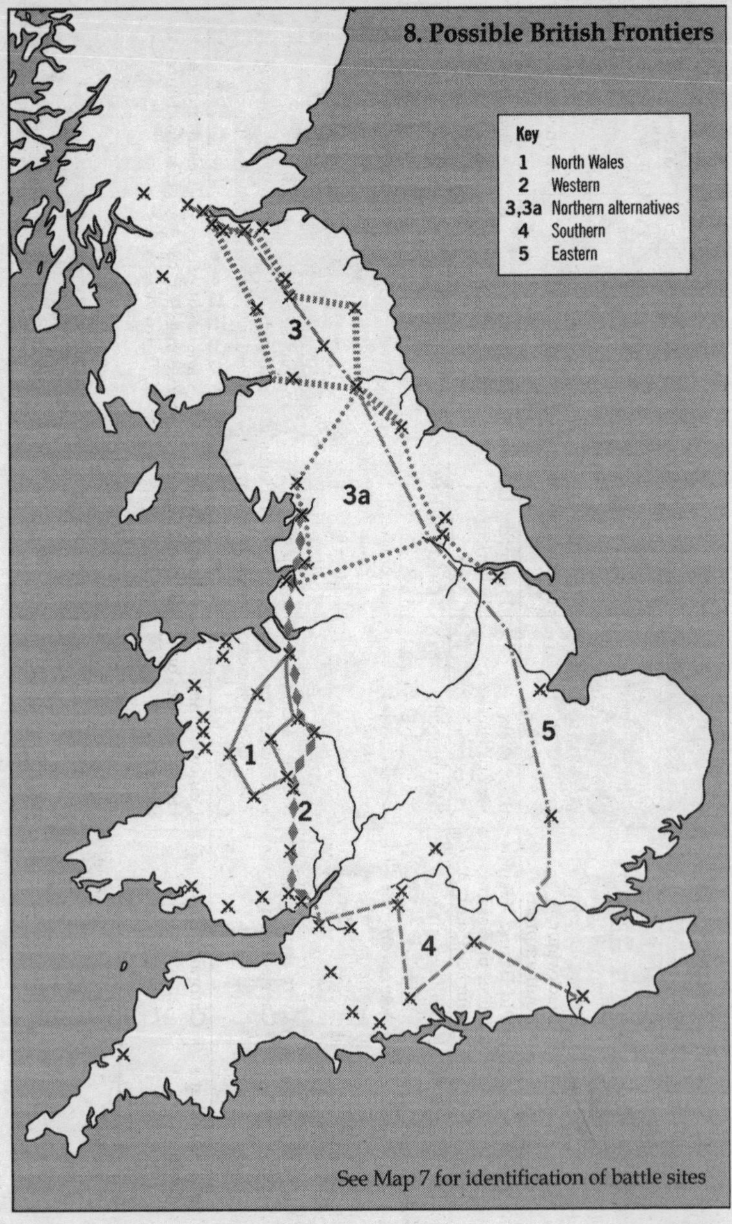
8. Possible British Frontiers
Key
1 North Wales
2 Western
3,3a Northern alternatives
4 Southern
5 Eastern
3
3a
1
2
5
4
See Map 7 for identification of battle sites

Table 7.1. Nennius's Battle Sites

Nennius's site	Southern frontier	Western frontier	Northern frontier	Eastern Frontier	North Wales
Mouth of River Glein	Glynde Reach, Lewes, Sussex	Lune, Lancaster; Clun, Shropshire	Glen, Northumberland	Glanford Brigg, Lincolnshire	Gleiniant, Trefeglwys, Powys
River Dubglas in Linnuis	Divelish/Devil's Brook, Dorset; Blackwater, Southampton	Douglas, near Preston, Lancashire	Devil's Water, Corbridge, Northumberland	Devil's Water, Corbridge, Northumberland	Dulas, Llandulas, Colwyn Bay, Gwynedd
River Bassas	Old Basing, Hampshire; or Bassingbourne, Cambridge	Baschurch, Shropshire	Dunipace, Camelon, Falkirk	Bassingbourne, Cambridgeshire	Baschurch, Schropshire
Forest of Celidon	Gellideg, nr Caerphilly, Gwent	Clun Forest, Shropshire	Hart Fell, Ettrick Forrest, Borders	Galtres Forest, York.	between Clywd and Conway, Gwynedd
Fort Guinnion	Wanborough, Swindon, Wiltshire	The Wrekin, Wroxeter, Shropshire	Binchester, Durham; or Stow-in-Wedale, Borders	Stow-in-Wedale, Borders	Gwynion, Llanarmon, Powys
City of the Legion	Caerleon	Chester	York or Carlisle	York	Chester
Bank of River Tribruit	Twrc estuary, near Caerleon, on Severn	Ribble estuary, Lancashire; or Twrc estuary, near Caerleon	Links of Forth, Stirling; or Fords of Frew, Kippen	Links of Forth, Stirling; or Fords of Frew, Kippen	?
Mount Agned at Breguoin	Catbrain, Bristol	Leintwardine, Herefordshire; or Ribchester, Lancashire	Edinburgh; or Eildon Hills; or High Rochester, Borders	Edinburgh; or Eildon Hills; or High Rochester, Borders	Leintwardine, Herefordshire
Mount Badon	Solsbury Hill, Bath; Liddington Castle, Swindon; Mynydd Baidan, Glamorgan	The Wrekin, Shropshire; Caer Faddon or Breidden Hill, Welshpool	Bowden Hill, Linlithgow	Bowden Hill, Linlithgow; or Liddington Castle, Swindon	Caer Faddon or Breidden Hill, Welshpool

[illegible] have deduced from our earlier chronology that Arthur's [illegible]le campaign, leading up to Badon, probably fell between 485 and 497 so if Nennius's battle list genuinely relates to Arthur and is not an amalgam of heroic battles, this map will help us focus more closely. We have five options. And we need to know who was ruling, or was the likely premier battle commander, in these locations during those years.

North Wales

The pattern of battles suggests conflict either between the territories of Gwynedd and Powys, or within Gwynedd, between the successors of Cunedda. The Saxons were still many years away from reaching the borders of Powys, and the threat from the Irish raiders, though still present, was no longer of such significance as to require so consolidated a campaign.

At this stage Gwynedd was not the united power it later became but was ruled by the sons and grandsons of Cunedda who governed from their hilltop forts in Anglesey and across the north of Wales. The principal ruler was Cadwallon Lawhir ("Longhand"). Early in his reign he was involved in a series of battles, where he combined forces with his uncle Ysfael against the Irish, who had settled on Anglesey in previous generations. Cadwallon took part in a famous battle called *Cerrig-y-Gwyddyl* ("Stones of the Irish"), where they hobbled their horses' front legs together so that they could only charge straight ahead. This was remembered in a Welsh Triad as one of the "Three Fettered Warbands".

Cadwallon appears in Geoffrey's story of Arthur as one of the four kings who bore golden swords at Arthur's coronation. This confirms that at least some tradition makes Cadwallon and Arthur contemporaries, but otherwise there is no firm evidence that Cadwallon fought either against or alongside Arthur.

Another candidate is Cadwallon's cousin Owain Danwyn, "White Tooth". Ruler of Gwynedd at Din Arth, he was the father of Cynlas the Tawny (Cuneglasus the Butcher), one of Gildas's tyrants, and was possibly murdered by his nephew Maelgwyn, son of Cadwallon, another of the tyrants. Graham Phillips and Martin Keatman, in *King Arthur, The True Story*, suggest that Owain is Arthur, noting that Owain was a contemporary of Arthur of Badon, that Arthur was murdered by his nephew, and that the rulers of Gwynedd were known as the 'Pendragons' (head dragons) of Britain.

The title Pendragon, whilst closely associated with Arthur and, more specially, his father Uther, was not held solely by the rulers of one territory. According to Laurence Gardner in *Bloodline of the Holy Grail*, the Pen Dragon or "Head Dragon" was the "Guardian of the Celtic Isle". The Pendragon was appointed by a council of Druid Elders, and the earliest recorded was Cunobelinus (Cymbeline). During the Roman occupation the title must have been little more than honorific, but once the Roman yoke was lifted the Pendragon was able to re-emerge. The holder would also be a powerful ruler of his own kingdom but, as the Pendragon, was also the personification of Celtic authority. He was not a battle commander, who, rather like the Roman *dux*, was the *guletic*, or *wledig*.

Gardner provides his list of the Pendragons in *Realm of the Ring Lords*. Those relevant to our period of scrutiny are listed below. Their dates are drawn from my own assessments in Chapter 3. I have added the names of the relevant *wledig*, according to Gardner, as well as other known *wledigs* [in brackets] not specified by Gardner.

Table 7.2. British Pendragons and Wledigs

Pendragon	Wledig
Eudaf Hen, *c*330–400	Macsen [Magnus Maximus] 383–388
Coel Hen, *c*355–425	[possibly also Coel Hen]
Vortigern, c400–455	Cunedda, *c*390–460
Cunedda, *c*390–460	Ceretic of Strathclyde, *c*400–470
Brychan of Brycheiniog, *c*430–500	Ambrosius, *c*425–495
Dyfnwal Hen, *c*455–525	[Amlawdd, *c*440–510]
Brychan of Manau, *c*480–550	[Casanauth, *c*480–550]
Maelgwyn of Gwynedd, *c*480–550	[Celyddon, *c*500–570]
Aedan mac Gabhran of Dál Riata, *c*534–608	Artúir, 559–596

Gardner shows that although the Pendragon inheritance follows a bloodline, this can pass through daughters as well as sons, and thus may not stay within one kingdom. For instance, Aedan mac Gabhran, of Irish descent, inherited the title because his mother was the daughter of Brychan of Manau, whose wife was the daughter of Dyfnwal Hen.

The Pendragon at the time of Badon, in the 490s, may have been Brychan of Brycheiniog, though he would have been old and unlikely to be present at the battle. Since we cannot be precise about individuals' lifespans, it's possible Brychan was dead by then and that Dyfnwal Hen, whom we shall meet later, was the Pendragon. It was not Owain White-tooth.

Phillips and Keatman treat Owain as a ruler of Powys, with his capital at Wroxeter, but the genealogies do not support this. Powys at this time was almost certainly ruled by Cadell (*see* Chapter 6), the servant of King Benli, who with the help of Germanus (or Garmon) assumes the kingship. Powys was still a single kingdom, as inherited from Vortigern, though it later split into North and South. Bartrum conjectures (based on the Benli story) that Cadell's fortress was in North Powys, at Llanarmon. Another suggestion, dating back to the seventeenth century, was that the descendants of Cadell (the Cadellings) lived at Gaer Fawr (the Great Castle), a massive hill fort just north of Guilsfield (Cegidfa), near Welshpool. Intriguingly, if you plot the likely Welsh sites for Arthur's twelve battles, all but one of them (the Twrc estuary for Tribruit) form a defensive square surrounding Guilsfield. It is a compelling thought that these battles might represent a campaign by Cadell to defend and rebuild the boundaries of Powys. Unfortunately, though archaeological evidence shows that this hillfort was restrengthened at the end of the Roman period, there is not much support for its continued occupation in the fifth or sixth centuries. If it was reoccupied it may have been only as a short-term defensive strategy.

A site nearby, though, holds more intriguing possibilities. Phillips and Keatman believe that Wroxeter was, at least for some time, the most important city within Powys, and the archaeology supports this. Ken Dark, in *Civitas to Kingdom*, states that "the evidence from Wroxeter does encourage us to suppose that this was, if not *the* political centre of the Powysian kingdom on the fifth century, at least one of them." Wroxeter was occupied through to the mid sixth century, but soon afterwards the population moved to the refuge of the hill fort at the Wrekin, just outside the Roman town. Wroxeter has long been proposed as Vortigern's town. Graham Webster confirms that in the centre of Wroxeter, in the mid fifth century, something like a grand country mansion was built for a "powerful character".

There is also a memorial stone, dating from this time, commemorating a king called Cunorix. It reads CUNORIX MAQUS MAQUI COLONE, and is usually translated as "Cunorix, son of Maquicoline". It has been dated as most likely of the late fifth century, probably 460–475. It is usually presumed to be a memorial to a visiting king, possibly one of the rulers of Dyfed, who was the guest of the head man in Wroxeter.

Cun- is a frequent prefix in Celtic names, such as Cunedda and Cunobelinus. The name Cunorix means "Hound King", and would convert into Welsh as Cynwrig, strikingly similar to Cerdic's son Cynric, suggesting the possibility that Cynric was named after one of Cerdic's relatives, perhaps an uncle, who might be commemorated here because he was one of the defenders of Wroxeter.

Maquicoline is an unusual compound name. It translates as "Son of the Holly". The equivalent word in Welsh for holly was *celyn*. Celyn was an occasional name, sometimes corrupted to Cuhelyn or Celynin. One of Gildas's brothers was called Celyn, but the name is not known for any king. Curiously, in the *Brut y Brenhinedd*, the name of Vortigern's grandfather, Vitalinus (Guethelinus), is copied as Cuhelyn. If we follow this fancy a little further, then Cunorix, as "the son of the son of" Cuhelyn, could be Vortigern himself. Vortigern means "supreme king", which could also be an interpretation of Cunorix.

Regardless of who Cunorix was, it is evident that Wroxeter was not only a major town in the fifth century, but one that was fit for a king who entertained kings. Someone would have succeeded to this estate after the death of Vortigern and his sons, and this can only have been the successor to the territory of Powys. Initially it may have been Ambrosius himself, ruling Powys from Wroxeter from the 460s to the 470s before Cadell took over.

This all rather temptingly makes Cadell a candidate for Arthur, one I have not seen previously suggested. One could even fancy Viriconium as the mythical Camelot, not by name, but as the most impressive surviving town in sub-Roman Britain. The archaeologists at Wroxeter stated that the town contains "the last classically inspired buildings in Britain". Christopher Snyder, in *An Age of Tyrants*, writes, "sub-Roman Wroxeter was a town worth protecting, with new structures and imported goods, worthy of a local lord and his guests."

This suggests something of far wider consequences than Cadell protecting Powys from the young upstart Maelgwyn. It suggests that Viriconium, in the hands of Cadell, served as a protection not just for Powys but for the whole of Wales, which brings us to the next option.

Western Frontier

The most remarkable aspect of the line connecting these battles is that it runs almost vertically north-south, much of it following what later became Offa's Dyke. It thus forms a natural frontier between Wales and beyond, reaching up into the old British kingdom of Rheged. It could easily be held from three forts – Caerleon in the south and Chester and Ribchester in the north, with Viriconium as the administrative centre. It would require a consortium of only three rulers, as in the 480s and 490s Chester was probably part of Powys. If we accept Cadell as the principal ruler in Powys, the ruler in Rheged was most likely Merchiaun (Mark) the Lean. The ruler in Gwent is more problematic as data is confusing. Table 3.7 suggests it would be Erb, one of those individuals who is no more than a name in a pedigree. The power in the area was either Brychan of Brycheiniog, or more likely Erb's predecessor Caradog, who was probably still alive.

Caradog is one of many with that name, but some believe that this is the real Caradog Vreichfras, not the descendant of a century later. Caradog was Arthur's senior counsellor whom we will discuss in more detail in the next chapter. Meirchion may have been the father of King Mark of the Tristan legend (*see* Chapter 13). This frontier would thus be held by four powerful rulers: Cadell, Brychan, Caradog and Meirchion. All of them could have been involved in battles holding the line in the name of the *Ardd Ri*, who at that time was Brychan.

The biggest problem with this proposal is why the frontier was here. Although today it runs remarkably close to the present border between Wales and England, there was no such division in the late fifth century. If there was any border, it was that between Britannia Prima and the other two southern provinces, which ran about thirty miles to the east. If, as we have suggested, Maxima Caesariensis had still sought to continue a Roman style of administration, whilst Flavia Caesariensis was becoming settled by the Saxons in the east, this border would be all the more significant to those in Britannia Prima.

There is, though, little evidence to show that the provinces survived much beyond the middle of the fifth century. Charts identifying the distribution of Saxon occupation by the late fifth century show them penetrating little further west than the line of Dere/Ermine Street, though with probable forays across the Midlands into eastern Powys which, at this time, stretched more into the centre of Britain.

The Dream of Rhonabwy, later included as part of *The Mabinogion*, talks of the battle of Badon as Caer Faddon, and places it near to Welshpool (*see* Chapter 8). Although the story dates from more than seven centuries after Arthur, it is clearly a memory of a major confrontation with the Saxons. It may not have been *the* Battle of Badon, as recalled by Gildas, but it must have been a significant battle at a place with a name sufficiently similar to Badon to become identified with it.

The battle of Caer Faddon probably took place in the late sixth century, a hundred years after Badon and twenty years after Gildas's death, though we can't be certain of that. Even before Gildas died the Saxon war machine had stirred again. In 556 Cynric and Ceawlin fought the British at *Beranbyrg* (Barbury Castle), close to Liddington Castle in Wiltshire. The date may not be wholly accurate, because the next victory isn't recorded until 571, when the West Saxons captured four towns in the Thames Valley. Then came the major defeat of the British at Dyrham in 577 followed by another at *Fethanleag* in 584 and "great slaughter" at Woden's Barrow (possibly Wanborough) in 592. All this is recorded in the *ASC*. We know that at the same time the Angles under Creoda were advancing across the British Midlands, carving out what became the kingdom of Mercia. Creoda died in 593 and there must have been many skirmishes, if not wholesale battles, before then, and certainly under his successor Pybba. So whereas the 480s and 490s saw the British rise up and force back the invaders, the 580s and 590s saw the reverse with the British slaughtered under a massive Saxon onslaught.

Under those circumstances the western frontier as shown in Map 8 takes on a new reality, but a century after Badon. This is the time of Artúir of Dyfed, Meurig of Gwent, Cynan of Powys, and Cynfor Host-Protector of the North. Cynan of Powys spent his time harrying his neighbours rather than fighting the Saxons. That was left to Cyndrwyn, a rival ruler of Pengwern, an outcrop kingdom of Powys, around Shrewsbury. Thanks to Cyndrwyn and his sons, including the famous Cynddylan, the men of Pengwern fought bravely to protect their lands against the Mercians. Cynfor Host-Protector doubtless rallied the Men of the North, though nothing is now remembered of his battles. In Gwent, Meurig and his famous father Tewdrig, who came back from retirement to fight one last battle against the Saxons, are long remembered in song. Meurig's son Athrwys possibly fought alongside them.

Between them, Meurig, Cyndrwyn and Cynfor could doubtless have held that frontier line and fought at those battles in Nennius's list. Yet, none is associated with them in legend, unless it is via Athrwys ap Meurig. We know virtually nothing about him, not even whether he succeeded to the kingdom of Gwent. He signed no charters as king, and the records show that Meurig, who had a long life, was succeeded by his grandson Morgan. This would, of course, fit in with Nennius's description of Arthur as a *dux bellorum*, and not necessarily a king. Perhaps Athrwys was killed in battle, and perhaps he fought alongside Cyndrwyn and Cynfor in holding the western frontier. If he did, those are not the names he is associated with in legend. And though Athrwys could not have fought at the Badon remembered by Gildas, he could have fought at Caer Faddon.

The western frontier is thus plausible a century after Badon, but not earlier.

Northern Frontier

One ruler dominated the north in the late fifth century. In the territory between the Walls the main force was Dyfnwal Hen,

Pendragon after the death of Brychan of Brycheiniog, and one of the most powerful warriors of his day. His grandfather was Ceretic of Strathclyde, and his sons became rulers of the territories between the Walls. One of his daughters married Brychan of Manau, possibly a son of Brychan Brycheiniog. His descendants were notably wealthy and later owned part of the legendary "ThirteenTreasures of Britain" sought by Merlin, including the halter of Clydno Eityn and the magic sword of Rhydderch Hael. Dyfnwal appears in the Irish stories about Cú Chulainn, in which he is known as Domnal, the warlike ruler of Scotland.

Dyfnwal's main opponents, apart from the Picts and the Scots, would have been the British tribes south of Hadrian's Wall, including the Gododdin and descendants of Coel, the Coelings. In contrast to Dyfnwal's descendants, the Coelings of that generation were poor. There was Merchiaun (Mark the Lean), his son Cinmarc the Dismal, and Mark's cousin Sawyl (Samuel) the Humble. However, Sawyl's cousin Einion was the father of Rhun the Wealthy, suggesting at least some change of fortune. How much of that might have been due to another cousin, Eliffer of the Great Host, is open to speculation.

Eliffer and his sons ruled the eastern Pennines, and thus were on the front line facing the rising menace of the Angles who, under Soemil, had laid claim to Deira, the area between the Humber and the Tees around the middle of the fifth century. Eliffer's father, Arthwys, must also have been involved in these battles. There would be few reasons or opportunities for the Coelings to venture north of the Wall unless threatened by Dyfnwal's sons. They had enough to cope with facing the Angles and the Irish. The pattern of battles in Map 7 is too haphazard to reflect any consistent campaign between the Coelings and the Gododdin, and is far more suggestive of battles between the Gododdin and Strathclyde marking Dyfnwal's territorial gains.

The epicentre of these battles is around the Eildon Hills and the Roman fort of Trimontium. This had ceased to be occupied by the end of the second century, but the Celtic fort at the top of one of the Eildon Hills showed evidence of reoccupation by the end of the fourth century. In *Arthur and the Lost Kingdoms*, Alistair Moffat has speculated that a Romano-British cavalry unit under Arthur re-established itself in this area, perhaps first at

Eildon but then further east at what became Roxburgh. This unit was primarily engaged against the advancing Angles. Moffat does not identify all of the sites from Nennius's list, suggesting sufficient in the area to presume that all belong there (though surprisingly he concedes that Badon probably was at Bath). There are certainly enough potential sites here to make this area a distinct possibility, whether it relates to Dyfnwal's expansionism or a cavalry unit holding back the Angles.

These sites mean that the battles were fought primarily on Gododdin soil, but if at this time the area was under the control of Dyfnwal and his sons, there is no room for anyone called Arthur. The only like-named individual in the region, the Coeling Arthwys, could not have managed a campaign this far north.

It is possible, though, to map out an alternative northern frontier. In *From Scythia to Camelot*, Linda Malcor and C. Scott Littleton propose a sequence that could have been fought by Lucius Artorius Castus against the Picts, around the year 185. They suggest that the campaign could have started at the fort of Ribchester (Breguoin), then under Castus's command, and from there along the Ribble to its estuary (Tribruit). The pursuit then moved south to a sequence of battles along the Douglas, before the Caledonii headed across the Pennines to York. Castus drove the Picts north to Binchester (Guinnion) and from there back across Hadrian's Wall where they met again at Yeavering Bell (River Glein). The Picts were now in full retreat, but Castus engaged them again in the Forest of Celidon before pursuing them north to the final victory at Dumbarton (Badon).

Malcor and Littleton don't offer a site for Bassas, but a site near Stirling would certainly fit their scenario. There are two concerns, however. Firstly, would this campaign be remembered three centuries later, by then somehow attributed to another whose own battles may have echoed those of Castus? And secondly, how does Badon fit into the timetable when it happened in the year of Gildas's birth? Badon (as Dumbarton) is the one weak link in an otherwise feasible proposal, and it raises again the possibility that Badon was not part of the same campaign, but the culmination of a series of battles against the Saxons.

Malcor and Littleton's proposal might also fit an alternative northern campaign. A campaign against the Angles could have started at York, and moved south along the Humber to face them in their heartland near Barton at Glanford Bridge (Glein) and then headed north to Binchester (Guinnion) and up to the Wall at Corbridge (one or more of the Dubglas battles). It would not need much of a trespass beyond the Wall to engage the Angles again in the Forest of Celidon. This may have marked the end of one campaign and could have been led by Eliffer of the Great Host from York, perhaps assisted by his father Arthwys. The threat then shifted to the West Coast with the Irish raiders. Battles could have taken place at Ribchester (Bregouin), along the Ribble Valley (Tribruit) and the River Douglas (thus causing a mental link with the previous campaign). This covers all of the sites except Bassas and Badon. Bassas, which we have suggested means "shallows", might relate to any of the shoreline in Morecambe Bay which was once above sea level but was later engulfed. And if Badon was a separate battle, and not part of this campaign, it need not have been in the north. This second campaign may well have been led by Arthwys in conjunction with Mark of Rheged.

There are other, later, events that may have caused these battles to become embedded in the Arthurian legend. The battle of Arderydd, for instance, which happened eighty years after Badon, in 573, was between Arthwys's grandsons, Gwenddoleu, Peredur and Gwrgi. The reasons behind this battle are uncertain but it suggests some climactic vendetta between the two sets of families. The fact that it happened north of Hadrian's Wall, in the territory of Rhydderch Hael, suggests that Gwenddoleu may have betrayed the Coelings and was now in the pay of the sons of Dyfnwal. Gwenddoleu was known for his wealth as he also had one of the Thirteen Treasures of Britain, a gold and silver chessboard. There is another tradition that states that the battle was between Gwenddoleu and Rhydderch, and that the sons of Eliffer were not involved. This may make more sense, as it suggests that one of the Coelings, who had become wealthy, saw an opportunity to gain territory from a young and as yet untried Rhydderch, with fatal consequences. Gwenddoleu was killed and his bard, Myrddin, went insane after the battle and fled into the Forest of Celidon.

Arderydd may have been remembered generations later rather like Camlann, and its closeness to Camboglanna on Hadrian's

Wall may have compounded the error. What's more, Arderydd is situated in the Forest of Celidon and thus may be the same as Nennius's seventh battle. The connection with Myrddin/Merlin adds further confusion. Add to this the memory that Dyfnwal was the Pendragon, and the mix could certainly add fuel to a tradition of a northern Arthur.

Gwenddoleu's cousin was Urien of Rheged who fought against the Angles in Northumbria during the 570s and 580s, with his cousins Gwallawg of Elmet and Morcant of Lothian. This included a major siege at Lindisfarne where, due to betrayal by Morcant, Urien was murdered. The disaster at Catraeth soon followed, the beginning of the end for northern resistance against the Angles. Urien's battles are commemorated in Taliesin's battle poem *Arise, Reget*, and these may include at least one that coincides with Nennius's list, the eleventh battle of Breguoin, "the halls of Brewyn." Otherwise Urien's battles do not overlap with Arthur's and since the end result is Arthur's victory as opposed to Urien's defeat, it suggests that Urien's campaign is not the source for the battle list. It could still, though, have blurred in the memory, with one sequence of battles ending in a betrayal becoming confused with another battle campaign which also, if you include Camlann, ends in betrayal. Urien features in the later Arthurian legends, but he stands suffiently bold as a possible Arthur himself.

Eastern Frontier

In chapter 5 I discussed Gildas's reference to "the unhappy partition with the barbarians" in *De Excidio*, and suggested that this boundary may have been delineated by the Roman Dere / Ermine Street, the modern-day A1. If we plot the battle sites against this road there is a surprising match. It would need to include a few dubious sites, such as those around Stirling, for Tribruit, and that at Stow for Guinnion, but otherwise follows several very feasible locales.

This frontier has the advantage of following Gildas's partition and of linking together the boundaries of the original Anglo-Saxon settlements in Bernicia, Deira, Lindsey and East Anglia. Apart from the problem of identifying this boundary around

London, it is otherwise supported by archaeological evidence which shows no extensive Saxon settlement west of that frontier until the mid sixth century.

The major problem is that this frontier runs the length of Britain and thus crosses several British kingdoms. Unlike the other frontiers, which are relatively self-contained and thus could be held by one chieftain, perhaps with the help of neighbouring kings, this one would require a significant consortium of kings. Yet this is exactly how Nennius describes it when he says that "Arthur, with the kings of Britain" fought the enemy. The individual best placed to work along this line would have been Arthwys of the Pennines since his territory, probably around the southern Pennines, was midway along this route. We have established that the original battles, under Vortimer, took place along the Humber estuary and this would be the obvious place for the battles to start around Brigg and York, locations also favoured by Geoffrey of Monmouth (*see* Chapter 9). There would have been a series of battles in the north, where the Angles were most strongly established, before other battles, doubtless encouraged by Aelle, erupted further south. Arthwys would have been reinforced here by the British rulers of Calchvynydd and Rhydychen, the territories around Oxford and the Chilterns, and it's possible that other battle sites with names now lost ought to be placed in this vicinity.

Badon need not be part of this frontier. The final battle could have marked a last ditch effort by the Saxons to force the British back. It could suggest a pincer movement by Aelle from the south plus the Saxons of Lindsey and East Anglia, perhaps under Octa (who Nennius tells us came south) who came down the Ridgeway or the Fosse Way into the British heartland. That defeat proved to the Saxons that they could not advance so far west and allowed the partition.

Southern Frontier

This frontier could have been controlled by a commander based at any of several major forts, not only those we have already discussed, including Caerleon in Gwent, Solsbury Hill near Bath, or Liddington Castle, near Swindon, but other strengthened hillforts such as South Cadbury, Glastonbury, and Cadbury-

Congresbury near Bristol, the first two with close Arthurian associations. To this we must add the Wansdyke and other defensive earthworks in the area which are the only firm signs of a genuine frontier. We can, to a degree, place the battle list along or close to this frontier and with connections to some of the known conflicts with the Saxons.

The first of the battles may well have taken place at Glyndebourne, near Lewes (Glein), defeating Aelle before moving along the coast to face another Saxon advance (attributed to Cerdic, but probably one of the other eponymous adventurers, such as Port or Wihtgar) at Blackwater (Dubglas) near the Solent estuary. Several engagements could have happened here allowing for a series of Saxon landings. The British may then have retrenched at Old Basing (Bassas), which formed the start of a defence across the south as Saxons now advanced from the north. Another battle at White Hills (Guinnion), Swindon, held the Saxons at bay and this may have ended the first series of assaults.

The second campaign may have started with some daring Saxon or Irish raids up the Severn and into south Wales, leading to battles at Pontardulais, Gellideg (Celidon), Caerleon (City of the Legion) and the Trwc estuary (Tribruit), before pushing the Saxons back across the Severn to Catbrain (Bristol) and the final engagement at Badon (either Bath or Liddington Castle).

This campaign could have started under Ambrosius, being perhaps the end of a much longer campaign by Ambrosius based at Cadbury. A young Arthur may have been in his ranks. Arthur could have taken over as commander of the second campaign. If so, this might suggest we would find some mention of Ambrosius rewarding Arthur as he hands over command. Although Pascent received lands from Ambrosius, as they were probably of the same generation, Pascent is unlikely to have taken over as commander. But Pascent's son is another matter. This was Riocatus, whom we have encountered before as Faustus's nephew.

Riocatus's name, meaning "king of battles", might imply that he became Ambrosius's military successor. Riocatus need not have succeeded his father by then; indeed, that may not have happened until around the year 500, after Badon.

Riocatus was the cousin of Cadell of Powys, known as "Gleaming Hilt", a strange cognomen which seems to suggest some gloriously decked hilt or scabbard to his sword. This is reminiscent of Arthur's sword Excalibur, because it was the scabbard, rather than the sword, that had magical qualities and would protect Arthur.

One might expect Ambrosius to be succeeded by his own son rather than Cadell, but although we know from Gildas that he had grandchildren, these may have been via a daughter. Alternatively, if Ambrosius was Riothamus, then his children may have lived in Armorica and inherited lands there.

Cadell of the Bright Sword and Riocatus, King of Battles, as joint successors to Ambrosius ruling from the one city in Britain that had not fallen into ruin – Viriconium – could well have become conjoined in later years as a legendary Arthur. If either of these, fighting under the banner of Ambrosius, led an army to Badon, with the final defeat of the Saxons, that would be enough to imprint that memory indelibly into the folklore of the British.

This is all highly conjectural and based on the flimsiest of evidence, but in the Arthurian world there is little else. This suggestion does fit a pattern of battles, and does provide a locale for a possible Arthur-like figure.

There are, of course, many other interpretations of these battle sites, both in terms of new locations or how the battle sequence may have run across the country. In *King Arthur, A Military History*, Michael Holmes discusses the Anglo-British battles and where Arthur's campaigns might be located. He generally follows the more traditional locations (Glen in Lincolnshire, Bath for Badon and so on) and allows Arthur free rein across the whole of Britain but in a series of battles spread over several years. He accepts Arthur as the High King successor to Ambrosius, but does not otherwise identify him beyond recognizing him as a great military commander.

Conclusion

Having explored all of the battles and dozens of sites we have been able to make a potential link between some sites and some individuals. Only one of these, Arthwys of the Pennines, has a name which may be resonant with Arthur, but we are, after all, looking as much for the victor of the key battle of Badon, whose memory may have become attached to a later Arthur. This has helped us identify several individuals, especially Dyfnwal, Cadell and Riocatus, who must have been alive at the time of Badon and probably fought there.

Each of the suggested frontiers has its strengths and weaknesses, though the patterns in North Wales and North Britain are not best placed for sustained campaigns against the Saxons. Neither is the western frontier, for all that a campaign could have been masterminded from Wroxeter. My own belief is that only the southern or eastern frontiers provide a plausible explanation for a sustained battle campaign. The eastern frontier has the advantage of linking to a known subsequent "partition" and allows for the likely presence of Arthwys of the Pennines. The southern frontier presents a better explanation for the hill forts in the south and a focused campaign against Aelle as *Bretwalda*.

Before we take this further, though, we need to remember that the battle list does not cover all of Arthur's exploits. For a more complete picture we must turn to the Welsh tales.

8

THE WELSH TRADITION – THE OTHER ARTHURS

So far, apart from the *Welsh Annals*, all of our information about Arthur has come from writings by English or Continental authors. When we turn to the Welsh record, a different Arthur emerges. In this section we will explore the relevant stories in the *Mabinogion* and other Welsh texts.

1. The Mabinogion

It may seem strange to include discussion of the *Mabinogion* as part of this "historical" section, and it is true that the stories do cross the divide, being more legend than fact. But, as we shall see throughout these explorations, there are factual elements, and the divide could be drawn almost anywhere. It is worth reflecting upon a comment by Gwyn Jones and Thomas Jones in their translation of the *Mabinogion* (Dent, 1949):

> . . . when we recall that Arthur was not a French, German or English, but a British king, it is not unreasonable to emphasize the significance of British material relating to him. British material, that is, uncontaminated by the Cycles of Romance, though necessarily affected by the vast complex of Celtic myth and legend.

The Celtic tales of Arthur incorporated into the *Mabinogion* are amongst the earliest to survive, certainly predating Geoffrey's

History, though not all necessarily surviving in written form from an earlier date.

The *Mabinogion* is a collection of Celtic tales, edited by Lady Charlotte Guest, with the help of Ioan Tegis who helped transcribe them into English, in 1846. She incorporated twelve in her first edition, although technically only the first four belong to the "Mabinogi", the stories about the hero Pryderi. It was Lady Charlotte who concocted the phrase "mabinogion" on a misunderstanding of the text. "Mab" means son, and the phrase is generally taken to mean "tales of youth". It has become a convenient tag for a collection of early Celtic tales, and so it will remain.

The stories incorporated into the *Mabinogion* come from two ancient collections, *Llyfr Gwyn Rhydderch* (*The White Book of Rhydderch*) which was committed to parchment in the early 1300s, and *Llyfr Coch Hergest* (*The Red Book of Hergest*), which was written down around 1400. Other versions of these stories survive in manuscript form from at least a century earlier, and were clearly part of an oral tradition long before that. But, as with the sources for Nennius and Geoffrey, since we lack the earliest versions we have no way of knowing how much they have been corrupted in the seven centuries since Arthur's day.

The four branches of the Mabinogi proper do not feature Arthur, although some of the characters reappear in the later tales. Here, I intend to discuss only two stories, *Culhwch and Olwen* and *The Dream of Rhonabwy*, which are of historical import. The other three, *The Lady of the Fountain*, *Peredur, Son of Evrawc* and *Gereint, Son of Erbin*, although they all feature Arthur, are related to the later romances told by Chrétien de Troyes and are discussed later.

2. Culhwch and Olwen

Culhwch and Olwen is the oldest of the texts used by Guest in her *Mabinogion*. Scholars believe it was written down in its final form around the year 1100, but the linguistic evidence suggests it reached a final oral form perhaps a century earlier. It thus predates Geoffrey's *History*, and is little more than a century later than Nennius. Yet, as we shall see, it bears no relationship to either.

The basic story can be summarised briefly, and illustrates how Arthur was perceived by the tenth and eleventh centuries. Culhwch, a cousin of Arthur, is born in a pigsty when his heavily pregnant mother Goleuddyd is frightened by the pigs. She gives birth but flees, and the baby is rescued by the swineherd and taken to the court of his father, Cilydd. After the death of Culhwch's mother, his father's new wife desires that her own daughter from a previous marriage should marry Culhwch. He refuses because he is still young, so his stepmother curses him and says that he will marry no one but Olwen, the daughter of the giant Ysbaddaden. Despite never meeting Olwen, Culhwch falls in love with her, and seeks the help of Arthur and his court to find her. The quest lasts a year and when at last Olwen is found, she agrees to marry Culhwch only if he carries out her father's wishes. She knows her father will refuse because when she marries, Ysbaddaden will die. Ysbaddaden sets Culhwch forty impossible tasks. These are achieved mostly by heroes from Arthur's court. Ysbaddaden dies, and Culhwch and Olwen are married.

It's a wonderful heroic tale full of adventure and larger-than-life characters. The supernatural elements no doubt grew in the telling, and more and more heroes were doubtless added, but there is no reason to suspect that the location of the story changed much because part of the story's strength lies in the knowledge of the locality. Let us therefore work through the people and places in the story, and see how much can be related to the historical elements we have already covered.

(a) **Amlawdd Wledig**

We learn at the outset that Culhwch is Arthur's first cousin. Culhwch's mother Goleuddydd was the daughter of Amlawdd Wledig, as was Arthur's mother Ygraine, and Rhieinwylydd, the mother of St. Illtud. Amlawdd has been accused of being a genealogical convenience in order to provide family links between individuals (*see* Table 8.1). If that were the case, however, someone would have had to invent him first, and why should later kings want descent from a fictional nobody? Amlawdd's name may have been corrupted, but it must have meant something at the time.

Table 8.1 Arthur's maternal family

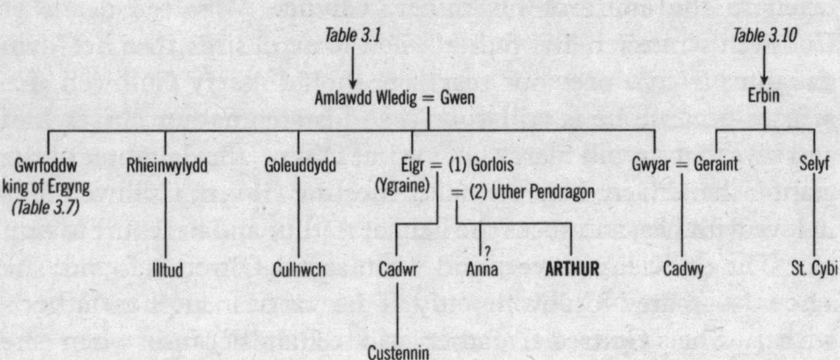

Peter Bartrum remarks that the name is unique in Welsh and seems to have a Nordic root, *Amlói*, or *Amleth*, the same as Shakespeare's Hamlet. There is a whole body of research, going back at least as far as 1880, which proposes that Hamlet/Amlethus was a variant of Anlaf, itself an Anglicisation of Olaf and that all these characters are represented in legend by Havelok the Dane. In this Anglo-Danish story, which became popular at the same time as the Welsh Arthurian legends, Havelok is a dispossessed Danish king (from the Danish settlements in England), who is serving as a scullion under the name of Cuaran in the court of King Godric of Lincoln/Lindsey.

Cuaran was the nickname given to Olaf Sihtricson, who became king of Jorvik (York) in 941, and ruled Danish Mercia (including Lindsey) until expelled by King Edmund of Wessex in 942. Olaf had been the son of an earlier Danish king of York, Sihtric, but, being a child when his father died, was smuggled out of England to relative safety in Ireland by his uncle Gothfrith (Godric).

There are some remarkable connections here. In the multilingual world of tenth century Britain, Olaf >Anlaf >Amlethus >Amlawdd would have been regarded as a hero, especially by the non-Saxons, and in later years, when his precise *floruit* had become confused, there would have been those who wanted to claim descent from him. In all likelihood, therefore, the name *Amlawdd* did not exist in the fifth century.

That does not mean that all of Amlawdd's "legendary" descendants also belong to the ninth century. Clearly St. Illtud does not. It simply means that Amlawdd might have been a ninth century hero transposed back in time as a convenient ancestor to various British (or non-Saxon) heroes. But it may also mean that some of his legendary descendants are from the ninth century. This is especially interesting because Olaf/Amlethus was the ancestor of the Norse kings of the Isle of Man. His great-great grandson was Godred Crovan ("White Hands"), who conquered Man in 1079 and established a dynasty that lasted for two hundred years. In later years Godred was remembered as King Gorry, and it's possible that his name passed into Arthurian legend as the name for the kingdom of Gorre, associated with Urien of Rheged.

There may, however, be another interpretation of the name Amlawdd. It is possible that it became confused with the name Emyr Llydaw. *Emyr* is not a personal name but a title, meaning "leader" (*amris*); thus Emyr Llydaw is "ruler of Llydaw." *Llydaw* was the Welsh name for Armorica (called Letavia in Latin), but it was also local to Wales. There is, for instance, a Llyn Llydaw, a lake in Snowdonia near a possible site for Camlann, close to Ambrosius's fort at Dinas Emrys. There is also a territory in southeast Wales, around Ystrad Yw between Brycheiniog and Ergyng, called Llydaw.

Llydaw may be derived from *Luyddog*, ("host" or "army"). This probably goes back to the time of Magnus Maximus, who withdrew many of the Roman forces from Britain to support his campaign in Gaul for the Imperial crown. The Welsh tale, *The Dream of Macsen Wledig*, also included in the *Mabinogion*, tells how Maximus married the daughter of Eudaf Hen, Elen Luyddog, or "Elen of the host". The name subsequently took on religious significance, but I suspect it originally referred to the army that was taken away from Britain. Magnus doubtless entreated Eudaf for his support, which was sealed by marriage to Elen. Maximus granted these soldiers territory in Armorica, and the name Llydaw followed. Whoever was commander of these troops may have been known as the Emyr Llydaw. In fact, the early king of Armorica, Budic, is called the son of Emyr Llydaw.

Does this help us identify Emyr Llydaw and Amlawdd? Amlawdd could either be a contraction of Em[yr] Llyd[aw], or a synonym. *Ymladdwr* is the Welsh for "fighter", or, more specifically, soldier. Amlawdd Wledig could, therefore, be the same title, "leader of soldiers", not unlike a *dux Britanniarum*. Amlawdd or Emyr Llydaw would therefore not be one individual but several. It would explain why Amlawdd seems to be the father of so many children.

The original Amlawdd may have returned to Wales at some stage, perhaps in the service of Owain Finddu or Vortigern. If he settled in northern Ergyng, the territory may have been called Llydaw after him. Later in *Culhwch and Olwen* we learn that the Men of Llydaw assembled at Ystrad Yw, near Crickhowell, in Gwent, to help Arthur. These men could have been a special force that had once been commanded by Amlawdd, Arthur's grandfather, and were now at Arthur's command.

Amlawdd is usually regarded as the father of a host of daughters, who, through marriages, became mothers of various early British notables. However, *Culhwch and Olwen* refers to two of Arthur's mother's brothers, who must therefore be sons of Amlawdd. These are Llygadrudd Emys and Gwrfoddw Hen, both of whom are killed during the boar hunt at Ystrad Yw, towards the end of the story. There is no separate record of Llygadrudd Emys (the name means "the red-eyed stallion"), but Gwrfoddw Hen is known. He was the last recorded king of Ergyng, and lived around the year 650. This certainly fits in with our speculation on Amlawdd.

(b) **Arthur's warriors**

When Culhwch arrives at Arthur's court, he is refused admittance and challenged by Arthur's head porter, Glewlwyd. The altercation of porter and visitor is evidently a set piece in Celtic folk history as it is also the basis for the poem *Pa Gur* (*Who is the gatekeeper?*), recounting the exploits of Arthur and his men, which we will return to later in this chapter.

Although Glewlwyd seems to have become forgotten in most Arthurian literature, he was clearly well known in Welsh tradition. He appears in several of the *Mabinogion* tales, where he is described as Glewlwyd Mighty Grasp, known for his size and strength. He is also remembered in the Welsh Triads as one of the "Three Unopposable Knights."

Culhwch is eventually admitted, and when he requests the aid of Arthur to find Olwen he recites the names of over 200 warriors and courtiers, and of twenty-one maidens. The list is an excuse to name the famous heroes of old and cannot be trusted as a true record of Arthur's men. It includes, for instance, heroes capable of super-human feats, such as Clust, son of Clustfeinad ("Ear, son of Hearer"), who could hear an ant stir from over fifty miles away even if it were buried seven fathoms deep, or Gwaddyn Oddeith ("Sole-blaze"), whose shoe soles could burn a swathe through any forest.

There are several names one would expect, such as Bedwyr, Cei and Gwalchmai, better known in the later tales as Sir Kay, Sir Bedivere and Sir Gawain. These are the most ancient names of Arthur's warriors, and we shall return to their stories. Other names reappear amongst Arthur's knights, converted into Norman French by Chrétien de Troyes. Arthur's bishop, Bedwini, for instance, becomes Sir Baudwin, Caradog becomes Sir Carados, Cynwyl becomes Sir Griflet, and Madog becomes Sir Mador. There are plenty of other examples, several of whom are included in the "Who's Who" (*see* Chapter 23).

Certain key names are missing. There's no Lancelot, although there is the warrior Llwch Llawwynniog ("Llwch of the Striking Hand"), who is believed by some to be the original Lancelot (*see* Chapter 17). There is no Merlin, although there is an enchanter called Menw, possibly Merlin's fictional prototype (*see* Chapter 15).

There are some unexpected names in the list, including Gildas, along with all of his brothers. We know that Gildas was a contemporary of Arthur, as he was born in the year of Badon, but one would not expect him to be close to Arthur. The list also includes Taliesin, "Chief of Bards". Taliesin is associated with

Arthur's court in other writings, including the Triads, but his appearance causes a problem with dates. Taliesin is more closely associated with the courts of Urien of Rheged, who ruled in the 570s, and of his son Owein, to whom Taliesin composed a eulogy. According to legend, Taliesin was summoned as a child to the court of King Maelgwyn. Maelgwyn died in 549, placing Taliesin's birth perhaps around 530–535. Since he apparently died at a great age, he may have lived as late as 610. This allows for him to have been present at the court of Arthur of Dyfed, who ruled in the 590s.

Returning to the list of warriors in *Culhwch and Olwen*, there are several interesting asides about a few otherwise little-known names. We learn, for instance, of Gwyn Hyfar, a name which, on the surface, sounds compellingly like Gwenhwyfar (Guinevere), but which apparently means Gwyn "the Irascible" or "the Modest". According to Gwyn and Thomas Jones' translation, Gwyn was "one of the nine who plotted the battle of Camlann." Lady Charlotte Guest translated this phrase as "the ninth man that rallied the battle of Camlann." Both opposing interpretations agree that Gwyn Hyfar was an overseer of Cornwall and Devon.

Among the list of warriors are various sons of Iaen, collectively described as "men of Caer Dathyl, kindred to Arthur on his father's side." Caer Dathyl is in north Wales, in the Lleyn Peninsula, and is mentioned in the *Mabinogion* as the stronghold of the ensorcelled Lord of Gwynedd, Math. Amongst the old documents known as the *Hanesyn Hen*, there is a list of the children of Iaen, including a daughter, Eleirch, who is described as the "mother of Cydfan ab Arthur". She is not described as Arthur's wife. We cannot be certain this is meant to be the same Arthur, but the spelling and connection are cause enough for thought.

(c) **Lost Lands**

One other name raises an interesting association with lost lands. There is a reference to Gwenwynwyn, called Arthur's "first fighter" or "champion", whose name appears in the Welsh Triads as one of the "Three Seafarers of Ynys Prydein." Though completely forgotten today, this hero has an interesting family history. Gwenwynwyn's grandfather was Seithennin, keeper of the sea-walls and flood-gates of Gwaelod, part of the territory (*Maes Gwyddno*) of Gwyddno Garanhir, one night Seithennin was drunk and failed to keep watch, and the lands flooded.

There are many legends of lost lands around Britain's coast, such as Lyonesse, the land believed to be buried between Lands End and the Scilly Isles off the southwest tip of Cornwall. But various Welsh sources mention other similar inundations. One such is in Cardigan Bay, which may well be Maes Gwyddno. There are several princes called Gwyddno causing confusion over the identity of Garanhir ("Long-Shanks"). There is a Gwyddno, Prince of Merionydd, who lived in the early seventh century, contemporary with Arthur of Gwent and Arthlwys of Ceredigion, but his link with the legend is a late assignment. Others suggest Gwyddno ap Cawrdaf, one of the Men of the North, who was thus a contemporary of Arthur of Dyfed.

Gwyddno's name is remembered in Porth Wyddno, listed in a Triad as one of the "Three Chief Ports" of Britain. This has been identified with Borth, north of Aberystwyth, on the borders of Dyfed and Ceredigion, which would connect Maes Gwyddno with lands believed lost in Cardigan Bay. However others suggest that it was a harbour on the River Conwy in North Wales or on the coast of Rheged which was buried when the waters of Morecambe Bay rose during the sixth century, perhaps as a consequence of the comet catastrophe of the 540s.

Gwenwynwyn must, therefore, have lived around 610–630, a century too late for Arthur of Badon, but not too late for Arthur of Dyfed. This great sailor would have earned his reputation because of the perils of the sea during the sixth century, not just the rising sea levels, but the constant battles with the Irish who remained a threat to the western coast of Wales, the very shores of Dyfed which the Irish had colonized in late Roman times when it was known as Demetia. Gwenwynwyn became the master of Arthur's fleet in Dyfed, a role that could easily see him classified as Arthur's champion.

The list includes one other member of Arthur's court, providing further evidence for the former existence of these flooded lands. This is Teithi the Old, "whose dominions the sea overran." One of the Welsh Triads places this kingdom, originally called Ynys Teithy, and later Kaerrihoc, in the west between Menevia and Ireland. *Menevia* is the old name for the town of St. David's on the western coast of Dyfed, suggesting that Ynys Teithy was an island or peninsula further out into the Irish Sea that was destroyed by flooding. It is difficult to provide a date for Teithi. It seems that Ynys Teithy was still referred to during the tenure of Oudoceus, archbishop of Llandaff, who held the prelacy from about 580 to 615 and was thus a contemporary of Arthur of Dyfed. Presumably the inundation of Ynys Teithi happened during this period. The Irish also remember him as Tethra, king of the Fomorians (*fo* meaning "under", and *mor* meaning "sea").

We can imagine a folk memory of these refugees from deluged lands living at the court of Arthur, and this may be how such tales as Tristan of Lyonesse began.

(d) **Camelot, Celliwic and the god Artaius**

Arthur's fabled castle Camelot does not appear in these Welsh tales – indeed, we have yet to encounter it at all. The list of notables at Arthur's court includes Glwyddyn the Craftsman, who is credited with building Arthur's Hall, called *Ehangwen* (meaning "expansive white"), and implying a beautiful white building seemingly too large to take in at once. This may not have been its real name, but rather how the hall was viewed. Later poems state that the hall shone with gold, so the image is of a bright shining palace, very similar to how Camelot is envisaged.

Arthur's Hall is placed in Celliwic, or Gelliwig, in Cernyw. The first of the Welsh Triads, "Three Tribal Thrones of Britain", lists Arthur's thrones as being at Mynyw, Celliwig and Pen Rhionydd. Because of Charlotte Guest's translation of Cernyw as Cornwall, people have been searching for Celliwic in the south-west, although no place by that name survives there. Various sites have been suggested, including Callington on the border of Devon and Cornwall, Castle Killibury, an ancient hill fort near Wadebridge, Callywith near Bodmin, and Willapark at Bossiney near Tintagel. Most of these are based solely on connections to ancient hillforts. Killibury is the most favoured, although none of these places has been adequately researched, and none has a logical Arthurian connection.

That there once was a Kelliwic in Cornwall is not disputed. There is a record of a Thomas de Kellewik in 1302, who lived at Gulval, north of Penzance. *Celli wig* means "the grove in the wood", and thus is a phrase that could have occurred in several places.

However, whilst there is no Celliwic in Cornwall, there are two in Wales. We have already established that Cernyw should not be translated as Kernow or Cornwall, but as Cernyw in South Wales, in Gwent, being the territory between Chepstow and Cardiff. In *Journey to Avalon*, Chris Barber and David Pykitt put forward the case that Gelliwig is the ancient hill fort now called Llanmelin, near Caerwent. The old name for Llanmelin was *Llan y Gelli* ("church of the grove"), but over time as the grove was forgotten and superseded by a mill, it became *Llanmelin* ("the church of the mill"). Barber and Pykett suggest that during that transition it would for a while have been known as Caer Melin, a name that Chrétien de Troyes corrupted into Caer-Malot, or Camelot. It is an intriguing argument, all the more so because nearby are the Bedwin Sands, named after Bedwini, bishop of Celliwic.

Barber and Pykett also suggest that Caerwent was Arthur's capital, not nearby Caerleon, and that Geoffrey of Monmouth mistook the two. Caerwent, the Roman town of Venta Silurum, was the former capital of the Silures, and thus more likely as the court for a post-Roman king of Gwent. The final link in the chain is that the Welsh Triads name Caradog Vreichfras as the chief elder of Celliwig, and Caradog was ruler of Ergyng in the sixth century.

The case for Llanmelin as Arthur's court sounds convincing on philological grounds. As yet, however, there is no archeological evidence to support it. An excavation in the 1930s showed it to have originated as a hill fort in the third century BC, with a progressive series of occupations and growth, particularly around 50BC. But it seems to have been abandoned around 75AD, and there is no evidence of post-Roman occupation. This is perhaps not surprising as from 75AD onwards the people would have come under Roman control and settled within Caerwent. The name Gelliwig survived amongst the Silures, and doubtless the location became a revered place, and thus a more suitable name in the tales for Arthur's court.

The other Gelliwig is in North Wales, on the Lleyn Peninsula. The name still survives as Gelliwig, with no corruption or revision. Its case is made by Steve Blake and Scott Lloyd in *The Keys to Avalon*. The name Gelliwig is still found in Gelliwig Farm, near Botwnnog, Pwllheli. There has long been a manor house on the site and it has never been excavated, so it is not known whether a Dark Age hall once stood there. The location seems remote for Arthur's main castle. We have already seen the Lleyn Peninsula associated with Vortigern, and his stronghold at Nant Gwrtheyrn was some ten miles northeast. We have also seen that Arthur had kindred at Caer Dathyl, which Guest connected to the village of Llanrwst, though it has also been linked to Caer Engan, near Penygroes, both of which are on the outskirts of Snowdonia.

Caer Dathyl was the stronghold of Math, son of Mathonwy, lord of Gwynedd, who is the eponymous protagonist in the fourth branch of the *Mabinogion*. This is a dark story of death, rape and rebirth. Central to it is Math's nephew Gwydion, whose brother Gilfaethwy lusts after Math's maidservant, Goewin. Gwydion contrives for Gilfaethwy to see Gowein, but the meeting ends in rape and Math punishes the brothers by turning them into different animals each year, in which guise they have to father young. In later mythology, the role of Gwydion was replaced by that of Artaius, a god of the air, who was worshiped in Gaul. Gwydion was a shape-changer and can be seen as a form of proto-Merlin. Artaius was originally a pastoral deity but, at the time of the great barbarian and Celtic post-Roman migrations, it seems that Artaius superseded Gwydion, coming to Britain possibly via Brittany. Between them Gwydion-Artaius became the god of rebirth, a Celtic sun-god who was worshipped at the time of the winter solstice.

Some have argued that the character of Arthur may have been a manifestation of Artaius. However, it is more likely that the original Arthur later became associated with Artaius, rather than the other way round. The association with Artaius doubtless also brought forth the shape-changing Gwydion aspect in the form of Merlin and his prototype Menw. There may have been a cult that worshipped Artaius on the Lleyn Peninsula, encouraging the association with King Arthur.

The Artaius connection may also have a link with the origin of Arthur's name. Firstly, and most mundanely, he may have been named after the god Artaius at birth. Secondly, his name may not have been Arthur, but he may have been dubbed that after his death by his followers because of the Artaius connection. Thirdly, he may not have been Arthur by birth but assumed the name during his lifetime in order to make the connection to the idea of re-birth, effectively being born again and giving new life to the British nation. This option gives significance to the idea of the once and future king, who had not died but would return. It also suggests a possible identity change. Perhaps Cadell or Riocatus, or even Ambrosius, could have taken on that epithet as symbolic of the change in fortune after Badon.

Since the name Gelliwig/Celliwic appears so prominently in *Culhwch and Olwen* it is a little surprising that Geoffrey did not use it in his *History*, preferring instead Caerleon. Surprising, because Geoffrey was aware of other items associated with Arthur, which he lifted directly from the story. When Culhwch first arrives at Arthur's Hall and before he invokes the roll call of names for his boon, Arthur refers to:

> Caledvwlch, my sword; and Rhongomyant, my lance; and Wynebgwrthucher, my shield; and Carnwenhau, my dagger; and Gwenhwyvar, my wife.

We have become used to the name of Arthur's sword being Excalibur, but in his *History* Geoffrey calls it Caliburn. The Welsh *caledvwlch* means "hard cut", and was almost certainly derived from the Irish sword *Caledbolg*, which belonged to Fergus mac Roich and which means "hard lightning". *Caliburn* itself is believed to be derived from the Latin *chalbys* for "steel." Geoffrey also calls Arthur's lance "Ron", describing it as "fit for slaughter;" the Welsh *Rhongomyant* means "slaying spear". Geoffrey did not pay too close attention, however, because he calls Arthur's shield Pridwen, whereas originally it was *Wynebgwrthucher*, meaning "face of evening". Pridwenn, or Prytwenn, as revealed later in *Culhwch and Olwen*, was the name of Arthur's ship, meaning "white form" or "fair shape".

(e) **The Cauldron of Dwrnach**

One of the impossible tasks set by Ysbaddaden involves the theft of the cauldron of Dwrnach. Like all cauldrons in Celtic folklore, it has special properties. In this case, the cauldron will not boil the food of cowards. A similar quest for a cauldron arises in the poem *The Spoils of Annwvyn*, and has many similarities to the episode in *Culhwch and Olwen*, suggesting that both came from the same source. These stories represent an early prototype for the story of the Quest for the Grail (*see* Chapter 16).

(f) **The Hunt of the Giant Boar**

Another of the forty tasks that Ysbaddaden set Culhwch was the hunt for the wild boar, Twrch Trwyth (*twrch* meaning "hog", and *trwyth*, or *triath*, "chief"). I suspect there was a deliberate pun here, as Trwyth can also mean "urine", so that the boar was known colloquially as "pig's piss".

Legend makes Trwyth the son of a king, Taredd Wledig, but because of his wickedness he had been turned into a boar, along with seven of his men, who are referred to as his piglets. The imagery is clearly allegorical for a prince who had become a violent and vile outlaw. Unfortunately, the name Taredd is not known outside the legend, and we cannot identify either him or his son.

Trwyth begins by terrorising Ireland, then crosses the sea to Dyfed and lays waste South Wales. Arthur and his heroes pursue the boar and drive him into the Severn estuary and eventually out into the open sea, but no more is heard of him. Thanks to Lady Charlotte Guest's original translation, the hunt seems to have taken place in Cornwall, but as discussed previously, Cernyw was along the southern shores of Gwent, west of Chepstow. That location makes far more sense than Cornwall, and provides a consistent route for the pursuit of Trwyth (*see map opposite*).

The pursuit falls into two distinct halves, the first confined to the territory of Dyfed, whilst the second takes place wholly in Gwent. Trwyth lands near St David's at Porth Clais, and is pursued around the coast to present-day Milford Haven, before

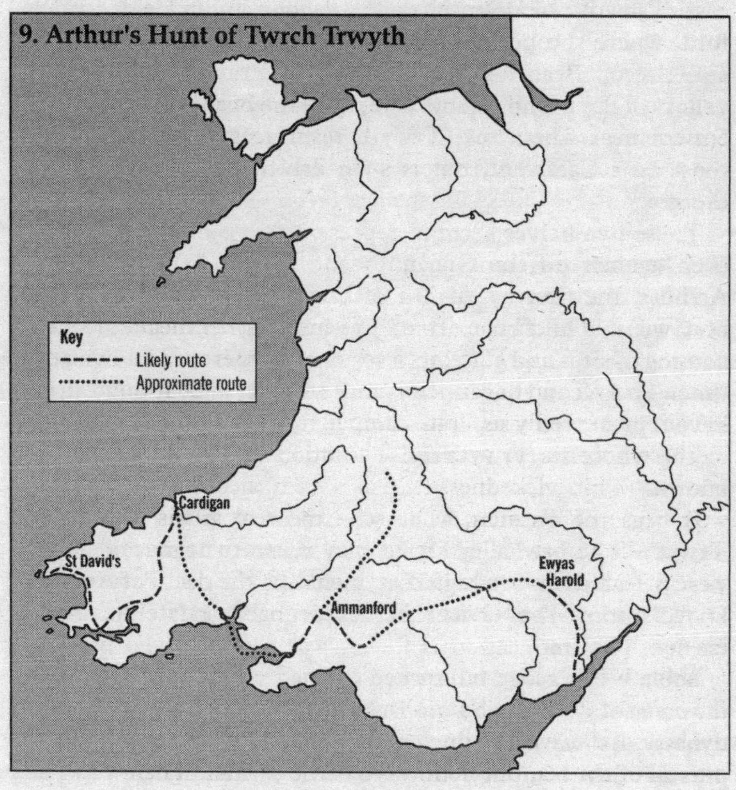

9. Arthur's Hunt of Twrch Trwyth

heading inland and up into the Preseli Mountains where, at Cwm Cerwyn, he slaughters many of Arthur's men, including Arthur's son Gwydre.

The pursuit of Trwyth then zig-zags out of the Preseli Mountains through Cardigan, and then the boar is lost to the east. Trwyth reappears in the Loughour Valley near Ammanford, where the hunt continues through the Black Mountains and Brecon Beacons, into the Vale of Ergyng and along the valleys of the Monnow and Wye, until the boar is driven into the Severn near Chepstow. Trwyth resurfaces along the Cernyw coast near Caerwent, but is soon driven out into the Severn estuary.

These two halves seem to represent two campaigns, perhaps even against different enemies and fought by two different Arthurs, the first by Arthur of Dyfed, the second by Arthur of Gwent. The first part of the hunt is very specific in its naming of sites and suggests a series of battles well known at the time. The second sequence is more vague, and, though it may have represented a separate campaign, by the time it was added to the whole story, its precise location was no longer so well known.

It begs the question as to who the real villain was behind Trwyth. The battles in Dyfed may relate to Irish raiders who were defeated but at a high cost, including the death of Arthur of Dyfed's son. The Gwent battles probably relate to another enemy. The implication is that it was a prince who was once of noble Welsh blood but turned renegade. This once again raises the name of Cerdic, who was British, yet founded the West Saxon dynasty. In *Journey to Avalon*, Barber and Pykitt suggest that the pursuit of the boar Trwyth was a battle against the Gewisse, and that Cerdic was their leader.

If Barber and Pykitt are correct, then whoever expelled Cerdic cannot have been Arthur of Gwent, who lived a full century after Cerdic. If we accept that Cerdic rose to power in the 530s, then his contemporary in Gwent was Nynnio, whilst Ergyng was ruled by Nynnio's brother Peibio. Both rulers are referred to in *Culhwch and Olwen* as the Ychen Bannawc, the "Horned Oxen", because God transformed them into oxen for their wickedness. Evidently they are not the heroes most likely to have expelled

Cerdic. Those would have been Riocatus or Cadell, who ruled the lands just to the north.

There is, in fact, a third boar hunt in the story. Culhwch is set the task of obtaining the tusks of the Chief Boar, Ysgithyrwyn. *Ysgithyr* means "tusk", so the name is really only an exaggeration for the Mighty Tusked Boar. Although at the start Arthur goes to the "west of Ireland" to seek the huntsman, Gwrgi Seferi, we are next told that Arthur "went into the North" to find Cyledyr the Wild, recorded as the son of Nwython (or Neithon, a Pictish name). The hunt for Ysgithyrwyn is conducted mainly by Caw, the father of Gildas, identified in the tale as being from Pictland. The records show a Caw ruling in the north at the time of Arthur of Badon, though he is usually associated with Strathclyde or Galloway. Galloway takes its name from the Gaels, or Irish, and thus Arthur's venture to the "west of Ireland" may not have been to Ireland at all, but to the islands off the west coast of Scotland which were then occupied primarily by Irish. Thus this hunt probably took place in Galloway, and may once have been an adventure relating to Caw and nothing to do with Arthur at all. In *The Figure of Arthur*, Richard Barber suggests that this boar hunt may have once been attributed to Arthur of Dál Riata, even though he lived a century later.

The likelihood is that by the time *Culhwch and Olwen* came to be written down, it had become a compendium, a grand epic tale of the adventures of all past heroes about whom the bards knew, linked together by the might and authority of Arthur. One example is the quest to obtain the blood of the Black Witch Orddu, at Pennant Gofud (the Valley of Grief) in the Uplands of Uffern ("Hell"). The brothers Cacamwri and Hygwydd at first try to seize Orddu, but are cast to the ground. Two more, Amren and Eiddyl, venture into her cave, but they suffer even worse. Now Arthur takes control, casting his knife into the cave and cutting Orddu in two. But it is Caw who takes the witch's blood, and thus probably Caw who was the original hero. In fact, during the course of this adventure Arthur is advised by his warriors that it is "unseemly" for them to see him fighting with the hag, as if this was an excuse for having Arthur present but not directly involved. Arthur has clearly been incorporated into this tale at a later stage and, in all likelihood, has been written into many of the other ones.

Culhwch and Olwen has raised a number of issues. The story seems to be set mid-way through Arthur's reign, in the 510s, and some of the characters do fit into that time scale. However, others, such as Taliesin, belong to the late sixth century, and their lives fit more comfortably with either Arthur of Dyfed or Arthur of Gwent. Arthur of Dyfed seems connected to legends about flooded lands, but Arthur of Gwent is more suited to one of the likely locations for King Arthur's fortress, Gelliwig or Caerwent. It has also opened up the possibility that Arthur's name may be related to Artaius, the Gaulish pastoral god. Finally, it may be that Arthur's name became a catch-all for the exploits of other heroes who preceded him, in particular Caw of Pictland and Cadell of Powys.

3. The Dream of Rhonabwy

The Dream of Rhonabwy is exactly what it says it is – an account of a dream. As such it has a strange, disconnected quality that can have little bearing on true history, and yet it raises some intriguing points. It probably wasn't composed until the late thirteenth century, its author looking back to what he clearly regards as a Golden Age that is threatening to fall apart.

The story starts with Madog, son of Mareddud, who "held Powys from end to end". This places the story at the start of Madog's reign, in 1132, for by the 1140s Powys was under threat from the expansionist regime of Owain Gwynedd. This makes the story contemporary with Geoffrey of Monmouth, and Geoffrey could well have known Madog, who was on friendly terms with the court of Henry I. It means that even if the story drew upon earlier tradition, it was composed some six centuries after Arthur and thus has no direct historical value. Yet because it describes the battle of Badon, it cannot be wholly ignored.

At the outset, Madog's brother Iorweth is jealous of his brother's power and goes on a rampage through Powys. Madog sends bands of warriors to track him down, one of whom is Rhonabwy. He and his companions spend the night in a dirty hovel, and Rhonabwy has a dream of the Arthurian age. The rest of the story describes that dream, a succession of unconnected visions of Arthur's warriors questing or in battle, while Arthur and Owain play a game similar to chess.

Rhonabwy finds himself and his companions travelling across the Plain of Argyngroeg, known today as Cyngrog, or Gungrog, just north of modern-day Welshpool, along the floodplain of the River Severn. One of the tributaries of the Severn here is called the River Camlad.

They are met by a knight who announces himself as Iddog ap Mynio, known as "Cordd Prydain", or "the Embroiler of Britain". While serving as messenger for Arthur the Emperor, he earned the name stiriring up strife between Arthur and his nephew Medrawd, thus causing the battle of Camlann. Although Arthur's messages to Medrawd were sincere, Iddog distorted them. He repented of his deeds and did seven years' penance. While they talk, Rhonabwy and Iddog are joined by Rhufon Befr (the "radiant"). He is also listed amongst Arthur's warriors in *Culhwch and Olwen*, and in one of the Welsh Triads as one of the "Three Fair Princes".

Continuing his dream-journey, Rhonabwy and his companions reach the ford of Rhyd y Groes and find a large encampment. There they see Arthur sitting with Gwarthegyd, son of Caw, and Bishop Bedwini. Various armies are arriving. Addaon ap Taliesin rides through the ford and splashes Arthur, causing Elffin ap Gwyddno to strike Addaon's horse with his sheathed sword. Both Elffin and Addaon appear in the genealogies, a generation apart. Their lives would have overlapped in the early 600s, and neither would be contemporary with Badon.

Then a tall and stately individual, identified as Caradog Vreichfras ("Stout-arm"), Arthur's chief counsellor and cousin, remarks that it is surprising that so great a host should be assembled in such a confined space, and that they should be here when they had promised to fight Osla Gyllellvawr ("Big Knife") at Badon that day. Arthur agrees that they must move on. They cross the ford, heading towards Cefyn Digoll, whilst Rhonabwy is told that the other troops he sees are the men of

Norway under the command of March, son of Meirchion, and the men of Denmark under the command of Edeyrn, son of Nudd. Soon after crossing the ford, they arrive below Caer Faddon, the site for the Battle of Badon.

This site cannot be far from Rhyd-y-Groes, perhaps an hour or two's march. Rhyd-y-groes is still marked on the Ordnance Survey map, though it is now the name of a farm. There was a ford here, over the Camlad, near Forden, where the river joins the Severn. Between Forden and Garthmyl was a fort called The Gaer, probably the old Roman fort of Levobrinta. A Roman road runs almost north-south along the Severn at this point, leading to Viriconium/Wroxeter. Arthur and his men almost certainly turned north along this road as it passes directly by Caer Digoll, now the Beacon Ring hill fort, as the story describes.

The army cannot have travelled much beyond Caer Digoll. Many years ago, Egerton Phillimore deduced that Caer Faddon was the name for the Black Bank spur of Long Mountain, just over two kilometres southeast of Buttington, near Welshpool. There are several hill forts and ancient settlements in this area, all possible candidates. Steve Blake and Scott Lloyd have suggested the likely sounding Breidden Hill, northwest of Middletown.

This territory is in Powys, not usually associated with Arthur, but which we have repeatedly encountered in relation to Cadell. Clearly the author of *The Dream of Rhonabwy* is remembering a famous battle in that area with which he has associated the name Badon, or Caer Faddon. But whether this is Arthur's Badon is another matter. The area has been the site of several battles; perhaps the most notable was that between the combined forces of Cadwallon of Gwynedd and Penda of Mercia, against Edwin of Northumbria, at Cefyn Digoll around the year 630. Cadwallon fought a further dozen battles across the north, leading to the defeat and death of Edwin. His victories were the last glory days of the British, and could easily have been remembered five hundred years later as an Arthurian conquest. In 893, a combined force of Welsh and Saxons under Alfred the Great defeated the Danes at Buttington. Gruffydd ap Llywelyn, in 1039, defeated Leofric of Mercia at Rhyd-y-Groes. This last battle would be within three generations of the composition of *The*

Dream of Rhonabwy, and would still be remembered. The author may have chosen that site in order to compare it with an Arthurian golden age, in a location known to have seen many decisive battles.

The *Welsh Annals* refer to a second battle of Badon in 665. The exact date can be confirmed by a reference to the Saxon celebration of Easter, which arose following the Synod of Whitby, called by Oswy, king of Northumbria in 664. As ever, the entry provides little information, not even who the combatants were. It refers to the death of Morgan, but does not say who he was or whether he died in the battle. He could be Morgan ap Athrwys, the ruler of Gwent and successor to Athrwys ap Meurig. Morgan was known as a warrior king, as much for his fighting within his borders as with the Saxons, although 665 is early for his death.

The *ASC* makes no reference to a second Badon any more than it did to the first, so it was probably an all-Welsh affair. The site in *The Dream of Rhonabwy* cannot be ruled out. Bards writing a century or two later could easily have linked the site of one battle with another, for although it is described as "the second battle of Badon", we should not automatically assume the two battles are in the same place. The possibility that Morgan ap Athrwys was killed at this second Badon makes it yet another tantalising link with the Arthur of legend. Moreover, the possibility that the two Badons were at the same site and in Powys is another, equally tantalising, link to Cadell.

The bizarre dream-like quality of the story is most evident when the battle is described by characters who appear while Arthur and Owain play chess. Eventually a truce is granted for a period of a month and a fortnight. The description of the battle, such as it is, does not match that recalled by Nennius, in which Arthur's men seemed to wipe out the enemy over a period of three days. That suggests these are not the same battles, and that the author of the tale chose it because it was associated with past victories.

When considering the truce, Arthur summons his counsellors, and there follows a list of over forty names. Also present, though not listed as one of the counsellors, is Rhun, son of Maelgwyn. Rhun was the powerful king of Gwynedd who ruled from around

549 until the 580s, and therefore a contemporary of Arthur of Dyfed (rather than Arthur of Gwent). The counsellors include Bishop Bedwini and Caradog Vreichfras, both linked with Arthur of Gelliwig in the Welsh Triads, Cador of Cornwall, Gwalchmei, Gwenwynwyn and Peredur Longspear. Cei is mentioned elsewhere, but not amongst the counsellors, and Bedwyr makes no appearance. Also mentioned are Dyrstan ap Tallwch, one of the earliest appearances of Tristan, although he otherwise plays no part in this story, and Llacheu, son of Arthur, remembered as Loholt in the romances.

4. Caradog Vreichfras

This is an appropriate moment to give further thought to Arthur's advisor Caradog Vreichfras, who has a significant role in this story, and appears in other Arthurian tales.

Caradog is described as Arthur's most senior counsellor, a position which allows him to speak his mind bluntly. He is portrayed as an acerbic character, not unlike that ascribed to Cei in the romances. His epithet, *Vreichfras*, means "strong-arm". Apparently Cardog's arm was broken in battle but mended more powerful than before. In the later French romances this became *Briefbras*, derived from *Brise-bras*, for "broken arm", but thereafter translated as "short arm" or "withered arm".

Cardog is associated with both Brycheiniog and Ergyng, plus the region known as Llydaw. He is infuriatingly difficult to date, because his name is so common and his ancestry confusing. He is usually made the son of Llyr Marini, who has no historical basis. The name seems to be a later fabrication to link Caradog with the god Llyr. The same legend makes his mother a fairy.

There are at least four Caradogs who appear in the pedigrees, and to whom the epithet *vreichfras* has become attached.

1. Caradog, father of Eudaf Hen, *fl.* 320s. Eudaf was Duke of the Gewisse in Ergyng and we may deduce that this Caradog was also a "ruler" (that is Roman magistrate) of Ergyng.

2. Caradog, father of Ynyr, *fl.* 420s, a possible king of Gwent. The pedigree of Ynyr is confusing and Caradog may have been his father or his son. Hence:
3. Caradog ap Ynyr, *fl.* 470s, a king of Gwent.
4. Caradog ap Gwrgan, *fl.* 590s, ruler of Ergyng.

The latter three seem to belong to the royal family of Gwent, so may all be descended from Eudaf and the first Caradog. We cannot dismiss the possibility that because one Caradog was known to be a ruler of Ergyng, tradition has linked all the others to that territory. But Caradog was such a popular name that it may well have passed down through a family, particularly one as noted as Eudaf's, which claimed descent from the original Ceretic, or Caratacus, ruler of the Catuvellauni at the time of the Roman invasion. Caratacus fled to the Silures in Gwent to mount a defensive campaign against the Romans, before being exiled to Rome with his brother Arviragus, who returned to Britain and settled among the Silures. There is thus a case to be made that Caradog became a family name of the rulers of the Gwentian Silures throughout the period of Roman occupation.

Of particular interest are (3) and (4), as one is contemporary with Arthur of Badon, and the other was probably alive, as a senior official, during the life of Arthur of Gwent. Most legends about Vreichfras have become too wrapped up in myth to be of value as history, but there is enough in *Culhwch and Olwen* and *The Dream of Rhonabwy* to suggest that a once great warrior was now a highly respected counsellor at Arthur's court.

The idea that Caradog and Arthur became enemies has no basis in these stories, and may have arisen from two factors. Firstly, the idea that Caradog may be the same person as Cerdic of the West Saxons. This is a very tempting idea and, if we accept the *ASC*'s original dates of Cerdic arriving in 495 and succeeding to the West Saxon kingdom in 501, it would make him a contemporary of Caradog ap Ynyr. However, we have determined that Cerdic lived at least a generation later. Perhaps Cerdic was related to Caradog, possibly as a nephew. That alone may make it sufficient for Caradog to be regarded as a traitor to Arthur, but any such arrangement may have been part of various peace or land treaties.

We might even go so far as to propose that Caradog is just old enough to have been Hengist's interpreter, but that is pure conjecture.

The other reason is because Caradog has also been called a ruler of Armorica, and may have deserted Arthur to establish a new kingdom over the sea (possibly explaining the *Llyr Marini* patronym, as both names mean "of the sea"). However, as we established earlier, Caradog conquered the territory of Llydaw between Ergyng and Brycheiniog, which is also the Welsh name for Armorica, and the two have become confused.

This may provide another connection with Cerdic. Cerdic is always called the leader of the Gewisse, whilst Eudaf Hen, son of the first Caradog listed above, was also called a duke, or *dux*, of the Gewisse. Could Caradog Vreichfras have inherited the title of duke of the Gewisse and, if so, what connection does this have to Cerdic?

There may be none. The simple answer may be confusion between the words Gewisse and Guuennessi. The first means "confederates" or "allies", and is usually taken to mean an army of mixed Romano-British and Germanic warriors, who were the band of mercenaries with which Cerdic carved out his kingdom. Cerdic's grandfather (or great-grandfather) was called Gewis, and his descendants became the Gewisse, or, more accurately, the Gewissingas. *Guuennessi* means "people of Gwent", of whom Eudaf was the *dux*, or more probably governor.

The confusion arises because Geoffrey of Monmouth called Vortigern a leader of the Gewisse. We know that Vortigern was descended from the men of Gloucester and established a dynasty in Powys, but was not himself from Gwent. He could, of course, have usurped the title, which would not have been out of character, or Geoffrey could simply have been mistaken.

However, we have seen that the first Saxon "adventus", perhaps at Vortigern's request, was around the year 428. Their leader was more likely to have been someone like Gewis than Hengist who, as we explore in the next chapter, comes later. If the Saxons became Vortigern's personal army they may have been known as the Gewisse, and Vortigern as their *dux*. The question arises as to whether there is a link between the

Gewisse and the Men of Llydaw, the "host" once commanded by Eudaf Hen. If there was confusion over Eudaf as both leader of the Gewisse and the Men of Llydaw might there not have been later confusion between Caradog and Cerdic in the same roles? Perhaps the Men of Llydaw and the Gewisse combined.

Either way at some stage Cerdic took command of the Gewisse, possibly the result of a conflict between Cerdic and his "uncle" Caradog, a conflict which would have been at about the time of the battle of Camlann. Could it be that Camlann, which was an internal squabble, was really a battle for the control of an elite army (an early concept of the Round Table) which Cerdic was able to wrest away from Arthur and Caradog, and out of which he created the kingdom of Wessex?

It is a shame to let facts get in the way of a good story, and all of this is entirely speculation based on nothing more than loose connections between names. However, let me throw in one further thought to allow speculation to ferment further.

If the *ASC* story of Cerdic is correct, then his early conquests in the 530s were in Hampshire and Wiltshire, north of Southampton. However, such archaeological evidence as there is for the early settlements of the West Saxon Gewisse places them in the upper Thames valley, between Dorchester and Swindon (close to two of the suggested sites for Badon). As the Gewisse became established, their name evolved into the Hwicce, the name of the province mentioned by Nennius as the location for Badon. This territory was later lost to the Mercians, who continued to hold Hwicce in high regard. Penda made Hwicce into a sub-kingdom, a bishopric was later established here, and Offa chose it as a site for one of his palaces. There was something special to the Saxons about the Hwicce, something now forgotten, but which may have had its roots in the Gewisse, Caradog and Cerdic.

Arthur's opponent at Badon in *The Dream of Rhonabwy* is given as Osla Gyllellvawr ("Big Knife"), usually interpreted as being Hengist's son Oisc, or Oisc's son Octha. In fact, *Osla* is remarkably similar to *Esla*, the son of Gewis, and therefore Cerdic's father or grandfather. If Esla and Osla were the same man, then Arthur's battle at Badon was against Cerdic's father. It has puzzled many authorities why, if Osla was Arthur's enemy at Badon, his name occurs in the long list of Arthur's warriors in the story of *Culhwch and Olwen*. But this might be so if Osla was really Esla, commander of the Gewisse for Llydaw, turned rebel. It would explain why Cerdic was believed to come from Llydaw (Armorica), when in fact he came from Llydaw (Ergyng), and how Eudaf, Vortigern and Cerdic could all be leaders of the Gewisse. And it might also explain the obvious reverence the Mercians had for the Hwicce, the "spiritual" descendants of the original Gewisse.

Tenuous though all these connections may be, they provide food for thought both as to the location of Badon and about its participants. The Arthur portrayed in *The Dream of Rhonabwy* does not seem to be either Arthur of Dyfed or Arthur of Gwent, despite the recurrence of several familiar names. The story has taken us into new territory, Powys, and thus made connections with its rulers and history.

Let us now turn to other Welsh texts to see what they say about Arthur.

5. Llongborth

In the *Black Book of Carmarthen* is a long elegy to another hero, Geraint, titled (possibly years later) *Geraint fil Erbin*. It includes the following verses.

In Llongborth, I saw the clash of swords,
Men in terror, bloody heads,
Before Geraint the Great, his father's son.
In Llongborth I saw spurs,
And men who did not flinch from the dread of the spears,
Who drank their wine from the bright glass.
In Llongborth I saw the weapons,
Of men, and blood fast dropping,
After the war cry, a fearful return.
In Llongborth I saw Arthur's
Heroes who cut with steel.
The Emperor, ruler of our labour.
In Llongborth Geraint was slain,

Brave men from the region of Dyvnaint,
And before they were slain, they slew.

Because the poem mentions Arthur, many have assumed that he was present at the battle, and that therefore the poem must belong to the sixth century. However, other translations interpret the key verse as follows:

In Llongborth I saw Arthur,
brave men hewed with steel.
Emperor, ruler of battle.

Although the poem has been attributed variously to Taliesin and Llywarch Hen, there is no evidence as to its author and consequently we do not know when it was composed. Therefore, we do not know which Geraint the poem refers to. The genealogies of Dumnonia list two Geraints, both sons of Erbin, although in the second case the Erbin connection may be an error on the part of a copyist (*see* Table 3.10). The second Geraint lived at the end of the seventh century, and the *ASC* records that in 710 the king of Wessex, Ine, fought against Geraint, "king of the Welsh". The Saxons referred to the British of Dumnonia as the "West Welsh", and this Geraint was probably the last independent king of Dumnonia.

The reference to Arthur has caused many authorities to presume it is contemporary with the Arthurian period, and must therefore relate to Geraint ab Erbin who not only appears in *Culhwch and Olwen* and *The Dream of Rhonabwy*, but also has his own *Mabinogion* story, *Geraint and Enid* (*see* Chapter 18).

The first Geraint is known as one of the "Three Seafarers of Ynys Prydein" in the Welsh Triads. He was the uncle of St Cybi who was born around the year 485 (according to Bartrum), so Geraint may have been born in the 460s, and therefore have been a contemporary of Arthur of Badon.

The word *Llongborth* means "port of the warships", rather pertinent if Geraint was one of the three seafarers. Some have suggested Portsmouth as a likely candidate for Llongborth, with the battle taking place at Portchester, just at the head of the natural harbour. This in turn has caused some to leap at the *ASC* entry for 501, which states:

> Here Port and his two sons, Bieda and Mægla, came with two ships to Britain at the place which is called Portsmouth and killed a certain young British man – very noble.

Could Geraint be this young nobleman? Unlikely, since as a major seafarer Geraint was not likely to be young, and he could well have been in his forties by 501. We cannot be sure that the *ASC* entry is genuine. The name Port is probably a back formation from Portsmouth (called *Portus* by the Romans). This does not preclude a Saxon and two sons landing there in 501 and doing battle or, indeed, a later scribe mistaking Llongborth for Portsmouth, so the date may be correct. However, there is no philological connection between Portsmouth and Llongborth. Also, if Geraint is more closely associated with Devon or Somerset, then Portsmouth, in Hampshire, is some way out of his territory.

Another suggestion has been Langport, in Somerset. In Saxon times it was called Longport, meaning "long market"; the word *portus* meaning both a naval port and a market place. Although now many miles inland, the river valleys of the Parrett and Cary were more navigable in Saxon times. Though it remains a credible site for a battle, as it is on the western limit of Saxon expansion in the sixth century, there is no evidence of any settlement at Langport before the year 880, nor is there evidence of any port or market there in the early sixth century.

Of more interest is Llamporth, in Wales. It is on the south side of Cardigan Bay near the village of Penbryn, where, even more strikingly, are sites called *Beddgeraint* ("the grave of Geraint"), and Maesglas, formerly *Maes Galanas* ("the field of the killing"). These sites have been identified both by Baram Blackett and Alan Wilson in *Artorius Rex Discovered*, and by Steven Blake and Scott Lloyd in *Pendragon*. The site, promising because of the Geraint connection, is also a wonderful natural harbour at what is now Tresaith, and it is in Dyfed, which ties in with the many previous Dyfed seafaring connections already explored in this chapter.

The major problem is that in referring to the death of Geraint, the poem says "Brave men from the region of Dyvnaint." *Dyvnaint*, meaning "dwellers in deep valleys", was the Celtic name for *Dumnonia*, which also means "deep ones", possibly linked to tin mining. Geraint seems inextricably linked to the West Country, even to the point that his son, Cado, is recorded in the *Life* of St Carannog as ruling in Devon.

The answer is almost certainly that although Geraint was a man of Dumnonia, he served at Arthur's court in Wales, probably in Dyfed. As a naval commander, he would have had no problem sailing between Dyfed and Devon, and Geraint probably retained close links with his home. But his main service to Arthur was in Wales, and it was there that he met his death.

It still begs the question as to whether the poem relates to Geraint the seafarer or the Dumnonian Geraint of 710. There are two factors. Firstly, the *ASC* does not record Ine as killing Geraint at that battle, and the *ASC* has never shied away from declaring such outcomes. Secondly, the battle of 710 was between Geraint and the Saxons, and if the site was Llamporth in Dyfed, as the evidence suggests, then the Saxons would not have been involved. A battle at Llamporth would have to have involved Geraint the Seafarer.

Dating the battle is more problematic. For Arthur and his men to have earned a sufficient reputation, it would need to have followed on from Arthur's campaign of the 480s and 490s, and is therefore probably post-Badon. If the battle was not against the Saxons, then the *ASC* entry is no longer relevant. Rather tellingly, towards the start of the poem, Geraint is referred to as the "enemy of tyranny", suggesting that the battle may have been against a local "tyrant" – the same word used by Gildas to describe his usurper kings. One of these, Vortipor, was the ruler of Dyfed and reigned from about 515 to 540. Geraint may have fought against Vortipor early in his reign, and lost. He would have been about 50 when Vortipor became king, and about 55 at the time of the battle of Camlann. Llongborth could have happened during those five years, with Geraint supporting Arthur against the rising tyrant kings.

On this basis, conjectural though it is, the Llongborth poem does seem to support an historical Arthur of Badon.

6. What Man?

There is a poem, which survives in an incomplete form, which is usually called *Pa Gur*, after the first two words of the first line. They translate as "What man is the gatekeeper?" The question seems to be asked by Arthur himself, because the gatekeeper, Glewlwyd Mighty Grasp, responds by saying "What man asks it?" and the response is "Arthur and worthy Cei."

We might at first seem to be back in *Culhwch and Olwen*, in which Culhwch also has an altercation with Arthur's gatekeeper Glewlwyd, but in fact we are in more chilling realms. Although it is not overtly stated, Arthur seems to be knocking on the door of the Other World, seeking admittance. Along with Arthur and Cei are "the best men in the world." Glewlwyd will not admit them unless Arthur states who they are, giving Arthur the opportunity to catalogue the names of his warriors and some of their heroic deeds.

The list has some telling names and even more revealing comments. The first name listed is Mabon ap Modron. Mabon appears in both *Culhwch and Olwen* and *The Dream of Rhonabwy*, renowned as a great hunter. Here he is described as "Uther Pendragon's servant." This is one of the few Welsh texts to refer to Uther Pendragon, who is otherwise believed to be an invention of Geoffrey of Monmouth's. The name invites us to ask when *Pa Gur* was written. It appears in the thirteenth century *Black Book of Carmrathen*, but Patrick Sims-Williams believes that the poem may date from around 1100 in its final form, possibly (but only just) predating Geoffrey's *History*. The reference to Uther Pendragon may have been added later, but it is a passing mention.

It's just possible that the line "Mabon, son of Modron, Uther Pendragon's servant", is suggesting that it was Modron who was the servant. Modron was Mabon's mother, not his father, and is regarded as the original of Morgan le Fay. Mabon's father is never named, and in *Culhwch and Olwen*, Mabon is taken from his mother as a baby and spirited away. This sounds remarkably like the legend of Arthur's birth. We could consider that Uther was really Mabon's father, making Mabon a counterpart of Arthur.

Later the poem refers to Manawydan, son of Llyr: "Manawyd brought home a shattered shield from Tryfrwyd." *Tryfrwyd* is the Welsh for Tribruit, a name given in Nennius's list of Arthur's battles. The poem continues:

On the heights of Eidyn
He fought with champions.
By the hundreds they fell
To Bedwyr's four-pronged spear
On the shores of Tryfrwyd,
Fighting with Garwlwyd.

This seems to place Tryfrwyd in the north, near Edinburgh (*Eidyn*). This is confirmed by the following stanza, which also makes a further reference to Arthur.

And Llwych of the Striking Hand,
Who defended Eidyn on the borders,
Its lord sheltered them,
My nephew destroyed them,
Cei pleaded with them,
While he slew them three by three.
When Celli was lost
Savagery was experienced.
Cei pleaded with them,
While he hewed them down.
Though Arthur was but laughing,
Blood was flowing
In the hall of Awrnach
Fighting with the hag.

Since Arthur has been narrating this poem until now, it seems strange that his name appears in the third person. Patrick Sims-Williams has suggested that the original wording, *aruthur*, may mean 'terrible' or 'strange', and that the poem is saying how frighteningly Cei was laughing as he hewed them down. There is a similar scene in *Culwch and Olwen*, in which Cei fights ferociously in the halls of Awrnach. Awrnach, or Wrnach, may be modern Cardurnock in the northernmost tip of Cumbria, about thirty km west of Carlisle. It was the site of an old Roman fort, and may have remained fortified under Coel and his descendants as a defence against the Irish.

If this is Arthur narrating first hand, then the reference to his nephew suggests Mordred, who was both Arthur's nephew and his incestuous son in the legends. In this part of the poem, the nephew's actions are linked with the loss of Celli, possibly Arthur's hall at Gelliwig, and thus may well relate to Mordred's treachery – or at least that of one of Arthur's nephews.

The poem also links Cei (Kay) with Arthur's son Llacheu, saying they "used to fight battles, before the pang of livid spears." One of the later stories says that Kay murdered Loholt (Llacheu), and the line in this poem is ambiguous since it is not clear if Cei and Llacheu are fighting against a common foe, or against each other.

What we have in *Pa Gur* are tantalising comments about the Arthur of legend that suggest that something of the historical Arthur is not far beneath the surface. Its relationship with the characters and events in *Culhwch and Olwen* may suggest that the two texts had a common origin, but the degree of factual evidence behind either is difficult to confirm. Whilst *Culhwch and Olwen* seems to relate more to the Arthurs of Gwent or Dyfed, *Pa Gur*'s northern references may hint at some memory of Arthur of the Pennines.

This leads us to one of the major poems of Celtic literature.

7. Catraeth

The earliest known reference to Arthur is usually cited as appearing in a series of elegies to dead warriors, *Y Gododdin* ("The Gododdin"), which celebrates the valour and bravery of those soldiers in their ill-fated battle at Catraeth. The poem credits itself to Aneirin, a contemporary of Taliesin who lived during the late sixth century, and who is described in one of the triads as the "prince of bards."

The original oral version was probably composed soon after the battle, with a written version existing by the 630s. The oldest surviving copy is included in a collection of poetry held in the

Cardiff Public Library known as *Llyfr Aneirin* (*The Book of Aneirin*), dating from around 1250. In fact, *Y Gododdin* survives in two forms, usually referred to as the A and B texts. The A text is longer and more complete, but the B text could well be an older, more contemporary version.

Ifor Williams, writing in 1938, suggested that Catraeth is the modern-day Catterick in Yorkshire, still the generally accepted view. Once the mighty Roman fort of Cataractonium, which covered a site of eighteen acres, it would still have been impressive in the sixth century.

The Gododdin, previously known as the Votadini, once occupied the territory stretching from Edinburgh and the Lothians down to Newcastle. By the end of the sixth century, their territory was being taken over by the Angles, who had established their own kingdoms of Bernicia and Deira in the former British territories of the Southern Gododdin and York. The Battle of Catraeth is usually seen as a last ditch effort to recover lost territory after the death of Urien. Urien, king of Rheged, is sometimes called the Lord of Catraeth, and presumably had at some time taken hold of territory east of the Pennines, perhaps in the domain of one of his rivals, Morcant of the Gododdin.

The raid, which is how the battle began, was a disaster for the Gododdin. According to Aneirin, who was not only an eyewitness but was captured at Catraeth (Version A, §46; B §48), only one Briton survived the battle (though elsewhere it appears that three survived). The rest were slaughtered, though they fought valiantly. In true heroic style, the Gododdin were wildly outnumbered. One translation gives their number as 300, whilst their enemy numbered 100,000 (A §10). Both numbers are probably poetic licence, but the Angles probably still outnumbered the Gododdin by ten to one.

The reference to Arthur comes at the end of version B, when describing the heroic death of one of the warriors. Translations of this verse vary: this version is by Joseph Clancy, in *Earliest Welsh Poetry*:

> He thrust beyond three hundred, most bold, he cut down
> the centre and far wing.

He proved worthy, leading noble men; he gave from his
herd steeds for winter.
He brought black crows to a fort's wall, though he was not
Arthur.
He made his strength a refuge, the front line's bulwark,
Gwawrddur.

This reference to Arthur is usually seized on as proof that Arthur existed, and that he was probably of the Gododdin. But the poem says no such thing. Clearly, the warrior Gwawrddur is being compared to Arthur, as some great standard of heroism but, despite his valour, "he was not Arthur." This does suggest that by the 590s Arthur was already a synonym for heroism. It is not clear if Arthur is dead or still alive. Arthur could have been remembered of old, and need not have been of the Gododdin himself. The warriors had been invited from all over Britain, and Aneirin's poem would have been heard throughout the surviving British kingdoms.

Some authorities have suggested that the Arthur referred to was Artúir mac Aedan, of Dál Riata. Artúir was killed in a battle with the Mæatae, possibly in 596. There is some dispute over the precise year. John Bannerman, in *Studies in the History of Dalriada*, believes it may have been as early as 590. If Artúir mac Aedan was dead by 590, and if it is to him that the poem refers, then it would be celebrating a past and glorious hero. If Artúir were still alive, however, the poem would enhance his status, as a British poet is commemorating British heroes in a tragic defeat, and comparing their heroism with that of a living warrior. One of the main arguments against Artúir mac Aedan being the Arthur of *Y Gododdin* is that it seems unlikely that the British would want to compare one of their own heroes, Gwawrddr, with an Irish/Gaelic warrior when the Irish had been their enemy for the last two centuries. However, the pedigrees suggest that Artúir's mother, one of Aedan's three wives, was the sister of a British king. Likewise, Aedan's own mother was purportedly Luan, daughter of Brychan of Manau. If these genealogies are correct, then Artúir was three-quarters British and therefore perhaps an acceptable "British" hero.

It has been suggested that the word "Arthur" may itself be a copyist's error, and that a scribe, coming across *aruthr*, copied it, either by accident or enthusiasm, as Arthur. If this were true, then the line would mean that despite his valour and heroic deeds, Gwawrddur was not terrible. But surely his battle fury must have been terrifying to behold. Whilst there may be instances when *aruthr* mutated to Arthur, this does not seem to be one of those cases.

Elsewhere the poem contains a more telling Arthurian reference, not usually cited. Verse 19 in Version A describes the heroics of Cadwal ap Sywno:

When Cadwal charged in the green of dawn a cry went up wherever he came.
He would leave shields shattered, in splinters.
Stiff spears this splitter would slash in battle, ripping the front rank.
Sywno's son, a wizard foresaw it, sold his life to purchase a high reputation.
He cut with a keen-edged blade, he slaughtered both Athrwys and Affrei.
As agreed on, he aimed to attack: he fashioned carcasses of men brave in battle,
Charged in Gwynedd's front line.

It is tempting to think that Athrwys might be either Arthwys of the Pennines or Athrwys of Gwent. However, if this battle dates to the 590s, by then Arthur of the Pennines was long dead and Arthur of Gwent had not yet been born.

Could it be that this verse recalls an earlier battle? A study of the poem suggests that it is an amalgam of eulogies, and not necessarily solely about the heroes of Catraeth. Cadwal would seem to be a man of Gwynedd, but he is not otherwise known. Even so, the episode may refer back to some ancient conflict between the descendants of Cunedda, once settled in Gwynedd, and their continued rivalry with the sons of Coel. Urien of Rheged was also a Coeling, and there are several references in *Y Gododdin* which suggest that the Coelings had sided with the Angles in a battle against the Gododdin.

The date of the battle is uncertain, with estimates varying from the 570s to the 590s. It would seem likely, though not absolutely certain, that it happened after the death of Urien (*fl.* 530–570). We know from Nennius that he was murdered during the siege of Lindisfarne at the instigation of Morcant (§63). The Bernician king at that time was probably Theodoric, who, if we take Nennius's account at face value, ruled from 571–578. However, an ambiguity in the text suggests that Urien may have been besieging Hussa, who reigned from 584–591. Therefore, Urien was either murdered in 591 when he was in sixties, or in 578 when he was in his fifties.

Since the battle of Catraeth happened soon after then it may have been in either 579/80 or 592/3 (the poem tells us the Catraeth raid was planned for a whole year). It is usually believed that the British defeat at Catraeth allowed Hussa's successor, Athelfrith, free reign in the North, and to start his invincible campaign to massacre the British and establish what became the Northumbrian kingdom. If so, then the battle happened in about 593 and the Arthur mentioned could well have been Artúir mac Aedan, who would have been too young in the late 570s.

If Catraeth had been such a victory for the Bernician kings, it is perhaps curious that there is no record of it in the *ASC*. The entry for 593AD records that Athelfrith succeeded to the kingdom, but there is no mention of a resounding slaughter of the Gododdin. Indeed, apart from a few not entirely accurate references to Ida, Aelle, and Athelfrith's father Athelric, there is no mention of the Northumbrians at all prior to 603. It is as if nothing much happened in the north until Athelfrith, who established the English in Britain.

Bede, however, noted that "no ruler or king had subjected more land to the English race or settled it, having first exterminated or conquered the natives." Evidently Bede knew of Athelfrith's near-genocide of the British, probably including the battle of Catraeth, but the fact that he doesn't mention it causes some authorities to suspect that Catraeth is not the same as Catterick, and was not even in northern Britain. Steve Blake and Scott Lloyd, in *The Keys to Avalon*, make the case – or rather reiterate one put forward by Dr John Gwenogfryn Evans in the early

1900s – that Catraeth was on the island of Anglesey, along the shores of the Menai Straits. They base this theory on a twelfth-century poem about the wars of Rhodri ap Owain Gwynedd, which refers to the "lands of Catraeth" in connection with Rhodri's battles in western Gwynedd. It is also unlikely that the Gododdin, clearly established as from Din Eidyn (Edinburgh), should travel all the way down to Anglesey to fight at Catraeth. It is far more plausible that men from Gwynedd would travel north to meet the Gododdin at Catraeth.

As far back as 1869, John Stuart Glennie suggested that Catraeth may be the same as the old name Calathros (*Calatria* in Latin and *Galtraeth* in British). The Irish Annals refer to Calathros as adjoining Cairpre (Carriber) on the Avon, just south of Linlithgow. *Gal-traeth* means "shore of sorrow", a suitable name for a memory of slaughter. To be on the shore and adjoining Carriber, it has to be north of Linlithgow on the shores of the Forth, possibly at Carriden. This is certainly a more logical location for warriors from Din Eidyn to venture into battle, as it is only some 25 km (16m) west of Edinburgh. The site suggests it is more likely to have been a battle against either the Picts or the Scots, rather than the Angles, although the Angles had themselves sometimes combined forces with the Picts in fighting a common enemy. It is difficult to understand, however, how Urien could be lord of Catraeth at somewhere so evidently part (or once part) of Gododdin territory. Nevertheless, this area has possible Arthurian connections because Bouden (or Bowden) Hill, one of the suggested sites for Badon, is just south of Linlithgow, near Torphichen. If Badon had been fought within a few miles of Catraeth, then the comparison of a warrior with Arthur becomes all the more potent. Arthur's tenth battle, Tribruit, could also have been fought in this vicinity.

Like so much else, *Y Gododdin* presents an enigma. The weight of evidence suggests a battle in the north and that the Arthurian reference is to a northern hero. If Arthur of Badon was already entering legendary status a century after Badon, he would have been remembered right across the British kingdoms. Even so, it seems hard to imagine that the Arthurs of Llongborth and of Catraeth are one and the same, and neither would seem to be

Arthur of Dyfed or Arthur of Gwent. Perhaps Arthur of the Pennines is at last showing his hand.

The most complete translation of the poem and its variants is *The Gododdin of Aneirin* edited by John T. Koch (University of Wales Press, 1997).

---

8. The Triads

The *Trioedd Ynys Prydein* ("The Triads of the Isle of Britain") are a series of records that function as mnemonics, to assist in remembering key names or events. They are always grouped in threes, such as the "Three Fair Princes" or the "Three Frivolous Bards", and sometimes a fourth name might be added as better (or worse) than all three. Triad No. 2, for instance, lists the "Three Generous Men" of Britain – Nudd, Mordaf and Rhydderch – and then says, "And Arthur himself was more generous than the three." This reads too much like a later addition to rectify the omission of Arthur, and references such as this are of no value at all. Only those triads that incorporate Arthur within the list and say something meaningful are worthy of consideration.

The triads turn up in various sources, primarily the *Red Book of Hergest* and the *White Book of Rhydderch*, but are part of a rigid oral bardic tradition, and some may date back to the sixth century. Tradition ascribes them to various bards such as Taliesin and Myrddin, but we now have no way of knowing who first wrote what, or when. Like all oral records they are subject to change over time, with new names substituted to reflect current thinking. Their reliability, six centuries after Arthur, is suspect, but just occasionally there may be some information, as much in what they don't say as what they do.

The translation and ordering of the triads has been rationalised by the work of Dr Rachel Bromwich in *Trioedd Ynys Prydein* (1978), and most quotes from triads now follow her numbering. She lists ninety-six triads, but other incomplete lists exist in different sequences suggesting that there are more. Nevertheless, for consistency I shall follow Dr Bromwich's numbering. Of those ninety-six, about twenty-six actually mention Arthur. However, some of these, such as the "Three Knights of Arthur's Court who won the Graal", are clearly late compositions. I've selected those few which do raise points of interest.

1. Three Tribal Thrones of Britain.
   - Arthur as Chief Prince in Mynyw, and Dewi as Chief Bishop and Maelgwyn Gwynedd as Chief Elder.
   - Arthur as Chief Prince in Celliwig in Cornwall, and Bishop Bytwini as Chief Bishop and Caradawg Strong-Arm as Chief Elder.
   - Arthur as Chief Prince in Pen Rhionydd in the North and Gyrthmwl Wledig as Chief Elder and Cyndyrn Garthwys as Chief Bishop.

This tells us the three principal courts of Arthur: Mynyw (St. David's), Celliwig (here sited in Cornwall because of the translation of Cernyw), and Pen Rhionydd. This last court has caused much conjecture. Its bishop, Cyndyrn Garthwys, is St Kentigern, and the reference to the North has caused most to suppose it is near Kentigern's bishopric in Glasgow. Since his parish covered most of Strathclyde and Rheged (Kentigern was the grandson of Urien of Rheged), Pen Rhionydd could have been anywhere in what is now Cumbria and Galloway. Bromwich, in her interpretation of the triads, has suggested it is the Rhinns of Galloway.

Depending on the location of Pen Rhionydd, this triad could be an accurate record of the three Arthurs. The Chief Prince of Mynyw was Arthur of Dyfed (though it is odd to see Maelgwyn of Gwynedd there). Arthur of Gwent ruled from Celliwig, and the third could relate to Arthur of the Pennines or Artúir of Dál Riata. The clue lies in identifying Gyrthmwl Wledig.

Although he appears in *The Dream of Rhonabwy* as one of Arthur's counsellors, he is seldom referred to. He is mentioned in the "Stanzas of the Graves", described as being "a chieftain of the North" but buried at Celli Frifael, which is in the Gower Peninsula in south Wales. His name appears in another triad as one of the "Three Bull Spectres" of Britain, suggesting that he had already passed into legend, and that there was some otherworld adventure involving his ghost. The mystery is not helped by his name, which was probably a melding of *Gwyrth-Mael*, or "Miracle Prince".

Curiously, the name *Gyrthmwl* appears in a poem composed by Heledd, the sister of Cynddylan, written sometime in the mid-seventh century.

> If Gyrthmwl were a woman, she would be weak today,
> her wail would be loud:
> she is whole, but her warriors are destroyed.

Ifor Williams has interpreted *Gyrthmwl* as a place name, and in fact it's one we've already encountered as Garthmyl, in Powys, close by the Roman fort of The Gaer, near Welshpool. It is from near here that Arthur leads his army to the battle of Caer Faddon in *The Dream of Rhonabwy*. Could it be that the composer of the triad confused the name of one of Arthur's strongholds with an individual? Or, more likely, was Garthmyl named after its lord? He may have been related to the Cadellings of Powys and commanded The Gaer on behalf of Arthur.

But how does this relate to "the North" and the parish of Kentigern? In his middle years, Kentigern allegedly moved to North Wales and founded a monastery at Llanelwy, now St. Asaph, in Gwynedd. This has since been rejected as a Norman fabrication, but the triad may have been repeating that fabrication, so that even though based on a false premise, the location may still be accurate. Twenty-five kilometres to the west of St. Asaph is Penrhyn. In *The Keys to Avalon*, Steve Blake and Scott Lloyd suggest that Pen Rhionydd ("Headland of the Maidens") is related to another locale, Morfa Rhianedd ("Seastrand of the Maidens"), which runs between Llandudno and Conwy. Located here is Deganwy, one of the courts of Maelgwyn Gwynedd.

The "North" would then seem to mean North Wales. Since Deganwy was Maelgwyn's stronghold, it seems odd to place him at Mynyw and Gyrthmwl at Deganwy. However, if we think back to Gildas's commentary upon Maelgwyn, we know that he first came to the throne by murdering an uncle, repented and went into a monastery, and then returned to his murdering ways. He probably usurped Deganwy in his later years, in the 530s or 540s, after Arthur's death. Near Borth is a stretch of shore called Traeth Maelgwyn where legend has it that Maelgwyn won his kingship.

This triad may be remembering, albeit awkwardly, a period when Arthur, as High King of Wales, appointed three sub-kings to govern Wales on his behalf. Maelgwyn took the west, Caradog the south and Gyrthmwl the east and north. This arrangement may not have lasted long because another triad, about the "Three Horse Burdens" of Britain, tells how Gyrthmwl's sons avenged his death when they attacked Dinas Maelawr, in Ceredigion. This has been idenitified as the fort of Pendinas, in Aberystwyth, suggesting conflict between Maelgwyn and Gyrthmwl.

9. Three Chieftains of Arthur's Court
   - Gobrwy son of Echel Mighty-thigh
   - Cadrieth Fine-Speech son of Porthawr Gadw
   - And Fleudur Fflam.

If ever there were three forgotten Arthurian names it must be these three. No legends have grown up around them, but they also appear in *Culhwch and Olwen* and *The Dream of Rhonabwy* as counsellors at Arthur's court. Since they are otherwise unknown, in all likelihood this triad has remained true and they probably were amongst Arthur's advisors. Cadrieth was also the name of one of the survivors of Catraeth, but there is no reason to presume they are the same person.

54. Three Unrestrained Ravagings of Britain
   - When Medrawd came to Arthur's court at Celliwig in Cornwall.
   - When Arthur came to Medrawd's court.
   - When Aeddan the Wily came to the court of Rhydderch the Generous at Alclud.

It is unfortunate that the name of Medrawd's court is not given but, in any case, the triad does no more than emphasise the rivalry between Arthur and Medrawd. The third line repeats a tradition that Aedan mac Gabhran, the future king of Dál Riata, took advantage of Rhydderch of Strathclyde. The legend recounts that Aedan incited a rebellion against Rhydderch, who was forced to flee to Ireland. Rhydderch returned, however, leading to the bloody battle of Arderydd in 574 (listed in the *Welsh Annals* under 575). The battle was between Rhydderch and Gwenddoleu, a renegade chieftain operating throughout Galloway and Rheged. Aedan allied himself with Gwenddoleu, whilst Rhydderch's men formed part of a confederate army organised by Peredur of York and his brother Gwrgi. Arderydd, also known as Arthuret, was evidently one of the great showdowns in British history. Gwenddoleu was killed and, so legend has it, his bard Myrddin went mad with grief and ran wild in the Caledonian forest. Aedan fled back to Dál Riata, whilst Rhydderch regained Strathclyde and became one of the great kings of the North.

59. Three Unfortunate Counsels of Britain.
   - To give place for their horses' fore-feet on the land to Julius Caesar and the men of Rome.
   - To allow Horsa and Hengist and Rhonwen into this Island.
   - The three-fold dividing by Arthur of his men with Medrawd at Camlan.

Here there may be a hint of memory of Arthur's fatal battle at Camlann, where, perhaps, his battle tactics were flawed. There have been few references to Camlann in our trawl through fabled history, but its memory permeates the triads, which dwell on the futility of the battle. One such reference is in Triad 53, the "Three Harmful Blows" of Britain, where it says: "The blow Gwenhwyfach struck upon Gwenhwyfar: and for that cause there took place afterwards the action of the Battle of Camlan." Gwenhwyfach, wife of Mordred, and her sister Gwenhwyfar/Guenevere quarrelled while collecting nuts. One sister struck the other and, from that, enmity arose between Mordred and Arthur, leading Mordred to abduct Guenevere and claim the kingdom, and to the final battle.

65. Three Unrestricted Guests of Arthur's Court, and Three Wanderers
    - Llywarch the Old
    - Llemenig
    - Heledd

Llywarch was cousin to Urien of Rheged. The Men of the North fought amongst themselves and Llywarch found himself hounded out of Rheged and reduced to poverty with most of his sons killed. He eventually settled in Powys in the late sixth century, where he died at an advanced age, a sad and somewhat lonely man. In one of his poems, he confirms that, "They welcomed me in the taverns of Powys, paradise of Welshmen." Llemenig is a shadowy character but one who might be a prototype of Lancelot (*see* Chapter 17). Heledd was the sister of Cynddylan, king of Powys in the mid-seventh century. This seems to suggest that Arthur's court was in Powys. By the time of Llywarch, the ruler of Powys was either Brochwel of the Tusks or Cynan the Cruel. Nevertheless, the court may still have been remembered as Arthur's.

73. Three Peers of Arthur's Court.
    - Rahawd son of Morgant
    - Dalldaf son of Cunyn Cof
    - Drystan son of March

Here are two more names that have faded into obscurity. Rahawd appears in Triad 12 as one of the "Three Frivolous Bards" at Arthur's court, along with Arthur himself! He also appears as one of Arthur's counsellors in *The Dream of Rhonabwy*, but otherwise his name is not known, and may be a late Norman addition. Dalldaf is another of Arthur's courtiers who appears in *Culhwch and Olwen*. Bartrum has suggested he may be the same as Doldavius, king of Gotland, whom we shall meet in Geoffrey's *History*. Drystan is another matter, as he is the well-known figure of Tristan (*see* Chapter 13).

The majority of the triads which mention Arthur are amongst the most fanciful and least historic, suggesting that they were added later as Arthur's legend grew. Elsewhere, triads in which one might expect to find Arthur in his role as High King do not mention him.

5. Three Pillars of Battle of Britain:
   - Dunawd son of Pabo, Pillar of Britain
   - Gwallawg son of Lleenawg
   - Cynfelyn the Leprous

We have encountered the first two in the battles in the North – indeed, Gwallawg is the nephew of Arthur of the Pennines who, had he really been a major force in the North, ought to feature in at least one triad. Cynfelyn the Leprous was also related, being a distant cousin, and may have earned the honour because of an unrecorded role at Arderydd. The following triad is similar.

6. Three Bull-Protectors of Britain.
   - Cynfawr Host-Protector
   - Gwenddoleu son of Ceidiaw
   - And Urien son of Cynfarch

These are also all Men of the North. Urien and Gwenddolau we have met. Cynfawr was the brother of Cynfelyn the Leprous, and although he is otherwise all but unknown, his epithet of "Host Protector", as identified by Bartrum, is similar to the Irish title "of the hundred battles", applied to the near legendary High King Conn. This suggests that Cynfawr, and no doubt Cynfelyn, were survivors of many battles in the North.

Yet Arthur is not amongst them, and if he had been such a Protector of the North, surely he would feature somewhere. Neither does he appear in the "Three Chief Officers" of Britain (Triad 13), who are Caradawg, Cawrdaf and Owain. He is not one of the "Three Battle Horsemen" (Triad 18), who include Caradog Vreichfras, or the "Three Enemy Subduers" (Triad 19), of whom one is Drystan/Tristan. Arthur is not even one of the "Three Battle Leaders" of Britain (Triad 25), who are Selyf ap Cynan, Urien of Rheged and, surprisingly,

Addaon, the son of Taliesin, whom we met in *The Dream of Rhonabwy*.

Whenever you expect to find Arthur in a triad, he isn't there, and when he does appear, it is usually as an echo of some aspect of his legend. Rather than the triads supporting the existence of Arthur, they tend to underscore the development of the legend in later years. Only three of them tell us anything pertinent about Arthur. Triad 1 shows how his administration was divided and where his three main courts were, Triad 65 suggests that he had a court in Powys, and Triad 59 reveals how he mismanaged his tactics at Camlann.

9. The Irish Annals

The Irish Annals are considerably more extensive than the Welsh, and it is strongly suspected that some of the *Welsh Annals* were rebuilt from the Irish ones many years later. The Irish Annals have little bearing on Arthurian history. They deal primarily with Irish history, and, although they do make occasional references to significant events in Britain, they are of little help in our deliberations.

Except, that is, for the following. There are six primary Irish Annals, starting with the *Annals of Inisfallen*, which survives from the eleventh century. The others are the *Annals of Ulster*, the *Annals of Clonmacnoise*, the *Annals of Tigernach*, the *Chronicum Scotorum* and the wonderfully named *Annals of the Four Masters*. Four of these have the following entry variously dated from the year 620AD (*Four Masters*), to 625/6 (*Scotorum* and *Inisfallen*). The most complete version is that in the *Annals of Clonmacnoise* (624):

> Mongan mac Fiaghna, a well-spoken man and much given to the wooing of women, was killed by Artúir ap Bicor, a Briton, with a stone.

A brief entry, but an intriguing one, which makes the point that Artúir was a Briton (sometimes translated as a Welshman), and therefore not Irish. Mongan is an historically recognized king, so there is no reason to presume his death from Arthur's missile is fabricated. That makes this Arthur very real, but we are in the period 620–626, a hundred years later than the events of Badon and Camlann.

The tale behind this Arthur takes us to one of the more famous legendary exploits of the Irish. Perhaps the best known of all of the Irish seafarers was Brendan, also known as Bran, the founding abbot of Clonfert. Brendan lived throughout the Arthurian period, around 486–575, and became immortalised through his travels, particularly the one recorded in the ninth-century poem, *The Voyage of Bran*. This includes an episode in which Bran meets Manannan mac Lir. Manannan tells Bran that his destiny is taking him to Ireland, where he will father a son, the future hero Mongan, with the wife of the king, Fiachna. The poem includes some predictions about Mongan, including the following quatrain:

'He will be - his time will be short -
Fifty years in this world:
A dragonstone from the sea will kill him
In the fight at Senlabor.

This prophecy was, of course, compiled by the bards many years after Mongan's death, but one wonders how significant the word "dragonstone" is. Did they mean a stone of the Pendragon?

The Voyage of Bran continues:

He will be throughout long ages
An hundred years in fair kingship,
He will cut down battalions, a lasting grave -
He will redden fields, a wheel around the track.
It will be about kings with a champion
That he will be known as a valiant hero,
Into the strongholds of a land on a height
I shall send an appointed end from Islay.
High shall I place him with princes,
He will be overcome by a son of error;
Moninnan, the son of Ler,
Will be his father, his tutor.

Does the "son of error" mean that Artúir ap Bicor was illegitimate? The poem also suggests that Mongan's killer would come from Islay. A later lament on the death of Mongan, attributed to the Ulster king Becc Boirche, also says:

Cold is the wind across Islay,
Warriors of Cantire are coming,
They will commit a ruthless deed,
They will kill Mongan son of Fiachna.

Islay was part of the kingdom of Dál Riata, carved out in Argyll and Kintyre ("Cantire") by the Irish from their own kingdom of Dál Riata, in Ulster. At the time of Mongan's death in 620–626, the king of the Kintyre Dál Riata was Eochaid Buide ("the Fair"), the youngest son of Aedan mac Gabhran. Eochaid's inheritance of the kingship was foretold by St Columba, when Aedan asked the missionary which of his four sons would succeed him. Columba declared that three of them, Artúir, Eochaid Find and Domangart, would pre-decease Aedan. It was the youngest, Eochaid Buide, who would succeed.

Artúir mac Aedan's name appears in the genealogies of the *History of the Men of Scotland* and, more significantly, his death is recorded in the *Annals of Tigernach*. Tigernach was the Abbot of Clonmacnoise in Ireland who died in 1088, but it is believed that he continued a set of annals maintained at the abbey since the year 544, when it was founded. They record the deaths of Artúir and Eochaid Find in 596 in a battle against the Mæatae north of the Antonine Wall, and therefore close to the territory of the Manau Gododdin. Their main fortress was at Dunmyat, in what became Clackmannanshire. Aedan of Dál Riata was expanding his regime and encountering conflicts on all sides. Although he was victorious over the Mæatae, it was at the cost of his sons Artúir and Eochaid Find.

The campaigns of Aedan hold some other tempting morsels. Though he was king of Dál Riata in Britain, Aedan was still subject to his Irish overlord in Ulster, Baetan mac Cairill, the most powerful king in Ireland at that time, who came to power in 572 and rapidly exerted his authority over the Dál Riatan settlement in Britain. Aedan was determined to keep his independence and, in 575, met Baetan in battle at Dun Baetan in Ulster. Aedan was defeated, and forced to pay homage to Baetan at Islandmagee, near Carrickfergus. Aedan's young son Artúir was present at Dun Baetan. Laurence Gardner, in *Bloodline of the Holy Grail*, tells us that this was the second battle at Dun Baetan (*see* Chapter 7). The first, in 516, had been between Aedan's father Gabhran, who augmented his troops with those of Ambrosius Aurelianus, and Baetan's father Cairill. The result was a remarkable victory for the Scots. Gardner believes it was this battle that Gildas recalls in *De Excidio*. The 574 battle is the one recalled by Nennius, but over time memories of the two have merged.

Aedan continued to do battle against the Ulster overlord. In 577, Baetan captured the Isle of Man, but was forced to retreat the following year. Baetan died, somewhat mysteriously, in 581, and in 582 Aedan, and presumably Artúir who would now have been aged about 23, succeeded in driving the remaining Irish out of Man and taking control of the island. Aedan remained a powerful ruler in the north throughout the rest of the sixth century, but met his match in 603 when he set out to teach Athelfrith of Northumbria a lesson. He was soundly defeated at Degsastan (probably Dawston, in Liddesdale). Bede records that he "took to flight with a few survivors while almost his entire army was cut down."

If Artúir mac Aedan died in battle in the year 596, he cannot be the Artúir who killed Mongan in 620. It would, in any case, be difficult to equate Artúir's father Aedan with Bicor. The implication of the reference to Islay and Kintyre is that Artúir ap Bicor was one of the Scottish Dál Riata, but would an Irish annalist refer to him as British? By this time we are four generations removed from Fergus, whose son Domangart was also born in Ireland, so we are at best only talking of grandchildren of settlers.

However, there had been Irish settlers in Kintyre for over a hundred years before Fergus established his separate kingdom, and these settlers would have interbred, and may well have been regarded as British by the Irish. If so, then we can go no further in our quest for Artúir ap Bicor. In all probability, he was a warrior in the army of Eochaid the Fair, who had been given his name in honour of Aedan's heroic son, and who in turn had his five minutes of fame.

Is there a case for looking further? Looking back to our pedigrees, we see that the only other contemporary Artúir was Artúir ap Pedr, who lived perhaps a little too early for this event. Like a Kintyre Arthur, this Artúir was also descended from Irish settlers, but by now over eight generations, so may well have been regarded as a Briton by the Irish.

In consulting this Arthur's pedigree in *The Expulsion of the Déisi*, we find that his father's name is given as *Retheoir*, which may mean "lance-man" or "lance wielder." This form of name may also equate with Bicor, which means "good throw" or "lucky throw". Thus the apparent patronymic *Bicor* may simply have been a nickname for Arthur, who after his success in killing Mongan became known as "Arthur of the lucky shot".

We can, perhaps, play this game a little further. At the same time that Artúir ruled Dyfed, his neighbour in Ceredigion was Arthfoddw ap Boddw, whose name may also incorporate a nickname, "Arth the lucky." Could "Arth the lucky" and "Arthur the lucky shot" be the same person?

We do not know enough about either Artúir of Dyfed or Arthfoddw ap Boddw to know why either might be fighting against Mongan in Ireland, or why they should be linked with Kintyre. The coasts of both territories were subject to attacks by Irish raiders and this may have been a retaliation, but it seems unlikely. I strongly suspect that Artúir ap Bicor is a red herring, though a useful one, because it does show that the name Artúir was perhaps becoming more prevalent by the seventh century.

We have now explored the vast majority of the Welsh Arthurian tradition. There are further minor references in other poems, but they tell us no more about an historical Arthur.

What is most obvious about the Welsh tales is that they provide none of that background supplied by Nennius, and later by Geoffrey. The Welsh stories tell us nothing of the background of Vortigern and Ambrosius, and nothing significant about Arthur's campaign against the Saxons. If anything, Arthur's battles seem to be against other British or Welsh warbands.

Badon is mentioned in *The Dream of Rhonabwy*, but not in the Triads, although Camlann does feature.

Furthermore, most of the dates relating to the Welsh Arthur are in the mid to late sixth century, and only a few, such as Geraint's, relate to the time of Badon.

Almost all of the references to Arthur in the Welsh tales relate to either Arthur of Dyfed or Arthur of Gwent, with perhaps a hint of Arthur of the Pennines. Only the elegies of Llongborth and Catraeth possibly contain a distant memory of the hero of Badon. The triads add little of merit, but we may again get a hint of Arthur's courts and of his battle tactics.

Despite the wealth of material, Arthur of Badon still eludes us. But now we turn to the man who will reveal all: Geoffrey of Monmouth.

9

THE CREATION OF ARTHUR – GEOFFREY'S VERSION

1. Geoffrey of Monmouth

Geoffrey of Monmouth's *Historia Regum Britanniae* (*History of the Kings of Britain*), completed around 1138 (thus more than six centuries after Arthur's time), was the work that really created the legend, taking a character known from folk tales and turning him into Britain's greatest hero. Even now, almost nine centuries after Geoffrey's work took the Norman world by storm, questions are still asked about its authenticity. Virtually every scholar treats Geoffrey's story as a fabrication, but it is peppered with enough tantalising facts to lure the reader into believing the rest. Over three hundred years have passed since Nennius compiled his *Historia Brittonum*, and in that time Britain had changed radically. The Saxon conquerors had themselves been conquered by the Normans seventy years earlier in 1066, many becoming serfs within the growing Norman empire. The Welsh remained independent, but although not conquered by the Normans were regarded as a vassal state. The Welsh nevertheless retained a fierce national pride, particularly strong under Gruffydd ap Cynan, king of Gwynedd, the most powerful ruler in Wales. Despite being held prisoner by the Normans at Chester for over ten years, Gruffydd continued to fight, although he was soundly defeated by forces under William II in 1098, and again by Henry I in 1114. For the rest of his life, which was long, Gruffydd ap Cynan strove to establish a national Welsh identity and heritage, becoming a patron of music and the arts, and bringing order to the bardic tradition. Gruffydd had a passion for bardic stories, and there is no doubt that during these years, especially the 1120s, his court was a cauldron for the formation of the Arthurian legend.

We know little about Geoffrey's early years. He calls himself Galfridus *Monumotensis*, or "of Monmouth", which probably means he was born there. Monmouth over the centuries has been claimed by both Wales and England. It was in the old kingdom of Gwent, or more accurately Ergyng, which places Geoffrey's childhood in the area where we know from Nennius that both Vortigern and Ambrosius, and therefore possibly Arthur, lived. Geoffrey doubtless grew up with the legends as part of his childhood, and apparently sometimes called himself Arthur, which may also have been his father's name. It is probable that his parents, or at least one of them, came from Brittany and that Geoffrey may have lived there for some years. We do not know when he was born, but it was probably in the 1080s, and he and his family may have returned to England from Brittany during the reign of Henry I, who became king in 1100.

We first learn of Geoffrey as a teacher and secular canon at St. George's College, Oxford, in 1129. The university did not yet exist, but Oxford was already becoming established as a seat of learning. Geoffrey was by then of sufficient status to be a witness to a charter, so he may have been there for most of the 1120s. He remained in Oxford until 1151 when he became bishop-elect of St. Asaph's in North Wales. He was ordained at Westminster Abbey in February 1152, but probably never visited St Asaph's due to the renewed conflict between the English and Welsh under Owain Gwynedd. Owain had taken advantage of an England weakened by civil war during the reign of Stephen to establish himself as the most powerful ruler in Wales. This conflict makes it clear that Geoffrey must have been regarded as a Breton rather than Welsh by his Norman peers, who would never have put a Welshman in charge of a bishopric. Nevertheless, Geoffrey's loyalties must have been divided, and this has to be borne in mind when studying his *Historia*.

Geoffrey probably worked for much of the 1120s and into the 1130s on the *Historia*, almost a fifth of which concentrates on the life and glory of King Arthur. He published separately, in 1134 or thereabouts, the *Prophetiae Merlini* (*The Prophecies of Merlin*), later incorporated into the *Historia*, and the *Vita Merlini* (*Life of Merlin*) in about 1150 (*see* Chapter 15).

It seems strange that a book that glorifies a hero of the British – the descendants of whom were now the Welsh – should prove so popular with the Normans. Geoffrey's work could be seen as a rallying cry to the Welsh to show that they had once had a hero capable of defeating the enemy. What they did once they could do again. The need to write his *Historia* could have been spurred by Gruffydd ap Cynan's desire to develop the bardic tales. Yet the book also had a strong message for the Normans, now settled in England for nearly a century. The Norman kings were still dukes of Normandy and, in a strange parallel with Arthur, William the Conqueror had been the duke (*dux*) who had become a king. More significantly, Britain had been treated as a rich but rather backward country by the French, who had a powerful heroic history in their own tales of Charlemagne, founder of the French Empire. In giving Britain Arthur, Geoffrey created a national hero who could rank alongside Charlemagne, and in whom the Normans, as conquerors of Britain, could take equal pride. Geoffrey's book was, therefore, as much propaganda as it was history, and it is as propaganda that it must be read. Equally, while teasing the facts out of the fancy is not easy, we should not dismiss it entirely as fiction. There is a confused but genuine history hidden amidst the myth.

Geoffrey's problem lay in organising that myth into a sequential history. In effect, what he did was to take all the facts and, like pieces of a jigsaw, tried to force them together into a story. Whilst forming a continuous narrative, the historical thread became jumbled, and the events or persons contemporary with Arthur are cast back in time and disconnected from him.

But where did Geoffrey get this information? So far, we have trawled through the surviving texts and none of them provides the degree of detail that Geoffrey does, particularly about Arthur. In both Nennius and the *Welsh Annals*, the Arthurian elements seem to be tucked in as extras, and not part of the natural flow. This is one reason why Geoffrey, even during his lifetime, has been accused of inventing most of his history. William of Newburgh, a far more fastidious historian than Geoffrey, who was writing his own history of Britain in the 1190s, accused Geoffrey with typical Yorkshire bluntness of having made it all up, "either from an inordinate love of lying or for the sake of pleasing the British."

There is a wonderful fourteenth century document called the *Polychronicon*, by Ranulf Higden, which says:

> Many men wonder about this Arthur, whom Geoffrey extols so much singly, how the things that are said of him could be true, for, as Geoffrey repeats, he conquered thirty realms. If he subdued the king of France to him, and did slay Lucius the Procurator of Rome, Italy, then it is astonishing that the chronicles of Rome, of France, and of the Saxons should not have spoken of so noble a prince in their stories, which mentioned little things about men of low degree. Geoffrey says that Arthur overcame Frollo, King of France, but there is no record of such a name among men of France. Also, he says that Arthur slew Lucius Hiberius, Procurator of the city of Rome in the time of Leo the Emperor, yet according to all the stories of the Romans Lucius did not govern in that time – nor was Arthur born, nor did he live then, but in the time of Justinian, who was the fifth emperor after Leo. Geoffrey says that he has marvelled that Gildas and Bede make no mention of Arthur in their writings; however, I suppose it is rather to be marvelled that Geoffrey praises him so much, whom old authors, true and famous writers of stories, leave untouched.

Did Geoffrey make it all up?

2. Geoffrey's ancient book

It is evident from the start that Geoffrey drew upon the works of Nennius and Gildas and upon other, more traditional, sources. In his lengthy dedication to Robert, Earl of Gloucester, the illegitimate son of Henry I and a supporter of Matilda during the civil war, Geoffrey states, with regard to his research:

> At a time when I was giving a good deal of attention to such matters, Walter, Archdeacon of Oxford, a man skilled in the art of public speaking and well-informed about the history of foreign countries, presented me with a certain very ancient book written in the British language. This book, attractively composed to form a consecutive and orderly narrative, set out all the deeds of these men, from Brutus, the first King of the Britons, down to Cadwallader, the son of Cadwallo. At Walter's request I have taken the trouble to translate the book into Latin, although, indeed, I have been content with my own expressions and my own homely style and I have gathered no gaudy flowers of speech in other men's gardens.

In other words, Geoffrey freely adapted this book into his own style. But what book was it? He doesn't name it, and evidently William of Newburgh did not know of it. Some have conjectured that it was Geoffrey's own invention, presenting the story as if derived from some long-lost factual source. However, he states that the book was given to him by Walter, Archdeacon of Oxford, and Walter, who died in 1151, was still alive at the time the *Historia* was issued. If there was no such book, then Walter was in on the hoax, and we are once again dangerously close to the territory of conspiracy.

Some have suggested that Geoffrey's book was the *Ystoria Britanica* (*see* Chapter 6), which introduced the character of Arthur/Riothamus. Whilst Geoffrey may well have consulted it, it is unlikely to have been his "very ancient book", as it was written in Latin and there was no need to translate it. Others claim that Geoffrey drew upon the *Brut y Brenhined* (*Chronicle of Kings*), though all known versions of this appear to be translations of Geoffrey's own *Historia* into Welsh. In some cases the translators added their own details to the text, thus providing variants, but there is no evidence that the *Brut y Brenhined* existed before Geoffrey's *Historia*.

Another suggestion is the ancient text known as the *Brut Tysilio* (*Chronicles of Tysilio*). There has been much dispute as to when these chronicles were first written. Tysilio was a sixth-century prince of Powys, son of Brochwel of the Tusks and great-grandson of Cadell. Legend has it that Tysilio yearned for the religious life, eventually fleeing to Brittany where he established a monastery. It is possible that this story represents two different Tysilios. In any case, neither Tysilio lived into the reign of Cadwaladr whose exploits conclude the *Brut Tysilio*, causing some to conjecture that the chronicle was continued by others. The copy in Jesus College, Oxford, is from the early 1500s, and thus post-dates Geoffrey's work. Intriguingly, copies of the *Brut* – including the one at Jesus – have a colophon which says:

> I, Walter, archdeacon of Oxford, translated this book from the Welsh into Latin and, in my old age, have again translated it from the Latin into Welsh.

One might puzzle as to why Walter should do that. Perhaps he had lost the original Welsh edition; and it is possible too that the Latin version from which he translated the book back into Welsh may not have been his own, but that undertaken by Geoffrey. If this is the case, it means – unfortunately – that the *Tysilio* translated back into Welsh would be derived from Geoffrey's work rather than from the original, which has us chasing our own tails!

There are many differences between the *Brut Tysilio* and Geoffrey's *Historia*, sufficient to suggest that they may both be translations of the same earlier text, but that the *Tysilio* is more faithful to the original. The noted archaeologist Flinders Petrie satisfied himself that the *Tysilio* was authentic and not a revision or contraction of Geoffrey's *Historia*. He argued that on a few occasions Geoffrey confirms that he is adding items, but that those elements are missing from *Tysilio*, whereas one would expect some reference to them if it were a direct translation. Others have noted that the versions of names used in the *Tysilio* show a closer relationship to the Celtic original, whereas some of those in the *Historia* could easily be scribal errors. An example appears in book *iii*.17, where Geoffrey refers to "Archgallo, the brother of Gorbonianus." In *Tysilio* this name appears as "Arthal". *Archgallo* is not a Latinisation of *Arthal*, but a misreading of the script, in which the *t* would have appeared as a Celtic Ꞇ, and easily misread for the letter *c*. Such an error is unlikely to arise in reverse.

Until an earlier version of *Tysilio* is discovered we will not know. Certainly the surviving text is sufficiently close to Geoffrey's, including many of his errors, asides and comments, that it would seem to be a direct translation, augmented and corrected in the light of their own knowledge and beliefs by later scribes.

My own belief is that Geoffrey did have an ancient text to work from, but that this was a miscellany rather like Nennius's, a hotchpotch of dates and legends and anecdotes which he endeavoured to rework into a single narrative. Clearly Geoffrey had no idea who Arthur was or when his period in history fell, but that did not stop him creating both an exciting story and a wonderful piece of propaganda.

3. Geoffrey's Vortigern and Ambrosius

Geoffrey tells the story of Britain separating from the Roman Empire and being attacked by Picts and Saxons, in much the same way as Gildas and Nennius do. After the abortive appeal to Agicus (Aëtius), Guthelinus (Vitalinus), Archbishop of London, turns to Aldroenus (*Aldwr* in British), ruler of Armorica/Brittany, and offers him the kingdom of Britain. Aldroenus admits that, although he once would have been interested, the present state of Britain offers no allure. However, Aldroenus suggests that his brother Constantine should return to Britain with two thousand soldiers on the understanding that if he frees Britain of its enemies, then he should inherit the crown.

Constantine is duly made king, marries a noblewoman whom Guthelinus himself had raised, and has three sons. The oldest, Constans, is promised to the church, and Aurelius Ambrosius and Uther are handed to Guthelinus to raise. Ten years pass, presumably in peace, until Constantine is killed by a Pict. A dispute arises over who should inherit the crown because Constans is now a monk and the other two are still children "in their cradles" (*vi.7*). Vortigern, whom Geoffrey calls "leader of the Gewissei," now appears on the scene (*vi.6*). He tells Constans that he will help him become king, crowns him, and becomes his advisor. With Constans a puppet ruler, Vortigern plots to become king himself. Other contenders for the throne –

the "older leaders of the kingdom", as Geoffrey calls them – were all dead, and Constans was Vortigern's only hurdle.

Vortigern assumes control of the treasury and places his own men in the major towns, telling them that there is fear of further attack from the Danes and Saxons. He also convinces Constans that he needs a bodyguard of select Pict soldiers. Vortigern, knowing that the Picts are untrustworthy, pays them handsomely, and then states that he plans to leave Britain. The Picts don't want him to go, and to keep him they murder Constans, presenting his head to Vortigern. Vortigern feigns anguish and has the Picts executed. Amidst suspicion that he planned it all, Vortigern crowns himself king.

Let's pause there a moment and consider how all this fits together. We should have one firm starting point, the letter to Aëtius, which we have dated to between 446 and 452, probably 451. Then follows Constantine's victory over the Picts, his coronation, marriage and raising children. Geoffrey says that ten years pass, but Constans is clearly older than ten, and old enough to be a monk. If Constans is about eighteen when Vortigern insinuates his way into the royal household and brings him (briefly) to the throne, that moves us on to 469. Ambrosius is still a baby, yet the chronology derived from Gildas and Nennius has him in the prime of manhood by now. Clearly Geoffrey is in error.

In all likelihood, Geoffrey confused Guthelinus's letter to Aëtius with the original plea to the Romans in 410, when Honorius abandoned Britain to its fate. Eighteen years added to 410 is 428, quite close to Nennius's date of 425 for Vortigern's rise to power. This is more satisfactory, because it allows Guthelinus, who is regarded as Vortigern's father (according to Nennius's genealogy), to be archbishop during these years and dead by 428.

However, we have to fit another sequence into this. In 410 Guthelinus had appealed to Aldroenus, whom he describes as the fourth ruler in line from Cynan who had been granted territory in Armorica by Magnus Maximus in 383. The four kings would be Cynan, Gadeon, Saloman, and then Aldroenus. Do we know enough about these semi-legendary rulers to date their reigns? The brothers Cynan and Gadeon, sons of Eudaf, may have ruled together, and would have been in their sixties and possibly older by the early 400s. Although Alain Bouchart and Bertran d'Argentré have assigned the dates 405–412 to Saloman's reign, these dates are highly dubious. The chronology of the various rulers of Armorica is almost impossible to piece together, and the details in Table 3.10 should be regarded with some circumspection.

We do not know the ancestry of Saloman, but we do know that of Aldroenus, called Aldwr by the British. Aldwr and his brother Constantine (Custennin) were the sons of Cynfor ap Tudwal, a chieftain in southern Cornwall who lived in the mid fifth century, a good generation or two adrift from Geoffrey's timescale. Cynfor has been identified with Cunomorus, whose name is inscribed on a stone at Castle Dore near Fowey. This Cunomorus is also associated with the Tristram legend, and is sometimes identified as King Mark. However, this Cunomorus lived later, in the early sixth century. Although Cynfor himself is unlikely to have migrated to Brittany, it is entirely possible for Aldwr to have done so. His brother has been called Custennin *Fendigiad* (the "Blessed") and Custennin *Waredwr* (the "Deliverer"), and is included in the list of "The Twenty-Four Mightiest Kings". Evidently this much-praised prince succeeded his father as king in the West Country, but must have spread further afield, as his name is associated with the founding of Chepstow, Warwick and Worcester. He was probably contemporary with Arthur of Badon (*see* Table 3.10), and thus is too late to fit into Geoffrey's timescale.

Geoffrey probably latched on to the name Constantine because of the usurper emperor who ruled from 408–411, whose son Constans was indeed murdered, by his general Gerontius. So Geoffrey took the real history of Constantine III and transplanted it onto the Dumnonian prince Custennin, with the evil Vortigern taking on the role of the commander Gerontius.

If we cannot place much credence in Geoffrey's Constantine and Constans, is it any more likely that Constantine was the father of Ambrosius and Uther? We have already seen the plausibility of an Ambrosius the Elder, of whom Vortigern was afraid, and since the younger Ambrosius was, according to Geoffrey, still a baby in 428, he is clearly not the antagonist at the battle of Guoloph in 437. Therefore, in Geoffrey's world, Ambrosius the Elder would be equal to Custennin/Constantine. The association of Custennin with Chepstow and Worcester is interesting as both these towns are in the Severn Valley, in the area of Gwent and the Gewisse, and would be associated with both Ambrosius and Vortigern. Though it is almost certainly oral tradition, it places Custennin in the right location. However, this would mean that either Custennin or his father Cynfor "wore the purple", to tally with Gildas's description. Clearly Constantine III, on whom Geoffrey's Constantine is based, did wear the purple, but Gildas would have regarded him as a usurper and a tyrant, and would not have heaped praise on him as he did on Ambrosius and his father. So we cannot accuse Gildas of confusing the Constantines as Geoffrey did. Custennin/Constantine does not fall neatly into the pattern of the Ambrosii, and Geoffrey's jigsaw is simply forcing the wrong pieces together.

So far, little that Geoffrey has written holds much water, yet his date for the birth of Ambrosius, around 427/428, is ideal for the chronology that has been developing. It would make Ambrose in his thirties and forties at the height of his glories in the 460s and 470s, and he could still, although elderly, have witnessed Badon. Unfortunately, there is nothing in the way of concrete evidence to support Ambrosius's birth at that date, so we remain in the realms of conjecture.

Returning to Geoffrey's narrative – with Vortigern's rise to power the young Ambrosius and Uther are taken to Armorica where they are welcomed by King Budicius (Budic), who ensures that they are properly cared for and educated. Meanwhile, in Britain, Vortigern's treachery is discovered, and he now lives in fear, knowing that Ambrosius and Uther are alive and may yet take their revenge.

There were several rulers of Armorica called Budic, but none at this time. The earliest, the grandson of Iahann Reeth (the possible Riothamus), did not reign until around 510. The *Brut Tysilio,* however, calls the ruler Emyr Llydaw. Emyr Llydaw, was not a name but a title – Leader of the Men of Llydaw, (a territory in northern Ergyng – *see* Chapter 8).

The Celtic *Stanzas of the Graves* credit this Emyr with a son, Beidawg Rhudd, a name that could easily be construed as Budic. The original story may have meant that Ambrosius and Uther were kept safe in Llydaw in Ergyng, not in Armorica. This would tie in with Nennius's claim that the young Ambrosius was found in Gwent.

Geoffrey next announces the arrival of Hengist and Horsa with a boatload of warriors. Vortigern, who is in Canterbury, agrees to meet them. Hengist explains that it is their country's tradition to draw lots now and again, sending the surplus population to look for new lands. So they set sail, and their gods have brought them to Britain. Vortigern is disappointed that they are pagan, but willing to negotiate. He suggests that if Hengist and his men offer to help him fight the Picts, he will consider their request. Soon afterwards the Picts cross the Wall into the North Country, and the Saxons join a British army to do battle. The Saxons are so powerful that the British hardly have to fight, and the Picts are soon defeated. Impressed, Vortigern grants Hengist and his men land in Lindsey.

Hengist reminds Vortigern that there is a faction keen to make Ambrosius king, and suggests bringing reinforcements from Saxony. In return, Hengist asks for a title. Vortigern refuses, but does grant him enough land to build a settlement. In due course Hengist builds his castle at Thanceastre (*Kaercarrei* in British). The name means Castle of the Thong, because Hengist measured out the land by a long leather thong, cut from the hide of a bull. There are places called Thong in Kent and Thwing in North Yorkshire, but Hengist's settlement is unlikely to be either of these. The most likely place is Caistor near Grimsby, for which the old Saxon name was Tunne-Caistor, and which was known to be an earlier British settlement called Caeregarry. Bede refers to the town, and notes that the town's name came from the monk Tunna, who lived in the late seventh century. Near to Caistor is Horncastle (previously *Hornecaestre*), which could equally have been Geoffrey's original source. Both towns are on the edge of the Lincolnshire Wolds in the territory of Lindsey, thus supporting the idea that this was the Saxons' first settlement, and not Thanet in Kent. Lindsey, like Thanet, was an island in those days, cut off from the surrounding land by marshy fens. Several village names in Lindsey, such as Firsby, Freiston and Friesthorpe, attest to early settlement by Friesians, Hengist's kinfolk.

Geoffrey's narrative continues, telling of the arrival of reinforcements in Britain, including Hengist's daughter whom he calls Renwein. The story continues as per Nennius, with a drunken Vortigern besotted by Renwein and desiring her as a wife even though he is already married. Hengist agrees, exchanging his daughter for the territory of Thanet, allowing for a second, more plausible settlement in Thanet.

Geoffrey now recounts the visit of Germanus and Lupus to Britain (*vi.13*). We know this to have happened in 429, and it seems scarcely credible that all that Geoffrey has recounted since Vortigern seized the throne could have happened in one year. Geoffrey gives no clue as to a time span, but the implication is that Ambrosius is old enough to have become a threat, and that we must have moved on perhaps twenty to twenty-five years, taking us to 448–453. Interestingly, this is the period often attributed to Germanus's second visit to Britain, although, as we established earlier, 436 is a more likely date. This passage appears in the *Brut Tysilio* as an interpolation, which suggests its compiler did not know where to place it and just guessed, so that if Geoffrey was drawing upon *Tysilio* he perpetuated the error.

Geoffrey's narrative follows closely the story in Nennius. Under the spell of Renwein, Vortigern gives in to Hengist's demands, and Hengist is allowed to bring in further reinforcements, including his sons Octa and Ebissa, and a man called Cherdic (spelled Chledric in *Tysilio*). This sounds suspiciously like Cerdic, and it is strange that Geoffrey, Tysilio and Nennius all mention him, as he does not reappear. Later, when referring to Cerdic of Wessex, Geoffrey calls him Cheldric. It is as if Cherdic had been introduced for a future story and then forgotten about, so that when Geoffrey picks up the thread again the name has changed. It is rather too late for him to be the same Ceretic as Hengist's interpreter, since Hengist seems to have coped well enough without him for the last decade or more. The *Tysilio* refers to Octa and Ebissa as Octa (or Offa), Hengist's son, and his uncle Ossa. *Ossa* may be a confusion for Horsa, although Ossa (or *Oisc/Aesc*) was also the name of Octa's son. It is also worth noting that the Offa who was the ancestor of the East Anglian kings was a contemporary of Octa (*see* Table 3.11), and, since the area around Lindsey was where Octa first settled, they could well have been related.

The growing Saxon forces unsettle the British and Vortigern's son Vortimer rebels. Commanding the British, he succeeds in defeating the Saxons and driving them back to the coast. Geoffrey notes the same battles as listed by Nennius, on the River Derwent, at Episford and on the sea-coast, from where they took refuge on Thanet.

The Saxons eventually sail away, but leave their women and children behind. Renwein, a folkloristic image of the evil stepmother, poisons Vortimer. Vortigern is restored to the throne, and Hengist returns to Britain, now supported by 300,000 troops. Although this figure is an obvious exaggeration, it is probably indicative of an overwhelming force. Vortigern convinces his fellow earls and counts to join him in a celebration of peace with the Saxons. What follows is the account of the "Night of the Long Knives", in which Hengist's men treacherously slay the British nobility (a figure is given later of 480 leaders [*viii*.5]). Only one man apart from Vortigern survives – Eldol (or Eidiol), Count of Gloucester, who, armed only with a stake, kills seventy men and escapes to tell the tale.

This section gives us two options. On the one hand, we can presume that Hengist arrived soon after Vortigern's accession, around 428/9, the date given by Nennius. The alternative is that the first wave of Saxons was pushed back, to return in a second major *adventus* during the 440s, and that this was when Hengist arrived. For many years, this has been most historians' standard interpretation. To resolve these two theories, we need to know more about Hengist.

4. Hengist

The name Hengist appears in both the epic poem *Beowulf* and the related fragment, *The Fight at Finnesburg*. In both tales Hengist is a prince of northern Frisia, driven into exile by interdynastic rivalries, who joins an army of Half-Danes, a mercenary warband led by Hnaef. While visiting Finn, king of the East Frisians, at Finnesburg, Hnaef is killed when a fight breaks out. The rest of the *Finnesburg* poem is lost, but an aside in *Beowulf* tells us more. After Hnaef's death Hengist became leader of the Half-Danes. They were forced to winter at Finnesburg, but the following spring, fighting resumed. This time, Hengist's men were victorious and Finn was killed. We do not know for certain that Geoffrey's Hengist and the Hengist of *Beowulf* are the same, but the respective descriptions of him as "banished" and an "exile" are suggestive, and it seems somewhat beyond coincidence that there would be two princes called Hengist exiled from Frisia at the same time.

Of course, this assumes that we are speaking of a real individual recorded in contemporary documents. Since we know no more about when any of these documents was composed, other than that it would have been at least three centuries later, then Hengist could simply have been a standardized hero dropped into any story as a recognizable character. The main argument against this is that Hengist is not central to *Beowulf*, but is mentioned as an aside, giving the story the feeling of authenticity. The legend of Hengist was so well known that it is almost certainly based on fact, and there is no reason to presume that the tales relate to more than one individual.

Unfortunately, neither *Beowulf* nor the *Finnesburg* fragment provides a date for these events, and testing the chronology of the genealogies also causes a dilemma. Hengist is regarded as the ancestor of the kings not only of Kent, but also of Swabia through another son, Harthwig (or Hartwake). Dates for the Swabian rulers are as uncertain as for the early Kentish kings, but a later king of Swabia, Bertold, is assigned the dates 568–633 with some degree of certainty. He was fifth in descent from Hengist, and allowing the usual average of 25–30 years per generation gives a mid-life date for Hengist of about 460.

We can compare this to the ancestors of the Icelingas, the tribe of Angles who settled in Britain under Icel. Icel's great-great-grandfather, Wermund, and Wermund's son Offa, are remembered in the heroic poem *Widsith* and in the Danish history by Saxo Grammaticus. Describing conflict between the Angles and the Saxons, these two works place Wermund's long reign towards the end of the fourth century. This would place Icel's mid-life at about 485. The genealogies make Icel contemporary with Hengist (*see* Table 3.11), which would give Hengist a prime-of-life of around 470–500, which overlaps with the previous calculation though could place him as much as a generation later.

We can also test it against Cerdic's ancestry. Amongst Cerdic's ancestors are Freawine and his son Wig, and both also feature in the life of Wermund as told by Saxo Grammaticus. From this we may calculate Wig's mid-life at around 400. Cerdic is four generations descended from Wig, making his mid-life around 510. We know that Cerdic is at least a generation later than Hengist, giving a mid-life for Hengist of around 480.

All of these calculations, no matter how vague the data they are based on, bring us to a mid-life date for Hengist of 460–490. According to the *ASC*, he was dead by 488. It is difficult to push his life back earlier.

If this is true, then it is impossible for Hengist to be the individual whom Vortigern welcomed to Britain in 428, and more plausible for him to belong to the second *adventus* in 449. It means we do not know who met Vortigern in 428 – if that date is correct – although Table 3.11 suggests it may have been any of a half-dozen names, including Soemil (who we know from Nennius was in Britain by 450) and, more intriguingly, Cerdic's great-grandfather Gewis (*see* page 210).

We could conjecture that although Saxons had been arriving and settling throughout the first half of the fifth century, the significance of the *adventus* under Gewis was that he became integrated into the British administration under Vortigern, most likely as some sort of personal bodyguard. This could have been in 428, and would have allowed for a generation to become established by the time of the second *adventus* in the 440s. Gewis and his army may subsequently have settled in Lindsey, but it is more likely that if they did serve as Vortigern's personal army their land would initially have been near Vortigern's court, possibly in or around London or, more likely, near Powys. Intriguingly, flowing down from the Berwyn Mountains in North Powys, and joining the River Vyrnwy just a few kilometres north of the Gaer Fawr hill fort at Guilsfield, is the River Tanat. It is possible that Gewis and his family were granted land in the Valley of the Tanat, a name which became confused with Thanet when Hengist and his followers claimed land there a generation later.

Before we set the above in stone, however, we need to follow the rest of Geoffrey's narrative. After the massacre of the British nobility, the Saxons release Vortigern, but only after his total capitulation and handing over of his townships. They capture London, York, Lincoln and Winchester, ravaging the countryside as they go. Vortigern flees to Wales and summons his magicians. Calling them "magicians" suggests that Geoffrey's narrative has now turned to fantasy, and that he is in fact paving the way for the introduction of Merlin. Geoffrey is recounting the same story as told by Nennius, except that Nennius uses the phrase "wise men", sometimes translated as "wizards". This is also the point at which Nennius introduces Ambrosius Aurelianus. Since Geoffrey had already introduced Ambrosius by this point, he adapted this section to introduce Merlin.

Merlin warns Vortigern that Constantine's sons, Aurelius Ambrosius (as Geoffrey calls him) and Uther, are sailing for Britain and will land the next day. Vortigern seeks safety in his castle at Genoreu, in Ergyng, usually identified as the hillfort at Little Doward, northeast of Monmouth, and near Symonds Yat, where the tiny village of Ganarew survives today.

Ambrosius and Uther arrive, and Ambrosius is crowned king. He demands the immediate death of Vortigern, marches on Genoreu and burns down the castle. Ambrosius then turns his attention to the Saxons. Having heard tales of his bravery and prowess, the Saxons retreat beyond the Humber. Hengist is encouraged when he discovers that Ambrosius's army is only some 10,000 men compared to his 200,000. Overconfident, Hengist advances south. The first engagement, at Maisbeli, goes in favour of the British. Hengist then flees to Cunungeburg (almost certainly Conisbrough, near Doncaster) for the showdown. *Maisbeli,* which has not been satisfactorily identified, means "the field of Beli", which could indicate a site of pre-Christian worship sacred to the earlier British king Beli, or it may be a field where the Beltane festival was celebrated. A possibility is Hatfield, the old name of which was Meicen, which had been a small Celtic territory in the locality of Doncaster.

After re-establishing his base at Gloucester, Ambrosius would have led his army along Ryknild Street, the main Roman road from Gloucester towards the Humber. Following this he would have passed through Conisbrough and Hatfield, all only a few kilometres inland from the original Anglo-Saxon settlements in Lindsey.

The battle of Cunungeburg is more evenly fought, and the Saxons might have won had not a further detachment of Bretons arrived. Eldol, the survivor of the massacre of the nobles, who has been looking for an opportunity to kill Hengist, is able to capture and subsequently behead him. A tumulus at Conisbrough has long been believed to mark Hengist's grave.

Geoffrey tells us that Hengist's son Octa flees to York, where he is besieged. Realizing that resistance is futile, Octa submits. Amazingly, he is pardoned, as is his kinsman Eosa, who has fled to Alclud (Dumbarton). Ambrosius grants them "the region near Scotland" (*viii.8*), which may be intended to mean Bryneich (Bernicia).

The most interesting thing about this section is how soon Hengist is killed after the death of Vortigern. Geoffrey's narrative can often take no cognisance of passing time, but here he makes it clear that events follow rapidly one after the other. If Geoffrey's source is accurate then we have to accept either that Vortigern lived longer than previously thought, or that Hengist died earlier, and not as late as 488. I mentioned earlier that the entries between 457 and 473 seem stretched out as if trying to fill a gap, and it does seem unlikely that Hengist's campaign really lasted for twenty-five years or more. However, these entries may also be subject to the nineteen-year discrepancy described elsewhere, in which case the *ASC* entry for 473 – which may mark Hengist's last victory – should be 454. This could mean that Hengist was killed in battle some time between 455 and 460. If this is true, then we have driven a wedge between Hengist and Aesc/Octa. The entry for 488, identifying Aesc as succeeding to the kingdom of Kent, makes no reference to him succeeding Hengist, and it would explain why the subsequent ruling family of Kent were called the Oiscingas and not the Hengistingas. In effect, Hengist was not Aesc/Octa's father, and may not have been related at all.

The next few sections we can skim. They tell of Ambrosius travelling to the destroyed cities and initiating a programme of rebuilding. He organises the burial of the massacred nobles at Kaercaradduc, which Geoffrey tells us is Salisbury. Ambrosius wants a permanent memorial to these noblemen, and consults Merlin. The result may be Stonehenge, although Geoffrey does not actually call it this, referring to it instead as the Giant's Ring.

He may have confused Stonehenge with the ring of Avebury, and likewise be confusing Avebury with Amesbury. He refers to the ring being built at the site of Mount Ambrius, where the nobles had been massacred. The origin of the name for Amesbury has long been associated with Ambrosius or, according to Geoffrey, with the monk St. Ambrius. It has been suggested that Ambrosius's coronation, which Geoffrey has take place at the stone circle at Mount Ambrius, may have been at Avebury, and that this originated the legend of the Round Table.

After the ceremony, Ambrosius appoints as his bishops Samson to the see of York and Dubricius to the City of the Legions. Establishing dates for Dubricius (*Dyfrig* in British) is difficult but important, because he is closely associated with Arthur. Samson's death is recorded – surprisingly specifically, but not necessarily accurately – as 28 July 565. We know that he was a contemporary of Gildas, who died around 572, and that both Samson and Gildas were pupils of Illtud, probably in the early 500s. Illtud was also the "instructor" of King Maelgwyn whom we have dated to the same period. Dubricius, a contemporary of Illtud's, ordained Samson as bishop. Thus Dubricius has to be alive around the year 500, and could not have died in 612 as noted in the *Welsh Annals*. He is closely associated with the territory of Ergyng, and, according to the scattered facts of his life recorded in the *Book of Llandaff*, was born at Chilstone ("Child's Stone") and raised in nearby Madley, Hereford. There was once a St. Dubricius's chapel at Lower Buckenhill, near Woolhope. Five charters in the *Book of Llandaf* were purportedly witnessed by Dubricius, although these span over a century. The earliest of them, a grant of land by King Erb of Gwent at Cil Hal near Harewood End, may be accurate (if a little doctored, as Dubricius is described as an Archbishop). This could well date to around 500. Bartrum suggests that Dubricius lived from around 465 to 521, whilst Nikolai Tolstoy dates his death to 532.

These dates for Samson and Dubricius are too late for them to have been appointed archbishops by Ambrosius in around 460, which is where we currently find ourselves in Geoffrey's chronology. If there is any truth in Geoffrey's claim that Ambrosius himself appointed them, the date would have to be closer to 500. Nothing in our analysis so far allows us to accept Ambrosius as ruling as late as 500, and he may well have been dead by then. Either Dubricius or Samson lived earlier (despite most other records suggesting they lived later), or Geoffrey has slipped a cog and jumped forward in time. As we shall see in Geoffrey's next section, he has almost certainly conflated two stories from different periods, and somehow Dubricius and Samson have been pasted on to Ambrosius, though they belong to a later time.

From this point on, Geoffrey's story lapses more into legend, suggesting that he switched his research from one set of old documents to another. It is now that he sows the seeds for the creation of Arthur.

5. Uther Pendragon

According to Geoffrey, Ambrosius's kingship is short-lived. Pascent, son of Vortigern, rises up against Ambrosius, first in league with an army of Saxons and then, following his defeat, with Gillomanius, or Gillomaurius, king of Ireland. Pascent offers a fortune to anyone who will rid him of Ambrosius, and a Saxon called Eopa (or Eppa), takes on the task. Disguised as a doctor, he succeeds in gaining access to Ambrosius, who is lying ill at Winchester, and poisons him.

This version is totally adrift from that told in Nennius (§48) which states that Ambrosius was beneficent towards Pascent and made him king of Vortigern's old territory. Nor is there any indication that Ambrosius was poisoned – Gildas would certainly have known if that were true, and used it as a further argument in his attack on his contemporaries.

What's probably happened here is that Geoffrey (or Tysilio before him) has confused two Pascents. Pascent was also the name of the son of Urien of Rheged who, unlike Vortigern's son, was a surly belligerent individual, remembered in the Welsh Triads as one of the "Three Arrogant Men" of Britain. Pascent ap Urien lived at the end of the sixth century, a hundred years after Vortigern. This explains not only the sudden shift in dates, and thus in the individuals, but in the locale of Geoffrey's next chapter. Pascent almost certainly raised a mercenary army, which quite probably included Irish and Saxon troops, but whether or not he sponsored a plot to poison someone whom Geoffrey regarded as Ambrosius, we cannot say. It has all the trappings of folklore, as well as Geoffrey's evident fondness for kings being poisoned.

It is always intriguing when Geoffrey drops real names into a story, as it implies a basis of truth. The name *Eopa* (variously spelled *Eoppa*, or *Eobba*) is known in historical documents as the father of Ida, the first Angle ruler of Bernicia, and thus ties in with our shift to the north. Since Ida's reign began around 547 or later, Eopa's heyday would have been in the 520s, again too late to have killed Ambrosius, but certainly contemporary with Dubricius and Samson. We can well believe that in the days of the Angle settlement of the north, a generation or two after Octa, Ida and his father would have been involved in many battles and dark deeds, possibly even in the murder (poison or otherwise) of one of the Men of the North.

Geoffrey tells us that Ambrosius's death is marked by a comet called the "dragon star", which is interpreted by Merlin as a good omen. Ambrosius's brother Uther defeats and kills Pascent and Gillomanius. Returning to Winchester, he is appointed as successor to Ambrosius. He adopts as his emblem the sign of the dragon, fashioned in the style of the comet, and from then on is known as Uther Pendragon.

Comets were not unusual in the fifth and sixth centuries. Gary Kronk, in *Cometography* (1999), lists fifty known observations during that time, mostly by Chinese astronomers, and it is not certain how many of these were evident to observers in Britain. Those of 467 and 520 may have been. One in 530 was so bright it was called "the Firebrand" by Byzantine astronomers, and is believed to have been a visitation by what we know as Halley's Comet. Another, in 539, was so long and pointed it was nicknamed "the Swordfish". A third, in 563, appeared during a total eclipse of the sun, and thus was visible during the day. Any of these may be Geoffrey's "dragon star", though there seem to be no records of any during the 470s and 480s, which is where we should be in Geoffrey's timeline.

Following Ambrosius's death, Octa believes he is now freed from his agreement. He raises an army, including the followers of Pascent and, with Eosa, lays waste to the north of Britain. Uther catches up with him at York, but the Saxon numbers are superior and the British are driven back to seek refuge in the foothills of Mount Damen, or Dannet. The likeliest survival of that name today is Damems, part of Keighley in Airedale. Damems is about forty miles from York, and so could be a day's hard riding. However, a later variant version of the *Historia*, compiled by the Welsh monk Madoc around the year 1300, states that Mount Damen "is Wingates, above the head of Chochem", presumably Windygates Hill in Northumberland, at the headwaters of the Coquet River. This is just north of the Roman fort of Bremenium at High Rochester, a very long way from York.

Advised by Gorlois, Duke of Cornwall, Uther attacks the Saxons at night. Surprised, they are defeated, and Octa and Eosa are taken as prisoners to London. Uther then tours Scotland, inspecting the damage caused by the Saxons. It is clear that Geoffrey has slipped ahead a century, and the story he is telling has nothing to do with Ambrosius or with Octa and Eosa. He has confused Octa's and Eosa's expedition with a much later battle for the north between the British and the Saxons, during the latter half of the sixth century.

Geoffrey is usually credited with "inventing" Uther. Certainly he made a major figure out of him, just as he did of Ambrosius, The name *Uthr*, or *Uthyr Pendragon*, does appear in other sources, albeit briefly. We've encountered one in the poem *Pa Gur*, which speaks of Mabon as the "servant of Uthr Pendragon". Uther is also mentioned in one of the Welsh Triads, the "Three Great Enchantments", which he is supposed to have taught to Menw ap Teirgwaedd. Menw, who appears as a shapechanger and magician in both *Culhwch and Olwen* and *The Dream of Rhonabwy*, is one of the "Three Enchanters" of Britain (Triad 27), and is arguably the prototype for Merlin. But for Menw to have learned an enchantment from Uther (rather than the other way round), suggests that Uther was of an older generation and very possibly regarded as something of a mage in his own right. Taliesin refers to Uther's son Madog, noting that before his death Madog's fortress was one of "abundance, exploits and jests", almost like Arthur's Camelot. Madog was in turn the father of the "golden-tongued knight" Eliwlod, who in another ancient poem speaks to Arthur from the grave in the form of an eagle.

Unfortunately, no surviving pedigree links Madog or Eliwlod with Arthur, even though they were his brother and nephew respectively. It suggests that Uther > Madog > Eliwlod existed independently as part of a much older tradition, and that Arthur was later grafted onto their stories, as he was onto so many hero tales.

Madog is a common Welsh name, and several Madogs appear in legend. According to one of the pedigrees Merlin, or more properly Myrddin, was the son of Madog Morfryn, himself the son of Morydd, a brother of Arthwys of the Pennines. Madog's cousin was Eliffer of the Great Host, and the Latin for Eliffer is Ele*uther*ius. It would be easy for these early pedigrees to have become confused, and for Madog to be treated as a son of Eleutherius. Madog's position in the pedigrees is far from clear, and it's entirely possible that he was one of Eliffer's sons. Another, later pedigree of the princes of Powys (*see* Table 3.9) shows a Merin, son of Madog, who lived in the early seventh century. Geoffrey could have mis-copied *Merin* as *Merlin*.

Geoffrey may originally have got the name Uther from Maximus's son Victor. *Victor*, in the sense of "victorious", may be rendered as *uabhar*, which means "proud" in Gaelic and is related to *aruthr*, the Brythonic for "terrible", as in a conqueror or tyrant. Geoffrey may also have made the leap to *Eleutherius*, which also means "famed" or "honoured", as in victor.

Eliffer was credited in the *Black Book of Carmarthen* with having had seven sons. One of the Welsh Triads, "Three Fair Womb-Burdens", refers to the triplets born to Eliffer's wife: Gwrgi, Peredur and Arddun. Arddun (pronounced *Arth-oon*) was a girl, but a later translation of this triad, now held at Jesus College, Oxford, and quite possibly once accessible to Geoffrey, corrupts *Arddun* to Arthur. Geoffrey, ever able to make two and two equal five, no doubt discovered this identification of [Ele]Uther[ius] as the father of Arthur, and that was all he needed. In reality, Arddun (some records call her Ceindrech) was not the daughter of Eliffer (*see* Chapter 3), but of Pabo, Eliffer's uncle.

Eliffer was justly famous in his day, as were his sons Gwrgi and Peredur, whose deaths in 581 were noted in the *Welsh Annals*.

Eliffer is exactly contemporary with Dubricius and Samson, although it is unlikely their paths crossed as his domain was in York, the setting for so much of Geoffrey's narrative. Eliffer's reign, from the 530s to the 550s, would have been one constant battle against the Angles, under Eopa, and doubtless against his fellow British as each ruler sought to protect his own territory. Eliffer was, for a while, the most powerful ruler in Britain, and there is no doubt that there would have been a period during his reign when he worked through the north, quelling his rivals. He might also have become king in either 530 or 539 at the time of a comet perihelion.

Returning to Geoffrey's narrative, we now enter familiar territory. After his tour of the north, Uther returns to London, and the following year holds a celebration of his victory, inviting all his nobles. These include Gorlois of Cornwall and his beautiful wife Ygerna, or Ygraine. Uther lusts after Ygerna and, affronted, Gorlois storms away from the festivities. Uther demands an apology, and when none is forthcoming, raises an army and ravages Cornwall. Gorlois's army is too small to face Uther's. He places Ygerna in safekeeping at Tintagel Castle and seeks refuge, with his army, at the hill-fort of Dimilioc. There still is a hill-fort and territory known as Domellic to the north of St Dennis in the middle of Cornwall. Another contender is the Tregeare Rounds, formerly called Castle Dameliock, an impressive earthwork near the hamlet of Pendoggett, just six miles south-west of Tintagel.

The siege of Dimilioc is deadlocked and Uther, pining for Ygerna, seeks the aid of Merlin. Merlin agrees to change the appearance of Uther into that of Gorlois so that he can gain access to Tintagel Castle. Uther/Gorlois is welcomed by Ygerna and taken to her bed, and that night Arthur is conceived. In the meantime, Uther's men attack Dimilioc and manage to take the fort, killing Gorlois. They are perplexed when they travel to Tintagel and find a man whom they believe to be Gorlois there. Uther changes back to his own self, and returns to capture Tintagel and Ygerna. They marry and have two children, Arthur and Anna.

This whole episode appears as an aside in Geoffrey's narrative, after which he returns to the story of Octa and Eosa. It was clearly drawn from a popular folk tale about Arthur rather than from any historical source. Geoffrey's story now leaps ahead fifteen years. Anna is married to King Loth of Lodonesia, though she cannot have been more than fourteen. During these years, the soldiers who guarded Octa and Eosa set their captives free, fleeing with them to Germany. They raise an army and once more return to plunder and ravage the north. Loth is put in charge of the British forces. The war is long and protracted with no victory to either side. Uther is furious and, though now old and "half dead", reprimands his nobles and leads his forces against the Saxons who are laying waste St Albans. In the ensuing battle, the British win and Octa and Eosa are killed. The Saxons retreat to the North and continue to harry the land. They send spies to watch Uther and, discovering his water supply, they poison it, thereby killing the king and hundreds of others.

6. Enter Arthur

Geoffrey places the showdown between Uther and the Saxons at St Albans. There is no specific historical reference to a battle here in the fifth century, but as we considered earlier with Gildas's *De Excidio*, St Albans, which remained a British enclave throughout the fifth century, was right on the edge of the division created post-Badon between the British and the Saxons, so would have been subject to periodic assaults from the Saxons. According to the *ASC*, Aesc/Octa died in 512, so in theory Geoffrey's narrative has now reached this year although many of the British characters he refers to lived half-a-century or more later.

However, if we try to follow a time line for Geoffrey's narrative we find we are much earlier, around the year 485. Our last "fixed" point was the death of Hengist around 457/460, the year of Ambrosius's coronation. Ambrosius's reign must have been long enough to see the start of a rebuilding programme, but unless Geoffrey has left out other detail, it cannot be much more than a decade, and we must presume in Geoffrey's timeline that Ambrosius's reign was over by the late 460s. Uther then quells the north, captures Octa and

Eosa, and seduces Ygerna, suggesting that Arthur's birth would be around 470. The deaths of Uther and Octa, fifteen years later, must be around 485. To push them as far as 512 would mean that Ambrosius's reign lasted nearly forty years, and since Geoffrey places his birth at around 426, he would by then have been 84. Uther, who was Ambrosius's younger brother and thus probably born around 428, would be nearly sixty in 485, which fits in with the narrative. However, this date is far too early for the death of Octa, which cannot be earlier than 512, and was most probably later. It is evident that Geoffrey's narrative has now split into two overlapping timelines as he seeks to fit later events into his earlier chronology.

It is at this point (Book 9), that Geoffrey commences the story of King Arthur. This is the original story, not the legend we know from the French romances and Malory.

Geoffrey relates that with the death of Uther, the Saxons become more invasive. A new leader is appointed, Colgrin (or Colgrim), who, with his brother Baldulf, has brought more forces from Germany and is laying waste to the far north. An urgent response is required, and the nobles wish to appoint Uther's son Arthur as their new king, even though he is only fifteen. He is crowned by Archbishop Dubricius at Silchester. Arthur promptly gathers together an army and marches on the Saxons at York, where Colgrim meets him with "a vast multitude", a combined army of Saxons, Scots and Picts. Their first battle is "beside the River Douglas", and the British are victorious. Colgrim flees, and Arthur pursues him to York and lays siege to the city. We have already discussed possible sites for these battles, derived from Nennius's list. It is evident that Geoffrey believed the river Douglas was near York.

Colgrim's brother is awaiting further reinforcements from Germany under the leadership of Cheldric, but learning of Colgrim's predicament he leads his troops overnight to York. He is attacked by Cador, Duke of Cornwall, in a vicious battle in which many are killed. Baldulf disguises himself as a minstrel and manages to get into York and be reunited with his brother. Arthur learns of the arrival of Cheldric's forces, and rather than face so large an army retreats to London.

Arthur calls upon Hoel, king of Brittany, who brings an army of 15,000 warriors to Britain. Geoffrey calls Hoel the son of Arthur's sister, but he had already stated that Anna, who was younger than Arthur, was married to Loth, and certainly could not have been married previously. According to Geoffrey, Hoel's father was Budic, the king who reared Ambrosius and Uther, and no direct relation to Arthur.

The Saxons Colgrim and Baldulf do not appear in other documents, which makes one wonder where Geoffrey found the names. I am convinced that he found most of his sources from old records, and though he may have elaborated some aspects of his stories the names are almost certainly based on genuine people. The name *Colgrim*, for instance, while it does not feature in the Anglo-Saxon histories, appears on some of the coins of Athelred the Unready and Canute in the early eleventh century, and was the name of the moneyer working at the Lincoln mint. The connection with Lincoln is interesting, because of the suggested site of Arthur's battles with Colgrim. *Colgrim* is actually a Norse name and so, once again, it seems likely that Geoffrey had found the name of a Scandinavian chieftain from a later vintage, who had nothing to do with the original Angle and Saxon settlement.

There are also some parallels between Baldulf and the Norse demi-god Balder, especially in the tale from Saxo Grammaticus's *History of the Danes* about the battle between Balder and the Danish king Høther (*III.69*). One night, during a pause in a violent battle, Høther disguises himself as a minstrel to infiltrate Balder's camp, and accidentally stumbles across Balder and kills him. In Geoffrey's story, it is Baldulf who disguises himself, but Geoffrey may have drawn his tale from the same source. The name *Høther* could have been treated by Geoffrey as Arthur.

The Norwegian philologist Sophus Bugge (1833–1907) believed that some of the sources for the early Scandinavian sagas were founded on Christian and Latin tradition imported to Scandinavia from England. Therefore, it is possible that some of the sources for Saxo's *History*, though told as Danish history, could owe their sources to earlier British events. Bugge suggested that Høther, in its original spelling *Höur*, could have been corrupted into Cador, and that Cheldric, or Cheldricus, may be a corruption of the Saxon king Gelderus, who was also defeated by Høther. As we shall see, there are various episodes from the early history of the Danes that have parallels, albeit slight, with Geoffrey's account.

Arthur and Hoel advance on Kaerluideoit (*Kaer-lwyd-coed* in *Tysilio*), which was being besieged by the Saxons. Geoffrey translates this as Lincoln, but it should be read as Lichfield (*Letocetum*). Making such an error shows that Geoffrey must have been working from an old document. Arthur lifted the siege and won a resounding victory, killing over six thousand Saxons. Though the town's name is supposed to mean "grey wood" (*llywd coed*), it was long believed to mean "field of corpses" (*lic feld*), referring to an ancient battle. It was called *Licitfelda* as early as 710. In his *Natural History of Staffordshire* (1686), Robert Plot relates the name to the martyrdom of a thousand Christians here following the death of St. Alban. But the arms of Lichfield represent three slain kings on a field, and seem more appropriate to some long forgotten battle, possibly Arthur's.

The survivors flee, pursued by Arthur. The armies meet again at Caledon Wood where Arthur is able to lay siege to the Saxons. Eventually he starves them out, and agrees to grant the Saxons their lives if they return to Germany and pay tribute. The Saxons sail away but soon change their minds, sail round Britain and land at Totnes in Devon, ravaging the countryside of the southwest as far as the Severn estuary. Then they lay siege to Bath. Arthur, furious at their duplicity and swearing revenge, rushes south, leaving Hoel, who had fallen ill, at Alclud.

Geoffrey describes Arthur's preparation for the battle. Arthur dons his golden helmet with a dragon's crest, and across his shoulders is his shield Pridwen, on which is painted a likeness of the Virgin Mary. His sword is Caliburn and his lance is Ron. Dubricius says a prayer, and the battle commences. The first day is deadlocked and the Saxons retreat to a nearby hill, still confident they will win by sheer weight of numbers. The next day Arthur and his men valiantly fight their way up the hill. Again, the battle seems deadlocked until Arthur, as Geoffrey describes it, goes berserk. Drawing his sword, Arthur rushes into the thick of battle, killing men with every blow – 470 in total, Geoffrey reports. Both Colgrim and Baldulf fall in the battle. Cheldric admits defeat and retreats, pursued by Cador who captures the Saxons' ships and hunts the men down relentlessly. Although the Saxons seek safety in the Isle of Thanet, still Cador pursues them and succeeds in killing Cheldric, whereupon the remainder surrender.

Arthur, in the meantime, has hurried back to Alclud, where Hoel is being besieged by Picts and Scots. His battles rage across Scotland, even up to Moray and Loch Lomond. Gilmaurius, the king of Ireland, arrives with reinforcements for his fellow Scots, but Arthur defeats him as well. Eventually the Scots are driven to famine by Arthur's tactics and, taking pity upon them, Arthur relents and grants a pardon.

Clearly in this section, Geoffrey's description of the battle of Bath is the same as Nennius's of Badon, complete with the description of Arthur's shield with the image of the Virgin Mary. In a way that is almost convincing, Geoffrey paints a picture of Arthur defending his realm at two extremes, in the far north and in the southwest, not dissimilar to the valiant efforts of King Harold in 1066, who after defeating the Norse at Stamford Bridge, then marched south to fight the Normans at Senlac Hill.

However, it is only two days' ride from Lichfield to Wroxeter (Viriconium) and on to Welshpool, where *The Dream of Rhonabwy* places Badon at Caer Faddon. The retreat by the Saxons to "Thanet" could be to the River Tanat, just west of Breidden. It would also tie in with Clun, just south of Wroxeter and east of the river Tanat, being the Forest of Caledon.

On the map opposite I have plotted the campaigns of Ambrosius, Uther and Arthur. With Arthur, I have taken the liberty of showing his campaign where I believe Geoffrey's "ancient book" meant. If we were to believe that he went from York to Lincoln to Caledon in Scotland, and then down to Bath, it would be nonsense. But if we accept a route from the Douglas in Lancashire, on to York, down to Lichfield, then over to the Clun Forest and Caer Faddon, then there is a clear and straightforward pattern. This theory would support an Arthur based at Wroxeter, Chester or York.

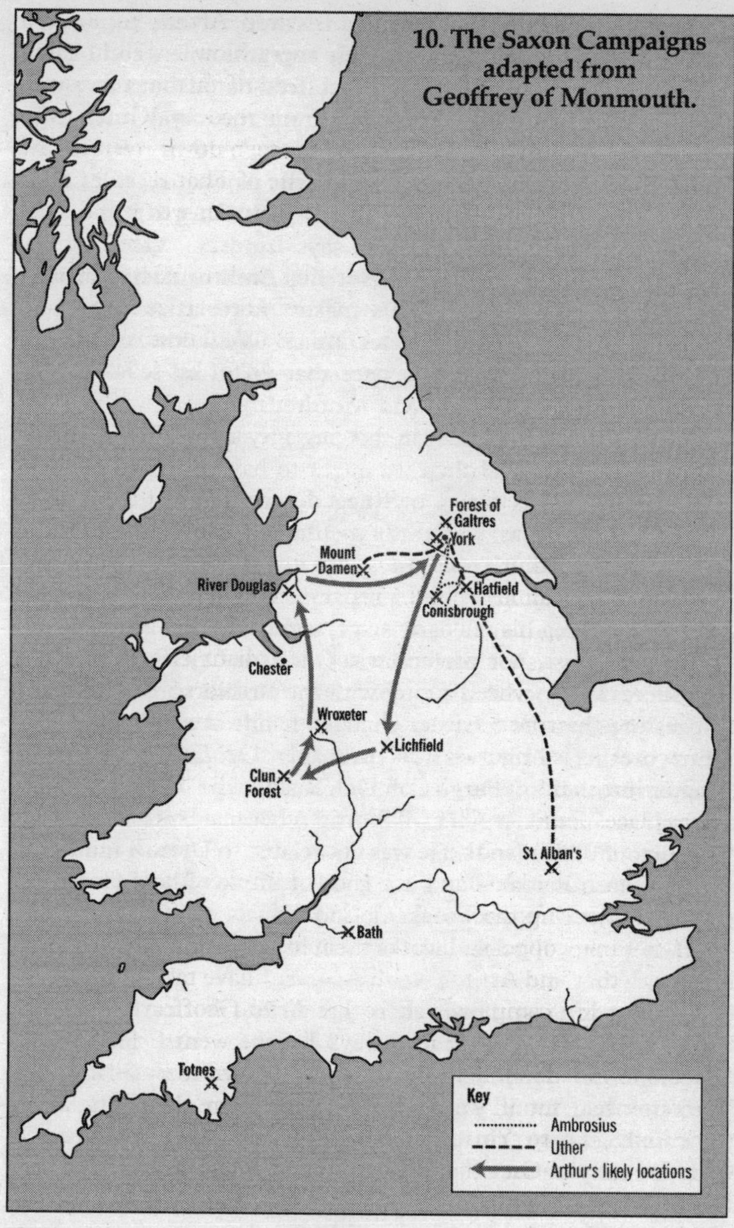
10. The Saxon Campaigns
adapted from
Geoffrey of Monmouth.
Forest of
Galtres
York
Mount
Damen
River Douglas
Hatfield
Conisbrough
Chester
Wroxeter
Lichfield
Clun
Forest
St. Alban's
Bath
Totnes
Key
Ambrosius
Uther
Arthur's likely locations

Having subjugated his enemies, Arthur returns to York to restore law and order in the city. He appoints a new archbishop, as Samson has been driven out. Geoffrey notes that there were three brothers in York descended from the royal line, Loth, Urien and Auguselus. To each of these, Arthur restores his kingdom: Auguselus (whom Tysilio calls Arawn) receives Scotland; Urien receives Murray (Tysilio says Rheged); and Loth (Llew) receives Lothian (Tysilio says Lindsey). Geoffrey also says that Loth, "in the days of Aurelius Ambrosius had married that King's own sister." This makes more sense than Loth marrying Arthur's young sister Anna. We know nothing of Ambrosius's sister, but it is here that Geoffrey says that she was the mother of Gawain and Mordred.

There is much to ponder in this passage. If the kings Geoffrey named were historical then we ought to have a record of them. The best known is Urien of Rheged, who reigned from about 570–590. Loth we have already mentioned, but it is interesting here that Tysilio makes him a ruler of Lindsey, rather than Lothian. Lindsey had been a separate kingdom but was taken over by the Saxons at an early stage, and its earliest attested ruler (if the genealogies are correct) was Crida (or Critta), in the 580s. His successors included a king with the British name Caedbaed, suggesting that the territory changed hands at some stage. The third brother, Auguselus, is probably Geoffrey's version of Angus, brother of Fergus of Dál Riata, who had established himself as ruler in Argyll in 498. Angus became chief of Islay and the surrounding islands. He was not related to Urien – indeed, he was not even British – and is a good example of how Geoffrey's *Historia*, like a sponge, soaks up individuals regardless of when and where they lived and works them into an apparently cohesive story.

Of most interest, however, is that Arthur is clearly operating from York, and York had always been the base for the *dux Britanniarum*. It is entirely possible, indeed very likely, that Geoffrey had found an ancient account of a campaign waged by a sixth century prince, still operating from York like the *dux* of old, and rallying the other princes – all of whom would have been his direct or distant cousins – against the Saxons. If this was the Arthur of the *Welsh Annals*, with the dates corrected as per

Gildas and Nennius, then we need to look for such a ruler in the period 480–500. Table 3.3 shows that at this time dominating the north were Arthwys of the Pennines and his son (some pedigrees suggest his brother) Eliffer of the Great Host. Eliffer could well have been based at York and we have also seen that his name is Latin was Eleutherius and that Geoffrey may have found a manuscript listing Eleutherius's son as Arthur. There is every possibility that Geoffrey had found a chronicle of the battles of Arthwys and Eleutherius and connected this to the works of Nennius and Gildas.

Circumstantial though this is, we nevertheless have names similar to Uther and Arthur, based in the area and period covered by Geoffrey, who were likely to have rallied fellow princes against the Saxons. Since we have also seen that Arthur could have fought at Breidden, the Caer Faddon of Welsh tradition, we may at last be seeing a pattern emerge.

Geoffrey continues by telling us that having set these matters to rights Arthur marries "the most beautiful woman in the entire island", Guenevere. According to Geoffrey, she is descended from a noble Roman family, and has been raised in the household of Cador. Cador is Arthur's half brother, son of Gorlois and Ygerna. Perhaps Guinevere had been Arthur's childhood sweetheart. Tysilio's version, however, says that it was her mother who was descended from the Roman nobility, and that her father was the hero Gogfran. Despite his hero status, we don't know much about Gogfran, or Ogrfan as he's often called. His home is variously placed at Aberysgyr (now Aberyscir), just west of Brecon or Caer Ogyrfan, the old name for Oswestry (*see* Gazetteer).

After his marriage, Arthur rebuilds his fleet and, with the coming of summer, sets off to take revenge against the Irish king Gilmaurius. Although Gilmaurius faces Arthur with a huge army, Arthur defeats him without any trouble.

Having subjugated Ireland, Arthur sails to Iceland, where he subdues the island, bringing immediate submission from the kings of "Gotland" and the Orkneys. Even assuming that Iceland was known to Irish navigators at this time, which has not been proven, it is not somewhere that Arthur or any other British ruler would be concerned with. In *Tysilio* this name is rendered as *Islont*, and it has been suggested by Peter Roberts, in his translation of Tysilio's *Chronicle*, that this means Islay, the island in the southern Hebrides ruled by the descendants of Fergus's brother Angus. It is far more likely that a sixth-century prince would be fighting the Irish Scotii in the Hebrides, and that Geoffrey is here recalling a campaign by a British warrior in the western and northern isles. It is also likely that this is where Geoffrey's "Irish" kings lived, amongst the Scotii of Kintyre.

However, it is worth noting that later, when Geoffrey lists all the notables attending Arthur's court, he refers to Malvasius, king of Iceland. *Malvasius* is Geoffrey's Latinization of Melwas, the king notorious in the Arthurian legends for the abduction of Guenevere. Melwas is usually described as the king of the Summer Country, or Somerset, but in Breton tales he was called the Lord of the Isle of Glass (Isle de Voirre), usually interpreted as Glastonbury, then an island in the Somerset marshes. Geoffrey may well have mistaken "glass" for "ice", and is really referring to Arthur's subjugation of Melwas. The story of Guenevere's abduction is not otherwise told by Geoffrey, but does appear in the *Life of Gildas*.

The use of the word *Gotland* by Geoffrey may seem strange at first. Tysilio uses Gothland, which normally means Sweden, when referring to that part of Scotland restored to Auguselus. By Geoffrey's day there had been considerable dispute between Scotland and Sweden and Norway (then one country) over ownership of the Hebrides and Orkneys. Most telling here is the story in one of the Icelandic sagas, of the ninth-century adventurer Ketil Flatnose, a Viking who had settled in the Norse kingdom of Dublin. King Olaf of Dublin, who had married Ketil's daughter, sent Ketil on a mission to rid the Hebrides of Danish pirates. Ketil was successful and set himself up as king of the Hebrides. After his death in about 870, his family left Britain and settled in Iceland. Ketil's grandson Thorstein later returned and established himself as a power in Caithness and Orkney.

However, Gotland is a corruption of Geatland. The Geats were a people of south Sweden, and were amongst those who settled in eastern England between the sixth and tenth centuries. Beowulf was king of the Geats, and it has been suggested that there may be a connection between the Geats and the later ninth-century kings of Mercia, starting with King Wiglaf in 827. Wiglaf does not fit comfortably into the genealogy of the Mercian kings, and it is possible that he was related by marriage and came from the vassal rulers of the sub-kingdom of Lindsey, in which case Geoffrey's reference to Geatland may be to the name by which Lindsey was known in the ninth and tenth centuries.

There was an earlier warlord whose battles followed this sequence. Aedan mac Gabhran, king of the Dál Riatan Scots, came to power in 574. In confirming his authority Aedan was in conflict with his Irish overlord Baetan map Cairill who defeated Aedan at Dun Baetan in that year. In 580, Aedan led a campaign to the Orkneys whose inhabitants were doubtless causing havoc around the Scottish Isles and, in 582, after Baetan's death, he conquered the Isle of Man. If we allow for Geoffrey to have confused Islay with the Isle of Man, we have both Arthur and Aedan in battle in Ireland, Man and the Orkneys. And accompanying Aedan on these campaigns would have been his son Artúir!

This northern theme continues in Geoffrey's next section. Apparently, after subjugating all the rebellious parts of Britain and Ireland, Arthur settles down to a reign of peace and harmony, a Pax Arthuriana. It is now that a code of courtliness and chivalry arises, and that Arthur's knights travel abroad, undertaking deeds of bravery. The other nations of Europe are so in awe of Arthur that they build major defences in case he should invade. Arthur reacts to this in what seems a sudden change of character. He becomes arrogant, and believes he can conquer Europe.

His first assault is on Norway. Geoffrey reveals that Loth, who is once again described as Arthur's brother-in-law, was the nephew of Sichelm, king of Norway. Sichelm had bequeathed Loth the kingdom but after Sichelm's death the Norwegians raised Riculf to the throne. Arthur invades Norway and in his usual manner sheds much blood, quells the country and is victorious. Both Norway and Denmark become subject to Arthur's growing imperial rule. Riculf is killed, and Loth becomes king.

The origins for this section of Geoffrey's narrative are not straightforward. Neither Norway nor Denmark existed as separate nations until a century or two after Arthur's day. It is possible that Geoffrey misunderstood Norway for *Norgales*, a common word in the Norman period for North Wales. But in any case, by Geoffrey's time both Norway and Denmark had proved themselves to be amongst the most powerful nations in Europe, through the domination of the Vikings. Both nations had ruled in Britain, most famously under Canute. Earlier, Alfred the Great had held on to Wessex by his fingernails when the Danes overran England, and his fight to defeat the Danes and recover his kingdom has some resonance with Arthur's story. After Alfred, England was divided for over a century with the Danes ruling half the country, and the Norse ruling, for a while, in York. Geoffrey probably knew this as history, and could have been influenced by Alfred's actions in presenting his own narrative.

There may be two other sources for this story, which Geoffrey wove together. At the time Geoffrey was writing, the Orkney Isles were still owned by Norway. In the early 980s, the earl of Orkney was Ljot, and his claim to the throne was disputed by his brother Skuli, who succeeded in raising the support of Kenneth II of Scotland. Ljot, however, won so convincingly that he laid claim to much of northern Scotland. Soon afterwards, he was killed in battle by Maelbrigte, uncle of Macbeth. Ljot's authority in northern Britain may well have echoed down the years, and Geoffrey might have linked the name with the following episode which took place in Gaul, at a time contemporary with Geoffrey's other stories of Arthur. Gregory of Tours tells the story in his *History of the Franks*, and, as he was directly involved, the story is wholly reliable. In the 570s, the Count of Tours was Leudast, the son of a slave who had risen to prominence under the patronage of the wife of Charibert, king of Paris. Leudast was a schemer, working one faction against another, but after Charibert's death he fell foul of Chilperic, king of Soissons, and was removed from office. Leudast then told Chilperic that Bishop Gregory was scheming to have the son of the late King Sigebert elevated to his former post. Chilperic saw through Leudast and had him cast into prison, but Leudast contrived with a priest called Riculf to spread stories to discredit Bishop Gregory. Leudast promised

Riculf that he would make the priest bishop in Gregory's place, but their plot was eventually uncovered after Riculf was tortured to within an inch of his life. Leudast fled, but later met his just deserts.

It is a remarkable coincidence to have both a Ljot and a Leudast (for which Geoffrey may have read Leodonus, or Loth) deprived of their titles and, in the latter story, a Riculf being promised the post of bishop. Further evidence that Geoffrey was drawing upon sources from the Frankish kingdoms comes with Arthur's next exploit.

After conquering Norway and Denmark, Arthur invades Gaul. The tribune of Gaul is Frollo, who after his defeat retreats to Paris, where Arthur lays siege. After a month, with the inhabitants starving, Frollo suggests that the outcome be decided by single combat. Frollo, a giant of a man, almost defeats Arthur, but in a final rally Arthur cleaves Frollo's skull in two.

Some have suggested that Frollo is Geoffrey's version of Rollo, the Viking adventurer who became first Duke of Normandy in 911. Rollo, or Hrólfur, was the great-great-great-grandfather of William the Conqueror. Geoffrey's picture of Gaul suggests that the territory, although technically under the sovereignty of the king of France, belonged to England by right of prior conquest. In portraying Gaul in such a way, it would be rather foolish of Geoffrey to suggest that it was conquered by defeating the same Rollo who was the ancestor of Henry I. It is also hard to believe that Geoffrey did not know that Rollo was Henry's ancestor, and he's unlikely to have adopted the name by choice.

In all likelihood, Geoffrey used the name from another source. There was a Roman family by the name of Ferreolus, who played an important role in the final days of the Empire and the development of the Frankish states. A member of this family was a tribune of Gaul in the 450s, and his son was occasionally referred to as Frolle. Frolle's son, Tonantius Ferreolus, was a patrician and three times Prefect of Gaul. Tonantius, a gifted diplomat, succeeded in gaining the support of the Visigoths in Rome's battle against the Huns. He also negotiated with the new Visigoth king, Thorismond, and saved the town of Arles from being sacked. Tonantius died in about 490, and thus was a contemporary of Clovis. Geoffrey may have chosen almost any of the Ferreoli, but the likeliest is Tonantius who, although he did not fight Thorismund in single combat, did negotiate with him one to one over a banquet, and thus lifted the siege of Arles. Geoffrey's imagination could make much of such material.

Geoffrey's narrative continues with Arthur's complete conquest of Gaul. He sends Hoel to take Poitou. Hoel is so successful that he also conquers Aquitaine and Gascony. Arthur's campaign takes nine years. He gives Neustria (Normandy) to his cupbearer Bedevere, and Anjou to his Seneschal Kay, as well as other provinces to other nobles. Satisfied, Arthur returns to Britain and decides to hold an imperial coronation at Caerleon.

The nine-year span is the first time-sensitive information Geoffrey has given since Arthur came to power. We have no clues to the time span of his original military campaign throughout Britain, or for the period when Arthur's reputation grows and the codes of chivalry are established. Logic would suggest that these must cover at least a decade, and probably two. To this we must add the nine-year Gallic campaign; thus, since Arthur was fifteen when he came to the throne, he must now be around 45, which would place us in about 515AD, according to Geoffrey's timeline.

All the great and the good attend Arthur's coronation. A few are worth mentioning here for the benefit of dating. Geoffrey lists four kings, all of whom we can date approximately. "Urian, king of Moray" is Urien of Rheged who ruled in the 570s. "Cadwallo Laurh, king of the Venedoti" is Cadwallon (Lawhir) "Long Hand" of Gwynedd, father of Maelgwyn, who ruled from about 500–534. "Stater, king of the Demetae" was more likely a title than a name. In Latin, *stator* is a magistrate's marshal. The name appears in the ancestry of Vortipor as a great-grandson of Constantine the Great, and although this pedigree is clearly confused, it would place Stater in the mid-fourth century. In *Tysilio* the name is given as Meurig, king of Dyfed, but this is clearly a late addition referring to an eleventh-century chieftain. Finally, there is "Cador, king of Cornwall" who lived in the early sixth century. Only Cador and Cadwallo are contemporaries, and fit within the time scale for Arthur that has been emerging. Also listed is Donaut map Papo (Dunod the Fat), who ruled a territory west of the Pennines in Yorkshire/Cumbria, which is now named Dent after him. He was present at the Battle of Arderydd in 573, making him a contemporary of Urien, and his death is given in the *Welsh Annals* in 595. Also named is Rhun ap Neithon, who was a prince of the Isle of Man, and lived around the 560s. Almost all of the names are of princes and nobles alive in the mid-to-late sixth century.

The celebrations last four days, and at the end Arthur receives an envoy from Lucius Hiberius, Procurator of the Republic, bearing a letter admonishing Arthur for not paying his tribute to Rome, and for attacking and claiming Roman territory in Gaul and the islands. Arthur is summoned to Rome to face a trial and due punishment. Failure to attend will lead to the invasion of his territories. Arthur refutes the demands, claiming that by the same token Rome should pay tribute to him because his forebears Constantine and Maximus had both once ruled Rome – another piece of Geoffrey's propaganda. Arthur believes it is time to teach Rome a lesson and plans to invade, amassing an army of over 180,000 troops.

When Lucius receives the answer to his letter, he determines to invade Britain and raises an army of over 400,000 troops, drawn from across the Empire.

Arthur sets off from Southampton, leaving behind Guenevere as regent and his nephew Mordred in charge of the island's defences. Upon landing in Gaul, Arthur undertakes a detour to fight a giant who is occupying the island of Mont-St-Michel and abducting maidens. Arthur soon despatches the giant and returns to the matter in hand. He encamps at Autun on the river Aube in Burgundy, and awaits Lucius's army. Arthur sends three envoys to parley with Lucius, including his nephew Gawain. Lucius's nephew Quintillanus taunts Gawain, who reacts by decapitating him. Gawain and the envoys are chased back to their army, though not before they have killed many of the Romans. A battle ensues and is described in immense detail, running to over twenty pages. Arthur is of course victorious, but at a cost. Amongst the casualties are Bedivere and Kay. Lucius Hiberius is also killed.

Who was Lucius? Although introduced as the Procurator of Rome, he is later identified as both the Emperor (*x.4*), and also simply as a general. Elsewhere, Lucius considers whether to wait for reinforcements from "the Emperor Leo" (*x.6*). As Geoffrey Ashe has analysed in *The Discovery of King Arthur*, only one Emperor Leo adequately fits this role, and this was Leo I, who was Emperor of the East in Constantinople, from 457 to 474. At that time the Empire in the West was in turmoil, with a succession of puppet emperors. One of these was Glycerius, who Ashe suspects may be Geoffrey's Lucius. He was emperor for little more than a year in 473/4.

Another suggestion is that Lucius is the Frankish king Clovis. Clovis succeeded his father as chief of the Salian Franks in 481, when he was only fifteen (the age that Arthur was). His rise to fame came in 486 when he defeated Syagrius, the Roman ruler of Northern Gaul and son of Aegidius. Over the next nine years (the same period as Arthur's campaign), Clovis pushed his authority south. His campaign to the west in Armorica was far more difficult, but he steadily extended his empire. In 507, the Eastern Emperor Anastasius elevated Clovis to the rank of consul, and in 509 he was declared sole ruler of the Franks. But his efforts had exhausted him and he died in 511, aged only 45. Clovis seems an ideal candidate for the source of Geoffrey's writings about Arthur. Much of what Arthur achieved seems to be modelled on Clovis's own campaigns, and his dates are almost identical to those that we have identified for Arthur. It is surprising, too, that Geoffrey should have Arthur fighting in Gaul and yet not encounter Clovis. One could argue that the name *Clovis*, an early form of *Louis*, could be mutated into *Lucius*, and that Arthur was fighting Clovis in his role as consul (*read* procurator) of Gaul.

This whole episode of Arthur's venture into France has to be seen in the light of events in Geoffrey's own lifetime. Henry I, youngest son of William the Conqueror, had grabbed the crown of England in 1100 while his brother Robert, the rightful heir, was involved in the Crusades. On his return in 1101, Robert invaded England, but Henry bought him off. Robert retained the duchy of Normandy, but Henry kept the kingship. Five years later, Henry invaded Normandy, captured and imprisoned Robert, and regained control of his father's lands. At the same time, Henry was in conflict with the Pope. Henry had appointed as archbishop of Canterbury the strong-willed Anselm, and Anselm was determined that only he, through papal authority, should be allowed to appoint bishops and other clergy. Henry disagreed. In 1103 Anselm went into self-imposed exile, and Pope Paschal II wrote to threaten Henry with excommunication. This communication from the Pope was similar to the letter received from Rome by Arthur. Henry eventually recalled Anselm, and reached a compromise whereby Anselm could appoint the bishops, but Henry retained authority over church lands. Meanwhile, Henry's campaign in France continued for over ten years, a combination of diplomacy and warfare culminating in the defeat of Louis VI (another suitable Lucius) in 1119. Through various marriages and alliances, Henry succeeded in controlling not only Normandy, but also Anjou and Maine.

In telling of Arthur's conquest of France, Geoffrey was finding precedents for Henry's position, and comparing Henry's achievements with those of Britain's greatest hero. There are even some parallels with Henry's final years and the breakdown of the world he had fought so hard to establish, but clearly this was an area in which Geoffrey would tread cautiously. It is perhaps pertinent that Geoffrey's work was not issued until after Henry's death, thus he was able to glorify Henry's reign whilst recognising the perils of kingship. Remember that the book was dedicated to Henry's eldest illegitimate son, Robert, Earl of Gloucester, and appeared in an England once again riven by civil war.

After defeating Lucius, Geoffrey tells us, Arthur winters in Gaul, preparing to march across the Alps into Rome the following summer. At this point, however, he receives news that Mordred has seized the crown and is living adulterously with Guenevere. Arthur entrusts Hoel with continuing his campaign against Rome, and returns to Britain, landing at Richborough. Mordred has entered into an alliance with the Saxon Chelric, promising him all the land between the Humber and Scotland, as well as Kent. He has also joined forces with the Picts and the Scots, and a confederate army of 80,000 troops advances to meet Arthur. It is a bloody battle and Gawain and Auguselus die, but Arthur's army is able to push back Mordred – or the "Perjurer", as Geoffrey calls him. Mordred retreats to Winchester. Guenevere, fearing the worst, flees from York to the City of the Legions (the *Tysilio* specifically says Caerleon), and withdraws to a nunnery.

Arthur marches to Winchester, and a second bloody battle ensues. Mordred loses the most men, and flees by ship to Cornwall. Arthur follows, and a third and final battle takes place at the "River Camblam" (*Camlan* in the *Tysilio*). Mordred is killed in the first onslaught, but the battle continues. Arthur, we are told, is mortally wounded and taken to the Isle of Avalon. He hands the crown over to Constantine, son of Cador. Avalon is usually identified with Glastonbury in Somerset, which was supposedly known as the Isle of Apples, or Ynys Afallach (*see* Gazetteer).

The final days of Arthur have their prototype in Henry I's last days. Henry had lost all male heirs to the throne. His second marriage was childless and he pinned his hopes on his daughter Matilda, but conflict erupted between Henry and Matilda's estranged husband Geoffrey of Anjou – a suitable Mordred in the eyes of the English nobles. Henry died before the war began, and the scene was set for civil war.

Mordred has since passed into legend as Arthur's nemesis. We will meet him again as Arthur's incestuous son, but that is the stuff of later tales and not the story as told by Geoffrey. The Welsh form of Mordred is *Medrod*, and intriguingly only one person by that name appears in the pedigrees accumulated by P.C. Bartrum in *Early Welsh Genealogical Tracts*. This is Medrawt ap Cawrdaf, grandson of Arthur's counsellor Caradog Vreichfras, and a contemporary of Athrwys of Gwent (*see* Table 3.7). We do not know whether Athrwys inherited the Gwentian throne, since he does not seem to have survived his father. It is possible that he was made a sub-king of Ergyng during his father's long reign, perhaps because Medrawt was too young to inherit, or perhaps because of a military necessity during the growing campaigns of the Saxons after their success at Dyrham in 577. If so, it is possible that once Medrawt reached maturity he might have sought to claim his patrimony, or, as implied in the Triads, a minor quarrel became a battle. Medrawt may well have killed Athrwys, which is why he did not become king.

Remarkably, Geoffrey provides a date for Arthur's passing:

"This in the year 542 after our Lord's incarnation." Geoffrey can only have calculated that date from the *Welsh Annals*, in which the battle of Camlann is given as year *xciii* (93), and which we have refined to 539. However, we now believe that date to be at least nineteen years out, and that it should be closer to 520. Earlier, we established that Arthur's coronation took place around 515, according to Geoffrey's timeline, and the Gallic/Roman campaign took at least two years, which brings as surprisingly close to 520. For all its vagueness and unlikelihood, there is a bizarre internal logic to Geoffrey's timeline that has taken us from the departure of the Romans in 410 to the fall of Arthur in 520. This suggests that Geoffrey must have been following a set of annals, perhaps a more complete version of the *Annales Cambriae*, which was subsequently lost.

Geoffrey tells us that Constantine continued in conflict with the sons of Mordred, who still headed a Saxon army. After a "long series of battles" the sons fled, one to London and one to Winchester, taking over those cities. Constantine regained the cities and killed Mordred's sons, both within churches. This was the sacrilege that Gildas recorded. Geoffrey cites this as happening around the time of the death of the saintly Daniel, bishop of Bangor, but his death is recorded in the *Annals* as *cxl*, or 586. Either Geoffrey misread the *Annals*, or he is referring to a possible later translation of Daniel's bones, though no other source refers to this.

Geoffrey states that Constantine died four years later, "struck down by the vengeance of God". The *Brut Tysilio* is far more specific and says that "in the third year of his reign Constantine himself was killed by Cynan Wledig." Geoffrey identifies this Cynan as Aurelius Conanus, another of the "whelps" whom Gildas decries. Geoffrey calls him Constantine's nephew, and states that Cynan killed another uncle who should have succeeded Constantine. The *Tysilio*, on the other hand, does not state that Constantine and Cynan are related, but agrees that Cynan/Conanus did kill an uncle and his two sons, who had a prior claim to the throne. Gildas called Conanus a parricide, so it is possible that he wiped out his father, his uncle(s) and his cousins. The *Tysilio* calls him "a young man, whose abilities were equal to the station, for he was prompt and spirited in war." However, his reign was brief and according to Geoffrey he died in the third year of his reign, or the second year, according to the *Tysilio*.

The next ruler was Vortiporius. He faced another onslaught of Saxons, whom he was able to defeat, and took control "of the entire kingdom." Geoffrey gives no length for his reign, but the *Tysilio* states four years.

Then came Malgo, or Maelgwyn Gwynedd. Geoffrey is generally full of praise for Maelgwyn, calling him "most handsome of all the leaders of Britain", who "strove hard to do away with those who ruled the people harshly." He was brave, generous and courageous, and became ruler of not only all of Britain, but also Ireland, Iceland, Gotland, Orkney, Norway and Denmark. However, he was "given to the vice of homosexuality." Geoffrey does not record Maelgwyn's fate, although the *Tysilio* does refer to him having died in a convent after seeing "the yellow spectre", or the plague. Unfortunately, neither source records the length of Maelgwyn's reign. After Maelgwyn, Geoffrey follows a catalogue of kings who sink into submission to the Saxons up to the death of Cadwaladr in the year 689, well beyond our period of interest.

We saw earlier that the end of Maelgwyn's reign is usually equated to the plague recorded in the *Welsh Annals* as occurring in the year 549. The length of his reign is uncertain, but it is commonly given as about fifteen years, starting in 534. Combining the data from Geoffrey and the *Tysilio*, the total span for the reigns of Constantine, Cynan and Vortiporius is about ten years, possibly more as Geoffrey does not state how long the battles with the sons of Mordred lasted. But ten to twelve years would seem about right overall. Previously we had reached the year 519/520 in Geoffrey's timeline, and the addition of ten to twelve years brings us to 529/532, certainly close enough to an uncertain 534 to link in with Maelgwyn's accession.

It is possible to recreate Geoffrey's internal chronology, adjusting his year of 542 by the nineteen-year discrepancy in the *Annals*. The result, like the ones extracted from Nennius, Gildas and the *ASC*, is not necessarily any more accurate, but it is one worth reviewing.

Table 9.1 An Arthurian chronology according to Geoffrey

410	End of Roman authority; appeal to Aldroenus; Constantine heads army; defeats Picts; made king.
410–426	Reign of Constantine. He marries and has three children: Constans (410), Ambrosius (425) and Uther (426).
426	Constantine dies; Constans made king under Vortigern's control.
428	Constans murdered; Vortigern king. Ambrosius and Uther smuggled to Brittany [Llydaw]. Arrival of Saxons [Gewis?].
428–440	Build up of Saxons, including arrival of Reinwen who marries Vortigern. Visit of Germanus and Lupus.
440s	Saxon wars. Vortimer deposes Vortigern and drives back Saxons.
449–455	Vortimer killed; Vortigern restored; return of Hengist. Massacre of nobles. Vortigern flees.
455–457	Ambrosius arrives; defeats and kills Vortigern. Made king. Defeats Hengist.
457–460	Rebuilding programme.
Late 460s	Ambrosius killed; Uther quells north. Octa and Eossa imprisoned.
c470	Birth of Arthur.
485–494	Uther poisoned; Arthur crowned. Octa and Eosa escape and are killed. Period of Arthur's battles.
495–506	Arthur's peaceful reign and rise of chivalry.
506–515	Arthur's Gallic campaign, culminating in imperial coronation.
516–520	Arthur's second Gallic campaign and march on Rome; Mordred's treachery; Arthur's return and fall at the battle of Camlann.
523	Death of Arthur in Avalon.
520–532	Reigns of Constantine, Cynan and Vortipor.

This timeline relates only to Geoffrey's narrative chronology and, of course, takes no account of individuals mentioned who existed at other times. The main difference between this chronology and the previous summary in Table 6.2 is the appearance of Uther. Geoffrey has Ambrosius killed after a short reign, whereas the assumption from the writings of Gildas and Nennius is that Ambrosius was the main British opponent to the Saxons during the 460s and 470s. Geoffrey also gives an earlier death for Hengist – indeed, his date for the death of Octa coincides with the *ASC*'s suggested date of 488 for Hengist's passing.

Whichever way we look at it, albeit from very shaky sources, Arthur's reign fits into the period 490–520. That does not mean that all of the events attributed to Arthur also have to fit into that period. Geoffrey's whole story from Vortigern to Arthur is clearly culled from a host of fragments and incidental sources which Geoffrey, in his desire to create a powerful narrative and a propaganda tool, together with his general misunderstanding of events, chose to piece together in a sequence that suited his purpose. In so doing he created the story of Arthur, and whilst we should not immediately dismiss everything that he says, because it does have a frustrating internal logic, neither should we accept anything. We must, however, admire Geoffrey's skill and imagination in creating a legend that has lasted a thousand years.

6. Conclusion

Geoffrey has clearly used six or seven different narrative sources, which he has interspersed with elements from Gildas, Nennius and the *Welsh Annals*.

(1) A chronicle, perhaps from Brittany, which traces the immediate post-Roman period, including the stories of Constantine and Ambrosius.
(2) A Welsh chronicle (linked with Nennius) for the story of Vortigern.
(3) A chronicle, also probably Breton, which is the story of Uther. This may be the same as (1).
(4) A northern chronicle of the sixth or seventh century, which traces the war between the Men of the North and the Saxons in the period 550–600. This may be the same one that Nennius knew and could have been written by Rhun ap Urien.
(5) Another northern chronicle (or the same as (4)) tracing the Viking invasion of Britain in the eighth and ninth centuries.
(6) A Gallic or Breton chronicle about the campaigns of Clovis and the Franks.
(7) A further chronicle, probably Welsh, which traces the battles between Arthur and Mordred.

Any of the above may not necessarily be a single or even a lengthy document. More likely they are fragments, perhaps of poems, annals and folktales. It is evident from the flow of Geoffrey's narrative that he was joining together accounts which he interpreted as relating to Arthur, but not necessarily the same Arthur. He also developed parallels with the reign of Henry I.

What seems evident from Geoffrey's account is that, despite his almost seamless narrative, the Arthur who fights the battles in the north is not the same Arthur who fights in Gaul, and neither is necessarily the Arthur who is the son of Uther and who meets his fate at Camlann. This suggests three, possibly four, prototypes for Arthur.

(1) An Arthur who was descended from the daughter or wife of Emyr Llydaw in Gwent (Llydaw being mistaken for Brittany), who lived in the late fifth century. This could have been the seventh century Arthur of Gwent by name but not necessarily by reputation as Geoffrey makes no reference to the Welsh tradition after Vortigern.
(2) An Arthur whose name was miscopied from Arddun, the child of Elifer (Eleutherius) of the North, and who lived in the mid sixth century. This name may subsequently have become fused with Elifer's father Arthwys (Arthur of the Pennines).
(3) Clovis, the king of the Franks, whose life parallels Arthur's.
(4) A later hero who fought the Viking invaders in the eighth and ninth centuries. The obvious contenders for this are Alfred the Great and Athelstan, whose battles against the Vikings have some similarity to Arthur's.

Since the crucial element is who Geoffrey believed fought at Badon, I suspect he found this in his Northern Chronicle, which he tried to blend with the elements in Nennius and Gildas. If it were ever possible to prove that either Arthwys ap Mar or Elifer fought at Lichfield and Caer Faddon, then we would have found Geoffrey's Arthur.

10

THE REAL KING ARTHUR – THE TWENTY CLAIMANTS

1. The Ground Rules

We have now covered all of the surviving historical and quasi-historical texts that relate to Arthur. Anything else we discuss in the later chapters is almost wholly drawn from legend, and whilst historical truths may remain deep down, they add nothing new to our understanding of the Arthur of history.

This means that in the last nine chapters we have touched upon the real Arthur – or Arthurs, because I believe it has become very evident that we are not dealing with one individual. The old tales retold by Nennius, those in the *Mabinogion*, and those by Geoffrey of Monmouth are a potpourri of historical characters, most of whom are known only by name. It was from these stories that the Arthur we have come to know grew in the telling, becoming the Arthur of Thomas Malory, but so far removed from the original as to be scarcely recognisable.

Which, of course, raises the question: will we recognise Arthur when we find him? What are the ground rules by which we can identify him? What key fact allows us to point at a figure in the line-up and say, "That's him"?

I said at the very start of this book that we have to find the right person in the right place at the right time. All of this exploration through the dim and often very vague pages of lost history has been about teasing out people's identities, and establishing when and where they lived. We have covered close on a thousand names and whilst this is only a very small fraction of all those living in the fifth and sixth centuries, it is a high proportion of the movers and shakers.

There is really only one criterion. The original Arthur, the one from whom all else flowed, has to be the victor of the first battle of Badon. Although we have not conclusively identified the site of Badon we have, thanks to Gildas, managed to fine-tune the date of Badon to between 493 and 497.

However, there is one strong caveat. Gildas, the one person who could have told us who was the victor at Badon, chose not to. As a consequence, we do not know who the victor was. However, what makes legends grow are not the facts, but what we *believe* to be the facts. So whilst the victor of Badon is the real origin of the Arthur legend, he does not have to be the original Arthur. Someone else may very rapidly have become associated with Badon so that the legend grew around him.

This happens quite often. Take, for instance, the Gunpowder Plot. If we were asked to name the chief conspirator, I suspect most of us would immediately name Guy Fawkes. But the mastermind was not Fawkes at all, but Robert Catesby. We know this because the details are fully documented, but that still doesn't stop us remembering Guy Fawkes above all others and, if it had happened many centuries earlier and all documentation was lost, we'd probably only remember Fawkes.

In the case of Arthur, history has been revised and rewritten so many times that virtually all we are left with is the version people wanted to remember. In that case, identifying the real Arthur may not mean identifying the victor of Badon, but identifying the person everyone *thinks* was the victor of Badon.

How, you may ask, do we know who they thought was the victor of Badon?

Because they told us. Gildas didn't directly, but gave us some clues. Nennius told us he was the victor of eleven other battles. *The Dream of Rhonabwy* tells us his chief counsellor was Caradoc Vreichfras, who is closely associated with Ergyng, and that his bishop was Bedwin, also named in the first of the Triads, which link Arthur, Bedwin and Caradoc with Celliwig in southern Gwent. However, the story places the battle of Caer Faddon in Powys, which though this may not be the original Badon, may be the one they associate with the victor. Geoffrey makes him the son and successor of Uther, the brother of Ambrosius. Uther and Ambrosius were allegedly the children of Constantine of Armorica, but we have surmised that this is not the Armorica known today as Brittany, but Llydaw in Ergyng.

Those are just some of the secondary pointers which help us home in. But let us first examine all of the contenders once again in chronological order to refresh our memories, and see who we can eliminate. The dates given are as per the tables in Chapter 3.

2. The Contenders

1. Lucius Artorius Castus (140–197)
He seems a rank outsider, but there is much about him that may have contributed to the legend. Littleton and Malcor put forward a compelling argument that the Sarmatian folktales of the Iazygian soldiers captured by Castus in Brittany and settled in Ribchester (Bremetennacum) could have contributed to the later Arthurian legend, particularly the story of returning Excalibur to the Lady of the Lake. They propose that Castus's campaign in the north reflects Nennius's sequence of battles, though their case for Dumbarton as Badon is perhaps the weakest element. Castus's exploits in Armorica possibly became associated with the character of Riothamus. Whilst Castus cannot be the original Arthur of Badon, his activities could certainly have encouraged the initial development of the legend.

2. Riothamus (430–500)
The idea that Riothamus might have been Arthur has apparently been around since at least 1175, when a monk at Orcamp Abbey in France made the connection. The current champion of the idea is Geoffrey Ashe in *The Discovery of King Arthur*. As Riothamus is another of those names that double as titles, and means "over king", he could as easily be Arthur, based on Ardd-ri, or "High King." Others have suggested that he was Ambrosius.

Because we have only a brief glimpse of Riothamus, and that entirely in Gaul and, for that matter, as the loser of a battle, not as a victor, he hardly stands out as a hero who would form the basis of legend. Some have equated him to the Breton King lahann Reeth, a name that may have been conflated with the later ruler

Ioanas Riotham. This may in turn be the Iaen of Caer Dathal whom the *Mabinogion* states were Arthur's kin.

The main problem with Riothamus also being Arthur of Badon, however, is one of timing. If Riothamus was Arthur, he would have to have been old enough to command troops in 469, and go on to be victorious at Badon around 493–497, and fight at Camlann in 514–518. His activities in Gaul could certainly have added further fuel to the flames of legend, but he is unlikely to be the victor of Badon.

3. Ambrosius Aurelianus (430–500)

This idea took root because Gildas, who was the first to name the battle of Badon, makes no mention of Arthur at all, but does name Ambrosius as leading the British in the lead-up to the battle. Gildas describes the victories as shifting between the British and the Saxons, "*usque ad annum obsessionis badonici montis*" or "all the way to the year of the siege of Mount Badon." It is clear that he was describing a span of some years from when Ambrosius took command to the eventual victory at Badon.

That alone does not rule out Ambrosius being the commander at Badon. The evidence shows that Ambrosius took command a few years after the Saxons had been driven home by Vortimer. Since Vortimer was dead and Vortigern disgraced, there was no other commander in charge until Ambrosius took control. We know that this has to be after 455, probably after 460 (*see* Table 6.2), but not long after. Ambrosius's campaign may even have run into the 480s, but to have one commander leading a battle campaign, no matter how intermittent, for thirty years is expecting much. Ambrosius is unlikely to have been born later than 435, which would make him 58 in 493 and nearly 80 at the time of Camlann. Ambrosius could still have been the victor of Badon, but he is unlikely to have been the Arthur of Camlann.

Ambrosius's dates coincide almost exactly with those of Riothamus, leading many to suggest that they are one and the same. If he had returned to Britain to continue his battles, this might explain why Riothamus is not heard of again in France. Frank D. Reno, in *The Historic King Arthur*, takes that extra step by making Ambrosius / Riothamus / Arthur all the same person, resulting in a rather aged Arthur. Reno suggests a birth year for

Ambrosius of 422 and that Arthur died in 518, making him 96. It is hard to imagine how he could have achieved anything at Camlann, let alone attempt to do battle with Mordred.

The only way that Ambrosius could be Arthur is if Ambrosius's campaign were shorter than Gildas implies, and therefore all of the preceding dates are shifted. This is a case to be argued, because we have already suggested that the main Saxon invasion, the second or third *adventus*, was not until the 470s, even the late 470s. We might imagine a campaign running from, say, 477 (Aelle's arrival) to 493, just sixteen years, which would not contradict Gildas. Still long, but perfectly manageable for one significant Roman. If Ambrosius was in his late twenties at the start of this, he would be 43 at Badon and 64 at Camlann.

However, this causes problems at the start of the fifth century. If Ambrosius was not born until 450, his father by then (if still alive) would have been in his sixties at least and though this is possible, it seems unlikely. This scenario would also rule out any possibility of Ambrosius being Riothamus.

So whilst we cannot rule out Ambrosius as being the victor of Badon, it is not realistic for him to have continued the Golden Age usually attributed to Arthur. Ambrosius must have handed over power to someone, and this leads us to our next contender or contenders.

4. Pascent (430–500)

If Arthur was Ambrosius's successor, we must consider Pascent, because Nennius tells us (§48) that when Ambrosius became king he installed Vortigern's eldest surviving son, Pascent or Pasgen, as ruler of the "provinces" of Builth and Gwrtheyrnion.

The use of the word "provinces" is intriguing as it has echoes of the old Roman term for one of the divisions of Britain. One might expect Ambrosius, upon becoming the High King (or, a true Roman, the vicarius), to appoint governors to the former Roman provinces.

If Ambrosius were mounting a retaliatory campaign against the Saxons he would have needed strong, trustworthy provincial governors and a reliable right-hand man. Pascent's descendants went on to rule Gwrtheyrnion and later Powys, so we must assume that Pascent was a reliable supporter of Ambrosius and not the rebel whom Geoffrey of Monmouth portrays.

So Pascent must be a part of the Arthur story, as he was one of the legitimate "kings" alive at that time. However, he was of the same generation as Ambrosius and would have been too old to fight at Badon, so I do not regard him as a serious candidate for Arthur. He may well have done the solid work of governing Britain while Ambrosius led the battle campaign, but administrators are never remembered.

It is the generation after him that is of more interest.

5. Cadell and Riocatus (both 460–530)

Pascent was in all likelihood succeeded by his son Riocatus. Ambrosius himself must have looked for a successor, not in Builth and Gwrtheyrnion where Pascent's line continued, but in Powys, which had been his central powerbase, governed from Wroxeter. I believe Ambrosius passed the succession on to Cadell (*see* Table 3.9).

Cadell has his own origin tale, as related by Nennius (*see* Chapter 6). It's a standard rags-to-riches folktale which may have some basis in reality. It is possible that, with Vortigern disgraced, Cadell had nothing to inherit and so did live initially as a scullion. He may well have been fostered, as was the Celtic custom, but to a poor family.

Cadell was probably born in the early 450s, and thus may have received Garmon's blessing around the age of 21 in the early 470s. He could have succeeded Ambrosius in the 480s and still only have been about forty at the time of Badon. His nickname, *Durnluc*, is usually translated of "gleaming hilt" or "hilt of light", significant with regard to Arthur's Excalibur.

The concept of the ruler of Viriconium, the last major city in Britain, wielding a bright sword and living in an area with which all of the battles have been associated, including Badon (at Caer Faddon), is a compelling one. There is certainly a sufficient case for Cadell to be considered as a serious contender as one of the characters behind the historical Arthur.

His cousin Riocatus may be equally significant. We know virtually nothing about him except that in his youth he must have entered the church, as he is referred to as a cleric in a letter by Sidonius to Bishop Faustus, Riocatus's uncle. Since he seems to have succeeded to the kingship of Gwrtheyrnion, or at least is included amongst the pedigrees of the kings of that land, he evidently did not stay in the church. We don't know exactly when Riocatus visited Faustus, but it was probably in the 470s when he may have still been a young man. The implications are that he may not have been ruling at the time of Badon, but could have inherited the kingdom soon after.

Nevertheless, someone who was alive at the time of Badon, who was called "king of battles" but was not himself a king, has much in common with Nennius's meagre description of Arthur. And Riocatus, like Cadell, was in the right place to have been able to fight a sequence of battles along the southern or western frontier.

6. Owain Danwyn (450–530) or Cynlas (480–560)
Owain Danwyn or "White Tooth" is put forward as a contender for Arthur by Keatman and Phillips in *King Arthur – The True Story*. I have already discussed their basic premise in Chapter 7 and have little to add here. Owain was contemporary with Badon and may well have fought there, but he was a minor ruler at Rhos. Although he lived at the right time, there are no other factors that would make him a likely candidate for Arthur.

On his website, <Arthur's Ring>, Mark Devere Davis puts forward several arguments to suggest that Owain's son Cynlas was Arthur. Most of these, like the proposals for his father, revolve around him living at the Fortress of the Bear, and make several other links with "bear" imagery. Davis highlights that Cynlas lusted after his wife's sister, a charge that was also brought against Arthur in later legend (with three Gueneveres). Davis also highlights Gildas's odd comment that Cynlas possessed "arms special to himself", which is suggestive of Excalibur.

From Gildas's tirade against Cynlas, it is apparent that he was a vicious despot who would not have been remembered as the heroic Arthur of Badon, or as a hero of any kind.

7. The Pendragons: Brychan (430–500) and Dyfnwal (455–525)
If we accept the date for Badon as being in the mid-490s, then

according to Table 7.2 the Pendragon was probably Brychan of Brycheiniog. Dyfnwal Hen would have been Pendragon at the time of the *Welsh Annals* date for Badon in 518. Neither Uther nor Arthur appears in the list of Pendragons as detailed by Laurence Gardner.

Most of Brychan's children entered the church; indeed, he is included in the Welsh Triad of the "Three Saintly Families" of Britain. According to legend, Gwynllyw of Gwent abducted one of Brychan's daughters, Gwladys, and Brychan pursued him in a violent fury. It needed Arthur, Cei and Bedwyr to stop the bloodshed. Although Arthur was probably added to this story later, it shows that there is no tradition suggesting that Brychan and Arthur are one and the same. Brychan did have a son called Arthen (460–530), the first example of an Arth- named child of a Pendragon. But he too entered the church. Cefn Arthur is on an old drovers' road near Llandovery.

As we have seen, Dyfnwal was a warrior who was a constant threat to those tribes south of the Wall. There is a pattern of battles related to Nennius's list that could represent an offensive against the Gododdin and Angles, and could place Badon in the north at Bowden Hill, near Linlithgow. Though this clearly had been the site of an ancient battle, nothing has yet suggested one as old as Badon, and the debris found there by the eighteenth-century antiquarian Sir Robert Sibbald is doubtless related to one of any number of battles in this area during Scotland's conflicts with England. Dyfnwal was obviously a powerful warrior, and he must have left behind significant memories, some of which may later have attached themselves to the Arthurian legend.

8. Vortipor (470–540) or Agricola (440–510)

Vortipor of Dyfed was a contemporary of Dyfnwal and may have operated in the same role in Wales as Dyfnwal did in the north. Vortipor was known as the "Protector". The title was not unique in Britain – Coel Hen had also used it, but probably with direct authority from Rome. With Vortipor, whilst he may have been pro-Roman, the title seems more one of conceit than of rank.

Vortipor is one of the kings singled out for criticism by Gildas who calls him the "bad son of a good king" and "spotted with wickedness". He may have been a better ruler in his youth but in his old age, when Gildas was writing, he was "defiled by various murders and adulteries." This included "the rape of a shameless daughter." Gildas does not say whether this was Vortipor's own daughter or "daughter" in a symbolic sense, such as a "daughter of Eve" or "daughter of the church". Others have interpreted it as a step-daughter. We know that later legends give Arthur an incestuous relationship with his sister, of which Mordred was the offspring. Arthur is not always the hero we like to imagine. Geoffrey of Monmouth portrays him as proud and vain in later years, defying Rome. In the later legends, as we shall see, he has moments of unprovoked violence and an adulterous relationship.

Since Gildas thought so ill of Vortipor, yet wrote of Badon as such a victory, does that mean that Vortipor could not have been the victor of Badon? Perhaps, but the opposite is as likely. If Gildas were going to castigate Vortipor then he would hardly want to name him as the victor of such an important battle. It would be surprising if Vortipor, as Protector, did not fight at Badon, which was the decisive battle against the Saxons. Perhaps Vortipor had not called himself the Protector at that stage. After all, if his father were still alive, and in his mid fifties, he probably also held the title – or at least the role – of Protector, and Gildas did at least praise him as a "good king."

We can almost certainly determine the coalition of kings. If the battle were in the south, then it probably involved Cadwallon Lawhir, Cadell, Riocatus, Rhain ap Brychan and perhaps Cynfor of Dumnonia. Agricola (Aircol) would have been the senior king though, because of his age, he may not have been involved in the majority of the fighting. That could well have been left to Vortipor as the *dux bellorum*.

Nennius tells us that Arthur fought "along with the kings". Gildas also calls Vortipor's father a king, but if Agricola also held the rank of Protector, he may have been regarded by later generations as over and above the kings.

In fact something like that may well have been felt by his son. Vortipor is, after all, a title, very similar in derivation to Vortimer – both names are rendered as Gwerthefyr in Welsh – and means "Over King". We do not know Vortipor's given name. His great-grandson was called Artúir, so we cannot dismiss the possibility that the name recurred in other generations, especially as his 4 x great grandfather also bore the prefix in Artchorp. Vortipor's title in Irish was Gartbuir, and it may just be possible that the Gaelic *b* was misread as an *h*, when written as *Gartbuir.*

Vortipor has perhaps one other surprise in store. In *Bloodline of the Holy Grail* Laurence Gardner makes several points about Artúir of Dyfed. I treat these separately below, but one is more relevant here. Gardner suggests that it is Artúir of Dyfed who died at Camlann in 537 or 538. Artúir lived too late for this, but Vortipor could well have died at around that time, and he is quite likely to have died in battle, despite his age. Our revised date for Camlann is 520, but this is based on its relationship to Badon. Supposing the Camlann entry in the *Welsh Annals* is correct at 538, Vortipor would then be in his mid sixties. There is some suggestion that Vortipor was in battle against his neighbour Ceredigion. That territory was between Demetia and Gwynedd, and Vortipor may have invaded Ceredigion many times in conflict against Gwynedd.

One of the likely locations for Camlann is in northern Ceredigion on the border with Gwynedd. Vortipor would have passed through here on his way to Gwynedd and that may be where he was ambushed and killed. We do not know Vortipor's fate but it was always more likely to have been in battle than peace. We do not know if he was killed by a nephew, but a family rivalry may well have been involved, if Vortipor had disposed of his wife and raped her daughter.

9. Cerdic (480–550) or Caradog (445–515)

This case is put forward by John C. Rudmin in "Arthur, Cerdic and the Formation of Wessex" available on the Camelot < celtic-twilight > website. Rudmin's argument is that Arthur, Cerdic and Caradog Vreichfras are all based on the same individual and he cites a number of comparisons. One of these is that Caradog's wife was Guignier, sister of Cador of Cornwall and, as we have seen, Arthur's future wife Guenevere had been raised in Cador's household. In the Welsh tales, Caradog's wife was Tegau Eurfron, though the stories about them are similar, further examples of how common characters (such as Cador) were thrown into the melting pot of legend. There may be more of a case to argue that Cerdic and Caradog are the same, or at least related, as we have explored, but it requires some manipulation to bring Arthur into that equation.

Caradog Vreichfras may well have fought at Badon, which is probably why he features so strongly in the later tales. Cerdic is unlikely to have been involved, on either side. If anything, Cerdic benefited from the collapse of Arthur after Camlann which, if it was in 538, saw Cerdic establish the West Saxon kingdom.

10. Urien of Rheged (*c*535–591)

There is a strong likelihood that Urien's battles against the Angles became fused in the folk memory with some of Arthur's battles. Urien is known to have scored a sequence of victories against the Saxons in a well-known battle list. Even though Badon was a victory for Arthur, Camlann was a defeat and betrayal, and Urien's death at Lindisfarne, betrayed by Morcant, would have echoed down the years. The *Northern Chronicle*, probably kept by his son Rhun, would have honoured Urien's victories along with others of the north (especially Arthwys, Eliffer and Peredur).

11. Athelstan (895–939)

The unsung hero of English history. While Alfred's greatness is rightly celebrated, that of his grandson, who ruled the English from 924 to 939, is often overlooked. Yet it was Athelstan who united Britain as none had previously. The main parallel with Arthur is that Athelstan had to conduct a campaign in the North to suppress both Welsh hostilities and the Norse in York. He also quelled a Cornish revolt under their king Hoel. He achieved a period of peace and prosperity in England never previously experienced. Although this is not the same as the post-Badon Pax Arthuriana, it does have parallels with Geoffrey's portrayal of how Arthur achieved peace. Also, after the Scots broke the treaty arrangement in 934, hostilities broke out which caused Athelstan first to devastate Scotland, just as Geoffrey described Arthur doing in his campaign, and then to meet a combined army of Scots and Vikings at Brunanburh in 937. All agree that this battle was the most decisive of all Saxon victories, and yet, like Badon, no one is really sure when Brunanburh was fought. All this happened two hundred years before Geoffrey wrote his

History, but considering his ability to confuse facts from any period, he may well have encountered a document about Athelstan's northern battles and, not knowing its origin, incorporated elements of it into his tale.

I shall now work through all of the individuals with any likely Arth– prefixed name, including some we have not yet discussed who I feel need to be mentioned if only to be dismissed. These are also presented in date order for the fifth and sixth centuries.

12. Arthwys ap Mar (450–520)
The number of sites in the north that could relate to Nennius's battle list is sufficiently tempting to suggest that there was an Arthur of the North, probably resident in Elmet, whose exploits against the Angles were long remembered.

Arthwys is the best situated to fight a campaign along the eastern frontier which, because of its association with Gildas's "partition", is the one most likely to be connected with Badon. Though it cannot be wholly discounted, Arthwys is unlikely to have fought as far south as Liddington, but if his territory were in Elmet, it would have been possible for him to bring reinforcements to a siege around the Breidden Hills or the Wrekin in Powys. In fact, if the Saxons had advanced that far west by the 490s, it would have been a certainty that the British in Powys would have looked to their northern cousins for aid. Just possibly, despite the other great and powerful at Badon, it was the northern prince who saved the day and entered legend. It may even be just as Geoffrey described it, with Arthwys pursuing the Saxons from Lichfield to a last-ditch battle in Powys.

13. Arthfael ap Einudd (480–550)
Arthfael appears in the *Life* of St. Cadog, who lived in the early sixth century. He is identified as a king of Glamorgan who granted Cadog land at what is probably modern-day Cadoxton, near Neath. His son Gwrgan the Freckled is also mentioned in Cadog's *Life*, when Cadog gives Gwrgan a sword given to him by Rhun ap Maelgwyn. Arthfael ruled close to Mynydd Baidan, where Blackett and Wilson identify Mount Badon, and he was almost certainly alive at the time of the battle. Arthfael is a

contemporary of Arthmael (St Arthmel), and their names are ostensibly the same, but there is no record that Arthmael ever ruled, even as a sub-king. The genealogy in which Arthfael appears is clearly corrupt and has probably picked up more than one pedigree. Unfortunately, no more is known.

14. Saint Arthmael (482–552)
Proposed by Chris Barber and David Pykitt in *Journey to Avalon*. Their idea is not so much who Arthur was but whom he became. The chronology only works if the dates in the *Welsh Annals* are correct for Badon and Camlann. It is also surprising that someone allegedly so well known could change identity so successfully and not be remembered by so many other notable holy men in Brittany, not least Gildas himself. Brittany had its own memories of Arthur, and centuries later his name evolved into Arzor. If the Bretons knew Arzor was really Arthmael, that would surely have found its way into the later legends.

15. Arthfoddw ap Boddw (540–610)
Suddenly there is a time leap. Despite the admitted roughness of our chronology, we have had a cluster of Arth- names in the mid-to-late fifth century, though no true Arthurs; but now there are none until the mid-to-late sixth century. Curiously, it is a gap that exactly encompasses the time of Arthur of Badon who, based on the limited evidence we have, must have lived from about 470 to 520, or to 540 if the later Camlann date is correct. The first new Arth- name seems to occur within a year or two of Arthur's death. Even more curiously, the first known is Arthfoddw, a name that means Arth the lucky or Arth the fortunate. Could Boddw of Ceredigion have named his son after Arthur in the hope that he would be fortunate? If so, then there must be another Arthur that we are missing or one whose real name we do not know. This is the gap filled precisely by Vortipor, Cadell and Riocatus.

We know nothing else about Arthfoddw. He is a name in the pedigrees of the rulers of Ceredigion. It may be pertinent that he chose to pass a similar name on to his son Arthlwys, of whom more below. That is the only example we have of successive generations with an Arth- name. It suggests to me that we have already passed the Arthur of Badon and that his name had left an impression.

16. Artúir ap Pedr (550–620)
We have at last reached the first individual whose name is genuinely "Arthur". The grandson of Vortipor, Artúir ruled Dyfed at the end of the sixth century. We are thus clearly a whole century after Badon so this Arthur can have no direct connection with the original historical Arthur.

Yet stories may have attached to him that later became grafted on to the composite Arthur of legend. We have already encountered several, most notably the hunt for the boar Trwyth. Stripping the story brings us back to a probable historical event, a series of battles against a brigand and his men who came from Ireland and first laid waste to parts of Dyfed before moving on to Gwent. The Gwent episode may relate to an entirely different historical event. The rulers of Dyfed were of Irish descent and they must have spent much of their time defending their lands from further Irish raiders. Also present in Arthur's court, in the tale of *Culhwch and Olwen*, are several survivors from lost lands, such as Gwenwynwyn, recorded as Arthur's champion, and Teithi the Old. The lost lands are believed to have been off the coast of Dyfed or Ceredigion, and perhaps to the north in Morecambe Bay. These locations could all be plausibly associated with the court of Artúir of Dyfed. Neither of them is of great significance in the later story of Arthur, and it is hard to imagine that Artúir of Dyfed played much part in fighting against the Saxons who, by his reign, were becoming firmly established in "England" and were enclosing the British into Wales.

In *Bloodline of the Holy Grail* Laurence Gardner tells us some unusual facts not recorded elsewhere. He tells us that Artúir of Dyfed was installed by Dubricius in 506. Dubricius was alive then but Artúir of Dyfed was not even a gleam in his father's eye. No matter how we play around with the dates in the Dyfed pedigree – probably the most reliable of all of them – it would be impossible to have Artúir of Dyfed alive earlier than 530. Also Dubricius is most unlikely to have installed a king in Dyfed since, as we have seen, his territory was soundly in Ergyng. The bishop of Dyfed was Dewi (St. David), whose dates are even more fluid than Dubricius's. In fact, opinion is shifting towards there having been two holy men called Dewi in Wales during the sixth century. The lesser known Dewi of Ergyng (who gave his name to Dewchurch, Dewsall and others), lived from perhaps 480 to 550 and was the companion of Dubricius and Gildas. The second, more famous St David of Dyfed lived from around 520 to 590 could quite possibly have inaugurated Artúir of Dyfed as king, perhaps in the 580s. Whether the earlier Dewi or even Dubricius enthroned a previous king of Dyfed, I have no idea, but 506AD would be a perfectly acceptable date for the accession of Vortipor, or Gartbuir as he may be remembered.

Gardner also tells us that Artúir of Dyfed's sister Niniane had married Ambrosius as part of a treaty to stop Dyfed's incursions into Powys. We know Niniane, also known as Nimue or Vivien, from the later legends as the lover of Merlin, as she has also been equated with the Lady of the Lake. Gardner makes her the mother of Merlin. If these elements are true they would again apply to an earlier ruler, such as Vortipor, as might Arthur's involvement at Camlann, which I have already discussed under Vortipor.

Nevertheless, with Artúir of Dyfed we start to see how some of the exploits of a real Arthur come together with the Arthur of legend and also show how both could be linked to a possible earlier "Arthur" in the form of Vortipor/Gartbuir.

17. Artúir mac Aedan (560–596)

This historically-attested character was recorded by Adomnán in his *Life of Columba,* written less than a century after the real events. Columba had, apparently, correctly foretold that Artúir would not succeed Aedan as king of the Dál Riatan Scots. Artúir met his fate in battle against the Picts, probably in 596. Laurence Gardner, though, who believes Artúir was the original Arthur, gives the date as 603. He believes that Artúir fought at both Camelon, near Falkirk, and Camboglanna on Hadrian's Wall. The battle at Camboglanna was savage, resulting in a rout that spilled over into a second battle at Degsaston [Dawston]. It was there that Artúir died, along with hundreds of his fellows. This was the decisive battle for the English that saw Athelfrith's domination of the north and the capitulation of the British and Scots. Aedan was a broken man after that.

Gardner makes Aedan the Pendragon of Britain and thus claims that Artúir is the only "Arthur" to have been born to a Pendragon. This is true if we exclude Arthen ap Brychan, previously cited. Although the exploits of Artúir are not fully recorded, many of his father's are, as he was, according to the authors of the *Biographical Dictionary of Dark Age Britain*, "one of the greatest warlords in the British Isles during the early Middle Ages". Although of Irish stock on his father's side, through his mother and grandmother he was of British stock and could claim descent from Dyfnwal Hen, so he was arguably more British than Irish. Aedan's wife was also British, which makes Artúir at least three-quarters British.

Aedan undertook several exploits in which Artúir would have been involved. He fought against his overlord Baetan mac Cairill in Ulster in 574, when Gardner maintains Artúir would have fought at Dun Baetan. Aedan then led a campaign against the Orkneys in 580, and conquered the Isle of Man in 582, a sequence of battles that closely follows Arthur's own, according to Geoffrey of Monmouth. It was not until the 590s, with his battles against first the Picts and then the Angles, that Aedan's golden touch began to fail, and it was at this time that Artúir died. Of course Geoffrey conveniently ignores this and moves on to another chronicle to explore Arthur's later adventures. But it seems likely that Geoffrey was influenced by Artúir mac Aedan's exploits as part of Arthur's early conquests. Some of these may translate into the battles in Nennius's list, especially those in Glen Douglas in Lennox.

Artúir ultimately failed in his battles against the Picts and there was no heroic accession to the throne. Artúir, therefore, also fits the criterion of a battle lord who fought alongside kings. Yet his victories were not his own, but his father's, and they did not herald a period of peace between the British and Saxons as achieved at Badon. Artúir is clearly one of the figures behind Arthur, but he's not the major one.

18. Arthlwys ap Arthfoddw (570–640)

Listed only for completeness. His father is included above, and the fact that Arthlwys inherited the Arth- prefix emphasises the growing significance of the name.

19. Artúir ap Bicor (590–660)
As discussed in Chapter 8, this Artúir immortalized himself through a lucky slingshot throw in killing the Irish champion Mongan, and with the Arthur name now gathering interest this exploit was yet another to add to the list of achievements. If the episode had reappeared in the legends it would have meant something, but as it didn't, we can only conjecture that Artúir's moment of fame, sufficient for him to be remembered in the Irish Annals, served to feed the rumour mill even more on the growing legend of Arthur.

20. Athrwys ap Meurig (610–680)
Of all the "Arthurs", this one is both the most promising and the most frustrating. Athrwys was a ruler of Gwent sometime in the seventh century, or possibly earlier. Blackett and Wilson, in *Artorius Rex Discovered*, date him 503–579, a century earlier than the date given in Table 3.7, whilst Barber and Pykitt, in *Journey to Avalon*, date him even earlier, 482–562. Since everyone has used the same pedigree, the difference is due to methods of dating. We know that his great-grandson Ffernfael died in 775, a date unlikely to be wrong, as the *Annals* in which that is recorded were brought into their final form only fifty years afterwards. Even if Ffernfael lived till he was 90, and was thus born in 685, and each respective father was 50 when their son was born, we could only push Athrwys's birth back to 535. There may be a missing generation but, in all probability, Athrwys was a seventh-century ruler, perhaps born as early as 600 or 590 at a push, but no earlier.

Although I have used the name Athrwys here, he only appears in one pedigree under that name. Elsewhere he is listed as Atroys, Adroes, Athrawes and Adros, scarcely names to cause confusion with Arthur.

Bartrum notes that whilst he appears frequently in the *Book of Llandaff* as a witness to charters and grants, he is never identified as a king. Possibly his father Meurig lived to a great age, as seems the case with several of the rulers of Gwent, and thus outlived Athrwys. This would support Nennius's remark that Arthur fought alongside kings but was not apparently king himself. Perhaps Athrwys served as regent in his father's old age, and was thus king in all but name, and he may have served as a sub-king of Ergyng.

There is a deed in the *Book of Llandaff* apparently witnessed by *Athruis rex Guenti regionis pro anima patris sui Mourici*, and though the grant may be accurate the other witnesses all date from the time of Dubricius, a hundred years earlier. The *Book of Llandaff* was not compiled until 1108, when the abbey needed to establish its rights over lands being appropriated by the Normans, and though it was drawn together from surviving documents doubtless much creativity was exercised in trying to reconstruct the more ancient and lost ones. It suggests that Athrwys was believed to be a contemporary of Dubricius and no one really knew which century that was.

Does all this necessarily matter? It certainly does, because Arthur of Gwent lived in the century or two before the tales of the *Mabinogion* and the *Welsh Annals* and other old documents were being created. He was the Arthur freshest in people's collective memories. He was far enough back for all history to be blended together (200 years might as easily be 400 in folk memory) but recent enough that the oral tradition remembered him fairly freshly. Thus all memories of Arthur could be pinned on to him.

However, Athrwys ap Meurig had to have been a memorable king in his own right in order for the blurring of memories to work. It would be no good if he were remembered as a coward or an imbecile. The memory of Athrwys ap Meurig could most easily be confused with Arthur of Badon if they had done something similar – something remarkably similar.

The clue to this may lie in the fact that at the time that the Arthurian legends were coming together, in the late eighth century, there was another Athrwys ruling Gwent, the great-great-grandson of Athrwys ap Meurig. This later Athrwys was the son of Ffernfael and ruled from about 775 to 800. This was when Offa ruled Mercia. At that time no other ruler in Britain mattered. Offa was the great king, the first to style himself "King of the English", with designs on becoming Emperor. He had come to power in 757 and defeated the Welsh at Hereford in 760. It is believed that part of the treaty was that Ergyng was taken over by Mercia, perhaps still administered by Ffernfael ap Ithel, but subservient to Offa. After Ffernfael's death in 775, it seems that Ergyng passed completely to the English. From 777 onwards Offa instigated a further series of raids into Wales, this time in retaliation for an offensive from Powys under Elisedd. Having asserted his authority Offa instigated the construction of the great earthwork known as Offa's Dyke and the building of this must have run throughout the reign of Athrwys ap Ffernfael. Although the Dyke did not run continuously into the south, as the Wye effectively formed the border, it was particularly strong around the border with Gwent. The ditch of the Dyke was on the western side, meaning it was there to stop the Welsh getting out. Wales was being hemmed in.

We know next to nothing about Athrwys ap Ffernfael, yet I am sure he is the key to the Arthurian legend. Here was a king who had lost part of his kingdom and was now being further humiliated by the greatest king Britain had known and was powerless to respond. What better way to save face than to revel in the glories of the past and to remember the great deeds of his ancestors?

What great deeds?

Well, there was one of great significance and that was the battle of Tintern Ford or, to give it its proper name, Pont y Saeson. Tintern had once been a royal fortress, and in the days of Tewdrig ap Llywarch it was one of the glories of the kings of Gwent. The story, as told in the *Book of Llandaff,* says that Tewdrig had ruled for many years and was old and tired. He wished to retire into the church and pass the governance to his son Meurig. Not long after, however, the Saxons invaded Ergyng and Meurig was under pressure. Tewdrig, who had a vision in which an angel told him he would be victorious but would himself be killed, came out of retirement, buckled on his sword and led his army to one last victory. It was the greatest victory of them all. As Archenfield Archaeology report, "This stopped their advance and South Wales was never again to be seriously threatened by the English people." This battle has strong resonances of Badon, perhaps even of Camlann, because, as prophesied, Tewdrig was injured by a lance and died three days later. He was buried at Matharn near Chepstow, close to Caradog Vreichfras's palace at Caldicot, and Caradog was probably present at that battle.

The battle of Tintern was as important to the kings of Gwent and Ergyng as Badon had been a hundred years earlier. Could

Athrwys of Gwent have been at the Battle of Tintern? If so, maybe some of the glory of that battle passed to him and over time, Tintern and Badon merged in the collective memory.

There has always been a problem dating this battle. Amazingly, it does not feature in the *Welsh Annals*, which may be a point in favour of arguing that by the time those *Annals* were compiled, memories of Tintern and Badon had started to blur. John Morris in *The Age of Arthur* suggested the battle may have happened in 584. After their victory at Dyrham in 577, when the Saxons defeated the rulers of Gloucester, Cirencester and Bath, the Saxons invaded the Severn Valley. The *ASC* reported a setback in 584 when Cutha was killed at Fethan Lea. The identity of that battle site has not been resolved to everyone's satisfaction. Both Stoke Lyne in Oxfordshire and Stratford-on-Avon have been suggested and Tintern can't be ruled out. However, other dates have been suggested. Sarah Zaluckyj in *Mercia* cites 597, whilst Hereford's own archaeological studies suggest around 620 or as late as 630.

It is unlikely to have happened much after the succession of Penda of Mercia, whose rise to power began in 626. The evidence suggests that Penda had an alliance with various Welsh princes, which he called upon as he fought his way to Mercian control. The battle would probably have been after Chester, which had been an overwhelming victory for the Northumbrians against the British. That defeat had been one of the factors that caused the Welsh to ally with Mercia. Chester also frustrates dating, but the prevailing view is that it happened in 615. The West Saxons were heavily on the offensive in the late 620s. Penda managed to defeat them with British help at Cirencester in 628. In all likelihood a West Saxon defeat by the Welsh at Tintern happened just before then, perhaps with Penda's help, in around 626. It could have been slightly earlier. It's unlikely to have been later.

If we suggest 626x628, that fits in remarkably well with our pedigrees in Table 3.7. Despite the problem in dating the Gwentian kings, that date exactly fits the lifespan for Tewdrig. It would also suggest that his grandson Athrwys could have fought at the battle. He was probably around twenty and it might have been his first major conflict.

Perhaps thereafter Athrwys fought alongside Penda. Perhaps

some of Nennius's battle list relates to Penda's climb to power between 626 and 633. Penda had combined forces with Cadwallon of Gwynedd who was on a personal vendetta of revenge against Edwin, king of Northumbria. Cadwallon and Edwin had apparently been childhood friends but when Edwin defeated Athelfrith and became king in 616 all that changed. Cadwallon succeeded to Gwynedd around the year 620. In that same year Edwin conquered and extinguished the British enclave of Elmet near Leeds, and doubtless refugees settled in Wales. This was probably the spark that lit the fire, as Cadwallon is supposed to have fought Edwin soon after and was soundly defeated. Geoffrey of Monmouth places the battle at Widdrington, near Morpeth in Northumberland, but it is unlikely that Cadwallon would have undertaken a battle so far from his base at that stage. Edwin continued the campaign through North Wales and into Anglesey. Cadwallon was driven to the very tip of the island and had to flee to Ireland (or possibly Brittany) where he remained in exile for seven years.

He returned in about 629 and it was then that his campaign of revenge began. An elegy to Cadwallon, *Marwnad Cadwallon*, talks of fourteen major battles and sixty musterings. The battle list is longer than Arthur's and includes a battle at Caer Digoll in Shropshire, close to the site for Caer Faddon in *The Dream of Rhonabwy*. At what stage Cadwallon and Penda joined forces is not clear. It may well have been from the start, with the mutual objectives of the extermination of Edwin and the conquest of Northumbria.

The culmination of the campaign happened on 12 October 632 at Hatfield, which is almost certainly Hatfield in Yorkshire, north of Doncaster – possibly the place that Geoffrey cited in his *History* for Ambrosius's defeat of Hengist. Here Penda and Cadwallon slaughtered the forces of Edwin of Northumbria, including Edwin himself and most of his family. The two did not leave it there. They went on a rampage through Northumbria, laying waste to the land, for a whole year. However, Cadwallon was caught by surprise at Heavenfield, near Hexham, by Hadrian's Wall and was killed by Oswald, son of King Athelfrith who had defeated the British at both Chester and probably Catraeth.

Had Cadwallon survived, the future of the British may have been very different. Cadwallon could have reclaimed much of the North for the British, but with his death the British resistance crumbled. The year 632/3 was their final triumph.

Perhaps Athrwys of Gwent was involved in it all. We know that Cadwallon had a huge force with him. The campaign could not have been supported by Penda's men alone. Cadwallon no doubt mustered British men in the North, but he needed large reserves to sustain his campaign for a whole year so far from Gwynedd. With Tewdrig dead and Meurig king, Athrwys was heir apparent but doubtless looking for battle experience. If he had helped in the victory at Tintern he now helped in the destruction of a kingdom.

We don't know if Athrwys was involved, but it would surprise me if he weren't. Cadwallon could not have achieved this with a force from Gwynedd alone, or even with the men of Powys. Gwent had already shown its prowess by defeating the Saxons at Tintern, and surely Cadwallon would have wanted some of that prestige for his army.

This is not to say that the legend of Arthur is based on the campaign of Cadwallon. Not at all. But when, in the 770s, Athrwys ap Ffernfael looked back to that Golden Age when the Welsh had proved they could defeat the English, who's to say that in pushing the case for the Arthur of legend he did not colour it with memories of Athrwys ap Meurig's victory at Tintern and the subsequent campaign that gave Wales glory and freedom?

It is only a proposal, but it would explain why Athrwys ap Meurig, who lived over a hundred years after Badon, and well beyond the traditional Arthurian period, might in any way be regarded as a candidate for the original Arthur. It explains why Arthur is shown as ruling from Caerwent (or Caerleon, as Geoffrey believed) and from Gelliwig, because that was Arthur of Gwent's base. It explains why so many of Arthur's court in *Culhwch and Olwen* and *The Dream of Rhonabwy* are people of Gwent, such as Bishop Bedwin and Caradog Vreichfras. Doubtless both were involved in the Battle of Tintern and the subsequent campaign of Cadwallon. It would explain the second half of the pursuit of the Boar Trwyth which takes place through Gwent. The victory at Tintern is close to the eventual expulsion of the Boar at the estuary of the Wye. It would also explain how Arthur's campaigns seem to shift between Wales and the North.

This does not mean that Geoffrey confused Cadwallon's campaign with Arthur's. The memories and histories of these still remained separate, but in Gwent the emphasis was changed so that Athrwys's role became more significant, and over a relatively short period of time this change in emphasis became fused with earlier tales of Saxons vanquished by the British. Athrwys, now treated as the victor at Tintern, also became the victor of Badon by association and the two histories merged.

If this is so, then Athrwys's victory at Tintern needed to be superimposed in people's memories over the victory at Badon, and it would help the argument if the victor at Badon was also called Athrwys or, as is possible, Arthwys of the Pennines. Perhaps the final picture is similar to Geoffrey's portrayal. Let me suggest the following.

Arthwys of the Pennines was fighting a sustained campaign against the Saxons along the eastern frontier. His forces were stretched to the south which allowed a retaliation by Aelle of the South Saxons who mounted his own campaign into the heartland of Britain. There could have been battles along the Ridgeway at Liddington or further north towards Lichfield. Aelle's forces, perhaps cut off from their retreat, pushed further west and were met by the coalition of kings – Cadell, Riocatus, Aircol, Vortipor, Caradog – along the western frontier, resulting in a siege at either the Wrekin or the Breidden Hills. Arthwys was able to bring his forces into play and wiped out the Saxon force. Aelle, Bretwalda of the Saxons, was killed, and thereafter the Saxons lacked a figurehead. The coalition of kings was now able to dictate a boundary which the Saxons could not cross, a boundary which Arthwys may have continued to patrol from his base in central Britain, which may well have been at Lichfield. Arthwys maintained a peace in Britain until his own death at the hands of the son of Sywno in the 530s. This is likely to have been near the frontier, perhaps at Camboglanna, which is why it would also be remembered in *Y Gododdin*.

Although Arthwys/Arthur was remembered as a great hero in the generations following, after two hundred years the where and the when had become blurred. By the time scribes tried to record the details in the Welsh Annals the dates had become confused. By now Athrwys ap Ffernfael's propaganda had done its work. His ancestor had become superimposed over Arthwys ap Mar and become a national hero. During this period other stories about other Arthurs became sucked into the story along with those of other heroes. By the time *Culhwch and Olwen* and its companion stories took their final form, heroes from throughout the fifth and sixth centuries had become Arthur's companions.

3. Rebuilding Arthur

The composite Arthur had been created, and continued to grow. It ought to be possible to show how this recomposition took place. I've already covered much of this above, so let's summarise it here. At this stage I am talking only about the Arthur from the *Mabinogion* and Geoffrey's *History*, and not the later Arthur of the romances, which is a whole other story. The suggestions included here are hypothetical but all are based on clear deductions made throughout this book.

Table 10.1. The Composite Arthur

Story as per Nennius, Geoffrey, etc.	**Possible original historical episode**
Uther disguised as Gorlois seduces Ygerna (*Geoffrey, viii.19*)	None. Pure legend, possibly based on the Irish legend of Manannan ap Lir's seduction of the wife of Fiachna and the birth of Mongan. The character of Uther as Arthur's father may be influenced by Eliffer/ Eleutherius of the North.
Arthur ascends throne at age 15, crowned by Dubricius (*Geoffrey, ix.1*)	Both Artúir mac Aedan and Athrwys ap Meurig may have been inaugurated into a command around the age of 15, Artúir as Wledig under Aedan and Athrwys as sub-king of Ergyng. However, probably the only ones who could have been inaugurated by Dubricius were Cadell or Riocatus.
Arthur's battle campaign against the Saxons (*Nennius §56; Geoffrey ix.1–3*)	Most recently Athrwys ap Meurig's involvement with Penda against Edwin but influenced by the campaign of Vortipor/Cadell/Riocatus in the fifth century and that by Arthwys ap Mar and Eliffer, plus Urien of Rheged against the Angles or Aedan and Artúir against the Picts and Angles. Possible influence by later campaigns of Alfred and Athelstan against the Danes.

Battle of Badon (*Gildas §26; Nennius §56; Geoffrey ix.4*)	Most recently Athrwys ap Meurig at Tintern, but originally the confederate kings under Aircol with Arthwys ap Mar's victory at either Breidden Hill (or the Wrekin) or Liddington Castle.
Arthur's follow-up campaign against Irish, Picts, Islay (Man?) and Orkneys (*Geoffrey ix.5–10*)	Aedan mac Gabhran's campaign in which Artúir mac Aedan was probably involved. May also be influenced by Athelstan's battle against the Scots.
Arthur's twelve years of peace (*Geoffrey ix.11*) More likely a generation of peace.	Followed Gwent's victory over Saxons at Tintern, but originally the victory by Aircol's alliance and Arthwys at Badon.
Hunt of the boar Trwyth (*Culhwch and Olwen*)	Dyfed episode drawn from Vortipor's or Artúir of Dyfed's battles against Irish raiders; Gwent episode probably based on Athrwys ap Meurig's forays against Saxons, or an earlier campaign to push Gewisse out of Ergyng.
Arthur's campaign against "Norway" and Gaul (*Geoffrey ix.11*)	Trigger for "Norway" was Athelstan's campaign at York and for Gaul was empire building by Henry I; Gaul's seed may have been influenced by Lucius Artorius Castus's campaign in Brittany, and possibly by Magnus Maximus's imperial campaign, but also merged with tales of Clovis and Ferreolus.
Arthur's special coronation (*Geoffrey ix.12–13*)	Probably invented by Geoffrey based on coronation of Norman kings, especially Stephen's, which he probably witnessed. But may have drawn origin from special coronation of Edgar at Bath in 973 or Offa's special ceremony in 787.
Arthur's campaign against Rome (*Geoffrey ix.14–x.13*)	Immediate trigger was excommunication of Henry I, but probably drew upon the imperial campaigns of Magnus Maximus and Constantine.
Treachery of Mordred (*Geoffrey xi.1*)	May have been premature death of Athwrys ap Meurig caused by involvement with his second cousin Medraut. Earlier betrayals, such as Urien's by Morcant, may also have influenced.
Battle of Camlann (*Geoffrey xi.2*)	We do not know where Athwrys ap Meurig died and there might well once have been a Camlann in Gwent. Otherwise may have been influenced by death of Artúir mac Aedan at Camboglanna, the possible death of Vortipor or Artúir of Dyfed at Camlan, or the slaying of Arthwys ap Mar, maybe also at Camboglanna.

SECTION 2

THE LEGEND GROWS

11

ARTHUR'S BONES

The success of Geoffrey's story about King Arthur is only too evident. Not only was his manuscript issued in thousands of copies – at least 200 survive to this day – but it created the Arthurian legend. The next chapters explore the many Arthurian tales that appeared between Geoffrey's *Historia* and the work we most associate with Arthur today, Malory's *Mort Darthur*. But first, we should look at one other feature created by Geoffrey's book that also survives to this day – the tourist industry.

Of the places most closely associated with Arthur in Britain, two stand out – Tintagel and Glastonbury. Ironically, they are the two with the least evidence of an Arthurian connection, and although Geoffrey placed Arthur's birth at Tintagel, he made no reference at all to Glastonbury. Arthur was taken to the Isle of Avalon after Camlann, and Geoffrey did not say where that was. All that changed in 1191, when some monks found the bones of Arthur.

Giraldus Cambrensis, or Gerald of Wales, is our source for this. He was purportedly a witness at the exhumation, although before we reveal his findings we need to consider how the exhumation came about.

Glastonbury Abbey had suffered greatly in a fire in 1184. During the late Saxon period, especially under the abbacies of Dunstan (942–955) and Athelwold (955–963), it was one of the great abbeys and schools of England. A monastic settlement had existed here since the late sixth century – Gildas was supposed to have been associated with it. For a period after the Norman

Conquest, the abbey lacked support and fell into disrepair. Much renovation, however, was carried out during the long abbacy of Henri de Blois (1126–1171), the brother of King Stephen, who was also Bishop of Winchester. Henri was known for his love of luxury, being perhaps the richest man in England, and although much of the building work enhanced the abbey's status, it also enhanced his comfort.

Within thirteen years of Henri's death, however, most of this improvement was lost through the great fire, including the library and its many rare books. Rebuilding work began immediately. Funds were forthcoming with royal patronage from Henry II.

Both Henry II and his queen, Eleanor of Aquitaine, were fascinated by the Arthurian legends. Their grandson, the future Duke of Brittany, was named Arthur when he was born on 29 March 1187. Arthur was next in line to the throne after Richard (who became Richard I in 1189 on Henry's death), and should rightfully have become king of England when Richard died on 6 April 1199, but his uncle John saw to it that Arthur would never succeed.

According to Gerald, Henry II had learned that the body of King Arthur was buried at Glastonbury. Even more, he was told they would find the body between two ancient tall pyramids in the abbey burial grounds. Henry had been told this by "some old British soothsayer", who may have been Welsh or Breton. We don't know when he learned of this, but it must have been late in his life, and probably around the time that Arthur was born. Henry is supposed to have passed word on to the abbot, but that cannot be so. At that time Glastonbury had no abbot. The post had not been filled after the last abbot, Robert of Winchester, died in 1178. Henry was more interested in appropriating the abbey revenues himself to finance his wars in France. He installed a friend, Peter de Marcy, to look after affairs, and this led to a major crisis within the abbey. In fact, it was under de Marcy that the great fire happened, and the circumstances behind it have never satisfactorily been resolved. De Marcy died soon afterwards.

Henry did not replace de Marcy, and instead put his Chief Justiciar, Ranulf de Glanville, in charge of the finances and of overseeing the rebuilding works. Henry may have told Ranulf about the possible burial place of Arthur – Ranulf was, after all, executor of Henry's will – but nothing seems to have happened before the King's death in July 1189. One might have thought that had Henry and Ranulf known about it, a search for the grave would have happened straightaway. Yet building works had been in hand for five years and it was not until early in 1191, eighteen months after Henry's death, that the search began.

In that time a lot had happened. After Henry's death his son Richard had no interest in Glastonbury other than its revenues to help finance his Crusade. He appointed an old friend, Henry de Sully, who had been abbot of Fécamp in Normandy, and who had been in charge of the rebuilding works there after that abbey had been destroyed by fire. De Sully had managed to turn Fécamp Abbey, with its precious relics, including the blood of Christ and a bone from the arm of Mary Magdalene, into one of the major centres of pilgrimage in Normandy.

Could he do the same for Glastonbury? Indeed he could. It was de Sully who ordered that the excavation be made for Arthur's body and it was he who selected the site, telling Gerald of Wales that he had learned this from the King himself. This was how Gerald reported the discovery in *Liber de Principis Instructione* ("On the Instruction of Princes"), which appeared two years later, in 1193.

> In our own lifetime Arthur's body was discovered at Glastonbury. Although legends had fabricated something fantastical about his demise (that he had not suffered death, and was conveyed, as if by a spirit, to a distant place), his body was discovered at Glastonbury, in our own times, hidden very deep in the earth in an oak-hollow, between two stone pyramids that were erected long ago in that holy place. The tomb was sealed up with astonishing tokens, like some sort of miracle. The body was then conveyed into the church with honour, and properly committed to a marble tomb. A lead cross was placed under the stone, not above as is usual in our times, but instead fastened to the underside. I have seen this cross, and have traced the engraved letters,

which were cut into it on the side turned inwards toward the stone, instead of facing outward and being visible. It read:

HERE LIES ENTOMBED KING ARTHUR, WITH GUENEVERE HIS SECOND WIFE, ON THE ISLE OF AVALON.

Many remarkable things come to mind regarding this discovery. For instance, he had two wives, of whom the last was buried with him. Her bones were discovered with those of her husband, though separated in such a way that two-thirds of the sepulchre, namely the part nearer the top, was believed to contain the bones of the husband, and then one-third, toward the bottom, separately contained the bones of his wife, wherein was also discovered a yellow lock of feminine hair, entirely intact and pristine in colour, which a certain monk eagerly seized in hand and lifted out; immediately the whole thing crumbled to dust.

There had been some evidence from the records that the body might be found there, and some from the lettering carved on the pyramids (although that was mostly obliterated by excessive antiquity), and also some that came from the visions and revelations made by good men and the devout. But the clearest evidence came when King Henry II of England explained the whole matter to the monks (as he had heard it from an aged British soothsayer): how they would find the body deep down, namely more than 16 feet into the earth, and not in a stone coffin but in a hollowed oak bole. The body had been placed so deep, and was so well concealed, that it could not be found by the Saxons who conquered the island after the king's death and whom he had battled with so much exertion while he was alive, and had nearly annihilated. That was why the lettering on the cross, which confirmed the truth, had been inscribed on the reverse side, turned toward the stone, so that it would conceal the secret of the coffin at that time and yet at some opportune moment or time, would ultimately reveal what it contained.

It should be noted also that the bones of Arthur's body that they discovered were so large that the poet's words seem to ring true: "Bones excavated from tombs are reckoned enormous." Indeed, his shin-bone, which the abbot showed to me, was placed near the shin of the tallest man of the region; then it was fixed to the ground against the man's foot, and it extended substantially more than three inches above his knee. And the skull was broad and huge, as if he were a monster or prodigy, to the extent that the space between the eyebrows and the eye-sockets amply encompassed the breadth of one's palm. Moreover, ten or more wounds were visible on that skull, all of which had healed into scars except one, greater than the rest, which had made a large cleft – this seems to have been the fatal one.

Gerald's description is detailed, as if he had been present, although some of the comments such as "his shin-bone, which the abbot showed to me", suggests that he had not seen the actual exhumation. In all likelihood Gerald visited Glastonbury afterwards, and his report was part of the "promotion" for the discovery.

The immediate question, though, is: how genuine was the discovery? Gerald's role in this is suspicious in itself, although whether he was part of the scheme or an innocent dupe is uncertain. In introducing the above item he said:

The memory of Arthur, the celebrated king of the Britons, should not be concealed. In his age, he was a distinguished patron, a generous donor, and a splendid supporter of the renowned monastery of Glastonbury; they praise him greatly in their annals. More than all other churches of his realm he prized the Glastonbury church of Holy Mary, mother of God, and sponsored it with greater devotion by far than he did the rest.

Where did Gerald get the information that Arthur was a noted patron of Glastonbury and mentioned in their annals? Some sixty years before this discovery, William of Malmesbury had been invited to Glastonbury to write a history of the abbey. A highly respected historian, Malmesbury had completed his own history of Britain, *Gesta Regum Anglorum* ("Acts of the English Kings"), in 1125, ten years before Geoffrey. Malmesbury, who had already had access to Glastonbury's archives when he completed that book, had written, "the tomb of Arthur is nowhere beheld, when the ancient ditties fable that he is yet to come." His *De Antiquitate Glastoniensis Ecclesiæ* ("On the Antiquity of the Church at Glastonbury") specifically mentions the Annals at Glastonbury but makes no mention of Arthur. In fact, no one had made any link between Arthur and Glastonbury until Geoffrey's colleague Caradog of Llancarfan wrote his *Life of Gildas* in the 1130s. In it he tells the story of Melwas, the king of the "summer country" who kidnapped Guenevere and held her at Glastonbury (presumably on the Tor). Arthur searched for her for a year before he learned of her whereabouts, whereupon he summoned up an army. Gildas and the abbot of Glastonbury intervened and Guenevere was restored to Arthur.

Malmesbury, though, had found no such references in his research. Neither, for that matter, had Abbot Dunstan, when he carried out major building works two centuries earlier. Even Geoffrey, never one to miss a trick, had made no reference to Glastonbury. He simply said that after Camlann Arthur was taken to the Isle of Avalon. Gerald of Wales, though, had something to say on that:

> What is now called Glastonbury was, in antiquity, called the Isle of Avalon; it is like an island because it is entirely hemmed in by swamps. In Welsh it is called *Inis Avallon*, that is, *insula pomifera*, "The Island of Apples", because the apple, which is called *aval* in the Welsh tongue, was once abundant in that place. After the Battle of Camlann, Morgan, a noble matron, mistress and patroness of those regions, and also King Arthur's kinswoman by blood, brought Arthur to the island now called Glastonbury for the healing of his wounds. Moreover, the island had once been called in Welsh *Inis Gutrin*, that is, *insula vitrea*, "The Island of Glass", and from this name, the invading Saxons afterwards called this place *Glastingeburi*, for *glas* in their language means *vitrum* or "glass", and *buri* means *castrum*, "castle" or *civitas*, "city".

No one before Gerald had suggested that Avalon was Glastonbury. He could only have got that idea from the abbot. Was Gerald in on the scheme? He was certainly a high flier. Born in 1145, he was the son of a Norman knight, Sir William de Barri. His mother Angharad was the granddaughter of Rhys ap Tewdwr, king of Deheubarth (1078–1093), through his daughter Princess Nesta, who was a mistress of Henry I. Nesta was notorious for her love life, and in 1109 was abducted by Owain ap Cadwgan, the hothead prince of Powys, causing a major political row between Henry and Owain's father. This could even have been the incident that inspired Caradog's story of the abduction of Guenevere.

Gerald believed he was destined for great things. Most of all he wanted to be made bishop of St. David's, in order to petition the Pope to raise the see to an Archbishopric and thus be independent of Canterbury. He was nominated for the post in 1176 but turned down by Henry II because of his Welsh blood. He refused two other bishoprics before he became involved at Glastonbury. One might suspect that Gerald was now seeking to ingratiate himself with Richard I. Unfortunately he never did achieve his goal, though he spent a lifetime trying. On the other hand, Henry de Sully rapidly received promotion, being elevated to the Bishopric of Worcester just a couple of years after his remarkable discovery at Glastonbury.

Aside from the fact that neither Dunstan nor Malmesbury had found any evidence of an Arthurian connection with Glastonbury – and they had access to the original documents before the fire – there are all manner of clues that show this to be one big hoax. The dimensions of the skull, for instance, particularly the distance between the eyes, is humanly impossible. The Latin lettering engraved on the cross was not contemporary with Arthur's day but was closer to the tenth or eleventh century. Some, including Leslie Alcock, have suggested that this may have been carried out in Dunstan's day when a mausoleum, known to have been on this same site, was demolished. Perhaps that had made reference to Arthur, and in order to salvage this a new cross was made. Unfortunately no record of this exists – and Malmesbury would have found it if it had. It is also hard to believe that Dunstan would not have made a more overt reference to this as by his day the legend of Arthur was already well known.

Then there was the matter of Excalibur. Later myth-makers, or mischief-makers, report that Richard I had presented the recently discovered Excalibur to Tancred, king of Sicily. Richard had left England for the Holy Land in July 1190, long before the excavation had started, and Gerald made no mention of Excalibur being found amongst the remains.

If we are to believe Gerald, there is still the question of whose remains these were and how the monks managed to find them that deep. They were, it is true, digging in the abbey's burial grounds, so one might have expected them to find remains, but there must have been considerable advance planning to have buried the cross. The size of the bones suggests that they may have belonged to a horse or an ox, but clearly no one would confuse a human skull with an animal's.

But apart from Gerald's report, we have no other "eyewitness" statements, and if Gerald was only repeating what the abbot told him, one might imagine there need have been no exhumation at all. However, in 1962 Ralegh Radford conducted a new excavation at the marked site of Arthur's grave and was able to verify that a previous excavation had happened. He also found some stone slabs which may have lined the ancient burial, but nothing else.

There were two other contemporary reports of the discovery, though dating them is difficult. Firstly, Ralph de Coggeshall recorded the event in his *English Chronicle*, finished in 1224. Curiously, Ralph implies that the site was discovered accidentally whilst they were burying another monk. Also his description of the wording on the cross omits all reference to Guenevere, stating simply HERE LIES THE FAMOUS KING ARTURIUS, BURIED IN THE ISLE OF AVALON. That was the same phrasing recorded by the chronicler at Margam Abbey in Glamorgan. The date of composition of that entry is disputed, some believing it to be contemporary with the event. With the exception of the wording on the cross, it reads similarly to Gerald's account and may even have been compiled from the same "press release" that Gerald had from the bishop. Bizarrely, the Margam Chronicle records that Mordred's remains had also been found!

The mystery might have been resolved. The cross survived long enough for the antiquary John Leland to see it on his visit in

1533. By that time the tomb of Arthur had been elaborately enhanced. This happened following a translation ceremony in 1278, marking a visit by Edward I. Leland's description of the wording on the cross agrees with Ralph de Coggeshall's. The cross itself was reproduced by another antiquary, William Camden, in the 1607 edition of his book *Britannia*, and it was this printing that enabled scholars to study the nature of the engraving. It also shows the abbreviated text, but Camden maintained that the other side of the cross contained the reference to Guenevere, although this contradicts Gerald's original claim that the wording was only on the one side, closest to the stone slabs. All of this suggests that the cross was created by the monks, a clever forgery, attempting to imitate an earlier form of lettering, but not one able to dupe modern scholarship. The reference to Arthur's second wife, which is a curious feature and one that tends to favour a genuine inscription, may well have upset the Church, and the wording was rephrased.

That was not all that upset the Church or, more especially, Richard I. He was unhappy with the belief held by the Welsh that Arthur was not dead but might return to help them in their hour of need. There had been Welsh unrest throughout the twelfth century, and the last thing Richard wanted, while away on his Crusade, was to have a Welsh revolt at home. A sound reason behind needing to find Arthur's bones, perhaps even greater than that of bolstering the revenues, was to prove once and for all that Arthur was dead.

Once again Gerald of Wales came to the rescue. In his original report he had noted the fantastical tales that Arthur might return, but a few years later, writing in *Speculum Ecclesiae* ("The Mirror of the Church"), he made the point emphatically:

> Furthermore, tales are regularly reported and fabricated about King Arthur and his uncertain end, with the British peoples even now believing stupidly that he is still alive. True and accurate information has been sought out, so the legends have finally been extinguished; the truth about this matter should be revealed plainly, so here I have endeavoured to add something to the indisputable facts that have been disclosed. After the Battle of Camlann . . . after

> Arthur had been mortally wounded there, his body was taken to the Isle of Avalon, which is now called Glastonbury, by a noble matron and kinswoman named Morgan; afterwards the remains were buried, according to her direction, in the holy burial-ground. As a result of this, the Britons and their poets have been concocting legends that a certain fantastic goddess, also called Morgan, carried off the body of Arthur to the Isle of Avalon for the healing of his wounds. When his wounds have healed, the strong and powerful king will return to rule the Britons (or so the Britons suppose), as he did before. Thus they still await him, just as the Jews, deceived by even greater stupidity, misfortune, and faithlessness, likewise await their Messiah.

The true story may never be fully known. The marble tomb was smashed and the remains destroyed in 1539 during Henry VIII's dissolution of the monasteries. The cross went missing sometime in the eighteenth century, though it, or a copy, was reputedly discovered in Enfield, of all places, in 1981. This was also believed to be a hoax though the finder, Derek Mahoney, refused to submit the item for analysis or to hand it over to Enfield Council, who maintained the item had been found illegally on one of their sites. Mahoney even served a prison service for contempt of court and later committed suicide. His copy of the cross was never found.

Whether true or false, Henry de Sully's discovery of Arthur's bones placed Glastonbury firmly on the pilgrim's map, in addition to the fact that they already claimed the relics of St. Patrick and St. Indract, and would later develop the story of Joseph of Arimathea and the Holy Grail. The Arthurian legend was gathering pace.

12

FROM MONMOUTH TO MALORY – THE CRUSADER DIMENSION

Between 1138, when Geoffrey completed his *Historia*, and 1470, when Malory wrote *Morte Darthur*, there was an explosion in Arthurian literature. Over one hundred and thirty different works appeared, excluding translations, variants, revisions or adaptations. About half of these appeared within the first century, and thereafter most of what followed were reworkings of the earlier stories. Nothing of any significance was added to the Arthurian saga after the 1230s.

Could this phenomenal outpouring be explained by the popularity of Geoffrey's work, which suited the politics of the courts of Henry I and King Stephen by enhancing their supremacy over the rival kings of France? Or were other factors at work? Factors which, in the process, created a new King Arthur – one far more powerful than the original – with an entire retinue of superheroes, the Knights of the Round Table.

This chapter will provide an overview of the stories that appeared in these three hundred and fifty years, and chart the key factors that created both the Arthur of legend and the mystery of the Holy Grail. Many names will keep recurring and become familiar, and we will find two major elements, without which we might never have seen the Arthurian phenomenon as we now know it. These were the Crusades and the Cistercian Order of monks.

The chart on the next few pages lists all of the major Arthurian tales and romances that appeared in these years. During those three and a half centuries everything we have come to know about

Table 12.1. Arthurian Literature and Events from Monmouth to Malory

Year (*all dates approx.*)	**General Arthurian or non-series tales and events**	**Lancelot Cycle**	**Perceval/Grail Cycle**	**Merlin Cycle**	**Gawain tales**	**Tristan tales**
1138	*History of the Kings of Britain*, Geoffrey of Monmouth					
1140s	*Lestoire des Engles*, Geffrei Gaimar					
1150s	*Roman de Brut*, Robert Wace			*Vita Merlini* (*Life of Merlin*), Geoffrey of Monmouth		The archetypal *Estoire de Tristan* (now lost)
1160s	*Erec et Enide*, Chrétien de Troyes *Lai du Cor* Robert Biket					Chrétien de Troyes's lost story of Mark and Iseult. *Tristan*, Thomas d'Angleterre
1170s	*Lanval*, Marie de France *Cligés* and *Yvain: Le Chevalier au Lion* Chrétien de Troyes	*Le Chevalier de la charrete* (The Knight of the Cart), Chrétien de Troyes, completed by Godefroi de Leigny				*Le Chèvrefeuil* (The Honeysuckle), Marie de France *Tristrant*, Eilhart von Oberge

Year (*all dates approx.*)	**General Arthurian or non-series tales and events**	**Lancelot Cycle**	**Perceval/Grail Cycle**	**Merlin Cycle**	**Gawain tales**	**Tristan tales**
1180s	*De Amore*, Andreas Capellanus *Erek*, Hartmann von Aue	Original Anglo-Norman *Lancelot*, now lost, which was basis for Ulrich's *Lanzelet*	*Conte du Graal*, Chrétien de Troyes		*Le Bel Inconnu* (The Fair Unknown), Renaud de Beaujeu	
1187	Arthur, Duke of Brittany, grandson of Henry II, born 29 March					
1191	Exhumation of Arthur's bones at Glastonbury					
1190s	*Brut*, Layamon *Owain* (or *The Lady of the Fountain*), anon	*Lanzelet*, Ulrich von Zatzikhoven	*Joseph d'Arimathie*, Robert de Boron *Perceval, First/Second Continuations*		*La Mule sans Frein* (The Bridleless Mule), Paien de Maisières	*Tristran*, Béroul *La Folie Tristan* (The Madness of Tristan), anon

Year (*all dates approx.*)	**General Arthurian or non-series tales and events**	**Lancelot Cycle**	**Perceval/Grail Cycle**	**Merlin Cycle**	**Gawain tales**	**Tristan tales**
1200s	*Iwein*, Hartmann von Aue *Fergus of Galloway*, Guillaume le Clerc		*Peredur*, anon. *Perceval* (now lost), Robert de Boron. *Parzival*, Wolfram von Eschenbach. *Perlesvaus* (*High History of the Holy Grail*), anon. *Bliocadran/ Elucidation Prologues*, anon	*Merlin*, Robert de Boron	*Le Chevalier à l'Épée* (The Knight of the Sword), possibly by Paien de Maisières	*Tristan*, Gottfried von Strassburg
1210s	*Wigalois*, Wirnt von Grafenberg *Meraugis de Portlesguez*, Raoul de Houdenc. *Yder*, anon. *Daniel of the Flowering Valley*, Der Stricker	*Lancelot do Lac*, anon. Prose *Lancelot*, and *Mort Artu* (Vulgate Cycle 1 and 3), anon	*Queste del Saint Graal* (Vulgate Cycle 2), anon	Prose *Merlin* (1), anon	*La Vengeance Raguidel* (The Avenging of Raguidel), Raoul	

Year (*all dates approx.*)	**General Arthurian or non-series tales and events**	**Lancelot Cycle**	**Perceval/Grail Cycle**	**Merlin Cycle**	**Gawain tales**	**Tristan tales**
1220s	*Jaufré*, anon. (French, Provençal). *Gliglois*, anon. *Durmart le Gallois*, anon.		*Perceval, Third Continuation*, Manessier; *Perceval, Fourth Continuation*, Gerbert de Montreuil. *Estoire del Saint Graal* (Vulgate Cycle 4), anon. Didot-*Perceval*, anon.	*Estoire de Merlin* (Vulgate Cycle 5), anon	*Les Enfances Gauvain* (The Youth of Gawain), anon.	*Tristrams Saga ok Ísöndar*, Brother Robert. *Tristan Ménestrel* (Tristan as Minstrel), Gerbert de Montreuil
1223	First known gathering of a "Round Table" pageant in Cyprus.					
1230s	*Mort Artu* (final part of *Roman du Graal* or Post-Vulgate Cycle), anon. *Palamedes*, anon.		*Estoire del Saint Graal* and *Quest del Saint Graal*, (both parts of *Roman du Graal* or Post-Vulgate Cycle), anon.	*Suite du Merlin* (including the Prose *Merlin*) (part of *Roman du Graal* or Post-Vulgate Cycle), anon.	*Diu Krône* (The Crown), Heinrich von dem Türlin *Livre d'Artus*, anon. *Mériadeuc* or *Le Chevalier aux deux épées* (The Knight of the Two Swords), anon.	*Tristan*, Ulrich von Türheim (continuation of Gottfried von Strassburg's *Tristan*). *Tristan als Mönch* (Tristan as Monk), anon.

Year (*all dates approx.*)	**General Arthurian or non-series tales and events**	**Lancelot Cycle**	**Perceval/Grail Cycle**	**Merlin Cycle**	**Gawain tales**	**Tristan tales**
1240s	*Garel of the Flowering Valley*, Der Pleier.					Prose *Tristan* (*Le Roman de Tristan de Léonis*) (First Version), anon.
1250s	*Geraint ab Erbin*, anon. *Wigamur*, anon. *Tandareis und Flordibel* and *Meleranz*, Der Pleier.				*Hunbaut*, anon. *The Perilous Cemetery*, anon.	Prose *Tristan* (Second Version), anon.
1260s	*Torec*, Jacob van Maerlant *Floriant et Florete*, anon. *Claris et Laris*, anon. *Beaudous*, Robert de Blois. *Roman de Laurin*, anon.		*Historie van den Grale*, Jacob van Maerlant	*Boec van Merline*, Jacob van Maerlant		

Year (*all dates approx.*)	**General Arthurian or non-series tales and events**	**Lancelot Cycle**	**Perceval/Grail Cycle**	**Merlin Cycle**	**Gawain tales**	**Tristan tales**
1270s	*Story of Meriadoc*, anon. *Roman de Roi Artus*, Rusticiano da Pisa. *The Marvels of Rigomer*, Jehan. *Escanor*, Girart d'Amiens.		*Der jüngere Titurel*, Albrecht.	*Les Prophécies de Merlin*, Richart d'Irlande.	*The Rise of Gawain*, anon.	
1280s	Likeliest period during which the Round Table at Winchester was made.		*Lohengrin*, anon.	*Arthour and Merlin*, anon. Earliest English romance about Merlin.	*Roman van Walewein*, Penninc and Pieter Vostaert	*Tristano Riccardiano*, anon. First Arthurian romance in Italian.
1290s	*Dream of Rhonabwy*, anon. *The Knight with the Sleeve*, anon.					*Sir Tristrem*, possibly by Thomas of Erceldoune (also known as Thomas the Rhymer)
1300s	*Moriaen*, anon.					
1310s	*Arthur and Gorlagon*, anon.					

Year (*all dates approx.*)	**General Arthurian or non-series tales and events**	**Lancelot Cycle**	**Perceval/Grail Cycle**	**Merlin Cycle**	**Gawain tales**	**Tristan tales**
1320s				*Merlijn-Continuatie*, Lodewijk van Velthem		
1330s	*Perceforest*, anon.		*Sir Percyvell of Galles*, anon. *Der nüwe Parzefal*, Philipp Colin and Claus Wisse			
1340s	*La Tivola Ritonda* (The Round Table), anon. *Ywain and Gawain*, anon.					
1348	Edward III initiates the Order of the Garter					
1380s	*Meliador*, Jehan Froissart. *Gismirante* Antonio Pucci. *Libeaus Desconus* and *Sir Launfal*, Thomas Chestre				*Sir Gawain and the Green Knight*, anon.	

Year (*all dates approx.*)	**General Arthurian or non-series tales and events**	**Lancelot Cycle**	**Perceval/Grail Cycle**	**Merlin Cycle**	**Gawain tales**	**Tristan tales**
1390s	Alliterative *Morte Arthure*, anon. *The Knight of the Parrot*, anon. "The Wife of Bath's Tale", Geoffrey Chaucer.				*The Awntyrs off Arthure*, anon.	
1400s	"Stanzaic" *Le Morte Arthur*, anon.				*Syre Gawene and the Carle of Carlyle*, anon.	*Saga af Tristram ok Ìsodd*, anon.
1420s	*The Avowing of King Arthur*, anon.					*Tristan*, Anton Sorg. First printed and illustrated Arthurian book.
1430s			*The History of the Holy Grail*, Henry Lovelich.	*Merlin*, Henry Lovelich.		
1440s					*Sir Gawan and Sir Galeron of Galloway*, anon.	

Year (*all dates approx.*)	General Arthurian or non-series tales and events	Lancelot Cycle	Perceval/Grail Cycle	Merlin Cycle	Gawain tales	Tristan tales
1450s				Prose *Merlin* (2), anon	*The Wedding of Sir Gawain and Dame Ragnell*, anon. *Gest of Sir Gawain*, anon.	
1470	*Le Morte Darthur*, Sir Thomas Malory; printed by Caxton in 1485 and in an illustrated edition by Wynkyn de Worde, 1498.					
1486	Arthur, son of Henry VII, born 20 September.					

Arthur and his world, about Merlin, Guenevere, Camelot and the Holy Grail, appeared and was tailored to fit the new image. The chart is divided into the main groupings of stories, and plot summaries will be given over the next six chapters. This chapter will provide an overview to show how these stories evolved, and why.

1. The Welsh background

We have already seen that between the eighth and the twelfth centuries wondrous tales about Arthur emerged, most being written down from oral tradition by the early 1100s. Arthur was raised from a mortal into the ranks of the great heroes, though he never became a fully-fledged god in the same way as such Scandinavian heroes as Thor (whose name has a striking similarity). Strangely, as time progresses and Arthur becomes the property of the Norman French, he reverts to being only too human, and it is the others, such as Lancelot and Gawain, who become super-human.

It is a fascinating transition because what usually captivates us about Arthur is not his historical origins, but the adventures of his court at Camelot and his ultimately tragic life. Arthur and his knights captured the mood and spirit of the times, and transformed a battle hero into Britain's greatest legend.

We have already discussed the early Welsh tales *Culhwch and Olwen* and *Pa Gur,* both of which portray Arthur in heroic and supernatural terms (*see* Chapter 8). Their Arthur is clearly different from the Arthur described by Nennius and Geoffrey of Monmouth, who portray him as a military leader with no unusual powers, although the mythical Arthur is lurking just offstage. In his section on the Wonders of Britain, Nennius refers to the stone at Carn Cafal that bore the imprint of Arthur's hound, and the tomb in Ergyng of Arthur's son, which is never the same size twice. Geoffrey includes Merlin's predictions and the story of Arthur fighting the giant at Mont-St.-Michel, an obvious Breton folktale that crept into his history. Yet all these are as nothing to what was emerging elsewhere.

Primary amongst the Celtic tales is *Preideu Annwvyn,* "The Spoils of Annwvyn", which tells of the attempt by Arthur and his men to rescue Gwair from an island fortress, and to find the pearl-rimmed cauldron owned by the Lord of Annwvyn. The story has some elements in common with the quest for the Holy Grail (*see* Chapter 16), but it is also an archetypal text for an Arthurian adventure, and may just relate to an heroic episode in Welsh history. As such, it is a crucial story in the mutation of the historical Arthur to the legendary one.

Whilst it would be an exaggeration to say that all Arthurian romances owe their origin to this story, of the surviving early Welsh tales this is the one that bears the closest resemblance to the key features of the later romances, including a quest, a rescue and a magical object. The adventure is not a total success, and was, in the words of the poet, "a woeful conflict". In fact, many of Arthur's adventures, and those of his knights, meet with failure and require some special heroism or magic to save the day.

The poem is attributed to Taliesin, who is supposed to be the narrator and one of the seven men who survived the journey. If he was indeed one of these men, there's little doubt that he would have composed a heroic poem to celebrate the achievement, although the poem is enigmatic enough to make one wonder whether Taliesin, or perhaps a later embellisher, was trying to say something else. If Taliesin, who lived from perhaps 530 to 610, experienced and wrote about this adventure in the 570s, it would fit into the reign of Artúir of Dyfed and, in fact, the poem does have connections with Dyfed.

The earliest surviving copy of *Preidu Annwvyn* dates from the early 1300s, when the flowering of Arthurian romance had already passed, but there is little doubt that the version we know today probably dates from the late ninth century, with oral versions existing before then. There would have been other heroic and mystical tales, not necessarily associated with Arthur, but of a kind that gradually formed into a body of work that influenced later storytellers. They would have borrowed from existing tales, and audiences for these stories would have looked forward to key passages and well-known episodes, just as we do today with formula action films. Unfortunately, all too few of those earlier tales have survived, and we only hear echoes of them in the stories.

Amongst the key passages are three well-known motifs: the

beheading test, the test for chastity, and the "loathly lady". All of these have origins in Celtic tales, and all of them become key elements in the Arthurian stories.

The beheading test is best known from its appearance in *Sir Gawain and the Green Knight*, but it also appears in several earlier Arthurian episodes, including the first continuation of Chrétien's *Perceval*, dating from the 1190s, in which the knight who takes up the challenge is none other than Caradog Vreichfras. The earliest known appearance of this challenge is in the Irish story *Fled Bricrenn* ("Bricriu's Feast"), from the Ulster Cycle, which dates from at least the eighth century. The earliest surviving manuscript is from around the year 1100. The original story would have been well known as it featured one of the great heroes, Cú Chulainn. Bricriu, a renowned troublemaker, has invited all the Irish heroes to a banquet. He promises to save the place of honour at the table for the knight he regards as the greatest of them all, but spreads dissension by telling each of three heroes that the place is reserved for him. Fighting breaks out, which is not resolved even after they petition the king of Munster. But then a giant stranger arrives at the royal palace, and challenges the three heroes to the beheading game, just as described in *Sir Gawain and the Green Knight*, except that here the return bout is on the following day. Two of the heroes chicken out, but Cú Chulainn takes up the challenge and is thus declared the greatest of the three.

The episode of the *Perceval* continuation in which this test appears is virtually a separate entity often called the *Livre de Caradoc*, which may have had a separate existence prior to its incorporation in that poem. Caradoc, a key figure at Arthur's court, appears in both *Culhwch and Olwen* and *The Dream of Rhonabwy*, and it is likely that the original version of the *Livre de Caradoc* was a Welsh tale which had drawn upon the Irish legend.

There is another episode in the *Livre de Caradoc* that is also a test, although of a different kind. Towards the end of the story, a youth arrives with a drinking horn, which will spill its contents over any man who drinks from it whose wife has been unfaithful. Only Caradoc passes the test. This episode was lifted almost entirely from the *Lai du Cor* by Robert Biket, which dates from the 1160s or earlier. The wife of Caradoc was Tegau Eurfron, listed in Triad 103 as one of the "Three Chaste Maidens" of Prydein. The same triad calls her "one of the three beauteous dames in the court of Arthur". Intriguingly, the list of the "Thirteen Treasures of Britain" includes the mantle of Tegau Eurfron, and one of the other versions of the chastity test is of a mantle that retains its beauty only on a faithful maiden. It is clear that legends about Caradoc were circulating in the Welsh world long before Biket's poem. Furthermore, although Biket places Arthur's court in Caerleon, he notes that Caradoc's wife had been born at Cirencester, and that the horn is still on display there. By the twelfth century Cirencester was no longer the major town it had been under the Romans, suggesting that it was not an obvious one for Biket to choose unless it was already associated with the legend of Caradoc and Tegau.

The "loathly lady" or *fier baiser* ("proud kiss") motif is perhaps best known from the *Wedding of Gawain and Dame Ragnell* and "The Wife of Bath's Tale" from the *Canterbury Tales*. In both cases, the hero agrees to marry a hideous hag in return for information, but discovers upon a kiss that she is the most beautiful woman in the world. The theme first appeared in *Le Bel Inconnu* ("The Fair Unknown"), by Renaud de Beaujeu, written in the late 1180s, in a slightly different form. A lady has been transformed into a serpent, but the young knight Guinglain is able to lift the curse with a kiss, and subsequently marries her. The motif can be traced back to the Irish tale, *The Adventures of the Sons of Eochaid Mugmedon*, in which Niall proves his suitability for kingship by kissing (and transforming) a hideous old hag. This tale was circulating by the 1020s and doubtless earlier, so was again well known by the time the Arthurian stories were taking shape.

In most cases, the authors of these early Celtic Arthurian tales are unknown – unless we accept the possible early roles of Taliesin or Llywarch Hen. However, one name has come down to us. Gerald of Wales, when not toadying up to the great and the good, wrote copiously, and refers to a great storyteller or "fabulator" who lived just before his time, called Bledhericus. Variants of that name crop up in other works. The Flanders poet Wauchier referred to a Bleheris, or Blihis, who knew of the Grail story, and the names Brandelis and Bleoberis feature as knights in the later romances. It is even conjectured (convincingly) that Bledhericus was the original of Merlin's mentor, Blaise.

Jessie L. Weston, in *From Ritual to Romance*, mentions a suggestion by Edward Owen of the Cymmorodorion Society that Bledhericus could have been "a certain Welsh noble" named Bledri ap Cadivor, a Welsh chieftain who lived near Carmarthen in Dyfed around 1080–1140. He was a *latemeri*, or interpreter, and it is understood that he was an intermediary between the Welsh and the Normans. Bledri also turned up at the court of Guillaume VII, count of Poitou (and IX of Aquitaine) in the 1110s or 1120s. Guillaume was the grandfather of Eleanor of Aquitaine, who was born at either Bordeaux or Guienne around 1120. Eleanor may even have heard these Arthurian stories directly from Bledri in her childhood, which would account for her lifelong interest in the subject.

The one story with which Bledri's name is associated is that of Tristan and Iseult (*see* Chapter 13). This was originally independent of the Arthurian story, and was not integrated until the prose *Tristan* of the 1240s. Bledri could have been the conduit for the Arthurian stories between Brittany, Wales and the Anglo-Norman world, reconstituting tales that had grown independently from a once-common source. Bledri was alive at the time of Geoffrey of Monmouth, and perhaps tales that Bledri recounted found their way to Geoffrey. Bledri is said to have compiled a collection of old tales about Gawain called *Le Grant Conte*, but no trace survives.

It is impossible to tell if Bledri or his counterparts were those who polished and refined *Culhwch and Olwen*, *Peredur*, *Geraint ab Erbin*, *Preideu Annwvyn* and *Le Livre de Caradoc*, all of which show that many independent Celtic Arthurian romances were circulating before Geoffrey compiled his *Historia*. Whilst Geoffrey was certainly aware of them, as a few of the elements found their way into his story of Arthur, he was not significantly influenced by them. However, with the mushrooming of interest in Arthur in the Anglo-Norman world, Geoffrey's successors looked to the old tales for ideas and inspiration, and the Arthurian legend began to grow.

2. The Alanic dimension

One of the less considered contributions to the Arthurian story, but one currently championed by C. Scott Littleton and Linda A. Malcor in *From Scythia to Camelot*, is the legends and stories of the Alans. The Alans were a Sarmatian tribe that rose to dominance in the latter years of the Roman Empire, whom we have already met in connection with Lucius Artorius Castus. They had steadily migrated from central Asia to settle in the Caucasus and around the northern shores of the Black Sea, with other groups settling in Persia. They gradually infiltrated eastern Europe, but were overwhelmed by the Huns and moved west, settling in France and Spain, whilst another group joined forces with the Vandals in North Africa.

The Alans that had remained in the Caucasus became the peoples now called the Ossetians. One of the most significant links between the Alans and the Arthurian legend comes from the Ossetian legend of Batraz's sword. Batraz, belonging to the group of warriors called the *Nartamongae* (Narts), has wreaked revenge upon those who killed his father, and, now satisfied, is prepared for his own death. He commands that his sword be thrown back into the sea. The sword is so heavy that his men hide it instead, but when Batraz asks them what they saw and they say nothing, he knows they have deceived him. He commands them again and this time they drag the sword to the sea and cast it in. At that point the sea bubbles blood red. They tell Batraz what they saw, and he dies fulfilled. The link with Arthur's final command for Excalibur is only too obvious. Whilst it is common in Celtic funeral tradition to cast swords and precious artefacts into lakes as offerings to the Otherworld, the eastern parallels with Bedivere's reluctance to throw Excalibur into the lake are pertinent.

There are other compelling parallels between the Sarmatian tales and the Arthurian romances. Lancelot has much in common with Batraz; both are raised by a fey-like female guardian associated with water, and are described as the best of all knights. Perceval, too, has parallels with the story of Kai Kosrau, as later told by the Persian poet Firdausi. Both are regarded as fools, both have lost their father and live in the forest, and both are encouraged to become warriors by their encounters with knights.

Perceval later learns that many of his ancestors bear the name Alan. There is also much similarity between the Tristan and Iseult story, and the Persian tale *Vîs u Râmîn* by Fakhr Ud-Din Gurgâni (*see* Chapter 13). Finally, the Cup of the Narts may be seen as a prototype Grail: it refills itself when empty; it can tell if anyone drinking from it is telling lies; and it can only be awarded to one amongst them who is without flaw.

The Alans established themselves across north-central France in those very territories that later developed the Arthurian romances, particularly Champagne, Normandy and Brittany. Through marriage, Alanic rulers claimed part of the kingdom of Brittany, the earliest ruling in the early 600s, and thus a contemporary of Athrwys of Gwent. Alain the Great established himself as king of Brittany in 888, and it was under his grandson Alain Barbetorte ("Twisted Beard") that Brittany became a duchy. The last of Barbetorte's descendants was Conan IV, whose daughter Constance married Geoffrey, son of Henry II and Eleanor of Aquitaine. Their son, who became duke of Brittany in 1187, was called Arthur.

Littleton and Malcor present a strong case for the Arthurian stories being a blend of Alanic and Celtic tales, each overlaying the other until their origins have become blurred. It is also probable that the original legends brought west by the Alans later found affinity with stories brought back by the Crusaders, and that these gave a greater depth and resonance to the growing Arthurian *mythos*.

Geoffrey may not have been aware of any of this when he completed his *Historia*, and it was for his successors to create the stories that we now know so well. His successors took two forms. There were those who translated and developed his *Historia*, and those who ignored history and went straight to the popular tales. It was the latter who developed the cycle of adventures, but not without some input from the former.

3. Wace and Layamon

Geoffrey's *Historia Regum Britanniae* had been a roaring success, and in his day there must have been several thousand copies circulating. Most were in Latin, but translations also started to appear. The earliest was by Geffrei Gaimar, who translated it into Anglo-Norman during the 1140s for Ralph Fitz Gilbert, in Lincolnshire. Gaimar brought the history up to the time of William II, titling it *Lestoire des Engles*. Unfortunately, his translation of Geoffrey's original *Historia* is now lost. It was soon superseded by a more significant version by Robert Wace, known as the *Roman de Brut*.

Wace was born in the first decade of the twelfth century, and was a Norman teacher and cleric who ended his days as a canon at the abbey of Bayeux in the late 1170s. He tells us that he was born on the island of Jersey and was educated at Caen, and also in the Ile de France before returning to Caen. We know from his surviving writings that he undertook independent research, mostly in Brittany, but also in parts of southern Britain, most likely the West Country. As a result, he brought his own thoughts to his translation. He did not simply invent material; rather, he stated his sources and at times questioned Geoffrey. He even refrained from translating the *Prophecies of Merlin* because he did not know how to interpret them.

Wace completed his work in 1155, and presented a copy to Eleanor of Aquitaine. With this royal audience in mind, Wace represented Arthur in a courtly style. This was not the full-blown courtliness of the later French romances, but one that removed Arthur from the sedateness of Geoffrey and the baseness of the Celtic tales. Arthur was portrayed as a king who was the equal, and in the mould of, the Anglo-Norman rulers. Most significantly, Wace introduced the Round Table:

> Arthur held high state in a very splendid fashion. He ordained the courtesies of courts and bore himself with so rich and noble a bearing that neither the emperor's court at Rome nor any other bragged of by man was accounted as aught besides that of the king. Arthur never heard speak of a knight in praise, but he caused him to be numbered of his household. [. . .] Because of these noble lords about his hall, of whom each pained himself to be the hardiest champion, and none would count himself the least praiseworthy, Arthur made the Round Table, of which the Bretons tell many fables. This Round Table was ordained of Arthur so

> that when his fair fellowship sat to meat their chairs should be high alike, their service equal, and none before or after his comrade. [. . .] From all the lands there voyaged to his court such knights as were in quest either of gain or worship. Of these lords some drew near to hear tell of Arthur's courtesies; others to marvel at the pride of his state; these to have speech with the knights of his chivalry; and some to receive of his largeness costly gifts.
>
> (Adapted from the translation by Eugene Mason, *Wace and Layamon*, Dent, 1912)

He was very likely describing Henry's court. Geoffrey's slightly more sober description is an interesting comparison:

> Arthur then began to increase his personal entourage by inviting very distinguished men from far-distant kingdoms to join it. In this way he developed such a code of courtliness in his household that he inspired peoples living far away to imitate him. The result was that even the man of noblest birth, once he was roused to rivalry, thought nothing at all of himself unless he wore his arms and dressed in the same way as Arthur's knights. [*ix*.11]

Geoffrey's account may have presented the "facts", but Wace's created the image. Although later romancers developed Wace's description, such as the idea that Arthur would not start one of his Holy Day meals before he had heard an account of some adventure, no one added anything of significance to change the basic impression. It was Wace who clothed Geoffrey's basic concept in pageantry for the romancers to embellish.

Wace also mentions the "marvellous gestes and errant deeds" attributed to Arthur. He goes so far as to say that, "They have been noised about this mighty realm for so great a space that the truth has turned to fable and an idle song." But, he also remarks, "the truth stands hid in the trappings of a tale." Wace understood that although it was no longer possible to separate fact from fiction, nevertheless deep down there was a basic truth. But this understanding does not stop him telling a good tale. He gives a rousing description of Arthur's battle against the giant of Mont-

St.-Michel, and of the fight against the Romans. He brings to life Arthur's final battle against Mordred, and develops the idea that Arthur will return. Whereas Geoffrey closes the life of Arthur with the noncommittal "[he] . . . was carried off to the isle of Avalon so that his wounds might be attended to", Wace adds that "He is yet in Avalon, awaited of the Britons; for as they say and deem he will return from whence he went and live again." Wace ends cautiously, saying "but nevertheless Arthur came never again." Henry II did not want to give the Welsh more fuel for rebellion.

Wace refers to the Round Table on three occasions. Twice he means specifically an item of furniture, but the third time, at the final battle, he refers to the deaths of "the knights of his Table Round, whose praise was bruited about the whole world," suggesting a knightly order of fellowship. This was an idea that would catch on throughout the kingdoms of the Middle Ages. When Edward III instigated the Order of the Garter in 1348, he was originally going to call it the Order of the Round Table. The concept of a "Round Table" as a gathering of knights for a tournament or pageant was also widely used. Its earliest such spectacle, as reported by Philippe de Navarre, was in 1223 when Jean d'Ibelin, Lord of Beirut, held a pageant in Cyprus for the knighting of his sons. Jean was related to the influential de Lusignan family amongst whom were the kings of Jerusalem, and had been Constable of Jerusalem from 1194. It is possible that Jean had seen what was supposed to be the Table of the Last Supper in the Holy Land. This was reputed to be round, and it features heavily in the Grail legend.

We do not know where Wace got the idea of a Round Table. He could well have heard of it in discussion at court from crusaders returning from the Holy Land, or amongst the fables of the Bretons. According to Peter Berresford Ellis, in *Celt and Greek*, it had become an established pattern at large gatherings for everyone to sit in an open circle with the most important individuals, usually the chieftain and the host, sitting at the centre. It was an obvious model to adopt, and if it also happened to fit in with the stories coming back from the Holy Land, so much the better.

Wace's work was every bit as popular as Geoffrey's, and likewise had its translators, including Layamon, a parish priest at Arley in Worcestershire, near Kidderminster, within sight of the Wrekin. Layamon was a Saxon, though his name indicates Scandinavian blood. Layamon embarked upon his translation, known simply as *Brut*, with great gusto. His final version, written in the 1190s, is, despite telling no additional story, a third longer than Wace's. It is simply full of rousing embellishments and flair that bring the story alive in the manner of such great Saxon and Danish stories as *Beowulf*. Layamon turns a history into a full story, complete with reported speech and detailed observation. He certainly doesn't let facts get in the way of a good tale. At his birth, the elves place Arthur under magical protection, and when he is wounded in the final battle it is the Elf Queen Argante who takes him to Avalon to be healed.

Layamon also greatly elaborates the reference to the Round Table. A fight breaks out in Arthur's hall over who should have precedence in dining, just as in *Bricriu's Feast*. A Cornish craftsman tells Arthur that he can make him a table that will seat 1600 men "all turn about", yet a table that could be taken with him and set up wherever needed. It doesn't take much to see that if all those men were seated around the outside of a circle, the table would be at least a hundred feet in diameter. However, Layamon also describes the seating as "without and within", suggesting that this may be an open circle with seating inside and out. Since it was portable it would consist of a series of interlocking trestle tables, which were the norm at most Saxon courts. Even so, it would require a significant number of tables (perhaps sixty or seventy), hardly ideal for transporting across country. But if Layamon was happy with elves magicking Arthur away, a table of such proportions clearly would present no problem.

Layamon completed his *Brut* sometime during the 1190s, by which time the Arthurian romances had taken a hold on the Anglo-Norman world. Others would continue to develop and adapt Geoffrey's *Historia*, mostly notably Robert Mannyng who incorporated his translation of Wace's *Brut* into the first part of *Story of England* (1328), and John Hardyng who used the Arthurian tales as a symbolic forerunner of the Lancastrian and Yorkist struggles in his *Chronicle* (1461). The intervening two hundred years, however, saw the historical Arthur eclipsed by the hero of legend.

4. Chrétien de Troyes

Wace tells us that at the time he was writing, in the early 1150s, tales of Arthur too numerous to mention were circulating throughout the Breton and Anglo-Norman world. Geoffrey and Wace were capitalising on an existing fascination amongst the general populace and re-presenting the legend in a form that related to the royalty and nobility of Europe.

Of particular significance was Wace's royal patronage, because it was the court of Henry II and Henry's network of relatives throughout Europe that would encourage the development of the Arthurian romance, partly for the sheer pleasure of the stories, but mostly because of what these stories signified for the Anglo-Norman world.

For the ladies, there were short pieces of courtly romance composed by Robert Biket and Marie de France. We don't know anything about Biket, but Marie de France clearly moved in royal circles. Her *lais* were dedicated to Henry II, whilst her collection of Aesopian fables, *Ysopet*, was dedicated to a Count William. William is usually identified as Henry's illegitimate son William Longespée, although if the fables were translated early enough he could be Henry's first-born, William, Count of Poitiers, a title inherited through his mother Eleanor of Aquitaine. William died in 1156, not three years old. Marie de France has never been properly identified, but one suggestion is that she was Henry's illegitimate half-sister, who was Abbess of Shaftesbury from 1181 to her death around 1216.

On a grander scale were the verse romances of Chrétien de Troyes, the man who effectively invented the genre. Geoffrey and Wace may have built the beacon, even added the fuel, but it was Chrétien who ignited it and its flames still shine nearly nine hundred years later. It was Chrétien who gave us Camelot and Lancelot and the Grail, along with dramatic adventures, mystical conundrums and the whole world of Arthurian chivalry and romance.

Chrétien's early work was all to do with romance, including translations of the love poems of Ovid. Not for him the harsh reality of a Dark Age Briton fighting for survival against the Saxons. In fact, Chrétien was not that interested in Arthur. He was more interested in stories of romance and peril that reflected the world around him, and how these stories might win the hearts of the ladies at court. What better means than the adventures of Arthur's knights? In this way Chrétien shifted the entire focus from warfare to romance.

Chrétien's initial inspiration may not have been the story of Arthur, but the parallel story of Tristan and Iseult. The *ménage à trois* between Mark, king of Cornwall, his young wife Iseult and his nephew Tristan was ripe for intrigue. At the start of *Cligés*, Chrétien tells us that he has written a romance about King Mark and the fair-haired Iseult. We can see here an obvious parallel with the other romantic threesome of Arthur, Lancelot and Guenevere. There had been no hint of this in any of the previous legends or histories, though there was a story of Guenevere's abduction by Melwas in Caradog's *Life of Gildas*, whilst Geoffrey and Wace refer to her abduction by Mordred. When Chrétien came to write about Lancelot and Guenevere in *Le Chevalier de la charrete*, which starts with her abduction by Meleagaunt (Caradog's Melwas), he grafted on to this the basic Mark/Tristan/Iseult formula and reworked it in an Arthurian milieu.

Before Chrétien gave this impetus to the Arthurian legend it had been the Tristan story that was gathering pace. Versions of the story were produced by Marie de France, Thomas d'Angleterre (a French poet at the court in London), Eilhart von Oberge (possibly from Brunswick) and Béroul (possibly from Normandy), from the 1160s to the 1190s, all drawing upon a now lost ur-*Tristan*, which may have been the original inspiration for all courtly romances. The best known of the versions of *Tristan* was that by Gottfried von Strassburg, written but not completed soon after the year 1200.

Chrétien's earliest surviving romances cleverly play around with the basic concept of love versus valour. *Erec et Enide*, begun in the late 1160s, is about a knight who wins a bride because of his daring and bravery, and settles down to married life. After his friends begin to believe that he has become a coward, he sets out again to prove himself. *Cligés*, from the early 1170s, tells of a knight who is in love with a woman who is promised to another. To forget about her, he goes to Arthur's court but is later reunited with his love, using a twist on the Tristan theme. In *Yvain: Le Chevalier au lion* (late 1170s), Yvain falls in love with the widow of a lord he has just killed. She agrees to marry him if he will stay with her and guard the castle and its spring. He does so, but soon yearns for adventure and risks losing his love in order to return to Arthur's court.

Chrétien's influence cannot be underestimated. Both *Erec et Enide* and *Yvain* reappeared in Welsh literature, and were grouped into the *Mabinogion*, renamed *Geraint ab Erbin* and *Owain* (also known as *The Lady of the Fountain*). Arguments have raged over whether the Welsh versions were based on Chrétien's stories, or if both drew their inspiration from a common Celtic story. My own view is that there must have been a Celtic original, either Welsh or Breton, because we find that Chrétien borrows so many of his names from the earlier tales. This must be the case for *Erec et Enide*, because at the end of Chrétien's story, when Erec sets out again on his quests, he takes Enide with him but behaves very strangely towards her. He will not let her speak and rebukes her if she does, even though she is trying to save Erec from danger. For a courtly romance, Erec is exceedingly uncourtly. The Welsh version makes more sense. In it, Geraint is led to believe that his wife has been unfaithful and so takes her with him on his adventures in order to keep an eye on her. It is probable that the original Celtic story was along these lines, and Chrétien adapted it for his own purpose, and that the Welsh version remained more faithful to the original. The Welsh versions are also notable for their lack of courtly intrigue. These are basic stories, clearly with no desire for all that romantic nonsense.

The stories *Erec* and *Yvain* also inspired the Arthurian romance in Germany, and at the same time established the reputation of Hartmann von Aue, who had the same impact in Germany as Chrétien did in France. Hartmann's version, *Erek,* is usually dated to the early 1180s, whilst *Iwein* was not completed until around 1202. There are parts of *Erek* which agree more with the interpretation of the Welsh *Geraint* than with Chrétien's. Since the Welsh version appearing in the *Mabinogion* had yet to be written, we can only assume either that Hartmann knew of an earlier proto-version, or that the Welsh adapter was aware of Hartmann's work.

It seems likely that it was the Tristan story that helped establish the courtly romance, which promptly sucked in the Arthurian story. Certainly by the 1180s the Arthurian setting so epitomized the courtly romance that when Andreas Capellanus wrote a treatise on courtly love, *De Amore*, he included within it a story by way of example, set at Arthur's court. Yet although Chrétien's first three romances include Arthurian characters and settings they were not essential to the story. Chrétien chose to include those elements because it was the vogue to do so. His main intent was to explore the idea of a knight torn between love and adventure, a story that had strong resonance at the time because of the demands on knights caused by the Crusades.

When Chrétien turned to matters more closely associated with Arthur, as with Lancelot, and Perceval and the Grail, he found it harder, so much so that he was unable to complete either story. *Le Chevalier de la charrete*, the proper title of the Lancelot story, was completed by Godefroi de Leigny, admittedly from an outline, whilst the Perceval story *Conte du Graal* was taken up by at least four "continuators". We do not know why Chrétien did not finish either story. *Conte du Graal* is regarded as the last of his stories, so he may not have lived to complete it. He may have left it incomplete because his patron, Philippe d'Alsace, Count of Flanders, died on the Third Crusade at Acre in June 1191. As for the Lancelot story, we know that he was writing *Yvain* at the same time, and it may be that he became too wrapped up in one to finish the other. Yet it is significant that he had problems developing a story beyond his basic formula.

Chrétien's patrons are important. The Lancelot story had been commissioned by Marie, countess of Champagne, daughter of Louis VII and his first wife Eleanor of Aquitaine. Marie was thus Henry II's stepdaughter. Marie's husband was Henri, count of Champagne, probably Europe's greatest diplomat of the period. In 1179 Henri, involved in the ill-fated attempt to relieve Tibériade from Saladin's forces, was captured by the Turks and only freed because of the intervention of the Byzantine emperor. His health was ruined, and he died soon after his return in March 1181. This must have affected Chrétien's work and might be a factor in why he did not complete *Le Chevalier de la charrete*. It may also be because he received more urgent commission to write the Grail story.

That commission came from Philippe d'Alsace, the flamboyant count of Flanders and a cousin of Henry II, who had returned from a visit to the Holy Land in 1179. Chrétien tells us that Philippe gave him a book and asked him to "tell in rhyme the finest story ever related in a royal court." We do not know what book that was. Was Chrétien trying the same literary device as Geoffrey of Monmouth? The answer is the same as for Geoffrey: why should Chrétien say something about his patron if it wasn't true? It is more likely that Philippe did have some book, perhaps in Latin, which he wanted adapted into Chrétien's courtly verse.

This means that Philippe already had an interest in the Grail. In fact, Philippe was a collector of relics, an interest that may have stemmed from his father Thierry, count of Flanders, who had joined the Second Crusade in 1147 and fought at Damascus. Thierry returned in 1150 with a bowl in which Joseph of Arimathea was reputed to have collected the blood of Christ from the cross. A special chapel was built for the bowl at Bruges, in Flanders, which is called the Chapel of the Precious Blood. Philippe had doubtless come across a story that he believed had some relevance to this relic, and it was from this interest that the Grail story began.

According to Noel Currer-Briggs in *The Shroud and the Grail*, the real reason for Philippe's visit to the Holy Land had been to secure a marriage between one of the sons of his favourite vassal Robert de Bethune, and one of the sisters of Baldwin IV, king of Jerusalem. Philippe's attempt failed, but he would have made some interesting connections in Jerusalem.

One of those he would have met was William, Archbishop of Tyre. William (*c*1130–1190) was also Chancellor of Jerusalem, effectively running the kingdom on behalf of the young Baldwin IV. He had been Baldwin's tutor, as well as principal advisor to Baldwin's father Amalric I. William had been born in the Holy Land, the son of a French or Anglo-Norman family who had settled there, and was fluent not only in French, English and Latin but also in Greek and Arabic.

As archdeacon, it was William who blessed the marriage in 1167 between Amalric and Maria Comnena, daughter of the Byzantine emperor Manuel. Currer-Briggs tells us that in 1171 Amalric visited Manuel in Constantinople, accompanied by William of Tyre, who recorded the event. We learn that Amalric (and possibly William) was given a full tour of the palace at Constantinople, and would have seen a very special relic we now call the Shroud of Turin.

There is little doubt that with his interest in relics Philippe of Flanders would have learned of the shroud from William. When Philippe returned from the Holy Land in 1178, he went via Constantinople. He may not have had an opportunity to see the shroud, but he would doubtless have tracked down other items, possibly including the book he gave Chrétien.

Of course, the shroud was not the first great relic to be seen in the East. In 1098, during the First Crusade, the monk Peter Bartholomew was supposed to have had a vision that led him to discover the Holy Lance in St. Peter's cathedral in Antioch. This was reputedly the spear which pierced Christ's body on the cross, variously called the Lance of Longinus (the name of the centurion) or the Spear of Destiny. Many were sceptical that this was the true spear – after all, one was also supposed to have found its way to the court of Charlemagne, whilst another (or a fragment of the same one) was in the church of Hagia Sofia in Constantinople. Nevertheless, the discovery of the lance was a spiritual boost to the Crusaders and spread dissension through the Muslim ranks, so no one investigated it too thoroughly.

Armed with a book, details of Philippe's father Thierry's pearl-rimmed relic, "Precious Blood", and the stories of the shroud and the Holy Lance, Chrétien had more than enough to inspire his story of Perceval and the Grail, (I discuss this in more detail in Chapter 16, and return to William of Tyre later). Suffice it to say that regardless of the interest that Chrétien's work had already created in the Arthurian romance, it was as nothing to the storm that would start with the appearance of the unfinished Grail Story.

We have seen that in the quarter century from 1155 to 1180 Chrétien's stories, especially *Erec* and *Yvain*, established the

Arthurian world as the preferred setting for the courtly romance for the next three hundred years. However, in terms of the development of the Arthurian legend as we know it, it was *Le Chevalier de la charrete* and *Conte du Graal* – stories inspired by the Crusaders through the influence of Henri de Champagne and Philippe d'Alsace – that were most important.

5. Robert de Boron and Wolfram

Le Chevalier de la charrete and *Conte du Graal* set in train a sequence of romances that within a generation would come together in the massive *Roman du Graal.* The story of Lancelot went through a slightly strange evolution (*see* Chapter 17), but the *Conte du Graal* was like a virus. Once it was released on the world there was no holding it back, perhaps all the more because it was left unfinished. Two poets – alas, their identities are uncertain – added their own versions of the ending, one following Gawain's story and one Perceval's, whilst the Welsh version, *Peredur*, cut it back to basics. The author of the second continuation was once believed to be Wauchier (or Gautier) de Denain, and although no clear attribution has been made no better candidate has come forth.

It was left to Robert de Boron to give new shape and direction to the Grail story. Robert produced at least three Arthurian romances, which gave some background to Chrétien's work. The only one that survives is the first, known as *Joseph d'Arimathie*, but which Robert may have called *L'Estoire dou Graal*. He followed this with *Merlin*, of which only a fragment survives, and probably wrote a now-lost *Perceval*, of which a version may survive in a later prose copy known as the Didot-*Perceval* (after the one-time owner of the manuscript). It was Robert who Christianised the Grail story; Chrétien had left it open to interpretation. Robert specifically links the Grail to the "vessel" at the Last Supper, and suggests that this vessel is more like a cup, since Joseph captures blood from Jesus's wounds in it after the body is removed from the cross. Chrétien had described the Grail as more of a dish, or platter. Robert also introduces the veil of Veronica, clearly influenced by the Shroud of Turin.

Robert did not go quite so far as to say that Joseph and the Grail came to Britain. The implication is that they went to the West, to the "vale of Avalon". Although Avalon was rapidly becoming associated with Glastonbury, it was not an immediate connection at the time. After all, Avallon in central France was only about a hundred kilometres away from the village of Boron, where Robert presumably lived or was born. Robert, probably at the wish of his patron, may have been making the claim that the Grail had come to the Holy Roman Empire, thus giving it a superiority over Flanders or England.

Robert is believed to have been a cleric in the court of Gautier de Montbéliard, in the territory of Montfaucon in the Jura. That might suggest that he was sufficiently removed from the courts of Champagne and Flanders to have no connection, but not so. In the world of the Crusades everyone was connected (*see* Tables 12.2 and 12.3). In 1202, he left for the Crusades and married Burgundia, daughter of Amalric II, king of Jerusalem and Cyprus. Burgundia's half-sister (and sister-in-law!) was Alice de Champagne, granddaughter of Marie de Champagne, and her uncle was Jean d'Ibelin, who would hold the first known Round Table pageant.

We don't know if Robert de Boron accompanied Gautier to Cyprus. It's possible, because *Joseph d'Arimathie* shows knowledge of the cultures of the Middle East, especially Georgia and Armenia, with which Amalric de Lusignan (Gautier's father-in-law) was connected, and where the Ossetian legends circulated. The Crusades and the European alliance in Palestine were becoming reflected in the growing Grail story.

Robert's purpose was to show how the Grail would eventually enable Arthur to recover Rome. From what we know of his *Perceval* and *Merlin*, Robert seems to have portrayed Merlin as the medium who helped engineer Arthur as the individual who would conquer Rome and regain it for the Holy Roman Empire. Although Robert doesn't say so, it seems evident that Arthur's conquest of Rome is intended to equate to a recovery of the Eastern Empire, Byzantium, which by the early 1200s had become a fragmented mess, carved up between the leaders of the Crusades and the Turks. The appalling Fourth Crusade in 1204, which served only to destroy Constantinople, may or may

Table 12.2 The Kings of Jerusalem

Note: dates given are for the reigns as king/queen of Jerusalem only

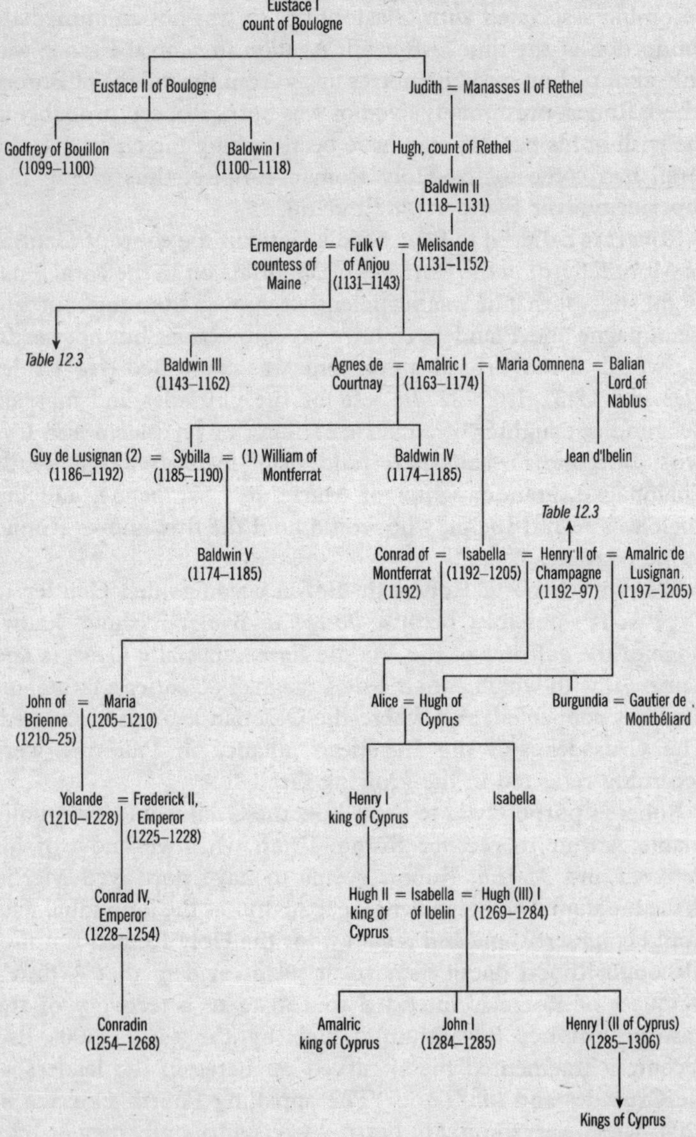

**Table 12.3 Constantinople and Jerusalem
The Angevin connection**

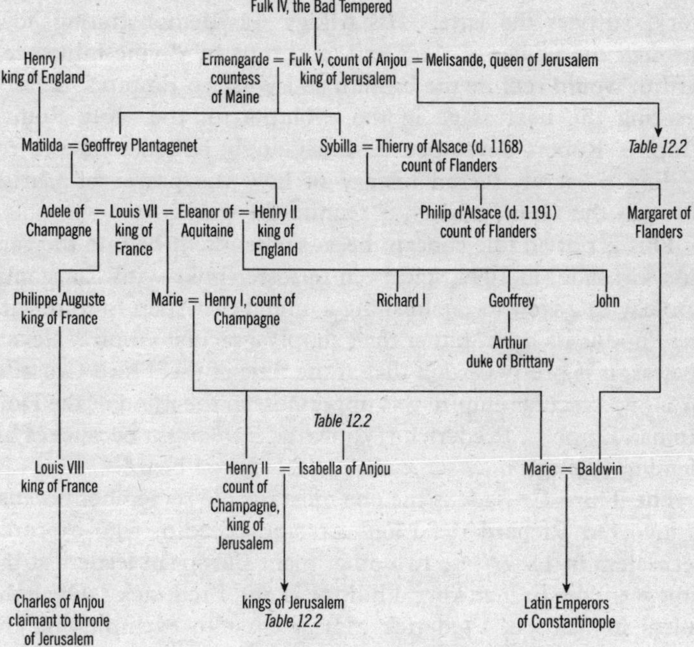

not have happened when Robert was working on his trilogy, and we cannot be sure if he was using the conquest of Rome as an analogy for recovering Jerusalem or conquering Constantinople, but I suspect the latter. His trilogy was demonstrating how, through the power of the Grail (and thus by divine influence), Arthur would reunite the Eastern and Western Empires, thereby creating the next stage in the evolution of the Holy Roman Empire. Robert developed an intriguingly linked sequence revealing a secret, sacred history of how the power of Christ, through the Grail, might yet reunite the world.

This is not an idle concept because the intent behind the very first Crusade, in 1096, had been to foster links with Constantinople with a view to establishing a united Christian Empire with the Pope as its head, rather than simply a secular empire. Nevertheless, it is pretty certain that at the time of the Third Crusade, in 1189, a secular empire was uppermost in the mind of the Holy Roman Emperor Frederick I, known as *Barbarossa* because of his flaming (though now somewhat grizzled) red beard.

The Third Crusade is the one most people remember because it involved Richard the Lionheart and Saladin, who captured Jerusalem in 1187. The two other main European leaders at the time were the French king, Philippe II and Frederick I. Of all the rulers in Europe, Frederick came closest to exemplifying the romantic image of the chivalric King Arthur. At the celebration of Pentecost in Mainz in 1188, Frederick was duly inspired and took the Cross. I strongly suspect that when Frederick led his vast army of some 100,000 men (Saladin believed it totalled a million!) out from Ratisbon in May 1189 – probably the largest and best equipped army ever to venture on a Crusade – he believed himself to be Arthur reborn. I also suspect that the latest generation of romancers had Frederick in mind when they wrote about Arthur.

Unfortunately, Frederick's crusade ended in disaster. The Byzantine Emperor Isaac Angelus had colluded with Saladin to hamper the overland route from Europe through Constantinople to the Holy Land, and Frederick's army had been forced to make a difficult crossing over the Bosporus, and through the mountains of Cilicia in southwest Turkey. Attempting to help his son, who was battling the Armenians at a bridge over the River

Calycadnus (modern Göksu), Frederick rode his horse across the river, but was carried away in the current and drowned. Although dispirited, Frederick's men took his body to the Holy Land and buried it at Antioch. However, just as in the legend of Arthur, rumours abounded that Frederick had not died but been washed away, and that he was presently sleeping and would return again to rule Germany.

Despite taking the Arthurian legend forward significantly by linking it to the legend of the Grail and Joseph of Arimathea, Robert was not a great writer, and his story is bland and straightforward. It required someone else to rework Chrétien's *Perceval* in a more inspired form, and that someone was Wolfram von Eschenbach. Wolfram referred to himself as a *minnesänger*, the German equivalent of a French troubadour. He joked about his own illiteracy, although that may simply mean he was not well versed in French or Latin. Wolfram probably came from somewhere near the town of Anspach, in Bavaria in southern Germany, and from about 1203 onwards was under the patronage of Hermann, Landgrave (count) of Thuringia, at his court at Wartburg in Eisenach. Hermann was a renowned patron of the arts, and we know that sometime around 1210 he commissioned Wolfram to translate the French *Aliscans* into the epic poem *Willehalm*. This non-Arthurian story of a young man's rise to knighthood and eventual retirement to a monastery is set against the background of Charlemagne's war against the Saracens, and was powerful Crusader fiction.

We do not know who commissioned Wolfram's *Parzival*, but Hermann probably played a part, since Wolfram was attached to his court at the time. The work appears to have been composed in two parts, since Wolfram stopped at the end of Book VI and asked for anyone else to continue it. He may have written these first six books at the behest of a patroness with whom he then fell out, and only continued the work when at the court of Hermann after 1203.

Like the continuators in Flanders, Wolfram was drawn to finish Chrétien's *Conte du Graal*. However, he was no slavish imitator. He even chides Chrétien's misuse of his source material, saying: "If Master Christian of Troyes has done wrong by this story, Kyot, who sent us the authentic tale, has good cause to be angry." Kyot, according to Wolfram, was a Provençal author and traveller who had found the manuscript – written in Arabic by an astronomer called Flegetanis – in Toledo. This may be a fictional device, but it gives an air of authenticity to a story that has many Arabic features. Wolfram's patrons, especially Hermann's son Ludwig who had been to the Holy Land with Henri of Champagne (the son of Marie, countess of Champagne), could easily have brought back any number of ancient documents. Wolfram used the idea of a more accurate source in order to explain the differences between his story and Chrétien's, and to allow it to develop along his own lines, whilst still contriving to relate it to the same subject. It was very effective.

There was a contemporary French writer, Guiot de Provins, but there is no reason to believe that Wolfram was suggesting Guiot as his source, despite the similarity of the name to *Kyot*, as nothing written by Guiot (a one-time *jongleur* turned monk who wrote social satire) has any connection with the Grail or the Holy Land. Yet Guiot did have some interesting connections. He was from Champagne (Provins is midway between Troyes and Paris), but had connections with Spain as one of his patrons was Pedro II of Aragon. Pedro's wife Maria was the granddaughter of the Byzantine Emperor Manuel. Guiot may well have known Chrétien, but there is no way of knowing if he knew Wolfram.

Another feature that suggests that Wolfram was following a previous script and not creating one is that his Parzival, rather than coming from Thuringia or Bavaria, is from Anjou. Chrétien makes no specific reference to Perceval's nationality. The implication is that he is either English or Welsh; indeed, most versions call Perceval *le Gallois*, "the Welshman". Making him an Angevin links him not only to the ruling house of England and Normandy, but more pertinently to the previous ruling house of Jerusalem. Fulk V, count of Anjou (whose son Geoffrey was the father of Henry II), had become king of Jerusalem through his marriage to Melisande, when her father Baldwin II died in 1131. He was succeeded by Amalric I.

The combined forces of the west never managed to regain Jerusalem after the Third Crusade, and the so-called kingdom remained in disarray, refocusing its "capital" at Acre. Fulk's line continued through his granddaughter Isabella, queen of Jerusalem, who married (amongst four husbands) Henri II of Champagne. After her death in 1205, at the time that Wolfram was writing *Parzival*, the kingdom passed through a sequence of daughters and husbands, until merging with the parallel kingdom of Cyprus.

In making Parzival an Angevin in search of the Grail castle, Wolfram was identifying the castle very clearly, to contemporary eyes, as a form of spiritual Jerusalem. It was not the same as Jerusalem, but was its spiritual counterpart. Parzival's adventures, and those of a more earthly Gawain, become joint quests to achieve control of the spiritual Jerusalem. Wolfram succeeds admirably in making the one an analogue of the other. All readers of *Parzifal* at the time would know what he was saying: that only the most devout and perfect Christian could achieve the Grail and, by inference, win the Holy War.

Parzival may even have become a way of excusing the creation and growth of the chivalric orders of knights in the Holy Land, the Knights Templar and the Teutonic Knights. Wolfram reveals that the Grail Knights are the "Templars", and that the Grail castle is a hidden fortress that governs the command of the west, sending out new lords to control tenantless lands. Wolfram's use of the world "Templars" or, more accurately, *Templeisen*, need not automatically mean the Knights Templar, since he is referring in general terms to those who guarded the Grail temple. But since he also dressed them in white surcoats with red crosses, the connection is inevitable.

However, the concept of the Grail Knights that Wolfram develops goes beyond the Templars, and becomes analogous to another order. The Teutonic Order of Knights, founded in 1190 and based at Acre, had been transformed in 1198 from a medical to a military order within the Knights Hospitaller. Their evolution into an independent order that fought on behalf of Christian rulers against pagan nations did not fully develop until after 1211, when Andrew, king of Hungary, hired them to combat the Kumans. Thereafter, the Teutonic Knights separated from the Knights Hospitaller and became mercenaries fighting in the name of God to protect Christians and to convert the pagans.

Wolfram makes a clever connection in the story. The symbol of the Teutonic Knights was a white surcoat charged with a black cross, covered by a dark blue mantle. The knight who becomes the Guardian of the Grail, Feirifiz (the illegitimate son of Parzival's father Gahmuret and the Arab queen Belacane of Zazamanc), is described as "particoloured", looking rather like a zebra, being half white and half black.

The Teutonic Knights were established under the auspices of Amalric II, king of Jerusalem. He was the fourth husband of Fulk's granddaughter Isabella, father-in-law of Gautier, Robert de Boron's patron and half brother of Jean d'Ibelin of the Round Table. The Master of the Teutonic Knights, at the time they developed their militaristic role in 1211, was Hermann von Salza. His family were vassals to Hermann of Thuringia on the Eisenach estate, and Salza had accompanied the Landgrave to the Holy Land in 1197, along with Henri II de Champagne. Hermann of Thuringia's son Ludwig married Elizabeth, daughter of Andrew of Hungary, whilst another son, Konrad, later became Grand Master of the Teutonic Knights.

There are too many coincidences here. Wolfram had finished working on *Parzival* by about 1210, concluding with the revelation that the Grail Knights secretly assisted dispossessed rulers against the pagans to protect the Christian faith. A year later, the new Master of the Teutonic Knights, who just happened to live on the estate where Wolfram was writing *Parzival*, set out to do exactly that in Hungary.

It is difficult to be certain which came first, as Wolfram may have been inspired by the concept of the Teutonic Knights, and worked their principles into *Parzival*. However, if Wolfram was also recounting his story of *Parzival* to Hermann of Thuringia, perhaps in the presence of Hermann von Salza, it suggests there must have been some interplay. I strongly suspect that Hermann of Thuringia used *Parzival* to help prepare the way for the new role of the Teutonic Knights by showing them as serving the holiest of purposes. The Grail Knights were not simply serving Christianity; they were protecting the Grail itself, the embodiment of Christ's spirit on earth. Under Wolfram, the Grail castle had become, on a spiritual plane, what the Papacy was on an earthly plane.

It is worth reminding ourselves that Wolfram did not write a further Grail poem. *Parzival* is complete in itself. Although

Arthur appears in the story, he has no significant role, although his nephew Gawain does, as an earthly counterpart to the spiritual quest of Perceval. *Parzival* is thus only a borderline Arthurian novel. Unlike Robert de Boron's work, which was looking toward a reunited Roman-Byzantine Empire, *Parzival* was looking to a united Papacy, and therefore did not need the Arthurian denouement.

At the same time as *Parzival* was being created, another writer, unfortunately anonymous, was also working from Chrétien's original and developing yet a third variant of the Grail story, usually called *The High History of the Holy Grail*, or *Perlesvaus*. It is a wholly allegorical version, far removed from Wolfram's secret history. Whereas the works by Chrétien, Robert de Boron and Wolfram were commissioned by the noble heads of Europe to promote and justify their activities in the Holy Land, *Perlesvaus* has the feel of a work produced by a member of the church to promote the spiritual and ethical aspects of the Grail. That suggests it was written by a learned monk or cleric, which is probably why it has remained anonymous, with no court poet claiming his hand or his patron. *Perlesvaus* lacks the inventiveness of Robert de Boron's work, the style of Wolfram's and the charm of Chrétien's, but what it has which those three lack is sincerity. It was composed by an individual who believed in what he was writing, not necessarily in a physical Grail, but in a spiritual goal. *Perlesvaus* was a book written not only to entertain, but to inspire and to provide a Christian foundation to the chivalric ideal.

Perlesvaus has some features that associate it with the Cathars, or Albigensians. It promotes the concept of self-determination, that an individual can transcend from earthly flesh, which the Cathars believed was corrupt, into the purity of the spiritual, through adherence to strict rules and disciplines. Because the Cathars did not conform to the church of Rome, they were considered heretics. This meant that Grail literature might also be considered subversive, but it appears that during this dangerous period everyone was preparing their own version of the Grail in order to achieve their own ends.

Because *Perlesvaus* gave a set of values in addition to a fascinating treatment of the Grail story, it provided a basis for the immense work that would come in the next decade, the most subversive and successful version of them all, the *Roman de Graal*.

6. The Vulgate Cycle

The success of the Grail stories, and the continued popularity of Chrétien's work, meant that by the second decade of the thirteenth century Arthurian stories were tumbling from every direction. The pseudonymous Guillaume le Clerc saw the same potential for political comment as the Grail writers in producing his Scottish adventure *Fergus of Galloway*, whilst the equally pseudonymous Paien de Maisières produced a slightly bawdy Gawain adventure in *Le Chevalier à l'Épée*. Many new knights came forward to share the limelight in *Wigalois*, *Meraugis*, *Yder*, *Jaufré*, and so on.

The proliferation of stories showed that a bedrock of tales had always been there, just ripe for the taking, amongst the Welsh and the Bretons and it seems every court poet, most of them French, but also German, Spanish, Italian, and even Norwegian, had a dozen or more Arthurian tales in their repertoire.

In addition to these writers, deep in the heart of Poitou someone was creating a masterpiece. The Vulgate Cycle, as it is called, runs to over 1,800 pages in translation (and that's just the first three books), and forms the basis of the Arthurian story as we know it. The title "Vulgate Cycle" is not very helpful; it was so named because of a similarity in form to the early Latin Bible, also called the Vulgate. More recently, scholars have called it the *Lancelot-Grail*, and it is steadily acquiring other names. My own preference is for these three volumes to be known as the *Roman de Lancelot*, but because the term Vulgate Cycle has become so attached, I shall still use that as and when suitable.

The first three books (later expanded to five) took a totally new approach. The author chose Lancelot as the central character, and the books tell of his life. The first book, *Lancelot*, tells of Lancelot's background and birth, his upbringing by the Lady of the Lake, his arrival at Arthur's court, his early adventures, including the capture of the Dolorous Garde, and his involvement in Arthur's war with Galehaut, who becomes Lancelot's firm friend. It also introduces Lancelot's love for Guenevere, and his relationship with Elaine of Astolat, which leads to the birth of Galahad. Along with a few mystical experiences, these last two facts are key to the second volume, the *Queste del Saint Graal*. This starts with the arrival of Galahad at Arthur's court, and the declaration by the knights that they would search ceaselessly for the Grail. The quest by Galahad serves as the framework for the quests by other knights, including Lancelot and Gawain, both of whom fail early, with only Bors and Perceval joining Galahad at the end. The third volume, *Mort Artu*, continues from the conclusion of the Grail quest, with the return of Bors to Arthur's court to tell the story. It charts the downfall of Arthur, from the plots by Agravain and Mordred to unveil Guenevere's adultery, the fracturing of the Round Table, the wars between Arthur and Lancelot, Mordred's usurpation of the throne, to the Battle of Camlann and the last days of the knights.

Although each book shows a different style, suggesting that they were written by different authors, there is a unified scheme to all three, which led Jean Frappier, writing in Loomis' *Arthurian Literature In The Middle Ages*, to suggest that the three books had an "architect" who plotted them all, and may even have written the *Lancelot*, but did not write all three. Curiously, the *Lancelot* is the one volume that has a separate life. There is an earlier version, *Lancelot do Lac*, which is not as long as the Vulgate *Lancelot*, taking events only as far as the end of the war with Galehaut, but which is otherwise identical. This was written only a few years before the Vulgate trilogy was started, and it's difficult to know where to draw the line. It is possible that *Lancelot do Lac* is a draft or early version of the Vulgate *Lancelot*, which was then extended when the Vulgate Cycle was conceived. We may well, therefore, have four authors, one of whom was also the grand "architect". First came the author of the original *Lancelot do Lac*, then the author who continued it as the Vulgate *Lancelot* (also known as the *Lancelot* Proper), and finally the two separate authors of the *Queste del Saint Graal* and the *Mort Artu*.

Curiously, all three books ascribe their authorship internally to Walter Map, yet all modern day scholars (with the exception of Noel Currer-Briggs) are adamant that Map could not have written them. There are three reasons for this. Firstly, Map was dead by 1209, and most evidence suggests that the Vulgate

Cycle was not started until 1215 at the earliest. Secondly, the stories show a limited knowledge of Wales and southern Britain, but a thorough knowledge of Poitou, where the trilogy is believe to have been composed. Thirdly, all three books are written from a Cistercian viewpoint and Map was vehemently anti-Cistercian. This last point is crucial to an understanding of the development of the Arthurian romance.

Map was born in or near Hereford, sometime around 1137. He regarded himself as English by birth but Welsh by association, and was probably of Welsh descent. He studied in Paris from 1154 to 1160, and thereafter was a clerk and justiciar to the court of Henry II, before becoming a canon of St. Paul's (and later of Lincoln and Hereford). He was Henry's representative at the Third Lateran Council in 1179, where he spoke out against the Waldensians (the followers of Peter Waldo who had denounced all wealth and may be seen as amongst the earliest Protestants). He was made archdeacon of Oxford in 1197, the post previously held by another Walter, the man who gave Geoffrey of Monmouth the "ancient" book to translate into Latin.

Map is known to have written a variety of works, but all that survives that is unarguably his is a collection of miscellaneous notes called *De Nugis Curialium* ("Courtier's Jottings"), consisting mostly of anecdotes and gossip, with Walter's wry observations on court life. It includes some poems and folk tales, and though there is nothing overtly Arthurian, there are short tales such as "Filii Mortue", about a knight who grieves after his wife's death but is then delighted to find her amongst a fairy host, which seems to have been the basis for the Breton *lai*, *Sir Orfeo*. That makes it possible, though not certain, that Map may have collected other folktales, and perhaps even composed items upon which later Arthurian stories were based. It has been claimed, though with no evidence, that Map may have written a Lancelot poem upon which *Lancelot do Lac* is based. Since the rest of the Vulgate *Lancelot* grew from the *Lancelot do Lac*, it might explain why Map's name is mentioned in the text. With Map's delight in court gossip, the idea of a story of adultery between queen and knight might have appealed to him. As Map served in the court of Henry II and Queen Eleanor, the subject of Arthurian tales would almost certainly have arisen.

So, all the circumstantial evidence is there, but it is sadly lacking in hard facts. Most damning of all is that Map was a close friend of Gerald of Wales, who, as we have seen, had written ingratiatingly about the exhumation of Arthur's remains at Glastonbury. Gerald refers to Walter several times in his writings, and it seems remarkable that Gerald makes no mention of Walter having written anything Arthurian. We must therefore concede that it is very unlikely that Walter Map wrote any of the Vulgate Cycle.

The question remains: why was this work attributed to him? Did his name give it a certain authority? Did he perhaps keep some records or other information that formed the basis of the cycle? I mentioned that Map attended the Lateran Council in 1179. Also there was William of Tyre, now archbishop, who had come to seek the Pope's support for a new Crusade. This was only a few months after Philippe d'Alsace had visited the Holy Land and met William. With Map's interest in folk tales, it is possible that he and William discussed similar matters. Noel Currer-Briggs is convinced that they did, and that Map composed the *Lancelot* Proper and the *Quest del Saint Graal* between 1183 and 1189 (when Henry II died), and the *Mort Artu* sometime after 1192, when he had finished *De Nugis Curialium*.

I am not convinced that Map wrote them. The variance in style is sufficient to suggest different authorship, but also there is something in what survives of Map's writings to suggest that he was not the type to write such a huge, sustained work. Someone who writes courtly jottings and anecdotes as much for fun as for any other purpose seldom produces a complicated, labyrinthine work of such magnitude. Also, someone renowned for speaking out against heretics and anyone who defied the Church would not then write a mystical, revelatory work containing some of the principles of those heretics.

This brings us to the matter of the Cistercians. Map's writings include several anti-Cistercian comments, primarily because he stood for the orthodox status quo and against any schism or fragmentation. However, his main argument against the Cistercians was their use of military force. He actually denounced them at the Lateran Council, remarking that, "Christ had forbidden Christians to use force and by using force the Templars had lost all the territory that the apostles had won by peaceful preaching." Map's argument was not against the Cistercian movement as such, but against what they had become.

The success and evolution of the Cistercians had been fast, and was due primarily to Bernard of Clairvaux (for whom the famous monastery and the breed of mountain dog are named). The Cistercians had been founded in 1098 by Robert of Molesme, who was related to the counts of Champagne. Robert had become dissatisfied with the practices undertaken by the Benedictines, obtained a dispensation to undertake reforms, and set up a new religious order at Cîteaux. Bernard joined the order in 1112, bringing a new vitality and charisma with him. New foundations were established, including one at Clairvaux in 1115, of which Bernard became the abbot. It was Bernard who championed the Knights Templar. At the Synod of Troyes in 1128, Bernard succeeded in securing official recognition of the Order and drew up the organisation's rules.

The first Cistercian pope, Eugenius III, was elected in 1145, and it was in response to his demands that, in the following year, Bernard made a rousing speech in the presence of Louis VII and Queen Eleanor, promoting the Second Crusade. Louis prostrated himself before Bernard and "took the Cross", a stage-managed affair if ever there was one. The Second Crusade was a disaster and Bernard, not understanding how it could have failed, believed it must be because of the sins of the Crusaders. He vowed to lead a new crusade himself, but was eventually talked out of it because of his ill health. He died soon after.

Over the next fifty years, the heads of the Cistercian order became more active and violent. Their condoning of the destruction of Constantinople in 1204 was another blot on an already saturated copybook.

Unfortunately, worse was to come. One of the heretical movements threatening the Catholic church were the Cathars, who claimed themselves as the "pure" ones, and railed against the corruption of the Catholic clergy and the pompousness of church doctrine. The Pope was determined to eliminate them, but all attempts failed. The last straw came when the Papal legate, Peter of Castelnau, was murdered in 1208, at the instigation – it was believed – of Raymond, count of Toulouse. The Pope sanctioned revenge and in 1209 Simon de Montfort, who was acting on behalf of the abbot of Cîteaux, Arnaud Amaury, seized Raymond's lands. The entire population of Béziers, over 20,000 men, women and children, were slaughtered. When de Montfort hesitated and asked the abbot how he would identify the heretics, Arnaud famously replied: "Kill them all. God will recognise His own."

By 1209, the same year that Walter Map died, the reputation of the Cistercians was exceedingly low. Might there be a way to redeem themselves? That must have been when someone turned his thoughts to the story of the Holy Grail. Although the Cistercians are not identified by name in the Vulgate Cycle, there are references throughout to the "white monks" and "white abbeys", as well as to procedures newly adopted by the Cistercians for confession and absolution. Roger Sherman Loomis, in *The Development of Arthurian Romance*, states: "Picture, then, the author as a monk in a white robe bending over a desk in a scriptorium or cloister, transforming the rough materials of chivalric fiction into an allegory of the search for God's grace."

The image may be sound, though a work of this scale must have required many monks, especially if they were producing several copies in addition to composing it. This project would have required approval by the abbot, possibly even the head of the order. It was a major project to redeem the Cistercians by featuring them at the centre of a holy quest conducted by the purest knight in the world, Galahad. Throughout the three books, it is repeatedly demonstrated that the smallest sin counts against you. Gawain, who has lustful thoughts, is soon ejected from the quest. Lancelot, once the greatest knight in the world, had sinned with Guenevere and could not achieve the quest. Each knight is put through many severe challenges to test their spiritual and moral resolve. Only then can they be rewarded with God's grace. What better way of making their case acceptable than for the Cistercians to claim that this is all the work of their greatest critic, Walter Map?

The powers that be had not finished with the Vulgate Cycle. Not long after its completion, two further books were added, by way of prequels. These were the *Estoire del Saint Graal* and the *Estoire de Merlin*. They effectively upgraded the first two books of Robert de Boron's trilogy, to serve as an historical introduction to the *Roman de Lancelot*. Even then the Cycle could not be laid to rest. By the 1230s, the five books had been revised as a new *Roman du Graal*, usually referred to as the Post-Vulgate Cycle. This was not hugely different from the original Vulgate Cycle except in one important respect, the addition of a new bridging section called the *Suite de Merlin*. This claims to be written by Robert de Boron, a claim that must be treated in the same way as the original Vulgate's pseudo-attribution to Walter Map.

The *Suite de Merlin* adds three significant elements: the Questing Beast, a new and cynical view of Arthur, and the "Dolorous Stroke." The Questing Beast is a strange hybrid creature that constantly bays like a pack of hounds, and is perpetually hunted by several knights. It seems that the very idea is representative of the Crusades. Here is something that, after more than a hundred years, seems to exist almost for its own sake, something which everyone makes an enormous noise over but which achieves very little. This interpretation is reinforced by the fact that the main questor of the beast, Pellinore, had in the earlier romances been a variant of Pelles, the Fisher King. In other words, the guardians of the Grail now seem locked into a never-ending quest that exists purely for its own sake.

In the Post-Vulgate cycle, Arthur is prepared to slaughter all newborn babies in order to rid himself of the prophesied threat to his kingship. Apart from the obvious Herod parallel, we now see an interpretation of the great Emperor destroying his off-spring kingdoms. That is effectively how the actions of the new Holy Roman Emperor, Frederick II, were seen. The grandson of Frederick Barbarossa, Frederick was heralded in his youth as *Stupor Mundi*, the "wonder of the world". A brilliant patron of arts and scholarship, he was really a Renaissance man two centuries too early. After twelve years of promises, Frederick eventually left for the Crusades in 1228, although he had to halt en route after catching the plague. Pope Gregory IX, who did not have a tenth of Frederick's intellect, excommunicated the emperor for failing to fulfil his promise. Frederick, with the contempt for authority that made him both brilliant and a victim of his own image, ignored the Pope and, once recovered, con-tinued to Acre. He was promptly excommunicated again, a fact which did not trouble him at all. A liberal at the time when all liberals were condemned, Frederick just continued to do what he had set out to do. He held a meeting with Saladin's nephew Nasir-ud-Din, Sultan of Egypt, and under the Treaty of Jaffa agreed a truce that saw the return of Jerusalem and other territory in Palestine to Christian control. He had achieved in a few weeks what no Crusader had achieved for forty years. Yet no one in the Western world seemed happy with this arrangement. It was seen as a weak truce rather than an outright victory, and, as Frederick was excommunicated, such a treaty could not really be accepted.

As a final irony, and a perfect example of the stupidity of the age, the authorities decreed that because Frederick was excommunicated, the entire city of Jerusalem was also threatened with excommunication if they had any dealings with him. Frederick remained untroubled. By right of his marriage three years earlier to Isabella of Jerusalem, Frederick was also King of Jerusalem, though this title passed in principle to his infant son Conrad, born in April 1228 (Isabella died a few days later). When Frederick entered Jerusalem on 17 March 1229, having been given the keys to the city by the Sultan, there was no one there to welcome him. So Frederick arranged his own coronation and crowned himself king the next day.

Returning to the Post-Vulgate Cycle, the "Dolorous Stroke" had, in fact, been a feature of all of the Grail stories, but its presentation kept changing. In the Vulgate Cycle, it occurred when the Pagan king Varlan took the Sword of the Strange Straps (itself a religious relic), and killed the Christian king Lambar. From that day the land was laid to waste until the coming of the Good Knight. In the Post-Vulgate version, it is the knight Balin who delivers the stroke. Effectively excommunicated by Arthur for killing the Lady of the Lake, Balin tries to prove himself in a series of quests, and at one stage fights an invisible knight. He manages to kill the knight, but is pursued by the knight's brother Pellam, the Fisher King. Chased through the Grail castle, Balin snatches up the Holy Lance and strikes Pellam with it.

The Dolorous Stroke was clearly a representation of the capture of Jerusalem by the Muslims, which initiated the Crusades. In the Vulgate version, it is described as a straightforward blow between East and West, but in the Post-Vulgate it is personalised and happens within the Grail castle. Since the Grail castle was effectively Jerusalem, and since Balin was an excommunicated knight, we may see here the writer of the Post-Vulgate cycle further criticising Frederick II, and suggesting that his actions would cause further destruction. The story continues with Balin fighting his brother Balan until both are killed, mirroring the battle that continued between Frederick and the papacy for much of the rest of his reign.

The growth in the Arthurian romance exactly parallels the period of the Crusades. A detailed analysis of all of the Romances, but particularly the works of Chrétien, de Boron, Wolfram and the Vulgate Cycle, relating all of the characters and events to people and circumstances in real life, has yet to be done, but I suspect we will find many parallels. Each author related events relevant to him, and thus there are several parallels to Arthur, Guenevere, Merlin, Lancelot and the Grail Knights. I have made my own interpretations in a few cases and have included those in the "Who's Who" section (*see* Chapter 23).

The Post-Vulgate cycle removes the main Lancelot episode, chiefly on grounds of length, but also because the need for the main Lancelot role had passed, as if the Crusades had sullied the reputation of the great knights. In fact, the day of the Crusades in the Holy Land had virtually passed with the loss of Jerusalem in 1244. At the time no one knew that Jerusalem would stay in Muslim hands, and there were further attempts to reclaim it, but no longer the consolidated efforts by the forces of Christendom. The last great crusader was Louis IX of France, later to become St. Louis, though his efforts also failed, as did those of Prince Edward, the future Edward I of England. Edward might have achieved results had not the death of his father caused him to return to England in 1272. Acre fell to the Mamluks in 1291 and that, effectively, brought an end to the Crusades.

It also brought an end to the mass of Arthurian romances. With the loss of the greater part of the Angevin Empire in France by the end of King John's reign, France was able once again to become French. The Angevin influence diminished, and with the crumbling of the Crusades the need for Arthur fell away. The champions of Christendom had failed to achieve their great goal, and they were now more concerned with internal affairs and tussles with their neighbours.

No new Arthurian story of any significance, apart from translations and reworkings, appeared for a century after the fall of Acre. Such as did appear were either parodies, like the anonymous "Knight of the Parrot", or stories that used the Arthurian setting to expose new problems. Most prevalent here were the land tenure wrangles in the Scottish borders that led to a flurry of Anglo-Scottish Arthurian stories featuring Gawain.

The only major work, itself a reworking of an old theme, but for once distinct and separate from the Arthurian cycle, was *Sir Gawain and the Green Knight*, regarded by many as the greatest Arthurian verse romance of all, certainly in English. Alas, its author, like those of all too many of these great works, remains anonymous.

Although interest in creating new Arthurian romances had faded, interest in the Arthurian world had not. Edward I was, in the words of Martin Biddle, "a passionate Arthurian". Writing sometime after 1316, the Dutch poet and chronicler Lodewijk van Velthem recorded a Round Table celebration held by Edward I in which the participants played the roles of the leading Arthurian knights. Biddle, in *King Arthur's Round Table*, has deduced that Lodewijk's account relates to one of two events. One was the celebrations at the time of Edward I's marriage to Margaret, daughter of Philip III of France, which happened at Canterbury in September 1299. The other is the celebrations in Winchester nine years earlier, in April 1290, for the imminent marriage of his daughter Joan of Acre to Gilbert de Clare, earl of Gloucester. If it was the latter, then this could well have been the event for which the Round Table, now displayed at Winchester, was made.

Records of these events are rare, but that does not mean that they did not happen. The next such event of interest was in 1344, when Edward III announced his intention to establish an Order of the Round Table "in the same manner and form as the Lord Arthur once King of England". That Arthur had fought the "English" was by now long forgotten. Edward's order did not come about, but the Order of the Garter was instigated in 1348. It is believed, however, again by Biddle, that with the 1344 announcement as the incentive, the Round Table at Winchester was moved from being an item of furniture to an icon, and raised to the wall. That simple act changed its significance considerably, as it became a symbol of greatness to behold rather than to use.

Few Arthurian romances had appeared during this period until *Sir Gawain and the Green Knight* sparked a revival of interest from the 1380s on. Most of these stories feature Gawain and are set in the north of England. They include *The Awntyrs off Arthure, The Carle of Carlyle* and probably the best known, *The Wedding of Sir Gawain and Dame Ragnell*, which may just have been an early effort by Malory. There were other efforts, such as the two renderings into English of the *Mort Artu* in verse form, known respectively as the "Alliterative" and the "Stanzaic" *Morte Arthur*.

The last great Arthurian work of the Middle Ages is also the one we know best and the one through which, in various modern versions or derivations, we come to know about Arthur – the *Morte Darthur* by Sir Thomas Malory. I shall discuss this and Malory in more detail in Chapter 19, but over the next few chapters I want to explore in more detail the main Arthurian characters and how they developed in the Arthurian romance.

13

TRISTAN AND ISEULT – THE ROMANCE BEGINS

Although Tristan, or Tristram as he became in English, is one of the best known Arthurian knights, he doesn't really belong in the Arthurian legend. He was not part of the original stories but infiltrated them via the first prose *Tristan* in the 1240s. The original story and characters had lives of their own.

1. The original Tristan

The name *Tristan*, or *Drystan*, is derived from the Pictish *Drust*, a name of obscure origin, but which may derive from the Celtic *drude*, meaning "druid", and may have been a title for Pictish priest-kings. There were several Pictish kings called Drust who lived during the Arthurian period (*see* Table 3.5).

The earliest is Drust mac Erp, ruler of the Picts from about 424 to 453, during whose reign Cunedda moved south to Wales, and the Pictish raid took place that led to the Alleluia victory of Germanus. Drust may also have been king at the time that an irate St Patrick wrote to Ceretic, the British ruler of Alclud, berating Ceretic's soldiers for capturing recently baptised Christians in Ireland, and selling them as slaves to the Picts.

The dates for Patrick have been subject to revision. His mission to Ireland is traditionally, based on the Annals, dated to 432 and he remained there until his death, c. 459–462. His letter to Ceretic is usually placed about halfway through that period, or about 447, towards the end of Drust mac Erp's reign. But the revised dates have Patrick's Irish mission starting in 456, and place his death in 493. This in turn places the letter to Ceretic in the early 470s. Fortuitously, the ruler of the Picts at this time was another "Drust", called Drest *Gurthinmoch*. This Drust ruled from about 468–498, which links him to the period of Arthur's battle campaign. The Tristan story includes an Irish warrior who exacts tribute from Tristan's uncle King Mark, thus suggesting a distant memory of Drest exacting tribute by way of slaves from the British or Irish.

There may be other clues in Scotland. Near Gatehouse of Fleet in Galloway is Trusty's Hill ("Drust's Hill"), which has some unusually carved Pictish stones yet is outside the traditional Pictish area, perhaps suggesting a successful Pictish raid on the British kingdom of Strathclyde. Near to Trusty's Hill is another hillfort, the Mote of Mark, which seems more than coincidence.

Whenever Tristan is mentioned in Celtic tales, he is given the patronymic *ap Tallwch*, the Brythonic form of the Pictish *Talorg*. The Pictish inheritance passed through the female line, usually through the sister of the preceding king, and, intriguingly, Drest *Gurthinmoch* was the grandson of the sister of Talorg ap Aniel.

There were several other Drests. Another by that name, Drest mac Giromt, ruled from about 513 to 533, and would have fought against the Gododdin. What is interesting about him is that his sister may have married Maelgwyn Gwynedd, since it has long been believed that the Pictish king Brude mac Maelchion was the son of Maelgwyn's union with a Pictish princess. There is one pedigree, recorded in *Bonedd yr Arwyr*, which connects Maelgwyn and a certain Trystan, giving Maelgwyn's mother Meddyf as Trystan's neice. However, this would make a distinction between Drest and Trystan.

There are two other cases in which the names Drust and Talorg come together. Drest mac Munait succeeded Talorg mac Mordeleg in 552. Though not apparently related, the names appear together in the Pictish king lists, and recorders may have presumed a father-son relationship. The second example is a Drust mac Talorcen, who ruled for one year from 781–782 and whose father went by the name of *Dubthalorc*, or Black Talorc. Although this is outside the Arthurian period, it is within a generation of the time when the Celtic oral legends started to come together during the reign of Merfyn Frych in the 820s.

The name Drust does have a Cornish connection, through the famous Tristan Stone just north of Fowey. Its worn inscription reads: DRUSTANS HIC IACET CUNOMORI FILIUS ("Here lies Drustan, the son of Cunomorus.") None of the Pictish Drusts had a father called Cunomorus. In fact, the one well-known Cunomorus, or Conmor, didn't even live in Britain, but in Brittany, in the 550s, and is remembered in the lives of various saints as a tyrant. He was a *Comes* (count), of Léon, who seized power over Domnonée, murdering the king, Ionas, or Jonas, and throwing the heir Iudwal into prison. He then married the king's widow, Leonore. There was considerable opposition to Conmor, including from Armel (one of the suggested manifestations of Arthur). Iudwal eventually recovered the throne, and Conmor was killed in battle. Gregory of Tours, the one reliable historian in all of this, makes him less of a tyrant and records that he gave sanctuary to Macliau, a neighbouring chieftain fleeing from his own brother. We also know that the usurped son Iudwal succeeded to the throne and that his grandson Judicaël flourished from about 610–640, thus dating Iudwal's youth to the 550s.

The hagiographer Wrmonoc, in the *Life of St. Paul Aurelian* (880s), refers to a King Marcus, also called *Quonomorius*, who might seem to be the same man as Conmor, but there is no evidence to support this. It is probable that Wrmonoc connected two contemporary rulers, one of Domnonée in Armorica, and one of Dumnonia in south-west Britain. The Dumnonian ruler is always referred to as March ap Meirchion, who lived in the 550s and 560s (*see* Table 3.10), certainly close enough to Conmor to suggest that they were contemporaries.

Conmor is the abbreviated Latin version of the Welsh *Cynfor*, and Cynfor ap Tudwal was March ap Meirchion's great-grandfather. It may be that, if Wrmonoc was working from a corrupt pedigree, he may have seen the names "March Cynfor" run together and made the wrong conclusion. Rachel Bromwich has suggested, in "The Tristan of the Welsh", included in *The Arthur of the Welsh*, that Cynfor may be the same man as the Cunomor on the Fowey stone. Cynfor is a generation earlier than Arthur of Badon, and if he were the father of an otherwise unrecorded Drust, that Drust could have been associated with

Arthur's warriors. However, he certainly would not be of the same generation as March's nephew.

There is one other place in the pedigrees where a similar conjunction of names appears, and this is amongst the descendants of Coel Hen (*see* Table 3.3). Urien of Rheged's father was Cinmarc, and his father was Merchiaun. The name March appears as Cinmarc, easily corruptible to Conmor. Cinmarc was known as "the Dismal", an epithet that may be appropriate to the Mark of legend, who had no wife and, until his courtiers forced him to, had no intention of marrying. This Cinmarc is exactly contemporary with Drest mac Giromt of the Picts, the uncle, as mentioned earlier, of Brude mac Maelchion. The name *Maelchion* could have been a corruption of Meirchion. If so, Brude's mother (Drest's sister) might have married Meirchion the Lean of Rheged, and Cinmarc would have been their son, and brother of Brude. This would make Drest the uncle of March, the exact reversal of the legend. Nevertheless, placing Mark/Cinmarc in the north does increase the chances of a Pictish union, and of him having had a son named Drust. If this were true, it would make him half-brother to Urien and Lot, a relationship not otherwise revealed in the legends.

There are few Celtic legends about March, and they are of no historical value. In one, March is imprisoned and, like the Birdman of Alcatraz, passes the time by teaching birds to fly. This legend is also associated with Alexander the Great, and was probably brought to Britain by the Romans, or may date to the time of the Crusades. The same legend says that he has the ears of a horse, but only his barber knows it, a story that probably arose because the name March means "horse".

The opening of *The Wooing of Emer* in the Ulster Cycle bears some similarity with Mark's story. Cú Chulainn is beloved by all, but has no wife. His friends implore him to marry, so Cú Chulainn sets out to woo Emer. Her father, Forgall the Wily, places a condition on any marriage, and Cú Chulainn has to complete a quest. A companion for part of his journey is Durst mac Serp (surely the Pict king, Drust mac Erp), but there any comparison ends.

As for Iseult, the name *Esyllt Fynwen* ("fair-neck") appears in *Culhwch and Olwen* as one of the ladies at Arthur's court, and reappears in the Welsh Triads as one of the "Three Faithless Wives" of Prydain. She is not remembered separately, however, and does not appear in any pedigree, so we may imagine her inclusion in *Culhwch and Olwen* is because her connection with Tristan was already an established legend.

A few independent Welsh legends survive about Tristan which depict him as a swineherd, and a particularly difficult one at that. He was minding the pigs of March when Arthur, Cei and Bedwyr came to him, and no matter what they tried, could not obtain a pig from him. Another tale tells how Tristan and Essyllt elope into the forest of Coed Celyddon, and Arthur has to seek them out. Tristan has a magical protection that kills anyone who draws his blood, and thus escapes unharmed. It needs the cunning of Gwalchmai (Gawain) to find Tristan and lure him back. Arthur gives Mark and Tristan a choice, saying that Esyllt can stay with one while the leaves are on the trees, and with the other when they are not. Mark chooses when the trees have no leaves, because of the long winter nights. But Esyllt argues that the holly, ivy and yew plants have leaves all year round, so she should be forever with Tristan.

These seem to be the few fragments that survive of a long-standing Tristan and Iseult legend, but there is insufficient evidence to show which Tristan or Mark they relate to, or when. Tristan, in any case, seems to be remembered in legend not just for his love of Iseult, but for the many disguises and schemes he employed to be with her. He may well be part of a much older "trickster" character common in most countries' folktales, and have nothing to do with a historical Mark and Iseult. The legendary King Mark may be a distortion of the Breton Conmor, who forcibly married the former king's widow, Leonore. The bare bones of that story could have evolved over time with other tales of tricksters and doomed love to develop into the legend.

In 1869, the German folklorist Karl Heinrich Graf noticed the similarity between the Tristan and Iseult story and the Persian story *Vîs u Râmîn*, written by Fakhr ud-Din Gurgâni around the year 1050. This was in turn derived from Parthian and Kurdish folklore, and the story could easily have been brought back from the Crusades around 1100, merging with a similar Welsh or Breton folktale. In *Vîs u Râmîn*, it is two brothers (Môbad and Râmîn) who love the same girl (Vîs), and there is even a talisman which binds Môbad to Vîs but renders him impotent. Râmîn tries all kinds of schemes to be with Vîs and is eventually banished. He asks for forgiveness, and is taken back by Môbad, who marries Vîs. This story has a happy ending, but otherwise there are parallels, which may have found resonances amongst the French troubadours, with the Celtic tale.

Whatever the circumstances, the evidence suggests that a basic story about Tristan and Iseult had evolved by the early 1100s. The Welsh interpreter Bledri is even credited with telling such a story, and that tale seems to have been picked up by a French troubadour living in London, known as Thomas d'Angleterre. Below I set out the original story in more detail, and then follow through the later versions to show how the tale became part of the Arthurian cycle of romances.

2. The original story

The original French story had nothing to do with King Arthur. It starts with Rivalin, king of Lyonesse, who falls in love with Blancheflor, the sister of Mark, king of Cornwall. Rivalin is killed in battle, and Blancheflor dies giving birth, naming her child Tristan. She leaves a ring by which Tristan will be recognised. He is at first raised by Rivalin's trusty marshal Roald, and his tutor Governal. He becomes well educated, and a good swordsman and harpist. After several youthful adventures, he is brought to the court of King Mark, where, because of the ring, he is recognised and made a knight. Tristan kills the Irish warrior Morholt, who has come to exact an annual tribute from Mark, but receives a poisoned wound himself. Believing he will die, he casts himself adrift in a boat but is washed up on the shores of Ireland, where he is cured by the queen (Morholt's sister) and her daughter Iseult, who believes he is a minstrel called Tantris. He returns to Britain, to his uncle's court. Mark is relieved that Tristan has survived. He wishes his nephew to succeed him, so determines not to marry. His court insists that he should, so Mark sets an impossible challenge. He says that he will marry the woman whose threads of hair two swallows have been fighting over. Tristran leads the quest, and although he does not want to go back to Ireland, a storm drives him there. He fights and defeats a dragon, but is overcome by the poisonous fumes. He is again revived by Iseult, who recognizes him and realizes that he had killed her uncle Morholt. She overcomes her desire to kill Mark because she wants to marry him, rather than her father's steward who is seeking her hand. Tristan and Iseult travel back to Cornwall together with Iseult's maid Brangwen, along with a love potion. However, Tristan and Iseult drink the potion by mistake and fall passionately in love. In some versions, the potion lasts forever whilst in others it wears off.

Although Iseult is married to Mark, she and Tristan meet secretly, though the dwarf Frocin forever tries to catch the couple out. Eventually Frocin succeeds when blood from an old wound of Tristan's stains Iseult's bed. They are condemned to death, but Tristan escapes and rescues Iseult who has been sent to die in a leper colony. They live frugally in the forest but Mark finds them, though he is again convinced of their innocence. They eventually return to court. Mark takes back his wife, although she must swear an oath of innocence and loyalty which, in different versions, becomes intriguingly contrived. Tristan is exiled, finally settling in Brittany in the service of Duke Hoel. He marries Hoel's daughter, Iseult of the White Hands, but in most versions promptly regrets it and rejects her. Tristan visits Iseult of Cornwall in disguise, but is wounded and poisoned. He sends for Queen Iseult with the message that if she is coming, the boat is to bear a white sail and, if not, a black one. Although she does come, Tristan's wife tells him it's a black sail, and he dies believing that Iseult has abandoned him. When Iseult arrives and finds he has died, she also dies immediately. Mark buries them together and from their tomb grow two intertwined vines.

3. The Romances

The foregoing version, with minor changes, was the one used in the following early romances. They differ more in the mode of telling than in the content. Thomas d'Angleterre, for instance, retained a more direct mood, concentrating on the love story and the impact on the individuals. His version has become known as the *version courtoise* (courtly version). Others focus on a story of adventure and daring, and are known as the *versions commune* (common versions). Until the time of the prose *Tristan*, the Arthurian references are minor, although Chrétien includes a reference to Tristan in *Erec et Enide*, drawing the name from *Culhwch and Olwen*. In this chapter and the next five I note available translations at the end of each work. No boxed entry signifies that there are no known translations or modern editions.

TRISTAN, Thomas d'Angleterre (French, *c*1160s) 2,755 lines survive.
The oldest surviving verse romance of the Tristan legend, probably originally drawing upon an older ur-*Tristan* document, now lost. Chrétien may have also drawn upon the same original for his romance, *Mark and Iseult*. Only about one-sixth of Thomas's poem survives, the main fragments telling how Mark discovers Tristan and Iseult together in an orchard and how Tristan is banished; it also covers Tristan's marriage to Iseult of the White Hands. Episodes dealing with Tristan's early life and how he met Iseult are lost. In this version, the effects of the love philtre are not limited to a specific period of time. Thomas omits Mark's forgiveness at the end, and any reference to the intertwining vines. Thomas's work served as the main source for the *Tristan* of Gottfried von Strassburg.

> Reconstructed by Joseph Bédier as *Le Roman de Tristan et Iseult* (Paris, 1902) and that version freely adapted into English by Hilaire Belloc as *The Romance of Tristan and Iseult* (George Allen, 1903). It was further developed by Paul Rosenfeld under the same title (Vintage, 1994). A prose translation by A.T. Hatto is included in *Tristan* by Gottfried von Strassburg (Penguin, 1967).

TRISTRANT, Eilhart von Oberge (German, between 1170–1190) fewer than 1,000 lines survive.
The oldest surviving Tristan romance for which we have anything approaching a full version. It differs in various respects from the traditional story. Here the love potion is potent at the outset and the lovers cannot bear to separate, but after four years its power wanes and they part amicably. Tristan becomes happily

married to Iseult of the White Hands, although the philtre retains enough power to make him seek out Queen Iseult. Eilhart's is the 'common' version, as he places emphasis upon the more lurid aspects of the tale, such as when Iseult is banished to the leper colony and the lepers have their evil way with her. Also at the end, although they are buried in one grave, Mark plants a rose-bush for Iseult and a grapevine for Tristan.
→ A prose version exists as *Historij von Herrn Tristrant und der schönen Isalden*, printed in Germany in 1483, somewhat toned down, but which enabled the original text of the poem to be reconstructed.

A translation by J.W. Thomas is *Eilhart von Oberge's Tristrant* (University of Nebraska Press, 1978).

LE CHÈVREFEUIL, Marie de France (French, 1170s) 118 lines
In this *lai* Marie recounts an episode in which the banished Tristan attempts to see the queen at a council the king has called. They are able to meet briefly in the forest. Marie likens them to the honeysuckle that clings to the tree – inseparable. She also remarks that she has known this tale for some time and has seen it written down.

Included in *The Lais of Marie de France* by Glyn S. Burgess and Keith Busby (Penguin, 1986) and *The Lais of Marie de France* by Robert Hanning and Joan Ferrante (Dutton, 1978). It is also in the new edition of *The Romance of Arthur* edited by James J. Wilhelm (Garland, 1994).

TRISTAN, Béroul (French, 1190s) 4,485 lines survive
A lengthy fragment survives, perhaps about half the original. Béroul favours the common version of Eilhart, though his use of humour at certain delicate moments suggests recognition of a more courtly mode. He has the philtre potent for only three years. King Arthur features in this version, and Iseult insists that he be present when she swears her oath of innocence and loyalty to Mark. Béroul emphasises the duplicitous nature of their relationship and emphasises the moral message of love, trickery and deception.

Available as *The Romance of Tristran* edited by Norris J. Lacy (Garland, 1989), which is also in the new edition of *The Romance of Arthur* edited by James J. Wilhelm (Garland, 1994).

LA FOLIE TRISTAN (The Madness of Tristan), anon. (French, 1190s) 998 lines
A poem set after Tristan's banishment, which has him disguised as a court fool in order to meet Iseult. He is so well disguised that even Iseult is unsure until Tristan is recognised by a hound.

A narrative version is included in *The Unknown Arthur* by John Matthews (Blandford, 1995).

TRISTAN, Gottfried von Strassburg (German, 1200s) 19,500 lines
This established the courtly version, championed by Gottfried. It emphasises the chivalrous nature of the story and concentrates on Tristan's upbringing and early adventures. However, Gottfried demonstrates that even though lovers may act falsely, God may still favour them if they are the victims of fate. The last section of Gottfried's poem, from the point when Tristan marries Iseult of the White Hands, was unfinished when he died. It was completed by Ulrich von Türheim *c*1235.

A prose translation by A.T. Hatto is *Tristan* by Gottfried von Strassburg (Penguin, 1967).

TRISTAMS SAGA OK ÍSÖNDAR, Brother Robert (Norwegian, 1226)
Although translated for the Scandinavian court (at the behest of King Haakon), and slightly reworked, this is the only surviving complete document of the courtly version. Brother Robert edited it for an audience not used to the courtly romances of Normandy and Germany, but otherwise it follows what is known of Thomas's version.

TRISTAN MÉNESTREL (Tristan as Minstrel), Gerbert de Montreuil (French, 1230s) and **TRISTAN ALS MÖNCH** (Tristan as Monk), anon (German, 1230s) 2,705 lines

Two similar poems featuring the 'disguise' motif in which Tristan adopts different disguises in order to see Iseult. Gerbert's version was inserted into his continuation of Chrétien's *Perceval*.

PROSE *TRISTAN*, anon. (French, first version 1240s, second version 1250s)
This is the first version to fully integrate the Tristan and Arthurian stories. It is clearly heavily influenced by the Vulgate Cycle, but also draws upon both the courtly and common strains of the Tristan story. Here, Tristan's father is Meliadus. His mother dies in childbirth, and Meliadus's new wife takes on the wicked stepmother role. She tries to poison Tristan but accidentally kills her own son. Tristan nevertheless asks that she not be punished. Meliadus is later murdered, and the young Tristan is raised by his tutor Governal at the court of King Pharamont of Gaul, before moving on to King Mark in Cornwall. The story then follows the traditional thread until after Tristan marries Iseult of the White Hands. When Mark discovers Tristan and Iseult's affair he determines to murder them. Tristan escapes, rescues Iseult from the lepers, and flees to Logres where he becomes involved with Lancelot, staying for a while at Joyeus Gard. He proves his worth as a knight, even besting King Arthur at a tourney, while his joust with Lancelot is declared a draw. He becomes a member of the Round Table, taking the seat previously occupied by Morholt, whom he had killed. This version is the first to introduce Dinadan and Palamedes as Tristan's companions. The Tristan > Iseult > Mark triangle serves as a parallel to the Lancelot > Guenevere > Arthur triangle, and Dinadan becomes the conscience that questions what is right or wrong in the Arthurian world.

Translation by Renee L. Curtis is *The Romance of Tristan* (OUP World Classics, 1994).

PALAMEDES, anon. though attributed to [the fictitious] Elie de Borron (French, 1240s)
Written between the two versions of the prose *Tristan*, this story begins at the time of Arthur's coronation, but otherwise the Arthurian world simply provides a background to a series of

rambling adventures of the fathers of Arthurian heroes, including Esclabor (father of Palamedes), Meliadus (father of Tristan), and Lac (father of Erec). Although written as a whole, and probably intended to develop an "elder" version of *Tristan* and *Lancelot*, the story is episodic and uncontrolled. It was usually printed in two halves. The first half, *Meliadus*, concerns the war between Meliadus and the king of Scotland, whose queen Meliadus has abducted. The second half, *Guiron le Courtois*, tells of the adventures of Meliadus in his search for Guiron, who had helped him win the war, and the various fortunes and misfortunes of Gurion.

→ A subsequent French version, known as the *Compilation* or *Roman de Roi Artus*, was made by Rusticiano da Pisa, friend and amanuensis of Marco Polo, sometime in the 1270s. Rusticiano's miscellany is like an anthology of Arthurian episodes, interpolated between and around the stories of Meliadus and Guiron, and including various stories of Tristan and Lancelot and a truncated story of Erec and Enide.

No modern version of *Palamedes* survives. The 1501 French edition of *Gyron le Courtoys* was reprinted in facsimile by Scolar Press (London, 1980) with an introduction by Cedric E. Pickford.

SIR TRISTREM, possibly by either Thomas of Erceldoune or Thomas of Kendal (English, *c*1290s) 3,344 lines.
The original Tristan story rendered in English. Although several names are changed it otherwise follows the traditional story and ignores the Arthurian embellishments.

The only surviving manuscript copy was reprinted in facsimile as *The Auchinleck Manuscript* by Scolar Press (London, 1977) with an introduction by Derek Pearsall and I.C. Conningham.

14

GAWAIN – THE FIRST HERO

Of all the warriors closely associated with Arthur, Gawain is the only one to appear in every story and legend, yet unlike Lancelot or Tristan, he has no separate story cycle of his own. He was always depicted as the most heroic until his career was eclipsed by Lancelot's and his reputation suffered. Curiously, Gawain's origins show just why that may have happened.

1. The original Gawain

In the Welsh tales, Gawain is *Gwalchmai ap Gwyar*, and is always referred to as the son of Arthur's sister. Since she is usually called Anna, Gwyar must have been his father. However, Gwyar is a female name. The only Gwyar in the pedigrees is the daughter of the ubiquitous Amlawdd Wledig (which would make her Arthur's maternal aunt), the wife of Geraint ab Erbin. Most pedigrees list Geraint as Arthur's cousin, but none show him as the father of Gwalchmai. So already we have a problem.

The later legends all make Gawain the eldest son of Lot. If we accept Gwyar as the proper name of Arthur's sister (rather than Anna) and that she married Lot, the brother of Urien, this would make Gawain a prince of Rheged. In later legends, such as that recorded by William of Malmesbury, Gawain – here called Walwen – is remembered as the ruler of Walweitha (Galloway), the northern part of Rheged. That would make Gawain the cousin of Owain, and these two knights are frequently associated in the early romances. Gawain would have been active in the latter half of the sixth century, and thus a contemporary of Artúir of Dyfed. He may well have been involved in most of the major battles in the North, including Arderydd and Catraeth, though he is not mentioned in either account. Some of the later tales covered below associate Gawain with Cumbria, and this may be part of a long-standing tradition.

William of Malmesbury mentions that the tomb of Walwen/Gawain had been found on the seashore at Rhos in North Wales. It was fourteen feet long. The *Stanzas of the Graves* records Gwalchmai's burial at Peryddon, which may be Periton, just south of Minehead in Somerset, but there is otherwise no association with Gwalchmai/Gawain in that area.

In *Culhwch and Olwen*, Gwalchmai is described as "the best of footmen [meaning a good traveller or scout] and the best of knights", and it is noted that he never returned home without achieving his quest. In later tales he is shown as courteous, friendly and chivalrous, always happy to let another take the credit for something he has achieved. He is also amazingly persuasive, and on many an occasion it is Gawain who will resolve a difficult problem. It is only in the late romances, such as the Prose *Tristan* and Malory, that Gawain's good nature is changed for that of a surly, irascible lecher, and this only in comparison to Tristan or Lancelot. In almost all other tales, he is the greatest of knights and serves as a yardstick against which the achievements of others are measured.

In many of the romances, Gawain's strength varies with the time of day and doubles by noon. His nickname, *Gwalltafwyn*, which means "hair like reins", is translated as "Golden Hair". Both of these attributes show that the character of Gwalchmai is based on a solar deity. In a remarkable piece of etymological analysis explored in *Celtic Myth and Arthurian Romance*, Roger Sherman Loomis showed that the derivation of Gwalchmai can be traced back to the legendary Irish hero Cú Roí mac Dáiri, whom Loomis also believes was based on a solar deity. Cú Roí was a king of Munster, and in the story *Fled Bricrenn* (discussed further below) it is Cú Roí who is the challenger in the beheading game with which Gawain is associated. Loomis shows that Cú Roí, sometimes written as Curi, would have been translated into Welsh as *Gwri*. In the list of warriors at Arthur's court in

Culhwch and Olwen is one Gwrfan *Wallt Afwyn*, "Wild Hair". Loomis shows that Gwrfan (which means "little man") becomes in turn Gwrvan, Gorvan, Gauvain and Gawain, whilst the epithet becomes Gwalltafwyn, Gwalltavwin, Galvagin, Galvain, Gawain, and that *Gwalltafwyn* is the origin of Gwalchmai, usually interpreted as "Hawk of May".

This means that Gawain appears in *Culhwch and Olwen* as both Gwrfan and Gwalchmai, but Gwrfan was already a derivation of another hero. His name was corrupted from Gwri *Wallt Eurin*, who appears in *Pwyll, Prince of Dyfed*, the first story of the *Mabinogion*. In that story Pwyll has a son who is stolen the night after he is born. At the same time Teirnyon, lord of Gwent Ys Coed, who is guarding his horses, discovers a baby boy left in swaddling clothes at his door. He calls the boy Gwri Golden-Hair. The boy grows rapidly, twice as fast as any other child. After four years the truth of his birth is discovered, and he is renamed Pryderi by his mother Rhiannon. He later succeeds his father as Lord of Dyfed. The four branches of the *Mabinogion* each tell us something about Pryderi, including how he wanders throughout Logres whilst under an enchantment and is trapped in a magic castle until released by Manawydan, and finally how he is killed in single combat by Gwydion.

There are various aspects of Gwri/Pryderi – such as his doubling in size, and, in the final tale in the *Mabinogion*, his refusal to sell any pigs until they have doubled in number – which are similar to Gawain's waxing strength, and which seem to support Loomis's assessment that they are one and the same. This means that Gawain is the same as the original, all-encompassing hero of the *Mabinogion*, the standard hero of Welsh legend. It explains why he appears in all the Arthurian stories, because he was the essential hero to resolve all quests. Regardless then of any historical basis to Gawain – and maybe Arthur of the Pennines did have a nephew called Gwrfan – the Gawain of the legend is drawn from an Irish sun deity via Pryderi.

2. Tales of Gawain

Although Gawain appears in every Arthurian story, he is not always the central character. He is usually the comparator against whom knights demonstrate their prowess. We might think of him as a universal standard of bravery. In the later Grail stories, he fails in the quest because he is too lustful, perhaps an indication that he was a primeval hero, and thus not suited to the Middle Ages. But in the early stories he goes a long way to succeeding, and it is possible that there were stories in which Gawain achieved the Grail, but which are now lost. Gawain was an ideal counterpart against which to measure the more spiritual attainment of Perceval, and it is unfortunate that in the later versions Gawain is supplanted by Bors.

There are some stories, however, in which Gawain has the central role. These include two superb adventures, *Diu Krône* and *The Rise of Gawain.* He appears in Geoffrey of Monmouth's *History* where he is portrayed both as the intermediary and the hothead, the two roles that epitomize him. Thankfully Gawain survived being pushed aside in the major Arthurian cycle of legends to rise again in what many regard as the finest of all Arthurian stories, *Sir Gawain and the Green Knight*, a story which clearly takes us back to his mythic origins.

LE BEL INCONNU (The Fair Unknown), Renaud de Beaujeu (French, late 1180s) 6,266 lines.

One of the earliest Arthurian-related "fair unknown" motifs. This phrase is so often applied to male heroes that it could as well be translated "The Handsome Stranger". In this case it is Guinglain, son of Gawain, who must free the daughter of the king of Wales, who has been transformed into a serpent and is being kept prisoner by two enchanters. He encounters many adversaries en route, but achieves his goal and his identity is revealed. The story was absorbed into the Arthurian saga via the first continuation of Chrétien's *Perceval*, in which Guinglain becomes Lionel (not the same as Lancelot's cousin), and was reworked by Robert de Blois with *Beaudous* (*c*1260s) and Thomas Chestre in *Libeaus Desconus* (*c*1380s). The best known "Fair Unknown" theme appears in Malory, with the story of Sir Gareth ("Beaumains").

A translation by Colleen Donagher is in *Le Bel Inconnu* edited by Karen Fresco (Garland, 1992). A narrative version is in *The*

Unknown Arthur (Blandford, 1995) and *The Book of Arthur* (Vega, 2002), both by John Matthews

LA MULE SANS FREIN (The Mule Without a Bridle), Paien des Maisières (French, late 1190s) 1,136 lines
A short poem written in such a clipped form as to be almost a parody of the Arthurian conventions, though, as most of these had yet to be established, this may be seen as an attempt to cash in on Chrétien's popularity by offering up other well-known but as yet undeveloped traditional material. The author's name – which translates as 'Pagan' – may itself be a pun on Chrétien (Christian).

A damsel comes to Arthur's court to seek help in the recovery of a mule bridle which has been stolen. Kay sets off but fails. Gawain takes up the challenge, and is able to use the damsel's magical mule. He overcomes a succession of challenges, including a revolving castle and a beheading game, before he triumphs.

Part of this story reappears in more detail in Heinrich von dem Türlin's *Diu Krône*.

Included in *Two Old French Gauvain Romances* edited by R.C. Johnston and D.D.R. Owen (Barnes & Noble, 1973). An abridged version is in *The Unknown Arthur* (Blandford, 1995) and *The Book of Arthur* (Vega, 2002), both by John Matthews.

LE CHEVALIER À L'EPÉE (The Knight with the Sword), anon. (*possibly* Paien des Maisières) (French, pre-1210) 6,182 lines.
Gawain is lost in a forest and accepts the hospitality of a knight at a castle. The knight even allows Gawain to spend the night with his daughter. Gawain discovers there is an enchanted sword suspended over the bed, but although it proves a trifle inconvenient, Gawain survives the night. The next day the knight is surprised to find Gawain alive, and so believes he must be the best of knights, and offers him his daughter in marriage. They marry, but while Gawain is away fetching the lady's hounds his bride is taken by another. Gawain challenges him, but although the bride chooses the other knight her hounds choose Gawain. Gawain defeats the suitor, and when his bride returns Gawain rebuffs her.

A translation is in *Three Arthurian Romances* by Ross G. Arthur (Dent, 1996). An abridged version is in *Secret Camelot* (Blandford, 1997) and *The Book of Arthur* (Vega, 2002), both by John Matthews.

LA VENGEANCE RAGUIDEL (The Avenging of Raguidel), Raoul (possibly but not conclusively Raoul de Houdenc) (French, 1210s), 6182 lines.

A longer poem which has as its overall framing device the separate quests by Gawain and Yder to avenge the death of the knight Raguidel. The two knights are selected because only Gawain can draw the lance from the dead body, and only Yder can remove his rings. They undergo various unrelated adventures, including some which seem to be echoes of *Le Chevalier à L'Epée*, such as when Gawain rescues the damsel Ydain from one ravisher only to lose her to another. When Gawain kills that rival, he takes Ydain back but soon rejects her. Gawain also rejects La Pucele del Gaut Destroit (the Maid of the Narrow Wood), she intends to decapitate him, but fails to recognise him when he returns. In fact, quite a few people fail to recognise each other in what is clearly an amalgam of tales brought together for effect, but not properly integrated. Gawain kills Raguidel's murderer Guengasoain, and Yder marries Guengasoain's daughter.

A translation is in *Sir Gawain: Eleven Romances and Tales* edited by Thomas Hahn (Kalamazoo, 1995), and extracts are in *King Arthur in Legend and History* edited by Richard White (Dent, 1997).

LES ENFANCES GAUVAIN (The Youth of Gawain), anon. (French, c1220s) 712 lines survive.

This is all that remains of a French romance on the youth of Gawain. Gauvain, the illegitimate child of Arthur's sister Morcades and her page Lot, is given to a knight, Gauvain le Brun, to raise, but le Brun sets him adrift in a casket and he comes into the care of a fisherman who takes him to Rome. There he is educated, knighted by the pope and earns a reputation in tournaments. There the fragments end, but it is clearly part of an old tradition about Gawain because Geoffrey of Monmouth also refers to

Gawain as having been sent as a child to Pope Sulpicius, who later dubbed him a knight (*ix*.11).

DIU KRÔNE, Heinrich von dem Türlin (Austrian, c1230s) 30,041 lines

A clever, creatively developed verse romance which brings much original thinking and treatment to various standard Arthurian themes. The poem is in two distinct halves, each made up of a series of interlinking adventures. But, as Heinrich intended by allusion in the title, which implies that each tale is like a jewel in a crown, all of the adventures come together to reflect a greater glory. That glory is essentially Arthur's court, which, as the story steadily unveils, remains a rock around which chaos and uncertainty lurk but never prevail. At the outset, a bizarre dwarf arrives at court with the drinking horn which enables the chastity test. It reveals that Guenevere was betrothed to a former love, Gasoein, who abducts her, and both Arthur and Gawain battle for her recovery. Gawain is the real hero of the poem as, when not seeking Guenevere, he is involved in a quest against a giant, and becomes beguiled by an enchanter. After Guenevere's recovery, he sets out on the Grail Quest after Parzival's failure. Although this is modelled to a degree on Chrétien and *Parzival*, Heinrich brings his own original interpretation to events, and even has Gawain succeed in the Quest. This adventure is itself interlaced with other marvels and Gawain's testing by Dame Fortune, all of which suggests that Heinrich is parodying the standard Arthurian motifs, whilst at the same time weaving a clever story. Were it not that *Diu Krône* does not take itself entirely seriously and was instantly overshadowed by the giant Vulgate Cycle, it might have been better remembered.

A translation by J.W. Thomas is *The Crown: A Tale of Sir Gawein and King Arthur's Court* (University of Nebraska Press, 1989). A short extract is in *King Arthur in Legend and History* edited by Richard White (Dent, 1997).

LIVRE D'ARTUS, anon. (French, late 1230s)

This is a variant prose but incomplete continuation of Robert de Boron's *Merlin*. It clearly borrows from the other continuations, including the Vulgate and Huth *Merlin*s, but adds its own interpretations, and substitutes Gawain for Lancelot as the main hero. Although it follows much of the plot of the Vulgate *Lancelot*, it weaves in several new stories and characters, but adds nothing to the overall concept. It has been suggested that this book may have had an earlier origin and been one of the archetypal texts behind the development of the Vulgate *Lancelot*, but most scholars no longer believe this.

A translation is in Volume 7 of the 8-volume *Vulgate Version of the Arthurian Romances* by H. Oskar Sommer (Carnegie Institution, 1908–16).

MÉRIADEUC, or LE CHEVALIER AUX DEUX EPÉES, anon. (French, late 1230s).
Lore, Lady of Garadigan, acquires a sword and belt from the corpse of Bleheri and puts it on, but then finds she cannot remove it. All attempts by Arthur's knights fail bar one, whose identity is not known, but who thereby wins a second sword. After freeing the Lady, the Nameless Knight departs but Lore proclaims she will marry no other man than him. Gawain is thus sent in search of the Nameless Knight. He undergoes various adventures, including undertaking single combat with the Nameless Knight without knowing who he is. At the end it is discovered that his name is Mériadeuc, and that he is the son of Bleheri, who had been killed unwittingly by Gawain. Mériadeuc had vowed to take his revenge upon his father's killer, but in the end all are reconciled and Mériadeuc weds Lore.

A translation is *The Knight of The Two Swords* by Ross G. Arthur and Noel L. Corbett (University of Florida Press, 1996).

HUNBAUT, anon. (French, *c*1250s), 3,818 lines.
A minor verse romance of passing interest. Gawain is sent by Arthur to demand the submission of the King of the Isles. He is accompanied by Hunbaut. The two deliver their message but on their return are separated. They each undertake various adventures, usually rescuing damsels, before both return to Arthur's

court. One episode involves the Beheading Test. The main interest of the story is how the chivalric and courtly demeanour of Hunbaut is contrasted against the coarser actions of Gawain.

> A French text of the poem but with an English introduction was published in Holland as *The Romance of Hunbaut* edited by Margaret Winters (E.J. Brill, 1984).

L'ATRE PÉRILLEUX (The Perilous Cemetery), anon. (Norman French, *c*1250s), 6,676 lines.
A highly derivative but no less entertaining romance with Gawain as the central character, although he remains nameless almost throughout. Arthur's new cup-bearer (interestingly, female, a parallel with the Grail bearer) is abducted by Escanor, and Gawain sets out to rescue her after Kay fails. He meets three damsels who believe that Gawain had been killed by three knights. He remains incognito, and promises to avenge Gawain. Much of the story takes place in a graveyard under the power of a demon who has trapped a maiden in a tomb. Gawain succeeds in beheading the demon and rescuing the damsel. He eventually also rescues the cup-bearer and defeats Escanor. Woven throughout the story are various episodes about resurrection and the reunion of hostile partners, suggesting that the origins of this story were in a Celtic legend of rebirth.

> A translation by Ross G. Arthur is available in *Three Arthurian Romances* (Dent, 1996).

DE ORTU WALUUANII (The Rise of Gawain), anon. (Anglo-Norman, late 1270s).
An unusual merger of later Arthurian romance with earlier Gawain tradition. Gawain is the illegitimate son of Arthur's sister Anna and King Lot, but is ignorant of his name and origins (as in the "Fair Unknown" motif). The infant is left in the care of merchants, along with a chest of treasure which also declares his true parentage, but he is stolen by another merchant, Viamandus, who raises him. Through his wiles, Viamundus secures the favours of the Roman emperor and becomes a senator, but dies suddenly when Gawain is twelve. Before his death, he reveals

Gawain's parentage to the emperor and pope. The emperor raises Gawain to a knight and he becomes known as the Knight of the Surcoat. He proves his military prowess in a war against the Persians in the Holy Land, an episode in which he also rescues the emperor's niece, and in which there is a description of a sea battle, unusual in Arthurian romance. Gawain wishes to help Arthur in his battles against his enemies and the emperor agrees, hoping this may bring the island of Britain back under Roman rule. As he nears Caerleon, Gawain is challenged by Arthur whom he defeats, along with Kay. Arthur welcomes Gawain to his court where he learns, from the emperor's message, that Gawain is his nephew. To prove Gawain's valour, Arthur takes him on an expedition against the Picts. Gawain excels himself and Arthur accepts him as a knight, and reveals his nephew's true parentage. The author of this story, who Loomis suspects was a cleric of English or Norman blood living in the Welsh marches, almost certainly also wrote the *Historia Meriadoci* (*see* Chapter 19).

A translation by Mildred Leake Day is *The Rise of Gawain* (Garland, 1984) and in the new edition of *The Romance of Arthur* edited by James J. Wilhelm (Garland, 1994). An abridged version is in *Secret Camelot* (Blandford, 1997) and *The Book of Arthur* (Vega, 2002), both by John Matthews.

ROMAN DE WALEWEIN, Penninc, completed by Pieter Vostaert (Dutch, *c*1280s), 11,198 lines.

A wonderfully inventive Dutch poem, almost certainly based on an earlier, now lost, story that may not have had anything to do with Arthur or even with Gawain (Walewein). A Floating Chessboard appears at Arthur's court, and, as mysteriously, disappears. Walewein vows to obtain it and follows it into a mountain crevice, which closes behind him. He has to battle dragons and cross a deep river before he finds the owner of the chessboard, King Wunder, but Wunder will only grant him the prize if Walewein gains for him the Sword with Two Rings. And so it continues, the success of each quest being dependent upon the achievement of another. Walewein is helped by a fox, who is really a transformed prince, and who will only be restored to his former self upon the achievement of another challenge.

A translation is *Roman de Walewein*, edited by David F. Johnson and H.M. Geert (Garland, 1992; revised Brewer, 2000), reprinted in *Legends of King Arthur* edited by Richard Barber (Boydell, 2001).

SIR GAWAIN AND THE GREEN KNIGHT, anon. (English, *c*1380s), 2,530 lines.
The "treasure of Middle English poetry", according to Laura Hibbard Loomis in *Arthurian Literature in the Middle Ages*, this is one of the finest of all Arthurian romances, and it is shocking to think that it has survived in just one single manuscript now held at the British Library. No author has been identified, although internal evidence suggests that he may have lived in Cheshire, and the Massey family of Dunham Massey may, according to local tradition, have some connection.

The poem is divided into four parts, or "fitts". The first is set at Arthur's court at Christmas, when Arthur refuses to start the feast until he has seen or heard of some marvel. At that point a green giant bursts into the hall riding a green horse and carrying a holly branch (in peace) and a green axe. He is contemptuous of the bravery of Arthur's court and demands a game. He challenges any knight to behead him with his axe on the understanding that he can have the return blow one year hence. Gawain accepts the challenge and beheads the knight who promptly retrieves his head, reminds Gawain of the terms, and leaves.

In the second part, Gawain is travelling north looking for the Green Chapel. He is offered hospitality at a castle and is invited to stay over Christmas until the appointed day. The third part tells of a strange exchange-of-winnings game. The host says he will give Gawain on three successive days whatever he acquires in his hunt, whilst Gawain must offer in return anything he has won at the castle. Each day the host's wife tries to seduce Gawain, but he refuses and simply receives kisses. On the third day he is given a green girdle. Gawain offers up the kisses to his host but keeps quiet about the girdle.

In the fourth part he heads to the Green Chapel, accompanied by a guide who tries to dissuade him. At the chapel he offers his neck to the green giant. The giant takes two swings at Gawain, stopping short each time, but on the third nicks the skin. Gawain is greatly relieved that he has survived, and learns that each swing of the axe was related to his honesty in giving up his winnings in the exchange game. The nick was because he had kept the girdle. The Green Knight reveals himself as his host, Sir Bercilak de Hautdesert, and tells him that the whole scheme was devised by Morgan le Fay in order to frighten Guenevere. He allows Gawain to keep the girdle, which he wears back to Arthur's court, after which all of the courtiers adopt the girdle as an emblem of honour.

This story is the best-developed treatment of the Beheading Test which had already appeared in several Arthurian tales, starting with the first continuation of *Perceval.* It can be traced back to the eighth-century Irish *Fled Bricrenn* ("Bricriu's Feast"), in which the mysterious green knight who challenges those at the feast is called Uath mac Imoman ("Horror, son of Terror"), and it is the hero Cú Chulainn who takes up the challenge.

Editions of this poem include that edited by J.R.R. Tolkien and E.V. Gordon (Oxford University Press, 1925; 1930; new edition, 1967), a modern translation by Brian Stone (Penguin Books, 1959), and a verse translation by Keith Harrison (Dent, 1998). The Tolkien-Gordon translation appears in *The Romance of Arthur* edited by James J. Wilhelm (Garland, 1994), and Harrison's is in *Legends of King Arthur* edited by Richard Barber (Boydell, 2001).

THE AWNTYRS OFF ARTHURE AT THE TERNE WATHELYN (The Adventures of Arthur at the Tarn Wadling), anon. (English, 1390s), 715 lines.

While on a hunting party Guenevere and Gawain become separated from the main party. In hostile weather, they see emerging from Tarn Wadling the ghost of Guenevere's mother, which pronounces dire warnings. Gawain asks specifically about the fate awaiting those who take lands not rightfully theirs. We now learn that a Scottish knight, Galeron, had lost his lands to Arthur through some deceit and that those lands had been given to Gawain. Galeron challenges Gawain to single combat but Arthur stops the fight, restores Galeron's lands and admits him to the Round Table.

Tarn Wadling was near High Hesket, a village south of Carlisle, but has long since been drained. The lands listed as Galeron's (Carrick, Cunningham, Kyle, Cumnock, Lanark, Loudon Hill) are all in Ayr and Galloway. This area had long been one of territorial disputes between the Lords of Galloway and the Scottish kings, and the problem took a further turn after 1306 across the entire Scottish borders with the "Disinherited". These were English knights who had been granted land in Scotland by Edward I, but found those lands confiscated by Robert the Bruce. These tales were almost certainly written for the dispossessed English nobility of the north, who looked to Edward I as their Arthur. A Scottish version of this poem was circulating by the 1440s under the title *Sir Gawan and Sir Galeron of Galloway*.

> The original, as "The Anturs of Arther", is in *Ywain and Gawain* edited by Maldwyn Mills (Dent, 1992). A modernised version was published as *The Awntyrs off Arthure*, edited by Helen Phillips (University of Lancaster, 1988). A prose adaptation as "The Adventure at Tarn Wathelyn" is in *The Unknown Arthur* (Blandford, 1995) and *The Book of Arthur* (Vega, 2002), both by John Matthews. Another version is in *The Knightly Tales of Sir Gawain* by Louis B. Hall (Nelson Hall, 1976).

SYRE GAWENE AND THE CARLE OF CARLYLE, anon. (English, *c*1400), 715 lines.

A short poem, part of which is lost, but part of which also exists in a later form. The later version may have been revised to conform with *Gawain and the Green Knight*, but the earlier version seems to have been derived from an older text. It has the same setting as *The Awntyrs off Arthure*. The inclusion of Bishop Baldwin harks back to the early Welsh tales. Gawain, Kay and Baldwin are lost after a day's hunting and take shelter at the hall of the notorious giant, the Carl of Carlisle. The poem then satirises the so-called courtly virtues of Arthur's court, showing both Kay and Baldwin as discourteous when the Carl imposes several tests of bravery. Gawain, however, remains upright and virtuous and is rewarded by the Carl. In the early version, the Carl is magically transformed back into human form, but in the later version Gawain achieves this by beheading the Carl. See also *The Avowing of King Arthur*.

The story is retold in *The Knightly Tales of Sir Gawain* by Louis B. Hall (Nelson Hall, 1976) and *Sir Gawain: Eleven Romances and Tales* edited by Thomas Hahn (Kalamazoo, 1995). A prose adaptation is in *Secret Camelot* (Blandford, 1997) and *The Book of Arthur* (Vega, 2002), both by John Matthews.

THE WEDDING OF SIR GAWAIN AND DAME RAGNELL, anon. (English, *c*1450s), 855 lines.

This verse romance is the culmination of both the "land dispute" theme and the "what-do-women-desire-most" problem, merged with the popular "Loathly Lady" motif. Once more the story starts with a hunt in Inglewood Forest. Arthur is confronted by the knight Gromer Somer Jour, who challenges Arthur with taking his lands and giving them to Gawain. Arthur promises reparation if the challenge can be deferred for a year. Gromer agrees, but only if in that time Arthur finds an answer to the question, what is it that women love best? Back at his court Arthur discusses the matter with Gawain, and they agree to search throughout the land for an answer. After much time, with no answer, Arthur returns to Carlisle. He encounters the most hideous woman he has ever seen, who identifies herself as Dame Ragnell (in some versions Ragnall). She promises to reveal the answer to the question provided she can marry Gawain. Gawain agrees, and Ragnell tells Arthur that what women most desire is sovereignty over men. Arthur tells Gromer, who also reveals that Ragnell is his sister, whom he despises now more than ever for he knows he has lost his lands. The wedding of Gawain and Ragnell goes ahead, and when Gawain kisses his bride she turns into a beautiful lady. She explains that he must decide whether he wants her beautiful by day and ugly by night, or vice versa. Gawain cannot choose and leaves the decision up to her, at which point she declares that she has gained what she most desired and thereafter she will remain beautiful by night and day. Ragnell becomes the mother of Guinglain but she dies after only five years.

Chaucer used a variant of the theme in "The Wife of Bath's Tale" (*c*1390), in which an unnamed Arthurian knight, who has raped a maiden, will be pardoned by the queen only if he can answer the question: what do women most desire? He likewise finds an old hag who has the answer, but demands that they marry. He also must choose whether she is to be ugly and faithful, or beautiful but unfaithful. It seems likely that Chaucer's version and the Gawain version both derive from some lost earlier version which could date back many centuries. A later ballad version of the Gawain story is *The Marriage of Sir Gawain* (late 15th century).

> The original text is *The Weddynge of Sir Gawen and Dame Ragnall* edited by Laura Sumner (Smith College, 1924) also available in *The Romance of Arthur* edited by James J. Wilhelm (Garland, 1994). A modern adaptation is in *The Knightly Tales of Sir Gawain* by Louis B. Hall (Nelson Hall, 1976). An abridged version is in *The Unknown Arthur* (Blandford, 1995) and *The Book of Arthur* (Vega, 2002), both by John Matthews.

GOLAGROS AND GAWANE, anon. (Scottish, *c*1490s), 1,362 lines.

A Scottish poem which miraculously survives in only one copy of the printed version (from 1508), with no known manuscript. It draws its source from two episodes in the first continuation of *Perceval*, but here places the emphasis on how Gawain's knightly virtue succeeds where ill manners fail. While they are travelling to the Holy Land, Arthur and his companions arrive at a beautiful city. Kay enters the town to obtain food but his usual ill temper means he is soon sent packing and Gawain must obtain the food. Later on their travels they come to a magnificent castle where the lord, Golagros, has striven to be independent of his sovereign. Arthur sends envoys to ask for Golagros's submission, but none succeeds and it is again left to Gawain to engineer a satisfactory conclusion. The story shows the continued influence of the territorial disputes in the Scottish borders.

The story is retold in *The Knightly Tales of Sir Gawain* by Louis B. Hall (Nelson Hall, 1976). An abridged version is in *Secret Camelot* (Blandford, 1997) and *The Book of Arthur* (Vega, 2002), both by John Matthews.

15

MERLIN – THE MAGIC AND THE MADNESS

1. Geoffrey's Merlin

The figure of Merlin is as mysterious as that of Arthur, if not more so. Whereas many will argue the case for an historical Arthur, there are fewer who can imagine a genuine Merlin. As a prophet and magician, he is the key that turns Arthur's tale from history into fantasy, and from fact into legend. As such, he cannot exist in a rational world. Yet Geoffrey of Monmouth did not create Merlin from nothing, although he did create the name. And, what's more, there was not one Merlin, but two.

Geoffrey introduces Merlin in two different texts. First, while he was writing his *Historia*, he was urged by Alexander, bishop of Lincoln, to translate and publish Merlin's *Prophecies*. As a result, Geoffrey issued the *Prophecies* in advance of the *Historia* in about 1134. He probably drew from several sources, few of which have survived, and embellished them with his own creativity, but his main source was almost certainly the poem *Armes Prydein* ("The Prophecies of Britain"). Although later attributed to Taliesin, this poem has been dated by Ifor Williams "without any hesitation" to 930, although much of the content derives from a century or two earlier. This poem refers to the *Dysgogan Myrdin* ("Prophecies of Myrddin"), and Geoffrey, seeking to convert Myrddin into Latin, halted at the obvious translation *Merdinus* because in Norman French, *merde* meant dung. Rather than go for the phonetic Merthin or a more literal translation – *Myrddin* translates as "sea fort" (*mor dinn*), which in Latin might be *Maridun* –

Geoffrey substituted an "l" to create Merlin. *Merle* is the old French for "blackbird", a bird that, while black, is far from sinister, unlike – say – a crow or raven.

Besides the reference to Myrddin in *Armes Prydein*, several poems were attributed to Myrddin, which, in translation, are "The Apple-trees", "The Greetings", "The Dialogue of Myrddin and Taliesin", "The Conversation of Myrddin with Gwenddydd his sister", "The Song of Myrddin in his Grave" and "Commanding Youth". The first three were included in the *Black Book of Carmarthen* which in its final form dates from about 1250, but which derives from sources at least two or three centuries earlier. These poems contain some prophecies, but they also contain more personal data. The prophecies, as Geoffrey developed them, do not concern us greatly in this book. They deal mostly with the domination of the British by the Saxons and the subsequent resurgence of the British. They can be linked to the idea of Arthur's passing, to return in time of need. As with all so-called "prophecies", however, these are often made to seem as if they relate to sometime in the distant future, when quite often they can be related to contemporary events, especially if the texts are more recent than they seem. Much attributed to a sixth-century Merlin seems far more apt to a ninth or tenth century soothsayer.

Geoffrey introduces Merlin by adapting the story from Nennius, and having Vortigern's men track down Merlin rather than Ambrosius. He makes Merlin the grandson of a king of Demetia (Dyfed). From the start, he was creating a false history for Merlin that would later cause him problems. However, at this stage Geoffrey's story fits his requirements neatly. He tells us that Vortigern, who is having problems building his fortress, is told to find a boy without a father. This his men do, encountering Merlin quarrelling with another boy in Kaermerdyn. There has been some suggestion that the name Myrddin was itself a mistake, derived from the British name for Carmarthen – *Caer Mirdin* derived from the Latin *Maridunum*, "fort by the sea". It is surprising that Geoffrey did not use the name of Menw, the enchanter in *Culhwch and Olwen*, who is wounded in the hunt for the Giant Boar. He is a shapechanger and a prototype for Merlin.

The rest of Geoffrey's story of Merlin (*see* Chapter 9) centres on how Merlin transforms Uther into Gorlois, leading to the seduction of Ygraine and the birth of Arthur. Geoffrey also has Merlin construct Stonehenge from stone magically brought from Ireland. Thereafter, however, Merlin vanishes from Geoffrey's story. The later episodes, such as the Sword in the Stone, Merlin's involvement with the Lady of the Lake, taking Arthur to receive Excalibur after his first sword is broken, and his death at the hands of Niniane, are all products of later writers, mostly Robert de Boron, and are discussed below.

Geoffrey evidently found more material about Myrddin, since he returned some years later, around 1150, to write his *Vita Merlini*. However, most of this contradicted what he had said before, because he had by now encountered tales about the real Myrddin. Geoffrey sought to bluff it out and managed to merge the two stories sufficiently to satisfy his patrons, including Alexander's successor as bishop of Lincoln, Robert de Chesney. But the joins creak rather, and have torn apart over the years.

It was in the *Vita Merlini* that Geoffrey drew upon the poems attributed to Myrddin and other ancient tales relating to the Battle of Arderydd in 573, which we covered in Chapter 7. We learn that Merlin has a wife, Gwendolyn, and that his sister Ganieda (Gwenddydd) is the wife of King Rodarch (Rhydderch Hael of Strathclyde). Geoffrey tells briefly of the rivalry between Peredur, "prince of North Wales", and Gwenddoleu, "king of Scotland", and of the ensuing battle in which Rhydderch was also involved. With the death of Gwenddoleu and of three or four of his brothers in the battle, Merlin loses his wits and rushes into the Caledonian forest. The queen, his sister, asks a travelling musician to find him. This he does, and through his music rids Merlin of his madness.

Merlin returns to court, but the sight of so many people threatens to turn his wits again. He desires to return to the woods, but Rhydderch will have none of this and has Merlin chained. Merlin becomes introspective and refuses to talk. However, when Merlin sees Rhydderch pluck a leaf from his wife's hair, he laughs. He refuses to explain why he laughed until released, and then reveals that Ganieda has been unfaithful. Ganieda believes she can prove her innocence by demonstrating Merlin's madness. She has a young boy disguised in three different ways and has Merlin predict how each boy will die. He makes three different predictions, the proof his sister needs to show he talks madness. It is only in later years when the child, then a young man, dies from all three causes that everyone recognizes Merlin's talent.

Meanwhile Merlin has returned to the woods, and it is from there that he utters various prophecies and where he also meets Taliesen. We learn from that meeting that Arthur had been taken to Avalon, the Isle of Apples, by Morgan and her sisters. We also learn that the steersman of the boat was Barinthus, already known in legend as "the Navigator", and associated with Manannan mac Lyr, the sea divinity related to the Isle of Man. As Barrind, he also appears in the story *The Voyage of St Brendan* as the sailor who first discovered the Blessed Isles and urged Brendan to go there.

Merlin remains in the woods till his final days, when he is joined by his sister and a disciple called Maeldin. We do not learn of his death, but from his own musings we can believe that when he died he wanted to be buried by an old oak tree that he had watched grow from an acorn.

Although Geoffrey fused these two Merlins into one, many knew this was not correct. The first to say so was Gerald of Wales, writing in about 1220, who said that there was one prophet Merlin Ambrosius (*Myrddin Emrys*), who lived in the time of Vortigern and Arthur, and another called Merlin Celidonius (after the forest) or Merlin Silvestris. Silvestris also means "of the trees", but Gerald believed this name had something to do with an air monster that Merlin encountered and which drove him crazy. This Merlin is also called Merlin the Wild (*Myrddin Wyllt*).

So were there two Merlins and, if so, were they both real? And what was Merlin's real name?

2. The original Merlin

At the time Geoffrey published his *Vita Merlini*, there were those who would have recognised in his portrayal of Merlin the identity of another mad man of the woods called Lailoken (or Llallogan by the Welsh). He lived at the time of St. Kentigern (*c*550–612), and was known as a troublemaker whose malicious plots resulted in the battle of Arderydd and the death of his lord, Gwenddoleu. He had a vision of angels casting spears at him (possibly Gerald's air monster), and declared that he would spend the rest of his life living with the beasts. He went mad and fled into the woods, but would occasionally appear on a rock overlooking Glasgow when Kentigern was preaching and utter his own predictions, including that of his own death. There are also notable parallels with Geoffrey's Merlin and his prediction of the young boy's triple death. Lailoken is kept in chains and refuses to speak until he reveals the queen's adultery. Infuriated, the queen arranges for some local shepherds to stone Lailoken to death, at which point he falls upon a sharp stake in a pond with his head in the water, and thus dies a triple death.

Whilst much of this may also be legend, there is no reason to doubt that at the time of Kentigern there was a wild man living in the forests near Glasgow who spouted prophecies. This would make him contemporary with the battle of Arderydd, and presumably he lived sufficiently long enough to earn a reputation. Geoffrey's version suggests that Merlin the Wild outlived King Rhydderch, but the king did not die until about 614 and it is questionable whether he was involved at Arderydd. This Merlin would also be contemporary with Artúir of Dyfed, although there is no reason why these two would have met. Geoffrey makes Merlin the grandson of a king of Dyfed, but this is almost certainly the sixth century equivalent of an urban myth, associating the name with Carmarthen.

There is, remarkably, a pedigree for Myrddin, albeit a late one. Triad 87, "Three Skilful Bards", distinguishes between the two Merlins, naming, in addition to Taliesin, Myrddin Emrys and Myrddin ap Morfryn. Even if we accept that this triad dates from after Geoffrey's work, he makes no mention of Myrddin's father Morfryn, a name which occurs elsewhere as the grandson of Mar (*see* Table 3.3). This gives him a possible life span of around 520–590, which fits in with the other known dates.

The question remains, however, as to whether Myrddin ap Morfryn is identical with Lailoken and, if so, why the two names? The name *Lailoken*, as *Llallogan*, apparently has the separate meaning as an ordinary noun, in addition to being a name, of "friend", or even "twin", suggesting a close friend. This raises the inevitable idea that perhaps Myrddin and Lailoken were twins and used this in some of their deceptions. Or that Merlin had a split personality, so that Lailoken was the Hyde to Myrddin's Jekyll. More feasible is that Lailoken was used as a nickname because Myrddin was so close to Gwenddoleu. The simplest explanation of all, of course, is that the pedigree was contrived after Geoffrey's account in order to legitimize Myrddin (although the family is that of Lailoken), and that there only ever was one Lailoken/Myrddin. However, this does not explain the existence of Myrddin by name in the Welsh tales and poems prior to Geoffrey. There must have been a Welsh Myrddin who later became confused (by Geoffrey) with Lailoken.

In *Bloodline of the Holy Grail*, Laurence Gardner explains the confusion by revealing that the name "Merlin" was a title, not a personal name, and was borne by the king's prophet or seer. According to Gardner, Taliesin had been the Merlin of Britain and was succeeded by Emrys, son of Ambrosius, who was the Merlin of Arthur. He also makes this Merlin the nephew of Artúir of Dyfed, whose sister Niniane had married Ambrosius. In this genealogical maze, Gardner makes Merlin Emrys the cousin of the Scots king Aedan (father of Artúir of Dál Riata). Thus in one knot Gardner ties together the Myrddin of Dyfed with Emrys Wledig (Ambrosius), along with the Scottish connection.

The noted Welsh scholar A.O.H. Jarman is convinced there only ever was one Myrddin, and that the evidence comes in the poem "The Conversation of Myrddin with Gwenddydd his Sister", often referred to simply as *Cyfoesi*. This poem, which is primarily a series of prophecies, dates from perhaps the tenth century and was used by Geoffrey in his *Vita Merlini*. The title identifies Myrddin as the brother of Gwenddydd, but during the poem the sister also refers to her brother, from whom she has now become estranged, as "my Llallogan Fyrddin". *Fyrddin* is the suffix of Carmarthen, known in Welsh as *Caerfyrddin*, evolving from *Caermyrddin*. Myrddin is thus given a joint name. Jarman's conclusion is that the name Myrddin had originally been created to identify the non-existent individual after whom Caermyrddin had gained its name – its derivation from the Latin having by then been forgotten. This Myrddin was then identified with the northern British Lailoken whose story had permeated down into Wales, but thanks to Geoffrey further confusing him with Emrys Wledig, Myrddin took on a new, though totally bogus, identity.

In truth, therefore, we must say that Myrddin never existed, but his alter ego Lailoken quite probably did. Whether the pedigree given to him (as Myrddin), showing a descent from Mar, is legitimate or bogus we cannot tell.

3. Merlin of the romances

Having created Merlin Geoffrey did surprisingly little with him. That in itself is an argument for showing that Geoffrey was working from other sources, and thus had no cause to weave Merlin further into the Arthurian legend. As a consequence Merlin's existence seems incomplete.

The spinners of the Grail legend found in Merlin the ideal individual to serve both as the prophet of the Grail and the means through which events leading to the Grail quest could be brought about after five centuries. This process was helped by Wace making Merlin the creator of the Round Table, and that was the link that Robert de Boron needed. The first part of Robert's trilogy, *Joseph d'Arimathie*, is discussed elsewhere (*see* Chapter 16). The second part is the following:

MERLIN, Robert de Boron (France, late 1190s or early 1200s) Only a fragment of Robert's original poem survives, but its content is preserved in the first part of the prose redaction known as the *Suite du Merlin* (or the *Huth Merlin*) from the 1230s and in the Dutch translation *Boec van Merline* by Jacob van Maerlant (completed by 1261).

Robert tells of Merlin's birth. Demons wish to create a prophet to rival Christ, a form of anti-Christ. An incubus impregnates the daughter of a wealthy man, but she confesses to her priest, Blaise, who by making the sign of the Cross at the child's birth is able to neutralize the evil. Nevertheless, the young Merlin, who has a hairy body, is still half-human, half-demon and has both perfect knowledge of the past and visions of the future. He thus knows the story of the Grail and of the future design for Arthur.

Robert then retells the story as related by Geoffrey of Monmouth dealing with Vortigern (here called Vertigier) and his tower, and the roles played by Merlin, the Pendragon (Ambrosius) and Uter. We see Merlin's role in aiding the Pendragon and creating the Round Table. The Round Table is a duplicate of the Grail Table, itself fashioned after the Last Supper Table. Merlin also works the glamour that allows Uter to appear to Ygerne in the guise of her husband. The story follows the traditional tale of Arthur's birth and upbringing to the point where he pulls the sword from the stone and proves himself the rightful heir.

A translation by Nigel Bryant is in *Merlin and the Grail* by Robert de Boron (Brewer, 2001).

ESTOIRE DE MERLIN or PROSE *MERLIN* (Vulgate Cycle), anon. (French, early 1230s).

This follows, so far as we know, Robert's original *Merlin* up to the point where Arthur is declared king, but then adds a variety of interlinked stories and a continuation, including how Arthur became the father of Mordred. Before Arthur pulled the sword from the stone he was infatuated with own half-sister, the wife of King Lot. Lot is called to a council of kings early one morning and leaves his wife asleep. Arthur climbs into her bed and she, in her half-sleep, believes him to be her husband, and Mordred is conceived. Anna learns the truth the next day, but the secret is otherwise not revealed. The story also tells how Leodegran, the father of Guenevere, had his evil way with his seneschal's wife, who then gave birth to a girl who was the exact image of Guenevere except for a birthmark like a king's crown in the small of her back. This explains the "false" Guenevere who appears in the Vulgate *Lancelot*. The plan to substitute the false Guenevere as Arthur's queen is also repeated.

We also see how Merlin sows the seed of his own doom when, disguised as a young squire, he travels through the Forest of Briosque and meets a beautiful young maiden called Vivian [Niniane]. He impresses her with his tricks and she wishes to learn magic from him. He agrees in return for her love.

We follow Merlin as he helps Arthur battle the rebel kings, the Saxons and Claudas in Gaul (*see* Chapter 17), the last of which is the background to the origins of Lancelot.

Finally Merlin tells Arthur that he is leaving. He visits his old mentor Blaise one last time and returns to Vivian with whom he wants to stay. He teaches Vivian all he knows, and she decides to keep Merlin all to herself. One day, in the Forest of Broceliande, while he sleeps, she conjures up a tower of stone about him that no magic can break and there he remains, trapped. She visits him every day to ensure that he has no desire to leave.

Arthur is upset at Merlin's departure and sends the knights to look for him. Only Gawain meets with any success, and hears Merlin's voice as he passes through the Forest of Broceliande, but is unable to see him. Merlin tells him what has happened and that it cannot be undone, and bids Gawain return to Arthur.

The story ends with the facts behind the birth of Lancelot, and leads directly into the Vulgate *Lancelot*.

→ An English verse adaptation was made by Henry Lovelich as *Merlin* (*c*1430s) which strengthens Merlin's role as a proto-John the Baptist to the advent of the Holy Grail. Merlin dictates the Grail book to Blaise and is instrumental in creating the Round Table as the third of the Grail tables. At about the same time, an anonymous author adapted the Vulgate *Merlin* in a version known as the Prose *Merlin*, which portrays Merlin as coming from northern Britain.

A full English translation of the Prose *Merlin* is not available but extracts will be found in *The Romance of Merlin* edited by Peter Goodrich (Garland, 1991), the new edition of *The Romance of Arthur* edited by James J. Wilhelm (Garland, 1994), and *The Lancelot-Grail Reader* edited by Norris J. Lacy (Garland, 2000).

SUITE DU MERLIN (Post-Vulgate Cycle), anon (French, late 1230s).

This is a more extensive version of the *Estoire de Merlin*, with several new episodes, many of them with a fantastic or satirical element, such as the Questing Beast, a hybrid monster which sounds like a pack of hounds and which everyone is keen to hunt for the thrill of the chase. The Beast was pursued mostly by Pellinore and, after his death, by Palamedes. It was in battle against Pellinore that Arthur broke his sword, the one pulled from the stone. As a consequence Merlin took him to see the Lady of the Lake and Arthur thereby acquired Excalibur. Although Arthur liked the sword Merlin advised him that it was the scabbard that held the power and that he would remain unharmed all the time he retained it. Morgan le Fay later schemed with Accolon of Gaul to kill Arthur. She stole Excalibur and gave a false Excalibur to Arthur. Arthur was only saved by the intervention of the Lady of the Lake. Although Arthur regained Excalibur, Morgan stole the scabbard.

The *Suite*'s version of Mordred's conception is different from that in the *Estoire*. Here it is placed a month after Arthur's coronation. Although Anna does not know she is Arthur's sister (in fact half-sister), Arthur presumably does, because he honours her due to her noble lineage. The *Suite* makes it clear that here Arthur has literally sown the seeds of his own destruction. The *Suite* shows Arthur in a further poor light when, after Merlin has predicted the birth of one whose actions will destroy the kingdom, Arthur gathers together all the newly born children and locks them in a tower. Herod-like, he had intended to have them killed, but a dream caused him to cast them loose in a ship which, thanks to God's guidance, washed up safely and the children were housed in the Castle of Boys. Unbeknown to Arthur, Mordred had not even made it to Arthur's tower. His boat was shipwrecked on its way to Arthur and Mordred; the only survivor, was rescued by a fisherman and raised by Nabur the Unruly with his son Sagremor.

The *Suite* tells a different version of the story of the "Knight of the Two Swords", this time incorporated as a *raison d'être* for the Grail Quest. As in the original story a lady comes to Arthur's court with a sword girded round her waist which she is unable to remove or even draw from its scabbard. Only a knight who is pure of heart can withdraw the sword, but whoever does so must return the sword to her. None of the knights can do it until Balin (here called Balain), a humble knight from the north, succeeds. Balin, however, keeps the sword. The Lady of the Lake comes to the court to ask for justice against Balin who killed her brother, but Balin uses his new sword to behead her. Arthur is outraged and Balin leaves Camelot in order to prove himself and gain Arthur's forgiveness. He takes part in Arthur's war against King Lot and shows great courage. Lot almost kills Arthur, but he is saved by Pellinor, who kills Lot, setting in train another sequence of events that will lead to Pellinore's own doom many years later.

Balin then sets out on the adventure that leads to the Dolorous Stroke. He takes a strange knight under his protection but the knight is killed by an invisible enemy. Merlin reveals that the invisible foe was Garlon the Red, brother of King Pellam. When Balin reaches Pellam's castle he succeeds in killing Garlon. Pellam pursues Balin in revenge and as he is chased through the castle Balin seizes a weapon to hand, which happens to be the Bleeding Lance. He strikes Pellam with it, wounding him through the thighs, and that is the Dolorous Stroke that lays the land to waste, and creates the need for the Grail Quest. Eventually Balin and his brother Balan kill each other in a duel. Merlin takes his sword, the one Balin had taken from the Lady of the Lake, and embeds it in a slab of marble which he magically sets to float around the world, to return when needed by Galahad.

In this version, the death of Merlin is made more sinister. Merlin loves Niviene but their relationship has not been consummated, and Niviene, who feigns love for Merlin to obtain as much knowledge as possible, has no wish to consummate it. Merlin tells Niviene of a couple who had loved each other madly and are buried together in a tomb in a house in the woods. He takes her there and shows her the couple under the stone slab of the tomb. Niviene has steadily been enchanting Merlin so that he weakens and that night she binds him and has him buried in the tomb and the stone replaced. Merlin lives long enough to tell Bagdemagus the story when he passes by some days later.

A full English translation of the *Suite de Merlin* is not available but extracts will be found in *The Romance of Merlin* edited by Peter Goodrich (Garland, 1991), the new edition of *The Romance of Arthur* edited by James J. Wilhelm (Garland, 1994), and *The Lancelot-Grail Reader* edited by Norris J. Lacy (Garland, 2000).

LES PROPHÉCIES DE MERLIN, Richart d'Irlande (French, 1270s).

Not related to Geoffrey of Monmouth's original work, this was purportedly a translation from Latin created for the Emperor

Frederick II, though it was in fact composed at least two decades after the Emperor's death. So whilst it appears to be predictions about political events in Italy and Palestine, it was really an opportunity for an after-the-event commentary, seeking political reform. There are some three hundred utterances apparently made by Merlin to various of his former colleagues, including many spoken from his tomb after he was incarcerated by Niniane.

> There is no full English translation but *Les Prophécies de Merlin* edited by Lucy Allen Paton (Oxford University Press, 2 vols., 1926) includes the original French text with a commentary in English.

ARTHOUR AND MERLIN, anon. (English, *c*1280s), 9,938 lines.

The earliest story of Merlin to be composed in English, a language that the author seems to have felt obliged to write in, rather than being comfortable with it. It may even have been composed by two poets, and certainly from two or more sources, as there is a sudden change of pace and mood following the crowning of Arthur. The poem follows the standard story of Merlin's birth, through his service to Uther, the creation of the Round Table, the birth and youth of Arthur and, after his coronation, his wars against the rebel kings.

> The text is edited with notes by O.D. Macrae-Gibson in *Of Arthour and Merlin* (Oxford University Press for Early English Text Society, 2 vols., 1973/79).

16

THE HOLY GRAIL

This book is only concerned with the Grail in how it relates to Arthur, and not whether the Grail exists and where it might be today. What we want to find out is how and why the Grail legend became so closely associated with Arthur, whether there might be any historical relevance, and how the Grail legend affected the stories and legend of Arthur. As we shall see, during the thirteenth century the Grail story dominated the Arthurian romance almost to the point of excluding Arthur himself, and concentrated on his knights, especially Lancelot, Gawain and Perceval. We need to explore the origins of the Grail legend and see what associations there may have been with Arthur before Chrétien de Troyes lit the fuse that began the Grail quest.

1. The origins of the Grail

The first reference to the Grail appears in Chrétien de Troyes's *Conte du Graal* written in the 1180s. I cover this story in detail below and mention it here in order to get a time fix and to see how Chrétien describes it. He says that the Grail was of "fine pure gold", and set with "precious stones of many kinds." He also says that the company are served from the Grail, and the overall impression is that he is describing a platter or tray. Although we have come to think of the Grail as a chalice, that description does not occur in Chrétien's work but only in Robert de Boron's. As the Grail story progresses, with its different interpreters, the Grail becomes several things including a container which seems to glow with the spirit of Christ. The word most commonly used to describe the Grail is a "vessel", clearly a container of some kind, but nothing more specific than that.

Thanks to Robert de Boron, the Grail became associated with the cup from which Christ drank at the Last Supper and with which he performed the sacrament with the wine representing his blood. After Christ's crucifixion, when Joseph of Arimathea was given custody of Christ's body, Robert de Boron states that he took a few drops of Christ's blood into the Grail and thus it became a symbol of rebirth and salvation. Anyone who was pure and free of sin and who could attain the Grail was thus assured of eternal life.

One matter is consistent, though – the Grail is able to feed all who are assembled with whatever they want and however much they want. This is an ancient concept and goes back at least as far as the Greek story of the horn of plenty, the cornucopia, which Zeus gave to Amalthea in gratitude for helping raise him, and which gave its possessor anything he desired. In the Christian story it equates to Christ's miracle of feeding the five thousand and in Celtic myth to Daghda's cauldron. The Daghda was one of the mightiest of Irish gods, the chief deity of the Tuatha Dé Danann, a magical race subsequently equated with the fairies. The Daghda had the power over life and death, represented by his club, a blow with one end of which meant death, and with the other meant life. He also had a cauldron which provided an inexhaustible supply of food. Both the club and the cauldron have their equivalents in the Grail story with the Holy Lance of Longinus and the Grail.

The cauldron had many mystical properties to the early Celts. It was seen as a symbol of rebirth, and cauldrons served as funerary urns for burial and rebirth in the Otherworld. In the second branch of the Mabinogion, *Branwen, Daughter of Llyr*, a cauldron is given to the Irish king Matholwch by Bendigeid Vran, from which the bodies of dead warriors, boiled overnight, arise as new the next day. Bendigeid Vran is better known as Bran the Blessed, and features in Robert de Boron's first Grail story as the Keeper of the Grail and the first Fisher King. According to the ancient pedigrees Bran was the father of Beli who married Anna, the cousin of the Virgin Mary (*see* Table 3.2). He was the ancestor of both Cunedda and Coel Hen, and thereby of most of the later British kings. Bran's grandson was Afallach, or Aballach, a name equated by some with Avalon. He appears in the *Quest of the Holy Grail* and in later stories as King Evelach, or Evelake.

In the tale of *Culhwch and Olwen*, Arthur's men are set many tasks by the giant Ysbaddaden. Amongst the treasures they must obtain is the basket of Gwyddno Garanhir, which could supply meat even if "the whole world should come together." Likewise the horn of Gwlgawd Gododdin will provide endless drink. They do not need to achieve all the quests in the end, though they do acquire the cauldron of Dwrnach Wyddel, which also seems to be a cauldron of plenty, but they have to fight for it. Bedwyr snatches the cauldron whilst Llenlleawc (regarded by some as the prototype of Lancelot) grabs Arthur's sword Caledvwlch and smites off Dwrnach's head.

The Welsh poem *Preideu Annwvyn*, which dates from around the late ninth century, involves a quest by Arthur and his men to recover the cauldron of the Lord of Annwvyn itself (*see* Chapter 12). Annwvyn represented the Otherworld. This cauldron is described as being rimmed with jewels, like the Grail. Being a cauldron of the Lord of the Otherworld, it too must have had qualities of rebirth, but in this story it is specifically stated that it will not cook meat as food for cowards, suggesting that it recognizes the hearts of the brave, just as the Grail recognises the pure in heart. Once again, the cauldron is not acquired easily. As in *Culhwch and Olwen* (this episode appears to have the same origin), Lleminawc/Llenlleawc wields a "sword of lightning" to snatch the cauldron. It is housed in a Glass Fort, also called Caer-Vanäwy (amongst other names), which means "Fort of the Divine Place", a suitable description for the Grail Castle. In *The Quest of the Holy Grail* the Grail Castle is called Corbenic. The name is believed to be derived from the Old French *Cor Benit*, meaning "blessed horn", another reference to the horn of plenty.

These few examples show that long before Chrétien established the mystery of the Grail there had been a Celtic tradition of an object with properties similar to a horn of plenty and a cauldron of rebirth. These stories also involve a seemingly impossible quest which may only be achieved by the bravest of men. The location of the treasure also has some mystical elements and seems to be situated in the land between our world and the next.

Besides the Grail itself one of the most striking images is that of the Waste Land. It does not appear in the earliest stories and takes different forms in the later ones. As I discussed in Chapter 12, the imagery has much to do with the concept of the Holy Land being laid waste during the Crusades. But it may also mean something closer to home. The *Anglo-Saxon Chronicle* records several periods of devastation leading up to and during the Civil War in England at the time of King Stephen. Here are two examples.

> 1125. On St Lawrence's Day there was so great a flood that many villages were inundated and men were drowned; bridges were broken down; the corn and meadows were completely laid waste, bringing hunger and death to men and livestock; and there was more unseasonableness in crops of every kind than for many years past.
>
> 1137. . . . they [the barons] levied a tax known as *tenserie* upon the villages. When the wretched people had no more to give they plundered and burned all the villages, so that you could easily go a day's journey without ever finding a village inhabited or a field cultivated . . . Wherever the ground was tilled the earth bore no corn for the land was ruined by such doings; and men said openly that Christ and His saints slept.

There is no doubt that such scenes were replicated across Europe, and memories of them would have been only too vivid among those reading the Grail stories. In the earliest the Waste Land is not caused by any supernatural means. It is simply that the Grail King, being wounded, is unable to tend his land. The imagery in Robert de Boron's *Perceval*, for instance, chillingly echoes that *ASC* entry for 1137, when Perceval rides through a deserted land.

As the scale of the Grail stories grew, so too did the curse upon the land, until we have an image of the whole of England laid waste, devastated until such time as the Good Knight can restore it. This same image stretches back throughout the history of England so consistently that it must have been indelibly ingrained upon the national consciousness. The harrying of the north had seen much land laid to waste by William the Conqueror and his barons. Before him there had been three centuries of Viking incursions and before them the wars between the Saxons and the Britons. This takes us back to the days of Arthur. We know from Gildas's description (§24) that Britain was like a wasteland in the years before Ambrosius led the resurgence (*see* Chapter 5).

This is why the Waste Land imagery is so appropriate to the Arthurian story and why it became associated with Arthur more closely than with any other Dark Age or medieval king. Arthur was the restorer of the Waste Land and would achieve it again through the purest of his knights. This was an image the Anglo-Norman kings were keen to foster during the Crusades – that they, as heirs to Arthur, were the saviours of Christendom.

In the Grail story that challenge is first put to Perceval. In the later Vulgate version it is Galahad who becomes the Grail Knight.

2. Perceval

Through all of the Grail stories Perceval is referred to as *le Gallois*, the Welshman. What's more, he is shown as someone ignorant of the world about him, because his mother had not wanted him to suffer the same fate as his father and brothers. It is Perceval's ignorance – innocence, really – that causes him, through no fault of his own, to fail to ask the right question at the Grail Castle. Perceval is thus symbolic of Everyman in the medieval mystery plays, who must be educated in the ways of the world and of the spirit in order to achieve divine grace. The entirety of the Grail story is based around that very concept of grace, so dear to the heart of the Cistercian order. Perceval, therefore, is seen as the everyday man who once had divine grace but who, through the sins of his forebears, has fallen into ignorance. As such, the Perceval of the story is based not on any one individual, but on everyone.

The name is itself significant. It comes from the old French

Perce Val, meaning "pierced valley". The story deals with a maimed Fisher King who, like Christ on the Cross, bears wounds caused by having been pierced by a sword or lance. By the time of the Post-Vulgate version discussed below, that is exactly what does happen when Balin strikes the Fisher King with the Holy Lance – the Dolorous Blow that lays all Christendom to waste. The "valley" relates to the Vales of Avalon, the land to which the Grail had been brought by Joseph of Arimathea and his brethren. To restore the land, Perceval must "pierce the vale", that is, enter the Grail Castle and solve the puzzle by asking the right question. That "piercing" would then heal the land, just as Jesus's final wounds allowed him to pass through death and on to resurrection.

When the Perceval story was adapted into Welsh, the translator chose to rename Perceval *Peredur*, meaning "hard spear"(from *peri* "spear" + *dur* "hard"), singularly appropriate for a lance or sword able to pierce. Whether that was the intention is not clear. Peredur was a well-known British hero from the time of Arthur whom we have already encountered. He was the son of Eliffer of the Great Host, brother of Gwrgi, and the victor of the Battle of Arderydd in 573. Peredur had the epithet *Paladr Hir*, "long spear". Another Peredur is mentioned in *Y Gododdin*, where he is known as *Arfau Dur*, "of the steel weapons". These probably refer to the same person. The Peredur of history was clearly a warrior of great renown and in that respect does not and could not equate in any way with Perceval. But what about the Peredur of legend?

What tends to be overlooked is that Peredur's name was transformed in Welsh legend to another much more famous name, Pryderi. Pryderi was the original hero of the *Mabinogion* and, as we have seen, under his natal name of Gwri was the original of Gawain. The renaming of Gwri as Pryderi is not properly explained in *Pwyll, Prince of Dyfed*, the first story in the *Mabinogion*, and indeed seems rather forced. It is more likely that amongst the original storytellers was one who conflated two stories, that of Gwri/Gawain and that of Peredur/Pryderi, and that other storytellers continued to narrate these adventures as relating to Gawain, and not Pryderi. This may account for why Gawain and Perceval are so closely associated in the Grail stories.

If we summarize the *Mabinigion* story *Manawydan, Son of Llyr*, mentally substituting the name Perceval for Pryderi, we encounter much that we will see again as we work through the Grail stories. At the start of the story Pryderi's father has died and Pryderi has become Lord of Dyfed. Manawydan marries Pryderi's widowed mother Rhiannon. Pryderi is married to Cigfa (who, if the pedigree is correct, is the niece of Vortigern). Pryderi agrees to share his inheritance of Dyfed with Manawydan. One evening, after they have feasted, they travel to Gorsedd Arberth (the Throne of Arberth). There is a peal of thunder, they are surrounded by a thick mist, and the place is filled with light. When they can see again they find that everything has disappeared – "neither house, nor beast, nor smoke, nor fire, nor man, nor dwelling; but the houses of the Court empty, desolate, uninhabited." It seems the whole of Dyfed has become deserted save for wild beasts. The four of them survive for two years by hunting and fishing but grow tired and go to Logres to seek work. Though they earn a living they have to keep moving on because of hostility from the local craftsmen. They return to Dyfed, which is still devoid of all but wild life, and continue to hunt.

One day, while out hunting with their dogs, they disturb a boar of pure shining white. They follow it to a lofty castle which looks new. The dogs follow the boar into the castle and all goes quiet. Against Manawydan's advice Pryderi goes into the castle to find his dogs. Inside the castle is empty except for a marble fountain. Beside the fountain is a golden bowl, suspended by four chains that seem to vanish into thin air. Taken by the quality of the bowl, Pryderi touches it, and immediately finds himself unable to move or speak. Manawydan waits till nightfall, then returns home. Rhiannon, annoyed at Manawydan's lack of action, sets out to the castle and discovers Pryderi, transfixed. The moment she touches the bowl to free him she is also trapped. Whereupon there is a clap of thunder, a mist falls, and the castle vanishes taking Pryderi and Rhiannon with it.

Manawydan and Cigfa try to survive on their own, and Manawydan sows several fields of corn. It grows, but when he inspects the first field he finds the corn devastated overnight. The following day the next field is devastated. The third night he stays up to watch over the last field and discovers a vast flock of mice swarming over it. He catches a mouse and determines to hang it as he would any other thief. While constructing the gibbet he is approached by a clerk, the first man he has seen in seven years. When the clerk learns what Manawydan is doing he offers to buy the mouse for a pound, but Manawydan will not sell. Then along comes a priest who offers Manawydan three pounds, but no luck. Finally, a bishop appears and offers Manawydan seven pounds. Still Manawydan will not budge. He now learns that the bishop is really Llywd ap Cilcoed who had cast an enchantment over the land in revenge for past ills he believed Pwyll had caused. Llywd wants the mouse because it is his pregnant wife, whom he had changed into a mouse along with all the other women of his court in order to devastate Manawydan's crop. Manawydan agrees, provided Llywd will lift the enchantment off the land and set Pryderi and Rhiannon free.

Several of these elements reappear in the Grail stories, including the Enchanted (Waste) Land, the mysterious (Grail) castle and the golden bowl (the Grail). We may also see a suggestion of the Siege Perilous in the Throne at Arberth (Narberth). One can perhaps read too much into it; the desolation of Dyfed as a punishment for the sins of the fathers may equate to the general sins of mankind for which the success of the Grail quest is the panacea.

Perhaps we can also see in Llywd the basis of the Fisher King. I suggest this not solely on the strength of this story (where I suspect that Llywd is also supposed to be the boar and thus the lure to the Castle, like the Fisher King) but also because Llywd reappears briefly in the story of *Culhwch and Olwen*. After Arthur and his men have obtained the magic cauldron of Dwrnach and returned to Dyfed, they arrive at the house of Llywd, which the text describes as "Mesur-y-Peir" ("the measure of the cauldron"). Any town by that name is now lost but Charlotte Guest suggests it might have been associated with Pwllcrochan ("the Pool of the Cauldron") near Pembroke, alas now almost entirely buried under an oil refinery. Llywd's own town is believed to be Ludchurch, near Narberth. The reference to "Mesur-y-Peir" begs the question as to whether Llywd thereafter became the guardian of the cauldron.

All of this is sufficient to show that there was plenty of material in the Celtic tales to serve as a basis for the Grail story. There may have been some eastern variant of these in the book Philip of Flanders gave to Chrétien. From then on the Grail story became the spiritual parallel of the Crusades. The following sets out all of the Grail romances in their order of appearance.

3. The Grail Romances

CONTE DU GRAAL (The Story of the Grail), Chrétien de Troyes (French, *c*1182), 9,234 lines

The longest of Chrétien's romances, and probably the most influential, it is also his most infuriating, as it was left unfinished and thus unexplained. It is from this that the whole Grail Cycle of stories has grown.

Perceval is a young country boy who has been kept in ignorance of worldly matters by his mother. He does not know his name, and it is not revealed until nearly halfway through the story. He does not know that his father and brothers met their deaths as knights, and knows nothing of knights, lords, ladies or the church. However, one day he sees some knights passing, their armour reflecting the sun so that he thinks them angels. This gives him the desire to be a knight and, much against his mother's wishes, he sets off for Arthur's castle. He sees his mother faint from despair but does not return. She has given him some words of advice, but like so much of the advice he receives throughout his adventures he either takes it too literally or misinterprets it, constantly giving the impression that he is a fool. Early in his travels he encounters a maiden asleep in a tent. He steals a kiss, takes her rings and also her food, puzzled that she is so affronted by this. When her lover returns he believes she has been unfaithful and vows to track down the young squire. Meanwhile, Perceval reaches Arthur's court where he is the subject of much ridicule, mostly as the butt for Kay's derision.

The queen had just been insulted by the Red Knight, who is leaving the court as Perceval arrives. Perceval desires the knight's red armour and asks Arthur if he may pursue the knight. A damsel, who had earlier laughed at Perceval, states her belief that he will be the greatest knight of all, but Kay derides and slaps her.

Perceval vows revenge. He follows and challenges the Red Knight and kills him, taking his armour. This gratuitous act has repercussions in some of the later stories.

Finding his way to Gornemant's castle, Perceval receives instruction in chivalry and combat, and is knighted. Gornemant advises Perceval not to ask too many questions at the risk of appearing ignorant. He travels to the castle of Beaurepaire, where Gornemant's niece Blancheflor lives, and where he defeats Clamadeu of the Isles who is besieging the castle. Perceval vows his love for Blancheflor and says he will return, but says he must first visit his mother.

After a day's journey he encounters a man fishing, who directs him to a magnificent castle where he can shelter for the night. Perceval is well received and given fresh clothing, and subsequently invited to dine with the lord of the castle. Perceval does not recognise the lord as the fisherman he saw earlier. He does, however, discover that the lord has been injured in some way. The lord presents Perceval with a fine sword. Perceval learns that only three such swords had been made and that this sword could never be broken save in one perilous circumstance. Perceval sits down to dine and witnesses the strange Grail procession. First into the room comes a youth holding a white lance with blood oozing from its tip. Perceval is puzzled, but heeding Gornemant's advice does not ask how or why this is happening. Next into the room come two youths bearing gold candelabra inlaid with black enamel, followed by a damsel who holds a grail of gold which shines so brightly that it makes the candles seem dim. Behind the damsel comes another maiden with a silver carving dish. These are laid on the table, but once again Perceval fails to query their nature or who is to be served from the Grail. The elaborate procession is followed by a sumptuous meal, after which host and guest both retire to bed. When Perceval awakes the next day he finds the castle empty and is unable to find a soul, not even someone to raise the drawbridge as he leaves.

Perceval encounters a young damsel whose lover has been killed. From her he learns that he has stayed at the castle of the Fisher King, and she admonishes him for not asking about the Grail or the lance. She asks Perceval his name, and this is the first time we learn it. We discover the damsel is his cousin, and she tells him his mother is dead. Perceval now pursues the knight who had killed her lover and after defeating the knight sends him back to Arthur's castle. There Arthur learns of Perceval's wanderings and sends knights out to recover him. They do not recognise him, and Perceval defeats Sagremor and Kay before Gawain recognises him and returns him to Arthur.

A few days later a "Loathly Damsel" (called Cundrie by Wolfram) arrives and berates Perceval, saying that had he asked the right question, the Fisher King would have been cured and his land would not be waste. "All these evils will be your doing," she tells Perceval. She invites any knights to accompany her on her quest to Proud Castle to rescue a besieged maiden. Many knights offer to go on the quest, including Perceval and Gawain, but before he can go Gawain is diverted in his quest.

The story now follows Gawain's adventures to clear his name of a charge brought by Guigambresil, of having killed his lord, the king of Escavalon, without issuing a challenge. We learn that Gawaine is armed with the sword Escalibor (Excalibur). En route he encounters other adventures and it is some time before he is able to enter upon what has become the Grail Quest. He is given leave of a year to quest for the Bleeding Lance, before he must return to fight in single combat with Guigambresil.

In the meantime, we learn that Perceval has spent five godless years wandering, perhaps trapped in some fairy realm, and seeming to have lost all understanding. He meets a hermit, who he learns is his uncle, and who tells him that the Fisher King is also an uncle. The reason that Perceval had been unable to ask the right question was because he was impure, having sinned by leaving his mother when she collapsed and not helping her. At this point Chrétien stops his story of Perceval, leaving it uncertain, and instead continues with Gawain's quest.

Gawain is led into the clutches of an evil damsel and an enchanted castle wherein lies the Bed of Marvels. Gawain is warned that anyone who lies on this bed will be killed. Gawain does so anyway, and manages to shield himself against five hundred arrows and a lion, which he kills. With this Gawain breaks the enchantment. Gawain then meets a knight called Guiromelant, who, although not recognising Gawain, regards him as his mortal enemy. From Guiromelant Gawain learns that the castle, the Rock of Champguin, also holds his own mother whom he has not seen for twenty years, and Arthur's mother Igraine, whom Arthur has not seen for sixty. When Guiromelant discovers who Gawain is he challenges him to a duel, but as Guiromelant is not armed Gawain agrees to hold it in a week's time. He sends a messenger to Arthur's court so that Arthur can be witness to the combat. At this point Chrétien's story ends, and the first continuation carries on.

→ **Peredur son of Efraug**. Although the Welsh version covers much the same territory as the first half of Chrétien's, it is severely truncated and loses much of its mystical aspect, except for the Grail element. There is no mystery about Peredur's name or identity, or that he is related to the Fisher King (who is not described as such). There is more about the nature of the sword presented to Peredur, which he breaks and repairs three times. The procession is led by two youths carrying the bleeding lance. They are followed by two maidens carrying the Grail (here called a salver) on which is a man's head swimming in blood. Peredur does not ask, nor is he told, what it all means. Neither is the castle deserted the next day. It is as if whoever copied or revised this story did not comprehend its significance and simply edited it as an ordinary adventure. It may well have been revised from an earlier story common also to Chrétien, in which case Chrétien had a far better understanding of its significance.

> The standard translations of Chrétien's works are both called *Arthurian Romances*, translated by D.D.R. Owen (Dent, 1987) and by William W. Kibler (Penguin, 1991).

PERCEVAL, FIRST CONTINUATION, anon. (French, c.1190s) 19,600 lines.

The author was once believed to be Gautier de Denain, but with no clear attribution the author is now termed Pseudo-Gautier. This continues exactly where Chrétien finished and doubles the length of the story, though does not bring it to a conclusion. Because Gawain is the hero it is sometimes called the *Gawain Continuation*.

Arthur responds to Gawain's summons and travels to the Castle Rock of Champguin where Gawain is trapped. Arthur witnesses the duel between Gawain and Guiromelant, and is reunited with his mother and sister. The various threads involving Guiromelant and Clarissant (Gawain's sister) are resolved, allowing Gawain to continue on his Grail Quest.

Gawain reaches the Grail Castle but finds a new challenge: he is asked to repair a broken sword, which he is unable to do. He sees the Grail Procession as Perceval had described. For the first time the vessel is actually called the Holy Grail and the maiden bearing it is weeping. Gawain finds a dead knight with a broken sword and learns that whoever can mend this sword can explain the mysteries of the Grail. However, Gawain is entranced and when he recovers finds himself in a field. The Grail Castle has disappeared.

Gawain returns to Escavalon to fight in single combat against Guigambresil, as previously agreed. Fortunately, Arthur is able to resolve the matter and Guigambresil marries Arthur's granddaughter. The continuation now gets rather lost in a series of other adventures, including Arthur's siege of the castle of Brun de Branlant who has refused to swear fealty, and a separate substantial story about Caradoc. Many believe it was once a separate story, referred to as the *Livre de Caradoc*. Caradoc is portrayed as the illegitimate son of Arthur's niece Ysave and the sorcerer Eliavrés, though he is long believed to be the genuine son of Caradoc, King of Nantes. He enters Arthur's court and takes up the challenge of the Beheading Game, which he survives because his opponent is his true father. There is much conflict between Caradoc and his parents who attach a deadly serpent to his arm which will gradually drain away his life force. This image suggests Caradoc had a withered arm which his French epithet *Briefbras* ("short arm") may also indicate. However, Caradoc is saved by Guigner, a maiden he had previously rescued. At the end Caradoc passes the drinking test as described in "The Lai of the Horn".

There is also a quest by Girflet to Proud Castle (the subject of the Loathly Damsel's request), where he is captured and imprisoned. In order to free him Gawain becomes involved in a series of single combats, which he wins. Only then does Gawain return to the Grail Castle. Gawain fails to mend the broken sword, but he learns that the Bleeding Lance was the one that pierced Christ's side at the Crucifixion. He does succeed in asking the right question about the Grail, but once again falls into an enchanted sleep and does not hear the answer. The *Continuation* ends with an unconnected episode about Gawain's brother Guerrehet (Gareth).

→ ***Gest of Sir Gawain*** (*c*1450). An English poem based on one of the episodes in the First Continuation, in which Gawain is interrupted by the brothers of a girl whom he is seducing. They each do battle with him but only one, Brandiles, is a match. Unable to complete their match they vow to meet again, but never do.

Available in *The Continuations of the Old French "Perceval"* (University of Pennsylvania Press, 5 vols., 1949-84). Extracts from all four are in *King Arthur in Legend and History* edited by Richard White (Dent, 1997), and are summarized at the end of *Chrétien de Troyes, Arthurian Romances* edited by William W. Kibler (Penguin, 1991). The separate Caradoc episode is in *Three Arthurian Romances* by Ross G. Arthur (Dent, 1996), and an abridged version is in both *Secret Camelot* (Blandford, 1997) and *The Book of Arthur* (Vega, 2002), both by John Matthews.

PERCEVAL, SECOND CONTINUATION, Gautier de Denain (French, *c*1190s) 13,000 lines.

In an attempt to wrap up previous unsatisfactory loose ends this story becomes overly episodic. Perceval finds himself on various quests, none of which he satisfactorily resolves. He also meets his sister and learns the truth about his mother's death, and becomes involved in a tournament at Proud Castle where he defeats many of Arthur's best knights. Most of these adventures are incidental to his main quest to recover a magic hound and the antlers of a white stag, which have been stolen from a maiden who declares her love for Perceval. He is not successful but does at length return to the Grail Castle. He restores the broken sword but a small notch remains, showing he has still not reached perfection and is thus not ready to learn the truth about the Grail. At this point Gautier abandons the story.

PERCEVAL, FOURTH CONTINUATION, Gerbert de Montreuil (French, late 1220s) 17,000 lines.

Although regarded as the fourth, this version fits best *before* the "Third Continuation". Apparently both were written at the same time, with neither author knowing what the other was doing. Both continuations show the influence of the works of Robert de Boron.

Perceval realizes that he has failed because he has still not expiated the sin of neglecting his mother. As he leaves the castle we realize we are no longer in the secular world but in some transitional semi-paradise. Perceval had almost reached perfection, but not quite. He tries to enter a garden, breaking his sword in the process, but though he learns that the Earthly Paradise is beyond he cannot enter. Perceval finds himself fighting demons and ghosts. He returns to his first love Blancheflor, and they marry but do not consummate their marriage in the belief that they must remain pure.

In contrast to Perceval's adventures, Gawain's are far more mundane and he now seems far removed from his quest for an answer to the Bleeding Lance. Perceval, however, at last makes it back to the Grail Castle and mends the Broken Sword completely.

PERCEVAL, THIRD CONTINUATION, Manessier (French, late 1220s) 10,000 lines.

This version brings the story-line to completion. Manessier leaps in with an explanation of the Broken Sword, which seems to be of more significance than the Grail. The sword had been used by a knight called Partinial to kill the Fisher King's brother, and wound the Fisher King. Perceval vows to kill Partinial, and much of the story is taken up with the quest to find him, during which time he encounters demons, and nearly kills Lancelot's brother Ector, though both Perceval and Ector are cured by an appearance of the Grail carried by an angel. Eventually Perceval defeats Partinial and returns to the Grail Castle with his head. He and the Fisher King have a meal at which the Grail procession again appears, and Perceval is at last accepted. The Fisher King now dies and a final vision of the Grail appears at Perceval's coronation as the new Fisher King. He rules for seven years before retiring as a hermit and the belief is that the Grail will be seen no more on Earth.

Between the first two and the last two Continuations, two *Prologues* appeared.

BLIOCADRAN PROLOGUE and **THE ELUCIDATION PROLOGUE**, anon. (French, early 1200s, post-Boron but pre-*Perlesvaus*) 800 and 484 lines respectively.

The first tells the story of Bliocadran, Perceval's father. All of his brothers have been killed in tournaments and although his wife pleads with him not to go, especially as the birth of their first child is imminent, he still leaves. He is mortally wounded and dies soon after. Bliocadran's widow takes her baby and flees to a remote wasteland forest in Wales. This prologue blends into the start of Chrétien's story by repeating the opening lines, though it also contradicts some of Chrétien's story, in that Perceval did have other brothers and sisters and his father was supposed to have died of grief over their deaths.

The second continuation, which may be of a later date, adds nothing substantive and tends to confuse. It implies that the castle of the Fisher King had become lost because twelve maidens, who served travellers from the local wells, were raped by King Amangon and his knights and their golden cups stolen. This is to be avenged by Arthur and his knights, and their exploits at the mysterious Proud Castle are seen as a parallel to those at the Grail castle. The author then explains the Grail mystery which, for a prologue, is unhelpful.

> The first prologue is available as *Bliocadran* edited by Lenora D. Wolfgang (Niemeyer, 1976), whilst the second is only available as *The Elucidation* edited by Albert W. Thompson (Institute of French Studies, 1931).

JOSEPH D'ARIMATHIE (or **L'Estoire dou Graal**), Robert de Boron (French, late 1190s) 3,514 lines.

This work reveals the origin of the Grail, imbuing it with Christian symbolism. Robert is the first to identify the Grail as the vessel used by Christ at the Last Supper, and to make the connection between the table of the Last Supper and Arthur's Round Table.

Joseph receives the Grail from Pilate and uses it to collect the blood of Christ when He is removed from the Cross. When Jesus's body disappears (after the Resurrection), Joseph is cast into prison. Jesus visits him, with the Grail, and tells him to continue commemorating the Last Supper in memory of Him. There are explicit instructions from Jesus as to what individual items mean, such as "the vessel of the sacrament will be a reminder of the stone tomb in which you laid me." All who see the vessel will have lasting joy and fulfilment for their souls, clearly meaning that those who believe in Christ will have everlasting life. At this stage Robert has done little more than repeat the message of the Gospels, but he now weaves that into the Arthurian myth.

Joseph is in prison for many years. Eventually the emperor Vespasian hears of the uproar over the death of Jesus and has it investigated, learning the story from Pilate. Pilate, in order to prove his story, has a search made for anything connected to Christ. In this process he finds Veronica, who has the cloth with which she wiped Christ's face on the way to the Cross, and which still bears an image of His face. The cloth heals Vespasian of his leprosy. Though this is not the same as the shroud of Turin, it is evidently based on the same cloth. Robert tells us that, "this image was the only thing they found which had touched Our Lord."

Joseph is now released and pardoned, and is reunited with his sister Enigeus and her husband Bron. They gather about them a following and leave Judea "into exile." All goes well at first but then their crops fail and Joseph believes it is because some of them have sinned. He is directed by the Holy Spirit to create a second table, in imitation of the one at the Last Supper, at which the service of the Grail will be celebrated. Bron, who becomes the Fisher King, is charged with collecting a fish to serve at the Grail table, but only those who are free of sin will be able to approach the table and enjoy the benefits of the meal. When a banished sinner tries to sit at the vacant place at the table, one that equates to where Judas had sat, he is "swallowed up" as if he had never existed.

Bron has twelve children but only one of these, Alain, will be the ancestor of the final keeper of the Grail. Bron and his successors, the Fisher Kings, become the guardians of the Grail and travel to the west, to the Vales of Avalon, to await the coming of the final keeper.

Robert continued his sequence of poems with *Merlin* (*see* page 401) before returning to *Perceval* which is treated below.

→ One of the more interesting translations is the Dutch *Historie van den Grale* by Jacob van Maerlant, completed in 1261. Maerlant took issue with Boron where he believed the work was at variance with the Gospels in how the apostles were dealt with by the Romans, and revised the text accordingly. Otherwise his translation is faithful.

> A translation by Nigel Bryant is in *Merlin and the Grail* by Robert de Boron (Brewer, 2001).

PERCEVAL, Robert de Boron (France, early 1200s)

None of this poem survives (and it may never have been completed) but it is believed that it was adapted as the prose version of part or all of it appears in the so-called Didot-*Perceval*, composed in the 1220s. That exists in two variant manuscripts (known as the D and E).

This version starts abruptly, with no information on Perceval's youth. We learn that his father is Alain le Gros, descended from Bron. Alain sends Perceval to Arthur's court where he proves himself in a grand tournament. Perceval begs to sit at the Siege Perilous, the forbidden seat at the Round Table and does so. This causes an Armageddon-like darkening of the skies and Arthur is admonished for allowing someone impure to sit at that seat. The voice also commands that the knights prove their valour so that they may be judged and the finest knight in the world identified. Only then may that knight be taken to the castle of the Fisher King and, by asking what the Grail is for and who is served with it, cause the Fisher King to be healed and the land made free of enchantment.

Much of what follows is drawn from Chrétien's story and the continuations, and may not have been in Robert's original scheme. Perceval has to undergo many perils before he achieves overall mastery and is directed by Merlin – now portrayed rather like Old Father Time – to the Grail castle where he cures the Fisher King and becomes the final keeper of the Grail. His actions restore the land, and Arthur is able to conquer Gaul and march on Rome. However, he is betrayed by Mordred and taken to Avalon. Merlin reveals these final facts to Perceval before himself disappearing into his "esplumior", a mystical word which seems to imply some future rebirth.

The full version is in *The Didot-Perceval* edited by William Roach (University of Pennsylvania Press, 1941). Another translation is *The Romance of Perceval in Prose* by Dell Skeels (Washington University Press, 1966). A translation by Nigel Bryant is in *Merlin and the Grail* by Robert de Boron (Brewer, 2001).

PERLESVAUS (or The High History of the Holy Grail), anon. (Flanders, early 1200s).

Perlesvaus is the earliest known prose Arthurian romance, an original composition not based on a verse romance, though clearly derived from the works of Chrétien and Robert de Boron. It was regarded by Sebastian Evans (*see below*) as the most complete and authentic text of the Grail story. It is certainly the purest version, and would undergo radical changes when developed as part of the Vulgate Cycle.

After a brief prologue on the Grail family and the origins of the Grail, the story opens with a languid King Arthur much in need of going adventuring. He sets out to visit a chapel in a forest to do penance but is admonished by the priest who says that he and his court, though once held in high regard, have now fallen into shameful repute. A malaise has settled over the land because a young knight who sheltered at the castle of the Fisher King failed to ask the right question when he witnessed the Grail. Returning from the chapel, Arthur is wounded in an encounter with a Black Knight. He is healed by a maiden who is seeking Perlesvaus and who further admonishes Arthur for his lack of positive guidance. She tells him the story of the origins of Perlesvaus, which is drawn from Chrétien's Perceval. As he continues his way through the forest a voice commands that he hold a court to consider how to right the world's ills.

Arthur calls the court, which is attended by all the knights save Gawain and Lancelot. They are visited by three maidens, one of them with a cart containing the heads of one hundred and fifty knights. She reveals that these knights met their fate because of the failure of Perlesvaus at the Grail castle. One of the other maidens brings a shield and a hound. The shield had once belonged to Joseph of Arimathea and was painted with the blood of Christ. She leaves these tokens to be retrieved one day by the Good Knight who, it is foretold, will heal the land.

When the maidens depart they meet Gawain who agrees to accompany the Maiden of the Cart. So begins Gawain's adventure, the first of a trilogy that will also include Lancelot and Perceval. Gawain's quest is initially to find the Good Knight. He fails to do so but his travels bring him to the Grail castle. He is unable to enter because of his sins, but is told he will be able to do so if he finds the Sword that had beheaded John the Baptist. Thus Gawain sets off on a further series of adventures, all of which he later learns have allegorical significance, and eventually wins the Sword. He returns and is admitted to the Grail castle. He dines, and witnesses the Grail procession, but is so overcome by the visions he sees that he fails to ask the right questions, at which point Gawain finds himself alone and leaves the castle.

Lancelot takes up the challenge. He has to pass the test of a beheading game, but finds his way to the Grail castle barred because of his love for Guenevere. Lancelot realises that he must track down the Good Knight Perlesvaus, who he believes is with his uncle Pelles. However, Perlesvaus has left Pelles and is involved in a series of battles, including rescuing his mother (who is still alive in this version). Perlesvaus also comes across the body of Arthur's son Loholt, killed by Kay who wished to claim credit for a giant Loholt had killed. There is much adventuring, and considerable symbolism in the respective quests by Gawain and Lancelot to find Perlesvaus and in his own adventures. Central to these is the battle for Castle Mortal whose king, the brother of the Fisher King, has been attacking the Grail castle. The king takes the castle, the Fisher King is killed, and the Grail vanishes. Perlesvaus, with the help of twelve hermit knights, retakes the castle.

The story now follows Arthur's own personal quest. Arthur

arrives at the Grail castle where he has a vision of the Grail in five forms of which only the last, as a chalice, is described. While Arthur is away Guenevere dies of grief over Loholt's death. Kay has fled to Brian des Iles in Brittany, who rises in revolt against Arthur. Brian is temporarily defeated and there is a final showdown in which Lancelot helps Arthur defeat Brian. Arthur, Gawaine and Lancelot all seek Guenevere's resting place at Avalon, which is revealed to be Glastonbury. Perceval has to defeat the Black Hermit, the last evil in the world. Perceval sails away from the Grail castle and is seen no more. He leaves the Castle in the hands of his cousin Joseus, but after long years he dies and the Castle falls into decay. Ever since, only two people have found the castle and returned, and they became saints.

The standard translation was *The High History of the Holy Graal* by Sebastian Evans (Dent, 1910) but this is now superseded by *The High Book of the Grail* by Nigel Bryant (Brewer, 1978).

PARZIVAL, Wolfram von Eschenbach (German, between 1204 and 1212) 25,000 lines
Although he promoted himself as illiterate and was criticised by Gottfried von Strassburg, Wolfram is generally regarded as the greatest of the German epic poets of the period. *Parzival* is effectively another continuation of Chrétien's *Perceval*, though Wolfram went to great pains to acknowledge his source as one Kyot of Provence. Most now believe this to be a fictional device, and that Wolfram needed a third party to "authenticate" the material he uses which differs from Chrétien's. According to Wolfram, Kyot's source was a manuscript in Arabic. *Parzival* does contain much Arabic colour and background, and Wolfram, as an itinerant knight, may well have picked up information from various sources, including knights returning from Jerusalem.

Although in structure *Parzival* follows the storyline of Chrétien's *Perceval*, there are some significant changes, including to Parzival's parents. His father Gahmuret was the younger son of the lord of Anjou, and, when his elder brother inherited the title, Gahmuret set out on worldly adventures. He spent time in Babylon and Arabia, even fathering a child, Feirifiz, by the queen of Zazamanc, before returning to the west and marrying Herzeloyde, queen of Waleis. Upon his brother's death, Gahmuret becomes lord of Anjou. He responds to a plea from the Baruc of Baghdad who is being attacked by the Babylonians, and dies in the conflict just days before Parzival is born. Mother and child flee into the remote forest until, captivated by the sight of knights, Parzival ventures forth into the world.

Wolfram often changes or provides names. Perceval's sweetheart becomes Condwiramurs, the Grail King is Anfortas and the Grail castle becomes Munsalvaesche, "the mountain of salvation". The Guardians of the Grail are the Templar knights. Parzival's experience at the Grail castle is similar to but more elaborate than previous descriptions, though he still fails to ask the right question. Parzival returns to Arthur's castle, is admonished by the ugly damsel, here called Cundrie the Sorceress, then both he and Gawain set off on their respective quests. Parzival wanders for nearly five years as if in a daze and eventually finds the retreat of the hermit Trevrizent (Parzival's uncle and the brother of Anfortas).

It is in Book 9 that Wolfram provides his interpretation of the Grail in what is an intensely mystical section. We learn that the Grail is a stone of power, the *lapsit exillis*. We also learn why the Fisher King Anfortas is wounded. He had fallen in love with a lady he had served and at a tournament was wounded in the genitals by a lance, the same one borne in the procession. However, it was prophesied that should a youth ask the right question of him about the Grail he would be cured, though could no longer serve as Grail King. In other words, the asking of the question, which had eluded Perceval in all of the versions to date, is the key to Perceval becoming the Grail King's successor. Trevrizent also reveals how the Grail serves as a secret organization despatching knights to become lords of disinherited lands.

Wolfram returns to follow Chrétien's storyline but as we approach the climax, which Chrétien left unfinished, Wolfram comes back into his own. Parzival's half-brother Feirifiz appears and he and Parzival do battle until Parzival recognizes his identity and the two are reconciled. Parzival and Feirifiz go jointly to the Grail castle. With his understanding Parzival is able to cure Anfortas, and the Grail King hands over his role to Parzival.

Feirifiz marries the Grail Bearer, Repanse. We even learn something of the future of Parzival's son Loherangrin.

Although Wolfram worked from the same material as Chrétien, he refashioned it from the spiritual to the hermetic, making it less a work of religious attainment and more of discovery and destiny. His light matter-of-fact touch would have allowed the reader to understand his own world whilst still being uplifted by the majesty of the subject. Wolfram doubtless planned to explore more of the Grail world, since he worked on another poem, *Titurel*, the name relating to a forebear of the Grail King. But he left that unfinished and it was completed in the 1270s as *Der jüngere Titurel*. Like the later epic poem *Lohengrin* (believed to be written by the otherwise-unknown Neuhäuser in the 1280s), it features no Arthurian characters so is only Arthurian by association.

→ The French Continuations (except the Fourth) were translated and reworked by Clause Wisse and Philipp Colin during 1331–1336 and incorporated between Books 14 and 15 as *Der nüwe Parzefal*, but their work adds nothing to the original.

> The standard translation is by A.T. Hatto (Penguin, 1980). A new translation is *Parzival with Titurel and the Love Lyrics* by Cyril Edwards and Julia Walworth (Boydell Press, 2004).

QUEST OF THE HOLY GRAIL, anon. (French, soon after 1215).

This is the second book in the original Vulgate Cycle and follows the Prose *Lancelot* (see next chapter), but is composed in an entirely different vein. It is clearly a spiritual quest with little relevance to earthly matters.

Camelot is visited on the day before Pentecost by a maiden who requests that Lancelot accompany her. She leads him to a nunnery in a forest where he is asked to knight a young man who is brought before him. This Lancelot does. Also present are Lancelot's cousins Bors and Lionel, who believe the young man is the son of Lancelot. All three return to Camelot. They discover, on the Seige Perilous, or Perilous Seat, a new inscription:

FOUR HUNDRED AND FIFTY-FOUR YEARS HAVE PASSED
SINCE THE PASSION OF CHRIST; ON PENTECOST,
THIS SEAT WILL FIND ITS MASTER.

They cover the inscription with a cloth. A squire rushes to tell King Arthur that a marble slab has floated down the river in which is embedded a sword. Arthur hurries to the scene with Lancelot, Gawain and Perceval. The sword has the inscription:

NO ONE WILL WITHDRAW ME FROM HERE
EXCEPT HE WHO WILL HANG ME AT HIS SIDE
AND HE WILL BE THE WORLD'S BEST KNIGHT.

Arthur, believing Lancelot to be the world's best knight, asks him to withdraw the sword. He refuses, knowing he will not succeed. Gawain is also loath to do so but Arthur insists. Neither Gawain nor Perceval can withdraw it. Lancelot sees it as ominous that Gawain has even tried and declares that he will rue the day.

They sit down for the Pentecostal meal. All the knights are present, including four crowned kings, and the only vacant seat is the Siege Perilous. No sooner have they completed their first course than all the castle doors and windows shut of their own accord, yet the dining hall remains light. An old man in a white cloak appears, leading a young knight in red armour, but without sword or shield. He is announced as the Desired Knight, descended from King David and the family of Joseph of Arimathea.

The knight is led to the Siege Perilous and when Lancelot removes the cloth he sees that the inscription now states THIS IS GALAHAD'S SEAT. Galahad reveals that he has come because the Quest for the Holy Grail will soon start. Arthur takes Galahad to the river, where the sword is still embedded in the marble slab. Galahad withdraws it easily, stating that he knew he would obtain a sword and so had not brought one. He now needs a shield.

A damsel riding by tells Lancelot that he is no longer the world's best knight and advises Arthur that they will soon be visited by the Grail. Arthur celebrates with a tournament and Galahad defeats all who stand against him.

While they dine that evening there is a clap of thunder, and the room is illuminated as if by the Holy Spirit. The Grail appears, but the room is so bright, and the Grail covered with a cloth, that no one can see it properly. It passes round the room and everyone finds their plates full with whatever food they desire. The Grail goes but no one sees how or where. Overcome by events, Gawain declares that he will not rest until he has seen the Grail. All the assembled knights (150), agree and swear an oath to seek the truth of the Grail. Arthur is distraught, realizing that this is the beginning of the end for the Round Table.

Although all the knights depart on their Quest the story concentrates on the actions of Gawain, Lancelot, Bors and Perceval and how Galahad's quest interacts with theirs. Each of the knights is tested and all, save Galahad, are found wanting, though at one stage Galahad fights with Lancelot and Perceval, not knowing who they are, and nearly kills them both. He hurries away before he can be recognised. Galahad's first encounter, however, is at the White Abbey. Bademagus and Yvain the Bastard had already reached it because Bademagus was interested in a shield which could not be taken from the abbey without its bearer being killed or maimed within a day or two. Galahad encourages them to take the shield, saying that if they fail he will use the shield himself. Bademagus takes the shield, despite a warning from the monks. A few leagues from the abbey he is challenged by a white knight, and receives a mortal blow.

The knight takes the shield back to the abbey and hands it to Galahad. The knight reveals that forty-two years after Christ's passion Joseph of Arimathea and his companions left Jerusalem and came to the city of Sarras, then ruled by the Saracen king Evalach, who was at war with his neighbour Tholomer. Joseph's son Josephus gave Evalach a shield marked with a red cross and told him that after three days, when he felt he was sure to be defeated, he was to reveal this shield. Evalach did so, and discovered that the shield bore the image of a crucified man. He recited the words that Josephus had told him and thereupon won the battle. A man whose hand had been amputated touched the shield and his hand was restored. Evalach took the shield to Josephus whose nose began to bleed. With his blood Josephus made the image of a cross on the shield. The shield is left in the safe keeping of Evalach to await the coming of the Good Knight, Galahad.

Galahad leaves Bademagus at the White Abbey and is accompanied by Bademagus's squire Melias, who wishes to become a knight. They reach a fork in the road, and learn that whoever takes the right turning will meet with certain death whilst only the world's greatest knight can take the left route. Melias, newly knighted, takes the left turning. He discovers a crown in a bush but when he takes it he is badly wounded by a knight. Galahad rescues him and takes Melias to an abbey to heal. There Melias learns that he had committed the sins of pride and presumption. As all of the knights proceed on the Quest they are to be tested and their sins discovered.

Galahad comes to the Castle of Maidens where seven brothers hold prisoner any maidens who pass their way. Galahad defeats the brothers and they all flee. Soon afterwards they meet Gawain who is travelling with his brother Gaheris and Yvain the Bastard. The seven brothers attack the knights but are soon killed. When they lodge for the night at a hermitage, the hermit admonishes Gawain for killing all of the brothers, which was not necessary to succeed in the Quest.

Lancelot, who had been travelling with Perceval, is now travelling alone. While resting he sees the arrival of a wounded knight who is healed by the appearance of the Grail. Lancelot tries to move but cannot. The knight's squire takes his armour. Only when they have gone can Lancelot move again. Lancelot tells this episode to a priest at a small chapel who explains that Lancelot will not achieve the Grail Quest because of his sin of adultery. He must first repent. Lancelot thereupon stays with the priest for five days to purge his sins and vows never to repeat them. When he leaves, and after a vision of his forebears, Lancelot enters a tournament. He chooses to fight on the side of the black knights, because they are losing, but he is unhorsed and captured. He learns that this was yet another test and that he should have fought on the side of the white knights, who represented the knights of heaven whilst the black knights were the soiled knights of earth. Confused and introspective, Lancelot wanders dazed for several days, putting up no fight when he in unhorsed by another knight. He finds himself hemmed in by cliffs and a river and there stops to await guidance from God.

Perceval, in the meantime, has come to a small chapel where

there is an old recluse. He discovers that she is his aunt who was once Queen of the Waste Land. She tells Perceval that his mother had died of a broken heart when he left her to become a knight. She also reveals that only three knights will complete the Grail Quest, Galahad, Bors and himself, but he will succeed only if he remains chaste. She explains to Perceval the significance of the Round Table, referring to the three great fellowships since the coming of Jesus Christ – the Table of the Last Supper, the Table of the Holy Grail, and now the Round Table.

When Perceval leaves his aunt he passes by an old abbey where he sees an incredibly ancient man lying upon a bed and wearing a crown. He asks one of the monks who he is and learns that he is none other than King Evalach himself, now called Mordrain, who had prayed that he would live until the Good Knight came.

Leaving the abbey, Perceval is attacked by bandits and though rescued by Galahad (though he does not know his identity) he loses his horse, and Galahad leaves before Perceval can follow. Perceval declares that he will do anything for a horse. A damsel appears who presents Perceval with a horse. Perceval becomes wary of the horse but mounts it in order to pursue Galahad. The horse, though, has a mind of its own and takes Perceval towards deep water. He is saved by crossing himself, otherwise he would have drowned. Perceval is rescued by a shipful of maidens and has to resist sexual temptation. Perceval prays to God and the ship and maidens vanish. Perceval is collected by another ship and a priest explains that, despite Satan's temptations, Perceval has passed the test.

Gawain, however, is struggling. He has joined forces with Hector, Lancelot's half-brother, hoping that together they might have more adventure. They challenge a knight and mortally wound him, only to discover they have wounded their friend Yvain the Bastard. Gawain is distraught and feels himself accursed. A holy man advises Gawain that he is too old and set in his ways for this Quest, expecting to find the solution in temporal matters rather than spiritual. He is told he should return to Camelot, but he cannot bear the thought of not being part of the Quest. Gawain tells the Holy Man that he will talk with him again but hurries to follow Hector. The two subsequently meet Galahad, though again they fail to recognise each other. Galahad severely injures Gawain, as Lancelot had foreseen when Gawain tried to remove the sword from the slab.

Bors is also undergoing his trials, beset by visions, in which he sees his brother Lionel being abducted and goes to his rescue but encounters a maiden being raped. Torn between the two, he saves the maiden but is too late to save Lionel. Bors carries Lionel's body to a castle for burial, but there a lady asks Bors to be her lover. Bors refuses even when the lady threatens to kill herself. Eventually his visions cease and a priest tells Bors that demons have been testing him but that he made the right choices. When he tracks down Lionel, his brother is furious that Bors had chosen to save the maiden and not him. Lionel attacks Bors and another knight, Calogrenant, intercedes and is killed. Lionel is struck by a firebolt. He survives but is no longer part of the Quest.

Bors and Perceval have survived their trials and meet Galahad at the sea's edge. Galahad is accompanied by Perceval's sister Dindrane. A crewless ship arrives. An inscription warns them that only those who are true to God can board. They board and discover a large bed on which is a sword, partly drawn from its scabbard. The sword has several inscriptions forewarning any potential user. Dindrane says that only one can draw the sword and she tells its history. Two generations earlier, the ship had arrived in Logres during a war between the Christian king Lambar, father of the Maimed King, and the pagan king Varlan. Varlan was near defeat when he saw the ship, leapt on board and found the sword. He rushed back into battle and killed Lambar, but when he returned to the ship for the scabbard he dropped down dead. From that day the land had lain barren, and the blow Varlan struck Lambar became known as the Dolorous Stroke. After studying the sword and its portents, Dindrane fastens the sword and belt to Galahad, revealing that this is the Sword of the Strange Straps. They explore the ship and learn that it was built by Solomon from the Tree of Life.

They leave the ship and come to a castle where they are attacked. The lady of the castle suffers from leprosy and a prophecy had told that the blood from a royal maiden would cure her. The townsfolk capture all maidens who pass by for their blood. Dindrane volunteers her blood, knowing that she will die. She asks of Perceval that her body be set adrift in a boat that will take her body to Sarras, where she wants to be buried in a tomb that would later house the bodies of Perceval and Galahad.

This they do. This same boat later passes Lancelot who still waits in grief by the river. He hears a voice telling him to board the boat and he discovers Dindrane with a note left by Perceval. He rejoices to learn that Bors, Perceval and Galahad are together, and hopes that some day he will meet his son. The boat carries him to a chapel where a knight awaits him and boards the boat. He discovers this is Galahad; at last the two meet and share thoughts and memories. They stay aboard for half a year, visiting strange lands, though the story tells nothing of their adventures.

At length Galahad departs, leaving Lancelot to continue his voyage to the Grail Castle. There Lancelot has a vision of the Grail but is so overcome that he passes into a coma that lasts for twenty-four days. He is eventually restored by King Pelles and returns to Camelot, having failed in his Grail Quest.

Galahad's travels bring him to the abbey where Perceval had seen King Mordrain (Evalach), and it is in his arms that Mordrain is at last able to die. He continues to travel throughout Logres for five years, now accompanied by Perceval, and at the end of that period they meet Bors.

The Grail company, again united, travel to Corbenic where Galahad restores the Broken Sword. Nine further knights arrive, three each from Gaul, Ireland and Denmark, so that twelve knights sit at the Grail Table. Josephus appears before them and conducts the ceremony of the Eucharist. Then he vanishes and from the Grail itself rises the Spirit of Christ. With blood from the Bleeding Lance, Galahad heals the Maimed King. Christ instructs Galahad that he is to take the Grail to Sarras. They feed from the holy Platter and are blessed by Christ before He vanishes.

Galahad, Perceval and Bors sail in the Ship of Solomon to Sarras, where Galahad cures a cripple. The boat carrying the body of Perceval's sister has also found its way to Sarras. However, the king of Sarras, Escorant, is suspicious and has them imprisoned. It is not until Escorant falls ill, after a whole year, that he releases them and pleads forgiveness. Galahad becomes the new king of Sarras. He rules for a year but prays to Christ to be released. He has one last vision from the Grail and then his soul departs. Bors and Perceval witness a hand reach down from Heaven to retrieve the Grail and the Bleeding Lance and from that day forth they are never seen again.

Perceval retires to a nunnery and dies a year later. He is buried beside his sister and Galahad. Bors, the last of the Grail knights, returns to Camelot and tells his story.

A translation with notes by Pauline Matarasso is available as *The Quest of the Holy Grail* (Penguin, 1969). Extracts are included in *The Lancelot-Grail Reader* edited by Norris J. Lacy (Garland, 2000).

ESTOIRE DEL SAINT GRAAL (The History of the Holy Grail) (Vulgate Cycle), anon. (French, *c*1230).
This is essentially Robert de Boron's *Joseph*, updated by incorporating the historical elements of the Grail from the *Quest of the Holy Grail*, already told in the Vulgate cycle. The story now forms a symbolical Christian history from the time of Jesus to the start of the Arthurian period. In the prologue, the author purports to be writing 717 years after Christ's Passion (that is, 750).

The story follows the basic outline of de Boron's work. Joseph of Arimathea is held in prison for 42 years until released during the reign of Vespasian. Recognizing that everyone is that much older (which de Boron fails to do), it is Joseph's son Josephus who becomes Keeper of the Grail and leads the mission out of Palestine. They take with them the Grail, which is now hidden within a box like the Ark of the Covenant. They go first to Sarras (the capital of the Saracens) where Joseph is able to convert the heathen king Evalach, who takes the Christian name Mordrain, whilst Evalach's brother-in-law becomes Nascien. Some of Mordrain's people refuse baptism and Josephus tries to rescue them from a demon, but he is attacked by an angel who wounds him in the thigh, though he is later healed, an early parallel of the later Maimed King. Nascien wishes to see the Grail but looks too closely inside the ark and is blinded. An angel later heals his blindness with the Bleeding Lance.

The company then divides and each has a series of adventures in various lands, before making their way eventually to Britain. The company are beset by temptations but prevail. The story tells of the Christianisation of the West, with Josephus in the role of St. Paul. We learn more about the magical Ship of Solomon and about the individual elements of the Grail, Sword and Lance. The Grail Table is created, which includes the seat reserved for only the most virtuous of heroes. When Moises sits there he is consumed by fire. After Josephus's death Alain, his cousin and the first of the Fisher Kings, becomes Guardian of the Grail and founds the Grail castle at Corbenic.

Finally we learn of the later Guardians of the Grail, as already recorded in the *Quest for the Grail*, including the story of the Dolorous Blow which created the Waste Land. The story ends with the death of Lancelot's grandfather, also called Lancelot. → An English verse adaptation was made by Henry Lovelich as *The History of the Holy Grail* (*c*1430s). It is fairly faithful to its original, but states that Joseph of Arimathea was buried at Glastonbury.

Extracts are included in *The Lancelot-Grail Reader* edited by Norris J. Lacy (Garland, 2000).

DER JÜNGERE TITUREL, Albrecht (*possibly, but not conclusively,* Albrecht von Scharfenberg) (German, early 1270s)
An intriguing variant version of the Grail drawing upon the work of Wolfram and essentially a completion of his unfinished *Titurel*. Although it uses as its core theme the love story of Parzival's cousin Sigune (whose death is one of the most poignant passages in *Parzival*) and the ill-fated Schionatulandaer, that is only a minor part of a work originally conceived on a grandiose scale. Titurel is the Grail King, his role announced by angels, who receives the Grail from Joseph of Arimathea. As in *Parzival*, the Grail is not a chalice but a stone, but a dish has been fashioned from it. Titurel takes the Grail to safety in a lost valley beyond impenetrable mountains and forests at Munt Salvasch, where he has built a magnificent temple which is described in loving detail. He guards the Grail for over four hundred years until the outer world becomes too hostile, when he sets forth with Parzival and takes the Grail to India, to the kingdom of Prester John.

A study and summary of the work is available in *The Art of Narration in Wolfram's* Parzival *and Albrecht's* Jüngere Titurel, by Linda B. Parshall (Cambridge University Press, 1981).

PERCEFOREST, anon. (Dutch, *c*1330s)
An audacious and brave attempt to completely recast the Matter of Britain into a new historical context set against a vast all-absorbing tapestry of legend, myth and folk tale that, in its first printed edition in Paris in 1528, ran to six thick folio volumes. In this version, the original line of British royalty descended from Brutus has died out and Alexander the Great conquers Britain and establishes his own royal house under his governor Perceforest. The main arc of the story extends from the betrayal of Britain to the Romans by Perceforest's son Betides, to its salvation through the Grail and the Christian faith being established in Britain. No complete English translation exists, but a projected twelve-volume French critical edition is currently being compiled.

SIR PERCYVELL OF GALES, anon. (English, *c*1330s), 2,288 lines.
An early English reworking of the Perceval story as told by Chrétien, but omitting the Grail element in order to develop the relationship between Perceval and his mother. Otherwise, the story follows the basic plot. Perceval becomes fascinated by knights, leaves his mother to go to Arthur's court, kills the Red Knight who had killed his father, and rescues and then marries Lufamour [Blancheflor]. He is then reunited with his mother who returns with him to his home with Lufamour, before Perceval eventually goes to the Holy Land. It thereby removes all mystical elements to convert it into a straightforward morality story.

The original English text is available in *Yvain and Gawain*, edited by Maldwyn Mills (Dent, 1992).

17

LANCELOT AND GUENEVERE – THE ROMANCE ENDS

Ask anyone to name one knight of the Round Table and they will almost certainly say "Lancelot". He became the greatest of all of Arthur's knights and eclipsed the stature of Arthur himself. The love affair between Lancelot and Guenevere is a major element in the story because it is this that leads to the sundering of the Round Table and the death of Arthur. Yet, through all this, Lancelot shines through. He is seen not as the offender but as the victim. He is a victim through his love for Guenevere, through his devotion to Arthur and through his desire to do good. Even though he may be super-human as a warrior and knight, Lancelot is intensely human in his failings.

Yet who was he? Arthur's other major knights – Bedivere, Kay, Gawain – had their origins in the Celtic tales and are instantly recognisable, but not so Lancelot. Was there an original on whom he was based?

1. The origins of Lancelot

The name Lancelot appears for the first time anywhere in line 1692 of Chrétien de Troyes's poem *Erec et Enide*, first composed towards the end of the 1160s. He is mentioned in passing and ranked as the third most renowned knight after Gawain and Erec. Yet when he next appears, anonymously, in *Le Chevalier de la charrete*, we discover he is a knight of exceptional valour. Within a few years *Lancelot do Lac* features him as the finest of all knights. It is also clear from Chrétien's story that he is only telling half the tale. There appears to be no reason why Lancelot keeps his identity a secret, and it was not until *Lanzelet*, a German version by Ulrich von Zatzikhoven, appeared a few years after *Erec et Enide* that there was any mention of his origins: he was stolen as a baby by a fey and brought up ignorant of his parentage. Yet this version has none of the love affair between Lancelot and Guenevere. That was Chrétien's invention, under instruction from Marie de Champagne, yet it is evident that he incorporated it into an existing legend, which may or may not have been about Lancelot as we came to know him, about a baby raised by a water sprite.

Such legends are common but we do not need to look far to find one directly within the Celtic Arthurian world. We have encountered Mabon ap Modron before. He was the mighty hunter who, in *Culhwch and Olwen*, helps hunt the Great Boar. He is also noted as a servant of Uther Pendragon in the poem *Pa Gur*. But who was he really? The name means "Son of the Mother", thus some have interpreted Mabon as the son of Mother Earth, the spirit of fertility. However, the land can be blighted and that is what happens to Mabon. Three days after his birth he is abducted, and no one knows where he is. Arthur and his men search for him and discover, from the oldest creature in the world, that Mabon is in a fortress in Caer Loyw (Gloucester) which can only be approached by water. Mabon is rescued by Arthur's forces and takes part in the hunt.

Lancelot likewise was abducted when only a few days old and raised by the Lady of the Lake in a fortress mysteriously surrounded by water and otherwise unapproachable. Unlike Mabon's, Lancelot's "imprisonment" was not harsh, because he was raised in the ways of chivalry, but he knows nothing of his parentage or origins, almost to the point of being frightened to know them. Like Mabon, we can consider Lancelot a great hunter inasmuch as he is unceasingly undertaking quests. As the son of Mother Earth, Mabon is seen as the eternal youth, which may be much of his appeal. Intriguingly the name of Melwas, the abductor of Guenevere, translates as "Prince Youth" (*mael gwas*).

If the character of Lancelot contains a faint folk memory of him likewise being a god of youth and fertility, it may also explain his relationship with Guenevere as perhaps representing a pre-Arthurian legend. There is little about Guenevere, or Gwenhwyfar, in the early Celtic tales. Her name means "white phantom" or "white shadow". She is mentioned in the Triads as the First Lady of the Island, but this is post-Arthurian. Geoffrey of Monmouth states that she was descended from a noble Roman family. In Marie de France's *Lanval* we see her portrayed as a seductress who, when spurned, turns vindictive. Her relationship towards Lancelot also waxes and wanes like the Moon, and it may well be that she is the embodiment of a distant lunar deity fighting for control of the Son of the Earth with Arthur in the role of the Sun.

If these ancient folk deities are distant forebears of Lancelot, what about his name? It is clearly not a Celtic name, nor is there anything similar in the Welsh tales. In his translation of the *Mabinogion* into French in 1913 Joseph Lot put forward the idea that Lancelot was derived from Llenlleawc, the character who wields the sword Caledvwlch in *Culhwch and Olwen* and wins the Cauldron of Plenty. There is a similar character in the *Preiddeu Annwvyn* whose name is spelled Lleminawc. Lleminawc, or Llemenig, crops up in several places. A Triad lists him as one of the "Three Unrestricted Guests" at Arthur's court and since the other two, Llywarch Hen and Heledd, are both refugees at the court of Powys, this may be the same for Llemenig. A surviving fragment of an otherwise lost poem about Cynddylan (Heledd's brother and a Prince of Powys in the mid-seventh century) calls Llemenig the "battle-hound of wrath, victorious in battle." He is described as the son of Mawan or Mawn, descended from Cadell Ddyrnllug of Powys. I have included him in Table 3.9. The pedigrees are slightly confused and he may be a generation earlier. Either way he would be contemporary with Artúir of Dyfed. The whole of this dynasty is associated with white, with Cadell of the Gleaming Hilt and Cynan of the White Chariot, and this may also be true of Llemenig, as it is of Guenevere.

Lot believed that Llenlleawc and Llemenig were one and the same, but that is by no means certain. One translation of *Preiddeu Annwvyn* places both characters in the story, but the most recent translation by John Koch suggests that the line translated as

"The sword of Llwc Lleawc" actually means "A sword of lightning slaughter".

Lot equated both these names with a third name, Llwch Llawwynniog, "of the Striking Hand", which may well relate to someone wielding a sword of "lightning slaughter". He is mentioned in *Pa Gur* as defending Eidyn's border. This character equates with the Irish god of the sun and lightning, Lugh *Loinnbheimionach*, "of the mighty blows". Lugh is described as a shining god of light, and Lancelot was first perceived in all white armour with a white crest.

The derivation, as suggested by Lot and developed by Loomis, is that the Bretons believed Llwch Llawwyniog and Llwch Lleminawc/Llenlleac were one and the same. They also believed that Llwch meant "lake". Llenlleac transmuted to Lancelin, a name in use in Brittany since the eleventh century, and that by degrees shifted to Lancelot of the Lake. I must confess that although I can imagine this might have happened I do not find it wholly convincing. Whilst Llemenig may be the source of the character he does not seem a likely source for the name. In Old Welsh *llain* means "blade" or "sword" and *lloyg* is "warrior" or "hero", so *Llainlloyg* is a composite that could corrupt to Lancelot.

The *–lot* suffix is a variant of *–let*, which means small or young, and the name is sometimes spelled Lancelet, so it may have meant "young hero" or "young sword". This would fit in with the motif of the Fair Unknown, a common theme in Arthurian romances. The Fair Unknown refers to an individual, almost always a youth, who arrives at Arthur's court ignorant of his birthright or family origins. He is often ridiculed and sets out to prove himself. He undergoes many challenges and adventures before discovering his origin. The Lady of the Lake keeps Lancelot ignorant of his past for as long as she can, as if learning his identity is a loss of innocence and youth.

Another possible derivation applies to the character of Lanzelet in the German version by Ulrich von Zatzikhoven. He has no knightly virtues, being raised by an evil water sprite intent on revenge and unleashed on the world pretty much as a killing machine and rapist. It is only once he has achieved her goals and come of age that he earns his name. Here it may well apply to the lands he has gained, since *Lanz* is the Old German for land, or at least that may be how the name was interpreted for Ulrich's story. It was purportedly based on an earlier legend, and doubtless one that Chrétien also knew but revised. Whatever story Chrétien used, there is little doubt that he originally modelled Lancelot on Tristan in order to create a parallel love triangle with Lancelot, Guenevere and Arthur.

There are other explanations for Lancelot's name, the most interesting being that by Linda Malcor and C. Scott Littleton in *From Scythia to Camelot*. They have explored the legends of the Alans, Sarmatians and Ossetians, all related tribes, and found many parallels between them and the Arthurian tales. They also suspect that the Alans may be the source of Lancelot's name. We have seen that the Alans became Kings and Dukes of Brittany and Counts of Vannes, and they also established themselves in the south of France, in Gascony and Toulouse. One of their centres was at Montauban in the old County of Lot. There is still a French département of that name but the old county was much larger and was one of the areas that suffered during the Albigensian Crusade as it was a centre for the Cathars. It does not take long to see that if there had been tales, now lost, of an heroic Alan of Lot, his name would have mutated from Alanus à Lot >Alans à Lot >Alanç-à-lot >Lancelot. It is more convincing than the derivation from Llemenig, all the more so since the name of the town of Alençon in Normandy has a similar source.

In *Bloodline of the Holy Grail*, Laurence Gardner provides a different derivation for Lancelot which succeeds in fusing a French origin with the Arthurian Cycle. He cites Lancelot's surname as del Acqs, "of the water", noting that this was a title attached to Mary Magdalen who purportedly died in Gaul in 63AD at Acquae Sextiæ (modern Aix-en-Provence). The title passed through the descendants of Mary and Jesus, the Fisher Kings, to the Counts of Toulouse and, through the female line, to the Comtesses d'Avallon. The first of these, Viviane del Acqs, is supposed to have married Taliesin and had three daughters. Ygerna became the mother of Arthur, Morgause (who married Lot) was the mother of Gawain, and Viviane, who married Ban, was the mother of Lancelot. Because of the title their names became anglicised as Ladies of the Lake. This makes Lancelot of French descent but also a cousin of Arthur.

This Messianic descent is of considerable relevance to Lancelot's involvement in the Grail story in the *Lancelot-Grail*, because it not only provides an interpretation of a purportedly true secret history of the continued bloodline of Jesus – the true *Sangreal* – but it also explains the significance of Lancelot's son Galahad.

Galahad is the child of Lancelot's relationship with Elaine, the Grail Maiden and the daughter of the Fisher King. This sinless child reunites the lines of descent from David and Joseph of Arimathea, and is thereby able to achieve the Grail Quest and heal the Land. The Vulgate *Lancelot* states that the name of Joseph of Arimathea's son was Galahad and, significantly, that was Lancelot's name at birth.

The name Galahad has long been recognised as a corruption of the Biblical name Gilead – in fact, both appear as Galaad in respective Vulgate texts. Galaad means "heap of testimony" and Roger Sherman Loomis determined that the phrase is an allusion to Jesus Christ who was the personification of the "heap of testimony" given by all the Old Testament prophets. Galahad thereby becomes a symbolic Christ on earth, a sinless child, born of sin, as all mankind is born of original sin. Loomis concludes that the use of the name was a stroke of genius by the author, and indeed it was. But it does not explain why Lancelot was originally given that name. One might deduce that Lancelot was perhaps destined to become Galahad, but was not ready and held a temporary name until his "baptism". The Lady of the Lake raised him as the perfect knight, but Lancelot failed because he sinned in his love for Guenevere and, as a consequence, like Moses, he was not allowed to enter the Promised Land. A new child, without corruption, was required. Galahad was also raised away from his family, in a nunnery, and although tempted on several occasions, he succeeded in remaining sinless and thus achieved the Quest.

Ingenious though this all seems it may not have been quite so faultlessly planned. Loomis, for instance, suspected that an earlier (now lost) Grail story has Gawain as the successful Grail Knight and that his name may have been corrupted to Galaan or Galaain. This would neatly counterbalance Balain, the knight who strikes the Dolorous Blow which gives rise to the Grail Quest. This might then suggest that the Grail Quest is a highly personalized story of redemption and self-fulfilment in which the sinful Gawain/Balain commits the "original" sin and, having gone through a rebirth, the pure Gawain/Galaad redeems himself. There may just have been a trace of this in the story of *Culhwch and Olwen*, where two sides of Gawain are suggested in the characters of Gwalchmai ap Gwyar and his brother Gwalchafed ap Gwyar. Sir John Rhys, in *Studies in the Arthurian Legend*, believes that Gwalchafed is the original Celtic name for Galahad, but few have supported this.

If, as some believe, Lancelot was a late substitute for Gawain in the story, then we may find the story having some vestige of the Gawain/Galahad partnership, but with Lancelot instead. There is indeed another character in the story with a similar name. This is Galehaut, King of the Far Isles. Galehaut is initially at war with Arthur but becomes such firm friends with Lancelot that he submits to Arthur and even joins the Round Table. Lancelot is distraught when Galehaut dies and not only builds a special tomb for him at his castle of Joyeuse Garde, but requests that when he dies he should be laid next to Galehaut. Galehaut, whose name means "High Prince", was probably the original Galahad alter ego of Gawain in the early (now lost) story, but once the "architect" of the *Lancelot-Grail* had the bit between his teeth he embellished the story way beyond its original plan. And in so doing, of course, created a masterpiece.

2. The real Lancelot

One query remains. If we dust aside for the moment the religious overtones of Lancelot's life and his possible Celtic or Alanic origins, we come back to the fact that not only did Marie de Champagne request the first story about Lancelot, she provided the *matiere et san* ("subject matter and treatment"). She may not have specified Lancelot as such, but she does seem to have wanted a story of heroic adventure and adulterous love, a love that seems to be condoned. This may have been an early strike for feminism, but it may also be something else. It is quite possible that the characters and events were all representative of people either at the Court of Champagne or at some rival court and Marie wanted to expose an adulterous relationship under cover of a story. The individuals at the time would have recognised themselves, but can we identify them today?

I suspect Marie had her mother in mind when thinking of Guenevere. Queen Eleanor, wife of Henry II of England and former wife of Louis VII of France, was one of the most beautiful women in Europe and one of the most influential. Duchess of Aquitaine in her own right, she was mother of one of England's most famous kings, Richard the Lionheart, and one of its most notorious, John. The love affairs of her youth were also the subject of gossip. Louis VII had adored his young wife (they were both only about sixteen when they married) but was jealous of the attention her beauty attracted. Soon after the birth of Marie, Louis banished the troubadour Marcabru from his court for being over familiar. Eleanor had at least two other affairs soon after, firstly with Geoffrey of Anjou and secondly, and most famously, with her uncle, Raymond of Poitiers, the handsome Prince of Antioch. Either of these may be seen as "her Lancelot", although both were older than her and neither really "rescued" her from abduction.

However, there was a famous abduction attempt in 1168, by which time Eleanor was 46 and past childbearing age. Henry had been punishing his rebellious Lusignan vassals, one of whom, Guy de Lusignan, attempted to kidnap Eleanor in order to gain concessions from Henry. Eleanor's bodyguard Earl Patrick ensured her swift escape, but he was stabbed and it was left to his nephew Sir William the Marshal to defeat the abductors single-handedly, though he was eventually captured. Marshal, tall with brown hair, was only twenty-two but had already led an eventful life and was a renowned champion of tournaments. His valour was recognised by the Queen who personally paid his ransom and later showered him with gifts. The later archbishop of Canterbury, Stephen Langton, called him "the best knight who ever lived", an epithet only too obvious in its day.

More recent events also had their echoes in the Arthurian saga. Henry had probably the most argumentative, ungrateful brood of children granted to any English king. They would all eventually rise up against him, prompted by the selfish Henry, known as the "Young King", though he would never actually reign, whom Henry II crowned as his successor in June 1170 and again in

August 1172. The Young King was unsatisfied with his grant of lands and authority and, urged on by his mother Eleanor, and by Louis VII of France, who saw this as an opportunity to defeat his old enemy, he rebelled against his father during the summer of 1173. He was supported in this by William Marshal, who also believed that the Young King had been treated badly by his father. Henry II soon came to realize that Eleanor had played a key part in this and had her imprisoned, first in Normandy and later, once all the rebellion had been quashed, in Old Sarum. There was even an invasion of England by forces from Flanders under the control of Robert, earl of Leicester, though it was a weak affair and soon defeated. If Robert had sought to be Mordred, he failed dismally.

Henry II and Eleanor were ideal models for Arthur and Guenevere. Not only were they great devotees of the Arthurian legends but their lives often mirrored the tales. There was even a great irony, in that Henry almost disowned his legitimate sons whom he came to regard as "bastards", whereas the one son who remained loyal to him and was very supportive during the rebellion was his eldest illegitimate son Geoffrey, then bishop of Lincoln and later archbishop of York. The one who ought to have become Mordred was Henry's greatest friend, whilst the sons he had once adored were all Mordreds in their hearts.

Eleanor's role as Guenevere continued to be followed to the letter. She was still in prison in England when Marie commissioned Chrétien to write his story of Lancelot and Guenevere. She would not be released until after Henry II's death in 1189, and the one sent to effect that release under instruction from Richard I was none other than William Marshal.

There is no evidence that William had an affair with Eleanor – he was too much the doyen of chivalry – though rumours arose, long after her death and completely false, that she had borne him a child. He remained intensely loyal to her for the rest of her life. Curiously, there was an incident in 1181 that further echoed the Lancelot story. The popularity of the Marshal caused the inevitable envy amongst others at court and a cabal formed against him. Rumours circulated that William was having an affair with the Young King's wife, Marguerite of France (daughter of Louis VII). William was distraught over the rumours and demanded of the Young King that he be allowed to fight in single combat anyone who would oppose him and if he lost he would be hanged for his crime. No one took up the challenge and the incident was laid to rest. William would go on to be Regent of England during the infancy of Henry III. He died in 1219 at the age of 73, having taken the habit as a Templar knight in his final days.

3. The Lancelot romances

The following are the Arthurian romances in which Lancelot features as the primary character. His Grail Quest is covered separately in the previous chapter.

LE CHEVALIER DE LA CHARRETE (**The Knight of the Cart**), Chrétien de Troyes (French, *c*1177) 7,134 lines.
The first story to mention Camelot and the first with Lancelot as the hero. At the outset a knight comes to Arthur's court saying that he holds many knights, nobles and ladies captive. He agrees to release them only if a knight escorts the Queen through the woods and can defeat Meleagant. Kay volunteers but is defeated and taken captive, with Guenevere, to Meleagant's castle at Gorre. Gawain sets out in pursuit and meets a knight who has himself done battle with Meleagant and whose horse is now near to death. Gawain does not recognise this knight as Lancelot. He gives Lancelot Kay's horse. Lancelot catches up with Meleagant's men but again his horse is killed. Lancelot meets a dwarf who agrees to take him in his cart to where the queen is held captive. Lancelot hesitates briefly because carts were used to convey criminals and he believes this will tarnish his reputation. Gawain is also offered a ride in the cart but refuses and follows on horseback.

They learn where the Queen is held prisoner. There are two ways in, via an underwater bridge or via a sword bridge. Gawain takes the underwater bridge while Lancelot heads to the sword bridge. He has several encounters on this journey, including a mystical episode in a monastery where he discovers the future graves of various knights and also learns of a magnificent tomb in which is buried one "who will deliver all those trapped in the kingdom from which none escapes." Lancelot is able to lift the slab to this tomb, though it needed the strength of ten. The monk is astonished and asks for Lancelot's name, but Lancelot will not reveal it. At this point Lancelot has a mystical vision of becoming the saviour of mankind, an early hint of the Grail story, but Chrétien does not pursue it, and it needed to wait for the Vulgate version to be explored in detail.

Lancelot has several temptations placed before him to stop him completing his quest but, aided by a young damsel, he makes it to and across the sword bridge. Meleagant challenges Lancelot to a duel which is postponed for a day to allow Lancelot's wounds to heal. The next day they are evenly matched but Lancelot's wounds hamper him. It is only then that someone in the crowd names him and, encouraged by the Queen, Lancelot defeats Meleagant but at the Queen's wish spares his life. Lancelot is surprised to find that the Queen rebuffs him and only later learns that it is because he had hesitated in getting into the cart and that his pride had come before his duty to the Queen. Later she relents and shares a night of passion with Lancelot, though it is Kay who is accused of adultery.

Meleagant is infuriated that Lancelot had spared him and challenges him to fight again a year hence. Before that time Meleagant captures Lancelot and incarcerates him in a tower without doors or windows. Lancelot is unable to fight the duel and Meleagant claims he is a coward. The damsel who had previously helped Lancelot tracks him down and secures his release. He returns to Camelot and fights and kills Meleagant.

The final section, from Lancelot's imprisonment, was completed by Godefroi de Leigny. Chrétien tells us that he was commissioned to write the piece by Marie de Champagne but something happened to stop him. The whole story is clearly an allegory about a knight overcoming temptation and pride in order that he can at last find union with Christ, in this case portrayed by Guenevere as the Virgin Mary. Since Chrétien followed this with the tale of Perceval he may have set Lancelot aside to rework the idea with the Grail.

> The standard translations of Chrétien's works are both called *Arthurian Romances*, translated by D.D.R. Owen (Dent, 1987) and by William W. Kibler (Penguin, 1991).

LANZELET, Ulrich von Zatzikhoven (Swiss, soon after 1194), 9,400 lines.
Apparently based on an Anglo-Norman book given to Ulrich by Hugh de Morville, though its provenance is not known. It differs significantly from the Lancelot tradition drawn upon by Chrétien and others.

The story begins along the lines of the "fair unknown" motif. Lanzelet is abducted when only two years old and is ignorant of his parentage. He is raised in the kingdom of a water-fey until he is fifteen, when she releases him on condition that he seeks revenge against a powerful knight who had wronged her long ago. Lanzelet slaughters his way through several lords, the prize being their lands and their daughters. One of them, Iblis, at some stage becomes his wife, even though Lanzelet continues his conquests. Now that he is of age, Lanzelet receives word from his mother and discovers his identity and that he is related to King Arthur. Word of his activities has reached Arthur and first Walwein (Gawain) and then Arthur go in search of him. At Arthur's court Lanzelet champions Ginover against the evil knight Valerin, but there is no adulterous love. Later, when Valerin abducts Ginover, Lanzelet is involved in her recovery, though it is achieved mostly through the help of the wizard Malduc.

> The only complete translation is *Lanzelet* by Kenneth G.T. Webster (Columbia University Press, 1951) but an abridged version is in *Secret Camelot* (Blandford, 1997) and *The Book of Arthur* (Vega, 2002), both by John Matthews.

LANCELOT DO LAC, anon. (French, soon after 1215)
This is the original version of what was expanded as the prose *Lancelot* and incorporated into what became called the Vulgate Cycle, and is treated below. This version ends with the death of Galahut after the war with Arthur but does not include the adventure with Morgan le Fay or the conception of Lancelot's son Galahad.
→ The Scottish adaptation, **Lancelot of the Laik** (late 1480s) is a hybrid of this and the Prose *Lancelot*. It omits the early adventures and the war between Arthur and Galiot (Galehaut)

and expands a political discourse which is but a few lines in the original into a much longer argument which alludes to the prevailing conditions in Scotland.

A translation of the original version by Corin Corley is *Lancelot of the Lake* by Elspeth Kennedy (Oxford University Press, 1989).

PROSE LANCELOT, anon. (French, soon after 1215)
This is the first of three romances, sometimes called the *Roman de Lancelot*, which together with *Queste del Saint Graal* and *Mort Artu* form what is usually referred to as the *Lancelot-Grail*. Though probably written by separate authors, these three seem to have been planned as a whole, perhaps by one unifying mind, though the scale of collaboration is uncertain. A decade or so later two further romances were added, *Estoire del Saint Graal* and *Merlin*, and together all five were known as the Vulgate Cycle, though at the time it was completed it seems to have been called *L'Estoire de Lancelot*.

At the start we are introduced to Lancelot's father, Ban king of Banwick, in France. Later in the story Banwick is associated with Bourges, though Malory subsequently says it was Bayonne. We also learn that Lancelot's mother is descended from the house of David. Their son is called Galahad, and whilst the author tells us that the name Lancelot will be explained, it is not. Ban was a vassal of Uther Pendragon and had assisted in driving King Claudas out of his lands, which were known as the Waste Lands. However, after Uther's death Claudas seeks revenge, regains his lands and destroys Ban's castle. Ban dies of a broken heart. On hearing of his death his brother Bors also dies, leaving two sons, Lionel and Bors the Younger.

The next day a woman arrives and takes Lancelot. She is Niniane, a fey who learned the magic arts from Merlin and who lives in a magical lake. Bors and Lionel in the meantime are looked after first by Pharien, a former vassal of Bors's father, and later by Claudas. Claudas believes he is all-powerful and considers attacking Arthur but first visits him in disguise. He is impressed with what he sees. Arthur has not been king for long and has only recently married Guinevere. He is still in battle against the rebel kings, in particular King Yon of Little Ireland (Corin Corley has suggested this means the Isle of Man but it may also mean Dál Riata), King Aguissant of Scotland (later described as Arthur's cousin) and the King of Galone (perhaps Galloway). Claudas returns to consider his plans.

In the meantime Lancelot is maturing. There is a lengthy description of his physical beauty including a forward reference to a remark by Guinevere that "if I were God, I should have made Lancelot just as he is." One of Niniane's maidens, Saraide, is sent to collect Lionel and Bors, and arrives in time to find them in conflict with Claudas, during which Claudas's only son is killed. Saraide turns the boys into hounds and the King's hounds into boys, and in the confusion is able to smuggle the boys away to the Lake where they are raised with Lancelot.

When Lancelot reaches eighteen he wishes to be a knight and the Lady of the Lake agrees to take him to King Arthur's court, though not before she tells him what she knows of the virtues of knighthood and chivalry. She also imparts some clues about the Grail, referring to Joseph of Arimathea and his son Galahad, and also to King Pelles of that line and his brother Alain. She decks Lancelot out in white and silver and gives him a magic ring that will break enchantments and help him find her again.

A retinue of over forty leave for Arthur's court, crossing to England to arrive at *Floudehoug*, which might possibly be Fleet, near Weymouth. It takes them four days to travel to a castle called Lawenor, which is 22 leagues from Camelot. This may be Lavernock, near Cardiff in South Wales, which at the time *Lancelot* was composed was known as *Lawernach*. The writer describes Camelot as a town, not simply a castle. When Arthur leaves to go hunting he exits by the Welsh Gate, suggesting that Camelot was close to Wales.

The Lady of the Lake hands Lancelot over to King Arthur who puts him in the care of Yvain to train him in the knightly arts. Ever impatient, Lancelot (whose name is still not revealed) states that he wishes to be knighted the next day. The court finds amusement in this, though Gawain can see the champion in him. Guinevere is puzzled by him, recognising that he is inhibited in her presence. He later asks if he may be her knight and she agrees.

At the knighting ceremony Arthur forgets to give Lancelot his new sword and Lancelot later receives his sword from the Queen, so placing him under an obligation to her.

Lancelot immediately volunteers for a challenge to fight on behalf of the Lady of Nohaut against the King of Northumberland who is after her land. He easily accomplishes this task even though he had been wounded in a confrontation on his way north. He also has to contend with Kay interfering with the combat.

After achieving his first challenge Lancelot goes adventuring and finds himself in a battle to regain the castle called Dolorous Garde. This becomes a siege of superhuman demands. Lancelot encounters a young maiden whose lover has been killed trying to capture Dolorous Garde. The castle is enchanted. It has two outer walls each manned with ten knights. Lancelot can only approach through a gate and fight one knight at a time, but every time that knight grows tired he steps back and another takes over. So the knights remain fresh while Lancelot tires. He learns that he has to complete his conquest before nightfall or he has to start all over again. Unable to complete that day he retires, anxious to fight the next. In one of the most vivid sequences in Arthurian romance, we see Lancelot fighting throughout the day, seeking to defeat each knight rather than let them escape to fight again. A damsel sent by the Lady of the Lake helps replace his shield, lance and helm, but still he fights. After defeating the first ten knights, he fights through to the second wall. The Lord of the Castle, Brandin of the Isles, is so overcome by Lancelot's bravery that he flees the castle. Lancelot, still fighting the next bank of ten knights, is unable to catch him. He defeats four more knights but the rest escape.

Lancelot is now in charge of Dolorous Garde but he learns that he must remain at the castle for forty days in order to rid it of its enchantments. He is also led to a cemetery that contains the graves not only of dead knights but of those yet to die. Here is a tomb with a heavy slab on which is written his identity. He alone manages to lift the slab, learns his name and that he is the son of Ban of Banwick. Only the damsel also sees the inscription, otherwise Lancelot retains the secret.

News of his victory spreads and Arthur and his knights come to Dolorous Garde to see for themselves. They are captured by the escaped knights, however, and there is further fighting until they are freed.

Not surprisingly Lancelot does not remain at Dolorous Garde for the necessary forty days, so the townsfolk lure him back on the pretext that they have captured Guinevere. Once returned, Lancelot determines to lift the curse, not by staying forty days, but by finding the source of the enchantment. This results in another astonishing sequence as Lancelot battles through various magical hurdles beneath the castle until he is able to release the demons. From that day on the castle is renamed Joyeuse Garde.

There has been much interest in where Lancelot's castle is located. The romance provides a location, stating that it is on a high rock alongside the River Humber near the town of Chaneviere. The land along the Humber is renowned for its flatness and there is certainly no rocky prominence. Malory suggested Bamburgh in Northumberland, perhaps because Nennius had called that site Din Garde, whilst others have suggested Alnwick or the castle rock at Edinburgh. However, the association with Brandin, or Brian, of the Isles may mean that it was either Peveril Castle in the Peak District or Knaresborough Castle in Yorkshire. Both of these fit the description and both were in the charge of the real Brian de Lisle during the reign of King John. Peveril Castle had to be wrested from Brian's hands as he refused to give it up.

In the meantime, Arthur has become involved in hostilities with Galehaut, the Lord of Sorelois and King of the Remote Isles. This first manifests itself in chivalrous manner with a tournament which Lancelot, though still wounded from his adventures, determines to attend. He still wishes to keep his identity a secret and though still accoutred in his white armour bears a different shield. Gawain determines to identify him but with little success. Lancelot fights bravely but is seriously wounded by Galehaut's cousin Malaguin, and returns into the care of the Lady of Nohaut. Meanwhile Gawain learns Lancelot's identity from one of the damsels of the Lady of the Lake and spreads the news around Arthur's court. Lancelot, in the meantime, recovers from his wounds and undertakes other adventures until he falls captive to the Lady of Malehaut. She also tries to find his identity but even though she travels to Arthur's court, she does not learn it.

By now Arthur is preparing for his battle against Galehaut. Lancelot begs to attend, and the Lady of Malehaut releases him on condition that he returns after the battle. Lancelot fights valiantly but Gawain is seriously wounded. Galehaut, realising his forces greatly outnumber Arthur's, gallantly withdraws and agrees to fight a year hence. Lancelot returns to his prison at Malehaut. Gawain, once he has recovered, sets out to find Lancelot but neither he nor any of the other knights are successful.

The year passes and time comes for the next battle against Galehaut. Lancelot again begs leave and the Lady agrees. This time Lancelot goes as a Black Knight so as not to be recognised. Once again Gawain is seriously injured but Lancelot fights so valiantly that Galehaut becomes intrigued by his identity. The two becomes friends and Lancelot agrees to fight on Galehaut's side on condition that if Arthur is on the verge of defeat, Galahaut should surrender. And so it happens.

Galehaut becomes firm friends with Lancelot, though still does not learn his identity. He does, however, learn of his adoration for Guinevere and it is Galehaut who arranges the assignation between Lancelot and Guinevere that leads to their love affair. Although Galehaut keeps their meetings secret the Lady of Malehaut guesses at Lancelot's love for the queen. In time, thanks to Guinevere, Galehaut and Malehaut become lovers.

Lancelot, now joined by his cousin Lionel as his squire, accompanies Galehaut back to his kingdom. From a later rather convoluted description, it seems that the kingdom of Sorelois is close to Arthur's kingdom, separated only by a narrow strait of water, suggesting that this may be Anglesey. The Faraway Islands may therefore be the Hebrides. From 1156 to 1164, Somerled ruled the Kingdom of Man and the Isles, which included all of the Hebrides. Thereafter the kingdom of Man included the Outer Hebrides, whilst the Inner Hebrides formed part of the Kingdom of the Isles.

Lancelot is distraught at being his separated from Guinevere and Galehaut shows him a retreat on the Lost Island. Gawain endeavours to track him down. He is joined by Lancelot's half-brother Hector. When Gawain and Lancelot eventually confront each other neither recognises the other and they do battle until

Lionel comes to the rescue. Gawain has been told by the Queen that Lancelot must do whatever Gawain asks of him, so at last Lancelot confirms his identity. They now receive news that Arthur is leading an army into Scotland to confront an invasion of Saxons and Irish, and Arthur begs that they join him.

They arrive to find Arthur besieging Saxon Rock which, it is revealed, was a castle once fortified by Vortigern. The text reveals that Saxon Rock is within twelve leagues of the town of Arestel, which may be a corruption of Arwystli, a district in southern Powys which borders on Vortigern's old province of Gwrtheyrnion. It would also be about twelve leagues from Dinas Emrys. It is at Arestel that Arthur meets the Saxon princess Gamille who lures him into her toils, and Arthur becomes a prisoner. This is an episode akin to Vortigern's love for Renwein.

Arthur's infidelity allows the author to develop Lancelot's affair with Guinevere. Guinevere had previously received a shield from the Lady of the Lake which depicts a knight and a lady in near embrace, but the shield is broken down the middle, separating the lovers. The Lady of the Lake says that once the Queen has consummated her relationship with her true lover the shield will mend, and that is how she finds it after her night with Lancelot.

Soon after, Lancelot is captured, along with Gawain, Hector and Galehaut, and spends several nights in prison during which time he goes crazy. Because of his condition he is released and recuperates with Guinevere. His madness is cured when he puts on the mended shield. Recovered, he sets off on a one-man crusade to free Arthur and his companions. With Lancelot back on the battle-field, Arthur's forces rally and they win the day. Released, and with Lancelot's story now revealed by Gawain, Arthur requests that Lancelot return to Camelot and become one of the Round Table. He agrees, but only because the Queen asks him. Galehaut also agrees to join the Round Table, though is unable to stay at Camelot because he still has lands to rule. However, when Galehaut returns with Lancelot to Sorelois he discovers that his castles are crumbling and fears this is a punishment from God because he dared to challenge Arthur.

There now follows the strange episode of the False Guinevere. A lady appears at court with a letter, accompanied by an elderly knight. The letter purports to be from the real Guinevere who had married Arthur but who on their wedding night had been captured and a False Guinevere, the real Guinevere's hand maiden, substituted for her. The facts are supported by the elderly knight, Bertilay. Before the Queen can deny the charges Gawain stands as her champion but as he refuses to fight an old knight Arthur agrees to put Guinevere on trial. Arthur is captured by Bertilay and drugged so as to love the False Guinevere. He consequently finds the Queen guilty and sentences her to be executed. Arthur's knights find this intolerable, particularly Gawain, and they defect from Arthur. When Lancelot learns of the Queen's predicament he sets out with Galehaut to rescue the Queen, which he does on the day set for her execution. With Arthur still under the influence of the drug, Lancelot and Galehaut take the Queen back to Sorelois for her protection, and there she and Lancelot continue their relationship. Arthur lives with the False Guinevere for over two years and it is not until she and Bertilay fall ill and confess that Arthur realizes his folly. Although reluctant to return to Arthur, Guinevere is eventually reconciled with the king.

The next adventure introduces Morgan le Fay. She has control over the enchanted Valley of No Return. Anyone who ventures into it who has been unfaithful becomes trapped. Gawain was abducted by Karados and held prisoner in the Dolorous Tower. To reach the Tower would-be rescuers have to pass through the valley. Yvain and Gawain's brother fail in their attempt, but Lancelot succeeds, though he disturbs Morgan asleep in her tent. She drugs Lancelot and steals the ring given to him by Guinevere, and sends it to Arthur saying that Lancelot is dying and that he confesses the sin of his love for the Queen. Guinevere is able to explain that her love was only for a valiant hero who had saved her and Arthur accepts this.

Galehaut believes that Lancelot is dying and becomes distraught. Although Morgan releases Lancelot he is too late to save Galehaut who has died of grief. Lancelot arranges for Galehaut to be buried at Joyeuse Garde so that he may also lie beside Galehaut when his time comes.

The next section follows Chrétien's original story, "The Knight of the Cart", about Guinevere's abduction by Meleagant and her rescue by Lancelot. It is told in more detail and, within the context of the whole story, provides greater insight into Lancelot's actions. This includes the episode where Lancelot enters a monastery and finds the tomb of Galahad, the son of Joseph of Arimathea. This name was withheld in Chrétien's earlier version, but here it becomes the link between Joseph (and the Grail, though that has yet to be introduced), Lancelot (whose baptismal name we now learn was Galahad), and Lancelot's future son. In this same episode the monks, amazed at Lancelot's strength in lifting the slab, take Lancelot to a cave where there is a second, more resplendent, tomb surrounded by fire. Lancelot is not allowed to approach the tomb. He will not succeed in the Grail Quest because he has sinned with the Queen. Lancelot also learns that his mother Helen is still alive and living in a nunnery.

The story moves on to the Grail episodes. There is a clear divide between the past set of adventures and the next set, the continuing link being Lancelot's affair with Guinevere. It is likely that the author melded together two or more earlier tales, such as Chrétien's *Lancelot* and *Perceval*, except that Perceval has now been sidelined and Lancelot has taken centre stage. Perceval appears later in the story as the younger brother of another Grail Quester, Aglovale.

After a series of minor adventures Lancelot is again missing from Camelot and the Queen believes he has been killed. Gawain and a party of knights set out to search for him. Most of the knights end up defeated by a giant of a knight called Tericam who throws them into prison. Gawain, however, first encounters Eliezer, son of King Pelles, the Fisher King, who tests Gawain to see if he can repair a broken sword. He can't. Gawain also encounters the fiery tomb, but is beaten back. Gawain finds his way to the Grail Castle, Corbenic, and undergoes further tests. First he is unable to rescue a damsel from a tub of boiling water. Then Gawain witnesses the Grail Procession when dining but is so overcome by the beauty of the Grail Maiden, King Pelles's daughter Elaine, that he fails to ask the right question. He then sleeps in the Adventurous Bed and, though attacked and wounded by a blazing lance and beset with terrible visions, he survives the night. His wound is cured by

Elaine with the Grail. Gawain, however, is forced to leave Corbenic in disgrace.

When Lancelot reaches Corbenic, however, he passes all the tests. He rescues the maiden from the boiling water. He also lifts the stone from another tomb which further confirms the prophecy that whoever lifts the stone will father a great knight. A fiery dragon is released which Lancelot soon kills. At the Grail dinner Lancelot also admires Elaine's beauty but not as lustfully as Gawain, though he still fails to ask the right question. Elaine falls in love with Lancelot and, through a potion provided by Elaine's governess Brisane, she tricks Lancelot into believing that she is Guenevere. The two spend the night together and Galahad is conceived.

Lancelot leaves Corbenic. Further adventures follow in which he kills Tericam and releases the knights, but he falls into a trap laid by Morgan le Fay and is imprisoned for over a year. He passes the time telling the story of his life in pictures on the prison walls. Eventually, through sheer brute strength, he escapes. He learns more about his past, discovers the tomb of his grandfather, also called Lancelot, and learns from a knight called Sarras of the birth of his son Galahad.

The story line finally turns full circle. Claudas is determined to declare war upon Arthur and sends various spies to Arthur's court to learn Arthur's strengths and weaknesses and to undermine the opposition. He incurs the wrath of Guinevere by insulting her. One of his nephews, Brumand, also believes that he can sit on the Perilous Seat at the Round Table which is reserved only for the purest knight in the world. Brumand is destroyed by fire the moment he takes the seat.

The storyline now reverts to Geoffrey of Monmouth's version of Arthur's assault on Gaul and Rome, except that in the Vulgate version it is all set in context. Arthur leads his army in war against Claudas. There are many set battles and the Romans send reinforcements to Claudas under Frollo. There is a long battle between Arthur and the Romans in which Lancelot is supreme. Rather than fight to the bitter end Frollo demands single combat with Arthur. Lancelot begs to fight in his place but Arthur declines and fights and defeats Frollo himself. It is the only episode in the whole of the Vulgate *Lancelot* where Arthur shows his true mettle and seems anything like the true Arthur of old, suggesting that this episode is drawn from an older tradition. The Romans retreat, Claudas flees, and Arthur grants Lancelot the lands he has won, so that he effectively regains his father's and uncle's lands of Benoic and Gaunes. It is now that Lancelot finds his mother just before she dies.

The story effectively ends there, but there is an epilogue that provides a link to the next novel. Guinevere learns of Lancelot's unfaithfulness with Elaine. Although she forgives him on learning of Elaine's trickery, Elaine, who has visited Camelot, once again succeeds in deceiving Lancelot. This time Guinevere discovers the two in bed and she banishes Lancelot from Camelot. He leaves, jumping naked through a window, and spends the next two years roaming mad through Logres, ending up as a court "fool" with King Pelles. Elaine cures his madness with the Grail and Lancelot is restored to Camelot. At the end he is introduced to his son Galahad, who spends his childhood in a nunnery.

This volume is followed in the Vulgate Cycle by *The Quest of the Holy Grail*, which is covered separately on page 429. It is then followed by the next work.

Extracts with interlinking notes are included in *The Lancelot-Grail Reader* edited by Norris J. Lacy (Garland, 2000).

LA MORT LE ROI ARTU (THE DEATH OF ARTHUR),
anon. (French, *c*1230)

After the metaphysical imagery of the Holy Grail, *The Death of Arthur* brings us back down to earth. So much so that you would hardly realise that Arthur and his knights had undergone such a spiritual adventure. Bors returns to Camelot and tells the story of the end of the Grail Quest. Arthur has taken a head count and noted that thirty-two of his knights had died in the Quest, with Gawain having killed eighteen of them. Gawain recognises this as a curse he has to bear, which will ultimately cause his downfall.

Life otherwise returns to normal. Arthur holds a tournament in Winchester to celebrate the end of the Quest. Lancelot says that he will not attend. Gawain's brother Agravain reveals to Arthur that Lancelot is having an affair with Guenevere, sowing doubt in

Arthur's mind that this may be why he does not want to attend the tournament. In fact, Lancelot had intended to go in disguise and when Arthur spots Lancelot in Winchester he is relieved. Gawain supports his friend and argues that Lancelot would never commit adultery. Gawain also discovers that a young Maid of Astolat is in love with Lancelot and it is her colours that Lancelot wears at the tournament. The Maid of Astolat is unnamed in the Vulgate. Malory calls her Elaine, but she is best known as the Lady of Shalott in Tennyson's *Idylls of the King*.

Lancelot is wounded at the tournament by his cousin Bors, and nursed back to health by the Maid of Astolat, who reveals her love for him, though he spurns her. Gawain tells Arthur of the Maid's love for Lancelot, believing that it is returned, and this satisfies Arthur that there can be no truth in Agravain's rumour. Guenevere becomes jealous of the Maid of Astolat and banishes Lancelot from Camelot. It is not until later, when the girl pines away and her body reaches Camelot on a barge floating down the river, that Guenevere realizes that Lancelot had remained faithful to her.

Arthur finds his way to the castle of his sister Morgan le Fay. Years before, when she held Lancelot here, he had painted the story of his life, including his love for Guenevere, on the walls of his cell. Arthur sees this and realizes Guenevere has been unfaithful.

In the meantime, Guenevere finds herself accused of murder. At dinner she would often hand a fruit to Gawain. Avarlan, a knight who hates Gawain, gives Guenevere a poisoned fruit knowing she will pass this to him. However, she gives it to Gaheris de Karaheu, who immediately dies. Gaheris's brother Mador accuses the Queen of murder and challenges her champion to combat, otherwise she must be burned at the stake. Because all of the knights have witnessed Gaheris's death, none of them will stand as her champion. Only Bors, who had admonished the Queen for sending Lancelot away, agrees to fight on her behalf unless a better champion appears. Lancelot does not know of the situation because he has been badly wounded by a hunter in the forest. He only learns of it once he has healed and then promptly returns to Camelot in disguise. He defeats Mador but refuses to kill him as Mador had once been his friend. Mador surrenders and the charges against the Queen are dropped.

Lancelot and Guenevere are reconciled and their love for each other becomes more open. Even Gawain has to accept it but neither he nor his brother Gaheriet will tell Arthur. However, his other brothers Agravain and Mordred have no such qualms. Arthur agrees to Agravain trying to trap Lancelot and Guenevere together. Arthur goes on a hunting trip but leaves Lancelot behind. Lancelot goes to Guenevere's apartment, but locks the door. Agravain tries to break in but cannot. Though unarmed, Lancelot opens the door, kills the first knight he sees, takes his sword and armour and fights his way out of the castle.

When Arthur returns Guenevere is imprisoned and condemned to be burned at the stake without trial. Lancelot rescues her, but in the fray he kills Agravain and accidentally kills Gaheriet. This incurs Gawain's wrath.

Lancelot takes Guenevere to Joyous Garde where he is besieged by Arthur. Lancelot refuses to bear arms against Arthur and will not defend himself when Arthur unhorses him. Hector comes to Lancelot's help. Arthur is unhorsed, but Lancelot refuses to allow the king's death and escorts him from the field.

The war continues for two months until the Pope intervenes, threatening to excommunicate Arthur. The Pope declares that the Queen should first be tried. Arthur still loves Guenevere and agrees to take her back provided Lancelot returns home to Gaul. Gawain, however, incites Arthur to continue the war. Arthur therefore leaves Mordred in charge of his court while he goes to Gaul.

Lancelot retains the upper hand and Arthur has no desire to continue. It is Gawain who insists on fighting and who challenges Lancelot to single combat. Reluctantly Lancelot accepts. It is a battle that lasts all day. Lancelot has the advantage in the morning but Gawain regains his strength at midday and only eventually tires by late afternoon. Gawain receives a violent head wound which brings him to his knees. He will not submit but Lancelot refuses to kill him.

Somewhat surprisingly at this stage, the author inserts the ages of the main characters. Gawain, he reveals, is 76, Lancelot is about 55, whilst Arthur is a remarkable 92.

There is no time to rest, as the Romans invade Gaul. The

fighting is short. Kay is killed, and Gawain's head wound re-opens. Arthur kills Lucius Hiberius and the Romans retreat.

Arthur receives news that Mordred has usurped the throne and attempted to marry Guenevere, having told her that Arthur was mortally wounded. She has escaped, though, and taken refuge in the Tower of London. Arthur returns to Britain, but Gawain is mortally ill. He sends a letter to Lancelot asking for forgiveness and telling him of events in Britain. On arrival in Britain Gawain dies and is buried at Dover.

On hearing of Arthur's arrival Mordred, who had been besieging the Queen at the Tower of London, retreats into the West Country. Guenevere flees to a nunnery. Arthur and Mordred meet in battle on Salisbury Plain in what proves a totally destructive battle. Arthur kills Mordred but Mordred also delivers a fatal blow. Although Arthur, Girflet and Lucan survive the battle, both Arthur and Lucan are severely wounded. Lucan dies when Arthur embraces him too vigorously.

Arthur and Girflet head towards the sea. Arthur commands Girflet to cast Excalibur back into a lake. Girflet disobeys twice. On the third time Girflet obeys and sees a hand rise from the lake, catch the sword, brandish it and withdraw it into the lake. Arthur commands Girflet to leave him. He looks back and sees a boat full of women, including Arthur's sister Morgan, take Arthur away. Girflet wanders in grief for three days till he returns to the Black Chapel to see if Lucan has been properly buried. He sees not only Lucan's tomb but Arthur's, and learns that the ladies had brought Arthur there. Girflet remains at the Black Chapel as a hermit, but dies eighteen days later.

Only now does Lancelot receive the news of Mordred's revolt and of the battle with Arthur. He hurries to Britain with Hector and his cousins. He learns that Guenevere had retired to a nunnery, but has died. Mordred's two sons have seized the kingdom. The elder, Melehan, kills Lancelot's cousin Lionel, and Bors kills Melehan, whilst Lancelot kills the younger son. Constantine becomes king of Logres.

Lancelot retires to a monastery with his cousin Bleoberis and becomes a priest. Bors returns to his kingdom in Gaul. Hector searches for Lancelot and, finding him, remains with him for four years until he dies. Soon after, Lancelot falls ill. Knowing he is about to die, Lancelot commands that he be taken to Joyous Garde and buried next to Galahaut, whom he had so loved. Bors arrives at the castle just in time for the funeral. Bors agrees to take Lancelot's place at the monastery and so he and Bleoberis spend their final years in the church, the last of the Knights of the Round Table.

→ The Middle English narrative poem called the Alliterative *Morte Arthure* (*c*1400; 4,346 lines) tells the story of Arthur's fate from the time he receives the summons from Emperor Lucius until his burial at Glastonbury. It adds a few original passages, such as Gawayn's single combat with the Greek knight Priamus, but otherwise follows the standard story. At about the same time, another poet developed the Vulgate version into a verse romance known as the Stanzaic *Le Morte Arthur* (*c*1400; 3,969 lines). Although shorter, it follows Arthur's decline from the tournament after the Grail Quest to Arthur's burial at Glastonbury. It includes most of the main episodes but excludes Arthur discovering Guenevere's affair via Lancelot's paintings, and the death of Mordred's sons after Arthur's death. In this version Bedwere is with Arthur at the end. This version was Malory's main source for the conclusion of *Morte Darthur*.

A translation by James Cable is *The Death of King Arthur* (Penguin, 1971). Both the Alliterative and Stanzaic poems are available in *King Arthur's Death* by Larry D. Benson (Bobbs-Merrill, 1974) and *King Arthur's Death* by Brian Stone (Penguin, 1988).

18

THE FORGOTTEN ADVENTURERS

The following includes all the remaining Arthurian romances that have not featured in the previous chapters. Most of the main heroes, especially Gawain, do appear but in lesser roles. The stories usually depict new heroes in one-off adventures which may depict or satirise people or events in their countries or origin. I have not included the many translations and adaptations of the main Arthurian stories that appeared throughout Europe at this time.

LAI DU COR (The Lay of the Horn), Robert Biket (French, c1160s) 580 lines.
An amusing short *lai* in which a fairy drinking horn will spill its contents on any drinker who has been cuckolded. This happens to Arthur and Guenevere admits she once gave a ring to another. Arthur is only reassured when the horn spills its drink on every other man save one, Garadue (better known as Caradog Vreichfras), who is awarded the lordship of Cirencester.

> The original text is in *The Anglo-Norman Text of Le Lai du Cor* edited by C.T. Erickson (Oxford: Blackwell, 1973). A prose version is in *Arthur King of Britain* edited by Richard L. Brengle (Appleton, 1964) and *King Arthur in Legend and History* edited by Richard White (Dent, 1997).

LANVAL, Marie de France (French, *c*1170) 646 lines.
Lanval is one of the poorer of Arthur's knights who believes he is

ignored by the king, though Guenevere has a passion for him. One day in the meadows Lanval sees two beautiful maidens who take him to their lady. He falls instantly in love with her and believes her the most beautiful woman in the world. She agrees to honour his love provided he never reveals anything about her. He does not know her name. Back at Carduel, Guenevere approaches Lanval but he rebuffs her saying that he loves another who is more beautiful. Guenevere tells Arthur that Lanval had attempted to seduce her. Lanval is arrested and, because he cannot reveal anything about his Lady, has no defence. Gawain believes him and tries to help. Just before his trial Carduel is visited by a series of damsels each more beautiful than the last, and the last is Lanval's Lady. She tells of Lanval's innocence and then leaves. Lanval goes with her and is never seen again. *Lanval* may have been based on an earlier story because another Breton *lai*, the anonymous *Graelent* (*c*1230s), though non-Arthurian, tells essentially the same story.

The story was rendered into several early English versions, the first of which is believed lost but which influenced in turn the anonymous *Sir Landeval* (*c*1230s) and *Sir Launfal* by Thomas Chestre (*c*1350).

> The text of both Marie de France's *Lanval* and Chestre's poem are in *Sir Launfal* edited by A.J. Bliss (Nelson, 1960). Recent versions include *The Lais of Marie de France* translated by Glyn S. Burgess and Keith Busby (Penguin, 1986) and *The Lais of Marie de France* translated by Robert Hanning and Joan Ferrante (Dutton, 1978). A prose version is in *The Unknown Arthur* (Blandford, 1995) and *The Book of Arthur* (Vega, 2002), both by John Matthews.

EREC ET ENIDE, Chrétien de Troyes (French, late 1160s) 6,958 lines.

Erec proves himself second only to Gawain as the most renowned knight at Arthur's court, but after he marries Enide he settles down to a routine life of marital bliss. His wife believes he may be losing his reputation, so to prove himself Erec takes her on a series of adventures. Despite proving his valour he is decidedly unchivalrous to his wife, not allowing her to talk and rebuking her whenever she does, even when warning him of danger.

The name of the hero is believed to be derived from the Breton chieftain Waroch. He was the son of Macliau who (as I mentioned in Chapter 13) had taken refuge with the equally infamous Conmor. After 577AD Waroch usurped territory across Armorica. Vannes fell to him in 578 and he renamed it Bro Waroch, "the Land of Waroch". His name was recorded by later chroniclers as Guerec and eventually Erec. Waroch is clearly not the character of Erec, though. For that we turn again to the relationship between Henry II and Eleanor. Henry had grown tired of the disorder in Brittany, which was supposed to be under the control of his vassal Conan IV. In July 1166 Henry deposed Conan, betrothed his son Geoffrey, duke of Brittany, to Conan's daughter Constance, and through her took control of the territory. Henry was thus symbolic of Waroch/Erec, and through Erec Chrétien could be satirical of Henry and Eleanor.

→ ***Gereint, Son of Erbin*** (*c*1250s). The Welsh version is similar, except that Gereint misunderstands Enide and believes she has been unfaithful, which is why he takes her on his adventures until she proves herself. This would explain why Gereint is so vile towards her, and suggests that Chrétien drew his story from an earlier common source.

→ ***Erek***, by Hartmann von Aue (German, late 1180s). Hartmann's version follows Chrétien's closely but is more intense. Erek loves his wife with a passion and for a while is more interested in lovemaking than in questing. When he realizes that he is losing the respect of his fellow knights he goes to the other extreme, keeping Enite at a distance while undertaking adventures. It is a while before he realizes her loyalty to him and they have a deeper, more spiritual love.

> The standard translations of *Erec et Enide* are by D.D.R. Owen in *Arthurian Romances* by Chrétien de Troyes (Dent, 1987) and by Carleton W. Carroll in *Arthurian Romances* by Chrétien de Troyes (Penguin, 1991).

CLIGÉS, Chrétien de Troyes (French, *c*1176) 6,784 lines.
The first third recounts the adventures of Cligés' father Alexander, son of the king of Greece and Constantinople, who proves

his courage in Britain, helping Arthur quell a rebellion. He is knighted and marries Gawain's sister Soredamors. Cligés is their only child. When Alexander's father is drowned his younger brother Alis usurps the throne.

Cligés grows to manhood and proves his valour fighting the Saxons. He falls in love with Fenice, daughter of the King of Germany, who is, however, given to Alis in marriage. She arranges for Alis to take a potion which makes him think he is enjoying his conjugal rights whilst Fenice remains a virgin. Cligés, in the meantime, travels to Britain where, in disguise, he defeats Arthur's champions, including Lancelot, though he draws with Gawain. He spends a year at Arthur's court and enjoys many adventures. Returning to Greece he meets up again with Fenice. She takes a potion which makes her feign death, and is thus able to escape from Alis and love Cligés. Alis dies soon after, and Cligés becomes King of Greece and marries Fenice.

Patrick Sims-Williams, in a talk given to the International Arthurian Society, suggested that the name Cligés may be derived from Glywys, the king of Glywysing. The character, though, is more contemporary. The Emperor of Byzantium at this time, who governed Greece and Constantinople, was Manuel Comnenus. The Comneni were a powerful family. Manuel's grandfather Alexius may well be both the Alexander and Alis of this story, as he started his reign a popular emperor but was despised by the end.

→ The late fourteenth century Middle English verse romance *Sir Cleges* has nothing to do with *Cligés*. It is set in the time of Uther Pendragon and concerns a knight who has fallen on hard times and is forgotten but whose virtue is eventually rewarded.

The standard translations of *Cligés* are those by D.D.R. Owen in *Arthurian Romances* (Dent, 1987) and by William W. Kibler in *Arthurian Romances* (Penguin, 1991). Kibler's translation also appears in the new edition of *Arthurian Romances* edited by James J. Wilhelm (Garland, 1994).

YVAIN: THE KNIGHT WITH THE LION, Chrétien de Troyes (French, *c*1177), 6,818 lines.

The story starts in Arthur's court at Carduel. Yvain learns from

Calogrenant of a remarkable spring in the Forest of Broceliande. If you draw water from the spring and pour it on an adjacent marble block it creates a mighty storm. Calogrenant did this and was challenged by Esclados the Red, the Guardian of the Spring. Esclados defeated Calogrenant but set him free. King Arthur vows to set out to fight Esclados for having challenged one of his knights but Yvain gets there first and mortally wounds Esclados. Pursuing the Guardian to his castle, Yvain is trapped but helped by the damsel Lunette, who gives him a magic ring which renders him invisible. Lunette's mistress, Laudine, widow of Esclados, is now fearful for their safety as the Spring needs a new Guardian. Yvain falls in love with her and agrees to marry her and be the new Guardian. Freshly armoured, he faces Arthur and his knights when they arrive at the Spring. Yvain defeats Kay but is recognised. Arthur is happy for Yvain. Gawain is attracted to Lunette and agrees to be her champion.

After several years Yvain grows tired of marital bliss and wishes to return to the Round Table for adventure. Laudine agrees that he may go for a year, but he must then return. However, Yvain so enjoys the adventuring life that he forgets the passage of time and fails to return. A damsel arrives with the message that Laudine has no desire to see him again and takes back Yvain's wedding ring. Yvain is distraught, loses his wits, and runs into the forest like a madman.

Yvain is saved by a countess whose maiden applies a magic ointment (from Morgan le Fay) which cures his madness. In return Yvain saves the countess from her wicked neighbour Count Alier, who has been taking her lands. The countess wishes Yvain would remain as her husband but he sets off on further adventures. He encounters a battle between a dragon and a lion and kills the dragon. The lion becomes Yvain's constant companion. From this moment Yvain and the lion are unconquerable although at one point, when Yvain takes on the giant Harpin, he has the lion confined to a castle because the giant claims the battle is uneven. Yvain is nearly defeated but the lion rescues him. The lion would seem to represent the strength that Yvain gains by drawing upon an inner reserve, probably meant to be the love of Christ, but possibly also the love of the chivalric ideal. Later Yvain again does battle with Gawain, as both are champions for opposing sides in a conflict. Thankfully they recognize each other, and Arthur uses his wisdom to reconcile the conflict. Eventually Yvain and Laudine are reconciled and Yvain lives on happily as the Guardian of the Spring.

→ ***Owain, or The Lady of the Fountain***. The Welsh version is identical, with the names changed, but is much truncated, with the adventures mere episodes rather than stirring tales. The second half, after Owain becomes Guardian of the Spring, is much reduced. He is also allowed to return to Arthur's court for only three months rather than a year.

→ ***Iwein***, by Hartmann von Aue (German, early 1200s). Very similar to Chrétien's but again more intense and passionate. When Iwein believes he has lost his wife, first his madness and then his adventuring are both reckless until he can come to terms with his responsibilities.

→ ***Ywain and Gawain***, anon. (English, 1340s) is the only surviving English version. It concentrates on the basic heroic story with all the courtly romance deleted. The original English text is available in *Yvain and Gawain*, edited by Maldwyn Mills (Dent, 1992).

> The standard translations of Chrétien's works are both called *Arthurian Romances*, translated by D.D.R. Owen (Dent, 1987) and by William W. Kibler (Penguin, 1991).

LAI DU CORT MANTEL (The Lay of the Short Mantle), anon. (French, *c*1200s).

Another tale of a chastity test, except that here a young man arrives with a beautiful cloak or mantle which every lady must try on. However, it will only fit those who have remained faithful to their husbands. Everyone fails the test except for a maiden who had at first not been at the court because she was ill. The lay is sometimes called *Le Mantel Mautaillié*.

> A translation by Marianne E. Kalinke is in the new edition of *Arthurian Romances* edited by James J. Wilhelm (Garland, 1994). An abridged retelling appears as "The Boy and the

Mantle" in *Secret Camelot* (Blandford, 1997) and *The Book of Arthur* (Vega, 2002), both by John Matthews.

LAI DU TYOLET, anon. (French, *c*1200s).
Most authorities believe this *lai* originally told a non-Arthurian story but was reworked to fit the new craze. Whether it borrowed from other Arthurian tales (chiefly the Perceval saga), or whether all were derived from an even earlier tale, is not certain. The *lai* falls into two halves. The first tells of the youth of Tyolet who, like Perceval, is raised in the woods, becomes captivated by knights and leaves his mother to go to Arthur's court. At court a damsel seeks Arthur's aid in obtaining the foot of a white stag. Various knights fail but Tyolet succeeds. However, he is attacked by a lion and left for dead, and another knight claims the prize. Gawain finds Tyolet and the impostor is revealed.

A translation by Jessie L. Weston is in *Guingamore, Lanval, Tyolet, Bisclavaret* (Nutt, 1900; reprinted Llanerch, 1994). An abridged version is in *Secret Camelot* (Blandford, 1997) and *The Book of Arthur* (Vega, 2002), both by John Matthews.

WIGALOIS, Wirnt von Grafenberg (German, early 1200s) 11,700 lines.
Perhaps inspired by Renaud's *Le Bel Inconnu*, this is a story in the "fair unknown" tradition. A strange knight offers Guenevere a magic girdle and states that should she choose not to keep it he will fight all knights who take up his challenge. She returns the girdle and, wearing it, the knight defeats all, including Gawain. He takes Gawain prisoner and returns to his faery realm where Gawain marries the knight's niece Florie. Gawain later returns to Arthur's court but when he tries to find the faery land and Florie he cannot. He is thus unaware that Florie has borne him a son, Wigalois.

Twenty years later Wigalois visits Arthur's court and passes the test of acceptance. Gawain becomes his mentor, neither knowing of their relationship. Wishing to prove himself, Wigalois becomes the champion of a maiden who needs help to free the castle of her mistress Larie from the heathen usurper Roaz.

Wigalois passes through various adversities and challenges, each more perilous than the last, during one of which he learns that Gawain is his father, and eventually defeats Roaz with God's aid. A water-wheel, which blocks Wigalois's access to Roaz's castle, and which is covered in swords and axes, stops when Wigalois prays for God's help. Thus the Christian has overcome the heathen. At the end Wigalois marries Larie in the presence of Gawain.

> A translation by J.W. Thomas is published as *Wigalois, the Knight of Fortune's Wheel* (University of Nebraska Press, 1977).

FERGUS OF GALLOWAY, Guillaume le clerc (*possibly* William Malveisin) (French, early 1200s), 6182 lines.
Though composed in French this poem may have been written in Scotland. D.D.R. Owen suggests it may have been by William Malveisin (d.1238), bishop of St Andrews from 1202, who would have known Alain of Galloway and others possibly associated with the work. Most notably the Lady Galiene may be the same as Galiena, daughter of the earl of Dunbar and Lothian and wife of Philip of Mowbray, Scottish ambassador to England in 1215.

Guillaume borrowed freely from the works of Chrétien. Fergus is a peasant who becomes smitten with the sight of knights and sets off to seek his fortune. He reaches Arthur's court where the sarcastic Kay sets him a quest to acquire the horn and wimple of Nouquetran guarded by the Black Knight. He falls in love with Galiene, the Lady of Lothian, but knows he must first complete his quest. He succeeds, but on his return finds that the Lady Galiene has been abducted and the story follows his search for her against many challenges. He is victorious and marries her. The story displays a light humour and is in all likelihood written about people and places known to Malveisin and the Lords of Lothian and Galloway.

> A translation by D.D.R. Owen is *Fergus of Galloway, Knight of King Arthur* (Dent, 1991).

MERAUGIS DE PORTLESGUEZ, Raoul de Houdenc (French, c1210s) 5,938 lines.
Possibly by the same author as *La Vengeance Raguidel*, and probably the same as the Beauvais knight Radulfus de Hosdenc. This poem of romantic rivalry cleverly weaves together playful adventures and a more serious quasi-mystical quest by Gawain to find the Sword of Strange Hangings (which was a key element in the Grail Quests). The main story line concerns the rivalry between Meraugis and Gorvain for the love of Lidoine and the various exploits Meraugis has to undergo to prove his worth.

> Extracts of a prose translation are included in *King Arthur in Legend and History* edited by Richard White (Dent, 1997).

YDER, anon. (French, 1210s) 6,769 lines.
A verse romance about Yder, an illegitimate squire who sets out to find his father Nuc, and falls in love with Queen Guenloie. He saves King Arthur who has been attacked but when Arthur is less than grateful Yder supports Talac de Rogemont, whose castle Arthur is besieging. Three times Yder defeats Kay, who takes his revenge by trying to poison Yder. He is healed by Guenloie and saves Guenièvre when she is attacked by a bear. He also fights a duel with his father before realizing who he is. He is accepted into the Round Table but Arthur becomes jealous of him because Guenièvre states that had she not married Arthur she would have married Yder. Yder successfully completes a quest for Guenloie and marries her, whilst his mother also marries his father. Yder seems a prototype for Lancelot and some have suggested that Guenloie was a variant for Guenevere.

> A translation is in *Yder* edited by Alison Adams (Brewer, 1983). An extract appears in *King Arthur in Legend and History* edited by Richard White (Dent, 1997).

DANIEL VON DEM BLÜHENDEN TAL (Daniel of the Flowering Valley), Der Stricker (German, *c*1215) 8,482 lines.
The young Daniel comes to Arthur's court and undertakes a series of quests against a supernatural foe. The story is one of adventure rather than courtly intrigue, and Arthur himself takes

part in the exploits, which include the abduction of the Queen. It is clearly influenced not only by the stories of Lancelot and Perceval but also such Greek and Roman stories as the tale of Medusa. What is most original about the story is that Daniel succeeds more by cunning than strength or force. Indeed the story seems to question current ideals of warfare.

→ The story was reworked as **Garel vom blühenden Tal** (Garel of the Flowering Valley) by Der Pleier (Austrian, *c*1240s) but with fewer Arthurian connections.

A translation of *Daniel* is in *Der Stricker: Daniel of the Blossoming Valley* by Michael Resler (Garland, 1990). A translation of *Garel* is in *The Pleier's Arthurian Romances* by J.W. Thomas (Garland, 1992).

JAUFRÉ, anon. (French, c1220s) 10,956 lines.

The only surviving Provençal Arthurian romance, this is a bright, lively, humorous tale of chivalry that verges on the parodic. Dates for its composition have varied from the 1180s to the 1220s, but the obvious familiarity with the work of Chrétien and the dedication to a young king of Aragon tend to favour dates either around 1204/5 or 1225.

The story is simple but compelling. Jaufré, whom most commentators see as a version of Chrétien's Girflet, sets out from Arthur's court to avenge both Arthur and the knight Melian against the brutal Taulat de Rogimon (see Yder). There are various adventures and misadventures and the inevitable love interest before all is brought to a satisfactory conclusion when Jaufré rescues and marries Brunissen.

It was first translated by Alfred Elwes as *Jaufré the Knight and the Fair Brunnisen* (Addey, 1856; reprinted Newcastle, 1979). More recent translations are *Jaufry the Knight and the Fair Brunnisende* by Vernon Ives (Holiday House, 1935) and *Jaufre: An Occitan Arthurian Romance* by Ross G. Arthur (Garland, 1992). An abridged version is "Jaufre" in *Secret Camelot* (Blandford, 1997) and *The Book of Arthur* (Vega, 2002), both by John Matthews.

GLIGLOIS, anon. (French, *c*1220s) 2,942 lines.
A courtly romance which just happens to be set at Carduel. The young Gliglois comes to Arthur's court, determined to be a knight, and becomes Gawain's squire. Both fall in love with the same maiden, Guenevere's handmaid Beauté, but whilst Gawain assumes she will love him because of his reputation, Gliglois works hard to prove his worth, and succeeds.

> Translated as *Gliglois* edited by Charles H. Livingston (Harvard University Press, 1932). An extract is included in *King Arthur in Legend and History* edited by Richard White (Dent, 1997).

DURMART LE GALLOIS, anon. (French, late 1220s/1230s) 15,998 lines.
Durmart is the son of the King of Ireland and Denmark, though his name suggests he is Welsh. A lusty young man, he needs to prove himself after having had an affair with the wife of his father's seneschal. Learning of the beauty of the Queen of Ireland he determines to win her hand. When they do meet he does not recognize her and continues in his quest. He is welcomed by Arthur's court, having rescued Guenevere from a brutish knight, but he refuses to join the Round Table until he has found his love. He finds her in Limerick under siege, but the culprit flees rather than combat Durmart. Rescued, the queen marries Durmart. At one stage the queen is accused of atheism whilst Durmart undertakes a pilgrimage to Rome. He also, surprisingly, sits at the Siege Perilous when he visits Camelot, even though that's against all the rules. The author was evidently modelling Durmart on Perceval, but the end result is unconvincing.

HISTORIA MERIADOCI (The Story of Meriadoc), anon. (Anglo-Norman, late 1270s).
A Latin prose romance, probably by the same author as *De Ortu Waluuanii*. It concerns Meriadoc, heir to the throne of Cambria in the days of Uther Pendragon. Meriadoc's father Caradoc is killed by his brother Griffin, who usurps the throne. Meriadoc and his sister Orwen are raised by the old king's huntsman. He becomes a knight at Arthur's court, and with Arthur's help wins

back his kingdom and brings his uncle to justice. Meriadoc, however, feeling he is not ready to rule, leaves the kingdom in the hands of his sister's husband Urien of Scotland, and returns to serve under King Arthur. He helps in the defeat of the Black Knight of the Black Forest which sets in chain a series of events that becomes Meriadoc's quest to help the Emperor of the Alemanni quell the many warring factions in Europe. Although he succeeds, Meriadoc is tricked by the German emperor and turns to the King of Gaul for his final victory. He is rewarded with many lands which he rules on behalf of the King of Gaul, who has now become the German emperor.

A translation is in *The Story of Meriadoc, King of Cambria* edited by Mildred Leake Day (Garland, 1988). An abridged version is in *The Unknown Arthur* (Blandford, 1995) and *The Book of Arthur* (Vega, 2002), both by John Matthews.

WIGAMUR, anon. (German, *c*1250s), 6,000 lines.
A minor verse romance which survives only in a few incomplete forms. It is derivative of the story of Lanzelet but otherwise has few recognizable Arthurian traits. Wigamur, the son of a king, is abducted in his youth and raised by a water fey. He becomes chivalrous and courteous, and enters the service of Arthur's uncle Yttra. He later accompanies Arthur in support of Queen Ysope, who is under siege by the heathen King Marroch. Wigamur discovers his true identity and marries his true love.

TANDAREIS UND FLORDIBEL, Der Pleier (Austrian, *c*1250s), 18,339 lines.
MELERANZ, Der Pleier (Austrian, *c*1250s), 12,834 lines.
Tandareis is a courtly romance of minor Arthurian association, of interest because it casts Arthur in a dark light. Tandareis is in love with Flordibel, but Arthur declares he will kill anyone who claims her love. The couple elope and Arthur pursues, but Gawain achieves an agreement. Tandareis has to prove himself on various quests abroad. He succeeds admirably but refuses to return to Arthur's court, even though Arthur now wants him back. All, though, eventually ends happily.

Meleranz is of even less Arthurian interest, though may be seen as the stereotypical romance. A young prince wants to become a knight at Arthur's court. On his way he falls in love with the young queen Tydomie. Meleranz continues to Arthur's court and after two years becomes a knight. Wishing to return to claim the hand of Tydomie, he undergoes various adventures and rescues Tydomie from the clutches of King Libers.

A translation of both poems is in *The Pleier's Arthurian Romances* by J.W. Thomas (Garland, 1992).

TOREC, Jacob van Maerlant (Dutch, *c*1262), 3,850 lines.
Almost certainly a translation of an anonymous French poem, *Torrez, le chevalier au cercle d'or*, which no longer survives, though we do not know what changes Maerlant wrought. A precious diadem is stolen from Torec's grandmother and he searches for it. It comes into the hands of Miraude who has vowed to marry the knight who will defeat all the other knights of the Round Table. Gawain conspires to help Torec by cutting the saddle girths of the knights so that Torec prevails.

FLORIANT ET FLORETE, anon. (French, *c*1260s), 8,278 lines.
Another stereotypical romance. Floriant is the posthumous son of the king of Sicily, who has been murdered by his seneschal. Floriant is abducted by Morgan le Fay who educates him in all the arts and sends him on a magic ship to Arthur's court. Hardly has he arrived than he learns that his true mother is being besieged by the seneschal in Sicily so returns, supported by Arthur. Floriant is victorious and marries Florete, daughter of the Emperor of Constantinople. Like Chrétien's Erec, Floriant is accused of idleness and so sets off across Europe to Britain with Florete, encountering many adventures including one where she saves him from a dragon. He settles down again in Sicily and, at the end, follows a white stag to Morgan's castle. The ending is missing.

An original French text is in *Floriant et Florete* by Harry F. Williams (University of Michigan Press, 1947) whilst a

French prose version is in *Le Roman de Floriant et Florete* edited by Claude M.L. Lévy (Éditions de l'Université d'Ottawa, 1983).

CLARIS ET LARIS, anon. (French, begun 1268), 30,370 lines.
Claris and Laris are two friends at the court of Arthur. Laris is abducted by the fey Madoine, and after much adventuring is rescued by Claris, who then marries Lidoine, widow of the King of Gascony. Laris professes his love for Marine, sister of Yvain. Marine's father King Urien is besieged by the king of Denmark, and is helped by the two friends along with Gawain and Yvain. Laris is taken prisoner, however, and it requires a fair amount of questing and adventuring, plus the help of Merlin, before he is found and marries Marine.

LES MERVEILLES DE RIGOMER (The Marvels of Rigomer), Jehan (French, *c*1270s), 17,271 lines.
A curious Arthurian romp written more like a parody. A maiden seeks the help of Arthur's knights to rid her mistress's castle of enchantment. The castle, called Rigomer, is purportedly in Ireland. Lancelot undertakes the task, and has many adventures before he reaches the castle, but contact with a magical lance deprives him of all power and he ends up as a scullion. Gawain and other knights have to rescue Lancelot and they too meet many strange and supernatural foes until at last Gawain triumphs. There is a separate quest where Arthur and Lancelot manage to right the wrongs done to the heiress of Quintefuele. The ending is missing but this does not detract from the overall gusto of the narrative.

A translation is *The Marvels of Rigomer* by Thomas E. Vesce (Garland, 1988).

ESCANOR, Girart d'Amiens (French, late 1270s), nearly 26,000 lines.
A romance dedicated to Eleanor of Castile and her husband Edward I, this is a stereotypical miscellany drawing upon Arthurian motifs to create two new stories. In the first, Kay falls in love with Andrivete of Northumberland but does not

declare his feelings, so has to rescue her when, after her father's death, she nearly enters into an enforced lowly marriage. The second has Gawain accused of murder and disinclined to challenge his accuser, Escanor le Beau. It is left to Galantivet to champion Gawain's honour. Escanor's uncle pursues Gawain but instead captures Galantivet's brother Gifflet, and only then is Gawain galvanised into action to save the day.

An extract appears in *King Arthur in Legend and History* edited by Richard White (Dent, 1997).

DIE RIDDERE METTER MOUWEN (The Knight with the Sleeve), anon. (Dutch, late 1290s), 4,020 lines.
A routine late verse romance, probably based on an earlier lost *lai* and only incidentally Arthurian. Miraudijs is a foundling raised in a monastery who comes to Arthur's court and is knighted. The love of his life is Clarette whose white sleeve he pennants from his lance, hence his nickname. He goes through the usual adventures, eventually discovering his parents, who wed, and marries Clarette.

MORIAEN, anon. (Dutch, early 1300s).
A Dutch romance which may have been based on a French original, and may have variant versions, because the surviving version incorporates some of the Dutch *Walewein*. It is an offshoot of the Perceval story and concerns Moriaen, a Moorish knight who is seeking his father, who in this version turns out to be Perceval's brother Agloval, but who in the original was probably Perceval himself. Walewein and Lancelot are also seeking Perceval for different reasons, and the three knights separate in order to complete their quest. Curiously it is Walewein's brother Gariet who eventually helps Moriaen find his father.

A translation by Jessie L. Weston was *Morien* (Nutt, 1901) reprinted as *The Romance of Morien* (Llanerch Press, 1996). It is also on the Celtic Twilight website <camelot.celtic-twilight.com>

ARTHUR AND GORLAGON, anon. (Latin, early 1300s).
Another tale which, like *Walewein*, is a blending of traditional folk tales with the Arthurian legend. Guenevere admonishes Arthur for kissing her in public and tells him he has no understanding of the nature of women. Confused, Arthur sets off secretly with Kay and Gawain to find an answer to the feminine psyche and is directed to the castle of Gorlagon, who tells Arthur the story of a lord who is turned into a werewolf by his unfaithful wife and who strives to retain his humanity despite his animal traits.

This was first translated by F.A. Milne in *Folk-Lore* vol. 15 (1904) and is reprinted in the anthologies *The Magic Valley Travellers* edited by Peter Haining (Gollancz, 1974), *Phantasmagoria* edited by Jane Mobley (Anchor Press, 1977), and *The Unknown Arthur* (Blandford, 1995) and *The Book of Arthur* (Vega, 2002), both by John Matthews.

MELIADOR, Jehan Froissart (French, completed 1388) 30,771 lines survive.
A late French verse romance written by Jehan Froissart at the request of Wenceslas, Duke of Luxembourg. Early in Arthur's reign Hermondine, daughter of the King of Scotland, declares that she will marry the knight who shows the greatest valour over the next five years. Various knights vie for her hand and there are frequent quests and tournaments but of course Meliador, son of the Duke of Cornwall, prevails.

GISMIRANTE, Antonio Pucci (Italian, 1380s)
Gismirante is the son of a former Round Table knight whose adventures help revive an otherwise moribund Arthurian court. He vows to find the most beautiful woman in the world, starting with a strand of her hair given him by a fairy. He undergoes many perilous adventures to find her and rescue her from an enchanted castle where she is held captive with other ladies by a giant. He of course wins her hand and they are married at Arthur's court.

LE CHEVALIER DU PAPEGAU (The Knight of the Parrot), anon. (French, 1390s)
A late French prose romance unusual in that for once Arthur is the hero and not one of his knights. Even stranger, Arthur is accompanied by a parrot in a beautiful gilded cage that both keeps him company and urges him on. Early in his reign, Arthur responds to a damsel's plea to help her mistress who is being oppressed by a knight. Arthur achieves his quest and meets a fascinating array of strange adversaries including a sea creature in the shape of a knight on horseback and a giant who is the son of a dwarf.

> A translation is *The Knight of the Parrot* by Thomas E. Vesce (Garland, 1986). A substantial extract is in *King Arthur in Legend and History* edited by Richard White (Dent, 1997). It is retold in *The Unknown Arthur* (Blandford, 1997) and *The Book of Arthur* (Vega, 2002), both by John Matthews.

THE AVOWING OF KING ARTHUR, anon. (English, *c*1400), 1,148 lines.
Like *The Carle of Carlyle* and *The Awntyrs off Arthure*, this story starts during a hunt in Inglewood Forest in Cumbria. It also features Arthur, Gawain, Kay and Baldwin. All four declare different vows. Arthur's is to slay a giant boar, Gawain's to stand guard all night at Tarn Wadling, Kay's to keep watch through the forest. Baldwin has three vows, unconnected with the hunt: not to be jealous of his wife, not to refuse food to anyone, and not to fear death. Arthur puts him to the test and he passes all three. Baldwin then recounts the past experiences that caused him to take these vows and these show Baldwin as a matter-of-fact, worldly-wise individual who has experienced life's vicissitudes.

> A translation by Roger Dahood is *The Avowing of King Arthur* (Garland, 1984). It is retold in *The Knightly Tales of Sir Gawain* by Louis B. Hall (Nelson Hall, 1976), *Sir Gawain: Eleven Romances and Tales* edited by Thomas Hahn (Kalamazoo, 1995) and in *The Unknown Arthur* (Blandford, 1997) and *The Book of Arthur* (Vega, 2002), both by John Matthews.

EACHTRA AN MHADRA MHAOIL (The Adventure of the Crop-Eared Dog), anon. (Irish, pre-1450)
One of several little-known Irish Arthurian stories which were circulating in the early fifteenth century but may have originated a century or more earlier. Though this has some elements in common with the Cumbrian Gawain stories, it otherwise gives full vent to the Celtic imagination. At the end of a day's unsuccessful hunting Arthur and his knights are challenged by a bejewelled knight with a lantern. None can defeat him, although Bhalbhuaidh (Gawain, though some translate it as Galahad) holds his own. The Knight of the Lantern disappears in a Druid mist but Gawain is determined to follow him and does so with the help of an earless dog who is really the King of India transformed. Their adventures take them right across the world, encountering wonder after wonder, until the Knight of the Lantern is caught and the curse lifted from the King of India.

The author provides some impressive statistics about Arthur's knights, referring to the twelve knights of the Round Table, twelve knights of the Council, twelve knights of activity, two-hundred-and-two score knights of the Round Table and seven thousand knights of the royal household: 11,076 knights in total. Arthur's court is called the Red Hall.

> This is translated in *Two Irish Arthurian Romances* by R. A. Stewart Macalister (Irish Texts Society, 1908, reprinted, 1998 with new Introduction). A new version is in *Secret Camelot* (Blandford, 1997) and *The Book of Arthur* (Vega, 2002), both by John Matthews.

CEILIDHE IOSGAIDE LEITHE (The Visit of the Grey-Hammed Lady) and **EACHTRA AN AMADAIN MOR** (The Story of the Great Fool), both anon. (Irish, pre-1450)
In the first a knight pursues a doe for three days but just as he is about to kill it the doe reveals herself as a beautiful woman. At Arthur's court she tells the other ladies that she has a tuft of grey hair behind her knee and when challenged by the court to show it she demands that all the ladies be examined. When they raise their skirts all the ladies except the visitor are punished for their immodesty by finding tufts of grey hair, and the knights have to

undergo various Otherworld adventures as a penance for their scepticism. The second is a retelling of the Perceval story blended with *Gawain and the Green Knight* but without the Grail theme.

The first is available in *The Book of Arthur* (Vega, 2002) by John Matthews. The second is in *The Arthurian Yearbook II*, edited by Keith Busby (Garland, 1992).

EACHTRA MHACAOIMH AN IOLAIR (The Adventures of the Boy Carried Off by an Eagle), Bríán Ó Corcráin (Irish, *c*1460s)

Although often associated with "The Adventure of the Crop-Eared Dog", this story has an identifiable author who claims, in his preface, to have been inspired by an earlier French story. A small baby is stolen by an eagle and dropped at Arthur's feet. He is raised at Arthur's court and undertakes many adventures to find his true heritage.

In *Two Irish Arthurian Romances* by R. A. Stewart Macalister (Irish Texts Society, 1908, reprinted, 1998).

19

MALORY – CAMELOT IN A PRISON CELL

If there's only one Arthurian romance that we know, it is the *Morte Darthur* of Thomas Malory. Why should that be? And why did Malory write it, since by his day the heyday of the Arthurian romance was over and nothing of much significance, besides *Gawain and the Green Knight*, had appeared for over two hundred years? In this chapter I want to see what Malory did and why, and to do that we need to find out who Malory was.

1. Malory

For centuries there has been uncertainty as to who Thomas Malory was. That's because there were at least nine people of that name alive at the time Malory claimed to have finished *Morte Darthur*, and although most of them can be ruled out for one reason or another there are two or three that might just have been the real Malory. But thanks to the extensive and quite remarkable detective work of P.J.C. Field, presented in *The Life and Times of Sir Thomas Malory*, there is now no argument that the author of the best known of all Arthurian works was Sir Thomas Malory of Newbold Revel, a manor in Warwickshire.

Field has deduced that Malory was born in about 1416, give or take a year. His father John Malory had been a sheriff of Warwickshire, a Member of Parliament and a Justice of the Peace, so Malory was born into a family of repute. Thomas Malory succeeded his father as a landowner, but clearly had further plans. By 1441 he had acquired a knighthood, and in 1445 became a Member of Parliament for Warwickshire.

In 1443 Malory seems to have had an altercation with a certain Thomas Smythe of Northampton. Charges brought against Malory were dropped, but in light of later developments we can already see that Malory was not a man to be trifled with. We may even see here the first indications of a bully or, perhaps, of an ambitious man unlikely to brook opposition. Whatever the nature of this assault, it was as nothing compared to what happened during a remarkable spree of violence in 1450–51.

Malory was apparently involved in an attempt to murder Humphrey Stafford, Duke of Buckingham, on 4 January 1450. It was over a year before Malory was arrested, and in that time he was accused of raping the same woman on two separate occasions, of extorting money by threat, of stealing cattle and of raiding the Duke of Buckingham's lodge, killing his deer and causing considerable damage. Even after he was arrested, he escaped and twice after that raided nearby Combe Abbey, stealing money. Most of these activities were carried out with a gang of accomplices, up to at least a hundred on the Abbey raid. None of these seems like the activities of a politically astute individual, but we have no idea as to either Malory's motives or the contextual circumstances of the crimes. We do not even know for sure whether he committed them all, or whether some may have been malicious charges. It nevertheless suggests that Malory was good at making enemies.

Malory was eventually arrested and cast into prison in London in January 1452, where he remained for the best part of eight years, though he was never brought to trial. He was bailed several times, and on one of those occasions went horse-stealing in East Anglia. He was also charged with various debts. With the passing years, a storm was gathering in England – the rivalry between the Lancastrians and the Yorkists. Henry VI, who had been a brilliant youth and of whom so much had been expected, had sunk into mental decline. In March 1454 Richard of York was made Protector of the Realm, a role he did not want to relinquish when the king recovered his wits the following February. Richard was dismissed and his arch-enemy, the Duke of Somerset, whom Richard had imprisoned, was released. Conflict broke out in May

1455 with the first Battle of St Albans, in which Somerset was killed. There was a period of reconciliation, and when Henry's mental illness returned that November, Richard of York was again protector.

However, Margaret of Anjou, Henry VI's queen and a formidable character in her own right, despised York and promoted her own favourite, the new Duke of Somerset, Henry Beaufort. Hostilities broke out at the Battle of Blore Heath in Shropshire, in September 1459, starting what became known as the Wars of the Roses. Although the fighting was instigated by the Lancastrians under Margaret of Anjou, the victors at Blore were the Yorkists, but the roles were reversed three weeks later at Ludford Bridge near Ludlow when, confronted by a Lancastrian force led by the king himself, many Yorkists defected. Richard, Duke of York, beat a hasty retreat to Ireland, whilst his second in command, Richard Neville, Earl of Salisbury, slipped away to Calais.

There was a resurgence the following June when the Yorkists, led by the Earl of Salisbury and his son the Earl of Warwick (both called Richard Neville, the latter best known as "the Kingmaker"), along with Edward, Earl of March (son of Richard of York, and the future Edward IV), met the Lancastrians at Northampton on 10 July 1460, in what proved to be a significant Yorkist victory. The king acceded to Richard of York's demands and Richard was made heir to the throne. That could have meant an end to it all had not Margaret of Anjou been so determined. She raised a major army in the north with the support of the new Duke of Somerset, the Duke of Northumberland and Lord Clifford, and overwhelmed the Yorkist army at Wakefield on 30 December 1460. At that battle Richard of York and the Earl of Salisbury were killed.

It was in the midst of this upheaval that Malory was released and pardoned. During the false calm of the autumn of 1460 he may have felt there was a chance to resume his old life, but with the battle of Wakefield everything changed. Driven by her success, Margaret of Anjou marched towards London and was met by the Yorkist forces under the Earl of Warwick at St. Albans on 17 February 1461. Outnumbered once again, the Yorkists were forced to retreat and Henry VI was reunited with his wife.

We do not know if Malory was present at that battle. One

would expect him to be on the Yorkist side, as it was the Yorkists who had pardoned him, and the Earl of Warwick was technically his liege lord. However, despite fighting against one's king being against all codes of chivalry and loyalty, the nature of the fighting in the Wars of the Roses caused many to consider that chivalry died in those days.

Malory almost certainly fought at the next battle, the bloodiest of the war – in fact, the bloodiest ever fought on British soil: Towton. The Lancastrians had retreated to their strongholds in the north rather than regain their grip on London. Edward, Earl of March, declared himself king on 4 March 1461, raised a new army and marched in pursuit. There were several conflicts en route but the main battle was fought just south of Tadcaster in Yorkshire on 29 March, in a snowstorm. It might have been a victory for the Lancastrians had not the forces of the Duke of Norfolk arrived in support of York and driven the Lancastrians back. It has been estimated that some 28,000 people, over half the combatants, died that day, most in that final retreat. Malory may have recalled that battle when, in describing Camlann, he wrote:

> And thus they fought all the long day and never stinted till the noble knights were laid to the cold earth; and ever they fought still till it was near night and by that time there was an hundred thousand laid dead upon the down.

Towton was the decisive victory, although there would be plenty of minor battles and skirmishes. It is known that Malory was in the army that headed north in October 1462 to capture the Lancastrian castles of Alnwick, Bamburgh and Dunstanburgh. When Malory came to write the final chapters in *Morte Darthur*, and lay Lancelot to rest, he said that, "some say Joyous Garde was Alnwick and others Bamburgh." These imposing castles clearly made a lasting impression on Malory. It was also on this campaign that he met Anthony Wydville (Woodville), later Earl Rivers.

Wydville, then only in his early twenties, was the brother of Edward IV's future queen, Elizabeth. He was on a rapid ascent to power, having been made Lord Scales that year, and succeeded his father as Earl Rivers in 1469. He was fascinated with the Arthurian world and acquired most of the major Arthurian romances for his library. He was a renowned champion at tournaments and was initiated into the Order of the Garter in 1466. He may well have imagined himself as a Lancelot. So far as we can tell he and Malory became close companions. It was probably through Wydville that Malory acquired his Arthurian interest and he may have had access to Wydville's library before entering prison for the final time. We know that Wydville later had a manuscript of Malory's *Morte Darthur* and that he was the major patron of Caxton, so it was quite probable that Wydville provided Caxton with a copy years later before coming to his own sticky end when he fell foul of Richard III.

We may see Wydville as Malory's direct inspiration but the 1460s became a decade of Arthurianism, possibly encouraged by the soldier-turned-historian John Hardyng. His verse-chronicle of Britain, first issued in 1457 for Henry VI, made an analogy between the Waste Land and Britain under a series of weak kings, a point he emphasised in the revised edition completed for Edward IV in 1464. Henry VI had been a devoutly religious man and his mental affliction was seen by some as a parallel to the maimed Fisher King. Edward, Warwick and others had no problems in seeing themselves as Grail Knights seeking to heal the Waste Land. Indeed, it worked in Edward's favour to be regarded as the new Arthur. Clerks were put to work to stimulate that view. John Hughes, in *Arthurian Myths and Alchemy*, draws attention to two Latin calendars compiled around 1461 and 1465, which look back over British history in the form of a series of prophecies. One of these, "A Prophecy of Merlin Concerning Henry VI", seems to have been deliberately contrived to show that Edward's rise to kingship was foreordained.

Edward IV encouraged Arthurian tournaments and spectacles. Much was made of the Round Table at Winchester as the hub of the Arthurian court, from which Edward and his knights set out to achieve their glorious deeds. Even before Edward had declared himself king, and some years before his marriage to Elizabeth Wydville, he had an illegitimate son whom he called Arthur Plantagenet. This Arthur, who became Viscount Lisle, outlived them all, surviving the next two reigns and even outliving Henry VII's first-born son Arthur, who died in 1502. Arthur Plantagenet died aged eighty in 1542.

With Edward turning his court into a new Camelot it was perhaps inevitable that someone would look again at the Arthurian romances, but I doubt anyone would have expected it to be Malory. Wydville was himself highly literate and eminently capable of the task, though he was perhaps too busy with state affairs. There was the chronicler William Worcester, or the Latin scholar Benedict Burgh, perhaps even Caxton himself.

Yet the circumstances under which Malory wrote the *Morte Darthur* were unusual. Sometime around 1468 he must have relapsed into his old ways because he was once again in prison, only it seems this time he had changed sides and become a Lancastrian sympathiser. Field conjectures that Malory had become involved in the Cornelius Plot, involving smuggling letters to Lancastrian agitators. It cannot have been so difficult a confinement since he was clearly kept provided with paper and ink and the source material he was adapting. In all probability his patron was Wydville, but Malory is silent on that score. Malory completed the work while still in prison, having been overlooked in two pardons. He finished *Morte Darthur,* he tells us, in the ninth year of Edward's reign, which places it between March 1469 and March 1470. Field estimates the work must have taken him two years, and although we do not know when he was imprisoned, it cannot have been much before June 1468 if he was genuinely involved in the Cornelius Plot. However, it has since been established that he was in Newgate Prison in Easter 1468, and may have been for some months earlier. In all probability, however, he may not have completed the work until the early part of 1470. He was eventually released in October 1470, when the Lancastrians surged back to power following a reversal of allegiance by Warwick. Alas, Malory did not live long to enjoy his freedom as he died on 14 March 1471, and was buried at the church of Greyfriars in Newgate.

If Malory undertook the work as a commission from Wydville, then we would need to consider Wydville's motives rather than Malory's, and considering the Arthurian splendour of Edward's court, it was more a matter of when rather than why. Malory, no doubt wrapped up in the same enthusiasm, clearly enjoyed the work – no one could complete something on that scale and with such passion without becoming totally immersed in it. Yet if

Malory had reverted to the Lancastrian cause, could he have had a motive different from Wydville's? Might he have seen Henry VI as Arthur and Edward IV as Mordred? Why else would he have written rather cynically in the last book of *Mort Darthur*:

> Alas, this is a great default of us Englishmen, for there may no thing please us no term. And so fared the people at that time, they were better pleased with Sir Mordred than they were with King Arthur; and much people drew unto Sir Mordred and said they would abide with him for better and for worse.

2. Caxton

William Caxton was born in Kent, probably in Tenterden, in around 1422. He was apprenticed to the London mercer Robert Large, who served as Lord Mayor in 1439–40, so early in his life Caxton was making influential contacts. He went to Bruges in Flanders in 1441, and served as governor of the association for English merchants in the Low Countries from 1462 to 1471. One of those significant small events that change history happened in October 1468 when, as head of a trade mission, Caxton visited Charles, Duke of Burgundy, who only three months earlier had married Margaret, sister of Edward IV. Also on that mission he would have met Anthony Wydville. Just over two years later Caxton became attached to the household of the Duke of Burgundy as a commercial advisor.

In 1469 Caxton had attempted to translate into English the popular French book, *Recuyell of the Histories of Troie* by Raoul Lefevre, which recounted many of the legends of ancient Greece. Caxton's French was poor, but, encouraged by Margaret of Burgundy, he persevered and finished it in 1471, presenting the duchess with the first copy. The task of producing further copies to meet the demand was onerous and, recalling a printing press he had seen in Cologne, Caxton acquired one and experimented. In 1475 he published his translation as the first book printed in English. The following year, under the patronage of Edward IV, Caxton returned to England and set up a printing office within Westminster Abbey. The first book he printed on

English soil was the second part of Lefevre's *Histories of Troie*, which he entitled *Jason*. Soon after, he published Wydville's own *Dicts and Sayings of the Philosophers*.

Caxton would never have met Malory, but the common link was Wydville. We don't know when Caxton received Wydville's copy of *Morte Darthur*, but it must have been before Edward IV died in April 1483, because Caxton tells us it was Edward who encouraged him to print it. Wydville doubtless lent him his own copy shortly before Edward's death, but Wydville's fate was also soon sealed. After Edward's death, he incurred the suspicions of Edward's brother, the future Richard III, who had Wydville executed in June 1483. It is possible that after Wydville's death Caxton acquired another variant copy of Malory's work.

For centuries the only known version of Malory's *Morte Darthur* was that published by Caxton, but in 1934 another version was found at Winchester College. It was deduced that neither of these versions was Malory's original, but had been slightly adapted by copyists in the decade since his death. The Winchester manuscript is, however, believed to be closer to Malory's original than Caxton's, as the printer took some liberties in rearranging some of the text and in removing some of Malory's references to himself. The Winchester version was eventually published by the Clarendon Press in 1967 as *The Works of Sir Thomas Malory*, edited by Eugène Vinaver. This showed that Malory had written the work as a series of self-contained books, rather than as the unified whole presented by Caxton.

By the time Caxton was readying the book to print, England was once again in upheaval. Edward IV had died somewhat mysteriously (he was still only 40) on 9 April 1483 and within ten weeks his brother Richard had assumed the throne as Richard III, after deposing Edward's young son Edward V, one of the two doomed Princes in the Tower. Richard's reign lasted just two years before he was killed at the Battle of Bosworth on 22 August 1485.

It was during those same two years that Caxton worked on adapting and printing the *Morte Darthur*. He completed it on 31 July 1485. On that very same day Henry Tudor set sail from Harfleur to claim the English throne, landing at Milford Haven a few days later. Richard III would have been too preoccupied to see a copy of *Morte Darthur* and, even if he had, may not have noticed a subtle change that Caxton made in Book 5, in which Arthur sails to do battle with the Emperor Lucius of Rome. While on his ship Arthur has a dream of a battle between a dragon and a bear, in which Arthur – the dragon – is shown to be victorious. Caxton changed "bear" to "boar". The white boar was Richard III's heraldic device, whilst Henry Tudor was represented by the Welsh dragon. Here Caxton, once a staunch Yorkist, betrayed his changed allegiance to the Tudors. Once again, the Arthurian stories meant something new to each generation. Doubtless as Caxton brought the book to press he saw Richard III as Mordred, who had stolen the kingdom from Edward/Arthur and imprisoned the queen. Richard, on the other hand, would have seen himself as the new Arthur, who had saved the kingdom from the final depraved years of his brother and was now conducting a crusade to improve the country's morals. This was probably why Caxton's preface includes a lengthy paragraph exhorting everyone to "Do after the good and leave the evil." Henry Tudor, in turn, perhaps saw himself as Uther Pendragon, ridding the kingdom of the enemy and establishing a new order. Just thirteen months after Bosworth, Henry's wife Elizabeth (daughter of Edward IV and Elizabeth Wydville) produced an heir to the throne, Arthur, Prince of Wales, the new hope for England.

3. Morte Darthur

The title *Le Morte Darthur*, lacking any punctuation as is usual for that period, was assigned to the work by Caxton. Malory's title was *The Whole Book of King Arthur and of His Noble Knights of the Round Table*. Although less accurate, Caxton's title is more memorable, but apparently he selected it by mistake, thinking that the title Malory gave to his final book was the title for the whole.

What Malory achieved, and what makes his work more memorable than most of its predecessors, is the unravelling of the intricate, interlacing work of the earlier romances, in which several stories run parallel to each other and the reader is taken in and out of them, reworking each as a separate continuous narrative. As a result, there is a greater concentration on the individual episodes, which helps to develop the characters. To produce this, Malory had to do a fair amount of rewriting, and in the process was able to bring his own thoughts and perspective to the whole cycle. Although he frequently deleted elements of the original, he added little, preferring more subtle changes that would make the story resonate with the period of Edward IV. However, the result is not just a collection of stories because, as Malory warmed to his theme, he constructed the sequence so that characters develop from book to book.

I do not intend to go through *Morte Darthur* in any detail. Not only is it readily available in several editions, but I have already discussed the story-lines in the preceding chapters. I would, however, like to highlight Malory's sources and such changes as he made to establish the Arthurian story as we now know it, and this is set out in the following chart. I've used for this the version from the Winchester Manuscript, as published in the edition called *Complete Works* (OUP, 1971), as this shows the original sequence of books.

Table 19.1. The sources for Malory's Morte Darthur

Book	*Source*	*Comments*
1. The Tale of King Arthur	The Post-Vulgate *Suite du Merlin.*	Caxton's Books I-IV. Malory dropped the material about Merlin's origins and fate and starts at the point where Uther and Ygraine meet, concentrating on Arthur's birth, the Sword in the Stone, the origins of the Round Table, the War with the Five Kings, the Questing Beast and adventures of Gawaine and Ywain.
2. The Tale of King Arthur and the Emperor Lucius	A condensation and major rewrite of the Alliterative *Morte Arthure* itself derived ultimately from Geoffrey of Monmouth's *History*	This was Malory's first book and is Caxton's Book V. Malory cut the original work by half and dropped the doom-laden ending so that it comes early in Arthur's reign rather as the climax in Geoffrey's work. It also builds up the role of Launcelot.
3. A Noble Tale of Sir Launcelot du Lake	Three episodes from the Vulgate Prose *Lancelot*	Caxton's Book VI. A much-reduced section selected to show Launcelot's prowess and chivalry. At this stage there is no hint of the adultery with Guenevere.

4. The Tale of Sir Gareth of Orkney	Malory's immediate source is unknown and was probably a now lost English poem based on the Fair Unknown motif. It owes much to Chrétien's story of *Yvain.*	Caxton's Book VII. Gareth is Gawain's brother but has yet to acquire knighthood and serves, incognito, in the kitchens where he is mocked by Sir Kay and known as Beaumains ("Fair Hands"). He begs a boon of Arthur and undertakes a quest on behalf of the Lady Linet to fight the Red Knight and wins his knighthood.
5. The Book of Sir Tristram de Lyones	The Prose *Tristan.*	Caxton's Books VIII-XII. Really a separate story out of sequence with the rest of the book, though he reworks the ending to lead into the Grail story
6. The Tale of the Sankgreal	The Vulgate *Queste del Saint Graal*	Caxton's Books XIII-XVII. Malory includes the origins of Galahad from the Prose *Lancelot* and then follows the original Grail quest closely.
7. The Book of Sir Launcelot and Queen Guinevere	Partly the Vulgate *Queste del Saint Graal* and partly the Vulgate *Mort Artu*	Caxton's Books XVIII-XIX. A mixture of stories that neatly develops the relationship between Launcelot and Guinevere starting with the episode of the "Poisoned Apple" from *Mort Artu,* the death of Elaine in "The Fair Maid of Astolat", and a fairly basic version of "The Knight of the Cart". Malory included a new story, "The Healing of Sir Urry", about a wounded knight who is cursed and can only be cured by the best knight in the world. The source for this story is unknown.
8. The Most Piteous Tale of the Morte Arthur	Partly the Vulgate *Mort Artu* and the English Stanzaic *Morte Arthur*	Caxton's Books XX-XXI. Follows the sources from the discovery of Guinevere's adultery through to the final battle and Arthur's end.

As this analysis shows, the only story that Malory created was "The Healing of Sir Urry", a self-contained episode of a Hungarian knight who, after killing his opponent, is sorely wounded in a joust. The opponent's mother, a sorceress, curses Urry that he shall wander the world, never to be healed other than by the best knight in the world. Urry is carried everywhere in a litter by his mother and sister for seven years, until at last they reach

Arthur's court. All the knights try to cure Urry and fail, but when Lancelot returns from his adventures he succeeds. In this episode, coming after the Grail Quest when Lancelot has failed as the purest knight, Malory has restored Lancelot to a state of grace. Clearly Lancelot was too important to him to have him become a lesser knight. Perhaps Malory saw himself as Urry, restored to favour years before by Sir Anthony Wydville (Lancelot) after his seven years in prison.

Although Arthur's world looked as if it was collapsing beyond Malory's prison walls, Malory could at least show that an individual might be redeemed. Throughout *Morte Darthur* there is a constant fluctuation between triumph and tragedy, a rise to glory followed by a fall from grace. Worldly fortunes may be won and lost but what is more important is spiritual fortune. Lancelot, the real hero of *Morte Darthur*, has to be redeemed even if all else fails. Lancelot is the conscience of the world that runs throughout *Morte Darthur*, and with the story of Urry, Malory was able to restore hope for the future.

20

THE VICTORIAN REVIVAL

For nearly four hundred years after Malory the Arthurian romance went into decline. With Malory's magnificent achievement now available in printed form, what more was there to do? The chivalric romance in general was steadily going out of fashion. There would be a few more great works, some of which drew upon Arthurian characters or motifs, such as Montalvo's *Amadis of Gaul* (1508) and Ariosto's *Orlando Furioso* (1516), but these are of marginal Arthurian interest, the last salvos in a war long won. Edmund Spenser would use a quasi-Arthurian world to epitomise the Elizabethan world of chivalry in his *Faerie Queen* (1590), but despite Arthur and Merlin being the main framing characters, and the mood being brilliantly evocative of the romances of old, it is clearly one step removed and not really an Arthurian work. Ironically, the character of Artegall may be based on Arthur of the Pennines, although Spenser would not have known that (*see* Chapter 23). Miguel de Cervantes so mercilessly, yet brilliantly, parodied the chivalric romance in *Don Quixote* (1605) that it sounded the death knell of the genre, which would not re-emerge until the time of Tennyson and the blossoming of the Victorian Pre-Raphaelite movement.

There follows a selective annotated checklist of those few works of interest in the period 1500–1800, during which time interest shifted to theatrical works, with John Dryden writing the first Arthurian opera. Few of these works have any relevance to the medieval romances, but instead hark back to a loose interpretation of Geoffrey of Monmouth's *History*. Anyone wishing more detail on this period of Arthurian literature should consult *The Flower of Kings* by James Douglas Merriman (University Press of Kansas, 1973).

1. Original Arthurian works, 1500–1800

This list is in chronological order, and includes only new works (not translations or reworkings) which deal wholly with the Arthurian world.

Arthur of Little Britain (London, *c*1530s). A translation by Sir John Bourchier [Lord Berners] of the French story *Artus de la Petite Bretagne*, which dates from the late fifteenth century. The eponymous Artus is not King Arthur, but the son of the duke of Brittany who, inspired by his namesake, undertakes a series of quests to break the enchantment on a castle and win the hand of the fair damsel Florence. Probably the earliest example of an Arthur-inspired fantasy.

I Due Tristani ("The Two Tristans"), anon. (Venice, 1555). This romance is in two parts. The first repeats the Tristan and Iseult story, but the second deals with their two children, also called Tristan and Iseult. After the lovers' deaths, young Tristan is welcomed by Mark (who believes him to be the son of Tristan's wife Iseult of the White Hands) and becomes king of Cornwall. He is welcomed by Arthur into the Round Table and suffers the unwelcome advances of Guenevere.

The Misfortunes of Arthur, Thomas Hughes and others (London, 1587). The earliest known Arthurian play, it was first performed before Elizabeth I at Greenwich on 28 February 1587. It follows Geoffrey of Monmouth's basic story of Arthur, but with Mordred as the son of Arthur and his sister Anne. Amongst Hughes's various collaborators was Francis Bacon. The play can be found on the internet at <www.lib.rochester.ed/camelot/hughes.htm> The most recent printing is edited by Brian Jay Corrigan (Garland, 1992).

The History of Tom Thumb, R.J. (usually treated as Richard Johnson) (London, 1621). One of the earliest English fairytales, not overly Arthurian but set in the time of King Arthur, which was obviously regarded in the seventeenth century as the "good old days". Merlin helps a barren couple have a child, the dwarf

Tom Thumb, who becomes an adventurer at Arthur's court. Available in many sources, including *The Classic Fairy Tales*, edited by Iona and Peter Opie (OUP, 1974). Henry Fielding freely adapted this for his play *Tom Thumb, a Tragedy* (London, 1730).

The Birth of Merlin, attributed to William Rowley (London, 1662). First performed in 1622, this play was posthumously published as a collaboration with William Shakespeare, but it is now believed that Rowley's collaborator was probably Thomas Dekker, though it was written as a sequel to *Hengist, King of Kent* (1615, also known as *The Mayor of Queensborough*), by Thomas Middleton. A motley jamboree-bag of a play about Merlin's role in the defence of Britain against the Saxons, more humour than history. Merlin's mother is called Joan Goe-Too't, and there's a courtier called Sir Nichodemus Nothing. The play was adapted with new material by R.J. Stewart, Roy Hudd and Denise Coffey, available as *The Birth of Merlin* (Element, 1989), whilst the original is on the internet at <www.lib.rochester.edu/camelot/rowley.htm>

King Arthur, or the British Worthy, John Dryden (London, 1691). A dramatic opera with music by Henry Purcell. An original work with only passing obligation to earlier sources, it has been described as more of a fairy extravaganza. Arthur and the Saxon chieftain Oswald battle against each other and against various perils to both win control of Britain and the hand of Emmeline, daughter of the duke of Cornwall. There are some imaginative scenes of sorcery including the summoning, by the Saxon magician Osmond, of an ice demon, the "Cold Genius", who can only be thawed by love. It was the most popular of Dryden's plays in his day. The latest printing is in *The Works of John Dryden*, edited by Vinton A. Dearing (University of California Press, 1997).

Prince Arthur (London, 1695) and **King Arthur** (London, 1697), Richard Blackmore. Two heroic verse poems intended to produce a national epic and written to celebrate William of Orange's victory over the Catholic James II in 1689. The first part draws parallels between William (Arthur) and James II (the Saxon Octa). As in Dryden's opera, they fight for the hand of the Princess Ethelina (Queen Mary, a symbol of England). The second book equates Arthur's battle against King Clotar with the British rivalry with Louis XIV. Blackmore, who was a moderately better doctor than a poet, received a knighthood for his efforts, but his works, considered too long-winded by most, faded into obscurity. *Prince Arthur* was reprinted by Scolar Press, 1971. Both poems are on the internet at <www.lib.rochester.edu/camelot/blakpa1.htm> and <www.lib.rochester.edu/camelot/blakka1.htm>

Merlin, or The Devil of Stonehenge, Lewis Theobald (London, 1734). A comic operetta with music by John Galliard. The first Arthurian Christmas pantomime, full of effects and melodrama and depicting Merlin as the villain.

Merlin in Love, Aaron Hill (London, 1760). Scarcely Arthurian, but an interesting depiction of Merlin as an old wizard with a long beard, dressed in a robe and wielding a magic wand, perhaps the earliest portrayal of what became a standard image. Apart from Merlin it has no Arthurian connections. Merlin tries to steal Columbine from Harlequin, and is turned into an ass. Described as a "pantomime opera", it was probably written as early as 1740, as Hill died in 1750.

Arthur, or the Northern Enchantment, Richard Hole (London, 1789). A verse romance which takes many liberties with Geoffrey's *History*. It follows the conflict between Arthur and Hengist, and is influenced by Dryden's play. The same applies to the gothic play *The Fairy of the Lake*, by John Thelwall (London, 1801).

Vortigern, William Henry Ireland (London, 1795). Passed off by Ireland as a newly discovered play by Shakespeare. It follows Vortigern's life as described by Geoffrey of Monmouth. It was staged at Drury Lane on 2 April 1796, but had such a foul reception that it closed after one performance. The play may be found on the website <www.vortigernstudies.org.uk>

2. Dawn of the Romantics

After Malory's *Morte Darthur*, the best-known Arthurian work is Alfred Tennyson's *Idylls of the King*, which catapulted the Arthurian story back into public consciousness and inspired the Victorian romantic fascination with the subject.

There were signs of a revival before Tennyson, the interest growing out of the late eighteenth century gothic revival from Germany. Tales by authors such as Ludwig Tieck and Baron de la Motte Fouqué, about brooding haunted castles and doomed knights, became all the rage. These works were not Arthurian, although it would not have taken much to make them so; a good example is Fouqué's long supernatural fantasy of the Crusades, *Der Zauberring* ("The Magic Ring", 1813). Their predecessor Christoph Wieland had started this movement, and amongst his works are *Merlin der Zauberer* ("Merlin the Magician", 1777) and *Geron der Adelige* ("The Noble Geron", 1777), the latter a blank verse adaptation of *Guiron le Courtois* (see *Palamedes*, page 377–8).

Walter Scott was fascinated by German romanticism, and mimicked it so well that some of his anonymously published works were believed to be translations from the German. He spent time editing a new edition of *Sir Tristrem* (Edinburgh, 1804), based on a thirteenth century work attributed to Thomas of Ercildoune. He incorporated an Arthurian story, "Lyulph's Tale", into his episodic verse romance *The Bridal of Triermain* (Edinburgh, 1813), which tells of Arthur's seduction by the witch Guendolen, who swears revenge when Arthur leaves her. Years later their daughter Gyneth arrives at Camelot, and reminds Arthur of his pledge that, should he have a daughter, she would marry the bravest of the Round Table knights. A tournament is declared which Gyneth turns into a bloodbath, until Merlin stops it and places Gyneth in a deep slumber in an enchanted castle. The next tale, "Sir Roland de Vaux", is set in the twelfth century with the eponymous knight in search of the enchanted castle. He wakes Gyneth, à la Sleeping Beauty. The story is available on several websites including <www.lib.rochester.edu/camelot/trierma.htm>

Scott wrote no more Arthurian tales, although *Ivanhoe* (1820) and his Crusader novels *The Betrothed*, *The Talisman* (both 1825) and *Count Robert of Paris* (1832) all evoke the atmosphere of the medieval romances.

With the impetus from Scott and growing interest from poets like William Wordsworth, and a new edition of Malory's *Morte Darthur* by Robert Southey in 1817, the Arthurian revival gathered pace. The first all-new Arthurian novel, and still one of the most original, was *The Misfortunes of Elphin* by Thomas Love Peacock (1829). Through his Welsh wife, Peacock had access to various Welsh texts long unknown to English readers. Uninfluenced by subsequent translations, he gave free rein to a very individualistic novel. Taliesin is the main character at Arthur's court in Caerleon, and the story includes the abduction of Gwenhyvar and the flooding of Gwaelod through Seithenyn's neglect. The story can be found at several websites, including <www.thomaslovepeacock.net>

3. Tennyson and the Pre-Raphaelites

Southey's edition of *Morte Darthur*, entitled *The Byrth, Lyf and Actes of King Arthur*, was the first new edition since 1634, and it proved very influential. It inspired not only Tennyson but, in time, William Morris and the Pre-Raphaelite movement. Tennyson encountered it while still a child and the effect stayed with him. From 1830, when he started "Sir Launcelot and Queen Guinevere", to 1889 with "Merlin and the Gleam", Tennyson spent a lifetime exploring, experimenting with and recreating a romantic but challenging view of the Arthurian world. Whilst idealising the imagery of Arthur, Guenevere and Lancelot, he also questioned it, forcing us to look again at what was happening. "The Lady of Shalott" (1832), his first published Arthurian poem, did that right from the start, telling of the final days and death of Elaine of Astolat, shunned by Lancelot and dying of a broken heart. Tennyson succeeds in depicting the beautiful world of "many tower'd Camelot", whilst thrusting into the forefront the image of betrayal and death.

Tennyson continued to explore Malory, creating a growing corpus of work. "Sir Galahad" contrasts the chastity and virtue of Galahad as a knight with his arrogance and compulsiveness as a man. "Morte d'Arthur" is an intensely moving account of Arthur's last hours, and includes Tennyson's version of the one image we all know from the Arthurian legend, that of Bedivere casting Excalibur back into the lake and the arm clad in white samite grasping the sword, brandishing it three times and withdrawing with it under the waters.

These poems, with others, including a revised version of "The Lady of Shalott", appeared in the two-volume *Poems* in 1842, which not only re-established Tennyson's flagging career but provided the final impetus for the Arthurian revival.

It was another ten years before Tennyson returned to the Arthurian world, this time with a group of four poems. The first two, "Vivien" and "Enid" (published together as *Enid and Nimuë*, 1857), contrasted two female perspectives. "Vivien" is a disturbing study of the seduction and betrayal of Merlin, showing the corruption that would destroy Camelot. "Enid", on the other hand, shows the devotion, fidelity and bravery of Gereint's wife in comparison to his own jealousy and cruelty. To these two Tennyson added "Guinevere", which portrays the queen's inevitably destructive turmoil caused by her dedication to duty and passion for Lancelot, and "Elaine", a different outlook on "The Lady of Shalott". These four, which showed the importance of the female influence on the world of chivalry, were issued in 1859 as *Idylls of the King*, a volume to which Tennyson would continue to add over the next thirty years. He was going to call the collection *The True and the False*, a description which more accurately reflects the contrasting female values, but which fails to convey the dream-like melancholia of *Idylls*.

The next edition of *Idylls* in 1870 contained four poems that Tennyson had issued in 1869 as *The Holy Grail and Other Poems*. In addition to "The Holy Grail" itself, a powerful study of individuals striving for perfection within a sinful world, the other three are "Pelleas and Ettarre", depicting a decaying post-Grail Camelot, "The Coming of Arthur", which explores attitudes towards Arthur's origin, and "The Passing of Arthur", a rewrite of the earlier "Morte d'Arthur". Writing "The Holy Grail" freed Tennyson's imagination. He had feared he might never achieve a successful version of the story that was both acceptable to Victorian values, and faithful to his concept of an Arthurian world riven by sin. Tennyson viewed the unceasing desire for perfection as ultimately self-destructive, which was the only way in which he could reconcile his Arthurian vision with the developing Victorian world. This balanced dichotomy influenced the remaining poems he would produce.

"The Last Tournament" (1871) shows the continued decay of

Camelot and of the knights, including the downfall of Sir Tristram. In contrast, "Gareth and Lynette" shows the power and virtue of the ideal Camelot. Some years later came "Balin and Balan" (1885) which, in Tennyson's version, is not the precursor to the Grail Quest but the start of Camelot's decline, emphasising the belief that self-denial and ignorance lead to destruction.

Tennyson produced one final Arthurian poem, not included in *Idylls*, which serves as a coda not just to that work but to most of his output. "Merlin and the Gleam" (1889) is a mixture of youthful ambition and the realism of old age, reflecting the need to pursue a dream whilst recognising a reality. That was Tennyson's view of Camelot. It was a Victorian ideal, which one should pursue but with caution, recognising that it contains the seeds of its own destruction.

Tennyson had placed much of the blame for Camelot's decay on the impossible demands made of men and women in an idealized society (the character of Guenevere suffers particularly badly). The fiery dynamo William Morris did not entirely agree.

Morris had discovered Tennyson's Arthurian world when he read "The Lady of Shalott" while studying at Oxford from 1853 to 1855. He was further inspired by Southey's edition of *Morte Darthur*, a copy of which he drew to the attention of his fellow student, Edward Burne-Jones, in 1855. Morris was still developing his concept of an idealized pre-industrial England, but whilst he delighted in Tennyson's work, he did not entirely agree with his portrayal of Guenevere. Morris began experimenting with several Arthurian poems, resulting in the publication of *The Defence of Guenevere and Other Poems* (1858). The title poem has Guenevere pleading with Gawain from the stake at which she is about to be burned, only to be rescued at the last moment by Lancelot. The passion with which Guenevere admits her adultery, revealing the tortured soul within, causes Gawain to turn away in pain. The anguish of unrequited love is further explored in "King Arthur's Tomb", in which Lancelot and Guenevere meet again after Arthur's death, filled with torment and guilt.

Like Tennyson, Morris portrays the difficulty of attaining the ideal, but whereas Tennyson explores it as a dream, Morris depicts it as a reality. He has no desire to provide excuses for not achieving a better world but instead recognises the problems and looks for solutions. "Sir Galahad" shows the immensity of the demands upon the knight to achieve the quest, and though others have failed, Galahad is able to succeed with the support of those others who were victorious – Bors, Perceval and Perceval's sister. This was Morris's depiction of the Pre-Raphaelite Brotherhood, which had Sir Galahad as their figurehead. The Brotherhood was founded in 1848 by William Holman Hunt, John Everett Millais and Dante Gabriel Rossetti amongst others, and though they had more or less disbanded by 1855, their spell lingered upon their disciples Morris, Burne-Jones, Arthur Hughes and Algernon Swinburne.

In 1857 Rossetti hired Morris and Burne-Jones to paint a series of murals from the *Morte Darthur* on the walls of the Oxford Union, an ill-fated project that shone briefly like a "highly-illuminated manuscript", according to Coventry Patmore. At the same time Rossetti, Millais and Hunt provided several Arthurian illustrations for the 1857 edition of Tennyson's *Poems*.

It was the dawn of the golden age of Arthurian art and poetry. The period from 1850 to 1910 would see some of the most beautiful and creative pictorial interpretations of Arthurian scenes. Following is a brief list of the major Arthurian artists and their key works. All are English unless stated otherwise.

Abbey, Edwin Austin (American; 1852–1911), Holy Grail murals for Boston Public Library, Boston, Mass. (1890–1901)

Anderson, Sophie (French; 1823–1903), *Elaine, or the Lily Maid of Astolat* (1870)

Archer, James (Scottish; 1823–1904). *Queen Guinevere* (1860), *La Mort D'Arthur* (1860), *King Arthur Obtains the Mystic Sword Excalibur* (1862), *Sir Lancelot Looks on Queen Guinevere* (1863), *The Parting of Arthur and Guinevere* (1865), *How Sir Lancelot and His Eight Fellows of the Round Table Carried Queen Guinevere from Amesbury to Glastonbury* (1869), *The Death of Arthur* (1872), *The Dying King Arthur on the Island of Avalon has a Vision of the San Grail* (1880), *King Arthur in the Quest of His Mystic Sword Excalibur* (1880), *La Mort D'Arthur* (1897)

Boughton, G.H. (1834–1905), *The Road to Camelot* (1898)

Burne-Jones, (Sir) Edward (1833–1898). *The Death of Merlin*

(1857) for the Oxford Union murals; paintings, *Sir Galahad* (1858), *The Beguiling of Merlin* (1874) and the Stanmore Hall tapestries (1891–94), depicting the Grail quest. He designed the scenery and costumes for J. Comyns Carr's stage production of *King Arthur* (1895) and provided a frontispiece for the Everyman edition of *The High History of the Holy Grail* (Dent, 1898 – not in the later printings). At his death he left incomplete the painting *Sleep of King Arthur in Avalon.*

Butler, Charles Ernest (1864–1933), *King Arthur* (1903)

Calderon, William (1865–1943), *Lancelot Discovered Sleeping* (1908)

Carrick, John Mulcaster (d.1878), *Le Morte D'Arthur* (1862)

Collier, John (1850–1934), *Guinevere a-Maying* (1897)

Corbould, Edward Henry (1815–1905), *Elaine the Lily Maid of Astolat* (1861), *Morte d'Arthur* (1864)

Cowper, Frank Cadogan (1877–1958), *La Belle Dame sans Merci* (1926), *Nimue Damosel of the Lake* (1924), *Lancelot Slays Sir Turquine*, *Legend of Sir Perceval* (1953), *Four Queens find Lancelot Sleeping* (1954)

Darvall, Henry (*fl*1848–1889), *Lady of Shalott* (1855), *Elaine* (1861)

Delville, Jean (Belgian; 1867–1953), *Tristan and Yseult* (1887), *Parsifal* (1890)

Dicksee, Frank (1853–1928), *The Passing of Arthur* (1889), *Chivalry* (1885), *La Belle Dame sans merci* (1902), *End of the Quest* (1921), *Yseult* (1901)

Draper, Herbert (1864–1920), *Lancelot and Guinevere* (1894), *Tristram and Iseult* (1901)

Duncan, John (1866–1945), *Tristram and Isolde* (1912)

Dyce, William (Scottish, 1806–1864), Frescoes for the Queen's Robing Room at the Palace of Westminster, including *The Vision of Sir Galahad* (1851), *King Arthur Unhorsed* (1852), *Sir Tristram Harping to La Belle Isolde* (1852), *Sir Gawain Swearing to be Merciful* (1854) and *The Admission of Sir Tristram to the Fellowship of the Round Table* (1864). His first design, *Knights Departing on the Grail Quest* (1849), was rejected.

Egley, William Maw (1826–1916), *Lady of Shalott* (1858)

Frampton, Edward Reginald (1870–1923), *Elaine* (1921)

Fripp, Charles Edwin (1854–1906), *Elaine* (1885)

Gilbert, John (1817–1897), *Sir Lancelot du Lake* (1886)
Gow, Mary L. (1851–1929), *Elaine* (1876)
Grimshaw, John Atkinson (1836–1893), *Elaine* (1877), *The Lady of Shalott* (1878)
Hacker, Arthur (1858–1919), *The Temptation of Sir Perceval* (1894)
Hughes, Arthur (1830–1915). *The Death of Arthur* (1857) for the Oxford Union murals; *The Birth of Tristram* (1862) for the Harden Grange stained glass windows; *The Brave Geraint* (1862), *La Belle Dame sans Merci* (1863), *Sir Galahad* (1870 and 1894), *The Lady of Shalott* (1873), *Gareth Overthrows the Red Knight* (1908)
Hunt, Holman (1827–1910), *The Lady of Shalott* (1850), and his drawings for the Moxon edition of Tennyson's poems (1857)
Leighton, Edmund Blair (1853–1923), *Tristan and Isolde* (1902)
MacNab, Peter (d.1900), *The Lady of Shalott* (1887)
Meteyard, Sidney (1868–1947), *"I'm Half Sick of Shadows" said the Lady of Shalott* (1913), *Tristan and Isolde*
Millais, William Henry (1828–1899), *Elaine, the Lily Maid of Astolat* (1862)
Morris, William (1834–1896). *Sir Palomides' jealousy of Sir Tristram* (1857) for the Oxford Union murals. Paintings, *Queen Guenevere* (1858) also called *La Belle Iseult*; *The Recognition of Tristram by La Belle Isoude* (1862) for the Harden Grange stained glass windows; tapestry *Vision of the Grail* (1891–94)
Paget, Henry Marriott (1856–1936), *Lady of Shalott* (1881)
Paton, Joseph Noel (Scottish; 1821–1902), *Sir Lancelot of the Lake* (1860), *Death Barge of King Arthur* (1865), *Sir Galahad's Vision of the Sangreal* (1880), *Sir Galahad and his Angel* (1884)
Pollen, J. Hungerford (1820–1902) *King Arthur obtaining the sword Excalibur* (1857) for the Oxford Union murals
Prinsep, Valentine Cameron (1838–1904), *Sir Pelleas Leaving the Lady Ettarde* (1857) for the Oxford Union murals
Riviere, Briton (1840–1920), *Elaine Floats Down to Camelot* (1860/3)
Rossetti, Dante Gabriel (1828–1882), *Sir Lancelot prevented by his sin from entering the Chapel of the San Graal* (1857) for the Oxford Union murals. Paintings, *Arthur's Tomb* (1854), *How Sir*

Galahad, Sir Bors and Sir Percival were Fed with the Grael (1864), *Tristram and Isolde Drinking the Love Potion* (1867); engraving, *Lady of Shallott* (1857). Drawings, *King Arthur and the Weeping Queens* (1857), *Queen Genever* (1858)

Sandys, Frederick (1832–1904), *Morgan-le-Fay* (1863), *Vivien* (1863)

Schmalz, Herbert Gustav (1856–1935), *Elaine* (1885)

Shaw, Byam (1872–1919), *The Lady of Shalott* (1898)

Spencer-Stanhope, John Roddam (1829–1908), *Sir Gawaine and the Damsels at the Fountain* (1857) for the Oxford Union murals; *Morgan le Fay*

Stillman, Marie Spartali (1843–1927), *Sir Tristram and La Belle Iseult* (1873)

Sullivan, Edmund Joseph (1869–1933), *The Lady of Shalott* (1899)

Wallis, Henry (1830–1916), *Elaine Floats Down to Camelot* (1861)

Waterhouse, J.W. (1849–1917), seven paintings of the Lady of Shalott from *The Lady of Shalott* (1888) to *I am Half Sick of Shadows* (1915), *Tristram and Isolde* (1916)

Watson Homer (Canadian, 1855–1936), *The Death of Elaine* (1877)

Watts, George Frederic (1817–1904), *Sir Galahad* (1862), *Britomart and her Nurse* (1878)

Whall, Veronica (1887–1967), 72 stained-glass windows in Arthur's Hall, Tintagel (1931–33)

Wheelwright, Rowland (1870–1955), *Enid and Gereint* (1907)

For those wishing to explore further, the authoritative works on Arthurian art are *The Arthurian Revival in Victorian Art* by Debra N. Mancoff (Garland, 1990), *The Legends of King Arthur in Art* by Muriel Whitaker (Brewer, 1990) and *The Quest for the Grail: Arthurian Legend in British Art 1840–1920* by Christine Poulson (Manchester University Press, 1999).

Tennyson's work encouraged others to visit the Arthurian world. In 1852, Matthew Arnold composed the first modern English treatment of the Tristan story, in the verse romance *Tristram and Iseult*, which includes, as a coda, Vivian's beguilement of Merlin.

Algernon Swinburne was also fascinated by the Tristan legend. An early attempt, "Queen Yseult", remained unfinished, but in 1882 Swinburne completed *Tristram of Lyonesse*. Swinburne believed that Tennyson had debased the purity of the original story, and that Arnold had been too basic. He wanted to restore to all its glory what he held as "the loveliest of medieval legends", showing Tristram as a doomed hero, a victim of fate. Swinburne also wrote *The Tale of Balen* (1896).

The story of Tristan also attracted the world of opera in the form of Richard Wagner. Wagner had already entered Arthurian territory, or at least Grail territory, with *Lohengrin* (1850), the story of Parsifal's son who comes to earth as a maiden's champion but is bound by the Grail oath to keep his anonymity, which is shattered when he is forced to give his name. Wagner would return to the Grail Quest with *Parsifal* (1882). But his first major Arthurian opera was *Tristan und Isolde* (1865), based loosely on Gottfried von Strassburg's romance though reduced to basics for dramatic effect. Wagner's characters are ruled by passion, hate turning to love, love turning to despair. *Tristan und Isolde* is perhaps more in the mould of *Romeo and Juliet* than an Arthurian romance, but its power demonstrates the allure the story had for the Victorians.

Wagner also pared *Parsifal* down in order to create a Christian allegory of a young innocent hero, Parsifal, who must overcome physical love to command a sacrificial love of mankind as a means of combating the evil sorcerer Klingsor, who has used the temptress Kundry to seduce Amfortas, guardian of the Grail.

In 1864 the West Country antiquary Robert Stephen Hawker, parson of Morwenstowe, published his own mystical poem of the Grail quest in *The Quest of the Sangraal*, the first of four planned parts, though no more appeared.

From poetry, art and music the Arthurian saga returned to the theatre with *King Arthur* by Joseph Comyns Carr, first performed at the Lyceum in London in January 1895. The first play to attempt an authentic adaptation of the Arthurian romance rather than using Geoffrey's *History*, it was an artistic and critical success. Burne-Jones designed the scenery and costumes, Sir Arthur Sullivan provided the incidental music. Henry Irving played Arthur to Ellen Terry's Guenevere.

Soon after the appearance of the first edition of *Idylls of the King*, James Knowles (later Sir James) completed his modern rendition of *Morte Darthur* as *The Legends of King Arthur and His Knights* (1862), which he dedicated to Tennyson. It led to a firm friendship with Tennyson, and the poet claimed that it was Knowles who encouraged him to return to the Arthurian world to continue the *Idylls*. Knowles's version proved extremely popular and encouraged other adaptations of Malory's work. There was a profusion of abridgments and adaptations of *Morte Darthur* from the late Victorian era onwards. Anyone interested in a detailed listing should consult *Sir Thomas Malory: An Anecdotal Bibliography of Editions 1485–1985* by Barry Gaines (1990).

Amongst these were some beautiful illustrated editions of both Malory and Tennyson. For *Idylls* these include Gustave Doré's famed artwork in the 1868 edition and Eleanor Fortescue-Brickdale's beautiful paintings for the Hodder & Stoughton 1911 edition. *Morte d'Arthur* includes those by Aubrey Beardsley (Dent, 1893/4), W. Russell Flint (Riccardi, 1910/11) and Arthur Rackham (Macmillan, 1917). The American Sidney Lanier adapted it as *The Boy's King Arthur* (Scribner, 1880), with a later edition illustrated by N.C. Wyeth (1917) being one of the most admired of all printings. In Britain, Andrew Lang adapted it as *Tales of King Arthur and the Round Table* (Longman, 1905), whilst in America Howard Pyle illustrated his own adaptations in four books, *The Story of King Arthur and His Knights* (1903), *The Story of the Champions of the Round Table* (1905), *The Story of Sir Launcelot and his Companions* (1907) and *The Story of the Grail and the Passing of Arthur* (1911).

This profusion of books, and there were plenty more, inevitably led to a parody of the Arthurian world which Mark Twain was only too happy to provide in *A Connecticut Yankee at the Court of King Arthur* (1889). It was not long before someone attempted to produce a genuine historical novel based on the true Dark Age world. This fell to William H. Babcock with *Cian of the Chariots* (1898), complete with extensive notes showing the thoroughness of his research. The modern Arthurian novel had arrived.

From then on authors began to produce their own original

versions of the Arthurian story, creating their own characters and worlds, not necessarily beholden to Malory or Geoffrey or Chrétien. This "modern" treatment of Arthur dominated the twentieth century, and the next chapter provides a working checklist of all major Arthurian novels.

SECTION 3

THE BIG PICTURE

21

SCRIBES OF THE ROUND TABLE: MODERN ARTHURIAN NOVELS

The twentieth century saw an explosion of novels either set in the Arthurian world, or featuring Arthurian characters in other settings. The production increased significantly after T.H. White completed his sequence *The Once and Future King* (1958), and shows no sign of abating. It is impossible here to list every book and story that has appeared over the last century. The most comprehensive bibliography of Arthurian texts is *The Arthurian Annals* compiled by Dan Nastali and Phil Boardman (OUP, 2004), whilst another useful compendium is *The Return from Avalon*, by Raymond H. Thompson (Greenwood Press, 1985).

The following list is in alphabetical order by the author's surname. Where known, authors' dates are provided. I have restricted coverage to books available in the English language and which are set in a recognizable Arthurian setting. An (h) after the title denotes those which take place in a realistic, historical Dark Age world; an (m) denotes those set in the quasi-historical world of the medieval romances but which still endeavour to be historical; and an (f) marks those that are fantasies, but still set in a form of historical milieu. I have not included standard retellings of Malory's *Morte d'Arthur*. I have excluded all works with a contemporary or science fiction setting unless it is directly related to one of the above. I have also excluded most time-shift stories, such as Mark Twain's *A Connecticut Yankee*, and those where Arthur and his knights are transported every which-where. Books for young adults are included (designated YA), but I have excluded those for young children.

I have listed the first publication details only, but have noted recently available reprints for books otherwise long out of print. US indicates that the book first appeared in the United States, UK in the United Kingdom. The list excludes poetry and drama but includes significant short story collections. The emphasis is on novels. I have asterisked (*) those titles which I believe should serve as a basic Arthurian library.

Although I have excluded poetry I must at least mention the following. No discussion of Arthurian-influenced works can omit reference to *The Waste Land* by T.S. Eliot (1922), even though he drew primarily upon Jessie Weston's study of the Grail legend, *From Ritual to Romance*, rather than directly from the stories. Nevertheless, Eliot's appropriation of the imagery of the desolation caused by the First World War shows the continued relevance of the Arthurian stories to the twentieth century. The same fusion of the traditional with the modern makes the three book-length poems by Edward Arlington Robinson of timeless relevance. The most traditional is *Tristram* (1927), for which he won the Pulitzer Prize, whilst the earlier *Merlin* (1917) and especially the highly spiritual *Lancelot* (1920) show the impact of World War I. Robinson, like Tennyson, sees the Arthurian heroes as seeking impossible ideals, which are more likely to be the cause of destruction than of salvation.

Attanasio, A.A. (b. 1951), *The Dragon and the Unicorn* (UK, 1994); *Arthor* (UK, 1995; US as *The Eagle and the Sword*, 1997); *The Wolf and the Crown* (US, 1998; UK as *The Perilous Order*, 1999); *The Serpent and the Grail* (US, 1999) (f)

The four books follow, to a degree, the basic pattern of Arthur's life, with a fifth-century setting, but Merlin, Morgan le Fay and the Grail receive a cosmic pseudo-scientific explanation. The 'Dragon' is the sentient power of the Earth, whilst the 'unicorn' is a spiritual Sun-being that takes on unicorn form when in touch with the Earth's dragon power. There are two opposing energy forces: the Fire Lords, or angels, who strive for order and progress and seek to stave off the impending Dark Ages in Europe, and the demons, one of whom, Lailoken, becomes the magus Merlin, the focus of the first book. His teacher, Bleys, was a Chinese pilgrim who has harnessed the power of the unicorn and become immortal. Arthor, or Aquila Regalia Thor, whose youth is covered in the second book, is none other than the Celtic hero Cuchulain, reborn in exchange for Uther Pendragon's soul. Unaware of his origins, Arthor is a violent, un-self-redeeming bully who rebels against his earthly destiny; it requires the intervention of Merlin to keep him on the true path. In the subsequent volumes, but especially in *The Wolf and the Crown*, Attanasio follows the Arthurian legend as we know it, but within his cosmological framework, portraying a demigodlike Arthor striving to keep order in a world of cataclysmic change.

(Note: Attanasio's *Kingdom of the Grail* (US, 1992) is not a grail story but an historical romance set during the Crusades.)

Atterton, Julian, *The Last Harper* (UK, 1983) (h)
YA novel about the youth of Taliesin, first called Gwion, who flees to Urien's court during the Saxon raids and is taught by Myrddin, whom he succeeds as bard. There are also some Arthurian references in *Knights of the Sacred Blade* (UK, 1989) set in twelfth-century Northumberland.

Babcock, William H. (1849–1922), *Cian of the Chariots* (US, 1890) (h)
The earliest novel to recreate an authentic sixth-century setting for Arthur's battle against the Saxons. Babcock has Caerleon at Leicester in the British Midlands and endeavours to locate all of Arthur's nine battles across Britain. This is on the internet at < www.lib.rochester.edu/camelot/cian.htm >

Baldry, Cherith (b. 1947), *Exiled from Camelot* (US, 2001) (m)
Cherith Baldry has long been Kay's champion, seeking to restore his reputation in several stories, and this novel is based on the episode in which Kay is believed to have killed Arthur's son Loholt. Kay is sent into exile and joins forces with a renegade knight who is seeking to undermine Camelot, forcing Kay to try and save Camelot and prove his innocence.

Barron, T.A. *The Lost Years of Merlin* (US, 1996) (f)
The first of YA series that looks at the teenage years of Merlin before the encounter with Vortigern. First known as Emrys, but with no memory, he is washed up on the Welsh coast and raised by a healer woman, Branwen, whom he later saves from being burned at the stake. He loses his sight but gains a "second sight". He begins a quest to find his origins and this takes him to the mythical Otherworld of Fincayra, where he learns that his real name is Merlin. His adventures, many drawn from Celtic legend, continue in *The Seven Songs of Merlin* (US, 1997), *The Fires of Merlin* (US, 1998), *The Mirror of Merlin* (US, 1999) and *The Wings of Merlin* (US, 2000). The fourth book takes Merlin into his future where he sees himself as an old man who encounters a young Arthur. The last two books also sowed the seed for the Great Tree of Avalon series which began with *Child of the Dark Prophecy* (US, 2004).

Berger, Thomas (b. 1924), *Arthur Rex* (US, 1978) (m)
An admirable attempt to update Malory, in a mock medieval tongue, and with much humour, bawdiness and irony. Also incorporates the story of Gawain and the Green Knight. In Berger's eyes, Arthur "was not historical but everything he did was true." Berger develops the relationship between the characters, especially Launcelot and Gawain, and explores the complexities of Morgan and Guinevere.

Borchardt, Alice, *The Dragon Queen* (US, 2001) (f)
First in a proposed trilogy, "Tales of Guinevere", by the sister of Anne Rice. It takes great liberties with the origins of Guinevere by presenting the unorthodox view of her as a sorceress, raised by a shape-shifter and a druid, who befriends and takes control over the dying breed of dragons, becoming a Boudicca-like warrior queen with magical powers. The second book is *The Raven Warrior* (US, 2003).

Borowsky, Marvin (1907–1969), *The Queen's Knight* (US, 1955) (m)
Screenwriter Borowsky's rather downbeat view of a slow-witted Arthur set up as a puppet king by the Lords of the Council but

who tries his best nonetheless. He succeeds to a degree thanks to the prowess of Lancelot and even wins Guinevere's respect, but has not the skills to succeed.

Bowers, Gwendolyn, *Brother to Galahad* (US, 1963) (m)
A YA novel about the Grail Quest and its aftermath as seen through the eyes of the Welsh Hugh of Alleyn, squire to Sir Galahad.

***Bradley, Marion** (1930–1999), *Mists of Avalon* (US, 1982) (h)
A significant bestseller which put the Arthurian world back into the market, this book retells the traditional story of Arthur but from the female viewpoint, primarily that of Morgaine, who here is both Arthur's half-sister and the mother of Mordred. Bradley paints strong characters and a believable world, in which the elder religions clash with Christianity and an easily manipulated Arthur finds kingship a constant series of dilemmas. A subsequent book, *The Forest House* (US, 1993), describing the fate of the Druids at the time of the Roman invasion, became a prequel to *Mists* by establishing Avalon as the centre of the Mother Goddess religion, and a successor to Atlantis. It introduces the character of Gawen whose fate is told in the sequel, *Lady of Avalon* (US, 1997), which bridges the gap between the other two books in three episodes tracing Gawen's reincarnations as the Defender of Britain. Since Bradley's death Diana L. Paxson has developed the series with *Priestess of Avalon* (UK, 2000) about Helena, the mother of Constantine the Great, and *Ancestors of Avalon* (US, 2004), which goes back to Atlantis.

Bradshaw, Gillian, *Hawk of May* (US, 1980), *Kingdom of Summer* (US, 1981), *In Winter's Shadow* (US, 1982), all three reissued in one volume as *Down the Long Wind* (UK, 1988) (h)
This increasingly bleak sequence features Gwalchmai (Gawain) as the main character, his struggles (rather than adventures) told from three different viewpoints. He tells his own story in the first book, from his youth and his flight to the Isles of the Blessed, to entering Arthur's service. The second, told by Gwalchmai's servant, concerns the clash between Gwalchmai as the Champion of the Light and his mother Morgawse as the Queen of Darkness

and his quest for his lost love Elidan. The third, told by Gwynhwyfar, shows Gwalchmai's growing despair for Arthur's court which turns to revenge when his son is killed. Bradshaw creates a believable historical Arthurian world seen from a new perspective.

Bulla, Clyde Robert (b.1914), *The Sword in the Tree* (US, 1956) (m)
When his father is reported dead and his uncle takes over his castle, young Shan seeks help from King Arthur in the form of Sir Gareth. The book was reprinted (Morrow, 2000).

Canning, Victor (1911–1986), *The Crimson Chalice* (UK, 1976), *The Circle of the Gods* (UK, 1977), *The Immortal Wound* (UK, 1978), all three reissued in one volume as *The Crimson Chalice* (UK, 1978) (h)
A partly successful attempt at creating a different historical background for Arthur (here called Arturo), only loosely connected to tradition. The first book follows the struggles of Arthur's parents (Baradoc and Gratia) against the Saxons, the second (and best) book follows Arthur's life up to Badon and enmity with Ambrosius, and the final volume, including the Grail quest, describes Arthur's inevitable decline. Arturo is shown as a rebel driven by destiny.

Carmichael, Douglas (b.1923), *Pendragon* (US, 1977; new edition, 2000) (h)
A strongly visualised historical novel of the first years of Arthur's reign working through each of the twelve battles, showing how Arthur (here Artorius) consolidates the kingdom, culminating in Badon Hill. Most of Arthur's warriors are present, even at this early stage, including Caius, Bedwyr and Lanceolatus. Guenevere is Vinavera, and the book explores the start of their relationship. Carmichael wrote a sequel, *The Last of the Dragons*, which remains unpublished, though an episode was reworked as the story "Madoc the Door Ward" in *The Mammoth Book of Arthurian Legends*, edited by Mike Ashley (UK/US, 1998).

Chadwick, Elizabeth, *First Knight* (US, 1995) (m)
The book of the film (*see* page 556).

Chant, Joy (b.1945), *The High Kings* (US, 1983) (m)
As if recounted by bards in Arthur's day, this is a series of stories based on the main characters in Geoffrey of Monmouth's *History*, from the arrival of Brutus to the time of Arthur. Only the final chapter, "Chief Dragon of the Island", covers Arthur.

Chapman, Vera (1898–1996), *The Green Knight* (UK, 1975), *The King's Damosel* (UK, 1976), *King Arthur's Daughter* (UK, 1976), all three reissued in one volume as *The Three Damosels* (UK, 1978) (m)
Although drawing its raw material from Malory and *Gawain and the Green Knight*, this series introduces new characters. Behind all three novels is Morgan le Fay's desire to destroy Arthur and his court, but pitted against her are not Arthur or his knights but three women. In the first book it is Vivian, granddaughter of Merlin, in the second it is Lynett (the Lady of the Fountain in the *Mabinogion*), and in the third it is Arthur's own daughter Ursulet, after Arthur's death. These were the first books to consider Arthur's decline from the female perspective. The last book became the basis of the animated feature film *Quest for Camelot*.

Chapman, Vera (1898–1996), *The Enchantresses* (UK, 1998) (m)
This follows the lives of the three sisters (triplets) Morgan, Morgause and Viviane, trained in witchery by Merlin, whose actions, some by design, others by chance, are all linked to the fate of their half-brother Arthur. The novel forms a greater framework for the earlier episodes in *The Three Damosels*.

Christian, Catherine (b.1901), *The Sword and the Flame* (UK, 1978; as *The Pendragon*, US, 1979) (m)
Essentially a retelling of the traditional story of Arthur from the viewpoint of Bedivere, with a degree of rationalisation to give the story verisimilitude. The role of the women at court is underplayed – Morgan surprisingly so – but the characters are finely realized.

Clare, Tom, *King Arthur and the Riders of Rheged* (UK, 1992) (h)
The author contends that Urien and his son Owain of Rheged were the actual leaders that performed the deeds attributed to Arthur (Arctures - The Northern Bear). Strongly Celtic, with many of the well-known characters and a magical atmosphere, the author's story is both credible and absorbing (*information courtesy of Larry Mendelsburg*).

Clarke, Lindsay (b.1939), *Parzival and the Stone from Heaven* (UK, 2001) (m)
Labelled "a grail romance retold for our time", this novel, which grew out of a radio play broadcast in 1995, follows faithfully Wolfram's original romance but presents it in a form that highlights many parallels to our lives today, points which Clarke delineates in a fascinating afterword. He contrasts the innocence and purity of Parzival with the earthiness of Gawain and the corruption of Arthur's other knights, creating a world every bit as familiar today as it was in Wolfram's time.

Closs, Hannah (1905–1953), *Tristan* (UK, 1940; US, 1967) (h)
A retelling of the story of Tristan and Isolde, but using modernistic techniques that heighten the intensity of the relationships between the individuals.

***Cornwell, Bernard** (b. 1944), *The Winter King* (UK, 1995), *Enemy of God* (UK, 1996), *Excalibur* (UK, 1997), known collectively as *The Warlord Chronicles* (h)
An individualistic retelling of the Arthurian story which shows the depth of Cornwell's research into both the whole Arthurian story – he uses many sources – and the military circumstances of the day. Cornwell creates a hitherto unknown narrator for the third-person perspective on events, Derfel, a Saxon slave who has grown up in Merlin's household. On one level he effectively takes the place of Bedivere, but on another he is the future of the land. After his death, Uther is succeeded by his lame grandson Mordred, still a child. Uther's illegitimate son Arthur becomes Mordred's guardian and Warlord of Dumnonia, determined to bring peace to Britain, especially in the conflict with Powys. The

trilogy describes the two basic struggles. Arthur faces conflict from without, from the Saxons, and conflict from within, the desire by Merlin to retain the old religion, to which end Merlin is seeking the ancient treasures of Britain, in particular the Cauldron. Merlin is Arthur's main enemy. In Cornwell's version Morgan le Fay is the wife of Archbishop Sansum, the figurehead for Christianity. All of the key episodes and set scenes are present, but they take on a different glow in the light of Cornwell's creativity.

(Note: Cornwell's Grail Quest series, *Harlequin* (UK, 2000), *Vagabond* (UK, 2002) and *Heretic* UK, 2003) is not Arthurian but is set during the Hundred Years' War, in which a soldier, Thomas of Hookton, has become involved in a search for the Grail.)

Cramer, James Douglas, *The Song of Arthur* (US, 2001) (f) Unusually, this is set after Camlann, during Arthur's final days in Avalon. As Arthur wrestles with his own conscience and memories, Percival (here Arthur's nephew) struggles with the idea of becoming king.

Crompton, Anne Eliot (b.1930), *Merlin's Harp* (US, 1995) (f) A YA book inspired by the idea that Gildas disliked Arthur because he had robbed churches for his war-chest. Gildas takes an untypically major role in this unusual treatment. It is the tale of Niviene, a Fey, daughter of the Lady of the Lake (Nimway), sister of Lugh (Lancelot), and apprentice to Merlin, who lives on the magical island of Avalon. The strife at Camelot threatens to endanger Avalon, and Merlin uses Niviene's special talents to help save the kingdom. There are two sequels, featuring the same characters but not bound as a trilogy. *Gawain and Lady Green* (US, 1997), whilst retelling the story of Gawain and the Green Knight, explores the conflict between Druidism and Christianity. In *Percival's Angel* (1999), Percival is shown as a human raised amongst the Fey whose quest is to develop his human side as a knight. The story really explores the anguish of coming of age and the loss of innocence.

Crossley-Holland, Kevin (b.1941) *The Seeing Stone* (UK, 2001), *At the Crossing Places* (UK, 2002), *King of the Middle Marc* (UK, 2003) (h/m)
Known as a poet and folklorist, Crossley-Holland has also written a simple guide for children to the Arthurian world in *The King Who Was and Will Be* (UK, 1999). His YA Arthurian trilogy is, predictably, refreshingly different. It is set at the time of Richard I and the Crusades. The hero is a young squire, Arthur de Caldicott, anxious to become a knight. Through his friendship with Merlin, the squire acquires the "seeing stone" which enables him to view Arthur's world. The trilogy then shows the growing parallels between the squire's world and Arthur's, especially once the squire accompanies his Lord on the Crusades. Crossley-Holland neatly retells the stories of both the Dark Age Arthur and the Arthur of the romances.

Cunqueiro, Alvaro (1911–1981), *Merlin and Company* (Spain, 1955; UK, 1996, trans. Colin Smith) (m)
Set in a timeless medieval Europe, built as much from the romances as from history, it depicts Merlin and Guinevere who have "retired" to Spain to escape their past but the kings and princes of Europe still demand their services.

Davies, Andrew, *The Legend of King Arthur* (UK, 1979) (h)
The book of the TV series (*see* page 557).

Deeping, Warwick (1877–1950), *Uther and Igraine* (UK, 1903) (h)
One of Britain's most popular novelists in his day, Deeping visited the Arthurian world four times, once with the time-shift novel *The Man Who Went Back* (UK, 1940). He significantly reworked the traditional story, which unfortunately anodised some of the relationships. In *Uther and Igraine*, we learn that Uther had first met her long before their encounter as described by Geoffrey of Monmouth. Igraine is a novice nun, driven out of her abbey when it is burned to the ground. She makes her way to Winchester where she meets Uther who is at that time disguised as the wandering knight Pelleas. Uther is shown as pious and caring, unlike the man of the legend. They become involved in

the war in Wales before the climactic scenes at Tintagel. *The Man on the White Horse* (UK, 1934) is set in 367AD in the last days of Roman Britain, and though it features people with Arthurian names and anticipates a hero who will fight the barbarians it is not directly Arthurian. Similarly, although Artorius appears in *The Sword and the Cross* (UK, 1957), the main character is Gerontius.

Dickinson, Peter (b.1927) *Merlin Dreams* (UK, 1988) (f)
A YA collection of nine stories and two poems plus interlinking material that helps piece together Merlin's life. In Dickinson's version Nimue has helped Merlin to rest in an enchanted sleep and he dreams various episodes in his life including most of the key traditional Arthurian moments, set in a well-visualized Celtic world.

Ditmas, E.M.R. *Gareth of Orkney* (UK, 1956) (m)
A YA book retelling, in slightly rationalised terms, Malory's story of Gareth "Beaumains". The same author's *Tristan and Iseult in Cornwall* (UK, 1969) is a non-fiction study.

Drake, David (b.1945) *The Dragon Lord* (US, 1979; revised, 1982) (h/f)
Set in the sub-Roman period it features Arthur as the leader of a band of mercenaries fighting the Saxons. But Arthur wants to be a genuine Dragon Lord and he sets Merlin the task of raising a dragon and the means of controlling it. Arthur's companions are known by the later names, such as Gawain and Lancelot, though the background is clearly Celtic.

Duggan, Alfred (1903–1964) *Conscience of the King* (UK, 1951) (h)
One of the more unusual historical novels told from the viewpoint of the renegade half Briton-half Saxon Cerdic/Coroticus, who was the son of Eleutherius. In a single-minded drive for survival and power Cerdic kills all who cross him, except for Arthur, and survives Badon to found the kingdom of Wessex.

Edwards, Rex, *Arthur of the Britons* (UK, 1975) (h)
The book of the TV series (*see* page 553).

Erskine, John (1879–1951), *Galahad* (US, 1926) (m)
The noted author of *The Private Life of Helen of Troy* enjoyed producing thinly disguised satires transposing the life and morals of the 1920s into historical settings. *Galahad*, sub-titled "enough of his life to explain his reputation", considers the tragic life of Elaine, the equivalent of the post-war "new woman", who desired Lancelot and craved a child which, when it grew to maturity and realised it was illegitimate, spurned its parents. Well written, the novel suffers by being too close to the era it is lambasting, but will doubtless regain its reputation for later generations. Erskine repeated his experiment with *Tristan and Isolde* (US, 1932), in which the Saracen knight Palamedes finds that the renowned chivalry of Arthur's court is but a veneer. He becomes involved in the Tristan > Isolde > Mark triangle, which is further complicated by Brangain's love for him. Erskine also wrote "Seven Tales from King Arthur's Court" (*American Weekly*, 1940), a series retold direct from Malory, with some twentieth century seasoning, which was not collected in book form.

Evans, Quinn Taylor, *Dawn of Camelot* (US, 1998) (f)
Evans (real name Carla Simpson) has written a six-book series of historical romances called "Merlin's Legacy". The first three feature the daughters of Merlin who have lived for centuries and have romantic entanglements in the times of the Vikings, Normans and Crusades. The fourth book, *Shadows of Camelot* (US, 1997), concerns Merlin's son Truan who travels back in time to help defend Camelot. *Dawn of Camelot* takes place at the time of Arthur and is the story of Merlin's sister Meg who falls in love with Arthur's childhood friend Connor. Merlin and Meg work together to protect Arthur so that he can save Britain. Its direct sequel, *Daughter of Camelot* (US, 1999), is about Meg and Connor's daughter Raine. Strictly for romance fans.

Faraday, W. Bernard (1874–1953), *Pendragon* (UK, 1930; reprinted US, 2002) (h)
A first-person account by Arthur of his battle to save Britain from the Saxons. The battle accounts are so vivid and the temper of the novel so passionate that it has been suggested that Faraday was

writing out his angst of his experiences in the First World War. It culminates in the Battle of Badon, which Faraday places at Badbury Rings.

Finkel, George (1909–1975), *Twilight Province* (Australia, 1967; as *Watch Fires to the North*, US, 1968) (h)
YA novel of how Bedwyr saves Artyr and how together they organise the Romano-British resistance. An original feature is their travels to Rome to acquire Thracian cavalry horses.

Fisk, Alan (b.1950), *The Summer Stars* (UK, 1992) (h)
The autobiography of Taliesin as he travels through Dark Age Britain.

Frankland, Edward (1884–1958), *The Bear of Britain* (UK, 1944; as *Arthur the Bear of Britain*, US, 1998) (h)
The story of Arthur's twelve battles across Britain and on to Camlann. Written during the War years it reflects the struggle for survival of the British against invasion. Frankland places Badon at Liddington Castle.

French, Allen (1870–1946), *Sir Marrok* (US, 1902) (m/f)
The story of Sir Marrok who, after his return from Arthur's wars against Rome, finds his wife has betrayed him, and is turned into a werewolf. The second half of the novel was reprinted in *The Mammoth Book of Arthurian Legends*, edited by Mike Ashley (UK/US, 1998).

Friesner, Esther (b.1951), *Up the Wall* (US, 2000) (f)
A collection of mostly humorous stories including "The Death of Nimuë" and "Three Queens".

Gemmell, David (b.1948), *Ghost King* (UK, 1988) (f)
Part of Gemmell's Sipstrassi series about Stones of Power, which are fragments of meteorites that confer special powers. The first, *Wolf in Shadow* (UK, 1987), takes place in the far future but this volume is set at the end of the Roman Empire and features the Warrior Culain (based on Cú Chulainn, though also a Merlin figure), known as the Lord of the Lance, and a young Uther

Pendragon (here called Thurso), who are fighting the Germanic invaders. Uther becomes High King but with the sequel, *Last Sword of Power* (UK, 1988), Uther's soul is trapped in Hell and a new leader must be found. The other books in the series move beyond the Arthurian period. Gemmell uses the Grail and Excalibur elements from the Arthurian legend to create an inventive heroic fantasy.

Gloag, John (1896–1981), *Artorius Rex* (UK, 1977) (h)
Arthur's rise and fall is told by Caius Geladius (Kay) to the Byzantine Emperor Justinian. Caius reports that Arthur is eventually abandoned by his companions as the local kings grow in strength.

***Godwin, Parke** (b.1929), *Firelord* (US, 1980) (h)
Godwin reconstructs a complex but plausible Celtic society in which the part-Pict Arthur has the vision and pragmatism to unite the defence against the Saxons. This is one of the best Arthurian novels, with credible characters and a believable culture. The sequel, *Beloved Exile* (US, 1984), is about the struggle by Guinevere and the remaining warriors to survive and ultimately integrate into what has become an alien Britain dominated by Saxons. *The Last Rainbow* (US, 1985), though treated as part of this sequence, takes place earlier and is the story of St Patrick, though it includes a meeting with Ambrosius Aurelianus (*see also* **Hawks, Kate**).

Greeley, Andrew M. (b.1928), *The Magic Cup* (US, 1979) (h)
Greeley retells what he believes is the original Grail story from Irish legends and includes his counterparts for Arthur (Cormac MacDermot), Guenevere (Finnabair) and Merlin (Columba).

Guler, Kathleen Cunningham, *Into the Path of Gods* (US, 1998), *In the Shadow of Dragons* (US, 2001) (f)
The first two volumes in the projected four-volume YA sequence, Macsen's Treasure. Set in the fifth century, before Arthur's reign, it is the story of the Welsh spy Marcus ap Iorweth and the psychic woman Claerwen who become involved in

Myrddin's quest for Macsen's Treasure, the sacred symbols of the British High Kings.

Haar, J. T. *Koning Arthur* [*King Arthur*], (Holland, 1967; US, 1973) (m)
A YA retelling of the Arthurian story but with the fantastic elements rationalised and with Modred (here Guinevere's brother) shown as the mastermind behind Arthur's demise. Rather too short for any depth of character it is, nevertheless, a sharply delineated storyline. Haar also wrote his version of *Parcival* (Holland, 1967), which has not been translated.

Hamilton, Lord Ernest (1858–1939), *Launcelot* (UK, 1926) (m)
An almost exact retelling of the Lancelot story from Malory, including the mock-archaic English, but overlaid with the shallow mores and conventions of the 1920s. Guenevere is depicted as the villain of the story whilst Launcelot appears as easily led.

Hanratty, Peter, *The Last Knight of Albion* (US, 1986), *The Book of Mordred* (US, 1988) (f)
Best read in reverse order of publication. *The Book of Mordred* is the story of Arthur's son in his own words, depicting a well meaning but misunderstood individual who is forced onto the Grail Quest to become a man. Here the Grail is Dagda's Cauldron. The second book is set twenty years after Camlann and follows the quest by Percevale, the last surviving Round Table knight, to find Mordred, who had created the Waste Land when he destroyed Arthur's realm. Anachronistically we learn at the end that these events all take place before the Roman conquest.

Hawks, Kate (pseudonym of Parke Godwin), *The Lovers* (US, 1999) (m)
A retelling of the story of Trystan and Yseult against the backcloth of Arthur's Britain. Told from the viewpoint of Sir Gareth who here was originally an Irish peasant, Deigh mac Diarmuid, but who becomes Lord Trystan's stablemaster before achieving knighthood.

Headlee, Kim, *Dawnflight* (US, 1999) (h)
The author wanted to revise the reputation of Guenevere by portraying her as a strong-willed warrior queen. Here she is the Pictish princess Gyanhumara, betrothed to the British warlord Urien, but soon to become the lover of Arthur. The story follows their relationship through Arthur's battle campaign, starting at Aberglein in Caledonia. Although marketed as a romance this is one of the more original of recent historical re-creations.

Herbert, Kathleen, *The Lady of the Fountain* (UK, 1982) (h)
Relocates the story into Cumbria, the true territory of the traditional story's hero, Owain of Rheged. Herbert also wrote a trilogy, *Queen of the Lightning* (UK, 1983), *Ghost in the Sunlight* (UK, 1986) and *Bride of the Spear* (UK, 1988). These are set in Northumbria in the early seventh century, thus a hundred years after Arthur of Badon, but feature memories of Arthur plus many historical characters associated with Geoffrey's Arthur. The trilogy tells the stories of various warrior queens of the north.

Hollick, Helen (b.1953), *The Kingmaking* (UK, 1994), *Pendragon's Banner* (UK, 1995), *Shadow of the King* (UK, 1997) known collectively as the Pendragon's Banner trilogy (h)
Another creative attempt at an historical Arthur. Set in the mid fifth century, and following Geoffrey Ashe's theory that Arthur was Riothamus, this series explores some interesting new avenues. Hollick makes Gwenhwyfar the daughter of Cunedda, and Arthur's second wife. His first was Winifred, daughter of Vortigern, by whom Arthur was the father of Cerdic. Bedwyr, Cei, Morgause and Morgaine all feature as does, unusually, Amlawdd, here portrayed as the brother of Melwas. Although not as convincing as some other historical re-creations, this trilogy is to be admired for its efforts to be original and authentic.

Housman, Clemence (1861–1955), *The Life of Sir Aglovale de Galis* (UK, 1905; slightly revised, UK, 1954; US, 2000) (m)
The story of the oft-neglected Sir Aglovale, brother of Lamorak and Percivale. Housman was a feminist and suffragette and came from a noted literary family; her brothers were the poets A.E. and Laurence. She uses Sir Aglovale as the vehicle for her own views

on a suppressive class-riddled society which was at its worst in Edwardian England. Edith Pargeter singled out the novel as "by far the finest work on an Arthurian theme since Malory".

***Hunter, Jim** (b. 1939), *Percival and the Presence of God* (UK, 1978, US, 1997) (m)
A clever reworking of the traditional story of Percival in which he undertakes a quest not only to rediscover the Grail Castle and correct his error over the unasked question, but also to find Arthur's court, which he believes may be a myth. By this simple twist Hunter creates a strikingly original work which is both a mystical allegory and a quest for self-fulfilment. Arthurian expert Raymond H. Thompson called it "unique" in Arthurian fiction for being a Christian existential novel.

James, Cary, *King & Raven* (US, 1995) (m)
A vivid and violent portrayal of murder and revenge at Camelot. Micah is a local peasant boy who witnesses the rape and murder of his sister by four of Arthur's knights. He seeks justice from Arthur but gets none and has to flee England or be killed himself by the knights. He returns years later from France as Sir Michel de Verdeur, but revenge is no easier and he becomes part of the downfall of Camelot.

James, John, *Men Went to Catraeth* (UK, 1969) (h)
A recreation of the battle of Catraeth as per *The Gododdin* with Aneirin as the leader of the Romano-British troops.

Johnson, Barbara Ferry, *Lionors* (US, 1975) (m)
The story of the young woman who fell in love with Arthur before he married Guinevere and bore him a child, in this case a blind daughter (in Malory it was the future knight Sir Borre).

Jones, Courtway (b.1923), *In the Shadow of the Oak King* (US, 1991), *The Witch of the North* (US, 1992), *A Prince in Camelot* (US, 1995), known collectively as the Dragon's Heirs trilogy (m).
An attempt to transpose a fairly faithful interpretation of Malory's story to fifth century Britain. The result is a strange

anachronistic mixture of Celtic and Norman-French names and some unusual identities for individuals. Pelleas, for instance, who recounts events in the first volume, is the illegitimate son of Uther and Brusen, sister of the King of the Picts. Guenevere is the daughter of Rowena and Vortigern. The second volume is told by Morgan le Fay and the third by Mordred. Despite certain anomalies and inconsistencies there are some vivid portrayals of the different cultures across Britain and how they contributed to both the rise and fall of Arthur.

Jones, Mary J., *Avalon* (US, 1991) (m)
Labelled as a lesbian Arthurian romance, this is the story of Argante, the child of Gwenhafyr and either Arthur or Lancelot, who has to be rescued from Arthur's wrath and grows up in Avalon, along with other women who seek refuge there, presided over by the Lady of the Lake. Projected as the first of three volumes.

Kane, Gil and Jakes, John, *Excalibur!* (US, 1980) (m)
Although this book runs to 500 pages, that still seems insufficient to cover all of Arthur's life and to allow for character and setting. As a result it feels fast-paced, yet it is controlled and succeeds where others fail at three times the length. There are a few changes, with the emphasis on Guinevere's relationship with Lancelot, which develops before her marriage to Arthur and this simmers its way through much of the book. One of the few novels to feature Amlawdd.

Karr, Phyllis Ann (b.1944) *The Idylls of the Queen* (US, 1982) (m)
Karr is known for her dedication to the Arthurian tale and has compiled the indispensable *The Arthurian Companion* (1983; revised, 2001). In *Idylls* she treats the poisoning of Sir Patrise as a murder mystery investigated by Sir Kay in order to clear Guinevere. In more humorous vein is *The Follies of Sir Harald* (US, 2001), in which the accident-prone and villainous Sir Harald encounters one problem after another when trying to get himself out of trouble.

Keith, Chester, *Queen's Knight* (UK, 1920) (m)
Develops the standard love story between Lancelot and Guenever, who have been lovers for many years. Morgan convinces Mordred that he is the true "Pendragon" and that he should take the throne for the good of the knights, who have become lethargic and indifferent to sin. After Mordred's coup, she plans to replace him with her only son Uwaine. When her plot fails, she kills herself. Keith was the pseudonym of Imogen Woodruffe Kemp (*information courtesy of Larry Mendelsberg and James Lowder*).

Kemp, Debra A., *The Firebrand* (US, 2003) (m)
The first volume in a projected series, *The House of Pendragon.* Set after the battle of Camlann it features Arthur's daughter Lin who goes into exile with Gaheris, one of the few surviving Knights of the Round Table. She and Gaheris marry and have a child called Arthur, to whom she begins to tell her story of how she was a slave in Mordred's household.

King, J. Robert, *Mad Merlin* (US, 2000), *Lancelot du Lethe* (US, 2001), *Le Morte d'Avalon* (US, 2003) (m)
Another trilogy that attempts to bring new twists to the standard story. Merlin is the main motivator in the first volume, but he has lost his identity and discovers that his fate is linked to that of the as-yet-unborn Arthur. The second volume explores Lancelot's traditional role whilst the final and strongest volume depicts Morgan le Fay's revenge upon Arthur for the death of her father.

Kleidon, Mitzi, *Rexcalibur* and *Eternity's Hope* (both US 2001) (f).
Of minor Arthurian interest but an original idea. Camelot's life essence was fed by a magic orchid maintained by Morgan but after Arthur's death she consigned the orchid to a distant place. Camelot is now a waste land and the new king waits for the descendants of the Round Table to find Camelot so that they can set out on the quest for the magic orchid.

***Lawhead, Stephen** (b. 1950), *Taliesin* (US, 1987), *Merlin* (US, 1988), *Arthur* (US, 1989), *Pendragon* (US, 1994), *Grail* (US, 1997)
The first three books were the original Pendragon Cycle. Reworking the origins of the Grail story and earlier Celtic legends,

Lawhead creates a new Christian myth. Avallach is the last king of lost Atlantis who has escaped the destruction of his land and settled in Britain, at Glastonbury. Avallach becomes the Fisher King and his daughter Charis the Lady of the Lake. She weds Taliesin and their son is Merlin. *Merlin* begins in the reign of Magnus Maximus and follows roughly the traditional story through to the birth of Arthur. The third volume is divided into three sections. The first, from the Sword in the Stone to the acquisition of Caledvwlch, is recounted by Pelleas, Prince of Llyonesse. The second, which follows Arthur's battle campaign, is told by Bedwyr. The final part, entitled "Aneirin", about Arthur's final days after Badon (here Baedun in Scotland), is told by Gildas. Though the Atlantis angle is alien to the original legend, Lawhead skilfully blends it with Celtic tradition to create one of the more convincing modern Arthurian novels. He has since added two more novels. *Pendragon* fits between sections 2 and 3 of *Arthur* and tells of further battle campaigns, especially the "forgotten war" against the Vandals. *Grail* weaves together the Grail Quest and the relationship between Gwenhwyvar and Llenlleawg. A sixth volume, *Avalon* (US, 2001), is set in the future with a possible return of Arthur to a corrupt Britain.

Lees, Frederick, *The Arthuriad of Catumandus* (UK, 1996) (h)
Catumandus is a Briton (we later learn he is one of Arthur's illegitimate sons) who is sent by the Byzantine Emperor Anastasius as an envoy to Britain, so we read something of a travelogue across Europe before he reaches Arthur's court. En route he meets Myrddin in Rome. Catumandus remains long enough in Britain to witness Arthur's downfall. All the usual characters appear and the story benefits from providing an outsider's view.

Lehmann, Ruth Preston (1912–2000), *Blessed Bastard* (US, 1997) (m)
An academic renowned for her knowledge of medieval Irish and Anglo-Saxon cultures, Lehmann has explored the character of Galahad, and how he might have been had he lived at the time of the historical Arthur. The book is as much psychological and spiritual as it is historical and provides some interesting twentieth-century insights on poor parenting.

***Lindsay, Philip** (1906–1958), *The Little Wench* (UK, 1935) (m)
Lindsay had set out to explore how love was the downfall of Arthur's kingdom. In his informative "Dedication", Lindsay tells us that he had planned to include much more, including elements of the Tristan and Iseult story, but instead he concentrated on Lancelot and Guinevere (the "little wench" of the title). The book is consciously set in the twelfth century and is a rich tapestry of the Arthurian court. It follows Malory with only minor changes and concludes with Lancelot and Guinevere's final meeting after Camlann. One of the best "modern" Arthurian romances.

McCaffrey, Anne, *Black Horses for the King* (US, 1996) (h)
Set in the years just before the first of Arthur's battles when a young Romano-Briton, Galwyn, flees from his uncle and joins the army of Lord Artos. McCaffrey used to breed horses in Ireland and the emphasis is on the role of the cavalry in Arthur's success.

McCormack, Patrick, *The Last Companion* (UK, 1997), *The White Phantom* (UK, 2000), *The Lame Dancer* (UK, due 2007), in the series "Albion" (h)
Set ten years after Camlann and narrated by one of the last survivors, Bedwyr, now called Budoc. In the first volume Budoc and a few companions try and keep safe the magic chalice, whilst in the second Budoc goes in search of Gwenhyfar. In the final volume, McCormack brings the Celtic and Saxon threads together in the conflict between Bedwyr and Cerdic. McCormack is brutally realistic about the period, at times almost too dark, developing a brooding atmosphere of gloom and despair, but with convincing historical detail.

McDowell, Ian (b.1958), *Mordred's Curse* (US, 1996), *Merlin's Gift* (US, 1997) (h)
Arthur's story through the embittered eyes of Mordred from the time he was first aware of Arthur as his uncle, when he glorified him, through his hatred for him and the final battle. Apart from Gawain no one is drawn in a good light, though

Mordred obviously perceives himself in a better light than others. Merlin is psychotic, Guinevere deceitful (she becomes Mordred's lover), Arthur overly pious and a better leader than a warrior. Powerfully written, but not for those who like their heroes unsullied.

McKenzie, Nancy, *The Child Queen* (US, 1994), *The High Queen* (US, 1995), both combined as *Queen of Camelot* (US, 2002) (h)
Inspired by Mary Stewart's work, McKenzie wanted to rediscover Guinevere in her true fifth century setting. It tells her life from childhood. The first book follows the traditional story of her love for Lancelot. The second book is more original. Realizing that she is barren Guinevere does what she can to raise Mordred, though with the same consequences as in the story we all know – Mordred rebels against his father. The characters are well drawn if somewhat idealized. The story ends with Guinevere's hope in Galahad. His story is told in *Grail Prince* (US, 2002), in which he determines to find the ancient treasures that will restore Britain to health, a quest he undertakes with Percival.

McKenzie, Nancy, *Prince of Dreams* (US, 2003) (h)
This retells the story of Tristan and Essylte, set in the years after Arthur's death when Merkion has become the High King.

Mallory, James, *The Old Magic* (US, 1999), *The King's Wizard* (US, 1999), *The End of Magic* (US, 2000) (m)
Based on the TV mini-series (*see* page 558).

Marshall, Edison (1894–1967), *The Pagan King* (US, 1959) (h)
Told by Arthur himself, who creates his own legend. Born Ambrosius, Arthur discovers that his father is Vortigern and that Modred is his half-brother, the real heir to the throne. In his youth Arthur sets off in travels across the wild countryside, which turns out to be a journey of both external and internal discovery till, as the victor of Badon, he becomes first King of Cambria and subsequently High King. But he later abdicates and journeys as a bard. He reconciles himself with Modred who is seen here as honourable. Despite, or because of, his significant

changes to the traditional story, Marshall creates a convincing if melancholic tale.

Massie, Allan (b.1938), *Arthur the King* (UK, 2003)
The second volume in what purports to be a lost history by the thirteenth century mage Michael Scott. The first, *The Evening of the World* (UK, 2001), has the Roman Marcus wandering across Europe during the days of the barbarian invasions, eventually reaching Britain. This second volume is surprisingly conventional, though the emphasis is placed on the machinations of Merlin and Morgan. It ends with Arthur's death.

Meaney, Dee Morrison, *Iseult: Dreams That are Done* (US, 1985) (m)
A retelling of the traditional story but from Iseult's viewpoint. Noble and idealistic, the lovers agree that, rather than hurt Mark, Tristan should go.

Middleton, Haydn (b.1955), *The King's Evil* (UK, 1995), *The Queen's Captive* (UK, 1996), *The Knight's Vengeance* (UK, 1997) known collectively as the Mordred Cycle (h)
Middleton's work is known for his ability to weave together reality and myth until they become indistinguishable and the Mordred Cycle is no exception. Here history becomes myth and vice versa, to the point where neither the reader nor the main characters can be totally sure of reality. Here, Arthur is murdered by Mordred at the end of the first book in revenge for having cast him (and all the other babies) adrift. Mordred returns to the sea and is rescued by Morgan, and their child is the new Arthur who will restore Logres. The third book tells some of the Arthurian story as we know it, but it is Mordred who is the eventual saviour. In turning the legend on its head, Middleton imbues it with a new meaning though one that he makes hard to swallow because it is couched in disturbing visions and language.

Miles, Rosalind (b.1943), *Guenevere: Queen of the Summer Country* (UK, 1999), *The Knight of the Sacred Lake* (UK, 2000), *The Child of the Holy Grail* (UK, 2001) (m)

The traditional Arthurian story told primarily from Guenevere's viewpoint. She is shown as a strong queen in her own right and the uniting of her lands with Arthur's brings about a powerful kingdom. Miles, known for her books set in the Elizabethan period, brings that same scheming Tudor mindset to develop various plots and counterplots by Guenevere, Merlin, Morgan, Agravain (who for once has a strong role) and Mordred, both in terms of personal gain and religious conflict, which gives the trilogy a recognisable reality.

Miles, Rosalind (b.1943), *Isolde, Queen of the Western Isle* (UK, 2002), *The Maid of the White Hands* (UK, 2003), *The Lady of the Sea* (UK, 2004) (h)
This trilogy explores the Tristan story and has arguably the strongest depiction of both Isolde and her Breton namesake in any modern treatment. Once again Miles brings her Elizabethan understanding to allow a deeper and less sentimental interpretation of this legend than usual.

Mitchison, Naomi (1897–1999), *To the Chapel Perilous* (UK, 1955) (m)
An Arthurian parody which retells the key events as if reported by newspaper journalists of the day. Mitchison uses the Arthurian motifs to satirize the growing popular journalism of the 1950s, but in so doing offers new insights on how the Arthurian story is perceived and can be interpreted.

Monaco, Richard (b.1940), *Parsival or a Knight's Tale* (US, 1977), *The Grail War* (US, 1979), *The Final Quest* (US, 1980), *Blood and Dreams* (US, 1985) (m)
The Grail Quest written with an awareness of the twentieth century's experience of war, especially the Second World War and Vietnam. Monaco has been criticized for the violence in the books, which he correctly defends as being present in the original, though the attitudes of Monaco's knights, especially Parsival's, are decidedly twentieth century. Parsival's inner anguish arises from his innate innocence being lost in a violent world and a struggle to recover that innocence. His difficulty in coping is contrasted with Gawain's natural, even cynical, approach to

survival. Monaco's books emphasise the hopelessness and despair of a violent world. Not for the squeamish.

Monaco, Richard (b.1940), *Runes* (US, 1984), *Broken Stone* (US, 1985) (f)
Monaco takes the Arthurian period back to the days of the early Roman empire, with Arthur being descended from Spartacus. Planned as one book, the second "half" is the more overtly Arthurian, but then promised a series which Monaco has chosen not to continue.

Moore, George (1852–1933), *Peronnik the Fool* (UK, 1921) (m)
A reworking of the Perceval story but drawn primarily from the French fairy tale in which an illiterate cowherd breaks his village's drought by his successful quest to Grey Castle. Moore's version is coloured by the loss of innocence following the Great War.

Munn, H. Warner (1903–1982), *King of the World's Edge* (US, 1939, 1966), *The Ship from Atlantis* (US, 1967), these two combined as *Merlin's Godson* (US, 1976), *Merlin's Ring* (US, 1974) (f)
Taking place after Camlann, this is a report by the Roman centurion Ventidius Varro (who had served in Arthur's army) to Rome about his subsequent adventures with his son Gwalchmai, and Myrdhinn, with the Aztecs. The story continues with the return of Gwalchmai, who finds himself trapped in Atlantis.

Newman, Robert, *Merlin's Mistake* (US, 1970), *The Testing of Tertius* (US, 1974) (f)
Two connected YA novels. In the first, two young knights accompany Tertius to help him find Merlin and reverse a spell placed on Tertius which gave him future sight. In the second, they become involved in a dark plot to destroy Britain, and have to rescue Merlin.

***Newman, Sharan** (b.1949), *Guinevere* (US, 1981), *The Chessboard Queen* (US, 1983), *Guinevere Evermore* (US, 1985) (f)
Newman was the first to write the Arthurian story from Guinevere's viewpoint. *Guinevere* tells of the future queen's childhood

and of the conflict between her Christian upbringing in a Romano-British family and the pagan beliefs of her nurse and of her mother's cousin Merlin. Merlin dislikes Guinevere and disapproves of her association with Arthur. The pagan aspect of Guinevere's beliefs is rendered physical in the form of the unicorn, which she is able to command and which becomes her "other self", though it fades as childhood innocence is lost. Guinevere's spiritual growth is represented by the character of Geraldus (the one anachronistic character in the novels) who serves as a form of inner conscience to Guinevere. The second book shows how Guinevere, now married to Arthur, is able to direct actions and exert her power if not her authority. The final volume follows her love affair with Lancelot and her fall from grace. Newman succeeds in portraying the gradual vanishing of the old pagan world and the emergence of the new, with Arthur as the lynchpin. Guinevere is torn between the two cultures just as she is torn between two loves.

Newport, Cris, *Queen's Champion* (UK, 1998) (f)
The Lancelot story retold from his viewpoint. The emphasis is on Lancelot's relationship with Guinevere. The main difference is the gay and lesbian element.

Norman, Elizabeth, *Silver, Jewels and Jade* (US, 1980) (f)
Of minor Arthurian interest. The story of Igraine before her life with Uther.

Nye, Robert (b.1939), *Merlin* (UK, 1978) (f)
Nye reminds us that Merlin was the spawn of an incubus and a virgin but that the devil's efforts to create an antichrist were thwarted when Merlin was christened. Throughout this book, called an "adult fairy tale", we have at the heart a story of the demon in us all. Nye's text serves to remind us just how much corruption, betrayal and infidelity there is in the Arthurian story. Previously Nye told the story of Taliesin in *Taliesin* (UK, 1966).

O'Meara, Walter (1897–1989), *The Duke of War* (US, 1966) (h)
A detailed account, as told by a young Romano-British girl, of Arthur's battle campaign at Badon against Aelle. Despite the

well-researched historical setting the usual core of Arthur's knights are present, including Lancelot. O'Meara places Badon at Liddington Castle.

Paterson, Katherine, *Parzival* (UK, 1998) (f)
Wolfram's *Parzival* retold for a YA readership.

***Paxson, Diana L.** (b.1943), *The Book of the Sword, The Book of the Spear, The Book of the Cauldron* (all US, 1999), *The Book of the Stone* (US, 2000) collectively called "The Hallowed Isle" (h/f)
The first work to draw upon the Sarmatian theory of the origin of some of the Arthurian legends, particularly that of Excalibur. Paxson fuses this with Celtic myth to produce an original sequence of stories which traces events from the end of Roman power (424) to Arthur's downfall (515). Paxson succeeds in retaining much of the original storyline but blends it with new ideas and characterisations to create a refreshingly original work. The second book has a unique portrayal of the Saxon Oesc. Paxson had earlier written a version of the Tristan story as seen through the eyes of Branwen in *The White Raven* (1988), and has continued Marion Bradley's Avalon series.

Peare, Catherine Owens, *Melor, King Arthur's Page* (US, 1963) (m)
A YA book that follows the misadventures of young Melor until he saves Arthur's life from the boar Troynt. A rare treatment of the Twrch Trwyth legend.

Phelan, Laurel, *Guinevere* (US, 1996) (h)
Purports to be the true story of Guinevere as discovered by the author under regression hypnosis. Since this is set in Celtic times but includes her affair with Lancelot we can classify it firmly under fiction. Another book of supposedly remembered Arthurian lives is *Camelot, the True Story* by Michael D. Miller (US, 1997).

Powys, John Cowper (1872–1963), *Porius* (UK, 1951) (h)
At least seven years in the writing and influenced by the imagery of the Second World War, this dense, brooding novel traces the

events of just one week in 499AD, when the Romano-Briton Porius must pull himself away from his family and the suspicious bigotry of his village and, under the influence of the anarchic Myrddin, join the army of Arthur. Ironically there is less of Arthur himself in this work than there is in the allegorical *A Glastonbury Romance* (UK, 1932), which has a contemporary setting.

Renzulli, Virgil, *Caliburn* (US, 2001) (f)
A short novel which focuses on the choice of an uncertain Arthur as king and events around the episode of the Sword in the Stone. It seeks to reveal the real story behind the legend.

Rice, Robert, *The Last Pendragon* (US, 1992) (h)
Marketed as a YA novel, this should be of wider interest. Bedwyr hid Caliburn rather than throw it into the lake and eleven years later he returns to Britain to seek the sword. He meets Medraut's son Irion, who looks just like Arthur. Irion urges Bedwyr to help in the fight against the Saxons but Bedwyr refuses, single mindedly seeking Caliburn while Irion tries to fight the cause.

Roberts, Dorothy James (1903–1990), *Launcelot, My Brother* (US, 1954), *Kinsmen of the Grail* (US, 1963) (m)
Two novels drawn from Malory. The first is the first-person account by Bors of Lancelot's life at Camelot, his Grail quest, his affair with Guinevere and the downfall of the Round Table. The second follows the Grail Quests by Gawain and Perceval. Both books provide a polished insight into the Arthurian world. Roberts had earlier written a similarly fine novel of the Tristram story, *The Enchanted Cup* (US, 1953), sympathetic whilst uncluttered.

Roberts, Theodore Goodridge (1877–1953), *The Merriest Knight* (US, 2001) (m)
This contains all the Arthurian stories written by Roberts for *Blue Book* between 1947 and 1951 plus the previously unpublished "Quest's End". Most of the stories fit into Roberts's humorous reconstruction of the adventures of the ever-cautious Sir Dinadan based on Malory. Also included is a related sequence of stories featuring the young knight Dennys ap Rhys and his

adventures with King Torrice. Witty and sophisticated, these provide a satirical glance at Camelot.

Robin, Harry, *I, Morgain* (US, 1995) (f)
Morgain looks back over her life and her attempts at revenge upon Arthur, the child of her mother's rape. Robin explores no new territory but provides a chilling image of Morgain, who seduces Arthur and bears him Mordred.

Rosen, Winifred, *Three Romances* (US, 1981) (m)
Rosen undertakes a modern interpretation of three different Arthurian romances, those of Gawain and Ragnell, Enid and Geraint, and Merlin and Niniane.

***Sampson, Fay** (b.1935), *Wise Woman's Telling* (UK, 1989), *White Nun's Telling* (UK, 1989), *Black Smith's Telling* (UK, 1990), *Taliesin's Telling* (UK, 1991), *Herself* (UK, 1992), all five combined in one volume as *Daughter of Tintagel* (1992; revised, US, 2004) (h)
This is the longest sustained work focusing on Morgan le Fay. Each volume provides a different viewpoint as her life progresses. We see her childhood through her nurse when she tries to kill the infant Arthur; we see her adolescence via the nuns at the remote convent where Morgan is banished; we see her early marriage to Urien via the smith who forges the special sword and scabbard; Taliesen reveals her later life as Modred grows to manhood; and finally Morgan looks back and tells her own story, and receives Arthur after Camlann. Based primarily on Malory but drawing on a wide variety of other early texts.

Seare, Nicholas, *Rude Tales and Glorious* (US, 1983) (m)
A minor item though, like Nye, it highlights the potential for immorality at Arthur's court. Two vagabonds (one of whom is revealed to be Lancelot) gain shelter by telling bawdy stories about Arthur and his knights.

Sharpe, Ruth Collier, *Tristram of Lyonesse* (US, 1949) (m)
A now dated and rather anachronistic retelling of the Tristram story.

***Shwartz, Susan** (b.1949), *The Grail of Hearts* (US, 1992) (f)
Drawing her inspiration from the various Grail romances but also inspired by the interpretation of Wagner, Shwartz explores the stories of Kundry, cursed because she laughed at the Crucifixion, and the sorcerer Klingsor who is endeavouring to gain the Grail. First Merlin and then the Grail knights are introduced after half way and then cautiously. This is a refreshingly different treatment that allows you to consider the Grail story from the inside out.

Springer, Nancy (b.1948), *I am Mordred* (US, 1998) (f)
A YA novel that concentrates on Mordred as a teenager. Told by him, this is the story of his anguish at knowing his fate, desperately torn between loving and hating his father. Mordred is painted as a sensitive, intelligent but severely troubled boy wrestling with destiny.

***Stewart, Mary** (b.1916), *The Crystal Cave* (UK, 1970), *The Hollow Hills* (UK, 1973), *The Last Enchantment* (UK, 1979), *The Wicked Day* (UK, 1983), the first three available in a single volume as *Merlin Trilogy* (US, 1980) (h)
The archetypal modern treatment that regenerated the interest in the potential for Arthurian fiction as a medium to explore beyond the traditional images. It remains one of the best interpretations. Merlin recounts his life. The first volume, drawn primarily from Geoffrey's *History*, tells of his childhood as the bastard son of Niniane, where he discovers he has second sight and uses this talent to help fulfil destiny. It ends with the birth of Arthur. *The Hollow Hills* (the first modern Arthurian novel to top both the US and UK bestseller lists) deals with Arthur's childhood, Merlin's quest for the Sword of Power, and ends with the Sword in the Stone. *The Last Enchantment* covers Arthur's battle campaign, Guinevere's abduction by Melwas (and rescue by Bedwyr, who becomes Guinevere's lover, rather than Lancelot, as in Sutcliff) and Merlin's final days as he tutors his successor Nimuë. *The Wicked Day* is the story of Mordred, portrayed here as another victim of destiny rather than as a villain. Although written as taking place in the Dark Ages (and Stewart provides useful notes to the appendix of each volume), the stories read with the mood of Malory.

Stewart wrote one other Arthurian novel, *The Prince and the Pilgrim* (UK, 1995), her milder form of a Grail Quest, but here focused on a Frankish fugitive (who may have the Holy Grail) and a prince seeking revenge for his murdered father who has been ensnared by Morgan le Fay.

Stone, Eugenia (1879–1971), *Page Boy for King Arthur* (US, 1949), *Squire for King Arthur* (US, 1955) (f)
Two YA novels about the peasant boy Tor who in the first rescues Lancelot and becomes Galahad's page and, in the second rescues Pellinore's son and becomes Pellinore's squire.

***Sutcliff, Rosemary** (1920–1992), *The Lantern Bearers* (UK, 1959), *Sword at Sunset* (US, 1963) (h)
These were Sutcliff's first Arthurian works, both seeking to fit the story into an historical context. Both have been reprinted as YA books though *Sword at Sunset* is more adult in treatment than her other interpretations. The first book deals with the departure of the Romans and the resultant struggle between Vortigern and Ambrosius. The young Artos appears towards the end. The story is told by Aquila, a Romano-British decurion who remains behind and joins Ambrosius's (and later Artos's) forces. He reappears in *Sword at Sunset*, though this is told in the first person by Arthur and is his memories from when he received the Sword of Maximus from Ambrosius till his final hours. Sutcliff remains faithful to the Celtic Arthur, so that Gwalchmai, Cei, Cador and Bedwyr are his primary companions, and it is Bedwyr who becomes Guinevere's lover. Arthur's major opponent is Cerdic. These two novels remain the best starting point for anyone wanting to read the story of the historical Arthur.

Sutcliff, Rosemary (1920–1992), *The Sword and the Circle* (UK, 1981), *The Light Beyond the Forest* (UK, 1979), *The Road to Camlann* (UK, 1981) (m)
These are a more traditional treatment for a YA readership, based primarily on Malory but incorporating Gawain and the Green Knight and Gawain and the Loathly Lady in the first book, which ends with the arrival of Percival. The second volume, written first, covers the Grail Quest and is by far the best and

most straightforward rendition of the story for any new reader. The third volume follows the *Mort Artu*, and includes Guinevere's abduction by Meleagaunce.

Sutcliff has written two other YA books of this period. *Tristan and Iseult* (UK, 1971) is a simple retelling of the basic story. *The Shining Company* (UK, 1990) is a retelling of *Y Gododdin*, about the Battle of Catraeth, set at least two generations after Arthur.

Taylor, Anna, *Drustan the Wanderer* (UK, 1971) (h)
A historical re-creation of Drustan and Essylt which may be more realistic but loses much of the glamour of the original.

Taylor, Keith (b.1946), *Bard* (US, 1981) (f)
The first in a series about Felimid, a wandering Irish bard whose harp has magical qualities. Felimid had fought for Artorius at Badon but thereafter the series follows his travels and occasional encounters with other Arthurian characters.

Telep, Peter, *Squire* (US, 1995), *Squire's Blood* (US, 1995) and *Squire's Honor* (US, 1996) (m)
A YA trilogy about young Christopher of Shores, a saddlemaker's son who aspires to knighthood. After a series of adventures he becomes Arthur's squire, but finds he has to refuse the knighthood he so wants because he had once fought briefly for the Saxons. The second volume is the best, where Telep follows the original idea of a character trying to unite the Britons and the Saxons whilst still protecting his lordship's kingdom. The final volume finds Christopher, dishonoured and accused of murder, trying to prove his innocence.

Timlett, Peter Valentine (b.1933), *Merlin and the Sword of Avalon* (UK, 2003) (f)
Drawing from all the romances, especially Robert de Boron, the Vulgate and Malory, this is the complete story of Merlin seen through the eyes of an occultist.

Tolstoy, Nikolai (b.1935), *The Coming of the King* (UK, 1988) (h)
The first in a still-to-be completed trilogy about Merlin, here the historical Myrddin who lived a century after Arthur of Badon.

Tolstoy, who has written a study of Merlin, *The Quest for Merlin* (UK, 1985), is rigorous in his authentic detail about Myrddin, but allows himself the latitude of developing more mystical means of linking Myrddin's life to other heroes and gods of legend. Arthur, long dead, does not appear in the book though Tolstoy plans to incorporate him retrospectively in the second volume.

Tranter, Nigel (1909–2000), *Druid Sacrifice* (UK, 1993) (h)
This is the story of Thanea and her son Mungo (St Kentigern) set in the second quarter of the sixth century. Tranter has followed one pedigree that makes Thanea the daughter of Loth and thereby sister of Gawain and niece of Arthur. The Arthurian element surfaces in the third section, which considers Mordred's rebellion (Mordred is shown as a pagan Pict rising up against the Christian Arthur) whilst Lancelot, who was king of Northumbria but who had been ousted by Ida of the Angles, is caught between the two factions. This section follows through to Arthur's death at Camlann (here at Camboglanna) when Arthur is succeeded by the aged Urien of Rheged.

***Treece, Henry** (1912–1966), *The Great Captains* (UK, 1956), *The Green Man* (UK, 1966) (h)
These may be seen as companion volumes telling different aspects of the same story. The first is the story of Arthur told in the context of a violent struggle for power and survival in a battle-torn Britain, drawing its background from Gildas. At the start, an ageing Ambrosius has care of his ward Medrodus, whom he has raised in the Roman way and expects to succeed him as Count of Britain. In the struggles that follow, the barbarian Artos is elected Battle Leader by the kings Vortipor, Cuneglassus and Caninus, leading to the inevitable rivalry with Medrodus, now renamed Medrawt. *The Green Man* is, unusually, the story of Hamlet/Amleth and thus the only novel which focuses on the shadowy character of Amlawdd. Arthur's world features as one of the trio of cultures that Amleth encounters. Bedwyr, Cei and Medrawt are Arthur's main companions. Treece also wrote the YA book *The Eagles Have Flown* (UK, 1954) which describes Arthur's battle campaign through

the eyes of two boys. Though less violent, it still depicts the harshness of the period.

Turner, Roy, *King of the Lordless Country* (UK, 1971) (h)
A less than convincing historical reconstruction in which Arthur rises to power within the Circle, a warrior band under the leadership of Gwenhwyfar. The story takes us to the battle of Badon.

Turton, Godfrey E., *The Emperor Arthur* (US, 1967) (h)
Retells the standard historical story within the context of a clash between the Roman church and paganism. Merlin is a pagan priest in league with the Saxons whilst the Church is wary of Arthur's power. The main characters however, perhaps because of the shortcomings of the narrator, Pelleas, seem amazingly naïve and rather impotent at controlling events.

Vance, Jack (b.1916), *Lyonesse* series with respective volumes subtitled *Suldrun's Garden* (US, 1983), *The Green Pearl* (1985), *Madouc* (US, 1989) (f)
These exotic and loquacious fantasies by Vance are more in the vogue of Lord Dunsany and really bear little relevance to the traditional Arthur. In effect Vance has created the legend of Lyonesse upon which Camelot was modelled. The stories are set two or three generations before Arthur in what became the mythical Elder Isles, and contain many Arthurian allusions including the prototype Round Table and less-than-holy Grail Quest.

Vansittart, Peter, *Lancelot* (UK, 1978) (h)
Lancelot tells his story from his childhood in late Roman Britain, his service under Ambrosius, his affair with Gwenhever and his association with the unpredictable Artorius. Lancelot is portrayed as an uncertain, questioning man challenging if accepting the role of Artorius. Along with *Parsifal* (UK, 1988), in which Vansittart's questing hero lives through two millennia, both works serve as a platform from which to consider one's identity and place within society.

Viney, Jayne, *The Bright-Helmed One* (UK, 1975) (h)
A multi-perspective view of Arthur, from one of his warriors, from his wife Winifrith and from Cei, the final part being the most successful in delineating Arthur's decline. Arthur comes across as remote, perhaps the inevitable fate of such a demanding destiny.

Wein, Elizabeth, *The Winter Prince* (US, 1993) (f)
A YA novel which explores the character and tempers of Medraut who, because he is illegitimate, is denied the succession, which goes to his half-brother Lleu. We find Medraut's jealousy drawing him to his enchantress mother Morgause, though he struggles with his conscience over which path he should choose. A fascinating exploration of dilemma and loyalty. The two sequels, *A Coalition of Lions* (US, 2003) and *The Sunbird* (US, 2003), follow Medraut's half-sister Goewin after Camlann, to Aksum (Ethiopia) where her cousin Constantine is Viceroy. Also there is Medraut's son Telemakos.

***White, T.H.** (1905–1964), *The Sword in the Stone* (UK, 1938), *The Witch in the Wood* (UK, 1939), *The Ill-Made Knight* (UK, 1940), later issued together with "The Candle in the Wind" as *The Once and Future King* (UK, 1958), *The Book of Merlyn* (US, 1977) (f)
Probably the best known Arthurian fiction, though it may be better known because of the animated film adaptation from *The Sword in the Stone*, a section of the book not representative of the whole. In the first Merlyn raises Arthur and we learn much through his education on the nature of the world about him, which has a timeless quality. It is light-hearted, with Merlyn a figure of fun, and does not prepare you for the second section, retitled "Queen of Air and Darkness" in the omnibus volume. Arthur fights his battles against his rebel kings whilst Morgause works her wiles, seducing Arthur. In the third section the characters shift towards the grotesque and we meet Lancelot, who is ugly and uncertain and as much a victim as everyone else. The final section replicates the *Mort Artu* but with the significant change that Arthur tries to replace feudality and knighthood with a form of government, a change that would happen to Malory's

world after his death – Malory even features in the book as Arthur's page. White was almost certainly reflecting upon the changing World Order as a result of the Second World War, a view that became even more evident in *The Book of Merlyn*, which the original publisher rejected, but which in tune with the times projected the helplessness of mankind to control themselves, a concept which is in accord with much of the Arthurian legend though oddly incongruous with White's original treatment. As a result, White's overall Arthuriad is inconsistent and anomalous, but by that very nature highlights the ambiguity of the Arthurian world.

Whyte, Jack (b.1943), *The Skystone* (Canada, 1992), *The Singing Sword* (Canada, 1993), *The Eagle's Brood* (Canada, 1994), *The Saxon Shore* (Canada, 1995), *The Fort at River's Bend* (Canada, 1997), *The Sorcerer: Metamorphosis* (Canada, 1997), *Uther* (US, 2001), *The Lance Thrower* (US, 2004), known collectively as "The Camulod Chronicles" (h)
This has now become the longest of all Arthurian narratives, although Whyte's original plan finished with Book 6. The original concept followed a vision from the time when a Roman officer and swordsmith, Publius Varro (who narrates the first two volumes), discovers the meteor, the Skystone out of which he forges the sword Excalibur, to the culmination of his hopes over a century later when Arthur Riothamus becomes High King. Varro established a Colony, called Camulod, which provided a central control to help protect the British after the departure of the Romans. With *The Eagle's Brood* the narrator becomes Varro's great nephew Merlyn, or Caius Merlyn Britannicus, cousin of Uther Pendragon, who continues Varro's grand plan. After Uther's death Merlyn becomes the protector of his infant son Arthur. It was Whyte's intention to stop with the crowning of Arthur, as he believed all that followed had been told. He has added one book, *Uther*, which relates events that run parallel with *The Eagle's Brood*, with two more volumes covering the role of Lancelot. Despite the detail of Whyte's grand scheme and the ingenuity of its development, some of the names he uses for new characters, such as Peter Ironhair and Derek of Ravenglass, jar with the Celtic and Roman names and spoil the overall effect.

Wolf, Joan, *The Road to Avalon* (US, 1988) (h)
A historical romance which explores the many relationships in Arthur's life and court but concentrates on his passion for Morgan, who here is treated as his aunt. There is no Lancelot in this version and Bedwyr is Gwenhwyfar's lover, as in Stewart's novels. Unusually, this book does have Merlin die (of a seizure) and we even witness his burial.

Woolley, Persia, *Child of the Northern Spring* (US, 1987), *Queen of the Summer Stars* (US, 1990), *The Legend in Autumn* (US, 1991) (m)
The story of Guinevere, drawn primarily from Malory. It follows the traditional story, although Guinevere is shown as a Princess of Rheged. Despite a Dark Age setting Woolley uses the standard form of names such as Bedivere, Lancelot and Tristan. The trilogy does not strike sufficiently new territory to make it memorable although the characters are well drawn and believable. Loosely adapted into the film *Guinevere* (1994).

Yolen, Jane (b.1939), The Young Merlin Trilogy, *Passager* (US, 1996), *Hobby* (US, 1996), *Merlin* (US, 1997) (m)
A YA trilogy which takes us through Merlin's childhood from age 8 to 12. There is little of the traditional tale of Merlin's origins here. He is abandoned in the woods at age 8, and adopted by a falconer who names him Merlin. His new family are killed in a fire which Merlin had dreamed and he discovers the prophetic nature of his dreams. He joins a travelling magic show which reaches Carmarthen where the story crosses with the legend of Vortigern and Ambrosius. Wandering again in the third book he encounters the wild folk of the woods and befriends a child called Cub, but whom Merlin calls Artus. Earlier Yolen had written *The Dragon's Boy* (US, 1990), which covers Artos's early teens, when he was fostered by Sir Ector. At a different level Yolen wrote a collection of memories and tales about Merlin, *Merlin's Booke* (US, 1986), which cast an idiosyncratic eye over his life.

Yolen, Jane (b.1939), *Sword of the Rightful King* (US, 2003) (f)
A YA novel and Yolen's variant version of the legend. Arthur's reign gets off to a less than auspicious start when someone else

pulls the sword from the stone. Yolen explores the close rivalry and affection between Arthur and Gawaine, whose mother Morgause plans to secure his future as king. Although all the characters and set scenes are present, they are all slightly askew so that nothing remains certain or predictable. Even Kay is likable.

Zettel, Sarah, *Sword of the Rightful King* (US, 2003) (f)
A forgotten episode in Gawain's career where he becomes the protector of the young woman Risa who is escaping from an evil sorcerer.

22

VISIONS OF CAMELOT – ARTHURIAN CINEMA

The number of Arthurian films grows steadily year by year, yet most continue to focus on a small range of subjects. They have either been routine costume dramas, concentrating on the love affair between Guinevere and Lancelot, usually alongside the treachery of Mordred, or they explore the Wagnerian world of Parsifal or the love affair of Tristan and Isolde. The alternative are the time-shift films, mostly based upon Mark Twain's *A Connecticut Yankee in King Arthur's Court*, which has been filmed at least ten times since the first in 1920, including the best known Bing Crosby version in 1949, listed below, plus other variants such as *Arthur the King* (1985), few of which have any merit.

The earliest surviving Arthurian film was an attempt to film Wagner's *Parsifal* in 1904. It was a brave effort, according to Kevin J. Harty, the authority on Arthurian films, but not entirely successful. *Parsifal* has been filmed at least five times, and in recent years it has become easy to acquire DVDs of fully staged productions. Tristan and Isolde was the subject of the next film, in 1909, produced in France and directed by Albert Capellani. Two other versions were produced in 1911 and 1920. Also, in 1909, Charles Kent produced the first film based on Tennyson's *Idylls*, *Launcelot and Elaine*, utilizing the subject that had so captivated artists over the previous few decades.

The first film to be based on Malory's work or possible elements of the Vulgate Cycle may well have been an Italian production, *Il Re Artù e I cavalieri della tavola rotonda*, directed by Giuseppe de Liguoro in 1910, but it seems that no print of the film survives. Other films of that decade, such as *Sir Galahad of Twilight* (1914) or *The Grail* (1915), used Arthurian imagery in contemporary settings, whilst Edison's *The Knights of the Square Table* (1917), uses the Arthurian concept to promote the Boy Scout movement.

The numerous versions of *Connecticut Yankee* kept the Arthurian wheel turning for the next thirty years and, apart from a Saturday-morning pictures serial, *The Adventures of Sir Galahad* in 1950, the first serious attempt to adapt the Arthurian legend did not come until MGM's major Cinemascope costume drama *The Knights of the Round Table* in 1953. This ushered in the era of the Arthurian swashbuckler, with *Prince Valiant* (1953) and *The Black Knight* (1954) and the British TV series *The Adventures of Sir Lancelot* (1956). However, apart from Cornel Wilde's *Lancelot and Guinevere* (1963), few of these films use the depth of the Arthurian story, preferring to use the basic imagery and superficial plot to present a standard medieval adventure film. It was not until the French *Perceval le gallois*, directed by Eric Rohmer in 1978, and the British *Excalibur*, from John Boorman in 1981, that two films appeared that treated their subject seriously and attentively.

The number of quality Arthurian films is still in the minority, but with more sophisticated techniques and more demanding audiences the definitive version may not be far away. Anyone interested in a more detailed study of Arthurian cinema should consult *King Arthur on Film* by Kevin J. Harty (McFarland, 1999), revised as *Cinema Arthuriana* (McFarland, 2002), and *Arthurian Legends on Film and Television* by Bert Olton (McFarland, 2000), which provides a detailed analysis of each film and TV episode. Harty's checklist of films is also on the Camelot website as <www.lib.rochester.edu/camelot/acpbibs/harty.htm>

The following lists all major Arthurian films and TV series from 1949 to date. As with the books it includes only those films set in an historical or chivalric Arthurian world and not in the modern day. The films are listed in alphabetical order of title. All films are in colour unless identified as black-and-white (b&w). Running time is given in minutes (m).

Adventures of Sir Galahad, The (Columbia, 1950, serial, 252m (15 episodes), b&w)
Director: Spencer Gordon Bennet. Screenplay: David Mathews, Lewis Clay, George H. Plympton.
Starring: George Reeves (Galahad), Nelson Leigh (Arthur), William Fawcett (Merlin), Charles King (Bors), Hugh Prosser (Lancelot), Jim Diehl (Kay), Marjorie Stapp (Guinevere), Pat Barton (Morgan), Leonard Penn (Modred).
A Saturday-morning serial with Galahad trying to find the lost Excalibur against a background of Saxon invasion.

Adventures of Sir Lancelot, The (UK TV series, Sapphire Films, 1956/7, 2 seasons, 30x30m episodes, first season b&w)
Directors: various, mostly Lawrence Huntington, Peter Maxwell. Writers: various, including H.H. Burns, Selwyn Jepson, Harold Kent, Leslie Poynton, John Ridgely.
Starring: William Russell (Lancelot), Ronald Leigh-Hunt (Arthur), Jane Hylton (Guinevere), Cyril Smith (Merlin), Robert Scroggins (Brian).
After earning his position at the Round Table Lancelot undertakes various quests in a quasi-medieval world as the Queen's Knight. Advanced TV series for its day, with some realistic fight scenes. Early episodes are now available on DVD.

Arthur of the Britons (UK TV series, 1972/3, 2 seasons, 24x30m episodes)
Directors: Peter Sasdy, Pat Jackson, Sidney Hayers, Patrick Dromgoole. Teleplays: primarily Terence Feely with Scott Forbes, Robert Banks Stewart, David Osborne, Jonathan Crown, David Pursall.
Starring: Oliver Tobias (Arthur), Brian Blessed (Mark), Rupert Davies (Cerdig), Michael Gothard (Kai), Jack Watson (Llud).
Marred only by its low budget, this was a good attempt to recreate the world of the Dark Ages with Arthur facing the Saxon invasion. The series ran in the US as *King Arthur, the Young Warlord* under which title selected episodes have been released on video (1996).

Arthur the King (US TV, 1985, 180m)
Director: Clive Donner. Screenplay: David Wyles.
Starring: Malcolm McDowell (Arthur), Edward Woodward (Merlin), Candice Bergen (Morgan), Rosalyn Landor (Guinevere), Rupert Everett (Lancelot), Joseph Blatchley (Mordred), Dyan Cannon (Katherine).
Present-day Katherine finds herself in Arthur's court which is in chaos. Main plots concern the efforts of Merlin and Niniane to restore order against Morgan and Mordred and Lancelot seeking to rescue Guinevere. Edited down to half length, it was released in video as *Merlin and the Sword* (1992).

Black Knight, The (Warwick/Columbia, 1954, 85m)
Director: Tay Garnett. Screenplay: Alec Coppel, Bryan Forbes.
Starring: Alan Ladd (John), Patricia Medina (Linet), André Morell (Sir Ontzlake), Peter Cushing (Sir Palamides), Anthony Bushell (Arthur), Patrick Troughton (Mark), Jean Lodge (Guinevere).
An early Irving Allen production. John, a blacksmith, disguises himself as the Black Knight and saves the Round Table from an attempted coup by King Mark and his Saracen allies.

Camelot (Warner/7 Arts, 1967, 179m)
Director: Joshua Logan. Screenplay: based on a stage play by Alan Jay Lerner adapted from the books by T.H. White.
Starring: Richard Harris (Arthur), Vanessa Redgrave (Guenevere), Franco Nero (Lancelot), David Hemmings (Mordred), Laurence Naismith (Merlyn), Lionel Jeffries (Pellinore).
A film adaptation of the Lerner & Loewe Broadway musical, which concentrates on Lancelot's affair with Guenevere. A video of the 1980 Broadway revival of the stage show was broadcast in 1982, still with Harris as Arthur, but with Meg Bussert as Guenevere and Richard Muenz as Lancelot.

Chevaliers de la table ronde, Les (Les Films si Jeudi, 1990, 230m), with sub-titles as *The Knights of the Round Table*
Director: Denis Llorca. Screenplay: Denis Llorca, Philippe Vialèles.

Starring: Maria Casarès (Viviane), Alain Cuny (Merlin), Michel Vitold (Fisher King), Nadine Darmon (Morgane).
Drawing from the Vulgate Cycle, this concentrates on the relationships between Merlin and Morgan and the Fisher King and Elaine.

Connecticut Yankee in King Arthur's Court, A (Paramount, 1949, 106m)
Director: Tay Garnett. Screenplay: Edmund Beloin.
Starring: Bing Crosby (Hank Martin/Sir Boss), Rhonda Fleming (Alisande), Cedric Hardwicke (Arthur), Murvyn Bye (Merlin), William Bendix (Sagramore), Henry Wilcoxon (Lancelot).
The best known and still enjoyable adaptation of Mark Twain's novel, complete with songs, though more of an Arthurian spoof than a serious recreation. Twain's novel was first filmed in 1920 and there have been many variants since. The latest is the TV movie *A Knight in Camelot* (1998), directed by Roger Young and starring Whoopi Goldberg as Dr. Vivien Morgan, which says enough.

Excalibur (Orion, 1981, 140m)
Director: John Boorman. Screenplay: Rospo Pallenberg.
Starring: Nigel Terry (Arthur), Gabriel Byrne (Uther), Nicol Williamson (Merlin), Helen Mirren (Morgana), Cheri Lunghi (Guenevere), Nicholas Clay (Lancelot), Robert Addie (Mordred), Paul Geoffrey (Perceval).
Still regarded as one of the best Arthurian films, this is a moody, angst-ridden film which attempts to meld the Malory story with a pagan background.

Fire and Sword (Von Fürstenberg, 1981, 84m)
English-title release of *Feuer und Schwert*. Issued in Eire as *Tristan and Iseult*.
Director: Veith von Fürstenberg. Screenplay: Max Zihlmann.
Starring: Christoph Waltz (Tristan), Antonia Preser (Isolde), Leigh Lawson (Mark), Peter Firth (Dinas), Christine Wipf (Brangane).
A faithful retelling of the Tristan and Isolde story.

First Knight (Columbia, 1995, 134m)
Director: Jerry Zucker. Screenplay: William Nicholson.
Starring: Sean Connery (Arthur), Richard Gere (Lancelot), Julia Ormond (Guinevere), Ben Cross (Malagant), Liam Cunningham (Agravaine), Christopher Villiers (Kay).
Takes some liberties in retelling the Arthur-Guinevere-Lancelot triangle. Includes Malagant's abduction of the Queen which develops into Malagant's assault upon Camelot and the death of Arthur. Effective battle scenes.

Gawain and the Green Knight (United Artists, 1973, 93m)
Director: Stephen Weeks. Screenplay: Stephen Weeks and Philip M. Breen.
Starring: Murray Head (Gawain), Nigel Green (Green Knight), Robert Hardy (Bertilak), Ciaran Madden (Linet), Anthony Sharp (Arthur).
A fairly faithful if lacklustre retelling of the medieval story merged with *The Lady of the Fountain*. It was remade to much the same script, though rather more trivialised, as *Sword of the Valiant* (Cannon, 1982, 102m) with Miles O'Keeffe as Gawain, Sean Connery as the Green Knight and Trevor Howard as Arthur.

Guinevere (US TV, Lifetime, 1994, 96m)
Director: Jud Taylor. Screenplay: Ronnie Kern, based on the books by Persia Woolley.
Starring: Sheryl Lee (Guinevere), Sean Patrick Flanery (Arthur), Noah Wyle (Lancelot), Donald Pleasance (Merlin), Brid Brennan (Morgan), Ben Pullen (Kai).
The feminist version of the story, told from Guinevere's viewpoint.

King Arthur (Touchstone, 2004, 126m)
Director: Antoine Fuqua. Screenplay: David Franzoni.
Starring: Clive Owen (Arthur), Keira Knightley (Guinevere), Ioan Gruffudd (Lancelot), Stephen Dillane (Merlin), Ray Winstone (Bors), Stellan Skarsgård (Cerdic).
The best attempt so far to create an authentic Dark Ages setting, despite the modern "feminist" and "freedom fighter" overtones.

An interesting portrayal of the conflict between the old Roman culture, the British and the Saxons.

Knights of the Round Table (MGM, 1953, 115m)
Director: Richard Thorpe. Screenplay: Talbot Jennings, Noel Langley, Jan Lustig.
Starring: Robert Taylor (Lancelot), Ava Gardner (Guinevere), Mel Ferrer (Arthur), Anne Crawford (Morgan), Stanley Baker (Modred), Felix Aylmer (Merlin), Gabriel Woolf (Percival).
An all-star big budget production for MGM's first wide screen Cinemascope costume drama, but the result, now very dated, is still a routine adaptation of Malory, redeemed by the always excellent Stanley Baker as the scheming Modred.

Lancelot and Guinevere (Emblem, 1963, 116m), released in US as *The Sword of Lancelot*
Director: Cornel Wilde. Screenplay: Richard Schayer and Jefferson Pascal.
Starring: Cornel Wilde (Lancelot), Brian Aherne (Arthur), Jean Wallace (Guinevere), George Baker (Gawaine), Michael Meacham (Modred), Mark Dignam (Merlin), Adrienne Corri (Vivien).
A serious attempt to make a quality adaptation of the last part of *Morte d'Arthur*, but it lacked the budget. Lancelot becomes Guinevere's champion and protects her against the murderous Modred (who here is Arthur's brother). Modred kills Arthur but Lancelot returns to save the kingdom.

Lancelot du Lac (Mara, 1974, 85m), released with sub-titles as *Lancelot of the Lake*
Director: Robert Bresson. Screenplay: Robert Bresson.
Starring: Luc Simon (Lancelot), Laura Duke Condominas (the Queen), Vladimir Antolek-Oresek (the King), Humbert Balsan (Gauvain), Patrick Bernard (Mordred).
Essentially a retelling of the Vulgate *Mort Artu*, events taking place in a collapsing Middle Ages.

Legend of King Arthur, The (UK TV series, 1979, 8x30m episodes)
Director: Rodney Bennett. Teleplay: Andrew Davies.

Starring: Andrew Burt (Arthur), David Robb (Lancelot), Felicity Dean (Guinevere), Steve Hodson (Mordred)
A worthy attempt to create an authentic historical Arthur still in keeping with the traditional story. Available on VHS and DVD.

Legend of Prince Valiant (US TV animated series, 1991–94, 65x30m episodes)
Executive Producers: David Corbett, Jeffrey Schon, William E. Miller. Story: David Corbett with Diane Dixon story editor.
Starring (voices): Robby Benson (Valiant), James Avery (Bryant), Tim Curry (Gawain), Efrem Zimbalist Jr (Arthur), Alan Oppenheimer (Merlin).
Cartoon series based upon the Hal Foster comic strip series.

Lovespell, see *Tristan and Isolt*

Magic Sword: Quest for Camelot (Warner Brothers, 1998, 86m) animated feature
Director: Frederik Du Chau. Screenplay: Kirk De Micco, William Schifrin, Jacqueline Feather, David Seidler, based on Vera Chapman's *The King's Damosel.*
Starring (spoken): Jessalyn Gilsig (Kayley), Cary Elwes (Garrett), Gary Oldman (Ruber), Pierce Brosnan (Arthur), John Gielgud (Merlin), Eric Idle & Don Rickles (two-headed dragon); with songs by Andrea Corr, Céline Dion.
Warner's first magic animated feature seeking to break into the Disney market, but the film suffers from too much indecision (they couldn't even agree on the title). A panel of scriptwriters distorted Chapman's original novel into an overly simplistic story of young Kayley and the blind boy Garrett trying to find the lost Excalibur and defeat the evil Ruber.

Merlin (US TV mini-series, Hallmark, 1998, 3x60m)
Director: Steve Barron. Screenplay: David Stevens.
Starring: Sam Neill (Merlin), Daniel Brocklebank (Young Merlin), Helena Bonham Carter (Morgan), Miranda Richardson (Mab), Paul Curran (Arthur), Lena Heady (Guinevere), Rutger Hauer (Vortigern), Jeremy Sheffield (Lancelot), Isabella Rossellini (Nimue), Jason Done (Mordred).

An ambitious but over-clever attempt to tell Merlin's life story and his pursuit of Nimue almost from cradle to grave, against the backcloth of the Arthurian legend, which sometimes seems to get forgotten.

Merlin: The Magic Begins (US TV mini-series, NBC, 1998)
Director: David Winning. Screenplay: Tom Richards, Christopher Roosen.
Starring: Jason Connery (Merlin), Deborah Moore (Nimue), Gareth Thomas (Blaze), Graham McTavish (Rengal), Paul Curran (Kay).
Only a token nod to the traditional story, this miniseries traces the adventures of Young Merlin, with his tutor Blaze, protecting the forest kingdom from the evil sorcerer Rengal. Received 15 Emmy nominations. Not to be confused with the other Merlin mini-series above.

Merlin and the Sword, see *Arthur the King*

Merlin of the Crystal Cave (UK TV, BBC, 1991, 6x30m episodes)
Director: Michael Darlow. Screenplay: Steve Bescoby, based on the novel by Mary Stewart.
Starring: George Winter (Merlin), Kim Thomson (Ninianne), Sam Hails (Arthur), Robert Powell (Ambrosius), Roger Alborough (Uther), Jon Finch (Vortigern).
Merlin seeks his father against the backdrop of the Saxon invasion. A fairly faithful adaptation of Stewart's novel. Edited slightly (164m) for video release (2000).

Mists of Avalon, The (US TV TNT, 2001, 3x60m episodes)
Director: Uli Edel. Screenplay: Gavin Scott based on the novel by Marion Bradley.
Starring: Anjelica Huston (Viviane), Julianna Margulies (Morgaine), Joan Allen (Morgause), Samantha Mathis (Gwenhwyfar), Edward Atterton (Arthur), Michael Byrne (Merlin), Mark Lewis Jones (Uther).
Although squeezed into three hours, this is a good adaptation of

Bradley's novel with strong imagery polarising the conflict between Avalon and Camelot, the Old Religion and the New, under the threat of the Saxons.

Monty Python and the Holy Grail (Python Pictures, 1975; 91m)
Director: Terry Gilliam & Terry Jones. Screenplay: the Monty Python team.
Starring: Graham Chapman, John Cleese, Michael Palin, Terry Jones, Terry Gilliam.
The perfect spoof. Arthur gathers together his knights but losing interest in Camelot they try and find the Grail.

Parsifal (Gaumont-TMS, 1982, 255m)
Director: Hans-Jürgen Syberberg. Screenplay: direct from Richard Wagner's opera.
Starring: Michael Mutter (Parsifal), Armin Jordan (Amfortas), Martin Sperr (Titurel), Edith Clever (Kundry), Aage Haugland (Klingsor).
The most complete attempt to film Wagner's *Parsifal*.

Perceval le gallois (Gaumont, 1978, 140m)
Director: Eric Rohmer. Screenplay: Eric Rohmer.
Starring: Fabrice Luchini (Perceval), André Dussollier (Gauvain), Marc Eyraud (Arthur), Marie-Christine Barrault (Guinevere), Michel Etcheverry (Fisher King), Arielle Dombasle (Blanchefleur).
A faithful adaptation of Chrétien's *Perceval*, including being told in verse, but here a completion allows Perceval to see the Grail. An authentic but unusual effort that uses stylized medieval backdrops.

Prince Valiant (20th Century Fox, 1954, 100m)
Director: Henry Hathaway. Screenplay: Dudley Nichols.
Starring: Robert Wagner (Prince Valiant), Brian Aherne (Arthur), Mary Phillips (Queen), James Mason (Sir Brack), Sterling Hayden (Gawain), Janet Leigh (Aleta).
Based on Hal Foster's well-known comic strip, this is really just an excuse for a swashbuckler in Camelot as Valiant fights for his kingdom and wins a place at the Round Table.

Prince Valiant (Constantin, 1997, 91m)
Director: Anthony Hickox. Screenplay: Michael Frost Beckner, Carsten Lorenz.
Starring: Stephen Moyer (Prince Valiant), Edward Fox (Arthus), Joanna Lumley (Morgan), Anthony Hickox (Gawain).
Valiant poses as Gawain (who is injured) to take Ilene to safety from the Vikings who are in league with Morgan to claim Excalibur and the throne.

Siege of the Saxons (Columbia, 1963, 85m)
Director: Nathan Juran. Screenplay: Jud Kinberg, John Kohn.
Starring: Ronald Lewis (Robert Marshall), Janette Scott (Katherine), Ronald Howard (Edmund), Mark Dignam (Arthur), John Laurie (Merlin).
A poor excuse for a swashbuckler though an interesting blend of Arthurian and Robin Hood legends. Edmund of Cornwall kills Arthur and usurps the throne, planning a forced marriage with Arthur's daughter Katherine, but all is saved by outlaw Robert Marshall.

Sword in the Stone, The (Disney, 1963, 79m) animated feature
Director: Wolfgang Reitherman. Screenplay: Bill Peet (songs by the Sherman Brothers)
Starring (voices): Karl Swenson (Merlin), Ricky Sorenson (Wart/Arthur), Sebastian Cabot (Sir Ector).
Pleasant children's adaptation of T.H. White's *The Sword in the Stone*, but it becomes too frivolous.

Sword of Lancelot, The, see *Lancelot and Guinevere*

Sword of the Valiant, see under *Gawain and the Green Knight*

Tristan and Isolde (20th Century Fox, 2004)
Director: Kevin Reynolds. Screenplay: Dean Georgaris.
Starring: James Franco (Tristan), Sophia Myles (Isolde), Rufus Sewell (Marke)
The latest attempt to get back to the original story.

Tristan and Isolt (Clar, 1979; 94m)
Director: Tom Donovan. Screenplay: Claire Labine.
Starring: Richard Burton (Mark), Nicholas Clay (Tristan), Kate Mulgrew (Isolt), Geraldine Fitzgerald (Branwyn), Kathryn Dowling (Yseult).
An Irish production, and a faithful rendition of the Tristan story.

23

FRIEND OR FOE? – AN ARTHURIAN WHO'S WHO

This book has shown that the Arthurian world is full of names, some well known, but many forgotten. A "Who's Who" of all of these names, both historical and fictional, would fill a book this size again. However, there are some key characters that I have not yet covered in any degree of detail. Although Chapters 13 to 18 look at Tristan, Gawain, Lancelot, Guinevere, Perceval and Merlin, plus a few other heroes from other romances, I have not yet discussed such other well known characters as Agravaine, Gareth, Bedivere, Kay, Mordred or Morgan le Fay, just to name a few.

The following therefore seeks to explore the other characters of note. It is not intended as a complete index to all Arthurian characters. For those who want a full directory I would recommend *The Arthurian Companion* by Phyllis Ann Karr (Green Knight, new edition, 2001), *Arthurian Myth & Legend* by Mike Dixon-Kennedy (Blandford, 1995), or for the complete afficionado *The Arthurian Name Dictionary* by Christopher W. Bruce (Garland, 1999). Here I want to cover those characters who either throw more light on the legend or allow us to explore further the Arthur of history.

The Knights of the Round Table

Before getting into the annotated listings, it might be useful to remind ourselves who the Knights of the Round Table were. The phrase is used rather glibly to cover just about every knight who appears in the Arthurian story, but strictly speaking only a core of knights were admitted to the Order of the Round Table. Numbers vary. In the Didot-*Perceval*, based on the work of Robert de Boron, the number is limited to twelve, which includes Arthur, with the thirteenth seat, the Siege Perilous, left vacant awaiting the perfect knight. This number is based on the number present at the Last Supper, with the thirteenth seat being that left vacant by Judas Iscariot. That seat is, of course, eventually filled by Galahad. Robert does not present a list of the eleven knights, but from his text it is possible to compile one, namely (in alphabetical order):

Bedivere	Lancelot
Erec	Mordred
Garries [Gareth]	Saigremor the Rash
Gawain	Urgan
Guirres [Gaheris]	Yvain
Kay	

Robert goes on to say that "the king presented 5,400 robes and devices of the Round Table" to all those present at the Feast of Pentecost. Clearly not all of those are knights, but it is evident that in Arthur's kingdom there are considerably more knights than those of the Round Table. Layamon's estimate in his *Brut* was 1,600. The Vulgate *Lancelot* states 150, a figure that Malory also gives in the Beaumains episode of *Morte Darthur*. Malory's knights (he names only 127) are listed in Table 23.1.

In the Welsh *Dream of Rhonabwy*, Arthur is accompanied by 41 counsellors, whilst earlier, when Culhwch swears by all those at Arthur's court in *Culhwch and Olwen* he recites a list of 220 names (some of them duplicates). These names include a few that reappear as knights in the romances, and cross-references are made in the following entries.

Another Welsh-derived document, the *Pedwar Marchog ar Hugain Llys Arthur*, dated to the fifteenth century, provides a list now called the "Twenty-Four Knights", which includes Arthur. The others are:

Aron	Blaes
Bors	Cadog
Cyon	Drudwas
Eiddilig	Eliwlod
Galahad	Glewlwyd
Gwalchmai	Hoel
Lancelot	Llywarch Hen
Menw	Mordred
Morfran	Nasiens
Owain	Perceval
Petroc	Sanddef
Tristan	

Many of the names are clearly derived from the Arthurian romances but some are of greater antiquity.

In *Erec et Enide*, Chrétien says that he could not name a tenth or even a fifteenth of all of Arthur's knights, and then lists 50, suggesting there must be more than 750 knights. He identifies the first ten knights in order of valour, though not all are given names. They are:

Gawain	The Ugly Brave
Erec	Meliant of Liz
Lancelot	Mauduit the Wise
Gornemant of Gohort	Dodinel the Wild
The Handsome Coward	Gandelu

Clearly, apart from Gawain, Erec and Lancelot, there is little consistency amongst the top knights, and there are others possibly better known today, such as Agravaine, Pellinore, Dinadan, Bleoberis and Lucan, who seem to be "also-rans" at this early stage.

By about 1516 names had been added to the places on the Round Table at Winchester. This seated 25 (including Arthur). The key list had now become:

Galahallt	Lamorak
Lancelot deulake	Bors de Ganis

Table 23.1. Malory's Knights of the Round Table from *Le Morte Darthur*

Aglovale	Edward of Orkney	Marrok
Agravaine	Epinogris	Melleaus de Lile
Aliduke	Erminide or Hermine	Melion of the Mountain
Anguish (King)	Fergus	Meliot de Logris
Aristause (Earl)	Florence	Meliagaunce
Arrok de Grevaunt or Degrevaunt	Gahalantine	Menaduke
Astamor	Gaheris	Mordred
Bagdemagus	Galagars	Morganore
Barant le Apres	Galahad	Nentres of Garloth
Baudwin	Galahaut	Nerovens
Bedivere	Galihodin	Ozanna le Cure Hardy
Bellangere le Beuse	Galihud	Palomides
Bellangere le Orgulous	Galleron of Galway	Patrise of Ireland
Belleus	Gareth	Pelleas
Blamore de Ganis	Gautere	Percivale
Bleoberis de Ganis	Gawaine	Perimones the Red Knight
Borre or Bohart le Cure Hardy	Gillemere	Persaunt
Bors de Ganis	Gingalin	Persides
Brandiles	Griflet le Fise de Dieu	Pertolepe the Green Knight (*i.e.* Bertilak)
Brunor le Noire or La Cote Male Tailée	Gromere	Petipase of Winchelsea
Brian de Listinoise	Guyart le Petite	Pinel le Savage
Carados (King)	Gromore Somir Joure	Plaine de Fors
Cardock	Harry le Fise Lake	Plenorius
Chaleins of Clarance (Duke)	Hebes	Priamus
Clarance (King) of Northumberland	Hebes le Renoumes	Reynold
Clarrus of Cleremont	Hectimere	Duke de la Rowse
Clegis	Helaine le Blank	Sadok
Cluddrus	Hervise de la Forest Sauvage	Sagramore le Desirous
Colgrevance	Hervise le Revel	Safere
Constantine	Ironside the Red Knight	Selises of the Dolorous Tower
Crosselm	Kay le Seneschal	Sentraile
Curselaine	Kay de Stranges	Servause le Breuse
Darras	King of the Lake	Suppinabilis
Degrane Saunce Velany	Ladinas de la Forest Sauvage	Tor
Dinadan	Lambaile	Tristram
Dinas	Lambegus	Ulbause
Dinas le Seneschal	Lamiel of Cardiff	Uriens of Gore (King)
Dodinas le Savage	Launcelot du Lake	Urre
Durnore	Lavaine	Uwaine le Blanche Mains
Driant	Lionel	Uwaine les Avoutres
Ector de Maris	Lovel	Villiars the Valiant
Edward of Carnarvon	Lucan the Butler	
	Mador de la Porte	
	Marhaus	

Gawain	Safer
Percivale	Pelleus
Lyonell	Kay
Trystram delyens	Ector de Maris
Garethe	Dagonet
Bedwere	Degore
Blubrys	Brumear
La Cote Male Tailee	Lybyus Dysconyus
Lucane	Aylnore
Palomedes	Mordrede

It is intriguing that some individuals come to the fore at certain times whilst others remain simply names, because all of them must have had some significance at some time. There is little doubt that when the French and German romances were at their peak of popularity the compilers added names that reflected individuals and events known to them and it is difficult to guess who they now meant. In the following I try and pierce the clouds where we can.

Here then is a Who's Who of the major Arthurian characters, both historical and legendary.

Aelle. The first Saxon Bretwalda, leader of the South Saxons, and Arthur's most likely opponent at Badon. *See* Chapter 7 for full discussion.

Aesc, *see* Oisc.

Aglovale. He first appears in the Vulgate *Quest del Saint Graal*, the eldest son of King Pellinore and thus the brother of Perceval and Lamorak. Aglovale has only a minor role, because much of his time is spent either defending his homeland or ruling a small kingdom in the Middle East. He had an affair with a Moorish princess and fathers a son, Moriaen. He is killed when Lancelot rescues Guinevere.

Agravain. One of the sons of King Lot and Margause and brother of Gawain. Although a valiant knight and handsome he is arrogant, scheming and generally disliked. Agravain looks out for his brothers but dislikes Lancelot and plots with Mordred to expose Lancelot's affair with Guenevere. It is his actions that lead ultimately to the downfall of the Round Table. Loomis believes his name was a corruption of Gware-van, meaning "Little Gware" and thus is the same as the knight described by Chrétien in *Erec et Enide* as Garravain of Estrangot. In the Welsh tales he appears as another manifestation of Gware Goldenhair, the basis of the same name who became Gawain. However, in character he may owe much to Rhufon the Radiant. In *The Dream of Rhonabwy* he is described as a handsome young man with yellow-red hair who dotes on Arthur and cannot bear the idea that Arthur should suffer loss of any kind. But he was also known as one of the "Three Arrogant Men" of Britain and the Stanzas of the Graves reports that he died young. Rhufon the Radiant is listed as the son of Dewrath or Dorath, a name not otherwise recorded. Curiously, a variant triad version of the "Three Arrogant Men" lists Rhun ab Einion instead of Rhufon and we find in *Culhwch and Olwen* that Rhufon ap Dorath is listed as Rhuawn ap Dorath, suggesting that his name may really be Rhun. Rhun ab Einion appears in Table 3.3 as a descendant of Coel and a nephew of Arthwys. Gawain, and by extension Agravain, is always identified as Arthur's nephew. This Rhun is known as Rhun the Wealthy, which may also explain why he was both radiant and arrogant. Regardless of name derivations, it is possible that the character of Agravain was drawn from this prince of the North. His territory of Estrangot is referred to elsewhere as the Strange Isle but is not otherwise identified. Rhun's territory was probably somewhere in the Southern Pennines around the Peak District, an isolated area in those days which may well have been regarded as Strange.

Agwisance, *see* Anguish.

Alynore. A name included on the Winchester Round Table. Many have puzzled over his identity because he does not appear in Malory or, for that matter, any other Arthurian text. It has been suggested it originally read Alymere and was changed in error when the inscriptions were repainted in 1789. Sir Alymere is still a minor knight. He is named just once in the Alliterative *Morte Arthure* as an "able knight" who fights alongside Arthur at the final battle. Each generation doubtless added their share of names and the likeliest candidate here is Aymer de Valence (*c*1270–1324), earl of Pembroke. Aymer was a nephew of Henry III and also related to the powerful de Lusignan family. His uncle, Aylmer de Lusignan, had been Bishop of Winchester from 1250 to 1260. Aymer de Valence was Commander of the English forces at Berwick in 1303 and defeated Robert the Bruce at both Methven in 1306 and Loudun Hill the following year. It is doubtless he who earned a reference in the Alliterative *Morte Arthure* and someone of influence must have perpetuated it in the Winchester Table.

Ambrosius Aurelianus. The one pre-Badon person named by Gildas in a passage that might just mean that Ambrosius was the victor at Badon, in which case he would have to be the historical Arthur. Because Gildas was ambiguous he has caused 1500 years of debate. *See* discussion in Chapters 5 and 10.

Amhar or **Amyr**. Recorded by Nennius as a son of Arthur, whom Arthur killed and buried in Ergyng and from whom the River Gamber takes its name. No explanation is given as to why Arthur killed his son. Amhar also appears in *Geraint ab Erbin* as one of the guardians of Arthur's bedchamber. He remains a mystery. We do not know who his mother was. Some have tried to equate him with Emyr Llydaw in which case he would, according to at least one source, be Arthur's brother-in-law. Arthur's better known son was Llacheu (*see entry*) also called Loholt.

Anfortas, *see* Fisher King.

Anguish or **Agwisance**. Both names appear separately in Malory but they are almost certainly the same person, both identified as a King of Ireland. He may be the same as the King with a Hundred Knights. At the outset, Agwisance or Aguysans was one of the kings who rebelled against Arthur at the start of his reign. Later we find him demanding tribute from Mark of Cornwall. Tristram killed Anguish's champion Marhaus, the queen's brother, but later, when Tristram is disguised, he and Anguish become good friends. Anguish was the father of Iseult. The name is usually suggested as a corruption of Angus or Oengus, a common name amongst the Irish kings and the Scottish kings of Dál Riata, who were of Irish descent. The earliest Angus of Dál Riata ruled from 736 to 750 and was already a king of the Picts. He claimed the Pictish throne after a series of battles against the former king, Drust (the Pictish form of Tristan). There was an earlier Oengus, king of Cashel, who was a contemporary of Vortigern rather than Arthur, and who was the first Irish king to be baptised a Christian, in 448. However, it should be noted that the early French romances translated the name of the Saxon Hengist as Hanguis or Hangus, and it would be easy for him to have become sucked into the story of the rebel kings.

Anna. Geoffrey introduces her as the younger sister of Arthur and the second child of Uther and Ygraine. Thereafter it gets a little complicated. He states that she married Lot of Lodonesia when she must have been about fourteen but soon after that he introduces her son (Arthur's nephew), Hoel of Brittany, who he says is the son of King Budic. Anna was not old enough to have been married before and have an adult child. Other sources clarify the problem and identify Hoel as the son of Gwyar, an earlier daughter of Ygraine and Gorlois. Geoffrey then further complicates matters by saying that Anna was the sister of Ambrosius rather than Arthur. This would make more sense chronologically because Anna's children include Gawain who is of much the same age of Arthur. However, the one consistent reference in all the tales is that Gawain is Arthur's nephew. This can only mean that Anna was not his younger sister, as Geoffrey first implies, but an older half-sister, and possibly the same as Gwyar. The Celtic tales always refer to Gawain as the son of Gwyar and Gwyar is a female name – though it means "gore" or "blood". The later romances gave Arthur three elder half-sisters, Morgawse (or Margause), Elaine (or Viviane) and Morgan, all of whom superseded Anna. The name Morgawse is almost certainly derived from Gwyar.

Antor, *see* Ector/Hector.

Artegall. Sir Artegall is best remembered not from any of the primary Arthurian romances but from Spenser's *Faerie Queen*. Yet there are many strong connections with the Arthurian legend. Merlin reveals Artegall to Britomart, daughter of King Rience, in his magic mirror. She falls in love with him and Merlin reveals that they will marry and be the ancestors of the Kings and Queens of Britain, meaning the Tudors. Artegall has thus become a substitute for Arthur. In Book V Artegall undertakes a quest to destroy the giant Grantorto and rescue Irena. Here Artegall, like Arthur, personifies Britain's right over Ireland. Irena represents Ireland and Grantorto the rebel uprising of 1580. Spenser had been involved with this as secretary to the Lord Lieutenant of Ireland, Arthur, Lord Grey of Wilton, who was believed to be the model for Artegall.

Whether by design or fortune Spenser drew upon an interesting name. Geoffrey of Monmouth, who muddled most names, refers to Artegall twice in two different ways. During Arthur's reign he is Artgualchar, the Earl of Guerensis (which Geoffrey says is now called Warwick), who attends Arthur's first council at Caerleon. Geoffrey had referred to the same individual earlier under the name Archgallo. He was one of the sons of Morvidus and had succeeded his elder brother Gorbonianus. Archgallo proved a ruthless, grasping king and was deposed, his brother Elidurus becoming king in his place. Five years later Elidurus encountered Archgallo wandering in the Forest of Calaterium and took pity on him. By subterfuge he convinced the peers to accept Archgallo as king again. He was crowned at York and this time his reign was glorious. He died after ten years and was buried in Leicester.

Although jumbled by Geoffrey, all of these names appear in Table 3.3. Gorbonianus is Germanianus, the son of Coel. Morvid is Mar (or Maeswig), Elidurus is Eliffer or Elidyr, and Archgallo is Arthwys. Folktale or garbled history, Geoffrey seems to be retelling a long-remembered story of the North which may bear a grain of truth about Arthwys. Geoffrey had mentioned the Forest of Calaterium earlier, placing it in Albany (Scotland), so it sounds the same as the Forest of Celidon, but J.A. Giles and others have suggested it was the Forest of Galtres, an old Royal Forest north of York, now long gone. Artegall/Archgallo may therefore be a manifestation of Arthur of the Pennines.

Arthur's sons. One of the tragedies of the Arthurian story is that Arthur and Guenevere had no children of their own and thus there was no line of succession. Nevertheless, Arthur is attributed with several sons, all presumably illegitimate, and each has their separate entry. See Amhar, Borre, Cydfan, Gwydre, Llacheu/Loholt, Merbis and Mordred.

Bagdemagus, Bademagus or **Bademagu**. We first meet him in Chrétien's *Lancelot* as Bademagu, the King of Gorre, a rather mysterious land regarded as something of an Otherworld. Bademagu's son Meleagaunt abducts Guenevere, but despite his rebellious son Bademagu remains courteous and keeps Guenevere safe as well as attending to the wounds of Kay and Lancelot. By the time we encounter him again in Malory, though, he has become more haughty. He storms off when Arthur makes Tor a knight of the Round Table instead of Bagdemagus. He calms down later, however, and is involved in the Grail Quest. In the original *Quest of the Holy Grail* Bagdemagus takes the Adventurous Shield from the White Abbey at Galahad's encouragement, even though he knows that anyone who does so shall die or be maimed. He is later defeated by the White Knight. It is evident that Bagdemagus does not survive the Quest, as his grave is seen and Arthur mourns his loss but Malory must have forgotten, for Bagdemagus speaks in support of Lancelot during the final days.

Chrétien placed Bademagu's capital at Bade or Bath, and as his name contains the same word it is likely that Chrétien believed he was a King of Bath. *Magu* may mean "magus" as in magician, or it could be a contraction of "magis" as in magistrate, so that the name means simply "Lord of Bath". Bagdemagus is made the nephew of Urien, who is also called King of Gorre, but was the king of Rheged. There is no name amongst his relatives or the later rulers of the Isle of Man close enough to have mutated into Bademagu.

Balin. With friends like Balin who needs enemies? Though able and courageous Balin is also impetuous and causes many problems, usually by killing first and thinking later. Already in trouble for having killed Arthur's cousin, and accused of killing the Lady of the Lake's brother, Balin promptly decapitates the Lady of the Lake and is consequently banished. He works his way back into Arthur's favour by capturing the rebellious king Ryons. He is also suspected of having killed the rebel king Lot (whose death is usually attributed to Pellinore). Balin's main role, though, is creating the Waste Land. In avenging the death of Sir Herlews he chases the invisible Sir Garlon back to King Pellam's castle, where he kills him. Pellam pursues Balin who grabs the Spear of Longinus in self-defence and wounds Pellam. This is the Dolorous Stroke that lays the land to waste and inaugurates the Grail Quest. Balin's death comes about when he fights his brother Balan and, in true Arthurian tradition, both knights are in different armour so neither recognises the other, and they kill each other. Balin was known as the Knight of the Two Swords and Merlin reforged one of these swords and set it in a marble slab to await Galahad. Loomis and others suggest that Balin's name, originally spelled Balaain, was derived from the same common source as Galahad's, originally spelled Galaad. Whether or no, there is the obvious balance between the two, with Balin creating the Waste Land and Galahad healing it. So, although Balin is called the son of the King of Northumbria, we need not seek a real Balin any more than we'll find a real Galahad.

Ban. King of Benwick or Benoic, brother of Bors and father of Lancelot and Ector de Maris. He supports Arthur in his battle against the rebellious kings but later loses his own lands to King Claudas and dies of a broken heart. Loomis has suggested that Ban of Benoic is a corruption of Bran the Blessed, which may explain the name but not the character. Claudas is almost certainly a memory of Clovis, and Gregory of Tours reported that "he encompassed the death of many other kings and blood-relations of his whom he suspected of conspiring against his kingdom." The original Ban was probably one such victim.

Baudwin. One of the few characters to survive from the original Celtic stories right through to Malory. Malory has him as the Constable of Britain who serves as governor while Arthur is in Europe at war against Rome. He accompanies Gawain on a number of exploits where they are all tested (*see* Chapter 14). He becomes a physician and retires to a hermitage. We meet him in all the Welsh tales and Triads as Bedwin or Bedwini, the Bishop of Gelliwic (*see* Chapter 8). Unlike many Celtic holy men, Bedwin does not seem to have left his mark on history. He was believed to be a Bishop of Llandaff but exactly when we don't know. Bedwin Sands off the coast of Gwent in the Severn are supposed to be named after him.

Bedivere or **Bedwyr**. In the Celtic tales Bedwyr was Arthur's constant companion, counted second only to Cei for valour. He was particularly noted for his skill with a spear. According to the poem *Pa Gur*, he fought at the battle of Tribruit. In *Culhwch and Olwen*, where he is involved in the quest for the Cauldron of Dwrnach, there is a reference to him being "one-handed". Geoffrey of Monmouth calls him Bedivere and makes him Arthur's Cup-bearer. He accompanies Arthur when he fights the giant at Mont-St-Michel. Arthur grants him the territory of Neustria (Normandy). He is killed at the battle of Saussy and buried at Bayeux. Surprisingly, despite his profile in the Welsh tales, Bedivere did not translate to the French romances, where most of his key tasks are assigned to others. Lucan becomes Arthur's cup-bearer and it is Griflet whom Arthur charges with returning Excalibur to the lake. However, the Stanzaic *Morte Arthur* grants that to Bedyvere, as does Malory, and as a consequence Bedivere remains one of the best known of Arthur's knights. Although he features so prominently in the Welsh tales, little else is said of him. He has no pedigree, though his father is sometimes noted as Bedrawt or Pedrawc. The best known Pedrawc was the son of Glywys, who became St. Petroc, so famous in his day that if Bedwyr were his son it would have been noted. There was, of course, Peder, the father of Artúir of Dyfed. This would make Arthur and Bedwyr brothers, which might account for why they were constant companions, but it is unusual that such a relationship is not mentioned when so many others seem to be Arthur's cousins. This very paucity of data seems to underline Bedwyr's historicity, in that he was remembered for what he was and did not mutate into legend. He was purportedly buried at Tryfan Hill in Gwynedd, near Bethesda. Bedwyr's Well or Spring, Ffynnon Fedwyr, is near Pontarddulais in Glamorgan, where there is also a Craig-y-Bedw.

Bertilak or **Bercilak**. The real name of the Green Knight in the story *Gawain and the Green Knight*, who was in league with Morgan le Fay. Something of a "jolly green giant", he's clearly a trickster, and a similar name, Bertilay, is given to the old knight who accompanies the False Guenevere in the Prose *Lancelot*. Loomis believes the name was derived from the Irish *bachlach*, meaning "churl" or "herdsman", which may be true for the name but it doesn't explain the trickster or challenger motif. Malory reinvents him as Pertolepe, one of four brothers (each associated with a different colour), who challenges Gareth after learning that Gareth had killed his brother Percard (the Black Knight). Gareth defeats him and Pertolepe pledges himself to Gareth thereafter, later becoming a Knight of the Round Table. He is killed during Lancelot's rescue of Guenevere.

Blaise. Confessor to Merlin's mother and Merlin's own mentor. He settled in Northumberland and there records Arthur's adventures as told him by Merlin. He was probably derived from the storyteller Bleheris.

Blamore, *see* Bleoberis.

Blanchefleur. The name used for both Tristan's mother and for Perceval's true love. Apparently the name "White Flower" was common in early French romances, presumably to signify purity. Tristan's mother died in childbirth. Perceval vows his love for Blanchefleur but has to leave her because of his concern for his mother. In Gerbert's *Fourth Continuation*, he does return to her and they marry. In Wolfram's *Parzival* her name becomes Condwiramurs.

Bleoberis or **Blubrys**. Brother of Blamore and cousin of Lancelot. Blamore is the more chivalric of the two. Bleoberis appears something of a rogue, demanding Sir Segwarides' wife as a boon, but he is defeated by Tristram. In the Vulgate *Mort Artu*, Bleoberis survives all perils and retires to a monastery with Bors, last of the Round Table knights. In Malory, both Blamore and Bleoberis end their days on Crusade. It has been suggested that the name Bleoberis (and that of Brandelis) is derived from the storyteller Bleheris, whose name was also rendered as Bledericus and who appears in Geoffrey's *History* as the Duke of Cornwall who defeated Athelfrith after the Battle of Chester.

Bohort, *see* Bors.

Borre, also known as Bohart le Cure Hardy ("the Strong Heart"). Arthur's illegitimate son by Lisanor or Lionors, and probably identical to Loholt (*see entry*). The name is so similar to Bohort that clearly at some stage it and Loholt became merged.

Bors or **Bohort**. Son of the Elder Bors, king of Gannes (or Ganis), brother of Lionel and cousin of Lancelot. Bors is one of the great knights and features heavily in the Prose Lancelot (*see* Chapter 17). He is also one of only three knights who succeed in the Grail Quest. The name is spelled as Bohors in some of the early texts and Loomis has deduced that it mutated, via Gohors, from the same original Celtic hero, Gwri Goldenhair, who inspired Gawain (*see* Chapter 14). Indeed, as the Grail romance developed Bors supplants Gawain, who might otherwise have become one of the Grail knights.

Brandelis. A popular name that crops up several times in the romances, also as Brandiles, Brandles, Brandilias, Brandis, Branduz and, via the last, as Brandin of the Isles. They are not necessarily always the same character, but they may have come together from two separate sources. He is probably best remembered from the First *Perceval* Continuation, in which he proves a match for Gawain. Malory serves him less well and has him trounced by Tristram and other knights in various jousts. He later declares himself hostile to Arthur and is killed in the fracas when Lancelot rescues Guenevere. The name is suggested as deriving from the Celtic deity Bran mac Lyr which became Bran de Lis > Brandelis. This same derivation points to Brandin/Brandus/Brian of the Isles being somehow connected. Brandin of the Isles was the Master of Dolorous Garde who was ousted by Lancelot. As Brian of the Isles he turns up in Malory as the Lord of Pendragon Castle whom Lancelot once again defeats. Like Brandiles, Brian becomes hostile to Arthur, even treacherous. He also has an affair with Niniane and learns some magic arts. This character is almost certainly based upon the historical Brian De Lisle (d.1234) who was one of King John's cronies. He held several castles throughout England, including Knaresborough and Peveril, and was forced to give them up after the death of King John. This same Brian is one of the likely candidates for the Sheriff of Nottingham in the Robin Hood story (he was the Forrester of Nottingham), thus providing an interesting link between Britain's two great legendary heroes.

Breuse Saunce Pyté, *see* Brunor.

Brian of the Isles, *see* Brandiles.

Bron. The original name for the Fisher King. *See entry and also* Chapter 16.

Brunor or **Breunor la Cote Male Tailée**, "the badly cut coat", also known as Brunor the Black. Brunor turns up at Arthur's court wearing the very coat in which his father had been hacked to death by Tristram (others say by Gareth). Kay, with his usual belligerence, gives him the nickname. His father was also called Brunor or Breuse and was so evil and violent that he was known as the Brown Knight Without Pity (Saunce Pyté). The son turns out to be very different from his father, bold, brave and bright. He saves the queen from a lion and undertakes a quest to help the lady Maledisant who first mocks him and then confesses her love for him; they later marry. After ousting Brian of the Isles, Lancelot makes Brunor Lord of Pendragon Castle. Brunor is the brother of Dinadan. Brunor's father is something of an enigma. In *Palamedes* he becomes confused with the knight known simply as Le Bon Chevalier, sometimes with the epithet "san Peor". He is an elder knight of the previous generation, highly regarded by Uther Pendragon, but he is held captive by the giant Nabon and loses his wits. There is a curious episode in which he explores a cave and finds the remains (plus a survivor) of the kings of old, all of whom seem to be giants. Although he recovers his wits he is later murdered by Briadan and Ferrant. Briadan is yet another version of Brandiles/Brian of the Isles, whilst Ferrant is almost certainly Alan Fergeant, Duke of Brittany (d.1112).

Calogrenant. The unlucky stooge of the Arthurian romance. It is his failure to defeat Esclados at the magical spring in Broceliande that sets Yvain on his first quest in Chrétien's tale. He gets the rough end of a joust in *Meraugis de Portlesguez*, and he gets in the way in *Queste del Saint Graal* when Lionel attacks Bors and is killed. He redeems himself slightly in *Claris and Laris* where, in the search for Laris, he succeeds in ridiculing Mordred. Loomis has suggested that his name is a conflation of *Cai-lo-grenant*, "Cei the grumbler", which is what Cei/Kay does well. Calogrenant doesn't really grumble, though; he's just something of a failure, which is increasingly how Kay is portrayed in the later romances. Calogrenant takes it a stage further. In some versions he is confused with Colgrevance, a knight who's little more than a name most of the time and whose moment of fame comes when, waiting the other side of the bedroom door where Lancelot and Guenevere are in bed together, he is killed when Lancelot rushes out. To add insult to injury, Lancelot then takes his armour and makes his escape. This knight is called Tanaguin in the Vulgate version.

Carados. There are two by this name; to avoid confusion, *see* **Karados** for the second. The first is a corruption of Caradog Vreichfras, Arthur's chief counsellor, who also turns up in later tales as Craddock or Cardock. He has his own adventures in the *Livre de Carados*. He is initially one of the rebellious kings but subsequently fights valiantly for Arthur and is killed in Gaul.

Cei, *see* Kay.

Cerdic. Leader of the Gewisse and founder of the West Saxon dynasty. It has been suggested that he was one of Arthur's opponents at Badon. Others suggest he may be the same as Caradog Vreichfras. He is discussed extensively in Chapters 4, 7 and 8.

Colgrevance, *see* Calogrenant.

Conmor or **Cunomorus**. Wrongly called Mark Cunomorus and identified as Mark, King of Cornwall in the Tristan story. In fact he was a Count of Léon who usurped power over Domnonée in the 550s. *See* Chapter 13.

Constantine. The name Constantine, made popular by the Roman emperor Constantine the Great, crops up several times in the Arthurian story. The Celtic version is Custennin, but in the Arthurian stories the name Constantine prevails. To clarify, here is a quick note on each of them.

(1) Constantine the Great, Roman emperor from 306–337, son of Constantius. Legend makes his mother Helena the daughter of Coel, Duke of Colchester.

(2) Constantine II, Roman Emperor of Britain and Gaul, 337–340, son of the above.

(3) Custennin, son of Magnus Maximus, claimed as ancestor of rulers of Dyfed (spurious). Legend makes him Overlord of Britain from 388 onwards, but there is no evidence for this and his fate is not known.

(4) Constantine III, Roman Emperor of Britain and Gaul, 407–411, not to be confused with the above, as he was apparently a soldier raised from the ranks.

(5) Constantine, brother of the Breton king Aldroenus. Geoffrey makes this Constantine become the first post-Roman British king. He may be a confused merging of (4) and (6).

(6) Custennin Fendigiad ("the Blessed"), believed to be a Prince of Dumnonia *c*470s.

(7) Custennin or Constantine of Dumnonia, *fl* 505–535, identified as son of Cador and treated as the successor to Arthur. He is the one castigated by Gildas.

Cunomorus, *see* Conmor.

Custennin, *see* Constantine.

Cydfan or **Kyduan**. Identified as a son of Arthur in the *Hanesyn Hen* batch of pedigrees. His mother is Eleirch, daughter of Iaen of Caer Dathyl – *Culhwch and Olwen* refers to the men of Caer Dathyl as being "kindred to Arthur on his father's side." Evidently Arthur was quite close to his relatives. We know nothing more about Cydfan or his relatives. Caer Dathyl is at the start of the Lleyn Peninsula, a location that suggests a connection with Artúir of Dyfed.

Cynwyl or **Cynfelyn**, *see* Griflet.

Dagonet. Arthur's court jester and the butt of everyone's jokes. Although knighted because Arthur believes him to be brave, Dagonet is really a coward, but goes so far as to dent his own shield to look as if he has been fighting. However, when pushed he will fight. He turns on Tristram in anger on one occasion (though is beaten by Tristram and goes mad), pursues Mark but dressed in Mordred's armour, and tracks down and kills Helior when he abducts Dagonet's wife.

Dinadan. Although he is the son of the evil Breuse Saunce Pyté, Dinadan is a likeable if lazy knight who sees no point in questing for the sake of it but first weighs up all the pros and cons. Dinadan rather likes practical jokes but can take as good as he gives. His appearances are always light hearted and he is particularly close to Tristram. However, he upsets Mordred and Agravaine and they kill him during the Grail Quest.

Drudwas or **Drydwas**. Listed in the Twenty-Four Knights of Arthur's Court but not amongst his Counsellors. He was known as one of the "Three Golden-Tongued Knights" of Arthur's court and no one could deny him his wishes. There is a story told about him called "The Birds of Llwch Gwin". Drudwas's sister was Arthur's mistress, and Drudwas schemed to have Arthur killed by some vicious birds. However Drudwas fell into his own trap and died. Drudwas is called the son of Tryffin, but this does not appear to be the Tryffen of Dyfed, grandfather of Vortipor. If the genealogies are correct, Drudwas may have been the nephew of Gwyddno Garanhir, who is discussed in Chapter 8.

Drust or **Drystan**, *see* Tristan.

Dubricius or **Dyfrig**. Bishop of Ergyng who lived *c*460-*c*530AD. According to Geoffrey he crowned Arthur. *See* discussion in Chapter 9.

Ector, **Hector** or **Antor**. The father of Kay, and Arthur's foster father. He is called Antor in the Vulgate *Merlin* and Ector in Malory, but in the earliest references to him in the Prose *Merlin* he is called Auctor, a name which some have suggested is merely a corruption of Arthur itself. Arthur has no idea that he has been fostered and is upset when he learns that Ector is not his real father. Ector fights on the side of Arthur against the rebel kings and against the Saxons, but we hear no more of him. In Welsh tradition Kay's father is Cynyr (*see* Kay).

Ector/Hector de Maris. One of the great knights of the Arthurian saga yet a strangely undervalued one. He is the illegitimate son of Ban of Benwick and the Damsel of les Mares, so is half-brother to Lancelot. He's also considerably more sensible than Lancelot, and although he can do little to curb Lancelot's impulsive actions, is always supportive of him. The name *Hektor* in the original Greek means "to resist", and that seems to be Ector's role here, to serve as a balance to Lancelot. In the Vulgate version Ector searches for Lancelot after the death of Arthur and spends his final days with him in the monastery. In Malory, however, by the time he finds Lancelot, the knight has just died. Ector ends his days on Crusade.

Elaine. There are several Elaines in the Arthurian story, including the mother of Lancelot, but two individuals are significant and I believe they were really both aspects of the same person though developed separate identities. The more important is Elaine of Corbenic, the Grail Maiden and the daughter of King Pelles. Pelles contrives, through a secret potion, to make Lancelot believe Elaine is Guenevere. The two sleep together and Elaine conceives Galahad. Their union reunites the lines of descent of David and Joseph. Although Lancelot is furious that he has been deceived he forgives Elaine and in fact is gullible enough to be deceived again, when Elaine visits Camelot. Elaine of Corbenic does not reappear; in fact she is supposed to have died while Lancelot was away on the Grail Quest. Guenevere had been intensely jealous of Elaine because of her beauty, and this same jealousy re-emerges in *Mort Artu* when Lancelot is healed of wounds sustained at a tournament by the Lady of Astolat, or Shalott. She is not named in the Vulgate, but Malory calls her Elaine, and these two Elaines could easily be one. Lancelot does not return Elaine's love and eventually she pines away and her body floats in a barge down the river to Camelot.

There were likewise two Elens or Helens in British tradition who became confused and merged to form the basis for Elaine of Carbonek. The primary one is Elen, daughter of Eudaf Hen, who married the Emperor Magnus Maximus. Through her Magnus gains acceptance as emperor in Britain; he even has a dream of her like some of the later Grail visions. Elen, as both a name and a character, became symbolic of the bride in whom is invested an inheritance, whether the "kingdom" of Britain or the Grail kingdom. This was further embellished by the memory of Helen, mother of Constantine the Great. Regardless of the facts, Helen had long entered legend as a British princess, daughter of Coel of Colchester, who became the mother of an Emperor. Constantine the Great, who brought Christianity to the Roman Empire, could be seen in the role of Galahad. Helen undertook a pilgrimage to Palestine and founded several churches as well as confirming the sites of most of the key holy places. She was also supposed to have discovered the True Cross, fragments of which were brought back to Britain. Helen thus became another manifestation of the Grail Maiden. There are many churches and sites dedicated to Elen/Helen in North Wales, primarily the Caernarfon area where Elen ferch Eudaf lived.

There is a third Elen in Geoffrey's *History*, the niece of Hoel of Armorica who is abducted by the giant of Mont-St-Michel.

Elidir, Eliffer or **Eleuther**. The names of three Men of the North. The most interesting is Eliffer of the Great Host, who was probably the son of Arthwys of the Pennines but who appears in some pedigrees as his brother. As Eleuther his name could easily be confused with Uther, especially when one triad gives him a child, Arddun, which becomes corrupted to Arthur. Although little written record survives of Eliffer's activities, it may well be that Geoffrey had a copy of a northern history and converted Eliffer's battles into Uther's. The other two are Elidyr the Stout, uncle of Urien of Rheged, and Elidir the Wealthy. The latter believed he was entitled to the kingdom of Gwynedd and invaded Anglesey, an action that resulted in Rhun's great march north. *See also* Artegall.

Eliwlod or **Liwlod**. Listed in the Twenty-Four Knights of Arthur's Court but not amongst his Counsellors. He was known as one of the "Three Golden-Tongued Knights" of Arthur's court, like Drudwas, but we learn little about him. He is supposed to be the nephew of Arthur.

Emyr Llydaw. One of the mystery men of fifth century British history. I have suggested that this was a title of the commander of the Gewisse, and also that he may be synonymous with Amlawdd Wledig. *See* Chapter 8 for discussion.

Erec. The hero of Chrétien's story *Erec et Enide* (*see* Chapter 18 for full discussion of name and character). Despite his prowess in that story Erec scarcely features in the later romances, which may be because Chrétien had created Erec out of Tristan and therefore his character was superfluous. It may be that Gareth also evolved from Erec's original name, Guerec, and superseded him. Erec does reappear on the Grail Quest in the Post-Vulgate version where he is killed by Gawain.

Ettard, *see* Pelleas.

Evalach or **Evelake**, also **Mordrain**. A pagan king of Sarras who is baptised by Joseph of Arimathea and adopts the name Mordrain. Mordrain's shield is painted with a cross from the blood of Josephus and this same shield is the one later used by Galahad after Bagdemagus takes it from the White Abbey. Mordrain survives through many generations until he is able to die in Galahad's arms. Whilst Mordrain is not himself a Fisher King or Grail King, his actions (with both the shield and the broken sword of Nascien, his brother-in-law) play a significant part in the Grail Quest. The name Evalach is derived from Afallach or Aballach, which appears in the pedigrees of the British kings (*see* Table 3.2). There he is the grandson of Bran the Blessed, whose counterpart Bron was the ancestor of the Fisher Kings. So although the legend and the tradition are at odds, the connection provides a holy authority to the British kings that would develop into the concept of the Divine Right of Kings. (*See entry on* Fisher King *below*.)

Fisher King or the **Rich Fisher**. The role of the Fisher King was originally that of the Guardian of the Holy Grail, but both the role and the individuals who hold the title change as the Grail story develops. As described by Robert de Boron in *Joseph d'Arimathie*, the first Fisher King was Bron, brother-in-law of Joseph. The name Fisher King arose because Bron had supplied the fish for the Last Supper and, via the Grail, the quantity of fish multiplied and could feed all present. Thereafter one of the roles of the Fisher King was to provide food (which may be seen as spiritual succour) to those who visit the Grail castle. Food is always plentiful because of the Grail. Bron's son Alain le Gros inherited the title and brought the Grail to the "isles in the West". In this version Alain's son Perceval is the final Fisher King, inheriting the kingship from his uncle, the hermit. Robert's time scale is clearly truncated, only allowing three generations from the time of Joseph to Arthur.

In the Vulgate Cycle, the Grail family was considerably enlarged, though there were still not sufficient generations. Here the title of Fisher King passed to Alain's nephew Aminadep (son of Joshua), and then passed through each generation to Catheloys, Manaal, Lambor and Pellehan to Pelles, whose daughter (called Elaine in later versions) bore Galahad to Lancelot. Pellehan

(Malory's Pellam) is wounded in the thigh and is thus known as the Maimed King, but in other versions the Maimed King and the Fisher King are not necessarily the same. Most of the names are derived from Bible patriarchs (*but see the separate entry on* Pelles).

In Wolfram's *Parzifal* the names change again. The title Grail King is preferred to Fisher King, and the first of these is Titurel. His descent is not explained, but in terms of generations he equates to Lambor. Titurel passes the role on to his son Frimutel, but although Frimutel is killed Titurel lives on, sustained by the Grail. Frimutel is succeeded by Anfortas whose sister Herzeloyde is Parzifal's mother. In this version Anfortas is the Maimed King (*see* Chapter 16 for the Grail story).

Frimutel, *see* Fisher King.

Gaheris or **Gaheriet**. The youngest son (variously third or fourth) of Lot and Morgause and brother of Gawain, Agravain and Gareth. The spelling of his name varies hugely and in some versions, such as Garriés, is sufficiently close to his brother Gareth (Gerrehés) to cause confusion and to suggest that the two were originally one. Loomis shows how all the names (including Gawain, Agravaine and even Bors) are derivations of Gwri (*see* Chapter 14). Gaheris serves as Gawain's squire until he is knighted. After Gawain he is Arthur's favourite nephew, suggesting that Arthur is oblivious to Gaheris's vicious streak. In fact, Gaheris is clearly troubled. He kills Pellinore in revenge for his father's death, and years later kills his own mother because she has taken Pellinore's son Lamorak as a lover. Gawain despatches Lamorak. At one stage Arthur even offers him Lot's kingdom of Orkney but Gaheris refuses until the Grail Quest is over. He is killed by Lancelot during his rescue of Guenevere, and it is this act that incurs Gawain's enmity and leads to the war with Lancelot.

There is another Gaheris of Karaheu who, in the Vulgate Cycle, eats the poisoned apple intended for Gawain, which leads to Guenevere being accused of murder. His brother is Mador. In Malory his name is changed to Patrise. Nevertheless, the similarity of the name, and that of his brother Mador to Gaheris's half-brother Mordred, suggests that at some stage there was a version in which it was Gawain's brother who died from poison.

Galahad or **Galaad**. The son of Lancelot and Elaine and the purest knight in the world, the only one able to achieve the Grail Quest (*see* Chapter 16). Lancelot's baptismal name was also Galaad, as was the name given to the younger son of Joseph of Arimathea. The name is derived from the Biblical Gilead.

Galehaut. Known as the High Prince, he was Lord of the Remote Isles and Surluse or Soreloise. He is ambitious and invades Arthur's lands, but is so overcome by Lancelot's prowess that he submits. Thereafter he and Lancelot are devoted friends, to the extent that when he believes Lancelot is dead he refrains from eating and dies. His story is told in Chapter 16. In some texts both his name and Galahad's are spelt Galahalt or Galeholt, showing that the names derive from the same source. So too may part of the character, since Galehaut becomes like another half of Lancelot, whose name was also originally Galahad. Bearing in mind that Galehaut had originally invaded Britain, it is possible that the basic character related to a real person, but not necessarily of Arthur's period. A likely candidate is the Dane, Thorkell the Tall. Galehaut is also tall. Thorkell's army invaded and decimated England in 1009, one of many Viking incursions at this time. But Thorkell did have some principles. When the Archbishop of Canterbury was murdered, Thorkell apologised and offered his army (for a fee) to Athelred to help protect England. He later became earl of East Anglia (under Canute).

Galeron or **Galleron**. A Scottish knight who is deprived unjustly of his lands and who challenges Gawain. For details *see* discussion of *The Awyntrs off Arthure* in Chapter 14.

Gareth or **Gueheret**. Son of Lot and Morgause and brother of Gawain, Agravaine and Gaheris. He is often confused with Gaheris in the French romances because of the similarity in names. In fact, in the French romances he and Gaheris could be interchangeable except that Gareth is perhaps more kindly and less impetuous. Gareth's name may have been derived from Guerec which would make him the same as Erec. Malory makes him into an entirely different personality and gives him the "Fair

Unknown" treatment. He comes to Arthur's court in disguise and works for a year in the kitchens. Kay nicknames him Beaumains. At the end of the year he seeks Arthur's boon and undertakes a quest for the scolding Lynette, an adventure told elsewhere as *The Lady of the Fountain*, and as part of Chrétien's *Yvain*. In Malory's version it is Gareth who kills the Brown Knight Without Pity (*see* Brunor). Gareth is killed with Gaheris when Lancelot rescues Guenevere.

Gawain or **Gauvain**. One of the earliest of Arthur's companions and amongst the greatest of all of his knights. He is discussed in detail in Chapter 14. It is worth adding here that Gawain and his three direct brothers run the whole spectrum of character types. Gawain is bold, brave and chivalrous (no matter how badly later story-tellers tried to blacken his name). Agravaine is the treacherous one, but with some semblance of valour. Gaheris is the bully with few, if any, scruples. Gareth, when not hiding behind the shadow of Gaheris, is the decent, quiet one who tries to do the right thing. The reason these four represent such extreme character traits is because they are all aspects of one original character, Gwri.

Geraint or **Gereint**. The hero of the Welsh stories called variously *Geraint son of Erbin* or *Geraint and Enid*. That story is discussed in Chapter 18. Geraint was an historical character; in fact, there were probably two of that name, and they are discussed in Chapter 8. He is ignored by the other romances but Malory gives him a token reference as Garaunt of Cameliard in Book X.

Gingalin, *see* Guinglain.

Girflet, *see* Griflet.

Gornemant of Gohort. In *Erec et Enide*, Chrétien calls Gornemant the fourth best knight yet, compared to the first three, Gawain, Erec and Lancelot, but we learn nothing more of him in that story. However, he reappears in Chrétien's Grail story, where we learn that he is the uncle of Blancheflor. He becomes Perceval's instructor in knightly techniques and codes of conduct. Unfortunately, one of his instructions, which Perceval follows to the letter, leads to all the aggravation of the Grail Quest, because he tells Perceval not to ask too many questions. As a consequence, when Perceval visits the Grail Castle he fails to ask the question that could heal the Maimed King and thereby cure the Waste Land. Gornemant desires that Perceval should stay a year and learn all the knightly arts but, because Perceval is anxious to leave, Gornemant gives him such instruction as he can and then knights him.

The fact that Chrétien rates this knight so highly and mentions him in his first story suggests that the name must have been known and circulating in other stories. Loomis says that Chrétien did not borrow the name from Geoffrey's *History*, but I suspect he did. Amongst the many people Geoffrey names as attending Arthur's coronation, which are really lists of names drawn from the pedigrees, is Coel's son Germanianus, but listed as Gorbonion map Goit, which could easily mutate into Gornemant de Gohort. Geoffrey had called Gorbonion earlier in his *History* as one of the pre-Arthurian British kings (without realizing who he really was), and had nothing but praise for him, saying, "there was no man alive who was more just than he or a greater lover of equity." Likewise Gornemant, whom Chrétien frequently calls a "worthy gentleman", has similar traits. In Wolfram's *Parzifal* he becomes Gurnemanz of Graharz, with the added complication that he has three sons and a daughter, Liaze, whom he hopes Parzifal will marry.

Griflet, **Girflet** or **Gifflet**. One of Arthur's most faithful knights and amongst the most valiant, listed by Chrétien in *Erec et Enide*, but falling outside the top ten. Griflet's one of those knights who's always there but is seldom the centre of attention, though he may be the same as the hero of the Provençal story *Jaufré*. Malory has him gallantly saving Guenevere during the war with the rebel kings, and from that he earns his knighthood. Otherwise Malory kills him off during Lancelot's rescue of Guenevere, but the Vulgate has Griflet, not Bedivere, as the knight who casts Excalibur back into the lake, and is the last to see Arthur alive. Griflet retires to a hermitage but soon after dies of grief. Often referred to as the "son of Do", Griflet is also called "le Fise de Dieu", or the son of God, suggesting he must once have been a holy man. He almost certainly equates with Cynwyl or Cynfelyn in *Culhwch and Olwen*, who was known as "the Saint". He was one of Arthur's twenty-four knights and one of the three survivors of Camlann, being the last to leave Arthur.

Guenevere or **Guinevere** or **Genievre** or **Gwenhwyfar**. The wife of Arthur and lover of Lancelot. She is discussed in detail in Chapter 16 and other episodes in her life appear in Chapter 18. The Triads note that Arthur had three wives, all called Gwenhwyfar though of different parentage, none of whom is the daughter of Leodegrance, her father in the romances. The Triad is really portraying three different images of Gwenhwyfar. In Celtic beliefs the figure three was of supreme importance, representing totality, just as the Church continues to represent God in triple form as Father, Son and Holy Ghost. The same tripleism was applied to Morgan (*see entry below*). The Vulgate did suggest the idea of a False Guenevere, purportedly a half-sister who claimed she was Arthur's original wife but had been abducted on their wedding night. Also, rather curiously, the Welsh form of her name, Gwenhwyfar, bears some comparison with Gwyn Hyfar, or "the Irascible", who is described in *Culhwch and Olwen* as the overseer of Cornwall and Devon and one of the nine who plotted the battle of Camlan. Possibly in the generations of storytelling, Guenevere took on a further, more scheming identity, a depiction which emerges strongly in some of the later romances.

The idea has been put forward, championed mostly by Norma Lorre Goodrich, that Guinevere was a Pictish princess and, in accordance with Pictish law, it was through the female bloodline that princes inherited the right to rule. There is a belief that Mordred was also a Pict and that Guenevere lived with Mordred as his mistress and is buried in Scotland at Meigle. The Alliterative *Morte Arthure* even goes so far as to make Guenevere the mother of Mordred's two sons, though tradition usually makes her sister Gwenhwyfach Mordred's wife. The fact that Arthur and Guenevere have no children is one of the factors that contribute to the unfaithfulness of both parties. One of the few consistent legends attached to Guenevere is that of her abduction, the earliest recorded being that by Melwas (*see* Chapter 11). This translated into the abduction by Meleagaunt in Chrétien's *Knight of the Cart*, and there are other abductions by Lancelot and Mordred. This would all support the argument that Guenevere was desired not for her beauty but because of her bloodline. It is all the more surprising, therefore, that neither the legend nor the romances say much about her ancestry or offer much clarity about her parentage. In Welsh tradition Gwenhwyfar's father was Ogrfan or Gogfran Gawr, and she was born at what is now Knucklas in Powys. In the Vulgate version it is Guenevere's father (Leodegran) who received the Round Table from Uther and passed it on to Arthur as part of the wedding dowry. Since the Round Table is linked to the Grail family, this would give Guenevere an even greater status. Whether descended from Roman nobility, the Grail family or Pictish stock, Guenevere was clearly a woman of importance.

Guinglain, Gingalin or **Gligan**. The son of Gawain and Dame Ragnell who is the archetypal "fair unknown" and hero of Renaud's *Le Bel Inconnu* (*see* Chapter 14).

Guiomar or **Guingamor**. He is first identified in *Erec et Enide*, where he is a guest at the wedding, as the Lord of the Isle of Avalon and Morgan le Fay's lover. The Vulgate version develops this by having Guenevere being annoyed at the relationship and banishing Guiomar from the court. This turns Morgan against Guenevere, and she seeks Merlin's help to learn witchcraft. His name is probably drawn from Gwyn ap Nudd, who features in the Celtic tales of Arthur, and is described as King of Avalon and Lord of the Fairies. His lover was Creiddylad (*see* Morgan *for more detail*).

Gwalchmai, *see* Gawain.

Gwenwynwyn. Called Arthur's First Fighter in *Culhwch and Olwen*. (*See* Chapter 8.)

Gwydre. Identified in *Culhwch and Olwen* as a son of Arthur who was killed in the Preseli Mountains during the hunt for the

Boar Trwyth. This is the only reference to Gwydre. It may be a confusion with Gwydre ap Llwydeu. Gwydre was stabbed by his uncle Huail (Gildas's brother), which resulted in a quarrel between Arthur and Huail, leading eventually to Huail's death. It may be that Arthur had adopted Gwydre, hence the reference to a son. Also, Gwydre is buried near the peak Cwm Cerwyn in the Preseli Mountains, suggesting that this may all refer to Artúir of Dyfed.

Gwyn Hyfar, *see* Guenevere.

Handsome Coward, The, *see* Sanddef.

Hector, *see* Ector.

Helena, *see* Elaine.

Hoel, Howel or **Hywel**. In Geoffrey's *History* he is treated as Arthur's nephew, the son of his sister and of Budic, King of Armorica. He assists Arthur in his battle against the Saxons and subsequently against the French at Poitou, when he also takes Gascony and Aquitaine, and later rallies the British at the Battle of Saussy. In all his battles he distinguishes himself and becomes known as Hoel the great. His niece Elen is killed by the giant of Mont-St-Michel. There is considerable confusion over who he was and I suspect that his name, which, as Hywel, is common in Welsh, was confused with the early Breton ruler Riwal, who established control of both the Breton province of Domnonée and the British province of Dumnonia some time in the early 500s. Later pedigrees tried to tie Riwal in with the ruling family of British Dumnonia but got everything out of synch. It is possible, in fact probable, that Riwal was related to that family and may have been descended from Cynan Meriadoc. Hoel is also associated with Hywel ab Emyr Llydaw, on the basis that Llydaw means Armorica and Emyr is a title for Budic. However, *see* Emyr Llydaw for further discussion.

Huail or **Hywel**. The brother of Gildas, who was executed by Arthur following an ongoing disagreement over the death of

Gwydre (Huail's nephew, who is also referred to as Arthur's son in some texts). Tradition has it that it was a long while before Gildas forgave Arthur, which is why Arthur is not mentioned in *De Excidio*. A stone commemorating Huail's death is in the market square in Ruthin.

Igraine, *see* Ygraine.

Iseult, Iseut, Isolde, Isoud, Esyllt or **Yseult**. Also called La Beale Isoud. She was the wife of King Mark and the lover of Tristan. Her story is told in Chapter 13, along with that of her namesake, Tristan's wife Iseult of the White Hands.

Ivain, *see* Owain.

Kai, *see* Kay.

Karados. Another of Morgan's allies, and a cousin of Guiomar. He commands the Dolorous Tower at the end of the Valley of No Return, which is controlled by Morgan le Fay. Anyone trying to get to the Tower has to pass along the Valley and it will only let pass those who have been faithful. Karados captures Gawain and after considerable difficulty Lancelot rescues Gawain and slays Karados. The name is a variant of Caradoc and is used in some texts for Caradog Vreichfras, but they are different characters. *See also* Carados.

Kay, Cai or **Cei**. In the romances he is Arthur's foster brother and the son of Antor/Ector. In Geoffrey's *History* he is Arthur's Seneschal, who performs valiantly in the campaign against Rome but is killed while rescuing Bedivere and is buried at Chinon. In the earlier Celtic tales, as Cai, he is amongst Arthur's most courageous heroes and features in all of the adventures. Most notably in *Pa Gur*, we learn about his exploits in Anglesey where he kills Palug's Cat. He has many characteristics. He can go for nine days and nights without sleep and can hold his breath under water for the same period. He generates such heat that even when it rains what is near him stays dry. His father says that he is headstrong and will not betray his feelings. He is known as Cai the Tall. The later romances change his character. He becomes bitter, surly, boastful and mocking. He seldom praises people but will always find fault. He remains courageous but seems poor in comparison to his fellow knights. Frequently it is Kay who volunteers for a quest only to fail so that another can achieve it. Kay remains loyal to Arthur and yet, in a strange change of character, we find that in *Yder* he tries to poison the eponymous knight, whilst in *Perlesvaus* he kills Arthur's son Loholt. Kay clearly has a bad temper because in one of the episodes in *Culhwch and Olwen*, Arthur jests at Cai suggesting he only killed a certain giant because he was asleep. Kay flies into a temper and thereafter will not stir himself to help Arthur. Yet he is regarded as the finest horseman at Arthur's court and even his horse Gwineu is counted amongst the "Three Lively Steeds" of Britain. In *Culhwch and Olwen* Cai is slain by Gwyddog, about whom we know nothing, and Gwyddog is promptly killed by Arthur.

The Celtic tales tell us that Cai is the son of Cynyr the Bearded, Lord of Penllyn. There is a peak called Caer Gai near Lake Bala. There had been a Roman fort nearby, at Llanuwchllyn, but that had long been abandoned, so that although Cai's name would appear to be Roman, a contraction of Caius, there is no reason to believe that he was raised in a Roman military camp as some have suggested. We are never told in the Welsh tales about Cai's wife, though in the Welsh version of *Tristram* we learn he is in love with Esyllt's handmaid Golwg. Yet he has two children, Garanwyn and Celemon, the latter of whom becomes one of the ladies at Arthur's court. In the later romances his wife is Andrivete, daughter of Cador of Northumberland.

Although the original Cai was almost certainly based on a historical character, we do not know who that was and no one of that name appears in the genealogies. Curiously, though, the Vulgate creates another Kay, called d'Estraus, who is made a nephew of Caradog Vreichfras, and it is just possible the writers had access to now-lost records that showed a relationship. The later Kay may have a prototype. Geoffrey, writing in the 1130s, has Kay created Duke of Anjou. The Count of Anjou at that time was Geoffrey Plantaganet, husband of the Empress Matilda. His father, Fulk V, was still alive and had become King of Jerusalem in 1131. But *his* father, Fulk IV, was known as Rechin, meaning "surly, ill-tempered". This Fulk was grumpy when he only inherited half the county of Anjou but soon drove out his brother, Geoffrey the Bearded. The epithets fit those of Kay and his father perfectly and the reputation of Fulk, who had died in 1109, would have been remembered by most of Geoffrey of Monmouth's generation.

Lady of Shalott, *see* Elaine.

Lady of the Lake. There seem to be two, possibly three, aspects of the Lady of the Lake as the stories progress, which reflect her changing role. She first appears as the foster mother and protector of Lancelot. Early on this character was switched with that of Morgan le Fay as the enchantress lover of Merlin. However, as Morgan developed in her own right (*see separate entry*), the Lady of the Lake took on the role of adviser and protector of Arthur and the adversary of Morgan. When named at all she is usually known as Niniane, with variants Nivienne or Viviane. The aspect who became Merlin's lover is also sometimes called Nimuë. Malory confuses the matter by creating a third Lady of the Lake, called Lile, who comes to Arthur's court to demand Balin's head because he has killed her brother. Balin promptly decapitates her. Lile is called the Lady of Avalon, but she is probably meant to be the Lady de l'Isle aux Phees who, in the story of Guyron, comes to Arthur to seek retribution for the death of her brother Pellinore.

The Vulgate tells us that the Lady of the Lake was the daughter of Dyonas and the niece of the Duke of Burgundy. Dyonas is treated as the son of Diana, the Roman goddess of the forest, but in fact he was developed from a Celtic deity, Dylan. He was a god of the sea, often pictured as a merman, and was the son of Gwydion and Arianrhod. Gwydion is discussed in Chapter 8 as the shape-changer prototype of Merlin. Niniane, therefore, developed as Merlin's granddaughter, a far more sensible relationship than being his lover, which explains why she came to supplant him and arranged for him to return to slumber in the forest. It also explains why she becomes the protector of Arthur.

In the Vulgate version Niniane's father Dyonas owns the Forest of Briosque in Brittany. Part of it had come through his marriage to the Duke's niece, and the remainder from Ban and Bors because of Dyonas's help during their war with Claudas. This relationship with Ban meant that with the king's death Niniane became the foster mother of Lancelot. As the "successor" to Merlin, Niniane saw her role in raising the perfect knight to achieve the Grail Quest, a plan that was thwarted by Morgan. *See* Chapter 17.

Lailoken, *see* Merlin.

Lambor, *see* Fisher King.

Lamorak. The son of King Pellinore (and therefore brother to Aglovale, Perceval and Elaine), regarded as one of the noblest of knights, and generally rated as third only to Lancelot and Tristram. His relationship with Tristram sours after Tristram spares him in a fight, which leads to an incident over the cuckhold's horn that nearly costs Iseult her life, but the two become reunited in the common fight against Nabon le Noir. Lamorak's fate is long sealed, though, because his father had slain King Lot and he incurred the further wrath of Gawaine and his brothers by becoming the lover of their mother Morgause. He is eventually killed by Gawaine.

Lancelot or **Launcelot**, *see* Chapter 17.

Lanval or **Launfal**. The hero of Marie de France's *lai, Lanval* (*see* Chapter 18).

Leodegrance or **Leodegan**. The father of Guenevere (*see entry*) in the romances, though her father was Ogrfan in Welsh tradition.

Leudonus, *see* Lot.

Lionel. The eldest son of King Bors and thus brother of Bors and cousin of Lancelot and Ector, he is raised with Lancelot by the Lady of the Lake. Lionel, who has a birthmark shaped like a lion on his chest, later fights and kills a lion soon after he is knighted.

Initially Lionel serves as Lancelot's squire, and rescues Lancelot when the knight does battle with Gawain. Impulsive and quick-tempered, Lionel has a vicious streak and seldom listens to reason. During the Grail Quest he nearly kills Bors because Bors follows his conscience and chooses to rescue a damsel rather than Lionel. In the fracas Calogrenant is killed. Lionel is amongst those captured by Tericam/Turquin until rescued by Lancelot. After the defeat of Claudas Lionel succeeds to his father's kingdom. He is killed by one of Mordred's sons in the battles that follow Camlann.

Lisanor, **Lyzianor** or **Lionors**. The mother of Arthur's son Loholt (*see* Llacheu).

Llacheu or **Loholt**. Possibly the only legitimate son of Arthur and Guenevere, although by the time of the Vulgate Cycle he had become an earlier, and illegitimate, son by Lisanor, daughter of Count Sevain. The Vulgate Cycle has Loholt die in the Dolorous Tower as a prisoner of Karados, but the *Perlesvaus* has him a victim of Kay's jealousy. Loholt has the odd habit of sleeping on the corpse of whomever he kills. Kay finds him on the body of the giant Logrin, beheads Loholt and claims the giant's death as his own. Malory calls him Borre, a name so similar to Bors, who is also called Bohort, as to suggest some confusion or even a connection. Since Loomis believes that Bohort evolved from Gohors > Gwri, the original super-hero who inspires Gawain, Agravaine and much else besides, it may be that Lohort is yet another manifestation of the original solar deity, though clearly a sleepy one.

Llacheu, however, does not seem to be a direct derivation of the same name. He was clearly highly regarded, Welsh texts treating him as one of the "Three Well Endowed Men" of Britain and noting that he was "renowned for his arts". He was also slain, but we do not know by whom. A much later reference states he met his death at Llechysgar, believed to be in Powys. It has also been suggested that Llacheu was killed at Llongborth and was the "young Briton of noble birth" recorded in the *ASC*. In neither case is there an associated grave name.

Llwch Lleminawc. Suggested as a Celtic prototype for Lancelot, though the name probably lent itself to Lucan. *See* Chapter 17 for discussion.

Llywarch Hen. The cousin of Urien of Rheged who ended up a refugee from his homeland as a guest at the Arthur's court. He later developed a reputation as a poet but this may be a confusion with Taliesin. He is remembered in Triad 65 (*see* Chapter 8).

Lohengrin. The son of Parzifal, according to Wolfram von Eschenbach.

Loholt, *see* Llacheu.

Lot or **Loth**. In Geoffrey's *History* he is the ruler of Lodonesia who marries Arthur's sister Anna, and is the father of Gawain and Mordred. He assists Uther in his battle against the Saxons. He loses his lands but following Arthur's victories they are restored. Subsequently Loth, as the nephew of Sichelm, king of Norway, becomes king of Norway with Arthur's aid. In the later romances his wife is Morgawse, and he has additional sons – Agravain, Gaheris and Gareth – plus two daughters, Soredamors and Clarissant. Lot is seen as antagonistic towards Arthur at the outset and subsequently joins the rebellion of the kings under Rience. He is killed in battle by Pellinore.

In Welsh tradition Lot is Lleuddun Luyddog, "Loth of the Hosts", and he is primarily remembered as the grandfather of St. Kentigern through his wayward daughter Taneu. Lleuddun is regarded as the eponymous founder of Lothian, and the later romances also treat Lot as the king of Lothian and Orcanie, usually translated as the Orkneys. Since Lleuddun's capital is remembered as Dinas Eidyn (modern Edinburgh), it would make sense to equate him with Lothian. However, the old British name for Leeds was Loidis or Lat, and the inhabitants were the Ladenses. Lot's sister Elfryddl married Eliffer of the Great Host, an epithet similar to Lot's, and it's possible that Loth may have succeeded to part of Eliffer's territory. Some pedigrees also list Loth as the brother of Urien, so he may have had some territory in northern Britain. This raises the question of his connection with the Orkneys. Some have suggested that there was a territory called Orcanie, either in Brittany or in northern Britain, though August Hunt has suggested it may be Archenfield, the old name for the area around the Forest of Dean. It may simply be that Lot's name was connected with Ljot, the Norse earl of Orkney, who ruled from 981–94.

Lucan. Arthur's butler, the son of Duke Corneus, cousin of Griflet and possibly brother of Bedivere. Although he tends to remain in the background the frequent references to his name show that he is at most major battles in the early days and is involved in the tourneys. He fights at Camlann and is severely wounded. When Arthur gives him his final embrace the wounds split and Lucan dies. His name, though not his character, is probably derived from the Celtic hero Llwch Lleminawc.

Lunette, Luned or **Lynet**. A cousin of Niniane, and sister of Lyones. She creates a fountain that causes storms. She becomes the wife of Gareth in Malory's version. Her story is told in Chrétien's *Yvain* and in the Welsh *The Lady of the Fountain.*

Mabon. As Mabon ap Modron he is listed amongst Arthur's counsellors in *Culhwch and Olwen*. However, he had also been spirited away at birth and his skills as a hunter are needed for Culhwch's series of tasks, so Arthur and his men track down Mabon in a prison approachable only by water. Mabon, or his mother, is also described as Uther Pendragon's servant. In the Prose *Tristram*, Mabon is seen as a sorcerer and student of Merlin and is called "le Noir". He is drawn from Maponus, the Celtic god of youth and music. Mabon probably equates to Mabuz whom Lanzelet aids in von Zarzikhoven's romance. *See also* Morgan.

MacArthur, Clan. The Scottish Clan MacArthur, also represented today by the Clan Campbell, claims descent from King Arthur through a son called Merevie or Smerbe or Smerevie or Merbis. This is almost certainly from Artúir mac Aedan of Dál Riata, who lived from 560–596AD. The line of descent to the earliest historical attested name runs Merevie > Ferrither > Duibne Mhor > Arthur OgFerrither > Duibne Falt Dhearg > Ferrither

> Duibne Dearg > Duibne Donn > Diarmind O'Duibne, who lived in the early tenth century. These eleven generations span about 300 years, and therefore this descent fits the time scale. Nothing is known of Merevie, whose name corresponds to the Welsh Meurig.

Mador or **Amador de la Porte**. One of Arthur's longest serving knights, since we are told in the Vulgate *Mort Artu* that he had served Arthur for forty-five years. Yet he is virile enough to fight Lancelot in single combat for an hour. This comes about because Mador's cousin Gaheris (Patrise in Malory) dies after eating a poisoned apple and Mador accuses the Queen of murder. Loomis suggests that Mador is drawn from the character of Mardoc, Gatekeeper to the Other World, but that role better suits Maduc le Noir, a knight who refuses to pay homage to Arthur but instead builds a fortress in the Forest of Sarpenic from where he strikes at and kills any of Arthur's company who pass. Intriguingly there is a Madog amongst the princes of Powys (*see* Table 3.9), who is named as one of the "Three Gate-Keepers" at the Battle of Perllan Fangor (believed to be the slaughter at Chester in 615).

Maduc le Noir, *see* Mador.

Maelgwyn. The king of Gwynedd who was considered by Gildas to be the most evil of the rulers he castigated. He is discussed in detail in Chapter 5. He was adopted into the later French romances as Malaquin le Gallois.

Malahaut, Lady of. From the same land as the King of the Hundred Knights, the Lady (rarely named but once called Bloie) appears in several romances but primarily the Vulgate *Lancelot*. *See* Chapter 17 for details.

Marc, **March** or **Mark**. Tristan's uncle and husband of Iseult. *See* Chapter 13.

Margawse, *see* Morgause.

Meleagaunt or **Melwas**. The son of Bagdemagus of Gorre who abducts Guenevere. This story first appeared in Caradog of

Llancarfan's *Life of Gildas* (*see* Chapter 11) and was rapidly drawn into the burgeoning Arthurian romance as the launchpad for Lancelot (*see* Chapter 17). Geoffrey of Monmouth had referred to Melwas as Malvasius, king of Iceland, though Iceland is a corruption of the Isle of Glass, regarded as Glastonbury. However, the few surviving fragments from earlier Welsh tradition that refer to him make him a Prince of North Britain, but he is not otherwise known.

Menw. An enchanter who is listed in the Twenty-Four Knights of Arthur's Court and amongst his Counsellors. He is involved in the hunt for the Boar Trwyth in *Culhwch and Olwen*, during which he became permanently scarred. He may be the prototype for Merlin.

Merbis or **Smerbe**, *see* MacArthur.

Merlin or **Myrddin**. *See* Chapter 15 for full discussion.

Mordrain, *see* Evelach.

Mordred. Originally treated as a legitimate son of Lot and Arthur's sister (*see* Anna *and* Morgause), but usually regarded as the illegitimate and incestuous son of Arthur and his half-sister. Mordred's story was developed in full in the Vulgate Cycle. Both versions of his conception and how Arthur tries to kill him as an infant are covered in Chapter 15, whilst his role in usurping the throne and his war with Arthur are covered in Chapter 17. Geoffrey's earlier version is in Chapter 9. Most romances show Mordred as a good knight in his youth, but once the truth of his birth is revealed he becomes troubled and his evil side takes over, especially once he pairs up with Agravaine. Mordred is credited with two sons but in the romances his wife is not named. In later Welsh tradition she is Gwenhwyfach, sister of Gwenhwyfar, and it is Mordred's reaction to an argument between the sisters that leads to Camlann, rather than him usurping the kingdom. Later tradition has the war arise because Arthur refuses to recognise Mordred as his heir. In Welsh he is called Medraut or Medrod. Only one other Medrod is listed in the pedigrees, and he is the grandson of Caradog Vreichfras and the father of St. Dyfnog. There is no reason to link the two, but tradition did because Dyfnog's mother is sometimes recorded as Gwenhwyfach. Both Mordred's children were murdered, probably by Constantine as implied by Gildas, though in the romances they are killed by Bors and Lancelot.

Morfran. According to *Culhwch and Olwen*, one of the three knights who survives Camlann, apparently because of his extreme ugliness as no one would approach him. Even so he is one of Arthur's counsellors and listed amongst his twenty-four knights. This may be the knight that Chrétien calls "the Ugly Brave".

Morgan, Morgain or **Morgen le Fay**. The enchantress of the Isle of Avalon who is shown throughout the legend as Arthur's adversary. Originally she is seen as Arthur's saviour, appearing only at the end of the story, along with her maidens, to bear Arthur away to Avalon and tend his wounds. She is sometimes called Argante, and was regarded as related to Arthur. Later texts, including Malory, make her his half-sister, along with Morgause and Elaine, and even contrive to have her seduce him to become the mother of Mordred. It is the Vulgate Cycle, particularly the Prose *Lancelot*, that introduces her as the beautiful but deadly fey who works through others to seek Arthur's downfall. These others include Accolon, Bertilak, Guingamor and Karados. Her main opponent is the Lady of the Lake, though before that role developed Morgan, as the Mistress of Avalon, was the prototype Lady of the Lake. Morgan became the fusion of several early myths and traditions. She is usually seen as a representation of the Morrigán, one of a group of Irish war-goddesses who seek to influence the outcome of battles by indirect means. These goddesses often appear in threes, as with Morgan and her two sisters. Morgan is also associated with the Nine Sisters of Avalon, though the only ones named are Moronoe, Mazoe, Gliten, Glitonea, Gliton, Tyronoe and Thiten.

The Morrigán also uses her sexual charms to achieve her plans. In the Irish legend of Cú Chulainn she seeks to allure the hero but when he spurns her she uses every means possible to destroy him. Morgan is also associated with the concept of the Divine Mother known as Modron. Later romances have Morgan as the wife of Urien of Rheged, and early Welsh tradition relates how Urien was beguiled by Modron ferch Afallach who bore him two children, Owain and Morfudd. Modron is also the mother of Mabon (*see entry*) who, in the early story *Lanzelet* appears as Mabuz, son of the Lady of the Lake.

In that last role Morgan is also seen as a healer. She provides a salve to help cure Erec in Chrétien's story, and in the equivalent Welsh story of Geraint she is shown in male aspect as Morgan Tud, Arthur's chief physician. Morgan's first lover Guingamor was called Lord of Avalon and is almost certainly based on Gwyn ap Nudd, whose lover was Creiddylad, mentioned in *Culhwch and Olwen* as the "maiden of most majesty" in all of Britain. Creiddylad was betrothed to Gwythyr but abducted by Gwyn, and this led to a war between the two which Arthur had to stop. More importantly, Creiddylad was regarded as the daughter of Llud Llawereint or Llud of the Silver Hand, the Welsh equivalent of the Irish Nuada Argatlam. Nuada is seen as a manifestation of Nodens, the British god of healing. There was a magnificent healing sanctuary dedicated to Nodens at Lydney in Gloucestershire, which was still in use into the early fifth century. It may be that the historical character upon which Morgan is based was a female healer at Lydney. We may even venture to conjecture whom this was. Vortimer had a daughter, Madrun, who may have retired to the sanctuary after her father's death. Later Welsh legend makes Madrun the founder of a church in Ardudwy while she was on a pilgrimage to Bardsey, and Bardsey, like Lydney, has a reputation as a healing sanctuary.

Morgause or **Margawse**. The half-sister of Arthur, who seems to have replaced Anna in the later narratives. She is the wife of Lot and mother of Gawain, Agravain, Gaheris and Gareth but, as revealed in the Vulgate Cycle, she sleeps with Arthur and becomes the mother of Mordred. After Lot's death she becomes the lover of Lamorak and is killed by her own son, Gaheris. In *Diu Krône* she is called Morchades, which links her name to Lot's kingdom of the Orkneys.

Morrigán, *see* Morgan.

Myrddin, *see* Merlin.

Nascien. The baptismal name of Seraphe, brother-in-law of Evalach/Mordrain. In the Vulgate Cycle, he is blinded when he looks too closely at the Grail but is healed by the Bleeding Lance. Nascien's later adventures involve Solomon's Ship and the Sword of David. His misuse of the latter causes it to break and Nascien to be wounded. Nascien is the ancestor of Lancelot and Galahad. One of his descendants is Galahad's guardian. The name also appears on the list of Arthur's twenty-four knights.

Nimuë, *see* Lady of the Lake.

Niniane, *see* Lady of the Lake.

Octa, *see under* Oisc.

Oisc or **Aesc**. The founder of the first Saxon dynasty in Kent, which was known as the Oiscingas. The *ASC* treats him as the son of Hengist. He may have fought at Badon and therefore may be the same as Osla Bigknife, but this is not definite. Bede has Octa as Oisc's son, but Nennius states that he was Hengist's son, so Octa may be Osla, and Oisc may have succeeded him. Osla might also be Esla, Cerdic's grandfather. *See* Chapters 4, 7, and 8.

Osla Bigknife, *see under* Oisc.

Owain, Owein, Ivain or **Yvain**. The son of Urien of Rheged who may have lived long enough to inherit the kingdom but who died soon afterwards, possibly at Catraeth. He is renowned in the battle poems of the North for having defeated the Angles (*see* Chapter 8). He is usually treated as the father of St. Kentigern. Owain mutated into the Arthurian romances, via Geoffrey's *History*, as Yvain, the Knight of the Lion (*see* Chapter 18). He is closely associated with Gawain and it is possible that the historical originals were cousins. He is the original tutor of Lancelot in the Vulgate version.

Palamedes or **Palomides**. A Saracen knight who is besotted with Iseult but never gains her hand. As a consequence, he ends up in various fights and altercations with Tristram. He also takes over from Pellinore in the never-ending pursuit of the Questing Beast. Palamedes has several brothers, including Safere and Segwarides. With Safere he helps rescue four brothers from Karados's Dolorous Tower. In the Prose *Tristram* Palamedes is wounded by Lancelot and later killed by Gawain, but Malory has him as an ally of Lancelot who accompanies him to France and becomes Duke of Provence. That last may have been a token gesture to Edward, Prince of Wales, son of Henry VI, who was still alive at the time Malory wrote *Morte Darthur*. Edward's mother Marguerite was the daughter of Rene the Good, King of Naples and Sicily, King of Jerusalem, Duke of Lorraine and, as it transpired, the last Count of Provence. Edward, as his eldest male grandson, might have succeeded him in that title had he not been killed at the Battle of Tewkesbury in May 1471.

Pellam or **Pellehan**. The king of Listinoise and both the Fisher King and the Maimed King. In the Post-Vulgate and Malory he is wounded by Balin with the Dolorous Blow. In some texts he is made the father of Perceval, but that is probably an error for his son Pelles (*see entry*). Loomis suggests that the name is a mutation of Beli, but all of the other Fisher King names are derived from the Biblical patriarchs, and Pellam could be derived from Peleg whose name means "division", as in his day the peoples of the Earth were divided.

Pelleas. A knight whose story seems an image of Tristan and Isolde. Pelleas is in love with Ettard but she does not return it. Gawain promises to win her over but instead takes the lady himself. Nimuë makes Pelleas fall in love with her and Ettard now becomes enamoured of Pelleas, but it's too late. Ettard dies of a broken heart.

Pelles. The son of Pellehan and father of Elaine. With the help of Brisen, Elaine's handmaiden, Pelles administers to Lancelot a potion that makes him believe Elaine is Guenevere, and as a result she conceives Galahad. *See* Fisher King.

Pellinore. Variously cited as the brother or cousin of Pelles and at times (as in the *Livre D'Artus*) confused with both him and Pellehan as the Fisher King. His wound arose because he doubted the wonders of the Grail and was punished by God. He becomes involved in the pointless pursuit of the Questing Beast. Pellinore is the father of Tor and of Elaine, who may be confused with Pelles's daughter. However, Pellinore fails to rescue Elaine while he is on a quest to find Nimuë, and as a result she dies. In the rebellion of the kings Pellinore kills Lot and is eventually killed by Gawain.

Perceval or **Percivale**. The original Grail knight. *See* Chapter 16 for full discussion.

Pertolepe, *see* Bertilak.

Ragnell, Dame. The name given to the Loathly Damsel, an ugly woman who is really a beauty in disguise who tests knights' loyalty and honesty. Gawain is usually on the receiving end. *See* Chapter 14.

Rhufon/Rhun the Radiant, *see* Agravain.

Rhydderch or **Ridderch Hael**. The king of Strathclyde whom some tales place at the battle of Arderydd. *See* Chapter 8 in particular.

Rience, Rion or **Ryon**. A king of Norgales (North Wales) and various other locales, who has fought and defeated eleven kings, each time adding their beards to his cloak. He intends to make Arthur's his twelfth. In the original Celtic legend Arthur fights and kills Rience (here called Rhitta or Ritho) in Snowdonia (one legend) or the Berwyn Mountains. Their struggle took place at Rhiw y Barfau ("Slope of Beards"). In Geoffrey's *History* he is a giant, which usually denotes a Saxon or Dane. In Malory it is Balin and Balan who capture Rience and deliver him to Arthur. There may be more to this story than first thought. The list of those at Arthur's court in *Culhwch and Olwen* includes Gormant ap Rhica who is Arthur's maternal half-brother. This might well have been a family squabble over inheritance. The town of Rhica, *Tref Rita*, was apparently in Gwent, north of Caerwent, near Llandegfedd.

Riothamus. A military leader and possibly king amongst the Bretons who may be the original Arthur. *See* Chapter 6.2 for discussion.

Safere or **Saphire**. Brother of Palamedes (*see entry*).

Sagremor or **Sacremors**. A knight related to the royal family of Constantinople although also called the son of the King of Hungary, or "Hongrie", which may be a pun on his insatiable hunger. Sagremor must have had an active metabolism as he is always leaping into action, seldom to great effect, and will throw himself into the heat of battle, and eat ravenously afterwards. Failure to eat makes him ill, so Kay nicknames him "le Mort jeune" ("the young dead"). It may also be reflected in his name, "sacred death". Chrétien, who first introduces Sagremor, may have based him on the character of Tall Atrwm in *Culhwch and Olwen* who apparently could never stop eating or drinking. Sagremor is killed in the final battle with Mordred. Curiously, in the Post-Vulgate *Merlin* Sagremor's father, Nabur the Unruly, rears the infant Mordred.

Sanddef. One of Arthur's twenty-four knights and one of the few survivors of Camlann, according to *Culhwch and Olwen*. He was known as "Angel Form" and no one dared attack him because he was so beautiful. He may be the equivalent of Chrétien's "Handsome Coward".

Taliesin. The name of a sixth-century bard to whom are credited many poems that refer to Arthur or his contemporaries. He even takes part in some of the adventures. His work is discussed in Chapter 8 and his main adventure in Chapter 12.

Terrican or **Turquin**. The brother of Karados who also captures knights, though he does not seem to be in league with Morgan. He is killed by Lancelot.

Tor. The illegitimate son of Pellinor, he is only young when he is brought by a cowherd to Arthur's court, but Arthur sees his potential and Tor soon proves himself. He is knighted and before long admitted to the Round Table, which annoys King Bagdemagus who thinks it is his turn. We only learn of a few of his adventures, the most notable of which involves his search for a hound and which includes him despatching the villainous Abelleus. Tor is killed during Lancelot's rescue of Guenevere. Chrétien almost certainly took his name from the Welsh sources, probably Twrch ap Perif, who appears in *Culhwch and Olwen* and as one of Arthur's counsellors in *Dream of Rhonabwy*. Twrch, of course, means boar or hog, as in the Twrch Trwyth, and evidently reflects Tor's lowly upbringing.

Tristan or **Tristram**. The lover of Iseult. *See* Chapter 13 for full discussion.

Turquin, *see* Terrican.

Ugly Brave, The, *see* Morfran.

Urien. A historical king of Rheged, and father of Owain. He lived at least two generations after Badon. Urien was famed for his battles against the Saxons, discussed in Chapter 8, and it's very likely that some of his battles were later grafted on to Arthur's battle list. Urien was murdered at the instigation of another chieftain called Morcant, a name that may have encouraged connections with both Mordred and Morgan. In the romances he is made king of Gorre.

Uther Pendragon. The father of Arthur whose life is told by Geoffrey of Monmouth. *See* Chapter 9 for discussion.

Uwaine, *see* Yvaine.

Vivian or **Viviene**, *see* Lady of the Lake.

Vortigern. The ruler of Britain who is accused of inviting the Saxons to Britain and of consorting with the enemy. His life is a preamble to the Arthurian story and, in Geoffrey's *History*, introduces Merlin. *See* Chapters 5, 6 and 9.

Vortimer. The son of Vortigern. *See* Chapters 5, 6 and 9.

Vortipor. A king of Dyfed known as the Protector, and a contemporary of Arthur of Badon. He is one of the kings castigated by Gildas. His life and Arthurian associations are discussed in Chapters 5 and 10.

Yder. The hero of his own verse romance (*see* Chapter 18). He seems to be a prototype of Lancelot, because Guenevere confesses her love for him. He remained a popular character, as he appears in several later romances. He dies during Arthur's Roman campaign. A Cornish legend about Yder (maybe another of that name) tells how he hurries ahead of Arthur to kill three giants on Brent Knoll in Somerset. He succeeds but dies of the effort. There is also a King Yder in the later romances, apparently a ruler of Cornouaille, who is one of the rebels who refuses to accept Arthur at the outset but who later fights valiantly on Arthur's behalf. It is easy to confuse the two.

Ygraine, **Ygerne** or **Igraine**. The wife of Gorlois, who is seduced by Uther and becomes the mother of Arthur. *See* Chapter 9.

Yseult, *see* Iseult.

Yvain. There are at least six knights by this name and possibly more, as not all identifications are obvious. The most famous of them was the legitimate son of Urien, who is covered under Owain. His half-brother, the illegitimate son of Urien and his seneschal's wife, is called Yvain li Avoutres ("the Bastard"). He appears in many of the key battles and quests but is killed by Gawain (who does not recognise him) during the Grail Quest. The other four all seem to be cousins and are Yvain de Lionel, Yvain li Dains (or l'Esclain), Yvain le Blanche Mains and Yvain du Cinel (or de Rivel).

24

LOST WORLDS – AN ARTHURIAN GAZETTEER

This is a quick guide to all sites in Britain with an Arthurian association, with a cross reference, where appropriate, to where that site may be discussed in more detail elsewhere in this book. It does not include sites outside Britain. Sites known only by their Arthurian names, such as Camelot, are listed separately at the start, with cross-references to suggested locales. All other sites are organized by county. I have only included those sites which have a direct link to the Arthurian legend so that many sites which have adopted such names as Arthur's Stone or Arthur's Table for a local landmark but with no known Arthurian link have been excluded. All of the possible battle sites are listed, but for a detailed discussion *see* Chapter 7.

Anyone wishing for a more detailed guide should refer to *A Guidebook to Arthurian Britain* by Geoffrey Ashe (Longman, 1980), reprinted and revised as *The Traveller's Guide to Arthurian Britain* (Gothic Image, 1997), and *A Traveller's Guide to the Kingdoms of Arthur* by Neil Fairbairn & Michael Cyprien (Evans, 1983), which also includes entries for Brittany.

LEGENDARY OR ARCHAIC NAMES

Agned. The site of Arthur's eleventh battle, according to Nennius. *See* Edinburgh and Melrose.

Astolat. Better known by its Tennysonian name Shalott, this place is variously called Ascalot or Escalot and was the home of Elaine, the Lady of Shalott. Malory placed it at Guildford, but only because he needed a site between Winchester and London. The oldest form of the name is Escalot which, if we remove the French prefix *Es*, becomes Calot. In Welsh this would have been Gwlodd or Caer Gwlodd, a name which appears in the poem *Preideu Annwvyn* as one of the epithets of the fortress of Annwn, the fairy fortress Caer Sidhi. Caer Gulodd, as it usually appears, means the Hidden Fortress, a suitable description for the Grail Castle. This suggests that the origins for both Astolat and Corbenic derive from the same source location even though they became two separate places. *See* Avalon.

Avalon. The Isle of Avalon was where, according to Geoffrey of Monmouth, Arthur's sword Caliburn was forged and where Arthur was taken to be healed. Geoffrey also tells us that Avalon was known as the Fortunate Isle or the Isle of Plenty. It is also known, according to William of Malmesbury, as the Isle of Apples, a translation of Ynys Afallach or Avallach. It came to represent the Otherworld, perhaps the visible portion of Annwn which was the Underworld. The name corrupted in the Grail legend to that of the King, Evelach or Evelake, whilst in the pedigrees Aballac was the son or grandson of Beli and ancestor of Coel and Cunedda. All of these names suggest an association with a halfway house to the Otherworld, a kind of portal to Heaven, and thus similar to, and possibly the source of, the Grail Castle. The location of Avalon (if not the source of the name) is almost certainly the same as Annwn. The poem *Preideu Annwvyn*, or "The Spoils of Annwn", gives eight names for the fortress to which Arthur sails to rescue Gwair and steal the magic cauldron. It is called Caer Sidhe ("fairy fortress"), Caer Pedryfan ("the four-cornered fortress"), Caer Feddyd ("Fort of the Gods"), Caer Rigor ("royal fortress"), Caer Wydr ("glass fort"), Caer Goludd ("hidden fortress"), Caer Fandwy ("High Fort"), Caer Ochren ("Fort of the Sides"). All describe not only a castle of some significance in size and form, but a castle of the gods. Annwn was the realm of the Celtic Gods which became Christianized as Avalon. It was evidently a place held as holy by the British.

Many places have been associated with Avalon, including Avallon in France, which may have helped cement the name, or the old Roman fort of Aballava (*see* Burgh by Sands). Of course neither of these is an island, although Robert de Boron in *Joseph d'Aramathie* refers to the "Vales of Avalon", suggesting Somerset, which by his day had become associated with Glastonbury (*see entry*). Other islands suggested are Anglesey, Arran, Bardsey, Lundy, Isle of Man and Iona, plus two islands off the Breton coast, Sein and Ile Aval. *See also* the entry for Lydney (Gloucestershire).

Badon. The site of Arthur's twelfth and most decisive battle. Many locations have been suggested but none with great certainty. These are discussed in detail in Chapter 7.

Bassas. Arthur's sixth battle, according to Nennius. *See* Baschurch (Shropshire), Falkirk (Scotland).

Bedegraine and **Brandigan**. In Malory's *Morte Darthur*, Arthur's first major battle against the rebellious kings is at Bedegraine, which was a castle friendly to Arthur but besieged by the rebels. Malory says that it is in Sherwood Forest but, as usual, he is probably confusing names. The centre of Sherwood Forest in Malory's day was not Nottingham but Ravenshead, the highest point, where the Forest Court sat. Nearby was Newstead Abbey on a promontory in the lake, just as Bedegraine Castle is described. Ravens are closely associated with Arthurian legend and the British word for Raven was *bran*. In Chrétien's *Erec et Enide*, the castle of Brandigan, built by King Evrain, is described as almost impregnable, on an island fifteen leagues wide and self sufficient in every way. Brandigan is clearly a corruption of *Branogenium*, the name of the Roman fort at Leintwardine. The name means literally "born of the raven", which may be a euphemism for "born of the king", Bran being the name of the early Celtic ruler. The name still exists in the areas as Brandon Camp, south of Leintwardine, which is surrounded by river tributaries and thus may be regarded as an island. It would be easy for Malory to believe that Ravenshead might also once have been called Brandigan, now further disguised as Bedegraine.

Benwick or **Benoic**. The kingdom of Lancelot's father, Ban, in France. There is a Benwick in Britain, near March in Cambridgeshire, but that name was originally *Beymwich*, which probably meant the "farm by the tree trunk", and it is an unlikely site for Lancelot's home. Another suggested site is Bannock near Stirling, site of the battle of Bannockburn. This derives from the

Celtic *Bannog*, for the peaked hill from which the burn flows. This may indeed have attracted the eye of the French, but the answer may be more prosaic than that. Littleton and Malcor make the point that Benwick or Banwick simply means the "wick" or farm/land of Ban, which is self-descriptive. Loomis believed that Ban de Benoic is a French version of Bran le Benoit, meaning Bran the Blessed. Either way Benwick is simply a descriptive placename and not a territory at all. There was an ancient castle at Banvou in Normandy that may have helped prompt the connection. *See also* Gannes.

Bregwyn. The site of Arthur's eleventh battle, possibly an alternative name for Agned. *See* High Rochester and Leintwardine.

Brocéliande. The ancient forest of central Brittany, famous for being where Merlin spent his final days with Nimuë and where he now lies entombed. Lancelot also spent his youth here at the lake at Comper. Wace, when writing his history, thought he ought to check out the forest but saw nothing. "A fool I returned; a fool I went," he wrote. All that now remains of the great old forest is the Forêt de Paimpont, between Rennes and Ploërmel. The Tomb of Merlin is on the north side near Comper. *See also* Forest of Dean (Gloucester).

Cameliard. The home of Guenevere and her father Leodegrance. Although this is usually placed in Cornwall (with links to the river Camel), Guenevere's home was traditionally in Wales at Knucklas (*see entry*). Just west of Knucklas is a mountainous region called Maelienydd and it has been suggested that the fortress at Knucklas may also have been known as Caer Maelienydd, which became Cameliard.

Camelot. The name of Arthur's principle castle and perhaps the most famous name in all Arthuriana. It first appeared in Chrétien de Troyes's story about Lancelot, *Le Chevalier de la Charrete*, written around 1177. He stated that Arthur "had left Caerleon and held a most magnificent court at Camelot", but otherwise gave no location. Not all of the French or German romancers mention Camelot, preferring Carduel. Most British sources list Caerleon, Gelliwig or Carlisle as Arthur's main courts. It was Malory who popularised Camelot and he is specific that it was Winchester (Book *xii*, Chapter *x*, Caxton edition), but he was only following the mood of the day when Edward IV promoted Winchester's Arthurian connections. Curiously Caxton, in his introduction to Malory's text, said that Camelot was in Wales and that "divers now living hath seen" its great stones and marvellous works. Since Chrétien had distinguished between Camelot and Caerleon, Caxton was probably referring to Caerwent, where the old Roman town was still visible. Barber and Pykitt suggest that the town of Llanmelin, which is almost part of Caerwent, may originally have been called Caermelin, which could have corrupted into Camelot.

Sixty years after Caxton's printing, John Leland identified Camelot with Cadbury Castle in Somerset, with its neighbouring villages of Queen Camel and West Camel. That has remained a popular site ever since, with circumstantial support coming from Alcock's archaeological survey in the late 1960s.

The name Camelot may have been derived from the Roman Camulodunum, modern-day Colchester. There is no evidence to suggest an Arthurian presence in Essex, least of all in any area close to the Germanic settlements, though it does appear that a British enclave subsisted into the fifth century around London and Essex. Nevertheless sub-Roman Colchester was never as resplendent as Caerwent or Wroxeter, the Roman Viriconium in Shropshire, which was the largest and most significant Roman town to see continued occupation throughout the fifth century. Both these towns, but especially Wroxeter, could have been sufficiently splendid during these violent times to be remembered as something special.

Camelford in Cornwall and Camelon near Falkirk have both been suggested solely on the similarity of the name. Camelford has no known building to support the claim. At Camelon, the Roman town was called Caermawr. No northern town was sufficiently beyond the battle zone to have been allowed to develop into a place of any appreciable luxury. If Camelot were meant to represent a specific place (and not just Chrétien's invention), it would need to be in the south and west, and not too far from Caerleon. Caerwent and Wroxeter would be the best possibilities, with Cadbury a close third.

Camlann. Arthur's final battle. Several sites have been suggested, all of which are discussed in Chapter 7. *See* separate entries on River Cam (Somerset) and Camlan (Gwynedd).

Carduel. At the start of *Yvain*, Chrétien refers to Arthur's court at "Carduel en Gales". This is usually translated as Carlisle, or *Caer Luel*, with Wales interpreted as covering all of the old British territories in western Britain. Marie de France also uses the name Carduel in her *lai*, *Lanval*, and it came to feature regularly in the French romances. The name may be related to Kerduel in Brittany, just north of Lannion, where there is an ancient château. It has been suggested that the Breton name derives from the holy man Tudual, but this seems unlikely. Tudual's monastery was at Tréguier, which is not too far from Kerduel, and there was no need for Tudual to have a separate hermitage.

Castle of Maidens. Another name for Mount Agned, according to Geoffrey of Monmouth; he was almost certainly referring to Edinburgh Castle.

Celidon. In Nennius's battle list the Forest of Celidon is noted as the site of Arthur's seventh battle. This is usually interpreted as the Caledonian Forest in the Scottish Borders, but there are other suggestions.

Celliwig, Gelliwig or **Kelliwic**. *See* Celliwic *under* Gwent.

Corbenic. The best known of the many names for the Grail Castle. The name is derived from the Old French *Cor Benit*, meaning "blessed horn", an allusion to the Horn of Plenty, clearly linking the Grail legend to the old Celtic beliefs. Since the Grail Castle is really not of this world but a halfway house to the Otherworld, it does not have an earthly counterpart and the castle meant something different to different romancers. Something that began as symbolic of Jerusalem later symbolised the Vatican but on a spiritual plane. *See also* Avalon.

Dolorous Garde or **Joyeuse Garde**. The name of Lancelot's Castle. We are told in the Prose *Lancelot* that this is on the Humber, but that is most unlikely. Malory suggested either Bamburgh or Alnwick, doubtless drawing upon tradition. Another suggestion is Edinburgh's Castle Rock, which Geoffrey of Monmouth, who believed it to be the site of the Castle of the Maidens, called Dolorous Mountain. Lancelot captures the castle from Brian/Brandin of the Isles, and there was a historical Brian of the Isles who held at different times Peveril Castle (*see* Castleton) and Knaresborough Castle, both of which were major castles at this time. Regardless of where the author intended it to be in Britain, it's possible that he had in mind a French castle. He may have used the Humber as the closest English equivalent to the great French estuary of the Gironde, just north of which, in the much rockier Charonne valley, was the once-impregnable castle of Taillebourg, where Eleanor of Aquitaine and Louis VII spent their wedding night. Forty years later its lord, Geoffrey de Rançon, was in rebellion against Richard, Duke of Aquitaine (the future Richard the Lionheart). Taillebourg was believed safe because it was hemmed in on three sides by mountains and the fourth side was well defended, but in a siege of a little over a week in July 1179 Richard captured the castle. It could well have been this remarkable victory that the author reworked into his story, portraying Richard as the new Lancelot. There is a Château de Joyeuse-Garde in Brittany along the Elorn Valley in la Forest-Landernau east of Brest. The buildings, of which only an arch and foundations remain, date from the eleventh century; it was probably renamed after Lancelot's castle.

Dubglas. The site of four of Arthur's battles, according to Nennius. There are many suggested sites under names the Douglas, Dulas or Blackwater.

Escalot, *see* Astolat.

Gannes. The kingdom of Lancelot's uncle Bors, and adjacent to Benwick. It is situated in France and most agree that Bors or Bohors of Gannes was a corruption of Gohors of Galles, who appears in the earlier Breton *Lay de Corn*. Galles is Wales, but may have been mistaken for Gaul. So Gannes is really a corruption based on an error for Gaul/France.

Glein. The site of Arthur's first battle, according to Nennius. There are several suggested sites, *see* Lancaster, Doddington, Wootton and Spalding.

Gorre or **Gore**. A kingdom ascribed to both Urien and Bagdemagus. It is also variously described as being surrounded by water, and accessible only by an underwater bridge and a sword bridge, as being near Bath and as being on the borders of Scotland, and near Sugales. Clearly there is some confusion here as well as perhaps both a metaphysical association and a geographical one. Loomis believed Gorre was symbolic of the Otherworld, but I suspect it was more prosaic than that. On the basis that Sugales means South Wales, some have suggested that Gorre is the Gower Peninsula in Glamorgan. The name is derived from *gwyr*, meaning hooked or curved. However, Urien's kingdom was Rheged, but it also extended to the Isle of Man. In Chrétien's time the former ruler of Man, Godred, was known as Old Gorry and, by extension, the name included the Isle of Man.

Guinnion. The site of Arthur's eighth battle. *See* Stow (Borders), Binchester and Llanarmon.

Joyeuse Garde, *see* Dolorous Garde.

Kynke Kenadon. The castle "upon the sands that marched nigh Wales", according to Malory, who has Arthur hold court here in the story of Beaumains (Caxton edition, book *vii*). It is usually identified with Caernarvon (Gwynedd), though it has been linked with Kyneton in Radnorshire even though that town has no shore.

Linnuis. The region of four of Arthur's battles at the River Dubglas, according to Nennius. The location is often interpreted as Lindsey in Lincolnshire, but there are other interpretations, such as Ilchester.

Listinoise or **Listineise**. The name of the Grail kingdom ruled by King Pellam, also called the Land of the Two Marches. Inasmuch as the Grail Castle, Corbenic, has no earthly counterpart, then neither does Listinoise. The name is sometimes translated as *Llys-yn-Nord*, a strange Norman-Welsh version of "castle of the north", but it could as easily be *Llys-y-nos*, "Castle of the Night" or, allowing for a clever play on words, *Llys-y-Nesu*. "Nesu", depending on its use, can mean to draw near or to move further away, an ideal description for the Grail lands.

Lyonesse. The kingdom of Tristan that was swallowed beneath the waves. Mordred is also alleged to have escaped here after Camlann. Tradition places it between the coast of Cornwall and the Scilly Isles but other versions make the Scilly Isles the remnants of Lyonesse or make Lyonesse closer to home and submerged beneath Mounts Bay off Penzance, with St. Michael's Mount being all that remains. Lyonesse was of sufficient size that it had 140 churches. There is a story that a terrific storm on New Year's Eve 1099 flooded lands off Cornwall and there was only one survivor. It has been estimated that if the sea level dropped by 10m then the Scilly Isles of Tresco, Bryher and Samson would become one island again, but with current sea-level changes this level would have been four thousand years ago. There is apparently a record that in the time of the Emperor Magnus Maximus the Scillies were referred to as one island. There are reports of other drowned lands around Britain's coast, especially in Cardigan Bay, and, as discussed in Chapter 8, survivors from these lands were supposed to be at Arthur's Court. There is a similar legend about the lost land of Ker-Ys off the coast of Brittany.

Pen Rhionydd. Identified in the first of the Welsh Triads as one of Arthur's three tribal thrones. The other two, at Celliwic and St David's, have been identified but Pen Rhionydd has caused problems, especially as it is said to be "in the north". Rachel Bromwich, in her translation of the Triads, suggests that it was the Rhinns of Galloway, making the connection with St Kentigern, who is listed as the Chief Bishop of Pen Rhionydd. I suspect that the Triad had itself drawn upon corrupt data and that "in the north" meant North Wales. I believe than Pen Rhionydd is the headland above Morfa Rhianedd, which are the sands (now a golf course) at Llandudno. Pen Rhionydd was the site of the court of Deganwy. The matter is discussed in detail in Chapter 8.

Sarras. Yet another version of the gateway to the Otherworld. Although described as a city of the Saracens (hence Sarras), it was from here that Galahad and the Grail were received to heaven. It was really a spiritual counterpart of Jerusalem. The king of Sarras is Evelach or Evelake, the name being a corruption of Afallach, which later formed into Avalon.

Senauden or **Sinadon**. This name occurs three times in different romances written in the 1190s. Firstly in *Le Bel Inconnu*, Renaud de Beaujeu has Gawain's son Guinglain come here after he has fought a knight and fallen in love with a fey on the Golden Isle. Here it is described as a Waste City and Guinglain has to fight a ghost. Later, in one of the Continuations of Chrétien's story of the Grail, Perceval states that he was born in Sinadon. In Chrétien's story he was raised in the wilds of Wales but the details of his birth are kept secret. Finally in Bèroul's version of *Tristan* Iseult sends her squire Perinis to find King Arthur and he learns that he is at Sinadon, where the Round Table "rotates like the Earth". The last is all too frequently translated as Stirling (suggested by William of Worcester in the 15th century), a most unlikely site since Perinis travels there from Caerleon in a relatively short time. Renaud's description of the Waste City admirably suits Segontium, the old Roman fort at Caernarvon, which many have suggested is Sinadon because of the phonetic similarity to Snowdon and because Guinglain's adventures reflect local folklore. The name Sinadon would have meant something to the Crusaders, because it was the name of a Christian temple built at Epidavros on the Argolid coast of the Greek Peloponnese in the 12th/13th centuries. The name may have been picked up by the Crusaders and adapted by the French romancers only remotely familiar with British sites. However, there is another site which may be more appropriate and link in with Renaud's reference to the Golden Isle. Just south of Dorchester in Oxfordshire is an Iron Age fort on an area known now as Wittenham Clumps but once called the Sinodun Hills. Dorchester had been a Roman city, deserted in the fifth century but soon occupied by the Saxons. Some of the earliest Romano-British cemeteries are in the area. It was over a century, though, before a new Dorchester started to rise from the ruins and there may have been orally transmitted memories of the ghost town of Dorchester. The French may have confused the Welsh *Dor*, which meant "walled town" with the French *d'or*, meaning "of gold". Dorchester was virtually an island in those days, ringed on three sides by the Thames and on the fourth by small streams, so it may well have been a Golden Isle to the French.

Shalott, *see* Astolat.

Sorelois. In *Lancelot du Lac* Galehaut is described as the lord of Sorelois and the Remote Isles. Sorelois is described as adjoining Arthur's kingdom, separated only by a strait of water which is deep and fast running. We also learn that Galehaut won it in battle against the nephew of the king of Northumberland. The anonymous author seems to be describing Anglesey, since not only does this fit the geographical description but he may have been recalling a vague memory of Cadwallon, ruler of Gwynedd, who eventually regained his land from Edwin of Northumbria who had driven him out of Anglesey. The Remote Isles might be the Isle of Man and the Outer Hebrides, which were a separate kingdom in the thirteenth century. Loomis believed that Sorelois was the Scilly Isles but these do not fit the description.

Tribruit. A river given by Nennius as the site of Arthur's tenth battle. It has been one of the hardest to identify and suggestions vary from the Fords of Frew near Stirling, to the estuary of the River Ribble, and the River Troggy near Caerleon.

ACTUAL LOCATIONS

ENGLAND

Cheshire

Alderley Edge. One of the sites where Arthur and his knights are supposed to be sleeping until they rise to defend their country again. *See also* Melrose.

Chester. The Roman fort of Deva and, from 87AD onwards, the home of the XX Valeria Victrix legion, the last legion to leave Britain. It is one of the probable sites for Arthur's ninth battle at the City of the Legion (*see also* Caerleon and York). It was the site of another major battle where the Angles of Northumbria, under Athelfrith, slaughtered the British of Powys under Selyf ap Cynan, in around 615. The victory gave Athelfrith total power across northern Britain and isolated the remaining British Men of the North from the Welsh.

Cornwall

Bodmin Moor. There are several sites. **Arthur's Bed** or **King Arthur's Bed**, a granite monolith on Trewortha Tor on the east of Bodmin Moor near the village of Berriowbridge. It was first recorded by the antiquarian William Borlase in 1754 but it had clearly been long in use by then. He noted that nearby are many eroded rocks, or "rock-basins", called **Arthur's Troughs**, which he used to feed his dogs. **King Arthur's Hall** is a stone enclosure east of St. Breward where the rise towards Garrow Tor passes marshy land called **King Arthur's Downs**. The "Hall" measures about 48m x 20m and is often waterlogged. It is stone lined so was probably a primitive reservoir to capture water from the Downs. Near Bolventor is **Dozmary's Pool**, suggested as the home of the Lady of the Lake and from where Arthur received Excalibur and to where Bedivere returned it. Since the nearest associated site for Camlann is at Camelford, almost ten km away across the Moor, it would have taken Bedivere some while to do it three times. **Callywith** on the outskirts of Bodmin, is one of several suggested sites for Arthur's court at Celliwic.

Callington. One of several suggested sites for Arthur's court at Celliwic. However, *see* Gelliwig *under* Gwent and Gwynedd.

Camelford. Suggested by Geoffrey of Monmouth as the site of the Battle of Camlann, at **Slaughter Bridge**; it has also been proposed as the site of Camelot (*see entry*) but on no basis beyond similarities of the name.

Fowey. Just north of Fowey, near Golant, is Castle Dore, an Iron Age hill-fort once believed to have been reoccupied in the sub-Roman period and to have been the home of King Mark (Cunomorus) of the Tristan legend. However, recent re-evaluation has ruled out the likelihood of post-Roman occupation. The legend had arisen because the French poet Béroul set the Tristan story at Lancien, interpreted as Lantyan, a village just north of Golant. It was further supported by the Tristan Stone, inscribed with the name of Drustan son of Cunomorus, which is south of Golant on the A3082 leading out of Fowey.

Kelliwic. The name given to Arthur's court and long believed to have been in Cornwall, mostly due to Charlotte Guest's translation of Cernyw as Cornwall. There was a Kellewic somewhere in Cornwall, possibly near Penzance, but it is a site long lost. However, *see* Gelliwig *under* Gwent and Gwynedd.

Pendoggett. 8km south of Tintagel on the B3314, just before Pendoggett, is the Iron Age camp called Tregeare Rounds, one of the sites suggested for Castle Dameliock, where Gorlois was killed. *See*, however, St. Dennis and St. Columb Major.

Porthleven. East of the town is The Loe or Looe Pool, a lagoon which some believe was the lake to which Bedivere returned Excalibur. There is, though, no nearby site associated with Camlann.

St. Columb Major. 4km east of the town is the ancient hill-fort of Castle-an-Dinas, suggested as the site where Uther's men besieged and killed Duke Gorlois. *See also* St. Dennis.

St. Dennis. Just west of the town is the farm of Domellick; the name is believed to be a survival of Dimilioc where, according to Geoffrey of Monmouth, Uther's men besieged and killed Duke Gorlois. An old manor of Dimelihoc is recorded here in the *Domesday Book*.

Tintagel. Thanks to Geoffrey of Monmouth, Tintagel has become indelibly imprinted on our consciousness as the birthplace of Arthur. It was here, according to Geoffrey, that Duke Gorlois of Cornwall had his castle and where Uther, disguised as Gorlois, seduced Ygerna. Tintagel is actually the name of the castle, not the village which was Trevena, though Tintagel has now superseded it. Since Geoffrey referred to Tintagel and not Trevena, there must have been a castle here in his day (Tintagel means "fort of the constriction", referring to the narrow neck of the peninsula on which it was built). The present castle, the ruins of which many still believe to be Gorlois's, was started in the 1140s by Reginald, illegitimate son of Henry I, when he was created earl of Cornwall in 1140. He was the brother of Robert, Earl of Gloucester, who was Geoffrey's patron. The castle wasn't completed until the 1230s, by the next earl, Richard, son of King John, one of the great Crusaders of the 1240s. Excavations in the 1930s, and again in the 1990s (which included the discovery of the Artognou inscription), showed that Tintagel had been a major site right through the Arthurian period, importing many high status goods from throughout the Roman world. Early thoughts that it might have been a monastery have been revised, and it is possible that it was a chieftain's stronghold. If so, the legends of Arthur's birth here cannot be entirely discounted. We have no idea where any of the Welsh princes were born, especially those who, like Cadell, may not have been native to the area.

Tintagel has its inevitable quota of such items as **Arthur's Quoit** and a **Round Table** and, after a difficult climb down to the beach, **Merlin's Cave**. Of more interest in the town itself are **King Arthur's Great Halls**, which include King Arthur's Hall and a Hall of Chivalry. These were created in 1933 by millionaire Frederick Thomas Glasscock (1871–1934), who founded a Fellowship of the Round Table and privately published several Arthurian books. The Hall was originally private but was opened to the public in 1993. It houses a granite Round Table, eight feet in diameter. The Hall of Chivalry contains a wonderful display of 72 stained-glass windows of Arthurian scenes, all by Veronica Whall.

Willapark, at Bossiney, just north of Tintagel, is one of several suggested sites for Arthur's court at Celliwic. Bossiney Mound, beside the Methodist Chapel, is supposed to be Arthur's Round Table. *See also* Gelliwig *under* Gwent and Gwynedd. East of Tintagel, 5km along the road to Davidstow, is **Condolden Barrow**, regarded locally as the burial mound of Arthur's half-brother Cador, Duke of Cornwall.

Wadebridge. The hill-fort at Castle Killibury is one of several suggested sites for Arthur's court at Celliwic. However, *see* Gelliwig *under* Gwent and Gwynedd.

Cumbria

Arderydd or **Arthuret**, *see* Carwinley.

Birdoswald. The modern name for Camboglanna, a Roman fort on Hadrian's Wall suggested as a site for the battle of Camlann.

Burgh by Sands. The site of the Roman fort of Aballava at the western end of Hadrian's Wall. It has been suggested that Aballava may later have been corrupted into Avalon. 20km to the west is **Cardurnock**, believed to be where Cei fought so viciously at the Halls of Awrnach. There was an old Roman fort here, though little evidence survives.

Camboglanna, *see* Birdoswald.

Carlisle. The Roman fort of Luguvalium which was raised to the capital of the *civitas* of Carvetiorum probably in the late second century. It may also have been the capital of the breakaway province of Valentia. As Roman authority declined this area gained an increasing degree of autonomy and it is likely that Carlisle formed the base for the later military rulers of the North, including Gwrwst, Merchiaun, Cynfarch and Urien. It is often cited as one of Arthur's principle courts but this is almost certainly because it was Urien's capital in Rheged. It may have been the site of Arthur's ninth battle at the City of the Legion. Carlisle later features in several early English poems and tales which feature Gawain, such as *The Carle of Carlisle* (*see* Chapter 14). *The Awyntrs off Arthure* is set at Tarn Wadling, which was near High Hesket just south of Carlisle. According to Malory, Guenevere's punishment, when she is to be burned at the stake, takes place at Carlisle, even though all preceding events had happened at Camelot.

Carwinley. The site of the battle of Arderydd or Arthuret, between Gwenddoleu and his kinsmen Peredur and Gwrgi in

573. Gwenddoleu was killed, and his bard Myrddin lost his wits and ran into the nearby Forest of Celidon. The site is virtually on the Scottish-English border on the banks of the River Esk and Liddel Water between the farms Lowmoat and Highmoat, less than a kilometre north-west of Carwinley (a corruption of Caer Gwenddoleu), north of Longtown.

Outhgill. 12km south of Kirkby Stephen stand the ruins of **Pendragon Castle**, built in the twelfth century by Hugh de Morville, one of the knights who murdered Thomas à Becket. This was at the height of the first wave of Arthur mania, and de Morville doubtless gave the castle its name out of self grandeur, suggesting it was the castle of Uther Pendragon. There was a local legend that Uther had attempted to alter the course of the River Eden that runs by the castle, but to no avail. There is no evidence of any previous occupation of the site in this lonely stretch of Mallerstang Common, but the name had its effect because Malory incorporated a reference to the Castle in *Morte Darthur*, making it the home of the renegade knight Sir Brian of the Isles whom Lancelot had ousted from Dolorous Garde and had to oust again for his vile deeds, giving the castle to Sir Brunor the Black. The castle is privately owned and not open to the public.

Penrith. The churchyard of St Andrew's contains the Giant's Grave, once believed to be the grave of Urien's son Owein. In fact the grave, which is actually two graves together, dates from the tenth century. Just south of Penrith at Eamont Bridge is an earthwork known as **King Arthur's Round Table**. It dates back at least to the Bronze Age and may once have been the site of a henge, though there is another henge close by at Mayburgh. With a circumference of almost 200m, it could accommodate at least 200 people and might at some stage have been used as a site of council, perhaps by Urien in whose kingdom it was. Just over a km to the east is the site of Giant's Cave by Brougham Castle. Here Lancelot is supposed to have slain the giant Tarquin who, with his brother Isir, was a cannibal. This is the site of the Roman fort Brocavum, one of the later fortifications which was in use from the second to the fourth century and could have been visited by Lucius Artorius Castus.

Derbyshire

Castleton. Here is Peveril Castle high up on the peak overlooking the town, a possible site for Lancelot's Dolorous Garde. It was established by William Peverel soon after the Norman Conquest and Henry II visited it in 1157. It was later in the care of Brian de Lisle, Constable of the Peak, who did not want to give it up after King John's death, and had to be taken by force by William de Ferrers, Earl of Derby. This episode may be replicated in the Vulgate Cycle by Lancelot's capture of the castle from Brandin of the Isles.

Devon

Lundy. The Isle of Lundy off the North Devon coast is associated with Annwn and Avalon. There has been evidence of occupation on the island since Neolithic times, but no direct links to Arthurian events.

Dorset

Badbury Rings. An Iron Age hill fort suggested as a possible site for Arthur's battle of Badon Hill. Its location, though, does not support this and there is a lack of any significant archaeological evidence.

Woolland, near Ilchester. Here at Bulberrow Hill are two rivers, the Divelish and Devil's Brook, that may equate to the site of Arthur's battles on the River Dubglas.

Durham

Binchester. The old Roman fort of Vinovium may be the site of Arthur's eighth battle at Fort Guinnion.

Gloucestershire

Forest of Dean. The main forest of southern Gwent and Ergyng, which may have been the British counterpart of the French Briosque and Broceliande. The name is derived from the Saxon word for "valley", *denu*, but there might be an earlier association if Lydney was Avalon (*see below*). The Forest of Briosque was owned by Dyonas, father of the Lady of the Lake, and may have been known to the British as the Forest of Dyonas.

Gloucester. Vortigern's family came from Gloucester. His grandfather Vitalinus is specially referred to as "of Gloucester" whilst his father was a high official in the town. Ambrosius the Elder may also have been an official. It remained inhabited throughout the fifth century and presumably into the sixth, as Conmail is referred to as a king of Gloucester when he was defeated at Dyrham in 577. Gloucester was where Mabon the Hunter was imprisoned and had to be rescued by Arthur in the story of *Culhwch and Olwen*.

Lydney. Between Chepstow and Gloucester, this was the site of a major healing sanctuary dedicated to the Romano-British god Nodens. It was built around the middle of the third century and remained in use into the early fourth century. Although of pagan origin, it may have continued to provide healing facilities to Christians. Although it no longer appears to be a physical island, as the name shows (Lydney, *Lida's Island*) it was once isolated by two streams, and would have been seen as an island haven in the woods tucked away from the real world (Nodens was also a god of the woods). Lydney could be the original Avalon. The Lydney complex was originally surrounded by lakes, and would be the obvious sanctuary for the Lady of the Lake. At Lydney hundreds of copper bracelets were found, which have long been associated with healing, and this may have been the basis of the ring that the Lady of the Lake gave to Lancelot.

Hampshire

Basing. Old Basing, south of Basingstoke, has been suggested as a possible site for Bassas, Arthur's sixth battle.

Charford. The favoured site for where Cerdic settled and fought his first battles, probably in the 530s and therefore after the Arthurian period.

Portchester. One of the suggested sites for Llongborth. However, *see* Llamporth in Dyfed.

Silchester. Between Reading and Basingstoke, this was the Roman town of *Calleva Atrebatum*. Although any Roman influence had ceased by the early fifth century, a Romano-British occupation seems to have continued right through the fifth and sixth centuries until a simple transition to Anglo-British occupation by the early seventh century. Somehow, perhaps because of a series of defensive ditches such as Grim's Dyke, Silchester managed to remain independent. The Saxon infiltration was minor and the town was eventually abandoned. It remains today the best preserved shell of all Roman towns. Intriguingly, Geoffrey of Monmouth has Arthur crowned here. This may be because there was some vague tradition of its British independence in the sixth century but I suspect it's more a case of language confusion. The old Welsh tales give Arthur's capital at Celliwig and *Celli* means a grove in a wood. The original Roman name *Calleva* meant "town in the woods", and it is believed that the prefix for Silchester came from the British adaptation to *Calle-cestre*. Curiously, although it is recorded as *Silcestre* in the *Domesday Book* (probably under Norman influence), by the next century it was back to *Cilcestre*. Geoffrey may have genuinely believed that Silchester was the old Celliwig.

Winchester. The Roman town of Venta Belgarum was the capital of the Belgae tribe and later became the capital of Wessex. Although there is evidence of continued Romano-British occupation in the early fifth century, it did not really re-emerge until the West Saxon king Cynegils established a new diocese here in 634 under Bishop Birinus. If it was occupied at all during the Arthurian period it was on a negligible scale. However, Malory chose to make Winchester the site for Camelot since it was here that Arthur's Round Table was displayed in the Great Hall. The Table is still on display.

Hereford & Worcester

Archenfield, *see* Ergyng.

Arthur's Cave, *see* Ganarew.

Dorstone. Between Dorstone and Bredwardine at the head of the Golden Valley is the impressive burial chamber called **Arthur's Stone**. The name really applies to the massive capstone. Although this area has many associations with Arthur the name is relatively recent; when it was first described in an antiquarian's report in 1728 it was called Artil's Stone. It is another Neolithic site dating back to at least 3500BC. The site is so significant, though, as a local landmark that it is tempting to think that in Arthur's day it could have been known as Arthur's stone to identify a meeting place.

Ergyng. This was one of the minor Welsh kingdoms that adjoined Gwent, and at times formed part of that kingdom. It was also in the front line of the Saxon and Angle advance across Britain, and much of what was Ergyng now falls into England in Hereford & Worcester (as Archenfield). Ergyng may well have formed a sub-kingdom of Gwent ruled by the heirs to Gwent and it has been suggested that Athrwys ap Meurig ruled as prince of Ergyng though he died too young to inherit Gwent. Caradog Vreichfras is also identified as a king or prince of Ergyng. Arthur's pursuit of the boar Twrch Trwyth took him through this part of Ergyng where the Dulas Brook, at Ewyas Harold, may be one of the sites for Arthur's second-to-fifth battles. 10km east of Ewyas Harold, at the delightfully named Wormelow Tump, is Gamber Head, which is the start of the River Gamber fed by the spring known once as Llygad Amr. This is where, according to Nennius, Arthur killed and buried his son Amr. There's no barrow visible today.

Ganarew. On the bend in the river near Symonds Yat is the hill fort of Little Doward which is where, according to Geoffrey of Monmouth, Vortigern was besieged and his fort burned down by Ambrosius. Below the hill near the river is **King Arthur's Cave**, though no one knows what the connection is.

Leintwardine. The Roman town here was **Bravonium** or **Branogenium,** and this might have corrupted into Breguein or Breguoin, the name of Arthur's eleventh battle. It probably also corrupted into Brandigan, the castle of King Evrian in *Erec et Enide*, a name that survives in Brandon Camp, a hill-fort to the south. *See also* Knucklas (Powys). The **Clun Forest**, north-west of the town, is a suggested site for the battle of Coed Celidon.

Hertfordshire

St. Albans. The Roman town of Verulamium was one of the first Christian towns in Britain. It remained occupied and functional as a British town throughout the fifth century and probably into the sixth. Germanus visited it in 429 and perhaps 436, and it must at some stage have been visited by Vortigern and Ambrosius. According to Geoffrey of Monmouth, the Saxons besieged it during Uther's reign. There are no direct Arthurian connections but as one of the major frontier towns during the Saxon settlement there may have been a confrontation here at some time.

Kent

Barham Down, south of Canterbury. According to Malory this was the site of a battle between Mordred and Arthur following Arthur's advance from Dover. There may have been a battle here between the British and the Saxons/Jutes in the early days of their settlement but that would be pre-Arthur, possibly part of Ambrosius's campaign. Malory may have tapped into a local tradition recalling that Barham was the site of the first battle between the Britons and the Romans under Julius Caesar in 54BC. The connection with Arthur may be because the name Barham derives from the Saxon *Bioraham* and Beora is the Saxon for "bear".

Dover. In Malory's *Morte Darthur*, Arthur fights Mordred here upon his return to Britain. Gawain, already wounded from an earlier battle with Lancelot, dies in the fighting and is buried in the Chapel of Dover Castle. Caxton refers to Gawain's skull being visible at Dover. This is all legend and has no basis in history. For another burial site for Gawain, *see* Bosherston in Dyfed.

Lancashire

Lancaster. Here, the estuary of the River Lune has been suggested as a possible site for Arthur's first battle.

Preston. The River Douglas joins the Ribble here and may be the site of Arthur's battles on the Dubglas. It is also a suggested site for the battle of Tribruit. East of Preston at **Ribchester** is the Roman fort of Bremetennacum, which was the main command of Lucius Artorius Castus. The name might also corrupt into Breguoin, the site of Arthur's eleventh battle.

Lincolnshire

Lindsey. This area, once known as Linnuis, is usually cited as the most likely for Arthur's four battles at the River Dubglas, even though there is no local river by that name. It was a locale settled early by the Angles and is referred to by Geoffrey of Monmouth in relation to Hengist. As discussed in Chapter 6, this area is more likely as the site of the earlier battles in Vortimer's or Ambrosius's campaign. *See also* Brigg.

Spalding. Near here the River Glen joins the River Welland and it is a suggested site for Arthur's first battle.

London

Although Malory places the episode of Arthur withdrawing the sword from the stone in London (probably at St. Paul's), and also has Guenevere seek refuge in the Tower of London (five hundred years before it was built), there are no historical sites in London with direct Arthurian connections.

Northumberland

Alnwick. Suggested by Malory as a possible site for Lancelot's castle Joyous Garde. *See also* Bamburgh.

Bamburgh. An impressive castle dominates the skyline here now and even without that it must have been an impressive site in Arthur's day. It was then known as *Din Guayrdi* and was probably the capital of the Southern Votadini. Malory suggested it as a possible site for Lancelot's Castle Joyous Garde. It was here that Ida established his capital in 547 or so. The area is associated with many battles between the British and Angles, some of which may have later become associated with Arthur's campaign. It was here that Urien was murdered during the siege of Lindisfarne in *c*590. Its present name is supposed to be derived from Bebba, the Pictish wife of Athelfrith, adopted soon after the defeat of the British at Catraeth.

Corbridge. At Dilston the Devil's Water may be one of the sites of Arthur's battles along the Dubglas.

Doddington. Near here the River Glen meets the River Till near Yeavering Bell. It has been suggested as a site for Arthur's first battle.

High Rochester. The old Roman fort of Bremenium, in British *Berwyn*, is one of the suggested sites for Arthur's eleventh battle at Bregouin. The seventh battle in the Forest of Celidon might also have been within this vicinity.

Oxfordshire

Dorchester. A possible site for the Golden Isle in Renaud's story *Le Bel Inconnu* and a possible site for Arthur's Round Table as described by Béroul in his story of Tristan, which sets Arthur's court at Sinadon. The Sinodun Hills, also known as Wittenham Clumps, are to the south of Dorchester.

Faringdon. Badbury Hill is a suggested site for Arthur's battle of Badon Hill.
Wootton. Near here the River Glyme joins the Dorn, a suggested site for Arthur's first battle.

Shropshire
Baschurch. Suggested as a possible site for Bassas, Arthur's sixth battle.
Clun. The Clun Forest is a suggested location for Arthur's seventh battle at the Forest of Celidon. It may also be related to his first battle on the River Glein.
Wroxeter. The site of the Roman fort at Viriconium, within site of the massive hill-fort of the Wrekin. Viriconium remained occupied well into the fifth century and even had improvements made and encouraged visitors. It may well have been the capital of Vortigern and Ambrosius, and even of Arthur, making it a possible site for Camelot. It has been suggested that Badon may have been fought here, at the Wrekin.

Somerset
Arthur's Bridge. Bridge over the river Alham near Ditcheat. It may be associated with Arthur's Lane, *see* Cadbury Castle.
Bath. One of the major towns of Roman Britain, *Aquae Sulis*, and the site suggested by Geoffrey of Monmouth (and perhaps Nennius) as the location for the siege of *Mons Badonicus*, which might have taken place on the surrounding hills at Bathampton Down or Solsbury Hill (*see* Chapter 7). Chrétien de Troyes, who had probably never been to Britain, refers to Bath/Bade as one of the cities of King Bagdemagus, *see* Gorre.
Brent Knoll, near Burnham-on-Sea. An imposing Iron Age hill-fort where the Romans also built a temple. William of Malmesbury tells a legend that the hill, then called the Mount of Frogs, was the home of three giants. Arthur set out to fight them but Yder went on ahead. By the time Arthur arrived Yder had killed the giants but had himself collapsed. The locality is also known as Battleborough, apparently after a battle between Alfred the Great and the Danes in 875, but it has been suggested that this could have been the site of one of Arthur's twelve battles, possibly Bregwyn.

Bristol. The suburb of Catbrain near Filton Airport has been suggested as being originally Cat-bregyon, which might be the same as Arthur's eleventh battle at Breguoin.

Cadbury Castle, a massive Iron Age hill fort at South Cadbury, which has been linked with Camelot ever since John Leland identified it in 1542, when he referred to it as "Camallate". The connection may have been derived from the nearby villages of **Queen Camel** and West Camel, which were known simply as *Camelle* in the Domesday Book and a century earlier as *Cantmael*. It is uncertain how long the locals had associated it with Arthur and Camelot but within the vicinity as you climb the hill are **Arthur's Well** and the crest is called **Arthur's Palace**. There are traces of an old track running from the hill towards Glastonbury, called **Arthur's Lane**.

A series of excavations, especially those under the direction of Leslie Alcock from 1966 to 1970 (one of the most thorough archaeological undertakings at any suspected Arthurian site), showed several periods of occupation stretching from around 3000BC to about 1000AD, with at least twelve distinguishable "settlements". The one during the Arthurian period was dubbed "Cadbury 11". It began in around 470 when there was a significant refortification of the hill after a period of disuse. At the summit, which the locals called Arthur's Palace, was found evidence of a timbered hall, measuring roughly 19m by 10m. The fortification of the hill was substantial and it was estimated that the site could house 1,000 warriors plus their families and workers.

The occupation at Cadbury lasted for at least two generations, to about 550, which is precisely the Arthurian period. The inevitable temptation is to suggest that the refortifications were instigated by Ambrosius and that the site continued to be occupied by Arthur. There is, alas, no direct evidence to support this, but it would be remarkable if Ambrosius were not connected, since we know from Gildas that his campaign started around the 460s/470s, and only a commander of some authority could have organised such a substantial fortification. There may be some clue in the name of Cadbury itself, as it means "Cada's fort." It is tempting to leap at Cada and imagine this may be Cador, Arthur's elder half brother, who was called Duke of Cornwall. Cada is more likely to be a Saxon name, though it could have been an adoption of a long-substantiated British name. Alcock provides full details of his excavation in *By South Cadbury is that Camelot* (London, 1972) with an update in *Economy, Society & Warfare Among the Britons and Saxons* (Cardiff, 1987).

Cam, the river that gave its name to the nearby towns of Queen Camel and West Camel near Sparkford. Camel Hill is to the north of the river whilst at Sparkford the Cam twists through a series of bends that might have earned the locale the name Camlann in Arthurian times. Cadbury Castle is little more than 1 km away.

Glastonbury. The purported Isle of Avalon and burial place of King Arthur. These and other associations connected with the Holy Grail, and the abduction of Guenevere by Melwas, did not appear until the late twelfth century. There is no earlier evidence for any Arthurian connections. *See* Chapter 11 for a full discussion.

Longport. One of the suggested sites of the battle of Llongborth. It is unlikely that an Anglo-British conflict would have happened here in Arthurian times, but it is certainly possible a century or two later. The stained glass in the east window of the parish church dates from the late fifteenth century, and it depicts a grail scene with Joseph of Arimathea carrying two cruets.

Queen Camel, *see* Cadbury.

Sussex (East and West)

Lewes. Just outside Lewes is Mount Caburn, a major British hill-fort. Below it is Glyndebourne, where the Glynde Reach may be the River Glen of Arthur's first battle. It is also a likely site for the British defeat of the Saxons under Aelle at *Mearcrædes burnam* in 485.

Pevensey. Here was the great Roman fort of *Anderitum*, built as part of the new Saxon Shore defences in the mid 290s. It may not have been occupied by the British during the early sub-Roman period but it was used as a retreat against the Saxons, probably after 477, and fell to Aelle after a terrible massacre in 491.

Selsey. Probable first landing site of Aelle in 477.

Wiltshire

Amesbury. Originally *Ambresbyrig*, "Ambre's stronghold", it has long been associated with Ambrosius Aurelianus, who may have used it as a fort in his campaign against the Saxons. Geoffrey of Monmouth also associates it with Ambrius, a monk who may have founded the monastery here in 979. According to Geoffrey the monastery was built on the site of the slaughter of Vortigern's nobles by the Saxons. Malory has Guenevere retire here as a nun and it is the site of her last meeting with Lancelot. Nearby is Stonehenge.

Badbury, *see* Liddington.

Liddington. Between here and Badbury is the significant Iron Age hill fort now called Liddington Castle but once called Badbury Castle. It is one of the more likely sites for Arthur's decisive battle of Badon.

Marlborough. Local legend suggests that the town's name is derived from Merlin's Mount, the name still given to a prehistoric mound in the grounds of Marlborough College. In the *Domesday Book* the town is recorded as Merleberg and was apparently derived from a similar personal name, *Mærla*.

Salisbury Plain. By the time of the Vulgate *Mort Artu* and Malory's *Morte Darthur*, this had become the site for Arthur's final battle at Camlann. There is nothing in the earlier legends to suggest that what was essentially an internal struggle was fought out here, though the Plain is a likely site for later conflicts between the British and the Saxons.

Yorkshire, North

Catterick. Believed by many to be the original site for the Battle of Catraeth as described in *Y Gododdin*. Not all agree with this. *See* Chapter 8 for discussion.

Knaresborough. Knaresborough Castle is on a cliff overlooking the town, and may be the site described for Lancelot's **Dolorous Garde**. It was built in the 1120s and became a favourite of King John, who used it as a base for hunting. He left it in the care of Brian de Lisle who may be the original of Brandin/Brian of the Isles in the Prose *Lancelot*.

Sutton on the Forest. Probably the centre of the old Royal Forest of Galtres. This may be the wood referred to by Geoffrey as the Forest of Calaterium, a name sufficiently close to Forest of Celidon to cause possible confusion. Arthur's seventh battle may have happened here.

York. The military capital of northern Britain during the Roman period and probably remained so for as long as a form of military command remained in the north. It may have been the base for Coel and his successors, certainly Peredur and possibly his father Eliffer and grandfather Arthwys. York features heavily in Geoffrey of Monmouth's story of Ambrosius and Uther. It is where Octa flees and is besieged, and where later Eosa defeats Uther. Geoffrey has Arthur's battle on the River Douglas at York against the Saxons. It is also from York that Geoffrey has Arthur allocate territories to his vassal kings.

SCOTLAND

Borders

Drumelzier. This tiny village in Upper Tweeddale is supposed to be where Merlin met his death and was buried. The burial site was believed to be just below the church where a small side stream, the Pausayl, meets the Tweed. However, the Tweed is suppose to have changed its course over the years so the exact spot may well be under the river. The B712 heads west of the village through Merlindale. This story almost certainly applies to Myrddin Wyllt or Lailoken, who lived wild in the Caledonian Forest for years and met a "triple" death as he himself had prophesied.

Melrose. Although the Arthurian connections here are all circumstantial, the combination gives food for thought. South of the town are the Eildon Hills, one of the suggested sites for Arthur's battle of Mount Agned. Several medieval romances refer to these hills as the Dolorous Mountains, which may also therefore link them to the Castle of the Maidens and to Lancelot's castle called Dolorous Garde. Arthur and his knights are supposed to be sleeping under the Hills awaiting their call to save Britain again. The fort at the top of the Hills was reoccupied in the fifth century and may have formed the base for a fighting unit. Other nearby localities are linked to Arthur's battles. Bowden Moor to the south-west is a suggested site for Badon (on name alone) whilst Stow in Wedale is linked to the battle of Fort Guinnion.

Stow, *see* Melrose.
Yarrow. Deep in the old Caledonian Forest the area of Hart Fell above Yarrow has been suggested as the possible site of Arthur's seventh battle.

Central Scotland

Falkirk. The Roman fort of Caermawr or **Camelon** has been suggested as a site for Camelot. Further north, where the B902 crosses the River Carron into Stenhousemuir, at the site of the old Carron Ironworks, used to be a Roman building known colloquially as **Arthur's O'en** or **Arthur's Furnace**. It was identified as such as far back as 1293, but the building is long gone and its significance lost. To the west of the town are the Hills of Dunipace, a site suggested, rather weakly, as the location for Arthur's sixth battle at Bassas.
Stirling. Stirling Castle was once believed to be Arthur's Castle, mostly because of a misinterpretation by William of Worcester of a reference to Arthur's court at Sinodun, which he took as a variance on Snowdon. Apparently Stirling was once known to the English as Snodun. In fact, in the twelfth century its name was recorded as Strevelin, an unlikely confusion with Sinodun. Below the castle heights, near the golf course, is an earthwork called the King's Knot, known colloquially as the Round Table. It was probably designed in the fifteenth century or so for tournaments in the area known as the King's Park.

The area around Stirling has some suggested sites for Arthur's battles. Stirling Castle itself has been suggested as the Castle of the Maidens and thus as the site for the battle of Mount Agned. The Links of Forth to the east of the town, south of the river, has been suggested for the Battle of Tribruit, whilst to the west of Stirling along the Forth at Kippen, the Fords of Frew have been proposed as the site for the battle of the River Bassas. None of these sites have much in their favour but as the three most difficult sites to identify they at least bear some consideration.

Dumfries & Galloway

Rockcliffe. South of Dalbeattie overlooking the inlet Rough Firt is the Mote of Mark, a hill-fort which was not only occupied in the sixth century but produced quality goods: jewels, brooches, harness fittings. Interestingly, 25km to the west at Gatehouse of Fleet is **Trusty's Hill** ("Drust's Hill") which contains some uniquely marked Pictish stones. It may suggest a deeper Tristan tradition here, relating to a raid by a Pictish leader, Drust, on a British encampment in Strathclyde.

Edinburgh and the Lothians

Edinburgh has several associations. The hill to the east of the capital, by Holyrood Palace, is called **Arthur's Seat** and may be the site of the original Votadini fort of Din Eidyn. This has led many to believe that Arthur was a prince of the Votadini, an idea seemingly supported by the reference to him in the poem *Y Gododdin*. The site has been known as Arthur's Seat from at least the 1400s. Geoffrey of Monmouth believed that Edinburgh was the site of the Castle of the Maidens and of Mount Agned, Arthur's eleventh battle.

Linlithgow. 5km south of Linlithgow off the A706 and before Lochcote Reservoir is Bowden Hill, suggested (on no better reason than name) as a possible site for the Battle of Badon. There are at least four Bowden Hills in Britain, including one near the Eildon Hills (*see* Melrose), plus a village in Wiltshire and a hill in Devon. None of these are serious contenders.

Perthshire

Arthurbank, *see* Meigle.

Arthurstone, *see* Meigle.

Barry Hill, *see* Meigle.

Meigle. The museum here has one of the carved stones from a tomb once displayed in the churchyard, which was claimed to mark the burial place of Guenevere. Local legend claims that she absconded with Mordred and Arthur had her put to death for adultery – some say she was torn to pieces by horses. Evidently there is an Arthurian tradition in the area because a few kms south-west along the A94 is a house called Arthurstone where once stood an Arthur's Stone, now lost. A little further along the road is the farm Arthurbank. Across the River Isla from Meigle, just beyond Alyth, is Barry Hill where Mordred's castle is supposed to have stood.

Strathclyde

Alclud. *See* Dumbarton.

Ben Arthur. A mountain at the head of Loch Long also known as The Cobbler. Its name may be associated with the Clan MacArthur and the Dál Riatan prince Artúir mac Aedan, and has thus been connected to the four battles fought by Arthur in the region of Linnuis.

Darvel. Near here the Glen Water meets the River Irving near Yeavering Bell. It has been suggested as a site for Arthur's first battle.

Dumbarton. The modern name for *Dun Breatann*, the Fort of the Britains, also called Alclud. It was the capital of the British kingdom of Strathclyde that managed to survive until the end of the ninth century, the last independent British enclave outside of Wales. Gildas was allegedly born here and his father Caw was a prince of Alclud in the late fifth century. Its major ruler during the Arthurian period was Dyfnwal the Old, who extended his territory across much of northern Britain between the Walls. Some of his exploits may have become subsumed into Arthurian legend. Geoffrey of Monmouth has Arthur lift a siege of Alclud by the Picts and Saxons. Later legend has this as the birthplace of Mordred, which would suggest that Lot was a Prince of Strathclyde. Lot appears amongst the descendants of Coel in Rheged and Galloway but the borders between Galloway and Strathclyde must always have been fluid.

Loch Lomond. According to Geoffrey of Monmouth, Arthur pursued an army of Picts and Scots to Loch Lomond where he trapped them on the islands in the loch. Whilst it is an unlikely site for Arthur of Badon it's a very possible site for Artúir mac Aedan of Dál Riata. He may have fought several battles in the area which might relate to Nennius's battle list which cites four battles in the region of Linnuis. The Roman geographer Ptolemy called this area Lindum.

WALES

*Clwyd (*Conwy, Denbighshire, Flintshire, Wrexham)

Deganwy. Here, at the mouth of the River Conway, was the fortress home of Maelgwyn, king of Gwynedd. Taliesin is supposed to have visited this court in his youth. Before Maelgwyn established this as his home it may have equated to Arthur's court of Pen Rhionydd, at that time governed by Gyrthmwl.

Llanarmon. In the Berwyn Mountains, this is the site of Carreg Gwynion, a possible site for Arthur's eighth battle at Fort Guinnion.

Llandulas, near Colwyn Bay. The River Dulas here may be one of the sites of Arthur's battles at the River Dubglas.

Mold. Just to the north-west is Maesgarmon, the possible site of the Alleluia Victory of Germanus in 429 or 436. The site may, though, be associated with St Garmon and therefore also connected with Cadell. *See* Moel Benlli in the next entry.

Ruthin. It has been suggested that Gildas did not mention Arthur in *De Excidio* because Arthur had killed Gildas's brother Hywel or Huail. That purportedly happened here in Ruthin. The story tells that in a duel at Caerwys (north of Ruthin) Hywel had wounded Arthur, causing him to limp. Arthur told Hywel to keep silent about the wound. Later, in Ruthin, Arthur disguised himself in order to meet a woman, but Hywel recognised the limp. Commenting upon it, Hywel broke his bond and Arthur had him arrested and executed. The execution stone is still on show outside Exmewe Hall in the Market Place.

In the Clwydian mountains north-east of Ruthin are two peaks of interest. **Moel Arthur** ("Hill of Arthur") is at the end of a valley called **Glyn Arthur** and is passed by Offa's Dyke long-distance path. It was occupied in the Iron Age, but it has not been excavated since 1849 and modern methods might discover more. South of Moel Arthur, 5kms east of Ruthin on a minor road heading up from Llanbedr-Dyffryn-Clwyd, is Moel Fenlli, also called **Moel Benlli**, the hill-fort of the tyrant Benlli who was destroyed by lightning, allowing Cadell to become king. Excavations in 1879 showed that this hill was occupied in the sub-Roman period. If, as I have suggested, Cadell is one of the candidates for the real Arthur, it may account for the names of these two, nearly adjacent, peaks.

*Dyfed (*Ceredigion, Carmarthenshire, Pembrokeshire)

Aberystwyth. On the outskirts is Llanbadarn Fawr, site of an early monastic settlement headed by Paternus (St. Padarn) in the early/mid sixth century. His *Life*, written in *c*1120, refers to

Arthur as a "tyrant", who visited Paternus and took a fancy to his tunic. When Paternus would not let him have it Arthur went into a rage and Paternus asked that the earth swallow him up, which it promptly did until Arthur had sought forgiveness. This may well be based on some incident relating to Artúir of Dyfed.

3kms south-east, off the A485 before Capel Seion, is **Nanteos House,** which for centuries was believed to house the Holy Grail, known as the Nanteos Cup, apparently brought to the place by the monks after the dissolution of Strata Florida Abbey. The Cup is now housed in a bank vault and visitors discouraged. Nanteos House, which passed out of the hands of the original owners in 1951, was again put up for sale in 2004.

Bosherston. This small village has several purported Arthurian connections. The trident-shaped lake, known as the Lily Ponds, was supposed to be where Bedivere returned Excalibur to the Lady of the Lake. However, there is no corresponding local site for Camlann and the lake was only created when the creek was dammed in the 18th century. South of the town is **St. Govan's Head.** Below the cliffs are the remains of a chapel where Govan is supposed to be buried. The name Govan has been connected with Gawain. The local church will tell you that Govan was Gobhan, a sixth-century blacksmith from Abergavenny who became a holy man, whilst as Gofan or Ouan he appears in the story of *Culhwch and Olwen* as one of the sons of Caw (and thus brother of Gildas) at Arthur's court. *See* Milford Haven.

Black Mountain. Arthur's pursuit of the giant boar Twrch Trwyth continued here as described in *Culhwch and Olwen*. It recommenced near Ammanford and headed across the Black Mountain towards the Brecon Beacons. North of Ammanford, near Pont-ar-llechau (on the A4069), is the hill **Pen Arthur**, below which, in the River Sawdde, are two large rocks, the biggest of which is called **Arthur's Quoit**, which he is supposed to have thrown from Pen Arthur. We may suppose that this area was the site of a battle associated with Arthur, possibly Artúir of Dyfed, but equally any of the Arthurian suspects, especially Vortipor.

Carmarthen. According to Geoffrey of Monmouth, this was the birthplace of Merlin, and the town was subsequently named after him as Caer Myrddin. In fact, the name was derived from the Roman name *Moridunum* which developed into Myrddin. In Geoffrey's day the town was called *Cair Mirdin*, and Geoffrey made the connection (albeit wrongly) with the bard Myrddin. The legend has stuck and there are the inevitable local landmarks. 4km east along the A40 is Bryn Myrddin ("Merlin's Hill"), an ancient hill fort, with which are associated Merlin's Wood, Merlin's Stone and, of course, Merlin's Cave, where he is supposed to be entombed. Heading south-west out of the town on the B4312 you will find Merlin's Quoit, a standing stone near the village of Llangain. **Carmarthen Museum** houses all that remains of Myrddin's Tree, that used to stand in the centre of the old town. It also houses the Vortipor Stone, which had been found at Castell Dwyran, and which is inscribed with the name of Vortipor, the ruler of Dyfed at the time of Arthur.

Haverfordwest. Originally Haverford, the town took its name from a ford over the River Cleddau, but it seems that just south of the town the small tributary of the Cleddau, called Merlin's Brook, required a bridge, now called Merlin's Bridge.

Llamporth. Near the village of Penbryn, this is a likely site for the battle of Llongborth.

Milford Haven. The Irish boar Twrch Trwyth passed through here, having come round the coast from St David's. This is probably a memory of an invading warband, probably Irish, that landed at Milford Haven and fought its way inland. The original Welsh name for the town was Aberdaugleddau, taken from the name of the river Cleddau, which means "sword". The name may signify a naval battle.

Narberth or **Arberth**. Features several times in the Mabinogion story *Manawydan son of Llyr* as the site of the Throne of Arberth and, by association, with the Siege Perilous and the Holy Grail. *See* Chapter 16.

Preseli Mountains. Now part of the Pembrokeshire Coast National Park, east of Fishguard, the Preseli Mountains must have more surviving standing stones per square km than anywhere else in Britain. It was from here that the blue stones came that were incorporated into Stonehenge, which Geoffrey attributes to the work of Merlin. The main Arthurian association here concerns Arthur's pursuit of the giant boar Twrch Trwyth which took them through Preseli. According to the story in *Culhwch and*

Olwen, there was a major confrontation at Cwm Cerwyn, which is today the highest peak at Foel Cwm Cerwyn (536m). It was in this conflict, which no doubt is a memory of a real battle perhaps between Artúir of Dyfed and an Irish warband, that Arthur's son Gwydre was killed. To the east of Cwm Cerwyn, between Glynsaithmaen and Cwm-garw, are two standing stones called Cerrig Maibion Arthur, "the Stones of the Sons of Arthur". Just west is Carn Arthur, sometimes called Bedd Arthur or Arthur's Grave. In the story Arthur continues the hunt, but maybe the cairn was built to mark the battle site. South of this site, at Glandy Cross, is a now despoiled stone circle called Meini Gwyr, "the leaning stones", also known as Buarth Arthur, "Arthur's enclosure". These three sites, being in such close proximity, despite being of much greater antiquity than Arthur, have clearly become associated with some major event, almost certainly in the reign of Artúir of Dyfed.

St. David's. Originally Mynyw, this is listed in the first Welsh Triad as one of Arthur's three tribal thrones governed, surprisingly, by Maelgwyn. It was also here that the Irish boar Twrch Trwyth first landed, at Porth Clais, and ravaged the land, working round the coast to Milford Haven before being pursued by Arthur and his men.

Tal-y-bont. A small village north of Aberystwyth. To the north of the village, down a side road leading towards Moel y Garn, is the grave of Taliesin, **Bedd Taliesin**.

Glamorgan/ Gwent

Caerleon. Identified by Geoffrey of Monmouth as Arthur's main court, the City of the Legion. It was the Roman *Isca Legionis*, the home of the Second Augustan Legion, and was one of the three permanently manned garrisons in Britain (*see* Chester and York). There were periods when the main force was elsewhere but it was in regular use from about 70AD to 350AD at the latest, and was being run down from about 300. It was probably already in a state of disrepair by the Arthurian period though the ruins would have been impressive, especially the bathhouse. The amphitheatre was the largest in Britain and encouraged the idea of this as Arthur's court and "round table". It is one of the contenders for the site of Arthur's ninth battle at the City of the Legion, though of the four it is the least likely. It is also unlikely to have had any significant Arthurian connections, the court of the rulers of Gwent being at Caerwent.

Caerwent. The Roman town of Venta Silurum, it was the tribal capital of the Silures, and continued as the capital of the kingdom of Gwent (Caerwent derived from *Caer Venta* and *Venta*, which meant "market" or "meeting place", became Gwent). The Roman town existed from about 90AD to 390AD, when it was systematically demolished. It had been refortified in the early 300s and was the only Roman town in Wales to have walls. Although Caerwent continued as the capital of Gwent the main court probably shifted outside the Roman area with some rebuilding to the north in what is now called Llanmellin. Barber and Pykett suggest that Llanmellin may, at the outset, have been known as Caermellin (before "fort of the mill" changed to "church of the mill"), and that Caermellin could have corrupted to Caermelot or Camelot (*see* Camelot). They also suggest that Llanmellin was originally Llan y Gelli and thus the original of Arthur's court at Gelliwig. The adjoining, and now much bigger, town of Caldicot was the home of King Caradog, probably Caradog Vreichfras. Caerwent remained the chief court of the kings of Gwent, certainly to the time of Athrwys ap Meurig, and the impressive ruins of the Roman fort would doubtless have raised its status as a town of importance amongst later visitors.

Gelliwig. The name of Arthur's court in the original Welsh tales. It was usually believed to be in Cornwall, but there are possible sites in Wales. Barber & Pykitt have proposed Llanmellin near Caerwent (*see entry*). *See also* under Gwynedd.

Lavernock. Possible site for the castle of Lawenor where Lancelot is supposed to have arrived in Wales in the Prose *Lancelot*. *See* Chapter 17.

Maesteg. South of the town is the mountain range of Mynydd Baidan, a possible site for the battle of Badon.

Pontarddulais. East of the town, north of Swansea, is Ffynnonfedw, Bedwyr's Well, and the ridge of Craig-y-Bedw looking down on Cwm Dulais, one of the many possible locales for Arthur's early battles.

Tredunnock or **Tredynog**. According to a legend told in the *Life* of St. Cadog, Arthur became incensed when he learned that

Cadog had given sanctuary to Llyngesog, who had killed three of Arthur's men. Arthur and Cadog negotiated from either side of the River Usk just below Tredunnock. The outcome of the debate was that Arthur would receive nine cows in redress but, clearly of a cussed nature, Arthur demanded that the cows be red and white. Cadog arranged for this and the cows crossed the river, but on the other side they turned into ferns. The origin of Tredunnock is *Tref Redinog*, "Fern Village".

Gwynedd and Anglesey

Aberdovey. On the hills north of the town, above Abertafol, is Carn March Arthur, the Cairn of Arthur's horse, where a stone is supposed to be imprinted with a hoofprint. The cairn is on the flanks of Mynydd y Llyn (Mountain of the Lake), and the lake is Llyn Barfog where Arthur is supposed to have killed a lake monster called an afanc.

Anglesey. The British name for the island was *Môn*, "mountain", referring to the headland of Holyhead, which in Arthur's time was called *Caergybi*, "fort of Cybi", named after the holy man St Cybi who lived from about 480 to 550. Anglesey was the last stronghold of the Druids whom Paulinus was seeking to destroy in his campaign in 60AD. It was in the territory of the Ordovices and was later the heartland of the Venedotians. It would have been the core territory of Cadwallon and his son Maelgwyn – Gildas's phrase for him, "Dragon of the Island", referred to Anglesey. The poem *Pa Gur* says that Cei came here to fight the giant cat Palug – later legend has Arthur fight the cat. There are several prehistoric sites that have attracted Arthur's name, especially the limestone pavement at Llanddona called Din Sylwy or **Bwrdd Arthur**, "Arthur's Table". It was a hill-fort in use into the Roman period. There is also **Ogof Arthur**, "Arthur's cave", near Llangwyfan, **Arthur's Quoit** at Llwydiarth Fawr and another near Moelfre, and **Arthur's Stone** near Llanfechell. The concentration of these names, including those on the mainland opposite, show a continued tradition with Arthur, possibly by association with the worship of the god Artaius. Anglesey is almost certainly the kingdom of Sorelois described in the Vulgate Cycle.

Bardsey Island. A small island off the point of the Lleyn Peninsula, called Ynys Enlli in Welsh. It was the site of a Celtic monastery founded in the mid-sixth century by Cadfan, and is closely associated with Merlin. Higden's *Polychronicon* claims that Merlin is buried here and that this was the site of a glass house that he built for Niniane. The suggestion of a glass house/ fort has linked Bardsey with Annwn in *The Spoils of Annwvyn* and by extension with Avalon. It may therefore have been the last resting place of Arthur. In *Journey to Avalon*, Pykitt and Barber claim that Bardsey was once called *Ynys Afallach*, the "isle of apples", and curiously, in the year 2000 it was discovered that the island did have the survival of an ancient stock of apples which may date back as far as the second abbott, Lleuddad, whose name still survives in gardens on the island. There are many caves around the southern tip of the island and in one of these Merlin is believed to be sleeping surrounded by the Thirteen Treasures of Britain. There is nothing historically to connect it with Arthur, but it was a Holy Island and the journey to it was treacherous, as described in *The Spoils of Annwryn*. Its Celtic name, *Ynys Enlli*, means the "isle of the currents".

Barmouth. A minor road leading north-east out of Barmouth ends at the farm of Sylfaen, just beyond which is a megalithic stone circle called **Cerrig Arthur**. It is not known how this came to be associated with Arthur.

Beddgelert. Tucked in a beautiful valley in the shadow of Snowdon, this is the nearest town to two significant Arthurian sites. 2km north-east on the A498 is the hill-fort Dinas Emrys, "Fort of Ambrosius", described by Nennius, where Vortigern was unable to build a stronghold and which required a human sacrifice. As a result a boy without a father was found, but he explained that the fort kept collapsing because of two battling serpents in a pool beneath the foundations, these being symbolic of the British and the Saxons. In Nennius's version that boy turns out to be Ambrosius, whilst Geoffrey reveals it to be Merlin. Vortigern grants the fort to Ambrosius/Merlin and builds his fort elsewhere. Excavations carried out by Dr. Savory in 1954–56 discovered that there really was a pool beside the fort, and that the stronghold dated from the mid-to-late fifth century, contemporary with Vortigern and Ambrosius. The current ruins on the hill are the remains of a twelfth-century castle and should not be confused with the original fort. No names were found to link it to a local ruler and since both Vortigern and Ambrosius are more closely connected with Gloucester and Powys, this seems too remote for them. It may have been occupied by one of the sons of Cunedda, possibly Dunod or Dunaut, as the territory around Dinas Emrys was called Dunoding.

Just north of Dinas Emrys is a pass called Cwm Llan, suggested as a site for Camlann. Just beyond it is Carnedd Arthur, a cairn supposed to mark Arthur's burial place. It looks down towards Llyn Lydaw where Bedivere is supposed to have returned Excalibur.

Bethesda. 10km south along the A5 is Llyn Ogwen and towering above the lake to the south is the Hill of Tryfan (994m). Somewhere on this hill is the reputed grave of Bedwyr.

Caernarvon. The Roman fort of Segontium was one of the major Roman strongholds in Wales, occupied almost continuously from around 78AD until troops were withdrawn by Magnus Maximus soon after 383. The fort is associated with Eudaf Hen, whose daughter married Magnus. Eudaf, as Octavius, may have been one of the later commanders here. Malory calls it Kynke Kenadon in Book VII (Caxton edition) of *Morte Darthur* where Arthur holds court one Pentecost and from where Gareth undertakes his adventure with Dame Lunet. It has also been identified with the Waste City of Senauden, but *see* Dorchester.

Dolgellau. To the east are two sites both called Camlan. One is on the A470 just north of Pentrewern. The other is about ten km along the same road at the junction with the A458 just south of Mallwyd. The name Mallwyd probably means "battle ground". Just north of Dolgellau is a river called Gamlan. All this suggests how common the name was and how difficult it is to isolate.

Dyffryn Ardudwy. A large burial chamber here is also known as Carreg Arthur or Arthur's Quoit. It is near one of the possible sites for Camlann.

Gelliwig, *see* Lleyn Peninsula.

Llanrwst. Charlotte Guest believed that the fortress of Math, Caer Dathyl, was "on an eminence" above this village, though no obvious site presents itself. There is a Pencraig Arthur a few kms to the north.

Llanuwchllyn. To the north of the town, at the southern end of Llyn Tegid (Lake Bala) was the Roman fort Caer Gai. The name means "Fort of Caius" and tradition has it named after Arthur's seneschal, Kay. It is also known as Caer Gynyr after Cynyr Ceinfarfog, Cai's father. The fort itself was only occupied between about 70 and130AD, but there is evidence of an associated "castle" still marked on the maps. Cai's father was known as the Lord of Penllyn, the name for the surrounding territory. Tradition suggests that the young Arthur was raised with Cai and thus spent his youth in this area. To the south, in the Berwyn Mountains, is Bwlch y Groes, where Arthur began his battle with King Rience.

Lleyn Peninsula. There are several sites of Arthurian interest. Near the southern tip, overlooking Bardsey Island (*see separate entry*) is **Rhiw**. The hill, Mynydd Rhiw (304m), has been the site of human habitation since the Stone Age and was also the site of a Bronze Age axe factory. There are many antiquarian sites around Rhiw but the one of Arthurian interest is also the most overlooked, **Gelliwig**, now the name of a farm between Rhiw and Botwnnog. Gelliwig was the name of Arthur's court in the Welsh tales and is usually placed in Cornwall. The name means "woodland grove", so was probably once common across Britain, but this site is the only place where it survives. There is no evidence that this was Arthur's court, but the many antiquities in the area show that it is a site of ancient interest that requires more investigation.

North-east of Rhiw, beyond Botwnnog, at the village of Garnfadryn, is the large hill-fort of **Carn Fadryn** (371m), believed to be named after Vortigern's granddaughter Madrun. It shows signs of having been occupied during the fifth century. Further north again, just beyond Nefyn, is **Nant Gwrtheyrn**, the Valley of Vortigern. Somewhere here, as the stream runs down from Llithfaen into Caernarvon Bay at Porth y Nant, is supposed to be the grave of Vortigern. It was described by Thomas Pennant in 1781 as a "high and verdant mount", still visible in 1905, but now lost. This clashes with the legend that he died at Ganarew in Gwent. If Vortigern died here then his citadel may well have been **Tre'r Ceiri**, on the eastern slopes of Yr Eifl (564m). This was occupied throughout the Roman period and possibly beyond, and still shows evidence of its strong fortification. The name means "Town of the Fortresses".

Returning to Rhiw, along the coast to the east is Abersoch and just north of the village is an old house called **Castellmarch** which has long been believed to be on the site of King Mark's castle. It more likely was a fort of horses, as "march" means horse.

Penygroes. Overlooking the town from the east at the start of the Nantlle Valley is the hill-fort of Caer Engan, suggested as a possible site for Caer Dathyl, a fort associated both with Math of the Mabinogion and with relatives of Arthur.

Powys

Aberyscir. One of the homes associated with Ogrfan, father of Guenevere (*see also* Knucklas). He may well have been connected with the Roman fort of Cicucium which was still occupied in the late fourth century. A hill-fort was just above the Roman one. Just to the north is the village of Battle, which takes its name from a battle in 1093 when the last of the independent Brecon princes, Bleddyn ap Maenyrch, was killed, but it serves to remind us that this was also the area of Arthur's pursuit of the Irish boar Twrch Trwyth and there were probably several battles nearby. Between Aberyscir and Brecon is the town of Cradoc, which may take its name from Caradog Vreichfras since this may have been part of the territory that he captured when he extended his territory from Ergyng across Llydaw into Breichiniog.

Brecon Beacons. This was the core of the old kingdom of Brycheiniog, ruled by Brychan. Arthur's pursuit of the giant boar Trwyth took him through the Brecon Beacons as described in *Culhwch and Olwen*. Most specific locations are vague until the hunt passes south into Gwent. The eastern part of the Brecon Beacons and the Black Mountains was known as Llydaw. *Culhwch and Olwen* refers to the men of Llydaw meeting at Ystrad Yw, a territory centred upon Llanbedr near Crickhowell. Llangors Lake to the north-west was also believed to be part of Llydaw. If so, then this is the territory often confused with Armorica, which was also known as Llydaw.

Builth Wells, *see* Rhayader.

Cradoc, *see* Aberyscir.

Knucklas. Little can now be seen of the ancient Castell y Cnwclas at Knucklas but this was long believed to be the home of Ogrfan, the father of Guenevere, and where she and Arthur married. This was probably the site of Guenevere's Cameliard. Ogrfan is associated with other sites in Wales, especially Aberyscir (*see above*).

Rhayader. Nennius records that during the hunt of the boar Twrch Trwyth, Arthur's hound Cabal (more likely his horse) left an imprint in a stone and Arthur left this as the topmost stone on a cairn. He records this as being at *Buallt*, the old name for Builth Wells, but the name survives, as Carn Gafallt, for a mountain south of Rhayader near the village of Elan.

Trefeglwys. It is here that the rivers Gleiniant and Trannon meet, suggesting a possible site for Arthur's first battle.

Welshpool. A focal point for several Arthurian sites such as those identified in *The Dream of Rhonabwy*. The plain on which the story starts, Argyngroeg, is to the north of the town, invariably now called Gungrog. The ford at Rhyd-y-groes, over the Camlad river, where Arthur's men gathered prior to the battle of Caer Faddon, is south-east of the town on the A490, 2km northwest of Chirbury. Arthur's warband moved north from here past Caer Digoll, which is the Beacon Ring hill-fort at Leighton. The battle site itself is just north of here, probably at the Breidden Hills. Due west from here, across the Severn, is the large hill-fort Gaer Fawr, which may have been one of Arthur's castles, linked to nearby Garthmyl, which may have been named after Arthur's vassal king Gyrthmwl.

25

FURTHER QUESTS – ARTHURIAN SOCIETIES AND WEBSITES

If you wish to pursue Arthurian research there are many avenues open to you.

The premier society is the International Arthurian Society (IAS) founded by Eugène Vinaver, Jean Frappier and Roger Sherman Loomis in 1948 for the promotion of the scholarly study of the literature, legends and iconography of King Arthur. It publishes an annual *Bibliographical Bulletin*. Being international, it has representatives in every country. Full details can be found at its website <www.dur.ac.uk/arthurian.society/contacts.htm>

The quarterly journal *Arthuriania*, published by Scriptorium Press, is available as part of the subscription for the North American Branch of the IAS, but it is also available separately. Enquiries should be sent to Arthuriana, Southern Methodist University, PO Box 750432, Dallas, Texas 75275–0432, USA or via their website <smu.edu/arthuriana/arthursubs.htm>

The *Arthuriana* website has a very helpful page of links to other Arthurian resources on the internet. It also provides access to the Arthurnet moderated e-mail discussion group, which can be contacted via <smu.edu/arthuriana/arthurnet.htm>

A new internet-based organisation is the Society for Arthurian Popular Culture Studies run by Michael A. Torregrossa as part of the King Arthur Forever website. It was established to foster research on Arthurian popular culture from all periods in which representations of the Arthurian legend appear. Its web address is <http://home.att.net/~torregrossa/>

The Heroic Age is a free on-line journal founded in 1998 and dedicated to the study of Northwestern Europe from the Late Roman Empire to the advent of the Norman Empire. The Publisher is Michelle Ziegler and the web address is <http://members.aol.com/heroicage1/homepage.html>

The major on-line research facility is The Camelot Project at the University of Rochester, established in 1995 to make available in electronic format a database of Arthurian texts, images, bibliographies and basic information. It is designed by Alan Lupack, Director of The Robbins Library, a branch of the Rush Rhees Library, and can be contacted at <www.lib.rochester.edu/camelot/cphome.stm>

Other websites of interest include:
"Early British Kingdoms" at <Britannia> run by David Nash Ford, and dedicated to "the history of all those little known kingdoms that existed in Britain during the Age of King Arthur", at <www.britannia.com/history/ebk/>
"Faces of Arthur", a companion site to "Vortigern Studies", both run by Robert Vermaat, is dedicated to the full range of interests in King Arthur and fifth century studies. At <www.geocities.com/vortigernstudies.org.uk/>
"Timeless Myths", which has a special section on the Arthurian romances and tales from Monmouth to Malory, at <www.timelessmyths.com/arthurian/index.html>
"Arthurian A2Z Knowledge Bank", part of the Mystical World Wide Web, for those who want a quick and easy A-Z guide to Arthurian names. Run by Mell Paul at <www.mystical-www.co.uk/arthuriana2z/index.htm>

BIBLIOGRAPHY

The following lists the major works I consulted in the preparation of this book.

1. History of the late Roman period to the sixth century

Alcock, Leslie, *Arthur's Britain* (London: Allen Lane, 1971)

Alcock, Leslie, *Economy, Society & Warfare Among the Britons & Saxons* (Cardiff: University of Wales Press, 1987)

Arnold, Christopher J. and Davies, Jeffrey L., *Roman and Early Medieval Wales* (Stroud: Sutton, 2000)

Barnwell, P.S., *Emperor, Prefects & Kings, The Roman West, 395–565* (London: Duckworth, 1992)

Bassett, Steven (editor), *The Origins of the Anglo-Saxon Kingdoms* (Leicester University Press, 1989)

Breeze, David J., *The Northern Frontiers of Roman Britain* (London: Batsford, 1982)

Cleary, A.S., *The Ending of Roman Britain* (London: Batsford, 1989)

Dark, Ken, *Britain and the End of the Roman Empire* (Stroud: Tempus, 2000)

Dark, K.R., *Civitas to Kingdom* (Leicester University Press, 1994)

Davies, Hugh, *Roads in Roman Britain* (Stroud: Tempus, 2002)

Davies, Wendy, *Wales in the Early Middle Ages* (Leicester University Press, 1982)

Dillon, Myles and Chadwick, Nora, *The Celtic Realms* (London: Weidenfeld & Nicolson, 1967)

Dornier, Ann, "The Province of Valentia", *Britannia* (13), 1982

Dumville, David N., *Britons and Anglo-Saxons in the Early Middle Ages* (Aldershot: Ashgate Publishing, 1993)

Ellis, Peter Berresford, *Celt and Saxon, The Struggle for Britain* AD 410–937 (London: Constable, 1993)

Evans, Stephen S., *Lords of Battle* (Woodbridge: Boydell Press, 1997)

Garmonsway, G.N. (editor, translator), *The Anglo-Saxon Chronicle* (London: Dent, 1953, 1972)

Gelling, Margaret, *The West Midlands in the Early Middle Ages* (Leicester University Press, 1992)

Giles, J.A., *Six Old English Chronicles* (London: Bell, 1891)

Giot, Pierre-Roland, Guigon, Philippe and Merdrignac, Bernard, *The British Settlement of Brittany* (Stroud: Tempus, 2003)

Hill, David, *An Atlas of Anglo-Saxon England* (Oxford: Blackwell, 1981)

Hood, A.B.E., *St Patrick, His Writings and Muirchu's Life* (Chichester: Phillimore, 1978)

Johnson, Stephen, *Later Roman Britain* (London: Routledge & Kegan Paul, 1980)

Jones, Michael E. and Casey, John, "The Gallic Chronicle Restored", *Britannia* (19), 1988

Kirby, D.P., *The Earliest English Kings* (London: Unwin Hyman, 1991)

Koch, John T., *The Gododdin of Aneirin* (Cardiff: University of Wales Press, 1997)

Laing, Lloyd and Jennifer, *Anglo-Saxon England* (London: Routledge & Kegan Paul, 1979)

Laing, Lloyd and Jennifer, *The Origins of Britain* (London: Routledge & Kegan Paul, 1980)

Laing, Lloyd, *Celtic Britain* (London: Routledge & Kegan Paul, 1979)

McClure, Judith and Collins, Roger (editors), *Bede, The Ecclesiastical History of the English People* (Oxford University Press, 1994)

Marsden, John, *Northanhymbre Saga, the History of the Anglo-Saxon Kings of Northumbria* (London: Kyle Cathie, 1992)

Maund, Kari, *The Welsh Kings* (Stroud: Tempus, 2000)

Mongan, Norman, *The Menapia Quest* (Dublin: Herodotus Press, 1995)

Moorhead, John, *The Roman Empire Divided, 400–700* (Harlow: Longman, 2001)

Morris, John, *The Age of Arthur* (London: Weidenfeld & Nicolson, 1973)

Morris, John (editor, translator), *Nennius, British History and the Welsh Annals* (Chichester: Phillimore, 1980)

Morris, John, *Arthurian Sources, Vol.2, Annals and Charters* (Chichester: Phillimore, 1995)

Morris, John, *Studies in Dark-Age History* (Chichester: Phillimore, 1995)

Muhlberger, Steven, "The Gallic Chronicle of 452 and its Authority for British Events", *Britannia* (14), 1983

Myres, J.N.L., *The English Settlements* (Oxford: Clarendon Press, 1986)

Newton, Sam, *The Origins of Beowulf and the Pre-Viking Kingdom of East Anglia* (Cambridge: Brewer, 1993)

Ó Cróinín, Dáibhí, *Early Medieval Ireland 400–1200* (Harlow: Longman, 1995)

Salway, Peter, *Roman Britain* (Oxford: Clarendon Press, 1981)
Snyder, Christopher A., *Sub-Roman Britain* (Oxford: Hadrian Books, 1996)
Snyder, Christopher A., *An Age of Tyrants* (Stroud: Sutton, 1998)
Stafford, Pauline, *The East Midlands in the Early Middle Ages* (Leicester University Press, 1985)
Swanton, Michael (editor, translator), *The Anglo-Saxon Chronicle* (London: Dent, 1996)
Thomas, Charles, *Christianity in Roman Britain to AD500* (London: Batsford, 1981)
Thompson, E.A., *Saint Germanus of Auxerre and the End of Roman Britain* (Woodbridge: Boydell Press, 1984)
Thorpe, Lewis (translator), *Gregory of Tours, The History of the Franks* (London: Penguin, 1974)
Vince, Alan (editor), *Pre-Viking Lindsey* (City of Lincoln, 1993)
Wacher, John, *The Coming of Rome* (London: Routledge & Kegan Paul, 1979)
Walker, Ian W., *Mercia and the making of England* (Stroud: Sutton, 2000)
Williams, Hugh (translator), *Gildas* (London: David Nutt, 1901).
Williams, Hugh (translator), *Two Lives of Gildas* (originally, 1889; reprinted, Felinfach: Llanerch, 1990)
Wilson, Roger J.A., *A Guide to the Roman Remains in Britain* (London: Constable, 4th edition, 2002)
Winterbottom, Michael (editor, translator), *Gildas, The Ruin of Britain and Other Works* (Chichester: Phillimore, 1978)
Wood, Ian, *The Merovingian Kingdoms, 450–751* (Harlow: Longman, 1994)
Yorke, Barbara, *Kings and Kingdoms of Early Anglo-Saxon England* (London: Sealby, 1990)
Yorke, Barbara, *Wessex in the Early Middle Ages* (London: Leicester University Press, 1995)
Zaluckyj, Sarah, *Mercia* (Almeley: Logaston Press, 2001)

2. Other historical studies, including the Crusades

Biddle, Martin, *King Arthur's Round Table* (Woodbridge: The Boydell Press, 2000)
Bouchard, Constance Brittain, *Holy Entrepreneurs: Cistercians, Knights and Economic Exchange in Twelfth-Century Burgundy* (Ithaca: Cornell University Press, 1991)
Crouch, David, *William Marshall, Knighthood, War and Chivalry, 1147–1219* (Harlow: Longman, 2002)
Hindley, Geoffrey, *The Crusades* (London: Constable, 2003)
Hughes, Jonathan, *Arthurian Myths and Alchemy — The Kingship of Edward IV* (Stroud: Sutton, 2002)

King, Archdale A., *Cîteaux and Her Elder Daughters* (London: Burns & Oates, 1954)
Nicolle, David, *The Crusades* (Oxford: Osprey, 2001)
Phillips, Jonathan, *The Fourth Crusade and the Sack of Constantinople* (London: Jonathan Cape, 2004)
Seward, Desmond, *The Monks of War* (London: Penguin Books, revised, 1995)
Urban, William, *The Teutonic Knights* (London: Greenhill, 2003)
Weir, Alison, *Eleanor of Aquitaine* (London: Cape, 1999)

3. Specific studies and speculations on Arthur and his world

Ashe, Geoffrey, *The Discovery of King Arthur* (Stroud: Sutton, revised edition, 2003)
Barber, Chris & Pykitt, David, *Journey to Avalon* (Abergavenny: Blorenge Books, 1993)
Barber, Richard, *The Figure of Arthur* (Cambridge: D.S. Brewer, 1972)
Barber, Richard, *King Arthur, Hero and Legend* (Woodbridge: Boydell Press, new edition, 1986, 1993).
Blackett, Baram and Wilson, Alan, *Artorius Rex Discovered* (Cardiff: King Arthur Research, 1985)
Blake, Steve and Lloyd, Scott, *The Keys to Avalon* (Shaftesbury: Element, 2000)
Blake, Steve and Lloyd, Scott, *Pendragon* (London: Rider, 2002)
Bruce, Christopher W., *The Arthurian Name Dictionary* (New York: Garland, 1999)
Carroll, D.F., *Arturius - A Quest for Camelot* (Goxhill: private, 1996)
Castleden, Rodney, *King Arthur, the Truth behind the Legend* (London: Routledge, 2000)
Chambers, E.K., *Arthur of Britain* (London: Sidgwick & Jackson, 1927)
Crawford, O.G.S., "Arthur and his Battles", *Antiquity* (35), 1935
Dames, Michael, *Merlin and Wales, a Magician's Landscape* (London: Thames & Hudson, 2002)
Davidson, Hilda Ellis (editor), Fisher, Peter (translator), *Saxo Grammaticus: The History of the Danes, Books I-IX* (Cambridge: Brewer, 1996)
Gidlow, Christopher, *The Reign of Arthur, From History to Legend* (Stroud: Sutton, 2004)
Gilbert, Adrian, Wilson, Alan and Blackett, Baram, *The Holy Kingdom* (London: Bantam Press, 1998)
Goodrich, Norma Lorre, *King Arthur* (New York: Franklin Watts, 1986), *Merlin* (Watts, 1988), *Guinevere* (HarperCollins, 1992), *The Holy Grail* (HarperCollins, 1992)
Grimbert, Joan Tasker (editor), *Tristan and Isolde, a Casebook* (London: Routledge, 2002)

Higham, N.J., *King Arthur, Myth-Making and History* (London: Routledge, 2002)
Holmes, Michael, *King Arthur, a Military History* (London: Blandford, 1996)
Kennedy, Edward Donald (editor), *King Arthur, a Casebook* (London: Routledge, 2002)
Lacy, Norris J. (editor), *The New Arthurian Encyclopedia* (New York: Garland, 1996)
Littleton, C. Scott & Malcor, Linda A., *From Scythia to Camelot* (New York: Garland, new edition, 2000)
Markale, Jean, *King of the Celts* (originally Paris, 1976) (Rochester, VT: Inner Traditions, 1994)
Markale, Jean, *Merlin, Priest of Nature* (originally Paris, 1981) (Rochester, VT: Inner Traditions, 1995)
Millar, Ronald, *Will the Real King Arthur Please Stand Up?* (London: Cassell, 1978)
Moffat, Alistair, *Arthur and the Lost Kingdoms* (London: Weidenfeld & Nicolson, 1999)
Phillips, Graham & Keatman, Martin, *King Arthur, the True Story* (London: Century, 1992)
Reid, Howard, *Arthur the Dragon King* (London: Headline, 2001)
Reno, Frank D., *The Historic King Arthur* (Jefferson, NC: McFarland, 1996)
Reno, Frank D., *Historic Figures of the Arthurian Era* (Jefferson, NC: McFarland, 2000)
Snyder, Christopher, *Exploring the World of King Arthur* (London: Thames & Hudson, 2000)
Tolstoy, Nikolai, *The Quest for Merlin* (London: Hamish Hamilton, 1985)
Turner, P.F.J, *The Real King Arthur* (Alaska: SKS, 1993, 2 vols)
Walters, Lori J. (editor), *Lancelot and Guinevere, a Casebook* (London: Routledge, 2002)
Wildman, S.G., *The Black Horsemen* (London: Baker, 1971)

4. Arthurian Legends, Romances, Literature, Art and Cinema

For specific romances see references in Chapters 13 to 18

Barron, W.R.J. (editor), *The Arthur of the English* (Cardiff: University of Wales Press, 2001)
Bartrum, P.C., *Early Welsh Genealogical Tracts* (Cardiff: University of Wales Press, 1966)
Bartrum, Peter C., *A Welsh Classical Dictionary* (Aberystwyth: National Library of Wales, 1993)
Bromwich, Rachel, Jarman, A.O.H., Roberts, Brynley F. (editors), *The Arthur of the Welsh* (Cardiff: University of Wales Press, 1991)

Coe, Jon B. and Young, Simon, *The Celtic Sources for the Arthurian Legend* (Felinfach: Llanerch, 1995)

Coghlan, Ronan, *The Encyclopedia of Arthurian Legends* (Shaftesbury: Element, 1991)

Dixon-Kennedy, Mike, *Arthurian Myth & Legend* (London: Blandford, 1995)

Dover, Carol, *A Companion to the Lancelot-Grail Cycle* (Cambridge: Brewer, 2003)

Field, P.J.C., *The Life and Times of Sir Thomas Malory* (Cambridge: Brewer, 1993)

Green, Miranda J., *Dictionary of Celtic Myth and Legend* (London: Thomas & Hudson, 1992)

Harty, Kevin J., *King Arthur on Film* (Jefferson, NC: McFarland, 1999)

Jackson, W.H. and Ranawake, S.A. (editors), *The Arthur of the Germans* (Cardiff: University of Wales Press, 2000)

Karr, Phyllis Ann, *The Arthurian Companion* (Oakland, CA: Green Knight, revised edition, 2001)

Koch, John T. with Carey, John, *The Celtic Heroic Age* (Aberystwyth: Celtic Studies Publications, 4th edition, 2003)

Loomis, Roger Sherman (editor), *Arthurian Literature in the Middle Ages* (Oxford: Clarendon Press, 1959)

Loomis, Roger Sherman, *Celtic Myth and Arthurian Romance* (New York: Columbia, 1927)

Loomis, Roger Sherman, *The Development of Arthurian Romance* (London: Hutchinson, 1963)

Lupack, Alan and Lupack, Barbara Tepa, *Arthur in America* (Cambridge: D.S. Brewer, 1999)

Luttrell, Claude, *The Creation of the First Arthurian Romance* (Evanston: Northwestern University Press, 1974)

Maier, Bernhard, *Dictionary of Celtic Religion and Culture* (Woodbridge: Boydell Press, 1997)

Mason, Eugene (editor, translator), *Arthurian Chronicles: Wace and Layamon* (London: Dent, 1962)

Matthews, John, *The Song of Taliesin* (London: Aquarian Press, 1991)

Merriman, James Douglas, *The Flower of Kings, A Study of the Arthurian Legend in England between 1485 and 1835* (Lawrence, KS: University Press of Kansas, 1973)

Padel, O.J., *Arthur in Medieval Welsh Literature* (Cardiff: University of Wales Press, 2000)

Roberts, Brynley F., *Brut y Brenhinedd* (Dublin Institute for Advanced Studies, 1971)

Roberts, Peter (translator), *The Chronicle of the Kings of Britain attributed to Tysilio* (originally 1811; facsimile reprint, Llanerch, 2000)

Thompson, Raymond H., *The Return from Avalon* (Westport, CT: Greenwood Press, 1985)

West, G.D., *French Arthurian Prose Romances* (University of Toronto Press, 1978)
Whitaker, Muriel, *The Legends of King Arthur in Art* (Woodbridge: D.S. Brewer, 1990)

5. The Holy Grail and other mystical/religious subjects

Barber, Richard, *The Holy Grail, Imagination and Belief* (London: Allen Lane, 2004)
Butler, Alan, *The Goddess, the Grail & the Lodge* (Alresford: O Books, 2004)
Cavendish, Richard, *King Arthur & the Grail* (London: Weidenfeld & Nicolson, 1978)
Currer-Briggs, Noel, *The Shroud and the Grail* (London: Weidenfeld & Nicolson, 1987)
Gardner, Laurence, *Bloodline of the Holy Grail* (Shaftesbury: Element, 1996)
Gardner, Laurence, *Realm of the Ring Lords* (Ottery St. Mary: Media-Quest, 2000)
Grigsby, John, *Warriors of the Wasteland* (London: Watkins, 2002)
Hutton, Ronald, *Witches, Druids and King Arthur* (London: Hambledon & London, 2003)
Loomis, Roger Sherman, *The Grail, from Celtic Myth to Christian Symbol* (originally 1963; London: Constable, 1992)
Owen, D.D.R., *The Evolution of the Grail Legend* (Edinburgh: Oliver & Boyd, 1968)
Phillips, Graham, *The Search for the Grail* (London: Random House, 1995)
Sinclair, Andrew, *The Discovery of the Grail* (London: Century, 1998)

6. Geographical studies

Ashe, Geoffrey, *The Traveller's Guide to Arthurian Britain* (Glastonbury: Gothic Image, 1997)
Ashe, Geoffrey, *The Landscape of King Arthur* (Exeter: Webb & Bower, 1987)
Cameron, Kenneth, *English Place Names* (London: Batsford, 1996)
Coates, Richard, *The Place-Names of Hampshire* (London: Batsford, 1989)
Fairbairn, Neil, *A Traveller's Guide to the Kingdoms of Arthur* (London: Evans Brothers, 1983)
Gelling, Margaret, *Place Names in the Landscape* (London: Dent, 1984)
Glennie, John S. Stuart, *Arthurian Localities* (originally 1869; reprinted Llanerch, 1994)

Hogg, A.H.A., *Hill-Forts of Britain* (London: Hart-Davis, MacGibbon, 1975)

Jackson, Robert, *Dark Age Britain, What to See and Where* (Cambridge: Patrick Stephens, 1984)

Matthews, John and Stead, Michael J., *King Arthur's Britain* (London: Blandford, 1995)

McKenzie, Peter, *Camelot's Frontier* (Morpeth: Longhirst Press, 1999)

Miller, Helen Hill, *The Realms of Arthur* (London: Peter Davies, 1970)

Mills, A.D., *Oxford Dictionary of British Place Names* (Oxford University Press, 1991, 2003)

Rahtz, Philip & Watts, Lorna, *Glastonbury, Myth and Archaeology* (Stroud: Tempus, 1993, 2003)

Rivet, A.L.F. and Smith, Colin, *The Place-Names of Roman Britain* (London: Batsford, 1979)

Room, Adrian, *The Penguin Dictionary of British Place Names* (London: Penguin, 2003)

Stobie, Denise, *Exploring King Arthur's Britain* (London: Collins & Brown, 1999)

ACKNOWLEDGMENTS

So much has been written about Arthur and his world that it is easy to become influenced by the thoughts and findings of others, no matter how much you try to remain independent. For that very reason I have consulted few people during the course of this book. I have made full use of the scholarship available both in the books listed in the Bibliography at the end of this book and on the websites listed in Chapter 25, and make specific acknowledgement here to the excellent work by Leslie Alcock, John Morris, Frank Reno and Richard Barber, as well as the contributors to Robert Vermaat's brilliant Vortigern Studies website.

However, every author needs a lifeline and I must give special thanks to Peter Berresford Ellis and Larry Mendelsberg. Both read through the manuscript at the final stage and offered helpful comments and observations. Peter Berresford Ellis also responded to my frequent pleas for help on the Celtic languages and translations whilst Larry Mendelsburg gave freely of his knowledge of Arthurian literature. I am exceedingly grateful to them both.

I must also thank Gary Kronk, who kindly made available to me cometary data updated from his book *Cometography* (Cambridge University Press, 1999); Dennis Lien of the University of Minnesota for researching data on artists and paintings; and Antony Wilson of York Coins for confirmation of data on Danish minters.

My thanks to my editors at Constable and Robinson, Krystyna Green and Peter Duncan, for their patience in letting me constantly revise the contractual delivery date while watching the book grow and grow.

And, of course, my thanks and gratitude to my wife Sue who puts up with my hours of isolation as I delve amongst "all those dead people", as she thinks of them, and then welcomes me back to the land of the living. To her I dedicate this book, with all my love and affection.

INDEX

This index covers Sections 1 and 2. The chapters in Section 3 are designed as individual indexes for authors, films, characters and sites and should be consulted in addition to the following. To avoid duplication the titles of stories and romances are entered under their English name wherever practical. Individuals known by a variety of names are entered under their most common form of name (e.g. Guenevere, Gawain).